THE KORAN

Translated from the Arabic by
J. M. Rodwell

Foreword and Introduction by
Alan Jones
The Oriental Institute, Oxford

PHOENIX

5 UPPER SAINT MARTIN'S LANE
LONDON
WC2H 9EA

A PHOENIX PAPERBACK

First published in Everyman in 1909
Reissued 1992 and 1994

This paperback edition published in 2009 by Phoenix, a division of
the Orion Publishing Group Ltd, Orion House
5 Upper St Martin's Lane, London WC2H 9EA

An Hachette UK company

Typeset by Deltatype Ltd, Birkenhead, Merseyside

Printed in Great Britain by Clays Ltd, St Ives plc

A CIP catalogue record for this book
is available from the British Library

www.orionbooks.co.uk

CONTENTS

NOTE ON THE EDITOR

ALAN JONES is Emeritus Fellow of Pembroke College, Oxford and of St Cross College, Oxford. After studying Classics, Arabic and Persian at Cambridge he moved to Oxford to study Turkish. He taught Arabic and Islamic Studies there from 1957 and retired as Professor of Classical Arabic in 2000. He is a specialist in pre-Islamic and early Islamic Arabic and in Quranic Studies, and, at a much later period, in the literature of Muslim Spain. He is just completing three volumes on the Qur'an: a translation, a commentary and a volume of background essays.

FOREWORD

The Koran, or, to give it its strict transliteration, the Qur'ān, is the sacred book of Islam. For Muslims it is the word of God revealed in Arabic by the archangel Gabriel to the prophet Muḥammad and thence to mankind. For them Muḥammad is the last of the prophets and thus the Qur'ān is the final expression of God's message to mankind.

Non-Muslims are unlikely to share this view, but they too will recognise that the Qur'ān is one of the most important and influential books known to mankind and that its influence is continuing to increase with the spread of Islam.

On that basis alone the Qur'ān is worthy of study, but its outstanding literary merit should also be noted: it is by far the finest work of Arabic prose in existence. Nevertheless, it has to be said that the Qur'ān is not an easy book to read. There are several reasons for this: the subject matter is complex and much of the language is highly charged; the order of the *sūras* (chapters) presents the contents in a way that those with no previous knowledge of the book often find confusing; the way material is presented within a *surā* is often surprising; the background of the work is very alien to the English-speaker; much of the power of the original is lost in translation – indeed most Muslims believe that the Qur'ān cannot be translated properly and therefore should not be translated at all.

These problems can be lessened, if not entirely removed, by a careful introduction. When Rodwell's translation was first published in 1861, he provided his own *Preface* for this purpose. He drew in part on traditional Arab sources but he was strongly influenced by European research of the time, particularly that of the German scholar Nöldeke. Unlike his translation, Rodwell's *Preface* has not withstood the test of time, and both it and some later introductory remarks by Professor G. Margoliouth are here replaced by my new introduction, which takes into account more recent scholarship. Some of Rodwell's obsolete notes have also been pruned.

There has been one other significant change. Rodwell arranged the *sūras* into what he thought was the proper chronological order. It is now realised that such an ordering is mistaken. As will be shown in the Introduction, the furthest one can go is to divide the *sūras* into four rough chronological groups. Any attempt to go further is fraught with difficulty and possibly misleading. The *sūras* have therefore been put back into the traditional order.

INTRODUCTION

THE ARABIAN PENINSULA AT THE TIME OF MUḤAMMAD'S BIRTH

Muḥammad is believed to have been born about 570 AD. As had long been the case, most of the Arabian peninsula was the domain of nomadic *bedu*, with occasional settlements where there was water, cultivation, trading or a cultic centre. The north-western, Syrian march was controlled by the Ghassānids, Arab vassals of the Byzantines; whilst to the north-east the Lakhmids of Al-Ḥīra, in what is now southern Iraq, were under the suzerainty of the Sassanians of Persia.

Only in the high upland – that of the Yemen in particular – was life anything other than harsh. The extreme climate was no less trying then than it is today, and from time to time there were earthquakes in the western mountains that rise from the Red Sea. The desert terrain, though healthy, was inhospitable, but malaria was endemic in most of the settlements, though apparently not in Mecca and the high, lush al-Ṭā'if.

Most trade that involved the *bedu* was local barter, but various commodities came from abroad. These included wine (from Syria, Iraq and Persia), weapons (spears etc. from India) and slaves (from Africa). There were long-distance caravan routes for spices and cloth from the Yemen to Syria and to Iraq, for which Mecca was a crucial staging point. There was also trade by sea along both the Arabian Gulf and the Red Sea. On the latter, Jedda, the port of Mecca some fifty miles distant, was also an important entrepôt.

The religious situation in the peninsula was complex. There were communities of Jews in the Yemen and in the Ḥijāz, and there were some Christians in the Yemen, particularly at Najrān. On the periphery there were large numbers of Christian Arabs in Syria (Monophysites) and in Iraq (Nestorians). In southern

Arabia several monotheistic cults had established themselves, including one to al-Raḥmān 'the merciful', a name that was to find prominence in the Qur'ān as one of the most favoured descriptions of God. In the Ḥijāz, in particular, idol-worship had developed in several settlements: Nakhla, al-Ṭā'if and, most important of all, Mecca. The *bedu* had little or no religion. Their poetry makes it clear that their basic belief was that Fate ruled their destiny and that sooner or later Fate would bring death. They knew about gods and idols, but there are lines of poetry that show that the gods, even Allah, were less important to the *bedu* than Fate. The people of the settlements appear to have had some conviction that visiting their idols and performing rituals, including animal sacrifice, might induce the idols to intercede with Fate on their behalf. These rituals have something of the appearance of pilgrimage, because they were normally held when the local population was swollen by influxes of visitors to annual fairs, the main purpose of which was trading. Surviving poetry makes it clear that such visitors did take part in the rituals, but this appears to be due more to their links with the people of the settlements and respect for their traditions than to firmly held religious belief.

Though the *bedu* seem to have had little expectation that Fate might be propitiated in this manner, they appear to have sought to avoid its final, fatal appearance in somewhat less formal ways, and divination and soothsayers (*kāhins*) were all popular. The *kāhins* had their own form of diction, a highly charged and often cryptic kind of prose, marked by rhythmic clauses and assonance. There were also two types of orators: tribal spokesmen, with an important role in inter-tribal relations; and itinerants preaching either a religious message or exhorting people to good. Finally there were storytellers who told and retold stories and legends of tribal life. All three kinds of prose were in the oral tradition. Writing, however, was known and used in the settlements for archival and legal purposes, but apart from a few scraps, all this prose material has disappeared. There can, however, be no doubt of its influence and importance in providing several types of prose discourse that were comprehensible over a wide area and were largely, though not entirely, free of dialectal features.

What has survived in a reasonable quantity is pre-Islamic poetry. This is often of the highest quality, for Arabic poetry was at its zenith from 525 to 650. Like storytelling, poetry was part of the fabric of tribal society, and poets were highly esteemed for their ability to sing the praises of their own tribe and feared for their ability to satirise or even curse. It was generally believed that each poet was inspired by his own individual inspirational spirit, a *jinn*.

The survival of considerable amounts of poetry, together with the later use made of it by commentators on the Qur'ān, has tended to divert attention away from the importance of the prose genres in paving the way for the Qur'ān. Yet the briefest comparison will show that poetry and the Qur'ān are not closely linked. For example, the treatment of such key factors as narrative and homily are totally different; it is only rarely and coincidentally that a Quranic phrase fits one of the metres of poetry; and though poetic diction does occur from time to time in the Qur'ān, normally when it is the most appropriate way of expressing an idea, it is not a major feature. For its part, the Qur'ān also strongly denies that Muḥammad was a poet or inspired by the *jinn*. The basic objection it makes is clearly to the assertion that must have been made by Muḥammad's Meccan opponents: that he was possessed by the *jinn* and not inspired by God.

Muḥammad

At the time of Muḥammad's birth, his home town Mecca was the most prominent of the settlements in the Ḥijāz. By the standards of the area it was a prosperous place, totally dominated by his tribe, the Quraysh, and deriving income not only from local and long-distance trade but also from those visitors who took part in the pilgrimage rituals in the town itself and at nearby Minā. It is now popular to suggest that the prosperity of Mecca had led to a materialism that was destroying the social cohesion of the town. The materialism was undoubtedly there – it is attacked in various passages in the Qur'ān – but the strength and tenacity of the Meccan opposition to Muḥammad for close on twenty years would not have been possible in a deeply divided society.

Very little is known of the first forty years of Muḥammad's life. Tradition has it that he was born into a respected rather than a rich family; that his father died before he was born and his mother when he was six; and that after her death he was looked after by his grandfather ᶜAbd al-Muṭṭalib and then his uncle Abū Ṭālib. In general terms this is confirmed by Qur'ān 93:6, 'Did he not find thee an orphan and gave thee a home?'

About 595 Muḥammad married Khadīja, a rich widow some years older than himself. They had several children, but only one of them, his daughter Fāṭima, was to survive him. Muslim tradition pictures Muḥammad engaged in trade and travelling to Syria both before and after his marriage, but this is uncertain. It would appear that as the years went by Muḥammad turned more and more towards monotheistic meditation, as a number of people in the area were doing. Eventually, around 610, he was convinced that he had been visited by the archangel Gabriel and ordered to preach God's message to the Arabs. After a brief period of uncertainty, when there was no further visitation, he had a similar experience and another revelation. From that time onwards Muḥammad was totally convinced that he was the Messenger of God, and his actions were based on that unswerving conviction. Whether he was right (as Muslims believe) or wrong (the view of non-Muslims) is immaterial. Occasionally he might have temporised, but his long-term goal never changed. And there were frequent revelations to fortify him in his work.

At first he preached in private to family and friends, converting the majority of them to the new religion. Eventually in 613 he began to preach in public. The response of the majority of Meccans was hostile and was to remain so. It has recently been fashionable to depict Meccan society as in social and economic decline; but if its long and active resistance to the new religion is an accurate gauge, it was a tough and determined community, bent on preserving its own privileged position, even if it was a bastion of idol-worship in the eyes of the nascent Muslim community.

Muḥammad continued to win over converts, but they were few in number, on average no more than two or three a month; and only occasionally did they include a prominent member of Quraysh. More than once Muḥammad tried to come to terms with the Meccans – the garbled story that has come down to us about the so-called 'Satanic verses' being connected with one of these (see 53:19–21). When the Meccans remained implacable he sent some of the converts to safer territory, certainly as far as the Yemen and possibly to Abyssinia. If anything, the situation worsened, particularly after the deaths of Khadīja and Abū Ṭālib in 618.

Muḥammad began to consider relocating the whole of the new community. In 620 he failed in negotiations for a move to al-Ṭā'if.

The next year, he met a group of people from Medina, his mother's home town, situated some 300 miles north of Mecca. Medina, or Yathrib as it was then known, was the home of two Arab tribes, Aws and Khazraj, and their three Jewish client tribes. It was a very large farming and trading settlement, but it had been in turmoil for a number of years, and in 616 Aws and Khazraj had actually fought a battle against each other. They now saw the possibility of inviting Muḥammad to Medina as a *ḥakam*, a wise man who would act as an arbiter between the factions. After lengthy negotiations, during which Muḥammad persuaded Aws and Khazraj to accept not only himself but his whole community, the migration to Medina, the *hijra*, took place, with Muḥammad himself finally arriving there in September 622. The difficulty that Muḥammad had faced in establishing the new religion at Mecca is indicated by the number of Emigrants: something over two hundred, followed by some stragglers.

The emigration to Medina was the decisive step in the struggle to establish the new religion, and it was soon chosen to mark the beginning of the Muslim era. The date is, incidentally, one of the very few for which there is external corroboration: a papyrus from Egypt bears a double date – year 22 of the *hijra* and a Greek equivalent of 643 AD.

Most of the Aws and Khazraj converted to Islam, with greater or lesser enthusiasm. The reverse was the case with the Jewish tribes. There were one or two converts, but the rest disdainfully rejected Muḥammad's claim to be a prophet. They were, however, party to a series of agreements drawn up principally with the clans of Aws and Khazraj that granted some political status in Medina to the Emigrants. Effective power remained with the leaders of Aws and Khazraj, a situation that was to alter little until 628. Some of these leaders were politically at some distance from Muḥammad, though they appear never to have challenged his religious claims. These opposition figures were not a cohesive group, but from time to time they caused Muḥammad considerable difficulties, and they are referred to in the Qur'ān as the *Munāfiqūn*, usually translated as 'hypocrites'.

However, these political difficulties seem to have been less pressing than the new community's economic ones. The Muslims from Aws and Khazraj, now called the *Anṣār* ('Helpers'), supported the Emigrants, but the latter still suffered the privations of a displaced group.

As soon as these initial problems began to ease, Muḥammad once more turned his attention to the Meccans, not merely, it would appear, because of the potential threat they posed, but because it was clear that his long-term aim of spreading his message among the Arabs could not be achieved in the face of Meccan opposition.

There was one conciliatory gesture when the direction to be faced in prayer, the *qibla*, was changed from being towards Jerusalem to being towards the Kaᶜba in Mecca. It was, however, more than offset by determined attempts to disrupt Meccan long-distance trading. After several unsuccessful attempts, a small Meccan caravan was intercepted and captured at Nakhla, between Mecca and al-Ṭā'if. Not long afterwards the Meccans heard that a much larger caravan on its way back from Syria was likely to be attacked. They sent a force of some 1,000 men to protect it. They met some 300 Muslims at Badr, not far from Medina, in a pitched battle in which the Muslims triumphed in March 624.

The victory, which was to become legendary in the annals of Islam, gave a considerable boost to the standing of Muḥammad in Medina, and when, shortly afterwards, they clashed with one of the Jewish tribes there, the Banū Qaynuqāᶜ, they were able to secure the consent of their Arab protectors the Khazraj for the expulsion of the Jewish tribe from the settlement.

The Meccans were roused to action by the defeat at Badr and in 625 they mounted a large expedition against Medina. A battle was fought on Mount Uḥud, one of the outlying parts of Medina. The Meccans gained the upper hand, and Muḥammad himself was wounded. However, for reasons that are unclear, but possibly logistical, the Meccans failed to press home their advantage. It was to prove a disastrous mistake for them.

Though Uḥud left Muḥammad with theological problems – defeat is not usually equated with divine support – it does not seem to have affected the political situation in Medina. However, the *bedu* tribes to the east became markedly hostile and cut down two small Muslim expeditions. Some months later the second of the Jewish tribes, the Banū l-Naḍīr, who had strong trading links with the *bedu*, clashed with the Muslims. They too were despatched northwards into exile.

The next year saw another expedition by the Meccans against Medina. Gathering all the support they could from the *bedu*, they set out to complete the business left unfinished at Uḥud. They were baulked by a series of trenches dug at strategic points in Medina, and after a month's ineffective siege they withdrew.

The retreat of the Meccans led to a dark episode at Medina. The third Jewish tribe, the Banū Qurayẓa, was accused of supporting the Meccans. As had been the case with the Banū Qaynuqāᶜ and the Banū l-Naḍīr, the decision about what to do with them lay with their Arab protecting tribe, in this case Aws. The judgement was savage; the men were to be killed and the women and children enslaved. With only a couple of reprieves the sentence was carried out.

The failure of the siege again led to a switch in allegiances among the *bedu*. More importantly, various prominent Meccans changed sides. A masterstroke by Muḥammad in 628 accelerated this process. He set out from Medina with a large group of followers to perform the pilgrimage at Mecca. What he had in mind was a modification of the old pagan rites, but, like the change of the *qibla*, it put Mecca at the centre of the new religion. The Meccans barred the way, but the confrontation ended in the truce of al-Ḥudaybiya that granted the Muslims the right to make the pilgrimage the next year.

Next year the Meccans did evacuate the city for three days and the Muslims were able to perform a pilgrimage. Before then, however, Muḥammad had led a large expedition and captured Khaybar, the next strategic settlement to the north of Medina. The population of Khaybar was largely Jewish, including many of those who had already been expelled from Medina. When they resisted, the settlement was taken by force, and those who had resisted were driven out.

The capture of Khaybar was part of a policy of pressure to the north that had started somewhat earlier and was to be pursued vigorously to the end of Muḥammad's life. It was also to lead to expansion northwards into Syria after his death. It appears to have been based on two aims: control of strategic routes and direct contact with northern tribes to convert them to Islam.

The period from the treaty of al-Ḥudaybiya to the death of Muḥammad was one of almost total success, the only reverse being the failure of one of the northern expeditions, to Mu'ta in what is now Jordan, in the autumn of 629. Tribes began to send delegations to Medina to negotiate allegiance to Muḥammad. His basic condition was always that they should become Muslims.

Towards the end of 629 there was an incident that led to the Meccans breaking the truce. Muḥammad assembled a large expedition and set out to deal with the Meccans once and for all. In the end, there was a negotiated surrender of the city (January 630).

Important though the capture of Mecca was, the region could not be secured without also dealing with the rival town of al-Ṭā'if and the Hawāzin, the large tribal confederation in the centre of whose lands al-Ṭā'if lay. The Muslims inflicted a crushing defeat on the Hawāzin in a pitched battle at Ḥunayn; but an attempt to besiege al-Ṭā'if was as fruitless as the Meccan siege of Medina had been. After only a fortnight the siege was called off, though it was not long before the people of al-Ṭā'if were won over by negotiation. Muḥammad then returned to Mecca and performed the lesser pilgrimage (the *ᶜumra*) and afterwards went back to Medina.

Most of Muḥammad's political activities were now centred on the lengthy process of negotiating with tribal delegations who came from increasingly distant parts of the Arabian peninsula. Political agreements appear to have been relatively easy to reach, but Muḥammad's main concern remained that the new adherents should become proper Muslims, and it became his practice to send Muslims from Medina back with the delegations to instruct them in the new faith.

He made one final expedition at the end of 630. It was to Tabūk, in furtherance of his northern policy. The size of the expedition, the largest he ever mounted, appears to have achieved his main aim, agreements with chiefs as far north as modern ᶜAqaba, without major bloodshed.

Muḥammad left Medina only once more, in March 632, to perform the pilgrimage at Mecca. There are indications that his health was beginning to fail and in June of that year, after a short illness, he died. As far as the Arabian peninsula was concerned he had achieved his goal of bringing the Arabs within the fold of Islam. Most of those outside were to follow shortly.

The Qur'ān

When reading the Qur'ān it is crucial to remember that the text was originally intended to be read aloud and that this is still its most effective form. Recitation to an audience gives the text a dimension that does not come across in silent reading, frequently showing up lines of thought that do not stand out clearly when one peruses the text. Translators often have to tackle this problem by adding to their translations bridging phrases that they normally draw from the numerous, and lengthy, commentaries on the Qur'ān that have been written over the centuries in Arabic.

FORM

In the standard form in which we have it today, the Qur'ān is divided into 114 chapters of very unequal length, called *sūras*. The *sūras* are the working units of the revelation. They are largely composite. All but one (*sūra* 9, which may well be unfinished) begin with the formula *bi-smi llāhi l-raḥmāni l-raḥīmi* 'in the Name of God, the Merciful, the Compassionate'; and in 29 *sūras* this formula is followed by a group of letters of the Arabic alphabet (e.g. *alif*, *lām*, *mīm*, found at the beginning of *sūras* 2, 3, 29, 30, 31 and 32), whose function is unknown but which seem to be of mystical import.

The text was originally revealed in pieces of varying length, most of them apparently containing a relatively short number of verses (*āyas*). There are vivid descriptions of Muḥammad's state during a revelation, but they are too brief for us to work out what happened. For example, an account that is traced back to one of his wives, ᶜA'isha, tells us, 'He was gripped by a spasm, and the sweat ran down him like pearls – and that on a winter's day', but that is all.

The basic revelations then took their places in the working units of the Qur'ān, the *sūras*, in a way which has never been understood. There are traditions that tell us that at Medina he would dictate to scribes and tell them how to arrange the revelations, sometimes inserting a new revelation into an older passage. A simplified and more pious tradition tells us that Gabriel used to go over the revealed text once a year with Muḥammad and that this happened twice during the last year of Muḥammad's life. Revelations are believed to have occurred over a period of years from 610 AD to Muḥammad's death in June 632 AD.

The Qur'ān was originally revealed orally, but in quite early passages it refers to itself as 'the Book', and there is some evidence of pieces being committed to writing whilst Muḥammad was still at Mecca. There is no evidence that he used scribes at Mecca, but in the later years at Medina he appears to have had a group of them, each with a special responsibility for a part of the text. It is not clear what happened to their material after Muḥammad's death, but in comparison with other religions the sacred text moved very quickly towards the form in which we have it today. A single version that rendered void a mass of variants that had arisen through widespread oral transmission was declared to be authoritative by the caliph ᶜUthmān some twenty years after Muḥammad's death, and to a very large extent the only changes that have taken place since that time are connected with the improvements in Arabic script that took place in the eighth century AD.

It has become traditional to divide the *sūras* into four or five periods: Early Meccan, Middle Meccan, Late Meccan and Medinan being the most popular schema. Though there is some justification for this, particularly as far as the Medinan period is concerned, it has two serious drawbacks: many of the *sūras* contain material from at least two periods, and the criteria for classification, particularly for the Middle Meccan and Late Meccan periods, are somewhat vague and impressionistic. Moreover, the groupings by and large ignore the composite nature of the *sūras*.

The grouping that is most widely known and referred to in the West is that of Nöldeke. It is of some use, provided that it is realized that such a grouping can act only as a rough guide and cannot be refined further. It also has to be said that it is no real advance on the traditional Muslim dating, on which it is heavily dependent. With the *sūras* put in numerical order to eliminate some of the pseudo-preciseness, his division of the Meccan *sūras* is:

Early Meccan:	1, 51–53, 55–56, 68–70, 73–75, 77–97, 99–109, 111–114 (48 *sūras*)
Middle Meccan:	15, 17–21, 23, 25–27, 36–38, 43–44, 50, 54, 67, 71–72, 76 (21 *sūras*)
Late Meccan:	6–7, 10–14, 16, 28–32, 34–35, 39–42, 45–46 (21 *sūras*)

It is only with the Medinan *sūras* that one can have any confidence about relating material in the *sūras* to external events. Even then there are a fair number whose position in the list is somewhat doubtful. The most common ordering, again first put forward by Nöldeke, is:

2, 98, 64, 62, 8, 47, 3, 61, 57, 4, 65, 59, 33, 63, 24, 58, 22, 48, 66, 60, 110, 49, 9, 5

(24 *sūras*)

The standard order, i.e. the one used in this printing, appears to have been drawn up precisely to avoid questions of chronology. The first *sūra* is short but ritually important. After that the *sūras* are arranged in rough order of length, from longest to shortest. This puts much of the material that is important for legal purposes early in the arrangement; but it has to be said that many readers find the lack of chronological guidance confusing. This is where an attempted ordering, such as that of Nöldeke set out above, is of some use. However, it is only with some of the Medinan *sūras* that it is possible to relate *sūras* to the events of Muḥammad's life.

STYLE

Stylistically the Qur'ān calls on four main registers that were current in seventh-century Arabia: the clipped, gnomic style of the *kāhins*, the admonitory, exhortative and argumentative style of the *khaṭībs*, the narrative techniques of the storytellers and the dramatic style of some poetry. In the Medinan period the verses containing social legislation appear to approximate to the style used in formal agreements.

It is the accepted view that much of the earliest material has a vigour that is terse and abrupt and that as time passed the terseness and to some extent the abruptness – and the verve – gradually diminished. The style thus broadened, eventually moving to the diffuse expression of the Medinan material. It is not unreasonable to see in this evolution of style differing mixtures of the registers of the soothsayers, preachers and storytellers and the eventual addition of the documentary style. But even the addition of the documentary style does not greatly diminish the oral and rhetorical nature of the other registers that gives the Qur'ān its distinctive linguistic stamp. It is the rhetorical focus that leads to one of the most characteristic features of the Qur'ān: the use of assonance to round off verses. The assonance may change after a few verses or remain constant throughout a longish *sūra*. Its use had almost certainly been made popular by soothsayers and preachers, but the scale of its use in the Qur'ān was new and remarkable. It is most striking in early material, particularly when the verses are short; but it is still effective in the late material at Medina when it may well be rounding off legal material composed in a flat documentary style. Unfortunately, there is no realistic possibility of conveying this feature in translation.

Two points of detail should be noted. Firstly, those reading the Qur'ān only in translation usually find the terse formulation of the early material difficult to follow. In reading this material, it helps if one remembers the oral nature of the revelation. Secondly, it is a point of both content and style that Muḥammad is at the centre of the revelation. In particular, he is the focal point for the dialectic that frequently occurs. Thus it is common to find passages that are introduced by the command 'Say'; and a high proportion of these are answers to clauses beginning 'they ask you' or 'they say', frequently referring to Muḥammad's opponents, sometimes to his followers. See, for example, 17:87: 'They will ask thee concerning the Spirit. Say, "The Spirit is by command of my Lord . . .".'

CONTENT

The central theme of the Qur'ān is the belief in one God, the merciful God who is the Creator of Heaven and Earth and all things and beings therein and whose omnipotence is to be seen everywhere in His signs (*āyāt* [as mentioned above, this word is also used to refer to individual verses of the Qur'ān]). Disobedience will lead to an apocalypse, which will be the prelude to the Day of Judgement. At the Judgement each individual will be judged and the righteous conveyed to Heaven and the unrighteous to Hell. Righteousness requires both belief and general rectitude.

Along with the passages that tell of God and His signs, there are also stories of peoples and prophets. Some of the earliest of these refer to Arabian legends: the destruction of the tribes of *ᶜĀd*, Thamūd and Madyan after they failed to respond to the messages of their prophets (Hūd, Ṣāliḥ and Shuᶜayb respectively). These stories were later to be afforced by other disaster/punishment stories drawn from Old Testament material: Noah and the flood, Lot and his people, and Moses and the Egyptians. In fact, Old Testament stories, often in a guise somewhat different from that in the Bible, dominate much of the narratives of the Qur'ān. Among the best known are: Adam and Eve; the Fall; the disobedience of Satan; Cain and Abel; Abraham; Isaac and Ishmael; Jacob, Joseph and his brothers; Moses, Aaron and the Israelites; Solomon and David; Jonah and Job. By far the most important of these prophetic figures are Moses, the leader who freed the Israelites from the yoke of the Egyptians and led them to the promised land, and Abraham, who, having turned his back on idolatry, built with his son Ishmael the Kaᶜba as a shrine to the one God.

There is much less material from the New Testament and Christian apocryphal sources. Apart from the story of Zacharias and the birth of John the Baptist and some references to the disciples (who are treated as a group and not named individually), the references are to Mary and, above all, to Jesus. The miraculous birth of Jesus is one of the signs of God, and mention is made of his ability to perform miracles such as raising the dead and healing the leper. However, Jesus is basically treated as one in the series of God's prophets, his description as *al-Masīḥ* 'the Messiah' apparently having little special force. The Qur'ān specifically rejects the doctrine of the Trinity (see, in particular, 5:17). It also denies the Crucifixion (4:157) at the beginning of a passage that appears to imply the following sequence of events: apparent death of Jesus, Ascension, and then, at some later time, second coming, natural death and general Resurrection.

There are some parables, but they are of little significance in comparison with the narrative material. The majority are in effect extended similes very similar to a form used with great success in early Arabic poetry (see, for example, 2:17, 2:19, 16:75, 16:112, 18:45, 24:35, 29:41, 30:28, 39:29, 66:10). For the rare longer parables see 14:24–7 (the good and bad trees); 18:32–44 (the two gardens); 36:13–32 (the unbelieving city); and 68:17–33 (the blighted garden).

In addition, *Sūra* 18 includes two stories from the Christian periphery to the north of Arabia: the so-called legend of the Seven Sleepers and extracts from the Alexander romance. There is also material that looks like traditional wisdom literature (cf. the material about Luqmān in *Sūra* 31).

The narratives are crucial in underpinning two doctrines that evolved during the period of revelation: the first, that God had sent a series of believing prophets to their peoples over the ages, all conveying the same message; and the second, that Muḥammad was the last in this series of prophets. Linked to this is the doctrine that Muḥammad is the prophet sent to the Arabs in particular and that his message is in Arabic *lisān ᶜarabiyy mubīn* 'clear Arabic language' (16:103, 26:195), *qur'ān ᶜarabiyy* 'an Arabic recitation' (12:2, 20:113, 41:3, 42:7, 43:3), *lisān ᶜarabiyy* 'Arabic language' (46:12), *ḥukm ᶜarabiyy* 'an Arabic judgement' (13:37).

In addition to biblical stories, there are a number of passages that are obviously parallel. From the Old Testament one may cite Q. 24:50 and Deut. 26:17; Q. 53:45 and 49 and 1 Sam. 2:6–7; Q. 53, 39–42 and Ezek. 18:20; and, at greater length, Q. 17:23–40 and Ex. 20:2–17/Deut. 5: 6–21. There are slightly more passages where the parallel is with the New Testament. See, for example, Q. 2:274 and Matth. 6:3–4; Q. 21:20 and Rev. 4:8; Q. 36:53 and 1 Thess. 4:16; Q. 48:29 and Mark 4:29; and, at greater length, Q. 2:49–64 and Acts 7:36–53. However, in none of these passages is there a close verbal relationship. There is more of that in such Semitic sayings as 'an eye for an eye' etc. (Q. 5:45 and Ex. 21:23–7) and 'before the camel will pass through the eye of a needle' (Q. 7:38 and Matth. 19:24); but it is only in Q. 21:105 'And now, since the Law was given, have we written in the Psalms that "my servants, the righteous, shall inherit the earth"' that we have a close parallel: Psalms 37:29 reads 'The righteous shall inherit the land and shall dwell therein for ever'. Remarkably the previous verse (Q. 21:104) 'On that day we will roll up the heaven as one rolleth up written scrolls' is a fairly close approximation to part of a quite separate verse (Isaiah 34:4) 'and the heavens shall be rolled together as a scroll'. However, by far the most interesting and instructive parallel is between *Sūra* 12 and Genesis 37–47: the story of Joseph. The Quranic narrative, which includes details from the *Midrash* as well as Genesis, may at first seem rather sketchy, but in Arabic terms it is beautifully judged and effective. It is, incidentally, the only longish *sūra* to be devoted to the telling of a single story.

As has been mentioned, exhortation to belief and rectitude is common from the earliest revelations onwards, but after the *hijra* it became necessary to offer more specific guidance on religious and legal matters.

Three of the five Pillars of Islamic faith (*arkān al-dīn*), witness to the one God (*shahāda*), prayer (*ṣalāt*) and alms-giving (*zakāt*), are mentioned in a fairly general way in Meccan material. Medinan material adds some detail about prayer: that it should be towards Mecca (2:142–50); that there should be ritual purification before prayer (4:43, 5:6), and so on, though the specific requirement to pray five times a day is nowhere mentioned. There is more detail on the two Pillars added in Medina, fasting (*ṣawm* 2, 183–5 and 187) and the pilgrimage (*ḥajj*, 2:196–200 and 203). There are passages too numerous to mention about fighting the infidel and the sharing of booty. Disturbances within the community are dealt with in passages on retaliation (e.g. 2:178–9, 4:92–3) and on theft (5:38). A less serious matter, but one dealt with severely, is usury (2:275–80, 3:130). There are regulations on bequests and inheritance (2:180–82, 5:106–8) and the assignment of debts (2:282–4). There are fifteen or so passages about marriage, and others about the position of women in society, of which 4:34 is now thought by many to be problematical. There is regulation of the calendar (9:36–7) and ten passages on food and drink. The two passages commenting on wine are an interesting example of how changes were sometimes gradually introduced, with the latest passage being deemed to abrogate previous ones. *Sūra* 2:219 reads, 'They question thee about strong drink and games of chance. SAY, "In both there is great sin, and utility for men, but the sin of them is greater than their usefulness".' In 5:90–91 this is sharpened to: 'Strong drink and games of chance are an abomination of Satan's handiwork. Avoid [this abomination] so that you may succeed. Satan seeks to cast enmity among you by means of strong drink and games of chance and to turn you from remembrance of God and from prayer.'

SOURCES

Orthodox doctrine renders discussion of the sources of the Qur'ān irrelevant for Muslims: the Qur'ān is the word of God. They are also able to dismiss discrepancies between the Bible and the Qur'ān by recourse to the doctrine that if there are differences between the Jewish, Christian and Muslim versions of the Scripture the Jews and the Christians have mangled the Message and Muslims have not. This doctrinal stance is, however, not without its problems. It is difficult to reconcile the very specific references to, for example, Muḥammad's family (cf., for example, Q. 33:28–33) with the belief that each prophet has received the same message.

For non-Muslims the Muslim standpoint is untenable, and non-Muslim scholars have given much thought to the question of how Muḥammad might have acquired his knowledge of the Bible. The most commonly accepted view is that Muḥammad received most of his information about biblical stories through informants who talked to him; that this material was digested, meditated on and then absorbed into what became the text. There are two passages in the Qur'ān itself that support this view. The first is Q. 16:103: 'We also know that they say, "Surely, a certain person teacheth him". But the tongue of him at whom they hint is foreign while this is in plain Arabic.' Secondly, Q. 25:4 reads: 'And the infidels say "This is a mere fraud of his own devising, and others have helped him with it, who had come hither with outrage and lie".' The allegation of fraud is strongly denied in Q. 25:6: 'Say, "He hath set it down Who knoweth the secrets of Heaven and Earth." '; but the question of help is ignored. It should be added that there is some corroboration in *ḥadīth* that Muḥammad received stories and information from various individuals, including Jews and Christians, and that the material he received from them found its way into Quranic form.

Be that as it may, the question of sources is one where there is an unbridgeable chasm between Muslim and non-Muslim. Tolerance requires us to recognise the chasm and to respect the views of those on the other side, wherever our basic stance may be.

The Qur'ān in English

The Qur'ān was first translated into English in 1649 by Alexander Ross, who based his work on the French version of André du Ryer. The first translation directly into English was that of Sale in 1734. Since that time there have been four important translations by non-Muslim scholars: Rodwell (1861), Palmer (1880), Bell (1937–9) and Arberry (1955); and there have been over thirty translations by Muslims, mainly from the Indian sub-continent. The best and most influential translation by a Muslim is undoubtedly that of a British convert, Muhammad Marmaduke Pickthall, which was first published in 1930. The translation of Ross has little interest other than its position as first in the field, but there is something of value in the others I have mentioned. Given the difficulties associated with translation of the work, all have strengths and weaknesses; but they are all worth consulting, something I would hesitate to say of those that I have not mentioned by name.

The strengths of Rodwell are very much the strengths of a nineteenth-century positivistic approach, which the reader will very soon see. Where he is much better than others is in his cross-referencing to biblical material, information that is crucial to one's understanding of the Qur'ān.

ALAN JONES

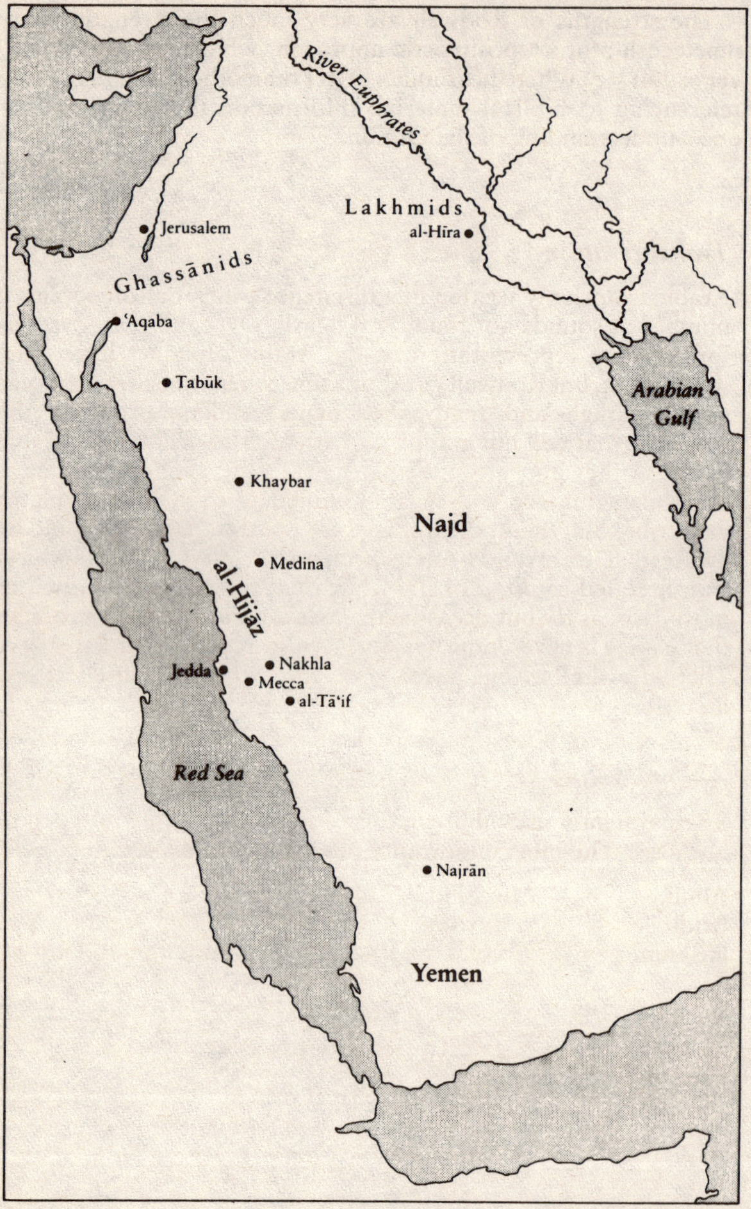
River Euphrates
Lakhmids
al-Hīra
Jerusalem
Ghassānids
ʻAqaba
Tabūk
Arabian Gulf
Khaybar
Najd
Medina
al-Hijāz
Nakhla
Jedda
Mecca
al-Tāʼif
Red Sea
Najrān
Yemen

NOTE ON THE TEXT

Transliteration

Arabic is not only written in a different script; it also contains a number of sounds not found in English. Over the years systems for accurate representation of the Arabic alphabet have been worked out, but Rodwell wrote at a time when transliteration was usually rough and ready. For many readers, probably the majority, that will not matter, and attempts to pronounce Arabic words as they appear on the paper will suffice. Those who have some acquaintance with Arabic script will probably be able to work out what the Arabic form of the word is, but they should be aware that Rodwell is often inconsistent; *ḍād*, for instance, is transliterated as *dh*, *d* or *ds*; while *dhāl* is also transliterated in most cases as *dh* but occasionally as *z*. There is also the problem that *hamza* is never indicated and '*ayn* scarcely ever and then as'. There are similar, but lesser, problems with his Hebrew transliteration.

Abbreviations

Sale frequently uses abbreviations for the sources he refers to in his notes. The most important ones are the following:

Abulf.	=	Abu l-Fidā', *al-Mukhtaṣar*
Beidh.	=	al-Baydāwī, *Commentary on the Qur'ān*
Hishami	=	Ibn Hishām, Biography of the Prophet (*Sīrat al-Nabiyy*)
Itq.	=	al-Suyūtī, *al-Itqān*
Tab.	=	al-Tabarī, *History*
Tirm.	=	al-Tirmidhī, *al-Jāmi*[c] *al-ṣaḥiḥ*
Wah.	=	al-Wāhidī, *Asbāb al-nuzūl*
Waq.	=	al-Wāqidī, *Kitāb al-Maghāzī*
Zam.	=	al-Zamakhsharī, *Commentary on the Qur'ān*

SUGGESTIONS FOR FURTHER READING

The following three books provide a background to the Qur'ān, a translation of the oldest Arabic biography of Muḥammad and an introductory book on Islam. They in turn will suggest further reading.

R. Bell, revised W. M. Watt, *Introduction to the Qur'ān*, Edinburgh 1970

A. Guillaume, *Life of Muhammad*, London 1955 (a translation of the Sīrat Rasūl Allāh of Ibn Ishāq [died 767 AD])

H. A. R. Gibb, *Islam*, London 1950

THE KORAN

SURA[1] I

MECCA – 7 VERSES

In the Name of God, the Compassionate, the Merciful[2]

Praise be to God, Lord of the worlds!
The compassionate, the merciful!
King on the day of reckoning!
Thee *only* do we worship, and to Thee do we cry for help.
Guide Thou us on the straight path,
The path of those to whom Thou hast been gracious; – with whom thou art not angry, and who go not astray.

SURA 2 – THE COW[1]

MEDINA – 286 VERSES

In the Name of God, the Compassionate, the Merciful

Elif. Lam. Mim.[2] No doubt is there about this Book: It is a guidance to the God-fearing,

Who believe in the unseen,[3] who observe prayer, and out of what we have bestowed on them, expend *for God;*

And who believe in what hath been sent down to thee, and in what hath been sent down before thee, and full faith have they in the life to come:

These are guided by their Lord; and with these it shall be well.

As to the infidels, alike is it to them whether thou warn them or warn them not – they will not believe:

Their hearts and their ears hath God sealed up; and over their eyes is a covering. For them, a severe chastisement!

And some[4] there are who say, 'We believe in God, and in the latter day:' Yet are they not believers!

Fain would they deceive God and those who have believed; but they deceive themselves only, and know it not.

Diseased are their hearts! And that disease hath God
increased to them. Theirs a sore chastisement, for that they
treated their *prophet* as a liar!
10 And when it is said to them, 'Cause not disorders in the earth:'
they say, 'Nay, rather do we set them right.'
Is it not that they are themselves the authors of disorder? But
they perceive it not!
And when it is said to them, 'Believe as other men have
believed;' they say, 'Shall we believe as the fools have
believed?' Is it not that they are themselves the fools? But they
know it not!
And when they meet the faithful they say, 'We believe;' but
when they are apart with their Satans[5] they say, 'Verily we hold
with you, and *at them* we only mock.'
God shall mock at them, and keep them long in their
rebellion, wandering in perplexity.
These are they who have purchased error at the price of
guidance: but their traffic hath not been gainful, neither are
they guided at all.
They are like one[6] who kindleth a fire, and when it hath
thrown its light on all around him . . . God taketh away their
light and leaveth them in darkness – they cannot see! –
Deaf, dumb, blind: therefore they shall not retrace their steps
from error!
Or like *those who, when there cometh* a storm-cloud out of
the Heaven, big with darkness thunder and lightning, thrust
their fingers into their ears because of the thunder-clap, for fear
of death! God is round about the infidels.
The lightning almost snatcheth away their eyes! So oft as it
gleameth on them they walk on in it, but when darkness closeth
upon them, they stop! And if God pleased, of their ears and of
their eyes would he surely deprive them: – verily God is
Almighty! O men *of Mecca*[7] adore your Lord, who hath created
you and those who were before you: haply ye will fear Him
20 Who hath made the earth a bed for you, and the heaven a
covering, and hath caused water to come down from heaven,
and by it hath brought forth fruits for your sustenance! Do
not then wittingly give peers to God.
And if ye be in doubt as to that which we have sent down to
our servant, then produce a Sura like it, and summon your
witnesses, beside God, if ye are men of truth:

But if ye do it not, and never shall ye do it, then fear the fire prepared for the infidels, whose fuel is men and stones:[8]

But announce to those who believe and do the things that are right, that for them are gardens 'neath which the rivers flow! So oft as they are fed therefrom with fruit for sustenance, they shall say, 'This same was our sustenance of old:' And they shall have its like given to them.[9] Therein shall they have wives of *perfect* purity, and therein shall they abide for ever.

Verily God is not ashamed to set forth as well the instance of a gnat[10] as of any nobler object: for as to those who have believed, they know it to be the truth from their Lord; but as to the unbelievers, they will say, 'What meaneth God by this comparison?' Many will He mislead by such *parables* and many guide: but none will He mislead thereby except the wicked,

Who, after its establishment, violate the covenant of God,[11] and cut in sunder what God hath bidden to be joined, and act disorderly on the Earth. These are they who shall suffer loss!

How can ye withhold faith from God? Ye were dead and He gave you life; next He will cause you to die; next He will restore you to life: next shall ye return to Him!

He it is who created for you all that is on Earth, then proceeded to the Heaven, and into seven[12] Heavens did He fashion it: and He knoweth all things.

When thy Lord said to the angels, 'Verily, I am about to place one in my stead on earth,'[13] they said, 'Wilt thou place there one who will do ill therein and shed blood, when we celebrate thy praise and extol thy holiness?' God said, 'Verily, I know what ye know not.'

And he taught Adam the names of all things, and then set them before the angels,[14] and said, 'Tell me the names of these, if ye are endued with wisdom.'[15]

30 They said, 'Praise be to Thee! We have no knowledge but what Thou hast given us to know. Thou! Thou art the Knowing, the Wise.'

He said, 'O Adam, inform them of their names.' And when he had informed them of their names, He said, 'Did I not say to you that I know the hidden things of the Heavens and of the Earth, and that I know what ye bring to light, and what ye hide?'

And when we said to the angels, 'Bow down and worship Adam,' then worshipped they all, save Eblis.[16] He refused and swelled with pride, and became one of the unbelievers.

And we said, 'O Adam! dwell thou and thy wife in the Garden, and eat ye plentifully there from wherever ye list; but to this tree come not nigh, lest ye become of the transgressors.'

But Satan[17] made them slip from it, and caused their banishment from the place in which they were. And we said, 'Get ye down, the one of you an enemy to the other: and there shall be for you in the earth a dwelling-place, and a provision for a time.'

And words *of prayer* learned Adam from his Lord: and God turned to him; for He loveth to turn, the Merciful.

We said, 'Get ye down from it, all together: and if Guidance shall come to you from me, whoso shall follow my guidance, on them shall come no fear, neither shall they be grieved:

But they who shall not believe, and treat our signs as falsehoods, these shall be inmates of the fire; in it shall they remain for ever.'

O children of Israel! remember my favour wherewith I shewed favour upon you, and be true to your covenant with me; I will be true to my covenant with you; me therefore, revere me! and believe in what I have sent down confirming your Scriptures, and be not the first to disbelieve it, neither for a mean price barter my signs: me therefore, fear ye me!

And clothe not the truth with falsehood, and hide not the truth when ye know it:[18]

40 And observe prayer and pay the legal impost, and bow down with those who bow.

Will ye enjoin what is right upon others, and forget yourselves? Yet ye read the Book: will ye not understand?

And seek help with patience and prayer: a hard duty indeed is this, but not to the humble,

Who bear in mind that they shall meet their Lord, and that unto Him shall they return.

O children of Israel! remember my favour wherewith I shewed favour upon you; for verily to you above all human beings have I been bounteous.

And fear ye the day when soul shall not satisfy for soul at all, nor shall any intercession be accepted from them, nor shall any ransom be taken, neither shall they be helped.

And *remember* when we rescued you from the people of
Pharaoh, who had laid on you a cruel chastisement. They slew
your male children, and let only your females live: and in this
was a great trial from your Lord:
And when we parted the sea for you, and saved you, and
drowned the people of Pharaoh, while ye were looking on:
And when we were in treaty with Moses forty nights: then
during his absence took ye the calf and acted wickedly:
Yet after this we forgave you, that ye might be grateful:
50 And when we gave Moses the Book and the Illumination[19] in
order to your guidance:
And *remember* when Moses said to his people, 'O my people!
verily ye have sinned to your own hurt, by your taking the calf
to worship it: Be turned then to your creator, and slay the
guilty among you;[20] this will be best for you with your
creator:' Then turned He unto you, for He is the one who
turneth, the Merciful:
And when ye said, 'O Moses! we will not believe thee until we
see God plainly;' the thunderbolt fell upon you while ye were
looking on:
Then we raised you to life after ye had been dead,[21] that
haply ye might give thanks:
And we caused the clouds to overshadow you, and we sent
down manna and quails upon you; – 'Eat of the good things we
have give you for sustenance;' – and they injured not us but they
injured themselves.[22]
And when we said, 'Enter this city,[23] and eat therefrom
plentifully at your will, and enter the gate with prostrations,
and say, "Forgiveness;" and we will pardon you your sins, and
give an increase to the doers of good:' –
But the evil doers changed that word into another than that
spoken to them,[24] and we sent down upon those evil doers
wrath from heaven, for that they had done amiss:
And when Moses asked drink for his people, we said, 'Strike
the rock with thy rod;' and from it there gushed twelve
fountains: each tribe[25] knew their drinking-place: – 'Eat and
drink,' said we, 'of what God hath supplied, and do no wrong
on the earth by licentious deeds:'
And when ye said, 'O Moses! we will not put up with one sort
of food: pray, therefore, thy Lord for us, that He would bring
forth for us of that which the earth groweth, its herbs and its

cucumbers and its garlic and its lentils and its onions:' He said, 'What! will ye exchange that which is worse for what is better? Get ye down into Egypt; – for ye shall have what ye have asked:' Vileness and poverty were stamped upon them, and they returned with wrath from God: This, for that they disbelieved the signs of God, and slew the Prophets[26] unjustly: this, for that they rebelled and transgressed!

Verily, they who believe (Muslims), and they who follow the Jewish religion, and the Christians, and the Sabeites[27] – whoever of these believeth in God and the last day, and doeth that which is right, shall have their reward with their Lord: fear shall not come upon them, neither shall they be grieved.

60 *Call to mind* also when we entered into a covenant with you, and lifted up the mountain[28] over you: – 'Take hold,' *said we*, 'on what we have revealed to you, with resolution, and remember what is therein, that ye may fear:'

But after this ye turned back, and but for God's grace and mercy towards you, ye had surely been of the lost! Ye know too those of you who transgressed on the Sabbath, and to whom we said, 'Be *changed into* scouted apes:'[29]

And we made them a warning to those of their day, and to those who came after them, and a caution to the God-fearing:

And when Moses said to his people, 'Verily, God bids you sacrifice a COW;'[30] they said, 'Makest thou a jest of us?' He said, 'God keep me from being one of the foolish.' They said, 'Call on thy Lord for us that He would make plain to us what she is.' He said, 'God saith, "She is a cow neither old nor young, *but* of the middle age – between *the two:*" do therefore what ye are bidden.'

They said, 'Call on your Lord for us, that he would make plain to us what is her colour.' He said, 'God saith, "She is a fawn-coloured cow; her colour is very bright; she rejoiceth the beholders."'

They said, 'Call on they Lord for us that He would make plain to us what cow it is – for to us are cows alike, – and verily, if God please, we shall be guided rightly:'

He said, 'God saith, "She is a cow not worn by ploughing the earth or watering the field, sound, no blemish in her."' They said, 'Now hast thou brought the truth:' Then they sacrificed her; Yet nearly had they done it not:

And when ye slew a man, and strove among yourselves about

him, God brought to light what he had hidden:

For we said, 'Strike *the corpse* with part of her.' So God giveth life to the dead, and sheweth you his signs, that haply ye may understand.

Then after that your hearts became hard like rocks, or harder still: for verily, from rocks have rivers gushed; others, verily, have been cleft, and water hath issued from them; and others, verily, have sunk down through fear of God: And God is not regardless of your actions.

70 Desire ye then that for your sakes[31] *the Jews* should believe?
Yet a part of them heard the word of God, and then, after they had understood it, perverted it, and knew that they did so.

And when they fall in with the faithful, they say, 'We believe;' but when they are apart[32] one with another, they say, 'Will ye acquaint them with what God hath revealed to you, that they may dispute with you about it in the presence of your Lord?' Understand ye their aim?

Know they not that God knoweth what they hide, as well as what they bring to light?

But there are illiterates among them who are unacquainted with the Book,[33] but with lies only, and have but vague fancies. Woe to those who with their own hands transcribe the Book corruptly, and then say, 'This is from God,' that they may sell it for some mean price! Woe then to them for that which their hands have written! and, Woe to them for the gains which they have made!

And they say, 'Hell fire shall not touch us, but for a few days:'[34] SAY: Have ye received such a promise from God? for God will not revoke his promise: or, Speak ye of God that which ye know not?

But they whose only gains are evil works, and who are environed by their sins, – they shall be inmates of the fire, therein to abide for ever:

But they who have believed and done the things that be right, they shall be the inmates of Paradise, – therein to abide for ever.

And when we entered into covenant with the children of Israel, *we said*, 'Worship none but God, and be good to your parents and kindred, and to orphans, and to the poor, and speak with men what is right, and observe prayer, and pay the stated alms.' Then turned ye away, except a few of you, and withdrew afar off.

And when we made a covenant with you that ye should not

shed your own blood,[35] nor expel one another from your abodes, then ye ratified it and yourselves were witnesses.

Then were ye the very persons who slew one another; and ye drove out a part of your own people from their abodes; ye lent help against them with wrong and hatred; but if they come captives to you, ye redeem them! – Yet it was forbidden you to drive them out.[36] Believe ye then part of the Book, and deny part? But what shall be the meed of him among you who doth this, but shame in this life? And on the day of the Resurrection they shall be sent to the most cruel of torments, for God is not regardless of what ye do.

80 These are they who purchase this present life at the price of that which is to come: their torment shall not be lightened, neither shall they be helped.

Moreover, to Moses gave we 'the Book,' and we raised up apostles after him; and to Jesus, son of Mary, gave we clear proofs *of his mission*, and strengthened him by the Holy Spirit.[37] So oft then as an apostle cometh to you with that which your souls desire not, swell ye with pride, and treat some as imposters, and slay others?

And they say, 'Uncircumcised are our hearts.' Nay! God hath cursed them in their infidelity: few are they who believe!

And when a Book had come to them from God, confirming that which they had received already – although they had before prayed for victory over those who believed not – yet when that Koran come to them, of which they had knowledge, they did not recognise it. The curse of God on the infidels!

For a vile price have they sold themselves, by not believing what God hath sent down, envious of God's sending down his grace on such of his servants as he pleaseth:[38] and they have brought on themselves wrath upon wrath. And for the unbelievers is a disgraceful chastisement.

And when it is said to them, 'Believe in what God hath sent down,' they say, 'In that which hath been sent down to us we believe:' but what hath since been sent down they disbelieve, although it be the truth confirmatory of their own Scriptures. SAY: Why then have ye of old slain God's prophets,[39] if ye are indeed believers?

Moreover, Moses came unto you with proofs of his mission. Then in his absence ye took the calf *for your God*, and did wickedly.

And when we accepted your covenant, and uplifted[40] the mountain over you, *we said*, 'Take firm hold on what we have given you, and hearken.' They said, 'We have hearkened and have rebelled:' then were they made to drink down the calf into their hearts for their ingratitude. SAY: A bad thing hath your faith commanded you, if ye be indeed believers.

SAY: If the future dwelling place with God be specially for you, but not for the rest of mankind, then wish for death, if ye are sincere:

But never can they wish for it, because of that which their own hands have sent on before them![41] And God knoweth the offenders.

90 And thou wilt surely find them of all men most covetous of life, beyond even the polytheists. To be kept alive a thousand years might one of them desire: but that he may be preserved alive, shall no one reprieve himself from the punishment! And God seeth what they do.

SAY: Whoso is the enemy of Gabriel – For he it is who by God's leave hath caused *the Koran* to descend on thy heart, the confirmation of previous revelations, and guidance, and good tidings to the faithful –

Whoso is an enemy to God or his angels, or to Gabriel, or to Michael, *shall have God as his enemy:* for verily God is an enemy to the Infidels.

Moreover, clear signs have we sent down to thee, and none will disbelieve them but the perverse.

Oft as they have formed an engagement *with thee*, will some of them set it aside? But most of them believe not.

And when there came to them an apostle from God, affirming the previous revelations made to them, some of those to whom the Scriptures were given, threw the Book of God behind their backs as if they knew it not:

And they followed what the Satans read in the reign of Solomon: not that Solomon was unbelieving, but the Satans were unbelieving. Sorcery did they teach to men, and what had been revealed to the two angels, Harut and Marut, at Babel.[42] Yet no man did these two teach until they had said, 'We are only a temptation. Be not then an unbeliever.' From these two did men learn how to cause division between man and wife: but unless by leave of God, no man did they harm thereby. They learned, indeed, what would harm and not profit them; and yet they knew that he who bought that art should have no part in the life to come! And vile the price for which they have sold themselves, – if they had but known it!

But had they believed and feared God, better surely would have been the reward from God, – if they had but known it!

O ye who believe! say not to our apostle, 'Raina'[43] (Look at us); but say, 'Ondhorna' (Regard us). And attend to this; for, the Infidels shall suffer a grievous chastisement.

The unbelievers among the people of the Book, and among the idolaters, desire not that any good should be sent down to you from your Lord: but God will shew His special mercy to whom He will, for He is of great bounty.

100 Whatever verses we cancel,[44] or cause thee to forget, we bring a better or its like. Knowest thou not that God hath power over all things?

Knowest thou not that the dominion of the Heavens and of the Earth is God's? and that ye have neither patron nor helper, save God?

Would ye ask of your apostle what of old was asked of Moses? But he who exchangeth faith for unbelief,[45] hath already erred from the even way.

Many of the people of the Book desire to bring you back to unbelief after ye have believed, out of selfish envy, even after the truth hath been clearly shewn them. But forgive them, and shun them till God shall come in with His working. Truly God hath power over all things.

And observe prayer and pay the legal impost:[46] and whatever good thing ye have sent on before for your soul's sake, ye shall find it with God. Verily God seeth what ye do.

And they say, 'None but Jews or Christians shall enter Paradise:' This is their wish. SAY: Give your proofs if ye speak the truth.

But they who set their face with resignation Godward, and do what is right, – their reward is with their Lord; no fear shall come on them, neither shall they be grieved.

Moreover, the Jews say, 'The Christians lean on nought:' 'On nought lean the Jews,' say the Christians: Yet both are readers of the Book. So with like words say they who have no knowledge.[47] But on the resurrection day, God shall judge between them as to that in which they differ.

And who committeth a greater wrong than he who hindereth

God's name from being remembered in his temples, and who hasteth to ruin them?[48] Such men cannot enter them but with fear. Theirs is shame in this world, and a severe torment in the next.

The East and the West is God's: therefore, whichever way ye turn, there is the face of God:[49] Truly God is immense and knoweth all.

110 And they say, 'God hath a son:' No! Praise be to Him! But – His, whatever is in the Heavens and the Earth! All obeyeth Him,

Sole maker of the Heavens and of Earth! And when He decreeth a thing, He only saith to it, 'Be,' and it is.

And they who have no knowledge say, 'Unless God speak to us, or thou shew us a sign . . . !' So, with like words, said those who were before them: their hearts are alike: Clear signs have we already shewn for those who have firm faith:

Verily, with the Truth have we sent thee, a bearer of good tidings and a warner: and of the people of Hell thou shalt not be questioned.

But until thou follow their religion, neither Jews nor Christians will be satisfied with thee. SAY: Verily, guidance of God, – that is the guidance! And if, after 'the Knowledge' which hath reached thee, thou follow their desires, thou shalt find neither helper nor protector against God.

They to whom we have given the Book, and who read it as it ought to be read, – these believe therein: but whoso believeth not therein, shall meet with perdition.

O children of Israel! remember my favour wherewith I have favoured you, and that high above all mankind have I raised you:

And dread the day when not in aught shall soul satisfy for soul, nor shall any ransom be taken from it, nor shall any intercession avail, and they shall not be helped.

When his Lord made trial of Abraham by commands which he fulfilled, He said, 'I am about to make thee an Imâm to mankind:' he said, 'Of my offspring also:' 'My covenant,' said God, 'embraceth not the evil doers.'

And remember when we appointed the Holy House[50] as man's resort and safe retreat, and said, 'Take ye the station of Abraham for a place of prayer:' And we commanded Abraham and Ismael, 'Purify my house for those who shall go in procession round it, and those who shall abide there for devotion, and those who shall bow down and prostrate themselves.'

120 And when Abraham said, 'Lord! make this secure land, and supply its people with fruits, such of them as believe in God and in the last day:' He said, 'And whoso believeth not, for a little while will I bestow good things on him; then will I drive him to the torment of the Fire!' An ill passage!

And when Abraham, with Ismael, raised the foundations[51] of the House, *they said*, 'O our Lord! accept *it* from us; for thou art the Hearer, the Knower.

O our Lord! make us also Muslims, and our posterity a Muslim people; and teach us our holy rites, and be turned towards us, for thou art He who turneth, the Merciful.

O our Lord! raise up among them an apostle[52] who may rehearse thy signs unto them, and teach them "the Book," and Wisdom, and purify them: for thou art the Mighty, the Wise.'

And who but he that hath debased his soul to folly will mislike the faith of Abraham, when we have chosen him in this world, and in the world to come he shall be of the Just?

When his Lord said to him, 'Resign thyself to me,' he said, 'I resign myself to the Lord of the Worlds.'

And this to his children did Abraham bequeath, and Jacob also, *saying*, 'O my children! truly God hath chosen a religion for you; so die not unless ye be also Muslims.'

Were ye present when Jacob was at the point of death?[53] when he said to his sons, 'Whom will ye worship when I am gone?' They said, 'We will worship thy God and the God of thy fathers Abraham and Ismael and Isaac, one God, and to Him are we surrendered (Muslims).'

That people have now passed away; they have the reward of their deeds, and ye shall have the meed of yours: but of their doings ye shall not be questioned.

They say, moreover, 'Become Jews or Christians that ye may have the *true* guidance.' SAY: Nay! the religion of Abraham, the sound in faith,[54] and not one of those who join gods with God!

130 Say ye: 'We believe in God, and that which hath been sent down to us, and that which hath been sent down to Abraham and Ismael and Isaac and Jacob and the tribes: and that which hath been given to Moses and to Jesus, and that which was

given to the prophets from their Lord. No difference do we make between any of them: and to God are we resigned (Muslims).'

If therefore they believe even as ye believe, then have they true guidance; but if they turn back, then do they cut themselves off *from you:* and God will suffice *to protect* thee against them, for He is the Hearer, the Knower.[55]

Islam is the Baptism of God, and who is better to baptise than God? And Him do we serve.

SAY: Will ye dispute with us about God? when He is our Lord and your Lord! We have our works and ye have your works; and we are sincerely His.

Will ye say, 'Verily Abraham, and Ismael, and Isaac, and Jacob, and the tribes, were Jews or Christians?' SAY: Who knoweth best, ye, or God? And who is more in fault than he who concealeth the witness which he hath from God? But God is not regardless of what ye do.

That people have now passed away: they have the reward of their deeds, and for you is the meed of yours; but of their doings ye shall not be questioned.

The foolish ones will say, 'What hath turned them from the kebla which they used?' SAY: The East and the West are God's. He guideth whom he will into the right path.

Thus have we made you a central people,[56] that ye may be witnesses in regard to mankind, and that the apostle may be a witness in regard to you.

We appointed the kebla which thou formerly hadst, only that we might know him who followeth the apostle, from him who turneth on his heels: The change is a difficulty, but not to those whom God hath guided. But God will not let your faith[57] be fruitless; for unto man is God Merciful, Gracious.

We have seen thee turning thy face towards every part of Heaven; but we will have thee turn to a kebla which shall please thee. Turn then thy face towards the sacred Mosque,[58] and wherever ye be, turn your faces towards that part. They, verily, to whom 'the Book' hath been given, know this to be the truth from their Lord: and God is not regardless of what ye do.

140 Even though thou shouldest bring every kind of sign to those who have received the Scriptures, yet thy kebla they will not adopt; nor shalt thou adopt their kebla; nor will one part of them adopt the kebla of the other. And if, after the knowledge

which hath come to thee, thou follow their wishes, verily then wilt thou become of the unrighteous.

They to whom we have given the Scriptures know him – *the apostle* – even as they know their own children: but truly a part of them do conceal the truth, though acquainted with it.[59]

The truth is from thy Lord. Be not then of those who doubt.

All have a quarter of the Heavens to which they turn them; but wherever ye be, hasten emulously after good: God will one day bring you all together; verily, God is all-powerful.

And from whatever place thou comest forth, turn thy face towards the sacred Mosque; for this is the truth from thy Lord; and God is not inattentive to your doings.

And from whatever place thou comest forth, turn thy face towards the sacred Mosque; and wherever ye be, to that part turn your faces, lest men have cause of dispute against you: but as for the impious among them, fear them not; but fear me, that I may perfect my favours on you, and that ye may be guided aright.

And we sent to you an apostle from among yourselves to rehearse our signs unto you, and to purify you, and to instruct you in 'the Book,' and in the wisdom, and to teach you that which ye knew not:

Therefore remember me: I will remember you; and give me thanks and be not ungrateful.

O ye who believe! seek help with patience and with prayer, for God is with the patient.

And say not of those who are slain on God's path[60] that they are Dead; nay, they are Living! But ye understand not.

150 With somewhat of fear and hunger, and loss of wealth, and
lives, and fruits, will we surely prove you: but bear good tidings to the patient,

Who when a mischance chanceth them, say, 'Verily we are God's, and to Him shall we return:'[61]

On them shall be blessings from their Lord, and mercy: and these! – they are the rightly guided.

Verily, Safa and Marwah[62] are among the monuments of God: whoever then maketh a pilgrimage to the temple, or visiteth it, shall not be to blame if he go round about them both. And as for him who of his own accord doeth what is good – God is Grateful, Knowing.

They who conceal aught that we have sent down, either of

clear proof or of guidance, after what we have so clearly shewn to men in the Book,[63] God shall curse them, and they who curse shall curse them.

But as for those who turn to me, and amend and make known the truth, even unto them will I turn me, for I am He who Turneth, the Merciful.

Verily, they who are infidels and die infidels, – these! upon them shall be the malison of God and of angels and of all men:

Under it shall they remain for ever: their torment shall not be lightened, and God will not even look upon them!

Your God is one God:[64] there is no God but He, the Compassionate, the Merciful.

Assuredly in the creation of the Heavens and of the Earth; and in the alternation of night and day; and in the ships which pass through the sea with what is useful to man; and in the rain which God sendeth down from Heaven, giving life by it to the earth after its death, and by scattering over it all kinds of cattle; and in the change of the winds, and in the clouds that are made to do service between the Heaven and the Earth; – are signs for those who understand.

160 Yet there are men who take to them idols along with God, and
love them with the love of God: But stronger in the faithful is the love of God. Oh! the impious will see, when they see their chastisement, that all power is God's, and that God is severe in chastising.

When those who have had followers[65] shall declare themselves clear from their followers after that they have seen the chastisement, and when the ties between them shall be cut asunder;

The followers shall say, 'Could we but return to life we would keep ourselves clear from them, as they have declared themselves clear of us.' So will God shew them their works! Sighing is upon them! but, forth from the fire they come not.

Oh men! eat of that which is lawful *and* good on the earth, but follow not the steps of Satan, for he is your avowed enemy:

He only enjoineth you evil and wickedness, and that ye should aver of God that which ye know not.

And when it is said to them, 'Follow ye that which God hath sent down;' they say, 'Nay, we follow the usages which we found with our fathers.' What! though their fathers were utterly ignorant and devoid of guidance?

The infidels resemble him who shouteth aloud to one who heareth no more than a call and cry! Deaf, dumb, blind: therefore they have no understanding.

Oh ye who believe! eat of the good things with which we have supplied you, and give God thanks if ye are His worshippers.

But that which dieth of itself, and blood, and swine's flesh, and that over which any other name than that of God hath been invoked, is forbidden you. But he who shall partake of them by constraint, without lust or wilfulness, no sin shall be upon him. Verily God is Indulgent, Merciful.

They truly who hide the Scriptures which God hath sent down, and barter them for a mean price – these shall swallow into their bellies nought but fire. God will not speak to them, or assoil them, on the day of the Resurrection: and theirs shall be a grievous torment.

170 These are they who have bartered guidance for error, and pardon for torment; But how great their endurance in fire!

This *shall be their doom*, because God had sent down 'the Book' with the very truth. And verily they who dispute about that Book are in a far-gone severance *from it*.

There is no piety in turning your faces towards the east or the west, but he is pious who believeth in God, and the last day, and the angels, and the Scriptures, and the prophets; who for the love of God disburseth his wealth to his kindred, and to the orphans, and the needy, and the wayfarer, and those who ask, and for ransoming; who observeth prayer, and payeth the legal alms, and who is of those who are faithful to their engagements when they have engaged in them, and patient under ills and hardships, and in time of trouble: these are they who are just, and these are they who fear the Lord.

O believers! retaliation for bloodshedding is prescribed to you: the free man for the free, and the slave for the slave, and the woman for the woman: but he to whom his brother shall make any remission,[66] is to be dealt with equitably; and to him should he pay a fine with liberality.

This is a relaxation[67] from your Lord and a mercy. For him who after this shall transgress,[68] a sore punishment!

But in this law of retaliation is your *security for* life, O men of understanding! to the intent that ye may fear God.

It is prescribed to you, when any one of you is at the point of death, if he leave goods, that he bequeath equitably to his parents and kindred. This is binding on those who fear God. But as for him who after he hath heard the bequest shall change it, surely the wrong of this shall be on those who change it: verily, God Heareth, Knoweth.

But he who feareth from the testator any mistake or wrong, and shall make a settlement between the parties – that shall be no wrong in him: verily, God is Lenient, Merciful.

O believers! a Fast is prescribed to you as it was prescribed to those before you, that ye may fear God,

180 For certain days. But he among you who shall be sick, or on a journey, *shall fast* that same number of other days: and as for those who are able *to keep it and yet break it*, the expiation of this shall be the maintenance of a poor man. And he who of his own accord performeth a good work, shall derive good from it: and good shall it be for you to fast – if ye knew it.

As to the month Ramadhan in which the Koran was sent down to be man's guidance, and an explanation of that guidance, and of that illumination,[69] as soon as any one of you observeth the moon, let him set about the fast; but he who is sick, or upon a journey, shall fast a like number of other days. God wisheth you ease, but wisheth not your discomfort, and that you fulfil the number *of days*, and that you glorify God for his guidance, and that you be thankful.

And when my servants ask thee concerning me, then will I be nigh unto them. I will answer the cry of him that crieth, when he crieth unto me: but let them hearken unto me, and believe in me, that they may proceed aright.

You are allowed on the night of the fast to approach your wives: they are your garment and ye are their garment.[70] God knoweth that ye defraud yourselves therein, so He turneth unto you and forgiveth you! Now, therefore, go in unto them with full desire for that which God hath ordained for you; and eat and drink until ye can discern a white thread from a black thread[71] by the daybreak: then fast strictly till night, and go not in unto them, but rather pass the time in the Mosques. These are the bounds set up by God: therefore come not near them. Thus God maketh his signs clear to men that they may fear Him.[72]

Consume not your wealth among yourselves in vain things, nor present it to judges that ye may consume a part of other men's wealth unjustly, while ye know *the sin which ye commit*.

They will ask thee of the new moons. SAY: They are periods fixed for man's *service* and for the Pilgrimage. There is no piety in entering your houses at the back,[73] but piety consists in the fear of God. Enter your houses then by their doors; and fear God that it may be well with you.

And fight for the cause of God against those who fight against you: but commit not the injustice of attacking them first: God loveth not such injustice:

And kill them wherever ye shall find them, and eject them from whatever place they have ejected you; for civil discord[74] is worse than carnage: yet attack them not at the sacred Mosque, unless they attack you therein; but if they attack you, slay them. Such the reward of the infidels.

But if they desist, then verily God is Gracious, Merciful.

Fight therefore against them until there be no more civil discord, and the only worship be that of God: but if they desist, then let there be no hostility, save against the wicked.

190 The sacred month and the sacred precincts are under the
safeguard of reprisals:[75] whoever offereth violence to you, offer
ye the like violence to him, and fear God, and know that God is
with those who fear Him.

Give freely for the cause of God, and throw not yourselves with your own hands into ruin; and do good, for God loveth those who do good.

Accomplish the Pilgrimage and the Visitation[76] of the holy places *in honour* of God: and if ye be hemmed in *by foes, send* whatever offering shall be the easiest: and shave not your heads until the offering reach the place of sacrifice. But whoever among you is sick, or hath an ailment of the head, must satisfy by fasting, or alms, or an offering. And when ye are safe *from foes*, he who contents himself with the Visitation of the holy places, until the Pilgrimage, *shall bring* whatever offering shall be the easiest. But he who findeth nothing *to offer*, shall fast three days in the Pilgrimage itself, and seven days when ye return: they shall be ten days in all. This is binding on him whose family shall not be present at the sacred Mosque. And fear God, and know that God is terrible in punishing.

Let the Pilgrimage be made in the months already known:[77] whoever therefore undertaketh the Pilgrimage therein, let him not know a woman, nor transgress, nor wrangle in the Pilgrimage. The good which ye do, God knoweth it. And provide *for your journey;* but the best provision is the fear of God: fear me, then, O men of understanding!

It shall be no crime in you if ye seek an increase from your Lord;[78] and when ye pour swiftly on from Arafat, then remember God near the holy monument; and remember Him, because He hath guided you who before this were of those who went astray:

Then pass on quickly[79] where the people quickly pass, and ask pardon of God, for God is Forgiving, Merciful.

And when ye have finished your holy rites, remember God as ye remember your own fathers, or with a yet more intense remembrance! Some men there are who say, 'O our Lord! give us *our portion* in this world:' but such shall have no portion in the next life:

And some say, 'O our Lord! give us good in this world and good in the next, and keep us from the torment of the fire.'

They shall have the lot which they have merited: and God is swift to reckon.

Bear God in mind during the stated days: but if any haste away[80] in two days, it shall be no fault in him: And if any tarry longer, it shall be no fault in him, if he fear God. Fear God, then, and know that to Him shall ye be gathered.

200 A man there is who surpriseth thee by his discourse concerning this life present. He taketh God to witness what is in his heart; yet is he the most zealous in opposing thee:

And when he turneth his back on thee, he runneth through the land to enact disorders therein, and layeth waste the fields and flocks: but God loveth not the disorder.

And when it is said to him, 'Fear God,' the pride of sin seizeth him: but he shall have his fill of Hell; and right wretched the couch!

A man, too, there is who selleth his very self out of desire to please God: and God is good to his servants.

O believers! enter completely into the true religion, and follow not the steps of Satan, for he is your declared enemy.

But if ye lapse after that our clear signs[81] have come to you, know that God is Mighty, Wise.

What can such expect but that God should come down to them overshadowed with clouds, and the angels also, and their doom be sealed? And to God shall all things return.

Ask the children of Israel how many clear signs we have

given. But if any man shall alter the boon[82] of God after it shall have reached him, assuredly God will be vehement in punishing *him*.

This present life is prepared for those who believe not, and who mock at the faithful. But they who fear God shall be above them on the day of resurrection; and God is bounteous without measure to whom He will.

Mankind was but one people;[83] and God sent prophets to announce glad tidings and to warn; and He sent down with them the Book of Truth, that it might decide the disputes of men; and none disputed but those to whom the Book had been given, after the clear tokens had reached them, – being full of mutual jealousy. And God guided those who believed to the truth of that about which, by his permission, they had disputed; for God guideth whom he pleaseth into the straight path.

210 Think ye to enter Paradise, when no such things have come upon you, as on those who flourish before you? Ills and troubles tried them; and so tossed were they by trials, that the Apostle and they who shared his faith, said, 'When will the help of God come?' – Is not the help of God nigh?

They will ask thee what they shall bestow in alms. SAY: Let the good which ye bestow be for parents, and kindred, and orphans, and the poor, and the wayfarer; and whatever good ye do, of a truth God knoweth.

War is prescribed to you: but from this ye are averse.

Yet haply ye are averse from a thing, though it be good for you, and haply ye love a thing though it be bad for you: And God knoweth; but ye, ye know not.

They will ask thee concerning war in the Sacred Month. SAY: To war therein is bad, but to turn aside from the cause of God, and to have no faith in Him, and in the Sacred Temple, and to drive out its people, is worse in the sight of God; and civil strife is worse than bloodshed. They will not cease to war against you until they turn you from your religion, if they be able: but whoever of you shall turn from his religion and die an infidel, their works shall be fruitless in this world, and in the next: they shall be consigned to the fire; therein to abide for aye.

But they who believe, and who fly their country, and fight in the cause of God may hope for God's mercy: and God is Gracious, Merciful.

They will ask thee concerning wine[84] and games of

chance. SAY: In both is great sin, and advantage also, to men; but their sin is greater than their advantage. They will ask thee also what they shall bestow in alms:

SAY: What ye can spare. Thus God sheweth you his signs that ye may ponder

On this present world, and on the next. They will also ask thee concerning orphans. SAY: Fair dealing with them is best;

But if ye mix yourselves up (in their affairs) – they are your brethren: God knoweth the foul dealer from the fair: and, if God pleased, he could indeed afflict you! Verily, God is Mighty, Wise.

220 Marry not idolatresses until they believe; a slave who believeth is better than an idolatress, though she please you more. And wed not your daughters to idolaters until they believe; for a slave who is a believer, is better than an idolater, though he please you.

They invite to the Fire; but God inviteth to Paradise, and to pardon, if he so will, and maketh clear his signs to men that they may remember.

They will also question thee as to the courses of women. SAY: They are a pollution. Separate yourselves therefore from women and approach them not, until they be cleansed. But when they are cleansed, go in unto them as God hath ordained for you. Verily God loveth those who turn *to Him*, and loveth those who seek to be clean.

Your wives are your field: go in, therefore, to your field as ye will; but do first some act for your souls' good: and fear ye God, and know that ye must meet Him; and bear these good tidings to the faithful.

Swear not by God, when ye make oath, that ye will be virtuous and fear God, and promote peace among men; for God is He who Heareth, Knoweth.

God will not punish you for a mistake in your oaths: but He will punish you for that which your hearts have done. God is Gracious, Merciful.

They who intend to abstain from their wives shall wait four months; but if they go back from their purpose, then verily God is Gracious, Merciful:

And if they resolve on a divorce, then verily God is He who Heareth, Knoweth.

The divorced shall wait the result, until they have had their courses thrice, nor ought they to conceal what God hath created in their wombs, if they believe in God and the last day; and it will be more just in their husbands to bring them back when in this state, if they desire what is right. And it is for the women to act as they (the husbands) act by them, in all fairness; but the men are a step above them. God is Mighty, Wise.

Ye may divorce your wives twice: Keep them honourably, or put them away with kindness. But it is not allowed you to appropriate to yourselves aught of what ye have given to them, unless both fear that they cannot keep within the bounds[85] set up by God. And if ye fear that they cannot observe the ordinances of God, no blame shall attach to either of you for what the wife shall herself give for her redemption. These are the bounds of God: therefore overstep them not; for whoever oversteppeth the bounds of God, they are evil doers.

230 But if the husband divorce her *a third time*, it is not lawful for
him to take her again, until she shall have married another husband; and if he also divorce her, then shall no blame attach to them if they return to each other, thinking that they can keep within the bounds fixed by God. And these are the bounds of God; He maketh them clear to those who have knowledge.

But when ye divorce women, and the time for sending them away is come, either retain them with generosity, or put them away with generosity: but retain them not by constraint so as to be unjust towards them. He who doth so, doth in fact injure himself. And make not the signs of God a jest; but remember God's favour towards you, and the Book and the Wisdom which He hath sent down to you for your warning, and fear God, and know that God's knowledge embraceth everything.

And when ye divorce your wives, and they have waited the prescribed time, hinder them not from marrying their husbands when they have agreed among themselves in an honourable way. This warning is for him among you who believeth in God and in the last day. This is most pure for you, and most decent. God knoweth, but ye know not.

Mothers, when divorced, shall give suck to their children two full years,[86] if the father desire that the suckling be completed; and such maintenance and clothing as is fair for them, shall devolve on the father. No person shall be charged beyond his means. A mother shall not be pressed unfairly for her child, nor a father for his child: And the same with the father's heir. But if they choose to wean the child by consent and by bargain, it shall be no fault in them. And if ye choose to have a nurse for your children, it shall be no fault in you, in case ye pay what ye promised her according to that which is fair. Fear God, and know that God seeth what ye do.

If those of you who die leave wives, they must await their state during four months and ten days; and when this their term is expired, you shall not be answerable for the way in which they shall dispose of themselves fairly. And God is cognisant of what ye do.

And then shall no blame attach to you in making proposals of marriage[87] to such women, or in keeping such intention to yourselves? God knoweth that ye will not forget them. But promise them not in secret, unless ye speak honourable words;

And resolve not on the marriage tie until the prescribed time be reached; and know that God knoweth what is in your minds: therefore, beware of Him; and know that God is Gracious, Mild!

It shall be no crime in you if ye divorce your wives so long as ye have not consummated the marriage, nor settled any dowry on them. And provide what is needful for them – he who is in ample circumstances according to his means, and he who is straitened, according to his means – with fairness: This is binding on those who do what is right.

But if ye divorce them before consummation, and have already settled a dowry on them, *ye shall give them* half of what ye have settled, unless they make a release, or he make a release in whose hand is the marriage tie. But if ye make a release, it will be nearer to piety. And forget not generosity in your relations one towards another; for God beholdeth your doings.

Observe strictly the prayers, and the middle[88] prayer, and stand up full of devotion towards God.

240 And if you have any alarm, then *pray* on foot or riding: but
when you are safe, then remember God, how he hath made you
to know what ye knew not.

And[89] such of you as shall die and leave wives, shall bequeath their wives a year's maintenance without causing them to quit their homes; but if they quit them *of their own accord*, then no blame shall attach to you for any disposition they may make of themselves in a fair way. And God is Mighty, Wise.

And for the divorced let there be a fair provision. This is a duty in those who fear God.

Thus God maketh his signs clear to you that ye may understand.

Hast thou not thought on those who quitted their dwellings – and they were thousands – for fear of death?[90] God said to them, 'Die:' then He restored them to life, for full of bounty towards man is God. But most men give not thanks!

Fight for the cause of God; and know that God is He who Heareth, Knoweth.

Who is he that will lend to God a goodly loan? He will double it to him again and again: God is close, but open handed also: and to Him shall ye return.

Has thou not considered[91] the assembly of the children of Israel after *the death of* Moses, when they said to a prophet of theirs, 'Set up for us a king; we will do battle for the cause of God?' He said, 'May it not be that if to fight were ordained you, ye would not fight?' They said, 'And why should we not fight in the cause of God, since we and our children are driven forth from our dwellings?' But when fighting was commanded them, they turned back, save a few of them: But God knew the offenders!

And their prophet said to them, 'Now hath God set (Talout) Saul king over you.' They said, 'How shall he reign over us, when we are more worthy of the kingdom than he, and of wealth he hath no abundance?' He said, 'Verily God hath chosen him to be over you, and hath given him increase in knowledge and stature; God giveth his kingdom to whom he pleaseth; and God is Liberal, Knowing!'

And their prophet said to them, 'Verily, the sign of his kingship shall be that the Ark shall come to you: in it is a pledge of security[92] from your Lord and the relics[93] left by the family of Moses, and the family of Aaron; the angels shall bear it: Truly herein shall be a sign indeed to you if ye are believers.'

250 And when Saul marched forth with his forces, he said, 'God will test you by a river: He who drinketh of it shall not be of my band; but he who shall not taste it, drinking a drink out of the hand excepted, shall be of my band.'[94] And, except a few of them, they drank of it. And when they had passed it, he and those who believed with him, the *former* said, 'We have no strength this day against (Djalout) Goliath and his forces:' But they who held it as certain that they must meet God, said, 'How oft, by God's will, hath a small host vanquished a numerous host! and God is with the steadfastly enduring.'

And when they went forth against Goliath and his forces, they said, 'O our Lord! pour out steadfastness upon us, and set our feet firm, and help us against the infidels!'

And by the will of God they routed them; and (Daood) David slew Goliath; and God gave him the kingship and wisdom, and taught him according to His will: and were it not for the restraint of one by means of the other, imposed on men by God, verily the earth had been utterly corrupted. But God is bounteous to his creatures.

Such are the signs of God: with truth do we rehearse them to thee, for one of the Sent Ones art Thou.

Some of the apostles we have endowed more highly than others: Those to whom God hath spoken, He hath raised to the loftiest grade, and to Jesus the Son of Mary we gave manifest signs, and we strengthened him with the Holy Spirit.[95] And if God had pleased, they who came after them would not have wrangled, after the clear signs had reached them. But into disputes[96] they fell: some of them believed, and some were infidels; yet if God had pleased, they would not have thus wrangled: but God doth what he will.

O Believers! give alms of that with which we have supplied you, before the day cometh when there shall be no trafficking, nor friendship, nor intercession. And the infidels are the wrong-doers.

God! There is no God but He; the Living, the Eternal; Nor slumber seizeth Him, nor sleep; His, whatsoever is in the Heavens and whatsoever is in the Earth! Who is he that can intercede with Him but by His own permission? He knoweth what *hath been* before them and what *shall be* after them; yet nought of His knowledge shall they grasp, save what He willeth. His Throne reacheth over the Heavens and the Earth, and the upholding of both burdeneth Him not; and He is the High, the Great!

Let there be no compulsion in Religion.[97] Now is the right way made distinct from error. Whoever therefore shall deny Thagout[98] and believe in God – he will have taken hold on a strong handle that shall not be broken: and God is He who Heareth, Knoweth.

God is the patron of believers: He shall bring them out of darkness into light:

As to those who believe not, their patrons are Thagout: they shall bring them out of light into darkness: they shall be given over to the fire: they shall abide therein for ever.

260 Hast thou not thought on him[99] who disputed with Abraham
about his Lord, because God had given him the kingdom?
When Abraham said, 'My Lord is He who maketh alive and
causeth to die:' He said, 'It is I who make alive and cause to
die!' Abraham said, 'Since God bringeth the sun from the
East, do thou, then, bring it from the West.' The infidel was
confounded; for God guideth not the evil doers:

Or how he[100] *demeaned him* who passed by a city which had been laid in ruins.[101] 'How,' said he, 'shall God give life to this city, after she hath been dead?' And God caused him to die for an hundred years, and then raised him to life. *And God* said, 'How long hast thou waited?' He said, 'I have waited a day or part of a day.' He said, 'Nay, thou hast waited an hundred years. Look on thy food and thy drink; they are not corrupted; and look on thine ass: we would make thee a sign unto men: And look on the bones *of thine ass*, how we will raise them, then clothe them with flesh.' And when this was shewn to him, he said, 'I acknowledge that God hath power to do all things.'

When Abraham said, 'O Lord, shew me how thou wilt give life to the dead!' He said, 'Hast thou not believed?' He said, 'Yes; but I have asked thee, that my heart may be well assured.' He said, 'Take, then, four birds,[102] and draw them towards thee, and cut them in pieces; then place a part of them on every mountain; then call them and they shall come swiftly to thee: and know thou that God is Mighty, Wise!'

The likeness of those who expend their wealth for the cause of God, is that of a grain of corn which produceth seven ears, and in each ear a hundred grains; and God will multiply to whom He pleaseth: God is Liberal, Knowing!

They who expend their wealth for the cause of God, and never follow what they have laid out with reproaches or harm, shall have their reward with their Lord; no fear shall come upon them, neither shall they be put to grief.

A kind speech and forgiveness is better than alms followed by injury. God is Rich, Clement.

O ye who believe! make not your alms void by reproaches and injury, like him who spendeth his substance to be seen of men, and believeth not in God and in the latter day. The likeness of such an one is that of a rock with a thin soil upon it, on which a heavy rain falleth but leaveth it hard: No profit from their work shall they be able to gain; for God guideth not the unbelieving people.

And the likeness of those who expend their substance from a desire to please God, and for the stablishing of their souls, is as a garden on a hill, on which the heavy rain falleth, and it yieldeth its fruits twofold; and even if a heavy rain fall not on it, yet is there a dew: God beholdeth your actions.

Desireth any one of you a garden of palms and vines through which rivers flow, in which he may have every fruit, and that old age should surprise him *there*, and that his offspring should be weakly, and that then a fiery violent wind shall strike it so that it shall be burned? Thus God maketh plain his signs to you that ye may reflect.

O ye who believe! bestow alms of the good things which ye
have acquired, and of that which we have brought forth for you
out of the earth, and choose not the bad for almsgiving,
270 Such as ye would accept yourselves only by connivance: and
know that God is Rich, Praiseworthy.

Satan menaceth you with poverty,[103] and enjoineth base actions: but God promiseth you pardon from himself and abundance: God is All-bounteous, Knowing.

He giveth wisdom to whom He will: and he to whom wisdom is given, hath had much good given him; but none will bear it in mind, except the wise of heart.

And whatever alms ye shall give, or whatever vow ye shall vow, of a truth God knoweth it: but they who act unjustly shall have no helpers. Give ye your alms openly?[104] it is well. Do ye conceal them and give them to the poor? This, too, will be of advantage to you, and will do away your sins: and God is cognisant of your actions.

Their guidance is not thine affair, O *Muhammad;* but God guideth whom he pleaseth. And the good that ye shall give in alms shall redound unto yourselves; and ye shall not give but as seeking the face of God; and whatever good thing ye shall have given in alms, shall be repaid you, and ye shall not be wronged. There are among you the poor, who being shut up to fighting for the cause of God, have it not in their power to strike out into the earth *for riches*. Those who know them not, think them rich because of their modesty. By this their token thou shalt know them – they ask not of men with importunity: and of whatever good thing ye shall give them in alms, of a truth God will take knowledge.

They who give away their substance in alms, by night and day, in private and in public, shall have their reward with their Lord: no fear shall come on them, neither shall they be put to grief.

They who swallow down usury, shall arise in the resurrection only as he ariseth whom Satan hath infected by his touch. This, for that they say, 'Selling is only the like of usury:' and yet God hath allowed selling, and forbidden usury. He then who when this warning shall come to him from his Lord, abstaineth, shall have pardon for the past, and his lot shall be with God. But they who return *to usury*, shall be given over to the fire; therein shall they abide for ever.

God will bring usury to nought, but will increase alms with usury, and God loveth no infidel, or evil person. But they who believe and do the things that are right, and observe the prayers, and pay the legal impost, they shall have their reward with their Lord: no fear shall come on them, neither shall they be put to grief.

O believers! fear God and abandon your remaining usury, if ye are indeed believers.

But if ye do it not, then hearken for war on the part of God and his apostle: yet if ye repent, ye shall have the principal of your money. Wrong not, and ye shall not be wronged.

280 If any one find difficulty in discharging a debt, then let there be a delay until it be easy for him: but if ye remit it as alms it will be better for you, if ye knew it.

Fear the day wherein ye shall return to God: then shall every soul be rewarded according to its desert, and none shall have injustice done to them.

O ye who believe! when ye contract a debt (payable) at a fixed date, write it down, and let the notary faithfully note between you: and let not the notary refuse to note, even as God hath taught him; but let him note it down, and let him who oweth the debt dictate, and let him fear God his Lord, and not diminish aught thereof. But if he who oweth the debt be foolish or weak, or be not able to dictate himself, let his friend dictate for him with fairness; and call to witness two witnesses of your people: but if there be not two men, let there be a man, and two women of those whom ye shall judge fit for witnesses: if the one of them should mistake, the other may cause her to recollect. And the witnesses shall not refuse, whenever they shall be summoned. And disdain not to put *the debt* in writing, be it large or small, with its time of payment: this will be more just for you in the sight of God, better suited for witnessing, and the best for avoiding doubt. But if the goods be there present, and ye pass them from hand to hand – then it shall be no fault in you not to write it down. And have witnesses when ye sell, and harm not writer or witness: it will be a crime in you to do this. But fear God and God will give you knowledge, for God hath knowledge of all things.

And if ye be on a journey and shall find no notary, let pledges be taken: but if one of you trust the other, let him who is trusted, restore what he is trusted with, and fear God his Lord. And refuse not to give evidence. He who refuseth is surely wicked at heart: and God knoweth your deeds.

Whatever is in the Heavens and in the Earth is God's: and whether ye bring forth to light what is in your minds or conceal it, God will reckon with you for it; and whom He pleaseth will He forgive, and whom He pleaseth will He punish; for God is All-powerful.

The apostle believeth in that which hath been sent down from his Lord, as do the faithful also. Each one believeth in God, and His Angels, and His Books, and His Apostles: we make no distinction between any of His Apostles.[105] And they say, 'We have heard and we obey. Thy mercy, Lord! for unto thee must we return.'

God will not burden any soul beyond its power. It shall enjoy the good which it hath acquired, and shall bear the evil for the acquirement of which it laboured. O our Lord! punish us not if we forget, or fall into sin; O our Lord! and lay not on us a load like that which thou hast laid on those who have been before us; O our Lord! and lay not on us that for which we have not strength: but blot out our sins and forgive us, and have pity on us. Thou art our protector: give us victory therefore over the infidel nations.

SURA 3 – THE FAMILY OF IMRAN[1]

MEDINA – 200 VERSES

In the Name of God, the Compassionate, the Merciful

Elif. Lam. Mim.[2] God! there is no god but He, the Living, the Merciful!

In truth hath He sent down to thee 'the Book,' which confirmeth those which precede it: For He had sent down the Law, and the Evangel aforetime, as man's Guidance; and now hath He sent down the 'Illumination.'[3] (Furkan.)

Verily for those who believe not in the signs of God, *is* a severe chastisement! And God is Mighty, the Avenger!

God! nought that is in Earth or that is in Heaven, is hidden unto Him. He it is who formeth you in your mothers' wombs. There is no god but He; the Mighty, the Wise!

He it is who hath sent down to thee 'the Book.' Some of its signs are of themselves perspicuous; – these are the basis[4] of the Book – and others are figurative. But they whose hearts are given to err, follow its figures, craving discord, craving an interpretation; yet none knoweth its interpretation but God. And the stable in knowledge say, 'We believe in it: it is all from our Lord.' But none will bear this in mind, save men endued with understanding.

O our Lord! suffer not our hearts to go astray after that thou hast once guided us, and give us mercy from before thee; for verily thou art He who giveth.

O our Lord! For the day of whose coming there is not a doubt, thou wilt surely gather mankind together. Verily, God will not fail the promise.

As for the infidels, their wealth, and their children, shall avail them nothing against God. They shall be fuel for the fire.

After the wont of the people of Pharaoh, and of those who went before them, they treated our signs as falsehoods. Therefore God laid hold of them in their sins; and God is severe in punishing!

10 Say to the infidels: ye shall be worsted, and to Hell shall ye be gathered together; and wretched the couch!

Ye have already had a sign[5] in the meeting of the two hosts. The one host fought in the cause of God, and the other was infidel. To their own eyesight, the infidels saw you twice as many as themselves: And God aided with his succour whom He would: And in this truly was a lesson for men endued with discernment.

Fair-seeming to men is the love of pleasures from women and children, and the treasured treasures of gold and silver, and horses of mark, and flocks, and cornfields! Such the enjoyment of this world's life. But God! goodly the home with Him.

SAY: Shall I tell you of better things than these, prepared for those who fear God, in His presence? Theirs shall be gardens, beneath whose *pavilions* the rivers flow, and in which shall they abide for aye: and wives of stainless purity, and acceptance with God: for God regardeth his servants –

Who say, 'O our Lord! we have indeed believed; pardon us our sins, and keep us from the torment of the fire;' –

The patient, and the truthful, the lowly, and the charitable, and they who seek pardon at each daybreak.

God witnesseth that there is no god but He: and the angels, and men endued with knowledge, stablished in righteousness, *proclaim* 'There *is* no god but He, the Mighty, the Wise!'

The true religion with God is Islam: and they to whom the Scriptures had been given, differed not till after 'the knowledge'[6] had come to them, and through mutual jealousy. But as for him who shall not believe in the signs of God – God will be prompt to reckon *with him!*

If they shall dispute with thee, then SAY: I have surrendered myself to God, as have they who follow me.

SAY to those who have received the Book, and to the common folk, Do ye surrender yourselves unto God?[7] If they become Muslims, then are they guided aright: but if they turn away – thy duty is only preaching; and God's eye is on His servants.

20 But to those who believe not in the signs of God, and unjustly slay the prophets, and slay those men who enjoin uprightness, – announce an afflictive chastisement.

These are they whose works come to nought in this world, and in the next; and none shall they have to help them!

Hast thou not marked those who have received a portion of the Scriptures, when they are summoned to the Book of God, that it may settle their differences? Then did a part of them turn back, and withdrew far off.

This – because they said, 'The fire shall by no means touch us, but for certain days:' – Their own devices have deceived them in their religion.

But how, when we shall assemble them together for the day of (which) *whose coming* there is no doubt, and when every soul shall be paid what it hath earned, and they shall not be wronged?

SAY: O God, possessor of all power, thou givest power to whom thou wilt, and from whom thou wilt, thou takest it away! Thou raisest up whom thou wilt, and whom thou wilt thou dost abase! In thy hand is good; for thou art over all things potent.

Thou causest the night to pass into the day, and thou causest the day to pass into the night. Thou bringest the living out of the dead, and thou bringest the dead out of the living; and thou givest sustenance to whom thou wilt, without measure.

Let not believers take infidels for their friends rather than believers: whoso shall do this hath nothing *to hope* from God – unless, indeed, ye fear a fear from them: but God would have you beware of Himself; for to God ye return. SAY: Whether ye hide what is in your breasts, or whether ye publish it abroad, God knoweth it: He knoweth what is in the heavens and what is in the earth; and over all things is God potent.

On that day shall every soul find present to it, whatever it hath wrought of good: and as to what it hath wrought of evil, it will wish that wide were the space between itself and it! But God would have you beware of Himself; for God is kind to His servants.

SAY: If ye love God, then follow me: God will love you, and forgive your sins, for God is Forgiving, Merciful. SAY: Obey God and the Apostle; but if ye turn away, then verily, God loveth not the unbelievers.

30 Verily above all human beings did God choose Adam, and Noah, and the family of Abraham, and the family of IMRAN, the one the posterity of the other: And God Heareth, Knoweth.

Remember when the wife of Imran said, 'O my Lord! I vow to thee what is in my womb, for thy special service. Accept it from me, for thou Hearest, Knowest!' And when she had given birth to it, she said, 'O my Lord! Verily I have brought forth a female,' – God knew what she had brought forth; a male is not as a female – 'and I have named her Mary, and I take refuge with thee for her and for her offspring, from Satan the stoned.'

So with goodly acceptance did her Lord accept her, and with goodly growth did he make her grow. Zacharias reared her. So oft as Zacharias went in to Mary at the sanctuary, he found her supplied with food.[8] 'Oh, Mary!' said he, 'whence hast thou this?' She said, 'It is from God; for God supplieth whom He will, without reckoning!'

There did Zacharias call upon his Lord: 'O my Lord!' said he, 'vouchsafe me from thyself good descendants,[9] for thou art the hearer of prayer.' Then did the angels call to him, as he stood praying in the sanctuary:[10]

'God announceth John (Yahia) to thee, who shall be a verifier of the word from God, and a great one, chaste, and a prophet of the number of the just.'

He said, 'O my Lord! how shall I have a son, now that old age hath come upon me, and my wife is barren?' He said, 'Thus will God do His pleasure.'

He said, 'Lord! give me a token.' He said, 'Thy token shall be, that for three days thou shalt speak to no man but by signs: But remember thy Lord often, and praise him at even and at morn:'

And remember when the angels said, 'O Mary! verily hath God chosen thee,[11] and purified thee, and chosen thee above the women of the worlds!

O Mary! be devout towards thy Lord,[12] and prostrate thyself, and bow down with those who bow.'

This is one of the announcements of things unseen by thee: To thee, *O Muhammad!* do we reveal it; for thou wast not with them when they cast lots with reeds[13] which of them should rear Mary; nor wast thou with them when they disputed about it.

40 *Remember* when the angel said, 'O Mary! Verily God announceth to thee the Word from Him: His name shall be, Messiah Jesus the son of Mary,[14] illustrious in this world, and in the next, and one of those who have near access to God;

And He shall speak to men alike when in the cradle and when grown up; And he shall be one of the just.'

She said, 'How, O my Lord! shall I have a son, when man hath not touched me?' He said, 'Thus: God will create what He will; When He decreeth a thing, He only saith, "Be," and it is.'

And he will teach him the Book, and the Wisdom, and the Law, and the Evangel; and he shall be an apostle to the children of Israel. 'Now have I come,' *he will say*, 'to you with a sign from your Lord: Out of clay will I make for you, as it were, the figure of a bird: and I will breathe into it, and it shall become, by God's leave, a bird.[15] And I will heal the blind, and the leper; and by God's leave will I quicken the dead; and I will tell you what ye eat, and what ye store up in your houses! Truly in this will be a sign for you, if ye are believers.

And I have come to attest the law which was before me; and to allow you part of that which had been forbidden you; and I come to you with a sign from your Lord: Fear God, then, and obey me; of a truth God is my Lord, and your Lord: Therefore worship Him. This is a right way.'

And when Jesus perceived unbelief on their part, He said, 'Who will be my helpers with God?' The apostles[16] said, 'We *will be* God's helpers! We believe in God, and bear thou witness that we are Muslims.

O our Lord! we believe in what thou has sent down, and we follow the apostle; write us up, then, with those who bear witness *to him*.'

And the Jews plotted, and God plotted: But of those who plot is God the best.

Remember when God said, 'O Jesus! verily I will cause thee to die,[17] and will take thee up to myself and deliver thee from those who believe not; and I will place those who follow thee above those who believe not, until the day of resurrection. Then, to me is your return, and wherein ye differ will I decide between you.

And as to those who believe not, I will chastise them with a terrible chastisement in this world and in the next; and none shall they have to help them.'

50 But as to those who believe, and do the things that are right, He will pay them their recompense. God loveth not the doers of evil.

These signs, and this wise warning do we rehearse to thee.

Verily, Jesus is as Adam in the sight of God.[18] He created him of dust: He then said to him, 'Be' – and he was.

The truth from thy Lord! Be not thou, therefore, of those who doubt.

As for those[19] who dispute with thee about Him, after 'the knowledge' hath come to thee, SAY: Come,[20] let us summon our sons and your sons, our wives and your wives, and ourselves and yourselves. Then will we invoke and lay the malison of God on those that lie!

This recital is very truth, and there is no god but God; and verily God is the Mighty, the Wise.

But if they turn away, then verily God hath knowledge of the corrupt doers.

SAY: O people of the Book! come ye to a just judgment between us and you – That we worship not aught but God, and that we join no other god with Him, and that the one of us take not the other for lords,[21] beside God. Then if they turn their backs, SAY: Bear ye witness that *we* are Muslims.

O people of the Book! Why dispute about Abraham,[22] when the Law and the Evangel were not sent down till after him? Do ye not then understand?

Lo! ye are they who dispute about that in which ye have knowledge;[23] but why dispute ye about that of which ye have no knowledge? God hath knowledge, but ye know nothing.

60 Abraham was neither Jew nor Christian; but he was sound in the faith,[24] a Muslim; and not of those who add gods to God.

They among men, who are nearest of kin to Abraham, are surely those who follow him, and this prophet *Muhammad*, and they who believe *on him*. And God is the protector of the faithful.

A party among the people of the Book would fain mislead you: but they only mislead themselves, and perceive it not.

O people of the Book! why disbelieve the signs of God, of which yourselves have been witnesses?

O people of the Book! why clothe ye the truth with falsehood? Why wittingly hide the truth?

Others of the people of the Book say: 'Believe in what hath been sent down to the believers, at daybreak, and deny it at its close' – Thus do they go back –

'And believe in those only who follow your Religion.' SAY: True guidance is guidance from God – that to others may be imparted the like of what hath been imparted to you. Will they wrangle then with you in the presence of their Lord? SAY: Plenteous gifts are in the hands of God: He imparteth them unto whom He will, and God is Bounteous, Wise.

He will vouchsafe His mercy to whom He will, for God is of great bounteousness.

Among the people of the Book are some, to one of whom if thou entrust a thousand dinars, he will restore them to thee: And there is of them to whom if thou entrust a dinar, he will not restore it to thee, unless thou be ever instant with him.

This – because they say, 'We are not bound to keep faith with the ignorant (Pagan) folk, and they utter a lie against God, and know they do so:'

70 But whoso is true to his engagement, and feareth God, – verily God loveth those that fear Him.

Verily they who barter their engagement with God, and their oaths, for some paltry price – These! no portion for them in the world to come! and God will not speak to them, and will not look on them, on the day of resurrection, and will not assoil them! for them, a grievous chastisement!

And some truly are there among them who torture the Scriptures with their tongues, in order that ye may suppose it to be from the Scripture, yet it is not from the Scripture. And they say, 'This is from God;' yet it is not from God: and they utter a lie against God, and they know they do so.

It beseemeth not a man, that God should give him the Scriptures and the Wisdom, and the gift of prophecy, and that then he should say to his followers, 'Be ye worshippers of me, as well as of God;'[25] but rather, 'Be ye perfect in things pertaining to God, since ye know the Scriptures, and have studied deep.'

God doth not command you to take the angels or the prophets as lords.[26] What! would he command you to become infidels after ye have been Muslims?

When God entered into covenant with the prophets,[27] he said, 'This is the Book and the Wisdom which I give you. Hereafter shall a prophet came unto you to confirm the Scriptures already with you. Ye shall surely believe on him, and ye shall surely aid him. Are ye resolved?' said he, 'and do ye accept the covenant on these terms?' They said, 'We are resolved;' 'Be ye then the witnesses,' said he, 'and I will be a witness as well as you.

And whoever turneth back after this, these are surely the perverse.'

Other religion than that of God desire they? To him doth everything that is in the Heavens and in the Earth submit, in willing or forced obedience! and to Him do they return.

SAY: We believe in God, and in what hath been sent down to

us, and what hath been sent down to Abraham, and Ismael, and Isaac, and Jacob, and the tribes, and in what was given to Moses, and Jesus, and the Prophets, from their Lord. We make no difference between them. And to Him are we resigned (Muslims).

Whoso desireth any other religion than Islam, that religion shall never be accepted from him, and in the next world he shall be among the lost.

80 How shall God guide a people who, after they had believed and bore witness that the apostle was true, and after that clear proofs *of his mission* had reached them, disbelieved? God guideth not the people who transgress.

These! their recompense, that the curse of God, and of angels, and of all men, is on them!

Under it shall they abide for ever; their torment shall not be assuaged! nor shall God even look upon them! –

Save those who after this repent and amend; for verily God is Gracious, Merciful!

As for those who become infidels, after having believed, and then increase their infidelity – their repentance shall never be accepted. These! they are the erring ones.

As for those who are infidels, and die infidels, from no one of them shall as much gold as the earth could contain be accepted, though he should offer it in ransom. These! a grievous punishment awaiteth them; and they shall have none to help them.

Ye shall never attain to goodness till ye give alms of that which ye love; and whatever ye give, of a truth God knoweth it.

All food was allowed to the children of Israel, except what Jacob forbad himself, ere the law was sent down; SAY: Bring ye then the law and read it, if ye be men of truth.

And whoso after this inventeth the lie about God: – These are evil doers.

SAY: God speaketh truth. Follow, therefore, the religion of Abraham, the sound in faith, who was not one of those who joined other gods to God.

90 The first temple that was founded for mankind, was that in Becca,[28] – Blessed, and a guidance to human beings.

In it are evident signs, even the standing-place[29] of Abraham: and he who entereth it is safe. And the pilgrimage to the temple, is a service due to God from those who are able to journey thither.

And as to him who believeth not – verily God can afford to dispense with all creatures!

SAY: O people of the Book! why disbelieve ye the signs of God? But God is witness of your doings.

Say: O people of the Book! why repel believers from the way of God? Ye fain would make it crooked, and yet ye are its witnesses! But God is not regardless of what ye do.

O believers! if ye obey some amongst those who have received the Scripture, after your very Faith will they make you infidels!

But how can ye become infidels, when the signs of God are recited to you, and his prophet is among you? Whoever holdeth fast by God, is already guided to a straight path.

O ye believers! fear God as He deserveth to be feared! and die not till ye have become Muslims.

And hold ye fast by the cord[30] of God, all of you, and break not loose from it; and remember God's goodness towards you, how that when ye were enemies, He united your hearts, and by his favour ye became brethren;

And when ye were on the brink of the pit of fire, he drew you back from it. Thus God clearly sheweth you his signs that ye may be guided;

100 And that there may be among you a people who invite to the
Good, and enjoin the Just, and forbid the Wrong. These are they with whom it shall be well.

And be ye not like those who have formed divisions, and fallen to variance after the clear proofs have come to them. These! a terrible chastisement doth await them,

On THE DAY when faces shall turn white, and faces shall turn black! And as to those whose faces shall have turned black '... What! after your belief have ye become infidels? Taste then the chastisement, for that ye have been unbelievers.'

And as to those whose faces shall have become white, they shall be within the mercy of God: therein shall they abide for ever.

These are the signs of God: we recite them to thee in truth: And God willeth not injustice to mankind.

Whatever is in the Heavens, and whatever is on the Earth is God's. And to God shall all things return.

Ye are the best folk that hath been raised up unto mankind. Ye enjoin the Just, and ye forbid the Evil, and ye believe in God:

And if the people of the Book had believed, it had surely been better for them! Believers there are among them, but most of them are perverse.

They will never inflict on you but a trifling damage; and if they do battle with you, they shall turn their backs to you: then they shall not be succoured.

Shame shall be stamped upon them[31] wherever found, unless they ally them with God and men! And the wrath of God will they incur, and poverty shall be stamped upon them! This – for that they believed not in the signs of God, and slew the prophets unjustly: This – because they rebelled, and became transgressors.

Yet all are not alike: Among the people of the Book is an upright folk, who recite the signs of God in the night-season, and adore:

110 They believe in God and in the latter day, and enjoin justice, and forbid evil, and speed on in good works. These are of the righteous.

And of whatever good ye do, ye shall not be denied the meed. God knoweth those who fear Him.

But as for the infidels, their wealth, and their children shall avail them nothing against God. They shall be the inmates of the fire, to abide therein eternally.

The alms which they bestow in this present life, are like a freezing wind, which falleth upon and destroyeth the cornfields of a people who have been to themselves unjust. God doeth them no injustice, but to themselves are they unjust.

O ye who have believed! form not intimacies among others than yourselves. They will not fail to corrupt you. They long for your ruin. Hatred hath already shewn itself out of their mouths, but more grievous is what their breasts conceal. The tokens thereof we have already made plain to you, if ye will comprehend.

See now! ye love them, but they love not you. Ye believe the entire Book. And when they meet you, they say, 'We believe;' but when they are apart, they bite their fingers' ends at you, out of wrath. SAY: 'Die in your wrath!' God truly knoweth the very recesses of *your* breasts.

If good befalleth you it grieveth them, and when ill lighteth on you, they rejoice in it. But if ye be steadfast and fear God, their craft shall in no way harm you. For God is round about their doings.

And *remember* when thou didst leave thy household at early morn, that thou mightest prepare the faithful a camp for the war;[32] – God heard, knew it –

When two troops of you became full of anxious thoughts, and lost heart, and when God became the protector of both! In God, then, let the faithful trust.

God had already succoured you at Bedr, when ye were the weaker! Fear God, then, that ye may be thankful.

120 Then thou didst say to the faithful, 'Is it not enough for you that your Lord aideth you with three thousand angels sent down from on high?'

Aye: *but* if ye be steadfast and fear God, and the foe come upon you in hot haste, your Lord will help you with five thousand angels in their cognisances![33]

This, as pure good tidings for you, did God appoint, that your hearts might be assured – for only from God, the Mighty, the Wise, cometh the Victory – and that He might cut off the uttermost part of those who believed not, or cast them down so that they should be overthrown, *defeated* without resource.

It is none of thy concern whether He be turned unto them in kindness or chastise them: for verily they are wrongful doers.

Whatever is in the Heavens and the Earth is God's! He forgiveth whom He will, and whom He will, chastiseth: for God is Forgiving, Merciful.

O ye who believe! devour not usury, doubling it again and again! But fear God, that ye may prosper.

And fear the fire which is prepared for them that believe not; and obey God and the apostle, that ye may find mercy:

And vie in haste for pardon from your Lord, and a Paradise, vast as the Heavens and the Earth, prepared for the God-fearing.

Who give alms, alike in prosperity and in success, and who master their anger, and forgive others! God loveth the doers of good.

They who, after they have done a base deed or committed a wrong against their own selves, remember God and implore forgiveness of their sins – and who will forgive sins but God only? – and persevere not in what they have wittingly done amiss.

130 As for these! Pardon from their Lord shall be their recompense, and gardens 'neath which the rivers flow; for ever shall they abide therein: And goodly the reward of those who labour!

Already, before your time, have examples been made! Traverse the earth, then, and see what hath been the end of those who treat *prophets* as liars.

This *Koran* is a manifesto to man, and a guidance, and a warning to the God-fearing!

And be not fainthearted, and be not sorrowful: For ye shall gain the upper hand if ye be believers.[34]

If a wound hath befallen you, a wound like it hath already befallen others: we alternate these days *of successes and reverses* among men, that God may know those who have believed, and that He may take martyrs from among you, – but God loveth not the wrongful doers –

And that God may test those who believe, and destroy the infidels.

Thought ye that ye should enter Paradise ere God had taken knowledge of those among you who did valiantly, and of those who steadfastly endure?

Ye had desired death ere ye met it. But ye have now seen it – and ye have beheld it – *and fled from it!*

Muhammad is no more than an apostle; other apostles have already passed away before him: if he die, therefore,[35] or be slain, will ye turn upon your heels?[36] But he who turneth on his heels shall not injure God at all: And God will certainly reward the thankful!

No one can die except by God's permission, *according to* the Book that fixeth the term *of life.*[37] He who desireth the recompense of this world, we will give him thereof; And he who desireth the recompense of the next life, we will give him thereof! And we will certainly reward the thankful.

140 How many a prophet hath combated those who had with them many myriads! Yet were they not daunted at what befel them on the path of God, nor were they weakened, nor did they basely submit! God loveth those who endure with steadfastness,

Nor said they more than this:[38] 'O our Lord! forgive us our sins and our mistakes in this our work; and set our feet firm; and help us against the unbelieving people.' And God gave them the recompense of this world, and the excellence of the recompense of the next. For God loveth the doers of what is excellent.

O ye who have believed! if ye obey the infidels, they will cause you to turn upon your heels,[39] and ye will fall back into perdition:

But God is your liege lord, and He is the best of helpers.

We will cast a dread into hearts of the infidels because they have joined gods with God without warranty sent down; their abode shall be the fire; and wretched shall be the mansion of the evil doers.

Already had God made good to you His promise, when by His permission ye destroyed *your foes*, until your courage failed you, and ye disputed about the order,[40] and disobeyed, after that *the Prophet* had brought you within view of that for which ye longed.[41]

Some of you were for this world, and some for the next.[42] Then, in order to make trial of you, He turned you to flight from them, – yet hath He now forgiven you; for all-bounteous is God to the faithful –

When ye came up the height[43] and took no heed of any one, while the Prophet in your rear was calling you *to the fight!* God hath rewarded you with trouble upon trouble, that ye might *learn* not *to* be chagrined at your loss of booty, or at what befel you! God is acquainted with your actions.

Then after the trouble God sent down security upon you. Slumber fell upon a part of you: as to the other part – their own passions stirred them up to think unjustly of God with thoughts of ignorance! They said – What gain we by this affair? SAY: Verily the affair resteth wholly with God. They hid in their minds what they did not speak out to thee, saying, 'Were we to have gained aught in this affair, none of us had been slain at this place.' SAY: Had ye remained in your homes, they who were decreed to be slain would have gone forth to the places where they lie: – in order that God might make trial of what was in your breasts, and might discover what was in your hearts, for God knoweth the very secrets of the breast.

Of a truth it was Satan alone who caused those of you to fail in duty who turned back on the day when the hosts met, for some of their doings! But now hath God pardoned them; For God is Forgiving, Gracious.

150 O ye who believe! be not like the infidels, who said of their
brethren when they had travelled by land or had gone forth to
war, 'Had they kept with us, they had not died, and had not
been slain!' God purposed that this *affair* should cause them
heart sorrow! God maketh alive and killeth; and God
beholdeth your actions.
And if ye shall be slain or die on the path of God, then
pardon from God and mercy is better than all your amassings;
For if ye die or be slain, verily unto God shall ye be
gathered.
Of the mercy of God thou hast spoken to them in gentle
terms. Hadst thou been severe *and* harsh-hearted, they would
have broken away from thee. Therefore, forgive and ask for
pardon for them, and consult them in the affair *of war*, and
when thou art resolved, then put thou thy trust in God, for
God loveth those who trust in Him.
If God help you, none shall overcome you; but if He
abandon you, who is he that shall help you when He is gone?
In God, then, let the faithful trust.
It is not the Prophet who will defraud you;[44] – But he who
shall defraud, shall come forth with his defraudings on the day
of the resurrection: then shall every soul be paid what it hath
merited, and they shall not be treated with injustice.
Shall he who hath followed the good pleasure of God be as
he who hath brought on himself wrath from God, and whose
abode shall be Hell? and wretched the journey thither!
There are *varying* grades with God: and God beholdeth
what ye do.
Now hath God been gracious to the faithful, when he raised
up among them an apostle out of their own people, to rehearse
unto them his signs, and to cleanse them, and to give them
knowledge of the Book and of Wisdom: for before they were
in manifest error.
When a reverse hath befallen you,[45] the like of which ye had
before inflicted, say ye, 'Whence is this?' SAY: It is from
yourselves. For God hath power over all things.
160 And that which befel you on the day when the armies met,
was certainly by the will of God, and that he might know the
faithful, and that he might know the hypocrites! And when
the word was 'Advance, fight on the path of God, or drive
back *the foe*,' – they said, 'Had we known how to fight, we

would have followed you.' Nearer were some of them on that day to unbelief, than to faith:

They said with their lips what was not in their hearts! But God knew what they concealed,

Who said of their brethren while themselves sat at home, 'Had they obeyed us, they had not been slain.' SAY: Keep back death from yourselves if ye speak truth.

And repute not those slain on God's path to be dead.[46] Nay, alive with their Lord, are they richly sustained;

Rejoicing in what God of his bounty hath vouchsafed them, filled with joy for those who follow after them, but have not yet overtaken them, that on them nor fear shall come, nor grief;

Filled with joy at the favours of God, and at his bounty: and that God suffereth not the reward of the faithful to perish.

As to those who after the reverse[47] which befel them, respond to God and the Apostle – such of them as do good works and fear God, shall have a great reward:

Who, when men said to them, 'Now are the Meccans mustering against you; therefore fear them!' it only increased their faith, and they said, 'Our sufficiency is God, and He is an excellent protector.'

They returned, therefore, with the favour of God, enriched by Him, and untouched by harm; and they followed what was well pleasing to God. And God is of great Munificence.

Only would that Satan[48] instil the fear of his adherents: Fear them not, but fear me if ye are believers.

170 Let not those who vie in haste after infidelity grieve thee:
Verily not one whit shall they injure God! God will refuse them all part in the life to come: a severe chastisement shall be their lot.

They truly who purchase infidelity at the price of their faith, shall not injure God one whit! and a grievous chastisement shall be their lot.

Let not the infidels deem that the length of days we give them is good for them! We only give them length of days that they may increase their sins! and a shameful chastisement shall be their lot.

It is not in God to leave the faithful in the state in which they are, until he sever the bad from the good:

Nor is God minded to lay open the secret things to you, but God chooseth whom he will of his apostles *to know them*.[49]

Believe, therefore, in God and his apostles: and if ye believe and fear God, a great reward awaiteth you.

And let not those who are niggard of what God hath vouchsafed them in his bounty, think that this will be good for them – Nay, it will be bad for them –

That of which they have been niggard shall be their collar on the day of the resurrection. God's, the heritage of the Heavens and of the Earth! And God is well-informed of all ye do.

Now hath God heard the saying of those who said: 'Aye, God is poor and we are rich.'[50] We will surely write down their sayings, and their unjust slaughter of the prophets; and we will say, 'Taste ye the torment of the burning.

This, for what your hands have sent before you; and because God will not inflict a wrong upon his servants!'

To those who say, 'Verily, God hath enjoined us that we are not to credit an apostle until he present us a sacrifice which fire out of Heaven shall devour,'

180 SAY: Already have apostles before me come to you with
miracles, and with that of which ye speak. Wherefore slew ye
them? Tell me, if ye are men of truth.

And if they treat thee as a liar, then verily apostles have been treated as liars before thee, though they came with clear proofs *of their mission*, and with Scriptures, and with the light-giving Book.

Every soul shall taste of death: and ye shall only receive your recompenses on the day of resurrection. And whoso shall scape the fire, and be brought into Paradise, shall be happy. And the life of this world is but a cheating fruition!

Ye shall assuredly be tried in your possessions and in yourselves. And many hurtful things shall ye assuredly hear from those to whom the Scriptures were given before you, and from those who join other gods with God. But if ye be steadfast, and fear God – this verily is needed in the affairs *of life*.

Moreover, when God entered into a covenant with those to whom the Scriptures had been given, *and said*, 'Ye shall surely make it known to mankind and not hide it,' they cast it behind their backs, and sold it for a sorry price! But vile is that for which they have sold it.

Suppose not that they who rejoice in what they have brought to pass, and love to be praised for what they have not done[51] –

suppose not they shall escape the chastisement. An afflictive chastisement doth await them,

For the Kingdom of the Heavens and the Earth is God's, and God hath power over all things.

Verily, in the creation of the Heavens and of the Earth, and in the succession of the night and of the day, are signs for men of *understanding* heart;

Who standing, and sitting, and reclining, bear God in mind, and muse on the creation of the Heavens and of the Earth. 'O our Lord!' *say they*, 'thou hast not created this in vain. No. Glory be to Thee! Keep us, then, from the torment of the fire.

O our Lord! surely thou wilt put him to shame whom thou shalt cause to enter into the Fire, and the wrong doers shall have none to help them.

190 O our Lord! we have indeed heard the voice of one that
called. He called us to the faith – "Believe ye on your Lord" – and we have believed.

O our Lord! forgive us then our sin, and hide away from us our evil deeds, and cause us to die with the righteous.

O our Lord! and give us what thou hast promised us by thine apostles, and put us not to shame on the day of the resurrection. Verily, Thou wilt not fail thy promise.'

And their Lord answereth them, 'I will not suffer the work of him among you that worketh, whether of male or female, to be lost. The one of you is the issue of the other.[52]

And they who have fled their country and quitted their homes and suffered in my cause, and have fought and fallen, I will blot out their sins from them, and I will bring them into gardens beneath which the streams do flow.'

A recompense from God! and God! with Him is the perfection of recompense!

Let not prosperity in the land on the part of those who believe not, deceive thee. 'Tis but a brief enjoyment! Then shall Hell be their abode; and wretched the bed!

But as to those who fear their Lord – for them are the gardens 'neath which the rivers flow: therein shall they abide for aye. Such their reception with God – and that which is with God is best for the righteous.

Among the people of the Book are those who believe in God, and in what He hath sent down to you, and in what He hath sent down to them, humbling themselves before God. They barter not the signs of God for a mean price.

These! their recompense awaiteth them with their Lord: aye! God is swift to take account.

200 O ye who believe! be patient, and vie in patience, and be firm,
and fear God, that it may be well with you.

SURA 4 – WOMEN[1]

MEDINA – 175 VERSES

In the Name of God, the Compassionate, the Merciful

O men! fear your Lord, who hath created you of one man (*nafs*, soul), and of him created his wife, and from these twain hath spread abroad so many men and WOMEN. And fear ye God, in whose name ye ask mutual favours, – and reverence the wombs *that bore you*. Verily is God watching over you!

And give to the orphans their property; substitute not worthless things of your own for their valuable ones, and devour not their property after adding it to your own; for this is a great crime.

And if ye are apprehensive that ye shall not deal fairly with orphans, then, of *other* women who seem good in your eyes, marry *but* two, or three, or four; and if ye *still* fear that ye shall not act equitably, then one only; or the slaves whom ye have acquired: this will make justice on your part easier. Give women their dowry freely; but if of themselves they give up aught thereof to you, then enjoy it as convenient, and profitable:

And entrust not to the incapable the substance which God hath placed with you for their support; but maintain them therewith, and clothe them, and speak to them with kindly speech.

And make trial of orphans until they reach the age of marriage; and if ye perceive in them a sound judgment, then hand over their substance to them; but consume ye it not wastefully, or *by* hastily *entrusting it to them;*

Because they are growing up. And let the rich *guardian* not even touch it; and let him who is poor use it for his support (eat of it) with discretion.

And when ye make over their substance to them, then take witnesses in their presence: God also maketh a sufficient account.

Men ought to have a part of what their parents and kindred leave; and women[2] a part of what their parents and kindred leave: whether it be little or much, let them have a stated portion.

And when they who are of kin are present at the division, and
the orphans and the poor, let them too have a share; and speak
to them with kindly speech.
10 And let those be afraid *to wrong the orphans*, who, should
they leave behind them weakly offspring, would be solicitous
on their account. Let them, therefore, fear God, and let them
propose what is right.

Verily they who swallow the substance of the orphan wrongfully, shall swallow down only fire into their bellies, and shall burn in the flame!

With regard to your children, God commandeth you to give the male the portion of two females; and if they be females more than two, then they shall have two-thirds of that which *their father* hath left: but if she be an only daughter, she shall have the half; and the father and mother of the deceased shall each of them have a sixth part of what he hath left, if he have a child; but if he have no child, and his parents be his heirs, then his mother shall have the third: and if he have brethren, his mother shall have the sixth, after paying the bequests he shall have bequeathed, and his debts. As to your fathers, or your children, ye know not which of them is the most advantageous to you. This is the law of God. Verily, God is Knowing, Wise!

Half of what your wives leave shall be yours, if they have no issue; but if they have issue, then a fourth of what they leave shall be yours, after paying the bequests they shall bequeath, and debts.

And your wives shall have a fourth part of what ye leave, if ye have no issue; but if ye have issue, then they shall have an eighth part of what ye leave, after paying the bequests ye shall bequeath, and debts.

If a man or a woman make a distant relation their heir, and he or she have a brother or a sister, each of these two shall have a sixth; but if there are more than this, then shall they be sharers in a third, after payment of the bequests he shall have bequeathed, and debts,

Without loss to any one. This is the ordinance of God, and God is Knowing, Gracious!

These are the precepts of God; and whoso obeyeth God and his prophet, him shall God bring into gardens beneath whose *shades* the rivers flow, therein to abide for ever: and this, the great blessedness!

And whoso shall rebel against God and his apostle, and shall break His bounds, him shall God place in the fire to abide therein for ever; and his shall be a shameful torment.

If any of your women be guilty of whoredom, then bring four witnesses against them from among yourselves; and if they bear witness *to the fact*, shut them up within their houses till death release them,[3] or God make some way for them.

20 And if two men among you commit the same crime, then punish them both; but if they turn and amend, then let them be: for God is He who turneth, Merciful!

With God himself will the repentance of those who have done evil ignorantly, and then turn speedily *unto Him*, be accepted. These! God will turn unto them: for God is Knowing, Wise!

But no *place of* repentance shall there be for those who do evil, until, when death is close to one of them, he saith, 'Now verily am I turned to God;' nor to those who die unbelievers. These! we have made ready for them a grievous torment!

O believers! it is not allowed you to be heirs of your wives against their will; nor to hinder them from marrying, in order to take from them part of the dowry you had given them, unless they have been guilty of undoubted lewdness; but associate kindly with them: for if ye are estranged from them, haply ye are estranged from that in which God placed abundant good.

And if ye be desirous to exchange one wife for another, and have given one of them a talent, make no deduction from it. Would ye take it by slandering her, and with manifest wrong?

How, moreover, could ye take it, when one of you hath gone in unto the other, and they have received from you a strict bond of union?

And marry not women whom your fathers have married: for

this is a shame, and hateful, and an evil way: – though what is past[4] may be allowed.

Forbidden to you are your mothers, and your daughters, and your sisters, and your aunts, both on the father and mother's side, and your nieces on the brother and sister's side, and your foster-mothers, and your foster-sisters, and the mothers of your wives, and your step-daughters who are your wards, born of your wives to whom ye have gone in: (but if ye have not gone in unto them, it shall be no sin in you to marry them;) and the wives of your sons who proceed out of your loins; and ye may not have two sisters; except where it is already done. Verily, God is Indulgent, Merciful!

Forbidden to you also are married women, except those who are in your hands as slaves: This is the law of God for you. And it is allowed you, beside this, to seek out wives by means of your wealth, with modest conduct, and without fornication. And give those with whom ye have cohabited their dowry. This is the law. But it shall be no crime in you to make agreements over and above the law. Verily, God is Knowing, Wise!

And whoever of you is not rich enough to marry free believing women, then let him marry such of your believing maidens as have fallen into your hands as slaves; God well knoweth your faith. Ye are sprung the one from the other. Marry them, then, with the leave of their masters, and give them a fair dower: but let them be chaste and free from fornication, and not entertainers of lovers.

30 If after marriage they commit adultery, then inflict upon them half the penalty enacted for free married women. This *law* is for him among you who is afraid of doing wrong:[5] but if ye abstain,[6] it will be better for you. And God is Lenient, Merciful.

God desireth to make this known to you, and to guide you into the ways of those who have been before you, and to turn Him unto you in mercy. And God is Knowing, Wise!

God desireth *thus* to turn him unto you: but they who follow their own lusts, desire that with great swerving should ye swerve! God desireth to make your burden light: for man hath been created weak.

O believers! devour not each other's substance in mutual frivolities;[7] unless there be a trafficking among you by your own consent: and commit not suicide: – of a truth God is merciful to you.

And whoever shall do this maliciously and wrongfully, we will in the end cast him into the fire; for this is easy with God.

If ye avoid the great sins which ye are forbidden, we will blot out your faults, and we will cause you to enter *Paradise* with honourable entry.

Covet not the gifts by which God hath raised some of you above others. The men shall have a portion according to their deserts, and the women a portion according to their deserts. Of God, therefore, ask his gifts. Verily, God hath knowledge of all things.

To every one have we appointed kindred, as heirs of what parents and relatives, and those with whom ye have joined right hands in contract, leave. Give therefore, to each their portion. Verily, God witnesseth all things.

Men are superior to women on account of the qualities with which God hath gifted the one above the other, and on account of the outlay they make from their substance for them. Virtuous women are obedient, careful, during *the husband's* absence, because God hath of them been careful.[8] But chide those for whose refractoriness ye have cause to fear; remove them into beds apart, and scourge them: but if they are obedient to you, then seek not occasion against them: verily, God is High, Great!

And if ye fear a breach between man and wife, then send a judge chosen from his family, and a judge chosen from her family: if they are desirous of agreement, God will effect a reconciliation between them; verily, God is knowing, apprised of all!

40 Worship God, and join not aught with Him in worship. Be good to parents,[9] and to kindred, and to orphans, and to the poor, and to a neighbour, whether kinsman or new-comer, and to a fellow traveller, and to the wayfarer, and to the slaves whom your right hands hold; verily, God loveth not the proud, the vain boaster,

Who are niggardly themselves, and bid others be niggards, and hide away what God of his bounty hath given them. We have made ready a shameful chastisement for the unbelievers,

And for those who bestow their substance in alms to be seen of men, and believe not in God and in the last day. Whoever hath Satan for his companion, an evil companion hath he!

But what *blessedness would be* theirs, if they should believe in God and in the last day, and bestow alms out of what God hath vouchsafed them; for God taketh knowledge of them!

God truly will not wrong any one of the weight of a mote; and if there be any good deed, he will repay it doubly; and from his presence shall be given a great recompense.

How! when we shall bring up against them witnesses from all peoples, and when we shall bring thee up as a witness against these? On that day they who were Infidels and rebelled against the prophet, shall wish that the earth were levelled with them! But nothing shall they hide from God.

O ye true believers,[10] come not to prayer when ye are drunken, but wait till ye can understand what ye utter; nor when ye are polluted, unless ye be travelling on the road, until ye have washed you. If ye be sick, or on a journey, or have come from the unclean place, or have touched a woman, and ye find not water, then rub pure sand, and bathe your face and your hands with it: verily, God is Lenient, Merciful.

Hast thou not remarked those[11] to whom a part of the Scriptures hath been given? Vendors are they of error, and are desirous that ye go astray from the way. But God knoweth your enemies; and God is a sufficient patron, and God is a sufficient helper!

Among the Jews are those who displace the words of their scriptures, and say, 'We have heard, and we have not obeyed. Hear thou, but as one that heareth not; and LOOK AT US;'[12] perplexing with their tongues, and wounding the Faith by their revilings.

But if they would say, 'We have heard, and we obey; hear thou, and REGARD US;' it were better for them, and more right. But God hath cursed them for their unbelief. Few only of them are believers!

50 O ye to whom the Scriptures have been given! believe in what we have sent down confirmatory of the Scripture which is in your hands, ere we efface your features, and twist your head round backward, or curse you as we cursed the sabbath-breakers:[13] and the command of God was carried into effect.

Verily, God will not forgive the union of other gods with Himself! But other than this will He forgive to whom He pleaseth. And He who uniteth gods with God hath devised a great wickedness.

Hast thou not marked those who hold themselves to be

righteous? But God holdeth righteous whom He will; and they shall not be wronged the husk of a date stone.

Behold how they devise a lie of God! Therein is wickedness manifest enough!

Hast thou not observed those to whom a part of the Scriptures hath been given?[14] They believe in Djibt and Thagout, and say of the infidels, 'These are guided in a better path than those who hold the faith.'

These are they whom God hath cursed: and for him whom God hath cursed, thou shalt by no means find a helper.

Shall they have a share in the kingdom who would not bestow on their fellow men even the speck in a date stone?

Envy they other men what God of his bounty hath given them? We gave of old the Scriptures and wisdom to the line of Abraham, and we gave them a grand kingdom:

– Some of them believe on *the prophet* and some turn aside from him: – the flame of Hell is their sufficing *punishment!*

Those who disbelieve our signs we will in the end cast into the fire: so oft as their skins shall be well burnt,[15] we will change them for fresh skins, that they may taste the torment. Verily God is Mighty, Wise!

60 But as for those who have believed, and done the things that
are right, we will bring them into gardens 'neath which the rivers flow – therein to abide eternally; therein shall they have wives of stainless purity: and we will bring them into aye-shadowing shades.

Verily, God enjoineth you to give back your trusts to their owners, and when ye judge between men, to judge with fairness. Excellent is the practice to which God exhorteth you. God Heareth, Beholdeth!

O ye who believe! obey God and obey the apostle, and those among you invested with authority; and if in aught ye differ, bring it before God and the apostle, if ye believe in God and in the latter day. This is the best and fairest way of settlement.

Hast thou not marked those who profess that they believe in what hath been sent down to thee, and what hath been sent down before thee? Fain would they be judged before Thagout, though commanded not to believe in him; and fain would Satan make them wander with wanderings wide of truth.

And when it is said to them, 'Accede to that which God hath

sent down, and to the apostle,' thou seest the hypocrites avert them from thee with utter aversion.

But how, when some misfortune shall fortune them, for their previous handywork? Then will they come to thee, swearing by God, 'We desire nothing but to promote good and concord!'

These are they whose hearts God knoweth. Therefore break off from them, and warn them, and speak words that may penetrate their souls.

We have not sent any apostle but to be obeyed, if God so will: but if they, after they have sinned to their own hurt *by unbelief*, come to thee and ask pardon of God, and the apostle ask pardon for them, they shall surely find that God is He who turneth *unto man*, Merciful.

And they will not – I swear by thy Lord – they will not believe, until they have set thee up as judge between them on points where they differ. Then shall they not find in their own minds any difficulty in thy decisions, and shall submit with entire submission.

Had we laid down such a law for them as 'Kill yourselves, or abandon your dwellings,' but few of them would have done it. But had they done that to which they were exhorted, better had it been for them, and stronger for the confirmation *of their faith*.

70 In that case we had surely given them from ourself a great recompense, and on the straight path should we surely have guided them.

And whoever shall obey God and the Apostle, these shall be with those of the Prophets, and of the Sincere, and of the Martyrs, and of the Just, to whom God hath been gracious. These are a goodly band!

This is the bounty of God; and in knowledge doth God suffice.

O ye who believe! make use of precautions; and advance in detachments, or, advance in a body.

There is of you who will be a laggard: and if a reverse befall you he saith, 'Now hath God dealt graciously with me, since I was not with you in the fight:'

But if a success from God betide you, he will say, as if there had never been any friendship between you and him, 'Would I had been with them! a rich prize should I have won!'

Let those then fight on the path of God, who barter this

present life for that which is to come; for whoever fighteth on God's path, whether he be slain or conquer, we will in the end give him a great reward.

But what hath come to you that ye fight not on the path of God, and for the weak among men, women and children, who say, 'O our Lord! bring us forth from this city[16] whose inhabitants are oppressors; give us a champion from thy presence; and give us from thy presence a defender.'

They who believe, fight on the path of God; and they who believe not, fight on the path of Thagout: Fight therefore against the friends of Satan. Verily the craft of Satan shall be powerless!

Hast thou not marked those to whom it was said, 'Withhold your hands awhile *from war;* and observe prayer, and pay the stated alms.' But when war is commanded them, lo! a portion of them fear men as with the fear of God, or with a yet greater fear, and say: 'O our Lord! why hast thou commanded us war? Couldst thou not have given us respite till our not distant end?' SAY: Small the fruition of this world; but the next life is the *true* good for him who feareth God! and ye shall not be wronged so much as the skin of a date stone.

80 Wherever ye be, death will overtake you – although ye be in
lofty towers! If good fortune betide them, they say, 'This is from God;' and if evil betide them, they say, 'This is from thee.' SAY: All is from God: But what hath come to these people that they are not near to understanding what is told them?

Whatever good betideth thee is from God, and whatever betideth thee of evil is from thyself; and we have sent thee to mankind as an apostle: God is thy sufficing witness.

Whoso obeyeth the Apostle, in so doing obeyeth God: and as to those who turn back from thee, we have not sent thee to be their keeper.

Moreover, they say: 'Obedience!' but when they come forth from thy presence, a party of them brood by night over other than thy words; but God writeth down what they brood over: therefore separate thyself from them, and put thou thy trust in God. God is a sufficient protector!

Can they not consider the Koran? Were it from any other than God, they would surely have found in it many contradictions.

And when tidings, either of security or alarm, reach them, they tell them abroad; but if they would report them to the apostle, and to those who are in authority among them, those who desire information would learn it from them. But for the goodness and mercy of God towards you, ye would have followed Satan except a few!

Fight, therefore, on God's path: lay not burdens on any but thyself; and stir up the faithful. The might of the infidels haply will God restrain, for God is the stronger in prowess, and the stronger to punish.

He who shall mediate between men for a good purpose shall be the gainer by it. But he who shall mediate with an evil mediation shall reap the fruit of it. And God keepeth watch over everything.

If ye are greeted with a greeting, then greet ye with a better greeting, or *at least* return it; God taketh count of all things.

God! there is no god but He! He will certainly assemble you on the day of resurrection. There is no doubt of it. And whose word is more true than God's?

90 Why are ye two parties on the subject of the hypocrites, when God hath cast them off for their doings? Desire ye to guide those whom God hath led astray? But for him whom God leadeth astray, thou shalt by no means find a pathway.

They desire that ye should be infidels as they are infidels, and that ye should be alike. Take therefore none of them for friends, till they have fled their homes for the cause of God. If they turn back, then seize them, and slay them wherever ye find them; but take none of them as friends or helpers,

Except those who shall seek an asylum among your allies, and those who come over to you – their hearts forbidding them to make war on you, or to make war on their own people. Had God pleased, he would have given them power against you, and they would have made war upon you! But, if they depart from you, and make not war against you and offer you peace, then God alloweth you no occasion against them.

Ye will find others who seek to gain your confidence as well as that of their own people: So oft as they return to sedition, they shall be overthrown in it: But if they leave you not, nor propose terms of peace to you nor withhold their hands, then seize them, and slay them, wherever ye find them. Over these have we given you undoubted power.

A believer killeth not a believer but by mischance: and whoso killeth a believer by mischance shall be bound to free a believer from slavery; and the blood-money shall be paid to the family of the slain, unless they convert it into alms. But if the slain believer be of a hostile people, then let him confer freedom on a slave who is a believer; and if he be of a people between whom and yourselves there is an alliance, then let the blood-money be paid to his family, and let him set free a slave who is a believer: and let him who hath not the means, fast two consecutive months. This is the penance enjoined by God; and God is Knowing, Wise!

But whoever shall kill a believer of set purpose, his recompense shall be hell; for ever shall he abide in it; God shall be wrathful with him, and shall curse him, and shall get ready for him a great torment.

O believers! when ye go forth to the fight for the cause of God, be discerning, and say not to every one who meeteth you with a greeting, 'Thou art not a believer'[17] in your greed after the chance good things of this present life! With God are abundant spoils. Such hath been your wont in times past; but God hath been gracious to you. Be discerning, then, for God well knoweth what ye do.

Those believers who sit at home free from trouble, and those who do valiantly in the cause of God with their substance and their persons, shall not be treated alike. God hath assigned to those who contend earnestly with their persons and with their substance, a rank above those who sit at home. Goodly promises hath He made to all. But God hath assigned to the strenuous a rich recompense, above those who sit still at home,

Rank of his own bestowal, and forgiveness, and mercy; for God is Indulgent, Merciful.

The angels,[18] when they took the souls of those who had been unjust to their own weal, demanded, 'What hath been your state?'[19] They said, 'We were the weak ones[20] of the earth.' They replied, 'Was not God's earth broad enough for you to flee away in?' These! their home shall be Hell, and evil the passage to it –

100 Except the men and women and children who were not able, through their weakness, to find the means *of escape*, and were not guided on their way. These haply God will forgive: for God is Forgiving, Gracious.

Whoever flieth his country for the cause of God, will find in the earth many under *like* compulsion, and abundant resources; and if any one shall quit his home and fly to God and his apostle, and then death overtake him, – his reward from God is sure: for God is Gracious, Merciful!

And when ye go forth to war in the land, it shall be no crime in you to cut short your prayers,[21] if ye fear lest the infidels come upon you; Verily, the infidels are your undoubted enemies!

And when thou, O *apostle!* shalt be among them, and shalt pray with them, then let a party of them rise up with thee, but let them take their arms; and when they have made their prostrations, let them retire to your rear: then let another party that hath not prayed come forward, and let them pray with you; but let them take their precautions and their arms. Pleased would the infidels be for you to neglect your arms and your baggage, that they might turn upon you at once! And it shall be no crime in you to lay down your arms if rain annoy you, or if ye be sick. But take your precautions.[22] Verily, God hath made ready a shameful torment for the infidels.

And when ye shall have ended the prayer, make mention of God, standing, and sitting, and reclining: and as soon as ye are secure, observe prayer; for to the faithful, prayer is a prescribed duty, and for stated hours.

Slacken not in pursuit of the foe. If ye suffer, assuredly they suffer also as ye suffer; but ye hope from God for what they cannot hope! And God is Knowing, Wise!

Verily, we have sent down the Book to thee with the truth, thou that mayest judge between men according as God hath given thee insight: But with the deceitful ones dispute not: and implore pardon of God. Verily, God is Forgiving, Merciful.[23]

And plead not with us for those who are self-deceivers; for God loveth not him who is deceitful, criminal.

From men they hide themselves; but they cannot hide themselves from God: and when they hold nightly discourses which please Him not, He is with them. God is round about their doings!

Oh! ye are they who plead in their favour in this present life; but who shall plead with God for them on the day of the resurrection? Who will be the guardian over them?

110 Yet he who doth evil, or shall have acted against his own weal,

and then shall ask pardon of God, will find God Forgiving, Merciful:

And whoever committeth a crime, committeth it to his own hurt. And God is Knowing, Wise!

And whoever committeth an *involuntary* fault or a crime, and then layeth it on the innocent, shall surely bear *the guilt of* calumny and of a manifest crime.

But for the grace and mercy of God upon thee, a party among them had resolved to mislead thee, but they shall only mislead themselves; nor in aught shall they harm thee. God hath caused the Book and the wisdom to descend upon thee: and what thou knowest not He hath caused thee to know: and the grace of God towards thee hath been great.

In most of their secret talk is nothing good; but only in his who enjoineth almsgiving, or that which is right, or concord among men. Whoso doth this, out of desire to please God, we will give him at the last a great reward:

But whoso shall sever himself from the prophet after that 'the guidance' hath been manifested to him, and shall follow any other path than that of the faithful, we will turn our back on him as he hath turned his back on us, and we will cast him into Hell; – an evil journey thither!

God truly will not forgive the joining other gods with Himself. Other sins He will forgive to whom He will: but he who joineth gods with God, hath erred with far-gone error.

They call, beside Him, upon mere goddesses! they invoke a rebel Satan!

On them is the malison of God. For he said, 'A portion of thy servants will I surely take, and will lead them astray, and will stir desires within them, and will command them and they shall cut the ears of animals;[24] and I will command them, and they shall alter the creation of God.'[25] He who taketh Satan rather than God for his patron, is ruined with palpable ruin:

He hath made them promises, and he hath stirred desires within them; but Satan promiseth, only to beguile!

120 These! their dwelling Hell! no escape shall they find from it!

But they who believe and do the things that are right, we will bring them into gardens beneath which the rivers flow; For ever shall they abide therein. Truly it is the promise of God: And whose word is more sure than God's?

Not according to your wishes, or the wishes of the people of the Book, shall these things be. He who doth evil shall be recompensed for it. Patron or helper, beside God, shall he find none.

But whoso doth the things that are right, whether male or female, and he or she a believer, – these shall enter Paradise, nor shall they be wronged the skin of a date stone.

And who hath a better religion than he who resigneth himself to God, who doth what is good, and followeth the faith of Abraham in all sincerity? And God took Abraham for his friend.

All that is in the Heavens and all that is on the Earth is God's: and God encompasseth all things!

Moreover, they will consult thee in regard to women: SAY: God hath instructed you about them; and His will is rehearsed to you, in the Book, concerning female orphans to whom ye give not their legal due, and whom ye refuse to marry; also with regard to weak children; and that ye deal with fairness towards orphans. Ye cannot do a good action, but verily God knoweth it.

And if a wife fear ill usage or aversion on the part of her husband, then shall it be no fault in them if they can agree with mutual agreement, for agreement is best. *Men's* souls are prone to avarice; but if ye act kindly and fear God, then, verily, your actions are not unnoticed by God!

And ye will not have it at all in your power to treat your wives alike, even though you fain would do so; but yield not wholly to disinclination, so that ye leave one of them as it were in suspense; if ye come to an understanding, and fear God, then, verily, God is Forgiving, Merciful;

But if they separate, God can compensate both out of His abundance; for God is Vast, Wise;

130 And whatever is in the Heavens and in the Earth is God's! We have already enjoined those to whom the Scriptures were given before you, and yourselves, to fear God. But if ye become unbelievers, yet know that whatever is in the Heavens and in the Earth is God's: and God is Rich, Praiseworthy.

All that is in Heaven and all that is in Earth is God's! God is a sufficient protector!

If he pleased, he could cause you to pass away, O mankind! and create others in your stead: for this hath God power.

If any one desire the reward of this world, yet with God is the reward of this world and of the next! And God Heareth, Beholdeth.

O ye who believe! stand fast to justice, when ye bear witness before God, though it be against yourselves, or your parents, or your kindred, whether the party be rich or poor. God is nearer than you to both. Therefore follow not passion, lest ye swerve from truth. And if ye wrest *your testimony* or stand aloof, God verily is well aware of what ye do.

O ye who believe! believe in God and his Apostle, and the Book which he hath sent down to his Apostle, and the Book which he hath sent down aforetime. Whoever believeth not on God and his Angels and his Books and his Apostles, and in the last day, he verily hath erred with far-gone error.

Verily, they who believed, then became unbelievers, then believed, and again became unbelievers, and then increased their unbelief – it is not God who will forgive them or guide them into the way.

Announce[26] to the hypocrites that a dolorous torment doth await them.

Those who take the unbelievers for friends besides the faithful – do they seek honour at their hands? Verily, all honour belongeth unto God!

And already hath He sent this down to you in the Book[27] 'WHEN YE SHALL HEAR THE SIGNS OF GOD THEY SHALL NOT BE BELIEVED BUT SHALL BE MOCKED AT.' Sit ye not therefore with such, until they engage in other discourse; otherwise, ye will become like them. Verily God will gather the hypocrites and the infidels all together in Hell.

140 They watch you narrowly. Then if God grant you a victory,
they say, 'Are we not with you?' and if the infidels meet with a success, they say to them, 'Were we not superior to you: and did we not defend you from those believers?' God shall judge betwixt ye on the day of the resurrection, and God will by no means make a way for the infidels over the believers.

The hypocrites would deceive God, but He will deceive them! When they stand up for prayer, they stand carelessly, to be seen of men, and they remember God but little:

Wavering between the one and the other – belonging neither to these nor those! and by no means shalt thou find a path for him whom God misleadeth.

O believers! take not infidels for friends rather than believers. Would ye furnish God with clear right to punish you?

Verily the hypocrites shall be in the lowest abyss of the fire: and, by no means shalt thou find a helper for them;

Save for those who turn and amend, and lay fast hold on God, and approve the sincerity of their religion to God; these shall be *numbered* with the faithful, and God will at last bestow on the faithful a great reward.

Why should God inflict a chastisement upon you, if ye are grateful, and believe? God is Grateful, Wise!

God loveth not that evil be matter of public talk, unless any one hath been wronged: God it is who Heareth, Knoweth!

Whether ye publish what is good, or conceal it, or pardon evil, verily God is Pardoning, Powerful!

Of a truth they who believe not on God and his Apostles, and seek to separate God from his Apostles, and say, 'Some we believe, and some we believe not,' and desire to take a middle way;

150 These! they are veritable infidels! and for the infidels have we prepared a shameful punishment.

And they who believe on God and his Apostles, and make no difference between them – these! we will bestow on them their reward at last. God is Gracious, Merciful!

The people of the Book will ask of thee to cause a Book to come down unto them out of Heaven. But a greater thing than this did they ask of Moses! for they said, 'Shew us God plainly!' and for this their wickedness did the fire-storm lay hold on them. Then took they the calf *as the object of their worship*, after that our clear tokens had come to them; but we forgave them this, and conferred on Moses undoubted power.

And we uplifted the mountain[28] over them when we made a covenant with them, and we said to them, 'Enter the gate adoring:' and we said to them, 'Transgress not on the Sabbath,' and we received from them a strict covenant.

So, for that they have broken their covenant, and have rejected the signs of God, and have put the prophets to death unjustly, saying the while, 'Our hearts are uncircumcised,' – Nay, but God hath sealed them up for their unbelief, so that but few believe.

And for their unbelief, – and for their having spoken against Mary a grievous calumny, –

And for their saying, 'Verily we have slain the Messiah, Jesus the son of Mary, an Apostle of God.' Yet they slew him not, and they crucified him not, but they had only his likeness.[29] And they who differed about him were in doubt concerning him: No sure knowledge had they about him, but followed only an opinion, and they did not really slay him, but God took him up to Himself. And God is Mighty, Wise!

There shall not be one of the people of the Book but shall believe in Him before his death, and in the day of resurrection, He will be a witness against them.

For the wickedness of certain Jews, and because they turn many from the way of God, we have forbidden them goodly viands which had been before allowed them.

And because they have taken usury, though they were forbidden it, and have devoured men's substance in frivolity, we have got ready for the infidels among them a grievous torment.

160 But their men of solid knowledge, and the believers who believe in that which hath been sent down to thee, and in what hath been sent down before thee, and who observe prayer, and pay the alms of obligation, and believe in God and the latter day, – these! we will give them a great reward.

Verily we have revealed to thee as we revealed to Noah and the Prophets after him, and as we revealed to Abraham, and Ismaël, and Isaac, and Jacob, and the tribes, and Jesus, and Job, and Jonah, and Aaron, and Solomon; and to David gave we Psalms.

Of some apostles we have told thee before: of other apostles we have not told thee – And discoursing did God discourse with Moses –

Apostles charged to announce and to warn, that men, after those apostles, might have no plea against God. And God is Mighty, Wise!

But God is himself witness of what He hath sent down to thee: In His knowledge hath He sent it down to thee. The angels are also witnesses: but God is a sufficient witness!

Verily, they who believe not and pervert from the way of God, have indeed erred with error wide of truth.

Verily, those who believe not, and act wrongfully, God will never pardon, and never will he guide them on path,

Than the path to Hell, in which they shall abide for ever! And this is easy for God.

O men! now hath an apostle come to you with truth from your Lord. Believe then, it will be better for you. But if ye believe not, then, all that is in the Heavens and the Earth is God's; and God is Knowing, Wise!

O ye people of the Book! overstep not bounds in your religion;[30] and of God, speak only truth. The Messiah, Jesus, son of Mary, is only an apostle of God, and his Word which he conveyed into Mary, and a Spirit[31] proceeding from himself. Believe therefore in God and his apostles, and say not, 'Three:' (there is a Trinity) – Forbear – it will be better for you. God is only one God! Far be it from His glory that He should have a son! His, whatever is in the Heavens, and whatever is in the Earth! And God is a sufficient Guardian.

170 The Messiah disdaineth not to be a servant of God, nor do the angels who are nigh unto Him.

And whoso disdaineth His service, and is filled with pride, God will gather them all to Himself.

And to those who believe and do the things that are right, will He pay them their due recompense, and out of His bounty will He increase them: but as for those who are disdainful and proud, with a grievous chastisement will He chastise them;

And none beside God shall they find to protect or to help them.

O men! now hath a proof come to you from your Lord, and we have sent down to you a clear light. As to those who believe in God and lay fast hold on Him, these will He cause to enter into his mercy and grace, and along the straight way unto Himself will He guide them.

They will consult thee. SAY: God instructeth you as to distant kindred. If a man die childless, but have a sister, half what he shall have shall be hers; and if she die childless he shall be her heir. But if there be two sisters, two-third parts of what he shall have shall be theirs; and if there be both brothers and sisters, the male shall have the portion of two females. God teacheth you plainly, that ye err not! God knoweth all things.

SURA 5 – THE TABLE

MEDINA – 120 VERSES

In the Name of God, the Compassionate, the Merciful

O Believers! be faithful to your engagements. You are allowed *the flesh of* cattle other than what is *hereinafter* recited, except game, which is not allowed you while ye are on pilgrimage. Verily, God ordaineth what he pleaseth.

O Believers! violate neither the rites of God, nor the sacred month *Muharram*, nor the offering, nor its ornaments,[1] nor those who press on to the sacred house seeking favour from their Lord and his good pleasure in them.

But when all is over,[2] then take to the chase: and let not ill will at those[3] who would have kept you from the sacred mosque lead you to transgress,[4] but rather be helpful to one another according to goodness and piety, but be not helpful for evil and malice: and fear ye God. Verily, God is severe in punishing!

That which dieth of itself, and blood, and swine's flesh, and all that hath been sacrificed under the invocation of any other name than that of God, and the strangled, and the killed by a blow, or by a fall, or by goring,[5] and that which hath been eaten by beasts of prey, unless ye make it clean *by giving the death-stroke yourselves*, and that which hath been sacrificed on the blocks of stone,[6] is forbidden you: and to make division *of the slain* by *consulting* the arrows,[7] is impiety in you. Woe this day on those who forsake your religion! And fear them not, but fear Me.

This day have I perfected your religion for you, and have filled up the measure of my favours upon you: and it is my pleasure that Islam be your religion; but whoso without wilful leanings to wrong shall be forced by hunger to transgress, to him, verily, will God be Indulgent, Merciful.

They will ask thee what is made lawful for them. SAY: Those things which are good[8] are legalised to you, and the prey of beasts of chase which ye have trained like dogs, teaching them as God hath taught you. Eat, therefore, of what they shall catch for you, and make mention of the name of God over it, and fear God: Verily, Swift is God to reckon:

This day, things healthful are legalised to you, and the meats of those who have received the Scriptures are allowed to you, as your meats are to them. And *you are permitted to marry* virtuous women who are believers, and virtuous women of those who have received the Scriptures before you, when you shall have provided them their portions, living chastely *with them* without fornication, and without taking concubines. Vain the works of him who shall renounce the faith! and in the next world he shall be of the lost.

O Believers! when ye address yourselves to prayer, wash your faces, and your hands up to the elbow, and wipe your heads, and your feet to the ankles.

And if ye have become unclean, then purify yourselves. But if ye are sick, or on a journey, of if one of you come from the place of retirement, or if ye have touched women, and ye find no water, then take clean sand and rub your faces and your hands with it.[9] God desireth not to lay a burden upon you, but he desireth to purify you, and He would fill up the measure of His favour upon you, that ye may be grateful.

10 And remember the favour of God upon you, and His covenant which He hath covenanted with you, when ye said, 'We have heard and will obey;'[10] and fear God; verily, God knoweth the very secrets of the breast.

O Believers! stand up as witnesses for God by righteousness: and let not ill-will at any, induce you not to act uprightly. Act uprightly. Next will this be to the fear of God. And fear ye God: verily, God is apprised of what ye do.

God hath promised to those who believe, and do the things that are right, that for them is pardon and a great reward.

But they who are Infidels and treat our signs as lies – these shall be mated with Hell fire.

O Believers! recollect God's favour upon you, when[11] certain folk were minded to stretch forth their hands against you, but He kept their hands from you. Fear God then: and on God let the faithful trust.

Of old did God *accept the* covenant of the children of Israel,[12] and out of them we raised up twelve leaders, and God said, 'Verily, I will be with you. If ye observe prayer and pay the obligatory alms, and believe in my Apostles and help them, and lend God a liberal loan, I will surely put away from you your evil deeds, and I will bring you into gardens 'neath which the rivers flow! But whoso of you after this believeth not, hath gone astray from the even path.'

But for their breaking their covenant we have cursed them, and have hardened their hearts. They shift the words *of Scripture* from their places, and have forgotten part of what they were taught. Thou wilt not cease to discover deceit on their part, except in a few of them. But forgive them, and pass it over: verily, God loveth those who act generously!

And of those who say, 'We are Christians,' have we accepted the covenant. But they *too* have forgotten a part of what they were taught; wherefore we have stirred up enmity and hatred among them that shall last till the day of the Resurrection; and in the end will God tell them of their doings.

O people of the Scriptures! now is our Apostle come to you to clear up to you much that ye concealed of those Scriptures, and to pass over many things. Now hath a light and a clear Book come to you from God, by which God will guide him who shall follow after his good pleasure, to paths of peace, and will bring them out of the darkness to the light, by his will: and to the straight path will he guide them.

Infidels now are they who say, 'Verily God is the Messiah Ibn Maryam (son of Mary)! SAY: And who could aught obtain from God, if he chose to destroy the Messiah Ibn Maryam, and his mother, and all who are on the earth together?
20 For with God is the sovereignty of the Heavens and of the
Earth, and of all that is between them! He createth what He will; and over all things is God potent.

Say the Jews and Christians, 'Sons are we of God and his beloved.' SAY: Why then doth he chastise you for your sins? Nay! ye are but a part of the men whom he hath created! He will pardon whom he pleaseth, and chastise whom he pleaseth, and with God is the sovereignty of the Heavens and of the Earth, and of all that is between them, and unto Him shall *all things* return.

O people of the Book! now hath our Apostle come to you to clear up to you the cessation[13] of Apostles, lest you should say, 'There hath come to us no bearer of good tidings, nor any warner.' But now hath a bearer of good tidings and a warner reached you. And God is Almighty.

And *remember* when Moses said to his people, 'O my people! call to mind the goodness of God towards you when he appointed Prophets among you, and appointed you kings, and gave you what never had been given before to any human beings:

Enter, O my people! the holy land which God hath destined for you. Turn not back, lest ye be overthrown to your ruin.'

They said, 'O Moses! Therein are men of might. And verily, we can by no means enter it till they be gone forth. But if they go forth from it, then verily will we enter in.'

Then said two men of those who feared *their Lord and* to whom God had been gracious, 'Enter in upon them by the gate: and when ye enter it, ye overcome! If ye be believers, put ye your trust in God.'

They said, 'O Moses! never can we enter while they remain therein. Go thou and thy Lord and fight; for here will we sit us down.'

He said, 'O my Lord, Verily of none am I master but of myself and my brother: put thou therefore a difference between us and this ungodly people.'

He said, 'Verily the land shall be forbidden them forty years: they shall wander in the earth perplexed. Fret not thyself therefore for the ungodly people.'

30 Relate to them exactly the story of the sons of Adam[14] when they each offered an offering; accepted from the one of them, and not accepted from the other. The one said, 'I will surely slay thee.' Said the other, 'God only accepted from those that fear Him.

'Even if thou stretch forth thine hand against me to slay me, I will not stretch forth my hand against thee to slay thee. Truly I fear God the Lord of the Worlds.

'Yea, rather would I that thou shouldest bear my sin[15] and thine own sin, and that thou become an inmate of the Fire: for that is the recompense of the unjust doers.'

And his passion led him to slay his brother: and he slew him; and he became one of those who perish.

And God sent a raven which scratched upon the ground, to shew him[16] how he might hide his brother's wrong.[17] He said: 'O woe is me! am I too weak to become like this raven, and to hide away my brother's wrong?' And he became one of the repentant.

For this cause have we ordained to the children of Israel that he who slayeth any one, unless it be a person guilty of manslaughter, or of spreading disorders in the land, shall be as though he had slain all mankind; but that he who saveth a life, shall be as though he had saved all mankind alive.[18]

Of old our Apostles came to them with the proofs *of their mission;* then verily after this most of them committed excesses in the land.

Only, the recompense of those who war against God and his Apostle, and go about to commit disorders on the earth, shall be that they shall be slain or crucified, or have their alternate hands and feet cut off, or be banished the land: This their disgrace in this world, and in the next a great torment shall be theirs –

Except those who, ere you have them in your power, shall repent; for know that God is Forgiving, Merciful.

O ye who believe! fear God. Desire union with Him. Contend earnestly on his path, that you may attain to happiness.

40 As to the infidels – if that they had twice the riches of the earth to be their ranson from torment on the day of resurrection, it should not be accepted from them! And a dolorous torment shall be theirs.

Fain would they come forth from the Fire; but forth from it they shall not come: and a lasting torment shall be theirs.

As to the thief, whether man or woman, cut ye off their hands in recompense for their doings.[19] This is a penalty by way of warning from God himself. And God is Mighty, Wise.

But whoever shall turn him *to God* after this his wickedness, and amend, God truly will be turned to him: for God is Forgiving, Merciful.

Knowest thou not that the sovereignty of the Heavens and of the Earth is God's? He chastiseth whom He will, and whom He will He forgiveth. And God hath power over all things.

O Apostle! let not those who vie with one another in speeding to infidelity vex thee; – of those who say with their mouths, 'We believe,' but whose hearts believe not; – or of the Jews – listeners to a lie – listeners to others – but who come not to thee. They shift the words *of the law* from their places, and say, 'If this be brought to you, receive it; but if this be not brought to you, then beware of it.' For him whom God would mislead, thou canst in no wise prevail with God! They whose hearts God shall not please to cleanse, shall suffer disgrace in this world, and in the next a grievous punishment;

Listeners to a falsehood and *greedy* devourers of the forbidden![20] If, therefore, they have recourse to thee, then judge between them, or withdraw from them. If thou withdraw from them, then can they have no power to injure thee. But if thou judge, then judge between them with equity. Verily, God loveth those who deal equitably.

But how shall they make thee their judge, since they possess already the Law, in which are the behests of God, *and have not obeyed it?* After this, they will turn their backs; but such are not believers.

Verily, we have sent down the law (Towrat) wherein are guidance and light. By it did the prophets who professed Islam judge the Jews; and the doctors and the teachers *judged* by that portion of the Book of God, of which they were the keepers and the witnesses. Therefore, *O Jews!* fear not men but fear Me; and barter not away my signs for a mean price! And whoso will not judge by what God hath sent down – such are the Infidels.

And therein[21] have we enacted for them, 'Life for life, and eye for eye, and nose for nose, and ear for ear, and tooth for tooth, and for wounds retaliation:' – Whoso shall compromise it as alms shall have therein the expiation *of his sin;* and whoso will not judge by what God hath sent down – such are the transgressors.

50 And in the footsteps of the prophets caused we Jesus, the son of Mary, to follow, confirming the law which was before him: and we gave him the Evangel with its guidance and light, confirmatory of the preceding Law; a guidance and warning to those who fear God; –

And that the people of the Evangel may judge according to what God hath sent down therein. And whoso will not judge by what God hath sent down – such are the perverse.

And to thee we have sent down the Book *of the Koran* with truth, confirmatory of previous Scriptures, and their safeguard. Judge therefore between them by what God hath sent down, and follow not their desires by deserting the truth which hath come unto thee. To every one of you have we given a rule and a beaten track.

And if God had pleased He had surely made you all one people; but He would test you by what He hath given to each. Be emulous, then, in good deeds. To God shall ye *all* return, and He will tell you concerning the subjects of your disputes.

Wherefore do thou judge between them, by what God hath sent down, and follow not their wishes! but be on thy guard against them lest they beguile thee from any of those precepts which God hath sent down to thee; and if they turn back, then know thou that for some of their crimes doth God choose to punish them: for truly most men are perverse.

Desire they, therefore, the judgments of the *times of* (pagan) ignorance? But what better judge can there be than God for those who believe firmly?

O Believers! take not the Jews or Christians[22] as friends. They are but one another's friends. If any one of you taketh them for his friends, he surely is one of them! God will not guide the evil doers.

So shalt thou see the diseased at heart speed away to them, and say, 'We fear lest a change of fortune befall us.' But haply God will of himself bring about some victory or event of His own ordering: then soon will they repent them of their secret imaginings.

Then will the faithful say, 'What! are these they who swore, by their most solemn oath, that they were surely with you?' Vain their works; and themselves shall come to ruin.

O ye who believe! should any of you desert His religion, God will then raise up a people loved by Him, and loving Him, lowly towards the faithful, haughty towards the Infidels. For the cause of God *will they* contend, and not fear the blame of the blamer. This is the Grace of God! On whom He will He bestoweth it! God is Vast, Omniscient!

60 Verily, your protector is God and His Apostle, and those who believe, who observe prayer, and pay the alms of obligation, and who bow in worship.

And whoso take God and His Apostle, and those who believe for friends, they truly are the people of God; they shall have the upper hand.

O ye who believe! take not such of those who have received the Scriptures before you, as scoff and jest at your religion, or the Infidels, for your friends, but fear God if ye are believers:

Nor those who when ye call to prayer, make it an object of raillery and derision. This they do because they are a people who understand not.

SAY:[23] O people of the Book! do ye not disavow us only because we believe in God, and in what He hath sent down to us, and in what He hath sent down aforetime, and because most of you are doers of ill?

SAY: Can I announce to you any retribution worse than that *which awaiteth them* with God? They whom God hath cursed and with whom He hath been angry – some of them hath He changed into apes and swine; and they who worship Thagout are in evil plight, and have gone far astray from the right path!

When they presented themselves to you they said, 'We believe;' but Infidels they came in unto you, and Infidels they went forth! God well knew what they concealed.

Many of them shalt thou see hastening together to wickedness and malice, and to eat unlawful things. Shame on them for what they have done!

Had not their doctors and teachers forbidden their uttering wickedness, and their eating unlawful food, bad indeed would have been their doings!

'The hand of God,' say the Jews, 'is chained up.'[24] Their own hands shall be chained up – and for that which they have said shall they be cursed. Nay! outstretched are both His hands! At His own pleasure does He bestow gifts. That which hath been sent down to thee from thy Lord will surely increase the rebellion and unbelief of many of them; and we have put enmity and hatred between them that shall last till the day of the Resurrection. Oft as they kindle *a beacon* fire for war shall God quench it! and their aim will be to abet disorder on the earth: but God loveth not the abettors of disorder.

70 But if the people of the Book believe and have the fear of
God, we will surely put away their sins from them, and will
bring them into gardens of delight: and if that they observe the
law and the Evangel, and what hath been sent down to them
from their Lord, they shall surely have their fill of good things
from above them and from beneath their feet. Some there are
among them who act aright; but many of them – how evil are
their doings!

O Apostle! proclaim all that hath been sent down to thee from thy Lord: for if thou do it not, thou hast not proclaimed His message *at all*. And God will protect thee from *evil* men: verily, God guideth not the unbelievers.

SAY: O people of the Book! ye have no ground to stand on, until ye observe the Law and the Evangel, and that which hath been sent down to you from your Lord.[25] The Book which hath been sent down to thee from thy Lord will certainly increase the rebellion and unbelief of many of them; but, be not thou troubled for the unbelievers.

Verily, they who believe, and the Jews, and the Sabeites,[26] and the Christians – whoever of them believeth in God and in the last day, and doth what is right, on them shall come no fear, neither shall they be put to grief.

Of old we accepted the covenant of the children of Israel, and sent Apostles to them. Oft as an Apostle came to them with that for which they had no desire, some they treated as liars, and some they slew;[27]

And they reckoned that no harm would come of it: – but they became blind and deaf! Then was God turned unto them: then many of them *again* became blind and deaf! but God beheld what they did.

Infidels now are they who say, 'God is the Messiah, Son of Mary;' for the Messiah said, 'O children of Israel! worship God, my Lord and your Lord.' Whoever shall join other gods with God, God shall forbid him the Garden, and his abode shall be the Fire; and the wicked shall have no helpers.

They surely are Infidels who say, 'God is the third of three:' for there is no God but one God: and if they refrain not from what they say, a grievous chastisement shall light on such of them as are Infidels.

Will they not, therefore, be turned unto God, and ask pardon of Him? since God is Forgiving, Merciful!

The Messiah, Son of Mary, is but an Apostle; other Apostles have flourished before him; and his mother was a just[28] person: they both ate food.[29] Behold! how we make clear to them the signs! then behold how they turn aside!

80 SAY: Will ye worship, beside God, that which can neither hurt nor help? But God! He only Heareth, Knoweth.

SAY: O people of the Book! outstep not bounds of truth in your religion; neither follow the desires of those who have already gone astray, and who have caused many to go astray, and have themselves gone astray from the evenness of the way.

Those among the children of Israel who believed not were cursed by the tongue of David,[30] and of Jesus, Son of Mary. This, because they were rebellious, and became transgressors: they forbade not one another the iniquity which they wrought! detestable are their actions!

Thou shalt see many of them make friends of the infidels. Evil the actions which their own passions have sent on beforehand; for God is angry with them, and in torment shall they abide for ever:

But, if they had believed in God, and the Prophet, and the *Koran* which hath been sent down to him, they had not taken them for their friends; but perverse are most of them.

Of all men thou wilt certainly find the Jews, and those who join other gods with God, to be the most intense in hatred of those who believe; and thou shalt certainly find those to be nearest in affection to them who say, 'We are Christians.' This, because some of them are priests and monks, and because they are free from pride.

And when they hear that which hath been sent down to the Apostle, thou seest their eyes overflow with tears at the truth they recognise therein, saying, 'O our Lord! we believe; write us down therefore with those who bear witness *to it*.

And why should we not believe in God, and in the truth which hath come down to us, and crave that our Lord would bring us into *Paradise* with the Just?'

Therefore hath God rewarded them for these their words, with gardens 'neath which the rivers flow; they shall abide therein for ever: this the reward of the righteous! But they who believe not and treat our signs as lies shall be the inmates of Hell-fire.

O ye who believe! interdict not the healthful viands which God hath allowed you; go not beyond this limit. God loveth not those who outstep it.[31]

90 And eat of what God hath given you for food, that which is lawful *and* wholesome: and fear God, in whom ye believe.

God will not punish you for a mistaken word in your oaths: but he will punish you in regard to an oath taken seriously.[32] Its expiation shall be to feed ten poor persons with such middling *food* as ye feed your own families with, or to clothe them; or to set free a captive. But he who cannot find means, shall fast three days. This is the expiation of your oaths when ye shall have sworn. Keep then your oaths. Thus God maketh his signs clear to you, that ye may give thanks.

O believers! surely wine and games of chance,[33] and statues, and the *divining* arrows, are an abomination of Satan's work! Avoid them, that ye may prosper.

Only would Satan sow hatred and strife among you, by wine and games of chance, and turn you aside from the remembrance of God, and from prayer: will ye not, therefore, abstain from them? Obey God and obey the Apostle, and be on your guard: but if ye turn back, know that our Apostle is *only* bound to deliver a plain announcement.

No blame shall attach to those who believe and do good works, in regard to any food they have taken, in case they fear God and believe, and do the things that are right, and shall still fear God and believe, and shall still fear him, and do good; for God loveth those who do good.

O ye who believe! God will surely make trial of you with such game as ye may take with your hands, or your lances, that God may know who feareth him in secret: and whoever after this transgresseth, shall suffer a grievous chastisement.

O believers![34] kill no game while ye are on pilgrimage. Whosoever among you shall purposely kill it, shall compensate for it in domestic animals of equal value (according to the judgment of two just persons among you), to be brought as an offering to the Caaba; or in expiation thereof shall feed the poor; or as the equivalent of this shall fast, that he may taste the ill consequence of his deed. God forgiveth what is past; but whoever doth it again, God will take vengeance on him; for God is mighty and vengeance is His.

It is lawful for you to fish in the sea, and to eat *fish*, as provision for you and for those who travel; but it is unlawful for you to hunt by land while ye are still on pilgrimage: fear ye God, therefore, before whom ye shall be assembled.

God hath appointed the Caaba,[35] the sacred house, to be a station for mankind, and the sacred month, and the offering, and its ornaments. This, that ye may know that God knoweth all that is in the heavens and on the earth, and that God hath knowledge of everything. Know that God is severe in punishing, and that God is Forgiving, Merciful.

The Apostle is only bound to preach: and God knoweth what ye bring to light, and what ye conceal.

100 SAY: The evil and the good shall not be valued alike, even though the abundance of evil please thee; therefore fear God, O ye of understanding! that it may be well with you.

O believers! ask us not of things which if they were told might only pain you; but if ye ask of such things when the *entire*

Koran shall have been sent down, they will be declared to you: God will pardon you for this, for God is Forgiving, Gracious.
They who were before you, asked concerning such things, and afterwards quickly disbelieved therein.

God hath not ordained anything on the subject of Bahira, or Saïba, or Wasila, or Hami;[36] but the unbelievers have invented this lie against God: and most of them had no understanding.

And when it was said to them 'Accede to that which God hath sent down, and to the Apostle:' they said, 'Sufficient for us is *the faith* in which we found our fathers.' What! though their fathers knew nothing, and had no guidance?

O believers! take heed to yourselves.[37] He who erreth shall not hurt you when ye have the 'guidance:' to God shall ye all return, and He will tell you that which ye have done.

O believers! let there be witnesses between you, when death draweth nigh to any of you, at the time of making the testament; two witnesses – just men from among yourselves, or two others of a different tribe from yourselves – if ye be journeying in the earth, and the calamity of death surprise you. Ye shall shut them both up, after the prayer; and if ye doubt them, they shall swear by God, 'We will not take a bribe though the party be of kin to us, neither will we conceal the testimony of God, for then we should be among the wicked.'

But if it shall be made clear that both have been guilty of a falsehood, two others of those who have convicted them thereof, the two nearest in blood shall stand up in their place, and they shall swear by God, 'Verily our witness is more true than the witness of these two; neither have we advanced anything untrue, for then should we be of the unjust.'

Thus will it be easier for men to bear a true[38] witness, or fear lest after their oath another oath be given. Therefore fear God and hearken; for God guideth not the perverse.

One day will God assemble the Apostles, and say, 'What reply was made to you?' They shall say, 'We have no knowledge, but Thou art the Knower of Secrets.'

When He shall say: O Jesus! Son of Mary! call to mind my favour upon thee and upon thy mother, when I strengthened thee with the Holy Spirit, that thou shouldest speak[39] to men *alike* in the cradle, and when grown up; –
110 And when I taught thee the Scripture, and Wisdom, and the Law, and the Evangel: and thou didst create of clay, as it were,

the figure of a bird, by my leave, and didst breath into it, and by my leave it became a bird; and thou didst heal the blind and the leper, by my leave; and when, by my leave, thou didst bring forth the dead; and when I withheld the children of Israel from thee, when thou hadst come to them with clear tokens: and such of them as believed not said, 'This is nought but plain sorcery;'[40]

And when I revealed unto the Apostles, 'Believe on me and on my Sent One,' they said, 'We believe; and bear thou witness that we are Muslims.'

Remember when the Apostles[41] said – 'O Jesus, Son of Mary! is thy Lord able to send down a furnished TABLE to us out of Heaven!' He said – 'Fear God if ye be believers.'

They said – 'We desire to eat therefrom, and to have our hearts assured; and to know that thou hast indeed spoken truth to us, and to be witnesses thereof.'

Jesus, Son of Mary, said – 'O God, our Lord! send down a table to us out of Heaven, that it may become a recurring festival to us, to the first of us and to the last of us, and a sign from thee; and do thou nourish us, for thou art the best of nourishers.'

And God said – Verily, I will cause it to descend unto you; but whoever among you after that shall disbelieve, I will surely chastise him with a chastisement, wherewith I will not chastise any other creature.[42]

And when God shall say – 'O Jesus, Son of Mary: hast thou said unto mankind – "Take me and my mother as two Gods, beside God?"' He shall say – 'Glory be unto Thee! it is not for me to say that which I know to be not the truth; had I said that, verily thou wouldest have known it: Thou knowest what is in me, but I know not what is in Thee; for Thou well knowest things unseen!

'I spake not to them aught but that which thou didst bid me – "Worship God, my Lord and your Lord;" and I was a witness of their actions while I stayed among them; but since thou hast taken me to Thyself, Thou hast Thyself watched them, and Thou art witness of all things:

'If Thou punish them, they are Thy servants, and if Thou forgive them . . .[43] Thou, verily, art the Mighty, the Wise!'

God will say – This day shall their truth advantage the truthful. Gardens shall they have 'neath which the rivers flow,

and remain therein for ever: God is well pleased with them and
they with Him. This shall be the great bliss.
120 Unto God belongeth the sovereignty of the Heavens and of
the Earth, and of all that they contain; and He hath power over
all things.

SURA 6 – CATTLE

MECCA – 165 VERSES

In the Name of God, the Compassionate, the Merciful

Praise be to God, who hath created the Heavens and the Earth, and ordained the darkness and the light! Yet unto their Lord do the infidels give peers!

He it is who created you of clay – then decreed the term *of your life:* and with Him is *another* prefixed term *for the resurrection*. Yet have ye doubts thereof!

And He is God in the Heavens and on the Earth! He knoweth your secrets and your disclosures! and He knoweth what ye deserve.

Never did one single sign from among the signs of their Lord come to them, but they turned away from it;

And now, after it hath reached them, have they treated the truth itself as a lie. But in the end, a message as to that which they have mocked, shall reach them.

See they not how many generations we have destroyed before them? We had settled them on the earth as we have not settled you, and we sent down the very heavens upon them in copious rains, and we made the rivers to flow beneath their feet: yet we destroyed them in their sins, and raised up other generations to succeed them.

And had we sent down to thee a Book written on parchment, and they had touched it with their hands, the infidels had surely said, 'This is nought but plain sorcery.'

They say, too, 'Unless an angel be sent down to him . . .' But if we had sent down an angel, their judgment would have come on them at once,[1] and they would have had no respite:

And if we had appointed an angel, we should certainly have appointed one in the form of a man, and we should have clothed him before them in garments like their own.[2]

10 Moreover, apostles before thee have been laughed to scorn: but that which they laughed to scorn encompassed the mockers among them!

SAY: Go through the land: then see what hath been the end of those who treated them as liars.

SAY: Whose is all that is in the Heavens and the Earth? SAY: God's. He had imposed mercy on Himself as a law. He will surely assemble you on the Resurrection day; there is no doubt of it. They who are the authors of their own ruin, are they who will not believe.

His, whatsoever hath its dwelling in the night and in the day! and He, the Hearing, the Knowing!

SAY: Other than God shall I take as Lord, maker of the Heavens and of the Earth, who nourisheth all, and of none is nourished? SAY: Verily, I am bidden to be the first of those who surrender them to God (profess Islam): and, be not thou of those who join gods with God.

SAY: Verily, I fear, should I rebel against my Lord, the punishment of the great day.

From whomsoever it shall be averted on that day, He will have had mercy on him: and this will be the manifest bliss.

If God touch thee with trouble, none can take it off but He: and if He visit thee with good – it is He whose power is over all things;

And He is the Supreme over his servants; and He is the Wise, the Cognisant!

SAY: What thing is weightiest in bearing witness? SAY: God is witness between me and you; and this Koran hath been revealed to me that I should warn you by it, and all whom it shall reach. What! will ye really bear witness that there are other gods with God? SAY: I bear no such witness. SAY: Verily, He is one God, and I truly am guiltless of what ye join with Him.

20 They to whom we have given the Book, recognise him (Muhammad) as they do their own children:[3] *but* they who are the authors of their own perdition are they who will not believe.

And who more wicked than he who inventeth a lie concerning God, or who treateth our signs as lies? Verily those wicked ones shall not prosper.[4]

And on 'the Day' we will gather them all together: then will we say to those who joined gods with God, 'Where are those companion-gods of yours, as ye supposed them?'

Then shall they find no other excuse than to say, 'By God our Lord! we joined not companions with Him.'

Behold! how they lie against themselves – and the *gods* of their own inventing desert them!

Some among them hearken unto thee: but we have cast veils over their hearts that they should not understand the *Koran*, and a weight into their ears: and though they should see all kinds of signs, they will refuse all faith in them, until when they come to thee, to dispute with thee, the infidels say, 'Verily, this is nothing but fables of the ancients.'

And they will forbid it, and depart from it: – but they are only the authors of their own perdition, and know it not.

If thou couldst see when they shall be set over the fire, and shall say, 'Oh! would we might be sent back! we would not treat the signs of our Lord as lies! we would be of the believers.'

Aye! that hath become clear[5] to them which they before concealed; but though they should return, they would surely go back to that which was forbidden them; for they are surely liars!

And they say, 'There is no other than our life in this world, neither shall we be raised again.'

30 But if thou couldest see when they shall be set before their Lord! He shall say to them, 'Is not this it[6] in truth?' They shall say, 'Yea, by our Lord!' 'Taste then,' saith He, 'the torment, for that ye believed not!'

Lost are they who deny the meeting with God until 'the Hour' cometh suddenly upon them! Then will they say, 'Oh, our sighs for past negligence of this *hour!*' and they shall bear their burdens on their back! Will not that be evil with which they shall be burdened?

The life in this world is but a play and pastime; and better surely for men of godly fear will be the future mansion! Will ye not then comprehend?

Now know we that what they speak vexeth thee: But it is not merely thee whom they charge with falsehood, but the ungodly gainsay the signs of God.

Before thee have apostles already been charged with falsehood: but they bore the charge and the wrong with constancy, till our help came to them; – for none can change the words of God. But this history of His Sent Ones hath already reached thee.

But if their estrangement be grievous to thee, and if thou art able to seek out an opening into the earth or a ladder into Heaven, that thou mightest bring them a sign . . . Yes! But if God pleased,[7] He would surely bring them, one and all, to the guidance! therefore be not thou one of the ignorant.

To those only who shall lend an ear will He make answer: as for the dead, God will raise them up; then unto Him shall they return.

They say, 'Unless a sign be sent down to him from his Lord . . .' SAY: Verily, God is able to send down a sign; but the greater part of them know it not.

No kind of beast is there on earth nor fowl that flieth with its wings, but is a folk[8] like you: nothing have we passed over in the Book:[9] then unto their Lord shall they be gathered.

They who gainsay our signs are deaf, and dumb, in darkness: God will mislead whom He pleaseth, and whom He pleaseth He will place upon the straight path.

40 SAY: What think ye? If the punishment of God were to come upon you, or 'the Hour' were to come upon you, will ye cry to any other than God? *Tell me*, if ye speak the truth?

Yes! to Him will ye cry: and if He please He will deliver you from that ye shall cry to Him *to avert*, and ye shall forget the partners ye joined with Him.

Already have we sent apostles to nations that were before thee, and we laid hold on them with troubles and with straits in order that they might humble themselves:

Yet, when our trouble came upon them, they did not humble themselves; but their hearts were hardened, and Satan prearranged for them[10] their course of conduct.

And when they had forgotten their warnings, we set open to them the gates of all things, until, as they were rejoicing in our gifts, we suddenly laid hold upon them, and lo! they were plunged into despair,

And the uttermost part of that impious people was cut off. All praise be to God, the Lord of the Worlds!

SAY: What think ye? If God should take away your hearing and your sight and set a seal upon your hearts, what god beside God would restore them to you? See! how we vary our wondrous verses (signs)! yet they turn away from them!

SAY: What think ye? If the punishment of God come on you suddenly or foreseen,[11] shall any perish except the impious?

We send not our Sent Ones but as heralds of good news and warners; and whoso shall believe and amend, on them shall come no fear, neither shall they be sorrowful:

But whoso shall charge our signs with falsehood, on them shall fall a punishment for their wicked doings.

50 SAY: I say not to you, 'In my possession are the treasures of God;' neither say I, 'I know things secret;' neither do I say to you, 'Verily, I am an angel:' Only what is revealed to me do I follow. SAY: Shall the blind and the seeing be esteemed alike? Will ye not then reflect?

And warn those who dread their being gathered to their Lord, that patron or intercessor they shall have none but Him,– to the intent that they may fear Him!

And thrust not thou away those who cry to their Lord at morn and even, craving *to behold* his face. It is not for thee in anything to judge of their motives, nor for them in anything to judge of thee. If thou thrust them away thou wilt be of the doers of wrong.

Thus have we made proof of some of them by others, that they may say, 'Are these they among us to whom God hath been gracious?' Doth not God best know the thankful?

And when they who believe in our signs come to thee, SAY: Peace be upon you! Your Lord hath laid down for himself a law of mercy; so that if any one of you commit a fault through ignorance, and afterwards turn and amend, He surely will be Gracious, Merciful.

Thus have we distinctly set forth our signs, that the way of the wicked might be made known.

SAY: Forbidden am I to worship those whom ye call on beside God. SAY: I will not follow your wishes; for then should I have gone astray, and should not be of the guided.

SAY: I *act* upon proofs from my Lord, but ye treat them as falsehoods. That *punishment* which ye desire to be hastened is not in my power; judgment is with God only: He will declare the truth; and He is the best settler of disputes.

SAY: If what ye would hasten on, were in my power, the matter between me and you had been decided: but God best knoweth the impious.

And with Him are the keys[12] of the secret things; none

knoweth them but He; He knoweth whatever is on the land and in the sea; and no leaf falleth but He knoweth it; neither is there a grain in the darknesses of the earth, nor a thing green or sere, but it is noted in a distinct writing.[13]

60 It is He who taketh your souls at night,[14] and knoweth what ye have merited in the day: then he awaketh you therein, that the set life-term may be fulfilled: then unto Him shall ye return; and then shall he declare to you that which ye have wrought.

Supreme over his servants, He sendeth forth guardians who watch over you, until, when death overtaketh any one of you, our messengers take his soul, and fail not:

Then are they returned to God their Lord, the True. Is not judgment His? Swiftest He, of those who take account!

SAY: Who rescueth you from the darkness of the land and of the sea, when humbly and secretly ye cry to Him – 'If thou rescue us from this, we will surely be of the thankful?'

SAY: God rescueth you from them, and from every strait: yet afterwards ye give Him companions!

SAY: It is He who hath power to send on you a punishment from above you, or from beneath your feet, or to clothe you with discord,[15] and to make some of you to taste the violence of others. See how variously we handle the wondrous verses, that haply they may become wise!

But thy people hath accused *the Koran* of falsehood, though it be the truth: SAY: I am not in charge of you: To every prophecy is its set time, and bye-and-bye ye shall know it!

And when thou seest those who busy themselves *with cavilling* at our signs, withdraw from them till they busy themselves in some other subject: and if Satan cause thee to forget *this*, sit not, after recollection, with the ungodly people:[16]

Not that they who fear God are to pass any judgment upon them, but the *object of* recollection is that they may *continue to* fear Him.

And quit those who make their religion a sport and a pastime, and whom this present life hath deceived: warn them hereby that every soul will be consigned to doom for its own works: patron or intercessor, beside God, shall it have none: and could it compensate with fullest compensation, it would not be accepted from it. They who for their deeds shall be

consigned to doom – for them are draughts of boiling water,
and a grievous torment; for that they believed not!
70 SAY: Shall we, beside God, call upon those who can neither
help nor hurt us? Shall we turn upon our heel after that God
hath guided us? Like some bewildered man whom the Satans
have spell-bound in the desert, though his companions call
him to the true guidance, with, 'Come to us!' SAY: Verily,
guidance from God, that is the true guidance; and we are
commanded to surrender ourselves to the Lord of the Worlds.

And observe ye the times of prayer, and fear ye God: for it is He to whom ye shall be gathered.

And it is He who hath created the Heavens and the Earth, in truth, and when He saith to a thing, 'Be,' it is.

His word is the truth: and His the kingdom, on the day when there shall be a blast on the trumpet: He knoweth alike the unseen and the seen: and He is the Wise, the Cognisant.

And *remember* when Abraham said to his father Azar,[17] Takest thou images as gods? Verily, I see that thou and thy people are in manifest error.

And thus did we shew Abraham the kingdom of the Heavens and of the Earth,[18] that he might be stablished in knowledge.

And when the night overshadowed him, he beheld a star. 'This,' said he, 'is my Lord:' but when it set, he said, 'I love not *gods* which set.'

And when he beheld the moon uprising, 'This,' said he, 'is my Lord:' but when it set, he said, 'Surely, if my Lord guide me not, I shall surely be of those who go astray.'

And when he beheld the sun uprise, he said, 'This is my Lord; this is greatest.' But when it set, he said, 'O my people! I share not with you the guilt of joining gods with God;

I turn my face to him who hath created the Heavens and the
Earth, following the right religion:[19] I am not one of those
who add gods to God.'
80 And his people disputed with him. – He said: 'Dispute ye
with me about God, when He hath guided me? And I fear
not the deities whom ye join with Him, for only by the will of
my Lord have they any power:[20] My Lord embraceth all
things in His knowledge. Will ye not then consider?

And how should I fear what ye have joined with God, since ye fear not for having joined with Him that for which He hath sent you down no warranty? Which, therefore, of the two parties is more worthy of safety? Know ye that?

They who believe, and who clothe not their faith with error,[21] theirs is safety, and they are guided aright.'

This is our reasoning with which we furnished Abraham against his people: We uplift to grades *of wisdom* whom we will; Verily thy Lord is Wise, Knowing.

And we gave him Isaac and Jacob, and guided both aright; and we had before guided Noah; and among the descendants of *Abraham*, David and Solomon, and Job and Joseph, and Moses and Aaron: Thus do we recompense the righteous:

And Zachariah, John, Jesus, and Elias: all were just persons:

And Ismael and Elisha and Jonas and Lot: all these have we favoured above mankind:

And some of their fathers, and of their offspring, and of their brethren: and we chose them, and guided them into the straight way.

This is God's guidance: He guideth by it such of his servants as he will: But if they join other gods with Him, vain assuredly shall be all their works.

These are they to whom we gave the Scripture and Wisdom and Prophecy: but if these *their posterity* believe not therein, we will entrust *these gifts* to a people who will not disbelieve therein.

90 These are they whom God hath guided: follow therefore their guidance. SAY: No pay do I ask of you for this:[22] Verily it is no other than the teaching for all creatures.

No just estimate do they form of God when they say, 'Nothing hath God sent down to man.' SAY: Who sent down the Book which Moses brought, a light and guidance to man, which ye set down on paper, publishing part, but concealing most; though ye have *now* been taught that which neither ye nor your fathers knew? SAY: It is God: then leave them in their pastime of cavillings.[23]

And this Book which we have sent down is blessed, confirming that which was before it; and in order that thou mightest warn the mother-city and those who dwell round about it. They who believe in the next life will believe in It, and will keep strictly to their Prayers.

But is any more wicked than he who deviseth a lie of God, or saith, 'I have had a revelation,' when nothing was revealed to him?[24] And who saith, 'I can bring down a book like that which God hath sent down'? But couldst thou see when the ungodly are in the floods of death, and the angels reach forth their hands, saying, 'Yield up your souls: – this day shall ye be recompensed with a humiliating punishment for your untrue sayings about God, and for proudly rejecting his signs!

'And now are ye come back to us, alone, as we created you at first, and ye leave behind you the good things which we had given you, and we see not with you your intercessors whom ye regarded as the companions of God among you. There is a severance between you now, and those whom ye regarded as partners with God have deserted you.'

Verily God causeth the grain and the date stone to put forth: He bringeth forth the living from the dead, and the dead from the living! This is God! Why, then, are ye turned aside from Him?

He causeth the dawn to appear and hath ordained the night for rest, and the sun and the moon for computing time! The ordinance of the Mighty, the Wise!

And it is He who hath ordained the stars for you that ye may be guided thereby in the darknesses of the land and of the sea! clear have we made our signs to men of knowledge.

And it is He who hath produced you from one man, and hath *provided for you* an abode and resting-place![25] Clear have we made our signs for men of insight.

And it is He who sendeth down rain from Heaven: and we bring forth by it the buds of all the plants, and from them bring we forth the green foliage, and the close growing grain, and palm trees with sheaths of clustering dates, and gardens of grapes, and the olive and the pomegranate, like and unlike.[26] Look ye on their fruits when they fruit and ripen. Truly herein are signs unto people who believe.

100 Yet have they assigned the Djinn to God as his associates, though He created them; and in *their* ignorance have they falsely ascribed to him sons and daughters. Glory be to Him! And high let Him be exalted above that which they attribute to Him!

Sole maker of the Heavens and of the Earth! how, when He hath no consort, should He have a son? He hath created everything, and He knoweth everything!

This is God your Lord. There is no God but He, the creator

of all things: therefore worship Him alone; – and He watcheth over all things.

No vision taketh in Him, but He taketh in all vision:[27] and He is the Subtil, the All-informed.

Now have proofs that may be seen, come to you from your Lord; whoso seeth them, the advantage will be his own: and whoso is blind to them, his own will be the loss: I am not made a keeper over you.

Thus variously do we apply our signs,[28] that they may say, 'Thou hast studied deep:' and that to people of understanding we may make them clear.

Follow thou that which hath been revealed to thee by thy Lord: there is no god but He! and withdraw from those who join other gods with Him.

Had God pleased, they had not joined other gods with Him: and we have not made thee keeper over them, neither art thou a guardian over them.

Revile not those whom they call on beside God,[29] lest they, in their ignorance, despitefully revile Him. Thus have we planned out their actions for every people; then shall they return to their Lord, and He will declare to them what those actions have been.

With their most solemn oath have they sworn by God, that if a sign come unto them they will certainly believe it; SAY: Signs are in the power of God alone; and He teacheth you not thereby, only because when they were wrought, ye did not believe.[30]

110 And we will turn their hearts and their eyes away from the truth, because they did not believe therein at first, and we will leave them in their transgressions, wandering in perplexity.

And though we had sent down the angels to them, and the dead had spoken to them, and we had gathered all things about them in tribes, they had not believed, unless God had willed it! but most of them do not know it.

Thus have we given an enemy to every prophet – Satans among men and among Djinn: tinsel discourses do they suggest the one to the other, in order to deceive: and had thy Lord willed it, they would not have done it. Therefore, leave them and their vain imaginings –

And let the hearts of those who believe not in the life to come incline thereto, and let them find their content in this, and let them gain what they are gaining.

What! shall I seek other judge than God, when it is He who hath sent down to you the distinguishing Book? They to whom we have given the Book know that it is sent down from thy Lord with truth. Be not thou then of those who doubt.

And the words of thy Lord are perfect in truth and in justice: none can change his words: He is the Hearing, Knowing.

But if thou obey most men in this land, from the path of God will they mislead thee: they follow but a conceit, and they are only liars.

Thy Lord! He best knoweth those who err from his path, and He knoweth the rightly guided.

Eat of that over which the name of God hath been pronounced, if ye believe in his signs.

And why eat ye not of that over which the name of God hath been pronounced, since He hath made plain to you what He hath forbidden you, save as to that which is forced upon you? But indeed many mislead others by their appetites, through lack of knowledge. Verily, thy Lord! He best knoweth the transgressors.

120 And abandon the semblance of wickedness, and wickedness itself.[31] They, verily, whose only acquirement is iniquity, shall be rewarded for what they shall have gained.

Eat not therefore of that on which the name of God has not been named, for that is assuredly a crime: the Satans will indeed suggest to their votaries to wrangle with you; but if ye obey them, ye will indeed be of those who join gods with God.

Shall the dead, whom we have quickened, and for whom we have ordained a light whereby he may walk among men, be like him, whose likeness is in the darkness, whence he will not come forth? Thus have the doings of the unbelievers been prepared for them.

Even so have we placed in every city, ringleaders of its wicked ones, to scheme therein: but only against themselves shall they scheme! and they know it not.

And when a sign cometh to them they say, 'We will not believe, till the like of what was accorded to the apostles of God, be accorded to us.' God best knoweth where to place his mission. Disgrace with God, and a vehement punishment shall come on the transgressors for their crafty plottings.

And whom God shall please to guide, that man's breast will He open to Islam; but whom He shall please to mislead, strait and narrow will He make his breast, as though he were mounting up into the very Heavens! Thus doth God inflict dire punishment on those who believe not.

And this is the right way of thy Lord. Now have we detailed our signs unto those who will consider.

For them is a dwelling of peace with their Lord! and in recompense for their works, shall he be their protector.

On the day whereon God shall gather them all together . . . 'O race of Djinn,' *will He say*, 'much did ye exact from mankind.' And their votaries from among men shall say, 'O our Lord! we rendered one another mutual services: but we have reached our set term, which thou hast set for us.' He will say, 'Your abode the fire! therein abide ye for ever: unless as God shall will.' Verily, thy Lord is Wise, Knowing.

Even thus place we some of the wicked over others, as the meed of their doings.

130 O race of Djinn and men! came not apostles to you from
among yourselves, rehearsing my signs to you, and warning you of the meeting of this your day? They shall say, 'We bear witness against ourselves.' This world's life deceived them; and they shall bear witness against themselves that they were infidels: –

This,[32] because thy Lord would not destroy the cities in their sin, while their people were yet careless.

And for all, are grades *of recompense* as the result of their deeds; and of what they do, thy Lord is not regardless.

And thy Lord is the Rich one, full of compassion! He can destroy you if He please, and cause whom He will to succeed you, as he raised you up from the offspring of other people:

Verily, that which is threatened you shall surely come to pass, neither shall ye weaken *its might*.

SAY: O my people! Act as ye best can: I verily will act my part, and hereafter shall ye know

Whose will be the recompense of the abode! Verily, the ungodly shall not prosper.

Moreover, they set apart a portion of the fruits and cattle[33] which he hath produced, and say, 'This for God' – so deem they – 'And this for his companions, whom we associate with Him.' But that which is for these companions of theirs, cometh not to God; yet that which is for God, cometh to the companions! Ill do they judge.

Thus have the companion-gods induced many of these, who join them with God, to slay their children, that they might ruin them, and throw the cloak of confusion over their religion. But if God had pleased, they had not done this. Therefore, leave them and their devices.

They also say, 'These cattle and fruits are sacred: none may taste them but whom we please:' so deem they – 'And there are cattle, whose backs should be exempt from labour.' And there are cattle over which they do not pronounce the name of God: inventing *in all this* a lie against Him. For their inventions shall He reward them.

140 And they say, 'That which is in the wombs of these cattle is allowed to our males, and forbidden to our wives;' but if it prove abortive, both partake of it. *God* shall reward them for their distinctions! Knowing, Wise is He.

Lost are they who, in their ignorance, have foolishly slain their children, and have forbidden that which God hath given them for food, devising an untruth against God! Now have they erred; and they were not rightly guided.

He it is who produceth gardens of the vine trellised and untrellised, and the palm trees, and the corn of various food, and olives, and pomegranates, like and unlike. Eat of their fruit when they bear fruit, and pay the due thereof on the day of its ingathering: and be not prodigal, for God loveth not the prodigal.

And there are cattle for burdens and for journeys. Eat of what God hath given you for food; and follow not the steps of Satan, for he is your declared enemy.

You have four sorts of cattle in pairs: of sheep a pair, and of goats a pair. SAY: Hath He forbidden the two males or the two females; or that which the wombs of the two females enclose? Tell me with knowledge, if ye speak the truth:

And of camels a pair, and of oxen a pair. SAY: Hath He forbidden the two males or the two females; or that which the wombs of the two females enclose?[34] Were ye witnesses when God enjoined you this? Who then is more wicked than he who, in his ignorance, inventeth a lie against God, to mislead men? God truly guideth not the wicked.

SAY: I find not in what hath been revealed to me aught forbidden to the eater to eat, except it be that which dieth of itself, or blood poured forth, or swine's flesh; for this is unclean or profane, being slain in the name of other than God. But whoso shall be a forced partaker, if it be without wilfulness, and not in transgression, – verily, thy Lord is Indulgent, Merciful!

To the Jews did we forbid every beast having an entire hoof, and of both bullocks and sheep we forbade them the fat, save what might be on their backs, or their entrails, and the fat attached to the bone. With this have we recompensed them, because of their transgression: and verily, we are indeed equitable.

If they treat thee as an impostor, then SAY: Your Lord is of all-embracing mercy: but his severity shall not be turned aside from the wicked.

They who add gods to God will say, 'If God had pleased, neither we nor our fathers had given him companions, nor should we have interdicted anything.' Thus did they who flourished before them charge with imposture, until they had tasted our severity! SAY: Have ye any knowledge that ye can produce to us? Verily, ye follow only a conceit: ye utter only lies!

150 SAY: Peremptory proof is God's! Had He pleased He had guided you all aright.

SAY: Bring hither your witnesses who can witness that God hath forbidden these animals; but if they bear witness, witness not thou with them, nor witness to the conceits of those who charge our signs with falsehood, and who believe not in the life to come, and give equals to our Lord.

SAY: Come, I will rehearse what your Lord hath made binding on you – that ye assign not aught to Him as partner; and that ye be good to your parents; and that ye slay not your children, because of poverty: for them and for you will we provide:[35] and that ye come not near to pollutions, outward or inward:[36] and that ye slay not anyone whom God hath forbidden you, unless for a just cause. This hath he enjoined on you, to the intent that ye may understand.

And come not nigh to the substance of the orphan, but to improve it, until he come of age: and use a full measure, and a just balance: We will not task a soul beyond its ability. And when ye give judgment, observe justice, even though it be the affair of a kinsman, and fulfil the covenant of God. This hath God enjoined you for your monition –

And, 'this is my right way.' Follow it then; and follow not *other* paths lest ye be scattered from His path. This hath he enjoined you, that ye may fear Him.

Then[37] gave we the Book to Moses – complete for him who should do right, and a decision for all matters, and a guidance, and a mercy, that they might believe in the meeting with their Lord.

Blessed, too, this Book which we have sent down. Wherefore follow it and fear God, that ye may find mercy:

Lest ye should say, 'The Scriptures were indeed sent down only unto two peoples before us, but we were not able to go deep into their studies:'[38]

Or lest ye should say, 'If a book had been sent down to us, we had surely followed the guidance better than they.' But now hath a clear exposition come to you from your Lord, and a guidance and a mercy. Who then is more wicked than he who treateth the signs of God as lies, and turneth aside from them? We will recompense those who turn aside from our signs with an evil punishment, because they have turned aside.

What wait they for, but the coming of the angels to them, or the coming of thy Lord Himself, or that some of the signs of thy Lord should come to pass? On the day when some of thy Lord's signs shall come to pass, its faith shall not profit a soul which believed not before, nor wrought good works in virtue of its faith. SAY: Wait ye. Verily, we will wait also.

160 As to those who split up their religion and become sects, have thou nothing to do with them: their affair is with God only. Hereafter shall he tell them what they have done.

He who shall present himself with good works shall receive a tenfold reward; but he who shall present himself with evil works shall receive none other than a like punishment: and they shall not be treated unjustly.

SAY: As for me, my Lord hath guided me into a straight path; a true religion, the creed of Abraham, the sound in faith; for he was not of those who join gods with God.

SAY: My prayers and my worship and my life and my death are unto God, Lord of the Worlds. He hath no associate. This am I commanded, and I am the first of the Muslims.

SAY: Shall I seek any other Lord than God, when He is Lord of all things? No soul shall labour but for itself; and no burdened one shall bear another's burden. At last ye shall return to your Lord, and he will declare that to you about which you differ.

And it is He who hath made you the successors of *others* on the earth, and hath raised some of you above others by various grades, that he may prove you by his gifts. Verily thy Lord is swift to punish. But He is also Gracious, Merciful!

SURA 7 – AL ARAF

MECCA – 205 VERSES

In the Name of God, the Compassionate, the Merciful

Elif. Lam. Mim. Sad.[1] A Book hath been sent down to thee:
therefore let there be no difficulty in thy breast concerning it: to
the intent that thou mayest warn thereby, and that it may be a
monition to the faithful.
Follow ye what hath been sent down to you from your Lord;
and follow no masters beside Him. How little will ye be
monished!
How many cities have we destroyed! By night, or while they
were in their midday slumber, did our wrath reach them!
And what was their cry when our wrath reached them, but to
say, 'Verily, we have been impious.'
Surely, therefore, will we call those to account, to whom an
Apostle hath been sent, and of the sent ones themselves will we
certainly demand a reckoning.
And with knowledge will we tell them *of their deeds*, for we
were not absent from them.
The weighing[2] on that day, with justice! and they whose
balances shall be heavy, these are they who shall be happy.
And they whose balances shall be light, these are they who
have lost their souls, for that to our signs they were unjust:
And now have we stablished you on the earth, and given you
therein the supports of life. How little do ye give thanks!
10 We created you; then fashioned you; then said we to the
angels, 'Prostrate yourselves unto Adam: and they prostrated

them all in worship, save Eblis: He was not among those who prostrated themselves.

To him said God: 'What hath hindered thee from prostrating thyself in worship at my bidding?' He said, 'Nobler am I than he: me hast thou created of fire; of clay hast thou created him.'

He said, 'Get thee down hence: Paradise is no place for thy pride: Get thee gone then; one of the despised shalt thou be.'

He said, 'Respite me till the day when *mankind* shall be raised from the dead.'

He said, 'One of the respited shalt thou be.'

He said, 'Now, for that thou hast caused me to err, surely in thy straight path will I lay wait for them:

Then will I surely come upon them from before, and from behind, and from their right hand, and from their left, and thou shalt not find the greater part of them to be thankful.'

He said, 'Go forth from it, a scorned, a banished one! Whoever of them shall follow thee, I will surely fill hell with you, one and all.

And, O Adam! dwell thou and thy wife in Paradise, and eat ye whence ye will, but to this tree approach not, lest ye become of the unjust doers.'

Then Satan whispered them to shew them their nakedness,
which had been hidden from them both. And he said, 'This
tree[3] hath your Lord forbidden you, only lest ye should become
angels, or lest ye should become immortals.'
20 And he sware to them both, 'Verily I am unto you one who
counselleth aright.'

So he beguiled them by deceits: and when they had tasted of the tree, their nakedness appeared to them, and they began to sew together upon themselves the leaves of the garden. And their Lord called to them, 'Did I not forbid you this tree, and did I not say to you, "Verily, Satan is your declared enemy."'

They said, 'O our Lord! With ourselves have we dealt unjustly: if thou forgive us not and have pity on us, we shall surely be of those who perish.'

He said, 'Get ye down, the one of you an enemy[4] to the other; and on earth shall be your dwelling, and your provision for a season.'

He said, 'On it shall ye live, and on it shall ye die, and from it shall ye be taken forth.'

O children of Adam! now have we sent down to you raiment to hide your nakedness, and splendid garments; but the raiment of piety – this is best. This is one of the signs of God, that man haply may reflect.

O children of Adam! let not Satan bring you into trouble, as he drove forth your parents from the Garden, by despoiling them of their raiment, that he might cause them to see their nakedness: He truly seeth you, he and his comrades, whence ye see not them. Verily, we have made the Satans tutelars of those who believe not.

And when *the wicked* commit some filthy deed, they say, 'We found our fathers practising it, and to us hath God commanded it' – SAY: God enjoineth not filthy deeds. Will ye speak of God ye know not what?

SAY: My Lord hath enjoined what is right. Turn your faces therefore towards every place where he is worshipped,[5] and call upon him with sincere religion. As he created you, to him shall ye return: some hath he guided, and some hath he justly left in error, because they have taken the Satans as their tutelars beside God, and have deemed that they were guided aright.

O children of Adam! wear your goodly apparel when ye repair to any mosque,[6] and eat ye and drink; but exceed not, for He loveth not those who exceed.

30 SAY: Who hath prohibited God's goodly raiment, and the healthful viands which He hath provided for his servants? SAY: These are for the faithful in this present life, but above all on the day of the resurrection. Thus make we our signs plain for people of knowledge.

SAY: Truly my Lord hath forbidden filthy actions whether open or secret, and iniquity, and unjust violence, and to associate with God that for which He hath sent down no warranty, and to speak of God that ye know not.

Every nation hath its set time. And when their time is come, they shall not retard it an hour; and they shall not advance it.

O children of Adam! there shall come to you Apostles from among yourselves, rehearsing my signs to you; and whoso shall fear God and do good works, no fear shall be upon them, neither shall they be put to grief.

But they who charge our signs with falsehood, and turn away from them in their pride, shall be inmates of the fire: for ever shall they abide therein.

And who is worse than he who deviseth a lie of God, or treateth our signs as lies? To them shall a portion *here below* be assigned in accordance with the Book *of our decrees*, until the time when our messengers,[7] as they receive their souls, shall say, 'Where are they on whom ye called beside God?' They shall say: 'Gone from us.' And they shall witness against themselves that they were infidels.

He shall say, 'Enter ye into the Fire with the generations of Djinn and men who have preceded you. So oft as a fresh generation entereth, it shall curse its sister, until when they have all reached it, the last comers shall say to the former, "O our Lord! these are they who led us astray: assign them therefore a double torment of the fire:"' He will say, 'Ye shall all have double.' But of this are ye ignorant.

And the former of them shall say to the latter, 'What advantage have ye over us? Taste ye therefore the torment for that which ye have done.'

Verily, they who have charged our signs with falsehood and have turned away from them in their pride, Heaven's gates shall not be opened to them, nor shall they enter Paradise, until the camel[8] passeth through the eye of the needle. After this sort will we recompense the transgressors.

They shall make their bed in Hell, and above them shall be coverings *of fire!* After this sort will we recompense the evil doers.

40 But as to those who have believed and done the things which are right (we will lay on no one a burden beyond his power) – These shall be inmates of Paradise: for ever shall they abide therein;

And we will remove whatever rancour was in their bosoms: rivers shall roll at their feet: and they shall say, 'Praise be to God who hath guided us hither! We had not been guided had not God guided us! Of a surety the Apostles of our Lord came to us with truth.' And a voice shall cry to them, 'This is Paradise, of which, as the meed of your works, ye are made heirs.'

And the inmates of Paradise shall cry to the inmates of the fire, 'Now have we found what our Lord promised us to be true. Have ye too found what your Lord promised you to be true?' And they shall answer, 'Yes.' And a Herald shall proclaim between them: 'The curse of God be upon the evil doers,

Who turn men aside from the way of God, and seek to make it crooked, and who believe not in the life to come!'

And between them shall be a partition; and on *the wall* AL ARAF[9] shall be men who will know all,[10] by their tokens, and they shall cry to the inmates of Paradise, 'Peace be on you!' but they shall not *yet* enter it, although they long to do so.

And when their eyes are turned towards the inmates of the Fire, they shall say, 'O our Lord! place us not with the offending people.'

And they who are upon Al Araf shall cry to those whom they shall know by their tokens, 'Your amassings and your pride have availed you nothing.

Are these they on whom ye sware God would not bestow mercy? Enter ye[11] into Paradise! where no fear shall be upon you, neither shall ye be put to grief.'

And the inmates of the fire shall cry to the inmates of Paradise: 'Pour upon us some water, or of the refreshments[12] God hath given you?' They shall say, 'Truly God hath forbidden both to unbelievers,

Who made their religion a sport and pastime, and whom the life of the world hath deceived.' This day therefore will we forget them, as they forgot the meeting of this their day, and as they did deny our signs.

50 And now have we brought them the Book: with knowledge have we explained it; a guidance and a mercy to them that believe.

What have they to wait for now but its interpretation? When its interpretation[13] shall come, they who aforetime were oblivious of it shall say, 'The Prophets of our Lord did indeed bring the truth; shall we have any intercessor to intercede for us? or could we not be sent back? Then would we act otherwise than we have acted.' But they have ruined themselves; and the deities of their own devising have fled from them!

Your Lord is God, who in six days created the Heavens and the Earth, and then mounted the throne: He throweth the veil of night over the day: it pursueth it swiftly: and *he created* the sun and the moon and the stars, subjected to laws by His behest: Is not all creation and its empire His? Blessed be God the Lord of the Worlds!

Call upon your Lord with lowliness and in secret, for He loveth not transgressors.

And commit not disorders on the earth after it hath been well ordered; and call on Him with fear and longing desire: Verily the mercy of God is nigh unto the righteous.

And He it is who sendeth forth the winds as the heralds of his compassion,[14] until they bring up the laden clouds, which we drive along to some dead land and send down water thereon, by which we cause an upgrowth of all kinds of fruit. – Thus will we bring forth the dead. Haply ye will reflect.

In a rich soil, its plants spring forth *abundantly* by the will of its Lord, and in that which is bad, they spring forth but scantily. Thus do We diversify our signs for those who are thankful.

Of old sent We Noah to his people,[15] and he said, 'O my people! worship God. Ye have no God but Him: indeed I fear for you the chastisement of the great day.'

The chiefs of his people said, 'We clearly see that thou art in a palpable error.'

He said, 'There is no error in me, O my people! but I am a messenger from the Lord of the Worlds.

60 I bring to you the messages of my Lord, and I give you friendly counsel; for I know from God what ye know not.

Marvel ye that a Warning should come to you from your Lord through one of yourselves, that he may warn you, and that ye may fear for yourselves, and that haply ye may find mercy?'

But they treated him as a liar: so we delivered him and those who were with him in the ark, and we drowned those who charged our signs with falsehood; for they were a blind people.

And to Ad[16] *we sent* their brother Houd.[17] 'O my people!' said he, 'worship God: ye have no other god than Him: Will ye not then fear Him?'

Said the unbelieving chiefs among his people, 'We certainly perceive that thou art unsound of mind; and we surely deem thee an impostor.'

He said, 'O my people! it is not unsoundness of mind in me, but I am an Apostle from the Lord of the Worlds.

The messages of my Lord do I announce to you, and I am your faithful[18] counsellor.

Marvel ye that a warning hath come to you from your Lord through one of yourselves that He may warn you? Remember how he hath made you the successors of the people of Noah, and increased you in tallness of stature. Remember then the favours of God, that it may haply be well with you.'

They said, 'Art thou come to us in order that we may worship one God alone, and leave what our fathers worshipped? Then bring that upon us with which thou threatenest us, if thou be a man of truth.'

He said, 'Vengeance and wrath shall suddenly light on you from your Lord. Do ye dispute with me about names that you and your fathers have given your idols, and for which God hath sent you down no warranty? Wait ye then, and I too will wait with you.'

70 And we delivered him, and those who were on his side, by
our mercy, and we cut off, to the last man, those who had
treated our signs as lies, and who were not believers.

And to Themoud *we sent* their brother Saleh. He said, O my people! worship God: ye have no other god than Him: now hath a clear proof *of my mission* come to you from your Lord, this she-camel of God being a sign to you: therefore let her go at large to pasture on God's earth: and touch her not to harm her, lest a grievous chastisement seize you.

And remember how he hath made you successors to the Adites, and given you dwellings on the earth, so that on its plains ye build castles, and hew out houses in the hills. And bear in mind the benefits of God, and lay not the earth waste with deeds of licence.

Said the chiefs of his people puffed up with pride, to those who were esteemed weak, even to those of them who believed, 'What! know ye for certain that Saleh is sent by his Lord?' They said, 'Truly we believe in that with which he hath been sent.'

Then said those proud men, 'Verily, we reject that in which ye believe.'

And they ham-strung the she-camel, and rebelled against their Lord's command, and said, 'O Saleh, let thy menaces be accomplished upon us if thou art one of the Sent Ones.'

Then the earthquake surprised them; and in the morning they were found *dead* on their faces in their dwellings.

So he turned away from them, and said, 'O my people! I did indeed announce to you the message of my Lord: and I gave you faithful counsel, but ye love not faithful counsellors.'

We also *sent* Lot, when he said to his people, commit ye this filthy deed in which no creature hath gone before you?

Come ye to men, instead of women, lustfully? Ye are indeed a people given up to excess.

80 But the only answer of his people was to say, 'Turn them out of your city, for they are men who vaunt them pure.'

And we delivered him and his family, except his wife; she was of those who lingered:

And we rained a rain upon them: and see what was the end of the wicked!

And we *sent* to Madian[19] their brother Shoaib. He said, 'O my people! worship God; ye have no other God than Him: now hath a clear sign come to you from your Lord: give therefore the full in measures and weights; take from no man his chattels, and commit no disorder on the earth after it has been made so good. This will be better for you, if you will believe it.

And lay not in ambush by every road in menacing sort; nor mislead him who believeth in God, from His way, nor seek to make it crooked; and remember when ye were few and that he multiplied you, and behold what hath been the end of the authors of disorder!

And if a part of you believe in that with which I am sent, and a part of you believe not, then wait steadfastly until God shall judge between us, for He is the best of judges.'

Said the chiefs of his people puffed up with pride, 'We will surely banish thee, O Shoaib, and thy fellow-believers from our cities, unless indeed ye shall come back to our religion.' 'What!' said he, 'though we abhor it?

Now shall we have devised a lie concerning God, if after he hath delivered us from your religion we shall return to it; nor can we return to it, unless by the will of God our Lord: our Lord embraceth all things in his ken. In God have we put our trust: O our Lord! decide between us and between our people, with truth; for the best to decide art Thou.'

And the chiefs of his people who believed not, said, 'If ye follow Shoaib, ye shall then surely perish.'

An earthquake therefore surprised them, and they were found in the morning *dead* on their faces, in their dwellings.

90 Those who had treated Shoaib as an impostor, became as though they had never dwelt in them: they who treated Shoaib as an impostor, were they that perished.

So he turned away from them and said, O my people! I proclaimed to you the messages of my Lord, and I counselled you aright; but how should I be grieved for a people who do not believe?

Nor did we ever send a prophet to any city without afflicting its people with adversity and trouble, that haply they might humble them.[20]

Then changed we their ill for good, until they waxed wealthy, and said, 'Of old did troubles and blessings befall our fathers:' therefore did we seize upon them suddenly when they were unaware.

But if that the people of these cities had believed and feared us, we would surely have laid open to them blessings out of the Heaven and the Earth: but they treated our signs as lies, and we took vengeance on them for their deeds.

Were the people, therefore, of those cities secure that our wrath would not light on them by night, while they were slumbering?

Were the people of those cities secure that our wrath would not light on them in broad day, while they were disporting themselves?

Did they, therefore, deem themselves secure from the deep counsel[21] of God? But none deem themselves secure from the deep counsel of God, save those who perish.

Is it not proved to those who inherit this land after its *ancient* occupants, that if we please we can smite them for their sins, and put a seal upon their hearts, that they hearken not?

We will tell thee the stories of these cities. Their apostles came to them with clear proofs of their mission; but they would not believe in what they had before treated as imposture. – Thus doth God seal up the hearts of the unbelievers –

100 And we found not of their covenant in most of them; but we found most of them to be perverse.

Then after them we sent Moses with our signs to Pharaoh and his nobles, who acted unjustly in their regard. But see what was the end of the corrupt doers!

And Moses said, 'O Pharaoh! verily I am an apostle from the Lord of the Worlds.

Nothing but truth is it right for me to speak of God. Now am I come to you from your Lord with a proof *of my mission*; send away, therefore, the children of Israel with me.' He said, 'If thou comest with a sign, shew it if thou art a man of truth.'

So he threw down his rod, and lo! it distinctly became a serpent.

Then drew he forth his hand, and lo! it was white[22] to the beholders.

The nobles of Pharaoh's people said, 'Verily, this is an expert enchanter:

Fain would he expel you from your land: what then do ye order to be done?'

They said, 'Put[23] him and his brother off awhile, and send round men to your cities who shall muster

And bring to thee every skilled enchanter.'

110 And the enchanters came to Pharaoh. Said they, 'Shall we surely be rewarded if we prevail?'

He said, 'Yes; and ye certainly shall be near my person.'

They said, 'O Moses! either cast thou down *thy rod* first, or we will cast down *ours*.'

He said, 'Cast ye down.' And when they had cast them down they enchanted the people's eyes, and made them afraid; for they had displayed a great enchantment.

Then spake we unto Moses, 'Throw down thy rod;' and lo! it devoured their lying wonders.

So the truth was made strong, and that which they had wrought proved vain:

And they were vanquished on the spot, and drew back humiliated.

But the *other* enchanters prostrated themselves adoring:

Said they, 'We believe on the Lord of the Worlds,

The Lord of Moses and Aaron.'

120 Said Pharaoh, 'Have ye believed on him, ere I have given you leave? This truly is a plot which ye have plotted in this my city, in order to drive out its people. But ye shall see in the end *what shall happen*.

I will surely cut off your hands and feet on opposite sides; then will I have you all crucified.'

They said, 'Verily, to our Lord do we return;

And thou takest vengeance on us only because we have believed on the signs of our Lord when they came to us. Lord! pour out constancy upon us, and cause us to die Muslims.'

Then said the chiefs of Pharaoh's people – 'Wilt thou let Moses and his people go to spread disorders in our land, and desert thee and thy gods?' He said, 'We will cause their male children to be slain and preserve their females alive: and verily we shall be masters over them.'

Said Moses to his people, 'Cry unto God for help, and bear up patiently, for the earth is God's: to such of His servants as

He pleaseth doth He give it as a heritage; and for those that fear Him is a happy issue.'

'We have been oppressed,' they said, 'before thou camest to us, and since thou hast been with us:' 'Perhaps,' said he, 'your Lord will destroy your enemy, and will make you his successors in the land, and He will see how ye will act *therein*.'

Already had we chastised the people of Pharaoh with dearth and scarcity of fruits, that haply they might take warning:

And when good fell to their lot they said, 'This is our due.' But if ill befel them, they regarded Moses and his partisans as (the birds) of evil omen.[24] *Yet*, was not their evil omen from God? But most of them knew it not.

And they said, 'Whatever sign thou bring us for our enchantment, we will not believe on thee.'

130 And we sent upon them the flood and the locusts and the kummal (lice) and the frogs and the blood, – clear signs[25] – but they behaved proudly, and were a sinful people.

And when any plague fell upon them, they said, 'O Moses! pray for us to thy Lord, according to that which he hath covenanted with thee: Truly if thou take off the plague from us, we will surely believe thee, and will surely send the children of Israel with thee.' But when we had taken off the plague from them, and the time which God had granted them had expired,[26] behold! they broke their promise.

Therefore we took vengeance on them and drowned them in the sea, because they treated our signs as falsehoods and were heedless of them.

And we gave to the people who had been brought so low, the eastern and the western lands, which we had blessed as an heritage: and the good word of thy Lord was fulfilled on the children of Israel because they had borne up with patience: and we destroyed the works and the structures of Pharaoh and his people:

And we brought the children of Israel across the sea, and they came to a people who gave themselves up to their idols. They said, 'O Moses! make us a god, as they have gods.' He said, 'Verily, ye are an ignorant people:

For the worship they practise[27] will be destroyed, and that which they do, is vain.'

He said, 'Shall I seek any other god for you than God, when it is He who hath preferred you above all other peoples?'

And *remember* when we rescued you from the people of Pharaoh they had laid on you a cruel affliction; they slew your sons, and let only your daughters live, and in this was a great trial from your Lord.

And we appointed a meeting with Moses for thirty nights, which we completed with ten other nights, so that his whole time with his Lord[28] amounted to forty nights. Then said Moses to his brother Aaron, 'Take thou my place among my people, and act rightly, and follow not the way of the corrupt doers.'

And when Moses came at our set time and his Lord spake with him, he said, 'O Lord, shew thyself to me, that I may look upon thee.' He said, 'Thou shalt not see Me; but look towards the mount, and if it abide firm in its place, then shalt thou see Me.' And when God manifested Himself to the mountain he turned it to dust! and Moses fell in a swoon.

140 And when he came to himself, he said, 'Glory be to thee! To
thee do I turn in penitence, and I am the first of them that believe.'

He said, 'O Moses! thee above all men have I chosen by my commissions, and by my speaking to thee. Take therefore what I have brought thee, and be one of those who render thanks.

And we wrote for him upon the tables a monition concerning every matter, *and said*, 'Receive them thyself with steadfastness, and command thy people to receive them for *the observance of* its most goodly *precepts:* – I will shew you the abode of the wicked.'

The unjustly proud ones of the earth will I turn aside from my signs, for even if they see every sign they will not believe them; and if they see the path of uprightness, they will not take it for *their* path, but if they see the path of error, for *their* path will they take it.

This, – for that they treated our signs as lies, and were heedless of them.

Vain will be the works of those who treated our signs, and the meeting of the life to come, as lies! Shall they be rewarded but as they have wrought?

And the people of Moses took during his absence a calf made of their ornaments, and ruddy like gold, and lowing.[29] Saw they not that it could not speak to them, nor guide them in the way?

Yet they took it *for a God* and became offenders!

But when they repented, and saw that they had erred, they said, 'Truly if our Lord have not mercy on us, and forgive us, we shall surely be of those who perish.'

And when Moses returned to his people, wrathful, angered, he said, 'Evil is it that ye have done next upon my departure. Would ye hasten on the judgments of your Lord?' And he threw down the tables, and seized his brother by the head and dragged him unto him. Said he, 'Son of my mother! the people thought me weak, and had well nigh slain me. Make not mine enemies to rejoice over me, and place me not among the wrong doers.'

150 He said, 'O Lord, forgive me and my brother, and bring us into thy mercy; for of those who shew mercy thou art the most merciful.'

Verily as to those who took the calf *as a god*, wrath from their Lord shall overtake them, and shame in this present life: for thus recompense we the devisers of a lie.

But to those who have done evil, then afterwards repent and believe, thy Lord will thereafter be Lenient, Merciful.

And when the anger of Moses was stilled, he took up the tables; and in their writing was guidance and mercy for those who dread their Lord.

And Moses chose seventy men of his people for a meeting appointed by us. And when the earthquake overtook them, he said, 'O my Lord! if it had been thy pleasure, thou hadst destroyed them and me ere this! wilt thou destroy us for what our foolish ones have done? It is nought but thy trial: thou wilt mislead by it whom thou wilt, and guide whom thou wilt. Our guardian, thou! Forgive us then and have mercy on us; for of those who forgive art thou the best:

And write down for us what is good in this world, as well as in the world to come, for to thee are we guided.' He said, 'My chastisement shall fall on whom I will, and my mercy embraceth all things, and I write it down for those who shall fear me, and pay the alms, and believe in our signs,

Who shall follow the Apostle, the unlettered[30] Prophet – whom they shall find described with them in the Law and Evangel. What is right will he enjoin them, and forbid them what is wrong, and will allow them healthful viands and prohibit the impure, and will ease them of their burden, and of the yokes which were upon them; and those who shall believe in him, and strengthen him, and help him,[31] and follow the light[32] which hath been sent down with him, – these are they with whom it shall be well.'

SAY to them: O men! Verily I am God's apostle to you all;

Whose is the kingdom of the Heavens and of the Earth! There is no God but He! He maketh alive and killeth! Therefore believe on God, and his Apostle – the unlettered Prophet – who believeth in God and his word. And follow him that ye may be guided aright.

And among the people of Moses there is a certain number[33] who guide others with truth, and practise what is right according to it.

160 And we divided *the Israelites* into twelve tribes, as nations; and we revealed unto Moses when the people asked drink of him – 'Strike the rock with thy staff:' and there gushed forth from it twelve fountains – the men all knew their drinking places. And we caused clouds to overshadow them, and sent down upon them the manna and the quails . . . 'Eat of the good things with which we have supplied you.' But it was not us whom they injured, but they injured their own selves:

And when it was said to them, 'Dwell in this city, and eat therefrom what ye will, and say "Hittat" (forgiveness), and enter the gate with prostrations; then will we pardon your offences, – we will give increase to the doers of good:'

But the ungodly ones among them changed that word into another than that which had been told them:[34] therefore sent we forth wrath out of Heaven upon them for their wrong doings.

And[35] ask them about the city that stood by the sea, when its *inhabitants* broke the Sabbath; when their fish came to them on their Sabbath day appearing openly, but came not to them on the day when they kept no Sabbath. Thus did we make trial of them, for that they were evil doers.[36]

And when some of them said, why warn ye those whom God would destroy or chastise with terrible chastisement? they said, For our own excuse with your Lord; and that they may fear Him.

And when they forgot their warnings, we delivered those who had forbidden evil; and we inflicted a severe chastisement on those who had done wrong, for that they were evil doers.

But when they proudly persisted in that which was forbidden, we said to them, 'Become scouted apes;' and then thy Lord declared that until the day of the resurrection, he would surely send against them[37] (the Jews) those who should evil entreat and chastise them: for prompt is thy Lord to punish; and He is Forgiving, Merciful.

And we have divided them upon the Earth as peoples: some of them are upright and some are otherwise; and by good things and by evil things have we proved them, to the intent that they might return to us.

And they have had successors to succeed them: they have inherited the Book: they have received the passing good things of this lower world,[38] and say, 'It will be forgiven us.' Yet if the like good things came to them *again*, they would again receive them. But hath there not been received on their part a covenant through the Scripture that they should speak nought of God but the truth? And yet they study its contents. But the mansion of the next world hath more value for those who fear God – Do ye not then comprehend? –

And who hold fast the Book, and observe prayer: verily, we will not suffer the reward of the righteous to perish.

170 And when we shook the mount[39] over them as if it had been a shadow, and they thought it falling upon them, . . . 'Receive, *said we*, with steadfastness what we have brought you, and remember what is therein, to the end that ye may fear God.'

And when thy Lord brought forth their descendants from the reins of the sons of Adam and took them to witness against themselves, 'Am I not,' said He, 'your Lord?' They said, 'Yes, we witness it.' This we did, lest ye should say on the day of Resurrection, 'Truly, of this were we heedless, because uninformed;'

Or lest ye should say, 'Our fathers, indeed, aforetime joined other gods with our God, and we are their seed after them: wilt thou destroy us for the doings of vain men?'

Thus make we our signs clear: that haply they may return to God.

Recite to them[40] the history of him[41] to whom we vouchsafed our signs, and who departed from them, so that Satan followed him, and he became one of the seduced.

Had we pleased, we had certainly thereby exalted him; but he crouched to the earth and followed his own lust: his likeness, therefore, is as that of the dog which lolls out his tongue, whether thou chase him away, or leave him alone! Such is the likeness of those who treat our signs as lies. Tell them this tale then, that they may consider.

Evil the likeness of those who treat our signs as lies! and it is themselves they injure.

He whom God guideth is the guided, and they whom he misleadeth shall be the lost.

Many, moreover, of the Djinn and men have we created for Hell. Hearts have they with which they understand not, and eyes have they with which they see not, and ears have they with which they hearken not. They are like the brutes: Yea, they go more astray: these are the heedless.

Most excellent titles hath God:[42] by these call ye on Him, and stand aloof from those who pervert[43] his titles. For what they have done shall they be repaid!

180 And among those whom we have created are a people who guide others with truth, and in accordance therewith act justly.

But as for those who treat our signs as lies, we will gradually bring them down by means of which they know not:

And though I lengthen their days, verily, my stratagem shall prove effectual.

Will they not bethink them that their companion *Muhammad* is not djinn-possessed? Yes, his office is only that of plain warner.

Will they not look forth on the realms of the Heaven and of the Earth, and on all things which God hath made, to see whether haply their end be not drawing on? And in what other book will they believe[44] who reject the Koran?

No other guide for him whom God shall mislead! He will leave them distraught in their wanderings.

They will ask thee of the Hour – for what time is its coming fixed? SAY: The knowledge of it is only with my Lord: none shall manifest it in its time but He: it is the burden[45] of the Heavens and of the Earth: not otherwise than on a sudden will it come on you.[46]

They will ask thee as if thou wast privy to it: SAY: The knowledge of it is with none but God. But most men know not this.

SAY: I have no control over what may be helpful or hurtful to me, but as God willeth. Had I the knowledge of his secrets, I should revel in the good, and evil should not touch me. But I am only a warner, and an announcer of good tidings to those who believe.

He it is who hath created you from a single person, and from him brought forth his wife that he might dwell with her: and when he had known her, she bore a light burden, and went about with it; and when it became heavy, they both cried to God their Lord, 'If thou give us a perfect child we will surely be of the thankful.'

190 Yet when God had given them a perfect child,[47] they[48]
joined partners with Him in return for what he had given them. But high is God above the partners they joined with Him!

What! Will they join those with Him who cannot create anything, and are themselves created, and have no power to help them, or to help themselves?

And if ye summon them to 'the guidance,' they will not follow you! It is the same to them whether ye summon them or whether ye hold your peace!

Truly they whom ye call on beside God, are, like yourselves, His servants! Call on them then, and let them answer you, if what ye say of them be true!

Have they feet to walk with? Have they hands to hold with? Have they eyes to see with? Have they ears to hear with? SAY: Call on these joint gods of yours; then make your plot against me, and delay it not.

Verily, my Lord is God, who hath sent down 'the Book;' and He is the protector of the righteous.

But they whom ye call on beside Him, can lend you no help, nor can they help themselves:

And if ye summon them to 'the guidance,' they hear you not: thou seest them look towards thee, but they do not see!

Make the best of things;[49] and enjoin what is just, and withdraw from the ignorant:

And if stirrings to evil from Satan stir thee, fly thou for refuge to God: He verily heareth, knoweth!

200 Verily, they who fear God, when some phantom from Satan
toucheth them, remember Him, and lo! they see clearly.

Their Brethren[50] will only continue them in error, and cannot preserve themselves from it.

And when thou bringest not a verse (sign) *of the Koran* to them, they say, 'Hast thou not yet patched it up?[51] SAY: I only follow my Lord's utterances to me. This is a clear proof on the part of your Lord, and a guidance and a mercy for those who believe.

And when the Koran is read, then listen ye to it and keep silence, that haply ye may obtain mercy.

And think within thine own self on God, with lowliness and with fear and without loud spoken words, at even and at morn; and be not one of the heedless.

Verily they who are round about thy Lord disdain not His service. They praise Him and prostrate themselves before Him.

SURA 8 – THE SPOILS[1]

MEDINA – 76 VERSES

In the Name of God, the Compassionate, the Merciful

They will question thee about THE SPOILS. SAY: The spoils are God's and the apostle's. Therefore, fear God, and settle this among yourselves; and obey God and his apostle, if you are believers.

Believers are they only whose hearts thrill with fear when God is named, and whose faith increaseth at each recital of his signs, and who put their trust in their Lord;

Who observe the prayers, and give alms out of that with which we have supplied them;

These are the believers: their due grade awaiteth them in the presence of their Lord, and forgiveness, and a generous provision.

Remember how thy Lord caused thee to go forth from thy home[2] on *a mission of* truth, and part of the believers were quite averse to it:

They disputed with thee about the truth[3] which had been made so clear, as if they were being led forth to death, and saw it before them:

And *remember* when God promised you that one of the two troops[4] should fall to you, and ye desired that they who had no arms should fall to you: but God purposed to prove true the truth of his words, and to cut off the uttermost part of the infidels;

That he might prove his truth to be the truth, and bring to nought that which is nought,[5] though the impious were averse to it:

When ye sought succour of your Lord, and he answered you, 'I will verily aid you with a thousand[6] angels, rank on rank:'

10 And God made this *promise* as pure good tidings, and to assure your hearts by it: for succour cometh from God alone! Verily God is Mighty, Wise.

Recollect when sleep, a sign of security from Him, fell upon you, and he sent down upon you water from Heaven that he might thereby cleanse you, and cause the pollution of Satan to pass from you, and that he might gird up your hearts, and stablish your feet by it:

When thy Lord spake unto the angels, 'I will be with you: therefore stablish ye the faithful. I will cast a dread into the hearts of the infidels.' Strike off their heads then, and strike off from them every finger-tip.

This, because they have opposed God and his apostle: And whoso shall oppose God and his apostle . . . Verily, God will be severe in punishment.

'This *for you!* Taste it then! and for the infidels is the torture of the fire!'

O ye who believe! when ye meet the marshalled hosts of the infidels, turn not your backs to them:

Whoso shall turn his back to them on that day, unless he turn aside to fight, or to rally to *some other* troop, shall incur wrath from God: Hell shall be his abode and wretched the journey *thither!*

So it was not ye who slew them, but God slew them; and those shafts were God's, not thine![7] He would make trial of the faithful by a gracious trial from Himself: Verily, God Heareth, Knoweth.

This *befel*, that God might also bring to nought the craft of the infidels.

O Meccans! if ye desired a decision, now hath the decision come to you.[8] It will be better for you if ye give over *the struggle*. If ye return *to it*, we will return; and your forces, though they be many, shall never avail you aught, for God is with the faithful.

20 O ye faithful! obey God and his apostle, and turn not away from Him, now that ye hear *the truth;*

And be not like those who say 'We hear,' when they hear not;

For the vilest beasts in God's sight, are the deaf, the dumb, who understand not.

Had God known *any* good in them, he would certainly have made them hear. But even if He had made them hear, they would certainly have turned back and withdrawn afar.

O ye faithful! make answer to *the appeal* of God and his apostle when he calleth you to that which giveth you life. Know that God cometh in between a man and his own heart, and that to him shall ye be gathered.

And be afraid of temptation: the evil doers among you will not be the only ones on whom it will light: And know ye that God is severe in punishment.

And remember when ye were few, and reputed weak in the land:[9] ye feared lest men should pluck you away; then was it that He took you in and strengthened you with his help, and supplied you with good things, that haply ye might give thanks.

O ye who believe! deal not falsely with God and his apostle; and be not false in your engagements, with your own knowledge:

And know that your wealth and your children are a temptation; and that God! with Him is a glorious recompense.

O ye who believe! if ye fear God he will make good your deliverance, and will put away your sins from you, and will forgive you. God is of great bounteousness!

30 And *call to mind* when the unbelievers plotted against thee, to detain thee prisoner, or to kill thee, or to banish thee: They plotted – but God plotted: and of plotters is God the best!

And oft as our signs were rehearsed to them, they said, 'Now have we heard: if we pleased we could certainly utter its like! Yes, it is mere tales of the ancients.'

And when they said, 'God! if this be the very truth from before thee, rain down stones upon us from Heaven, or lay on us some grievous chastisement.'

But God chose not to chastise them while thou wast with them, nor would God chastise them when they sued for pardon.

But because they debarred *the faithful* from the holy temple, albeit they are not its guardians, nothing is there on their part why God should not chastise them. The Godfearing only are its guardians; but most of them know it not.

And their prayer at the house *of God* is no other than whistling through the fingers and clapping of the hands – 'Taste then the torment, for that ye have been unbelievers.'

The infidels spend their riches[10] with intent to turn men aside from the way of God: spend it they shall; then shall sighing be upon them, and then shall they be overcome.

And the infidels shall be gathered together into Hell,

That God may separate the bad from the good, and put the bad one upon the other, and heap them all up and put them into Hell! These are they who shall be lost.

SAY to the infidels: If they desist *from their unbelief*, what is now past shall be forgiven them; but if they return *to it*, they have already before them[11] the doom of the ancients!

40 Fight then against them till strife be at an end, and the religion be all of it God's. If they desist, verily God beholdeth what they do:

But if they turn their back, know ye that God is your protector: Excellent protector! excellent helper!

And know ye, that when ye have taken any booty, a fifth[12] part belongeth to God and to the Apostle, and to the near of kin, and to orphans, and to the poor, and to the wayfarer, if ye believe in God, and in that which we have sent down to our servant on the day of the victory,[13] the day of the meeting of the Hosts. Over all things is God potent.

When ye were encamped on the near side of the valley, and they were on the further side, and the caravan was below you, if ye had made an engagement *to attack*, ye would have failed the engagement; but *ye were led into action notwithstanding*, that God might accomplish the thing *destined* to be done:

That he who should perish might perish with a clear token[14] *before him*, and that he who liveth might live with it. And verily, God Heareth, Knoweth.

Remember when God shewed them to thee in thy dream, as few: Had he shown them numerous, ye would certainly have become fainthearted, and would certainly have disputed about the matter – But from this God kept you – He knoweth the very secrets of the breast –

And when, on your meeting, he made them to appear to your eyes as few, and diminished you in their eyes, that God might carry out the thing that was to be done.[15] To God do all things return.

Believers! when ye confront a troop, stand firm and make frequent mention of the name of God, that it may fare well with you:

And obey God and his Apostle; and dispute not, lest ye become fainthearted and your success go from you; but endure with steadfastness, for God is with the steadfastly enduring.

And be not like those *Meccans* who came out of their houses insolently and to be seen of men, and who turn others from the way of God: God is round about their actions.

50 When Satan prepared their works for them, and said, 'No man shall conquer you this day; and verily I will be near to help you:' But when the two armies came in sight, he turned on his heel and said, 'Ay, I am clear of you: ay, I see what ye see not:[16] ay, I fear God; for God is severe in punishing.'

When the hypocrites and the diseased of heart said, 'Their Religion hath misled the *Muslims:*[17] But whoso putteth his trust in God . . . Yes, verily God is Mighty, Wise!

If thou didst see, when the angels cause the infidels to die! They smite their faces and their backs, and – 'Taste ye the torture of the burning:

This, for what your hands have sent on before you:' – and God is not unjust to his servants.

Their state is like that of the people of Pharaoh and of those before them who believed not in the signs of God: therefore God seized upon them in their sin! God is Mighty, severe in punishing.

This, because God changeth not the favour with which he favoureth a people, so long as they change not what is in their hearts; and for that God Heareth, Knoweth.

Their state is like that of the people of Pharaoh, and of those before them who treated their Lord's signs as lies. We therefore destroyed them in their sins, and we drowned the people of Pharaoh; for they were all doers of wrong.

The worst beasts truly in the sight of God are the thankless who will not believe;

They with whom thou hast leagued, and who are ever breaking their league, and who fear not God!

If thou take them in war, then, by the example of their fate, scatter those who shall follow them – that they may be warned:

60 Or if thou fear treachery from any people, throw back *their treaty* to them as thou fairly mayest,[18] for God loveth not the treacherous.

And think not that the infidels shall escape Us! They shall not weaken *God*.

Make ready then against them what force ye can, and strong squadrons whereby ye may strike terror into the enemy of God and your enemy, and into others beside them whom ye know not, *but* whom God knoweth. All that you shall expend for the cause of God shall be repaid you; and ye shall not be wronged.

And if they lean to peace, lean thou also to it; and put thy trust in God: for He is the Hearing, the Knowing.

But if they seek to betray thee, God will be all-sufficient for thee. He it is who hath strengthened thee with His help, and with the faithful, and hath made their hearts one. Hadst thou spent all the riches of the earth, thou couldst not have united their hearts; but God hath united them, for He is Mighty, Wise.

O prophet! God, and such of the faithful as follow thee, will be all-sufficient for thee.

O prophet! stir up the faithful to the fight. Twenty of you who stand firm shall vanquish two hundred: and if there be an hundred of you they shall vanquish a thousand of the infidels, for they are a people devoid of understanding.

Now hath God made your work easy, for he knoweth how weak ye are. If there be an hundred of you who endure resolutely, they shall vanquish two hundred; and if there be a thousand of you, they shall vanquish two thousand[19] by God's permission; for God is with those who are resolute to endure.

No prophet hath been enabled to take captives until he had made great slaughter in the earth. Ye desire the passing fruitions of this world, but God desireth the next life *for you*. And God is Mighty, Wise.

Had there not been a previous ordinance[20] from God, a severe chastisement had befallen you, for *the ransom* which ye took.

70 Eat therefore of the spoils ye have taken what is lawful and good; and fear God: God is Gracious, Merciful.

O prophet! say to the captives who are in your hands, 'If God shall know good[21] to be in your hearts, He will give you good beyond all that hath been taken from you, and will forgive you: for God is Forgiving, Merciful.'

But if they seek to deal treacherously with you – they have already dealt treacherously[22] with God before! Therefore hath He given you power over them. God is Knowing, Wise.

Verily, they who have believed and fled their homes and spent their substance for the cause of God, and they who have taken in the prophet and been helpful to him, shall be near of kin the one to the other. And they who have believed, but have not fled their homes, shall have no rights of kindred with you at all, until they too fly their country. Yet if they seek aid from you on account of the faith, your part it is to give them aid, except against a people between whom and yourselves there shall be a treaty. And God beholdeth your actions.

The infidels lend one another mutual help. Unless ye do the same, there will be discord in the land and great corruption.

But as for those who have believed and fled their country, and fought on the path of God, and given the prophet an asylum, and been helpful to him, these are the faithful; Mercy is their due and a noble provision.

And they who have believed and fled their country since, and have fought at your side, these also are of you. Those who are united by ties of blood[23] are the nearest of kin to each other. This is in the Book of God. Verily, God knoweth all things.

SURA 9[1] – IMMUNITY

MEDINA – 130 VERSES

An IMMUNITY from God and His Apostle to those with whom ye are in league, among the Polytheist Arabs! (those who join gods with God).

Go ye, therefore, at large in the land four months: but know that God ye shall not weaken;[2] and that those who believe not, God will put to shame –

And a proclamation on the part of God and His Apostle to the people on the day of the greater pilgrimage, that God is free from *any engagement* with the votaries of other gods with God as is His Apostle! If, therefore, ye turn to God it will be better for you; but if ye turn back, then know that ye shall not weaken God: and to those who believe not, announce thou a grievous punishment.

But this concerneth not those Polytheists with whom ye are in league, and who shall have afterwards in no way failed you, nor aided anyone against you. Observe, therefore, engagement with them through the whole time *of their treaty:* for God loveth those who fear Him.

And when the sacred months[3] are passed, kill those who join other gods with God wherever ye shall find them; and seize them, besiege them, and lay wait for them with every kind of ambush: but if they shall convert, and observe prayer, and pay the obligatory alms, then let them go their way, for God is Gracious, Merciful.

If any one of those who join gods with God ask an asylum of thee, grant him an asylum, that he may hear the Word of God, and then let him reach his place of safety. This, for that they are people devoid of knowledge.

How shall they who add gods to God be in league with God and with His Apostle, save those with whom ye made a league at the sacred temple? So long as they are true to you, be ye true to them; for God loveth those who fear Him.

How *can they?* since if they prevail against you, they will not regard in you either ties of blood or faith. With their mouths will they content you, but their hearts will be averse. The greater part of them are perverse doers.

They sell the signs of God for a mean price, and turn others aside from his way: evil is it that they do!

10 They regard not in a believer either ties of blood or faith; these are the transgressors!

Yet if they turn to God and observe prayer, and pay the impost, then are they your brethren in religion. We make clear our signs to those who understand.

But if, after alliance made, they break their oaths and revile your religion, then do battle with the ring-leaders of infidelity – for no oaths are binding with them – that they may desist.

What! will ye not fight against those *Meccans* who have broken their oaths and aimed to expel your Apostle, and attacked you first? Will ye dread them? God is more worthy of your fear, if ye are believers!

So make war on them: By your hands will God chastise them, and will put them to shame, and will give you victory over them, and will heal the bosoms of a people who believe;

And will take away the wrath of their hearts. God will be turned unto whom He will: and God is Knowing, Wise.

Think ye that ye shall be forsaken as if God did not yet know those among you who do valiantly, and take none for their friends beside God, and His Apostle, and the faithful? God is well apprised of your doings.

It is not for the votaries of other gods with God, witnesses against themselves of infidelity, to visit the temples of God. These! vain their works: and in the fire shall they abide for ever!

He only should visit the temples of God who believeth in God and the last day, and observeth prayer, and payeth the legal alms, and dreadeth none but God. These haply will be among the rightly guided.

Do ye place the giving drink to the pilgrims, and the visitation of the sacred temple,[4] on the same level with him who believeth in God and the last day, and fighteth on the way of God? They shall not be held equal by God: and God guideth not the unrighteous.

20 They who have believed, and fled their homes, and striven with their substance and with their persons on the path of God, shall be of highest grade with God: and these are they who shall be happy!

Tidings of mercy from Himself, and of His good pleasure, doth their Lord send them, and of gardens in which lasting pleasure shall be theirs;

Therein shall they abide for ever; for God! with Him is a great reward.

O Believers! make not friends of your fathers or your brethren if they love unbelief above faith: and whoso of you shall make them his friends, will be wrong doers.

SAY: If your fathers, and your sons, and your brethren, and your wives, and your kindred, and the wealth which ye have gained, and merchandise which ye fear may be unsold, and dwellings wherein ye delight, be dearer to you than God and His Apostle and efforts on his Path, then wait until God shall Himself enter on His work:[5] and God guideth not the impious.

Now hath God helped you in many battlefields, and, on the day of Honein,[6] when ye prided yourselves on your numbers; but it availed you nothing; and the earth, with all its breadth, became too straight for you:[7] then turned ye your backs in flight:

Then did God send down His spirit of repose[8] upon His Apostle, and upon the faithful, and He sent down the hosts which ye saw not, and He punished the Infidels: This, the Infidels' reward!

Yet, after this, will God be turned to whom He pleaseth; for God is Gracious, Merciful!

O Believers! only they who join gods with God are unclean! Let them not, therefore, after this their year, come near the sacred Temple. And if ye fear want,[9] God, if He please, will enrich you of His abundance: for God is Knowing, Wise.

Make war upon such of those to whom the Scriptures have been given as believe not in God, or in the last day, and who forbid not that which God and His Apostle have forbidden, and who profess not the profession of the truth, until they pay tribute out of hand,[10] and they be humbled.[11]

30 The Jews say, 'Ezra (Ozair) is a son of God';[12] and the Christians say, 'The Messiah is a son of God.' Such the sayings in their mouths! They resemble the saying of the Infidels of old! God do battle with them! How are they misguided!

They take their teachers, and their monks, and the Messiah, son of Mary, for Lords[13] beside God, though bidden to worship one God only. There is no God but He! Far from His glory be what they associate with Him!

Fain would they put out God's light with their mouths: but God only desireth to perfect His light, albeit the Infidels abhor it.

He it is who hath sent His Apostle with the Guidance and a religion of the truth, that He may make it victorious[14] over every other religion, albeit they who assign partners to God be averse from it.

O Believers! of a truth, many of the teachers and monks do devour man's substance in vanity, and turn them from the Way of God. But to those who treasure up gold and silver and expend it not in the Way of God, announce tidings of a grievous torment.

On that day their *treasures* shall be heated in hell fire, and their foreheads, and their sides, and their backs, shall be branded with them . . . 'This is what ye have treasured up for yourselves: taste, therefore, your treasures!'

Twelve months is the number of months with God,[15] according to God's book, *since* the day when He created the Heavens and the Earth: of these four are sacred: this is the right usage: But wrong not yourselves therein; attack those who join gods with God in all, as they attack you in all: and know that God is with those who fear Him.

To carry over a sacred month to another, is only a growth of infidelity. The Infidels are led into error by it. They allow it one year, and forbid it another, that they may make good the number of months which God hath hallowed, and they allow that which God hath prohibited. The evil of their deeds hath been prepared for them *by Satan:* for God guideth not the people who do not believe.

O Believers! what possessed you, that when it was said to you, 'March forth on the Way of God,' ye sank heavily earthwards? What! prefer ye the life of this world to the next? But the fruition of this mundane life, in respect of that which is to come, is but little.[16]

Unless ye march forth, with a grievous chastisement will He chastise you; and He will place another people in your stead, and ye shall in no way harm Him: for over everything is God potent.

40 If ye assist not *your Prophet* . . . God assisted him formerly, when the unbelievers drove him forth, in company with a second only![17] when they two were in the cave; when *the Prophet* said to his companion, 'Be not distressed; verily, God is with us.' And God sent down His tranquillity upon him, and strengthened him with hosts ye saw not, and made the word of those who believed not the abased, and the word of God was the exalted: for God is Mighty, Wise.

March ye forth the light and heavy *armed*,[18] and contend with your substance and your persons on the Way of God. This, if ye know it, will be better for you.

Had there been a near advantage and a short journey, they would certainly have followed thee; but the way seemed long to them.[19] Yet will they swear by God, 'Had we been able, we had surely gone forth with you:' they are self-destroyers! And God knoweth that they are surely liars!

God forgive thee! Why didst thou give them leave *to stay behind*, ere they who make true excuses had become known to thee, and thou hadst known the liars?

They who believe in God and in the last day will not ask leave of thee to be exempt from contending with their substance and their persons. But God knoweth those who fear Him!

They only will ask thy leave who believe not in God and the

last day, and whose hearts are full of doubts, and who are tossed up and down in their doubtings.

Moreover, had they been desirous to take the field, they would have got ready for that purpose the munitions of war.[20] But God was averse to their marching forth, and made them laggards; and it was said, 'Sit ye *at home* with those who sit.'

Had they taken the field with you, they would only have added a burden to you, and have hurried about among you, stirring you up to sedition; and some there are among you who would have listened to them: and God knoweth the evil doers.

Of old aimed they at sedition, and deranged thy affairs, until the truth arrived, and the behest of God became apparent, averse from it though they were.

Some of them say to thee, 'Allow me *to remain at home*, and expose me not to the trial.' Have they not fallen into a trial *already?* But verily, Hell shall environ the Infidels!

50 If a success betide thee, it annoyeth them: but if a reverse betide thee, they say, 'We took our own measures before:' and they turn their backs and are glad.

SAY: Nothing can befall us but what God hath destined[21] for us. Our liege-lord is He; and on God let the faithful trust!

SAY: Await ye for us, other than one of the two best things?[22] But we await for you the infliction of a chastisement by God, from himself, or at our hands. Wait ye then; we verily will wait with you.

SAY: Make ye your offerings willingly or by constraint; it cannot be accepted from you, because ye are a wicked people:

And nothing hindreth the acceptance of their offerings, but that they believe not in God and His Apostle, and discharge not *the duty of prayer* but with sluggishness, and make not offerings but with reluctance.

Let not, therefore, their riches or their children amaze thee. God is only minded to punish them by means of these, in this life present, and that their souls may depart while they are unbelievers.[23]

And they swear by God that they are indeed of you, yet they are not of you, but they are people who are afraid *of you:*

If they find a place of refuge, or caves, or a hiding place, they assuredly turn towards it and haste *thereto*.

Some of them also defame thee in regard to the alms; yet if a part be given them, they are content, but if no part be given them, behold, they are angry!

Would that they were satisfied with that which God and His Apostle had given them, and would say 'God sufficeth us! God will vouchsafe unto us of His favour, and so will His Apostle: verily unto God do we make our suit!'

60 But alms are only *to be given* to the poor and the needy,[24]
and those who collect them, and to those[25] whose hearts are won *to Islam*, and for ransoms, and for debtors, and for the cause of God, and the wayfarer. This is an ordinance from God: and God is Knowing, Wise.

There are some of them who injure[26] the Prophet and say, 'He is *all* ear.' SAY: An ear of good to you! He believeth in God, and believeth the believers: and is a mercy to such of you as believe:

But they who injure the Apostle of God, shall suffer a dolorous chastisement.

They swear to you by God to please you; but worthier is God, and His Apostle, that they should please Him, if they are believers.

Know they not, that for him who opposeth God and His Apostle, is surely the fire of Hell, in which he shall remain for ever? This is the great ignominy!

The hypocrites are afraid lest a Sura should be sent down concerning them, to tell them plainly what is in their hearts. SAY: Scoff ye; but God will bring to light that which ye are afraid of.

And if thou question them, they will surely say, 'We were only discoursing and jesting.' SAY: What! do ye scoff at God, and His signs, and His Apostle?

Make no excuse: from faith ye have passed to infidelity! If we forgive some of you, we will punish others: for that they have been evil doers.

Hypocritical men and women imitate one another.[27] They enjoin what is evil, and forbid what is just, and shut up their hands.[28] They have forgotten God, and He hath forgotten them. Verily, the hypocrites are the perverse doers.

God promiseth the hypocritical men and women, and the unbelievers, the fire of Hell – therein shall they abide – this their sufficing portion! And God hath cursed them, and a lasting torment shall be theirs.

70 Ye act like those who flourished before you. Mightier were they than you in prowess, and more abundant in wealth and children, and they enjoyed their portion: so ye also enjoy your portion, as they who were before you enjoyed theirs; and ye hold discourses like their discourses. These! vain their works both for this world and for that which is to come! These! they are the lost ones.

Hath not the history reached them of those who were before them? – of the people of Noah,[29] and of Ad, and of Themoud, and of the people of Abraham, and of the inhabitants of Madian, and of the overthrown cities? Their apostles came to them with clear proofs *of their mission:* God would not deal wrongly by them, but they dealt wrongly by themselves.

The faithful of both sexes are mutual friends: they enjoin what is just, and forbid what is evil; they observe prayer, and pay the legal impost, and they obey God and His Apostle. On these will God have mercy: verily, God is Mighty, Wise.

To the faithful, both men and women, God promiseth gardens 'neath which the rivers flow, in which they shall abide, and goodly mansions in the gardens of Eden. But best of all will be God's good pleasure in them. This will be the great bliss.

O Prophet! contend against the infidels and the hypocrites, and be rigorous with them: Hell shall be their dwelling place! Wretched the journey thither!

They swear by God that they said no such thing: yet spake they the word of infidelity, and from Muslims became unbelievers! They planned what they could not effect;[30] and only disapproved *of it* because God and His Apostle had enriched them by His bounty! If they repent it will be better for them; but if they fall back *into their sin*, with a grievous chastisement will God chastise them in this world and the next, and on earth they shall have neither friend nor protector!

Some there are of them who made this agreement with God – 'If truly He give us of His bounties, we will surely give alms and surely be of the righteous.'

Yet when he had vouchsafed them of His bounty, they became covetous thereof, and turned their backs, and withdrew afar off:

So He caused hypocrisy to take its turn in their hearts, until the day on which they shall meet Him – for that they failed their promise to God, and for that they were liars!

Know they not that God knoweth their secrets and their private talk, and that God knoweth the secret things?

80 They who traduce such of the faithful as give their alms freely, and those who find nothing to give but their earnings, and scoff at them, God shall scoff at them; and there is a grievous torment *in store* for them.

Ask thou forgiveness for them, or ask it not, *it will be the same*. If thou ask forgiveness for them seventy times, God will by no means forgive them. This, for that they believe not in God and His Apostle! And God guideth not the ungodly people.

They who were left at home were delighted to stay behind God's Apostle, and were averse from contending with their riches and their persons for the cause of God, and said, 'March not out in the heat.' SAY: A fiercer heat will be the fire of Hell.' Would that they understood this.

Little, therefore, let them laugh, and much let them weep, as the meed of their doings!

If God bring thee back *from the fight* to some of them, and they ask thy leave to take the field, SAY: By no means shall ye ever take the field with me, and by no means shall ye fight an enemy with me: ye were well pleased to sit at home at the first crisis: sit ye *at home*, then, with those who lag behind.

Never pray thou over anyone of them who dieth, or stand at his grave[31] – because they believed not in God and His Apostle, and died in their wickedness.

Let not their riches or their children astonish thee: through these God is fain only to punish them in this world, and that their souls should depart while they are still infidels.

When a Sura was sent down with 'Believe in God and go forth to war with His Apostle,' those of them who are possessed of riches demanded exemption, and said, 'Allow us to be with those who sit *at home*.

Well content were they to be with those who stay behind: for a seal hath been set on their hearts so that they understand not:–

But the Apostle and those who share his faith, contend *for the faith* with purse and person; and these! *all* good things await them: and these are they who shall be happy.

90 God hath made ready for them gardens 'neath which the rivers flow, wherein they shall remain for ever: this will be the great bliss.

Some Arabs of the desert came with excuses, praying exemption; and they who had gainsaid God and His Apostle sat at home: a grievous punishment shall light on such of them as believe not.

It shall be no crime in the weak, and in the sick, and in those who find not the means of contributing, to stay at home, provided they are sincere with God and His Apostle. Against those who act virtuously, there is no cause of blame: and God is Gracious, Merciful:–

Nor against those, to whom when they came to thee that thou shouldst mount them, thou didst say 'I find not wherewith to mount you,' and they turned away their eyes shedding floods of tears for grief, because they found no means to contribute.

Only is there cause of blame against those who, though they are rich, ask thee for exemption. They are pleased to be with those who stay behind; and God hath set a seal upon their hearts: they have no knowledge.

They will excuse themselves to you when ye come back to them. SAY: Excuse yourselves not; we cannot believe you: now hath God informed us about you: God will behold your doings, and so will His Apostle: to Him who knoweth alike things hidden and things manifest shall ye hereafter be brought back: and He will tell you what ye have done.

They will adjure you by God when ye are come back to them, to withdraw from them: Withdraw from them, then, for they are unclean: their dwelling shall be Hell, in recompense for their deserts.

They will adjure you to take pleasure in them; but if ye take pleasure in them, God truly will take no pleasure in those who act corruptly.

The Arabs of the desert are most stout in unbelief and dissimulation; and likelier it is that they should be unaware of the laws which God hath sent down to His Apostle: and God is Knowing, Wise.

Of the Arabs of the desert there are some who reckon what they expend *in the cause of God* as tribute, and wait for some change of fortune to befall you: a change for evil shall befall them! God is the Hearer, the Knower.

100 And of the Arabs of the desert, some believe in God and in
the last day, and deem those alms an approach to God and to

the Apostle's prayers. Are they not their approach? Into His mercy shall God lead them: yes, God is Indulgent, Merciful.

As for those who led the way, the first of the Mohadjers,[32] and the Ansars, and those who have followed their noble conduct, God is well pleased with them, and they with Him: He hath made ready for them gardens under whose *trees* the rivers flow: to abide therein for aye: this shall be the great bliss:

And of the Arabs of the desert round about you, some are hypocrites: and of the people of Medina, some are stubborn in hypocrisy. Thou knowest them not, *Muhammad:* we know them: twice[33] will we chastise them: then shall they be given over to a great chastisement.

Others have owned their faults, and with an action that is right they have mixed another that is wrong. God will haply be turned to them: for God is Forgiving, Merciful.

Take alms of their substance,[34] that thou mayst cleanse and purify them thereby, and pray for them; for thy prayers shall assure their minds: and God Heareth, Knoweth.

Know they not that when his servants turn to Him with repentance, God accepteth it, and that He accepteth alms, and that God is He who turneth, the Merciful?

SAY: Work ye: but God will behold your work, and so will His Apostle, and the faithful: and ye shall be brought before Him who knoweth alike the Hidden and the Manifest, and He will tell you of all your works.

And others await the decision of God; whether He will punish them, or whether He will be turned unto them: but God is Knowing, Wise.

There are some[35] who have built a Mosque for mischief[36] and for infidelity, and to disunite the faithful, and in expectation of him[37] who, in time past, warred against God and His Apostle. They will surely swear, 'Our aim was only good:' but God is witness that they are liars.

Never set thou foot in it.[38] There is a Mosque[39] founded from its first day in piety. More worthy is it that thou enter therein: therein are men who aspire to purity, and God loveth the purified.

110 Which of the two is best? He who hath founded his
building on the fear of God and the desire to please Him, or he
who hath founded his building on the brink of an undermined

bank washed away by torrents, so that it rusheth with him into the fire of Hell? But God guideth not the doers of wrong.

Their building which they[40] have built will not cease to cause uneasiness in their hearts, until their hearts are cut in pieces.[41] God is Knowing, Wise.

Verily, of the faithful hath God bought their persons and their substance, on condition of Paradise for them *in return:* on the path of God shall they fight, and slay, and be slain: a promise for this is pledged in the Law, and in the Evangel, and in the Koran – and who more faithful to his engagement than God? Rejoice, therefore, in the contract that ye have contracted: for this shall be the great bliss.

Those who turn to God, and those who serve, who praise, who fast, who bow down, who prostrate themselves, who enjoin what is just and forbid what is evil, and keep to the bounds[42] of God . . .[43] Wherefore bear *these* good tidings to the faithful.

It is not for the prophet or the faithful to pray for the forgiveness of those, even though they be of kin, who associate other beings with God, after it hath been made clear to them that they are to be the inmates of Hell.

For neither did Abraham ask forgiveness for his father, but in pursuance of a promise which he had promised to him: but when it was shewn him that he was an enemy to God, he declared himself clear of him. Yet Abraham was pitiful, kind.

Nor is it for God to lead a people into error, after he hath guided them aright, until that which they ought to dread hath been clearly shewn them. Verily, God knoweth all things.

God! His the kingdom of the Heavens and of the Earth! He maketh alive and killeth! Ye have no patron or helper save God.

Now hath God turned Him unto the Prophet and unto the refugees (Mohadjers), and unto the helpers (Ansars),[44] who followed him in the hour of distress, after that the hearts of a part of them had well nigh failed them.[45] Then turned He unto them, for He was Kind to them, Merciful.

He hath also *turned Him* unto the three[46] who were left behind, so that the earth, spacious as it is, became too strait for them; and their souls became so straitened within them, that they bethought them that there was no refuge from God but unto Himself. Then was He turned to them, that they might be

turned *to Him*, for God is He that turneth, the Merciful.
120 Believers![47] fear God, and be with the sincere.

No cause had the people of Medina and the Arabs of the desert around them, to abandon God's Apostle, or to prefer their own lives to his; because neither thirst, nor the labour, nor hunger, could come upon them when on path of God;[48] neither do they step a step which may anger the unbelievers, neither do they receive from the enemy any damage, but it is written down to them as a good work. Verily, God suffereth not the reward of the righteous to perish.

Nor give they alms either small or great, nor traverse they a torrent, but it is *thus* reckoned to them; that God may reward them with better than they have wrought.

The faithful must not march forth all together to the wars: and if a party of every band of them march not out, it is that they may instruct themselves in their religion, and may warn their people when they come back to them, that they take heed to themselves.

Believers! wage war against such of the infidels as are your neighbours, and let them find you rigorous: and know that God is with those who fear him.

Whenever a Sura is sent down, there are some of them who say, 'Whose faith hath it increased?' It will increase the faith of those who believe, and they shall rejoice.

But as to those in whose hearts is a disease, it will add doubt to their doubt, and they shall die infidels.

Do they not see that they are proved every year once or twice? Yet they turn not, neither are they warned.

And whenever a Sura is sent down, they look at one another. . . . 'Doth any one see you?' then turn they aside. God shall turn their hearts aside, because they are a people devoid of understanding.

Now hath an Apostle come unto you from among yourselves: your iniquities press heavily upon him. He is careful over you, and towards the faithful, compassionate, merciful.
130 If they turn away, SAY: God sufficeth me: there is no God
but He. In Him put I my trust. He is the possessor of the
Glorious Throne!

SURA 10 – JONAH, PEACE BE ON HIM!

MECCA – 109 VERSES

In the Name of God, the Compassionate, the Merciful

Elif. Lam. Ra.[1] These are the signs of the wise Book!

A matter of wonderment is it to the men *of Mecca*, that to a person among themselves We revealed, 'Bear warnings to the people: and, to those who believe, bear the good tidings that they shall have with their Lord the precedence merited by *their* sincerity.' The unbelievers say, 'Verily this is a manifest sorcerer.'

Verily your Lord is God who hath made the Heavens and the Earth in six days – then mounted his throne to rule all things: None can intercede with him till after his permission: This is God your Lord: therefore serve him: Will ye not reflect?

Unto Him shall ye return, all together: the promise of God is sure: He produceth a creature, then causeth it to return again – that he may reward those who believe and do the things that are right, with equity: but as for the infidels! – for them the draught that boileth and an afflictive torment – because they have not believed.

It is He who hath appointed the sun for brightness, and the moon for a light, and hath ordained her stations that ye may learn the number of years and the reckoning *of time*. God hath not created *all* this but for the truth.[2] He maketh his signs clear to those who understand.

Verily, in the alternations of night and of day, and in all that God hath created in the Heavens and in the Earth are signs to those who fear Him.

Verily, they who hope not to meet Us, and find their satisfaction in this world's life, and rest on it, and who of our signs are heedless; –

These! their abode the fire, in recompense of their deeds!

But they who believe and do the things that are right, shall their Lord direct aright because of their faith. Rivers shall flow at their feet in gardens of delight:

10 Their cry therein, 'Glory be to thee, O God!' and their salutation therein, 'Peace!'

And the close of their cry, 'Praise be to God, Lord of all creatures!'

Should God hasten evil on men as they fain would hasten their good, then were their end decreed! So leave we those who hope not to meet Us, bewildered in their error.

When trouble toucheth a man, he crieth to us, on his side, or sitting, or standing; and when we withdraw his trouble from him, he passeth on as though he had not called on us against the trouble which touched him! Thus are the deeds of transgressors pre-arranged for them.

And of old destroyed we generations before you, when they had acted wickedly, and their Apostles had come to them with clear tokens *of their mission*, and they would not believe: – thus reward we the wicked.

Then we caused you to succeed them on the earth, that we might see how ye would act.

But when our clear signs are recited to them, they who look not forward to meet Us, say, 'Bring a different Koran from this, or make some change in it.' SAY: It is not for me to change it as mine own soul prompteth. I follow only what is revealed to me: verily, I fear, if I rebel against my Lord, the punishment of a great day.

SAY: Had God so pleased, I had not recited it to you, neither had I taught it to you. Already have I dwelt among you for years, ere it *was revealed to me*. Understand ye not?

And who is more unjust than he who coineth a lie against God, or treateth his signs as lies? Surely the wicked shall not prosper!

And they worship beside God, what cannot hurt or help them; and say, 'These are our advocates with God!' SAY: Will ye inform God of aught in the Heavens and in the Earth which he knoweth not? Praise be to Him! High be He exalted above the deities they join with Him!

20 Men were of one religion only:[3] then they fell to variance: and had not a decree (of respite) previously gone forth from thy Lord, their differences had surely been decided between them!

They say: 'Unless a sign be sent down to him from his Lord . . .' But SAY: The hidden is only with God: wait therefore: I truly will be with you among those who wait.

And when after a trouble which had befallen them,[4] we caused *this* people to taste of mercy, lo! a plot on their part against our signs! SAY: Swifter to plot is God! Verily, our messengers note down your plottings.

He it is who enableth you to travel by land and sea, so that ye go on board of ships – which sail on with them, with favouring breeze in which they rejoice. But if a tempestuous gale overtake them, and the billow come on them from every side, and they think that they are encompassed therewith, they call on God, professing sincere religion: – 'Wouldst thou but rescue us from this, then will we indeed be of the thankful.'

But when we have rescued them, lo! they commit unrighteous excesses on the earth! O men! assuredly your self-injuring excess is only an enjoyment of this life present: soon ye return to us: and we will let you know what ye have done!

Verily, this present life is like the water which we send down from Heaven, and the produce of the earth, of which men and cattle eat, is mingled with it, till the earth hath received its golden raiment, and is decked out: and they who dwell on it deem that they have power over it! *but*, Our behest cometh to it by night or by day, and we make it as if it had been mown, as if it had not teemed only yesterday! Thus make we our signs clear to those who consider.

And God calleth to the abode of peace;[5] and He guideth whom He will into the right way.

Goodness[6] itself and an increase of it for those who do good! neither blackness nor shame shall cover their faces! These shall be the inmates of Paradise, therein shall they abide for ever.

And as for those who have wrought out evil, their recompense shall be evil of like degree, and shame shall cover them – no protector shall they have against God: as though their faces were darkened with deep murk of night! These shall be inmates of the fire: therein they shall abide for ever.

And on that day will we gather them all together: then will
we say to those who added gods to God, 'To your place, ye and
those added gods of yours!' Then we will separate between
them: and those their gods shall say, 'Ye served us not:[7]
30 And God is a sufficient witness between us and you: we cared
not aught for your worship.'

There shall every soul make proof of what itself shall have sent on before, and they shall be brought back to God, their true lord, and the deities of their own devising shall vanish from them.

SAY: Who supplieth you from the Heaven and the Earth? Who hath power over hearing and sight? And who bringeth forth the living from the dead, and bringeth forth the dead from the living? And who ruleth all things? They will surely say, 'God:' then SAY: 'What! will ye not therefore fear him?

This God then is your true Lord: and when the truth is gone, what remaineth but error? How then are ye so perverted?

Thus is the word of thy Lord made good on the wicked, that they shall not believe.

SAY: Is there any of the gods whom ye add to God who produceth a creature, then causeth it to return to him? SAY: God produceth a creature, then causeth it to return to Him: How therefore are ye turned aside?

SAY: Is there any of the gods ye add to God who guideth into the truth? SAY: God guideth into the truth. Is He then who guideth into the truth the more worthy to be followed, or he who guideth not unless he be himself guided? What then hath befallen you that ye so judge?

And most of them follow only a conceit: – But a conceit attaineth to nought of truth! Verily God knoweth what they say.

Moreover this Koran could not have been devised by any but God: but it confirmeth what was revealed before it, and is a clearing up of the Scriptures – there is no doubt thereof – from the Lord of all creatures.

Do they say, 'He hath devised it himself?' SAY: Then bring a Sura like it; and call on whom ye can beside God, if ye speak truth.

40 But that which they embrace not in their knowledge have they charged with falsehood, though the explanation of it had not yet been given them. So those who were before them brought charges of imposture: But see what was the end of the unjust!

And some of them believe in it, and some of them believe not in it. But thy Lord well knoweth the transgressors.

And if they charge thee with imposture, then SAY: My work for me, and your work for you! Ye are clear of that which I do, and I am clear of that which ye do.

And some of them lend a ready ear to thee: But wilt thou make the deaf to hear even though they understand not?

And some of them look at thee: But wilt thou guide the blind even though they see not?

Verily, God will not wrong men in aught, but men will wrong themselves.

Moreover, on that day, He will gather them all together: They shall seem as though they had waited but an hour of the day! They shall recognise one another! Now perish they who denied the meeting with God, and were not guided aright!

Whether we cause thee to see some of our menaces against them *fulfilled*, or whether we *first* take thee to Ourself,[8] to us do they return. Then shall God bear witness of what they do.

And every people hath had its apostle.[9] And when their apostle came, a rightful decision took place between them, and they were not wronged.

Yet they say, 'When will this menace be made good? Tell us if ye speak truly.'

50 SAY: I have no power over my own weal or woe, but as God pleaseth. Every people hath its time: when their time is come, they shall neither retard nor advance it an hour.

SAY: How think ye? if God's punishment came on you by night or by day, what portion of it would the wicked desire to hasten on?

When it falleth on you, will ye believe it then? Yes! ye will believe it then. Yet did ye challenge its speedy coming.

Then shall it be said to the transgressors, 'Taste ye the punishment of eternity! Shall ye be rewarded but as ye have wrought?'

They will desire thee to inform them whether this be true? SAY: Yes! by my Lord it is the truth: and it is not ye who can weaken Him.

And every soul that hath sinned, if it possessed all that is on earth, would assuredly ransom itself therewith; and they will proclaim their repentance when they have seen the punishment: and there shall be a rightful decision between them, and they shall not be unjustly dealt with.

Is not whatever is in the Heavens and the Earth God's? Is not then the promise of God true? Yet most of them know it not.

He maketh alive and He causeth to die, and to Him shall ye return.

O men! now hath a warning come to you from your Lord, and a medicine for what is in your breasts, and a guidance and a mercy to believers.

SAY: Through the grace of God and his mercy! and in this
therefore let them rejoice: better is this than all ye amass.
60 SAY: What think ye? of what God hath sent down to you for
food, have ye made unlawful and lawful? SAY: Hath God
permitted you? or invent ye on the part of God?

But what on the day of Resurrection will be the thought of those who invent a lie on the part of God? Truly God is full of bounties to man; but most of them give not thanks.

Thou shalt not be employed in affairs, nor shalt thou read a text out of the Koran, nor shall ye work any work, but we will be witnesses over you when ye are engaged therein: and not the weight of an atom on Earth or in Heaven escapeth thy Lord; nor is there aught that is less than this or greater, but it is in the perspicuous Book.

Are not the friends of God, those on whom no fear shall come, nor shall they be put to grief?

They who believe and fear God –

For them are good tidings in this life, and in the next! There is no change in the words of God! This, the great felicity!

And let not their discourse grieve thee: for all might is God's: the Hearer, the Knower, He!

Is not whoever is in the Heavens and the Earth subject to God? What then do they follow who, beside God, call upon deities they have joined with Him? They follow but a conceit, and they are but liars!

It is He who hath ordained for you the night wherein to rest, and the lightsome day. Verily in this are signs for those who hearken.

They say, 'God hath begotten children.' No! by his glory!
He is the self-sufficient. All that is in the Heavens and all that
is in the Earth is His! Have ye warranty for that asser-
tion? What! speak ye of God that which ye know not?
70 SAY: Verily, they who devise this lie concerning God shall
fare ill.

A portion have they in this world! Then to us they return! Then make we them to taste the vehement torment, for that they were unbelievers.

Recite to them the history of Noah,[10] when he said to his people, – If, O my people! my abode with you, and my reminding you of the signs of God, be grievous to you, yet in God is my trust: Muster, therefore, your designs and your false gods, and let not your design be carried on by you in the dark: then come to some decision about me, and delay not.

And if ye turn your backs on me, yet ask I no reward from you: my reward is with God alone, and I am commanded to be of the Muslims.

But they treated him as a liar: therefore we rescued him and those who were with him in the ark, and we made them to survive the others; and we drowned those who charged our signs with falsehood. See, then, what was the end of these warned ones!

Then after him, we sent Apostles to their peoples, and they came to them with credentials; but they would not believe in what they had denied aforetime: Thus seal we up the hearts of the transgressors!

Then sent we, after them, Moses and Aaron to Pharaoh and his nobles with our signs; but they acted proudly and were a wicked people:

And when the truth came to them from us, they said, 'Verily, this is clear sorcery.'

Moses said: 'What! say ye of the truth after it hath come to you, "Is this sorcery?" But sorcerers shall not prosper.'

They said: 'Art thou come to us to pervert us from the faith in which we found our fathers, and that you twain shall bear rule in this land? But we believe you not.'

80 And Pharaoh said: 'Fetch me every skilled magician.' And
when the magicians arrived, Moses said to them, 'Cast down what ye have to cast.'

And when they had cast them down, Moses said, 'Verily, God will render vain the sorceries which ye have brought to pass: God prospereth not the work of the evil doers.'

And by his words will God verify the Truth, though the impious be averse to it.

And none believed on Moses but a race among his own people, through fear of Pharaoh and his nobles, lest he should afflict them: For of a truth mighty was Pharaoh in the land, and one who committed excesses.

And Moses said: 'O my people! if ye believe in God, then put your trust in Him – if ye be Muslims.'

And they said: 'In God put we our trust. O our Lord! abandon us not to trial from that unjust people,

And deliver us by thy mercy from the unbelieving people.'

Then thus revealed we to Moses and to his brother: 'Provide houses for your people in Egypt, and *in* your houses make a Kebla, and observe prayer and proclaim good tidings to the believers.'

And Moses said: 'O our Lord! thou hast indeed given to Pharaoh and his nobles splendour and riches in this present life: O our Lord! that they may err from thy way! O our Lord! confound their riches and harden their hearts that they may not believe till they see the dolorous torment.'

He said: 'The prayer of you both is heard: pursue ye both therefore the straight path, and follow not the path of those who have no knowledge.'

90 And we led the children of Israel through the sea; and Pharaoh and his hosts followed them in eager and hostile sort until, when the drowning overtook him, he said, 'I believe that there is no God but he on whom the children of Israel believe, and I am one of the Muslims.'

'Yes, now,' *said God:* 'but thou hast been rebellious hitherto, and wast one of the wicked doers.

But this day will we rescue thee with thy body that thou mayest be a sign to those who shall be after thee:[11] but truly, most men are of our signs regardless!'

Moreover we prepared a settled abode for the children of Israel, and provided them with good things: nor did they fall into variance till the knowledge (the Law) came to them: Truly thy Lord will decide between them on the day of Resurrection concerning that in which they differed.

And if thou art in doubt as to what we have sent down to thee, inquire at those who have read the Scriptures before thee.[12] Now hath the truth come unto thee from thy Lord: be not therefore of those who doubt.

Neither be of those who charge the signs of God with falsehood, lest thou be of those who perish.

Verily they against whom the decree of thy Lord is pronounced, shall not believe,

Even though every kind of sign come unto them, till they behold the dolorous torment!

Were it otherwise, any city, had it believed, might have found its safety in its faith. But it was so, only with the people of JONAS. When they believed, we delivered them from the penalty of shame in this world, and provided for them for a time.

But if thy Lord had pleased, verily all who are in the earth would have believed together. What! wilt thou compel men to become believers?

100 No soul can believe but by the permission of God: and he shall lay his wrath on those who will not understand.

SAY: Consider ye whatever is in the Heavens and on the Earth: but neither signs, nor warners, avail those who will not believe!

What then can they expect but the like of such days *of wrath* as befel those who flourish before them? SAY: WAIT; I too will wait with you:

Then will we deliver our apostles and those who believe. Thus is it binding on us to deliver the faithful.

SAY: O men! if ye are in doubt as to my religion, verily I worship not what ye worship beside God; but I worship God who will cause you to die: and I am commanded to be a believer.

And set thy face towards true religion, sound in faith, and be not of those who join other gods with God:

Neither invoke beside God that which can neither help nor hurt thee: for if thou do, thou wilt certainly then be one of those who act unjustly.

And if God lay the touch of trouble on thee, none can deliver thee from it but He: and if He will thee any good, none can keep back his boons. He will confer them on such of his servants as he chooseth: and He is the Gracious, the Merciful!

SAY: O men! now hath the truth come unto you from your Lord. He therefore who will be guided, will be guided only for his own behoof: but he who shall err will err only against it; and I am not your guardian!

And follow what is revealed to thee: and persevere steadfastly till God shall judge, for He is the best of Judges.

SURA 11 – HOUD

MECCA – 123 VERSES

In the Name of God, the Compassionate, the Merciful

Elif. Lam. Ra.[1] A book whose verses are stablished in wisdom and then set forth with clearness – from the Wise, the All-informed –

That ye worship none other than God – Verily I *come* to you from Him charged with warnings, announcements;

And that ye seek pardon of your Lord, and then be turned unto Him! Goodly enjoyments will He give you to enjoy until a destined time, and His favours will He bestow on every one who deserves his favours.[2] But if ye turn away, then verily I fear for you the chastisement of the great day.

Unto God shall ye return, and over all things is he Potent.

Do they not doubly fold up their breasts, that they may hide themselves from Him?

But when they enshroud themselves in their garments, doth He not know *alike* what they conceal and what they shew?

For He knoweth the very inmost of their breast.

There is no moving thing on earth whose nourishment dependeth not on God; he knoweth its haunts and final resting place: all is in the clear Book.

And He it is who hath made the Heavens and the Earth in six days: His throne had stood ere this upon the waters,[3] that He might make proof which of you[4] would excel in works.

10 And if thou say, 'After death ye shall surely be raised again,' the infidels will certainly exclaim, 'This is nothing but pure sorcery.'

And if we defer their chastisement to some definite time, they will exclaim, 'What keepeth it back?' What! will it not come upon them on a day when there shall be none to avert it from them? And that at which they scoffed shall enclose them in on every side.

And if we cause man to taste our mercy, and then deprive him of it, verily, he is despairing, ungrateful.

And if after trouble hath befallen him we cause him to taste our favour, he will surely exclaim, 'The evils are passed away from me.' Verily, he is joyous, boastful.

Except those who endure with patience and do the things that are right: these doth pardon await and a great reward.

Perhaps thou wilt suppress a part of what hath been revealed to thee, and wilt be distressed at heart lest they say, 'If a treasure be not sent down to him, or an angel come with him . . .' But thou art only a warner, and God hath all things in his charge.

If they shall say, '*The Koran* is his own device,' SAY: Then bring ten Suras like it[5] of your devising, and call whom ye can to your aid beside God, if ye are men of truth.

But if they answer you not, then know that it hath been sent down to you in the wisdom of God only, and that there is no God but He. Are ye then Muslims?

Those who choose this present life and its braveries, we will recompense for their works therein: they shall have nothing less therein than their deserts.

These are they for whom there is nothing in the next world but the Fire: all that they have wrought in this life shall come to nought, and vain shall be all their doings.

20 *With such can they be compared* who rest upon clear proofs from their Lord? to whom a witness from him reciteth the Koran, and who is preceded by the Book of Moses, a guide and mercy? These have faith in it: but the partisans of *idolatry*, who believe not in it, are menaced with the fire! Have thou no doubts about that Book, for it is the very truth from thy Lord. But most men will not believe.

Who is guilty of a greater injustice than he who inventeth a lie concerning God? They shall be set before their Lord, and the witnesses shall say, 'These are they who made their Lord a liar.' Shall not the malison of God be on these unjust doers,

Who pervert others from the way of God, and seek to make it crooked, and believe not in a life to come? God's power on earth they shall not weaken; and beside God they have no protector! Doubled shall be their punishment! They were not able to hearken, and they could not see.

These are they who have lost their own souls, and the deities of their own devising have vanished from them:

There is no doubt but that in the next world they shall be the lost ones.

But they who shall have believed and done the things that are right, and humbled them before their Lord, shall be the inmates of Paradise; therein shall they abide for ever.

These two sorts of persons resemble the blind and deaf, and the seeing and hearing: shall these be compared as alike? Ah! do ye not comprehend?

We sent Noah of old unto his people: – 'Verily I come to you a plain admonisher,

That ye worship none but God. Verily I fear for you the punishment of a grievous day.'

Then said the chiefs of his people who believed not, 'We see in thee but a man like ourselves; and we see not who have followed thee except our meanest ones of hasty judgment, nor see we any excellence in you above ourselves: nay, we deem you liars.'

30 He said: 'O my people! how think you? If I am upon a clear revelation from my Lord, who hath bestowed on me mercy from Himself to which ye are blind, can we force it on you, if ye are averse from it?

And, O my people! I ask you not for riches: my reward is of God alone: and I will not drive away those who believe that they shall meet their Lord: – but I see that ye are an ignorant people.

And, O my people! were I to drive them away, who shall help me against God? Will ye not therefore consider?

And I tell you not that with me are the treasures of God: nor do I say, "I know the things unseen;" nor do I say, "I am an angel;" nor do I say of those whom you eye with scorn, No good thing will God bestow on them: – God best knoweth what is in their minds – for then should I be one of those who act unjustly.'

They said: 'O Noah! already hast thou disputed with us, and multiplied disputes with us: Bring then upon us what thou hast threatened, if thou be of those who speak truth.'

He said, 'God will bring it on you at His sole pleasure, and it is not you who can weaken him;

Nor, if God desire to mislead you, shall my counsel profit you, though I fain would counsel you aright. He is your Lord, and unto Him shall ye be brought back.'

Do they say, 'This Koran is of his own devising?' SAY: On me be my own guilt, if I have devised it, but I am clear of that whereof ye are guilty.

And it was revealed unto Noah. Verily, none of thy people shall believe, save they who have believed already; therefore be not thou grieved at their doings.

But build the Ark under our eye and after our revelation: and plead not with me for the evil doers, for they are to be drowned.
40 So he built the Ark; and whenever the chiefs of his people passed by they laughed him to scorn:[6] said he, 'Though ye laugh at us, we truly shall laugh at you, even as ye laugh at us; and in the end ye shall know

On whom a punishment shall come that shall shame him, and on whom shall light a lasting punishment.'

Thus was it until our sentence came to pass, and the earth's surface[7] boiled up. We said, 'Carry into it one pair of every kind, and thy family, except him on whom sentence hath before been passed, and those who have believed.' But there believed not with him except a few.

And he said, 'Embark ye therein. In the name of God be its course and its riding at anchor! Truly my Lord is right Gracious, Merciful.'

And the Ark moved on with them amid waves like mountains: and Noah called to his son – for he was apart – 'Embark with us, O my child! and be not with the unbelievers.'

He said, 'I will betake me to a mountain that shall secure me from the water.' He said, 'None shall be secure this day from the decree of God, save him on whom He shall have mercy.' And a wave passed between them, and he was among the drowned.

And it was said, 'O Earth! swallow up thy water;' and 'cease, O Heaven!' And the water abated, and the decree was fulfilled, and the Ark rested upon Al-Djoudi; and it was said, 'Avaunt! ye tribe of the wicked!'

And Noah called on his Lord and said, 'O Lord! verily my son is of my family: and thy promise is true, and thou art the most just of judges.'

He said, 'O Noah! verily, he is not of thy family: in this thou actest not aright.[8] Ask not of me that whereof thou knowest nought: I warn thee that thou become not of the ignorant.

He said, 'To thee verily, O my Lord, do I repair lest I ask that of thee wherein I have no knowledge: unless thou forgive me and be merciful to me I shall be one of the lost.
50 It was said to him, 'O Noah! debark with peace from Us, and with blessings on thee and on peoples *to be born* from those who are with thee; but as for other and *unbelieving* peoples, we will give them their good things in this world, but hereafter shall a grievous punishment light on them from us.

This is one of the secret Histories: we reveal it unto thee: neither thou nor thy people knew it ere this: be patient thou: verily, there is a *prosperous* issue to the God-fearing.

And unto Ad *we sent* their Brother HOUD. He said, 'O my people, worship God. You have no God beside Him. Ye only devise a lie.

O my people! I ask of you no recompense for this: my recompense is with Him only who hath made me. Will ye not then understand?

O my people! ask pardon of your Lord; then be turned unto Him: He will send down the heavens upon you with copious rains:

And with strength on strength will He increase you: only turn not back with deeds of evil.'

They said, 'O Houd, thou hast not brought us proofs *of thy mission:* we will not abandon our gods at thy word, and we believe thee not.

We can only say that some of our gods have smitten thee with evil.' Said he, 'Now take I God to witness, and do ye also witness, that I am clear of your joining other gods

To God. Conspire then against me all of you, and delay me not.

For I trust in God, my Lord and yours. No single beast is there which he holdeth not by its forelock. Right, truly, is the way in which my Lord goeth.

60 But if ye turn back, I have already declared to you my
message. And my Lord will put another people in your place, nor shall ye at all hurt Him; verily, my Lord keepeth watch over all things.'

And when our doom came *to be inflicted*, we rescued Houd and those who had like faith with Him, by our special mercy: we rescued them from the rigorous chastisement.

These men of Ad gainsaid the signs of their Lord, and rebelled against his messengers, and followed the bidding of every proud contumacious person.

Followed therefore were they in this world by a curse; and in the day of the Resurrection *it shall be said* to them, 'What! Did not Ad disbelieve their Lord?' Was not Ad, the people of Houd, cast far away?

And unto Themoud we sent their Brother Saleh: – 'O my people! *said he*, worship God: you have no other god than

Him. He hath raised you up out of the earth, and hath given you to dwell therein. Ask pardon of him then, and be turned unto him; for thy Lord is nigh, ready to answer.'

They said, 'O Saleh! our hopes were fixed on thee till now:[9] forbiddest thou us to worship what our fathers worshipped? Truly we misdoubt the *faith* to which thou callest us, as suspicious.'

He said, 'O my people! what think ye? If I have a revelation from my Lord to support me, and if He hath shewed his mercy on me, who could protect me from God if I rebel against him? Ye would only confer on me increase of ruin.

O my people! this is the she-Camel of God, and a sign unto you. Let her go at large and feed in God's earth, and do her no harm, lest a speedy punishment overtake you.'

Yet they hamstrung her: then said he, 'Yet three days more enjoy yourselves in your dwellings: this menace will not prove untrue.'

And when our sentence came to pass, we rescued Saleh and those who had a like faith with him, by our mercy, from ignominy on that day. Verily, thy Lord is the Strong, the Mighty!

70 And a violent tempest overtook the wicked, and they were found in the morning prostrate in their dwellings,

As though they had never abode in them. What! Did not Themoud disbelieve his Lord? Was not Themoud utterly cast off?

And our messengers came formerly to Abraham with glad tidings. 'Peace,' said they. He said, 'Peace,' and he tarried not, but brought a roasted calf.

And when he saw that their hands touched it not,[10] he misliked them, and grew fearful of them. They said, 'Fear not, for we are sent to the people of Lot.'

His wife was standing by and laughed;[11] and we announced Isaac to her; and after Isaac, Jacob.

She said, 'Ah, woe is me! shall I bear a son when I am old, and when this my husband is an old man? This truly would be a marvellous thing.'

They said, 'Marvellest thou at the command of God? God's mercy and blessing be upon you, O people of this house; praise and glory are His due!'

And when Abraham's fear had passed away, and these glad

tidings had reached him, he pleaded with us for the people of Lot. Verily, Abraham was right kind, pitiful, relenting.

'O Abraham! desist from this; for already hath the command of thy God gone forth; as for them, a punishment not to be averted is coming on them.'

And when our messengers came to Lot, he was grieved for them; and he was too weak to protect them,[12] and he said, 'This is a day of difficulty.'

80 And his people came rushing on towards him, for aforetime had they wrought this wickedness. He said, 'O my people! these my daughters will be purer for you: fear God, and put me not to shame in my guests. Is there no rightminded man among you?'

They said, 'Thou knowest now that we need not thy daughters; and thou well knowest what we require.'

He said, 'Would that I had strength to resist you, or that I could find refuge with some powerful chieftain.'[13]

The Angels said, 'O Lot! verily, we are the messengers of thy Lord: they shall not touch thee: depart with thy family in the dead of night, and let not one of you turn back: as for thy wife, on her shall light what shall light on them. Verily, that with which they are threatened is for the morning. Is not the morning near?'

And when our decree came *to be executed* we turned those *cities* upside down, and we rained down upon them blocks of claystone one after another, marked[14] by thy Lord himself. Nor are they far distant from the wicked *Meccans*.

And we sent to Madian[15] their brother Shoaib. He said, 'O my people! worship God: no other God have you than He: give not short weight and measure: I see indeed that ye revel in good things; but I fear for you the punishment of the all-encompassing day.

O my people! give weight and measure with fairness; purloin not *other* men's goods; and perpetrate not injustice on the earth with corrupt practices:

A residue,[16] the gift of God, will be best for you if ye are believers:

But I am not a guardian over you.'

They said to him, 'O Shoaib! is it thy prayers which enjoin that we should leave what our fathers worshipped, or that we should not do with our substance as pleaseth us? Thou forsooth art the mild, the right director!'

90 He said, 'O my people! How think ye? If I have a clear revelation from my Lord, and if from Himself He hath supplied me with goodly supplies, and if I will not follow you in that which I myself forbid you, do I seek aught but your amendment so far as in me lieth? My sole help is in God. In Him do I trust, and to Him do I turn me.

O my people! let not your opposition to me draw down upon you the like of that which befel the people of Noah, or the people of Houd, or the people of Saleh: and *the abodes* of the people of Lot are not far distant from you!

Seek pardon of your Lord and be turned unto Him: verily, my Lord is Merciful, Loving.

They said, 'O Shoaib! we understand not much of what thou sayest, and we clearly see that thou art powerless among us: were it not for thy family we would have surely stoned thee, nor couldest thou have prevailed against us.'

He said, 'O my people! think ye more highly of my family than of God? Cast ye Him behind your back, with neglect? Verily, my Lord is round about your actions.

And, O my people! act with what power ye can *for my hurt:* I verily will act: and ye shall know

On whom shall light a punishment that shall disgrace him, and who is the liar. Await ye; verily I will await with you.'

And when our decree came to pass, we delivered Shoaib and his companions in faith, by our mercy: And a violent tempest overtook the wicked, and in the morning they were found prostrate in their houses

As if they had never dwelt in them. Was not Madian swept off even as Themoud had been swept off?

Of old sent we Moses with our signs and with incontestable power to Pharaoh, and to his nobles – who followed the behests of Pharaoh, and, unrighteous were Pharaoh's behests.

100 He shall head his people on the day of the Resurrection and cause them to descend into the fire: and wretched the descent by which they shall descend!

They were followed by a curse in this world; and in the day of the Resurrection, wretched the gift that shall be given them!

Such, the histories of the cities which we relate to thee. Some of them are standing, others mown down:

We dealt not unfairly by them, but they dealt not fairly by themselves: and their gods on whom they called beside God availed them not at all when thy Lord's behest came to pass. They did but increase their ruin.

Such was thy Lord's grasp[17] when he laid that grasp on the cities that had been wicked. Verily his grasp is afflictive, terrible!

Herein truly is a sign for him who feareth the punishment of the latter day. That shall be a day unto which mankind shall be gathered together; that shall be a day witnessed *by all creatures.*

Nor do we delay it, but until a time appointed.

When that day shall come no one shall speak a word but by His leave, and some shall be miserable and others blessed.

And as for those who shall be consigned to misery – their place the Fire! therein shall they sigh and bemoan them –

Therein shall they abide while the Heavens and the Earth shall last, unless thy Lord shall will it otherwise; verily thy Lord doth what He chooseth.

110 And as for the blessed ones – their place the Garden! therein shall they abide while the Heavens and the Earth endure, with whatever imperishable boon thy Lord may please to add.

Have thou no doubts therefore concerning that which they worship: they worship but what their fathers worshipped before them: we will surely assign them their portion with nothing lacking.

Of old gave we Moses the Book, and they fell to variance about it. If a decree *of respite* had not gone forth from thy Lord, there had surely been a decision between them. Thy people also are in suspicious doubts about the Koran.

And truly thy Lord will repay every one according to their works! for He is well aware of what they do.

Go straight on then as thou hast been commanded, and he also who hath turned to God with thee, and let him transgress no more. He beholdeth what ye do.

Lean not on the evil doers lest the Fire lay hold on you. Ye have no protector, save God, and ye shall not be helped *against Him.*

And observe prayer at early morning, at the close of the day, and at the approach of night; for the good deeds drive away the evil deeds. This is a warning for those who reflect:

And persevere steadfastly, for verily God will not suffer the reward of the righteous to perish.

Were the generations before you, endued with virtue, and who forbad corrupt doings on the earth, more than a few of those whom we delivered? but the evil doers followed their selfish pleasures, and became transgressors.

And thy Lord was not one who would destroy those cities unjustly, when its inhabitants were righteous.

120 Had thy Lord pleased he would have made mankind of one religion: but those only to whom thy Lord hath granted his mercy will cease to differ. And unto this hath He created them; for the word of thy Lord shall be fulfilled, 'I will wholly fill hell with Djinn and men.'

And all that we have related to thee of the histories of these Apostles, is to confirm thy heart thereby. By these hath the truth reached thee, and a monition and warning to those who believe.

But say to those who believe not, 'Act as ye may and can: we will act our part: and wait ye; we verily will wait.'

To God belong the secret things of the Heavens and of the Earth: all things return to him: worship him then and put thy trust in Him: thy Lord is not regardless of your doings.

SURA 12 – JOSEPH, PEACE BE ON HIM

MECCA – 111 VERSES

In the Name of God, the Compassionate, the Merciful

Elif. Lam. Ra.[1] These are signs of the clear Book.

An Arabic Koran have we sent it down, that ye might understand it.

In revealing to thee this Koran,[2] one of the most beautiful of narratives will we narrate to thee, of which thou hast hitherto been regardless.

When Joseph said to his Father, 'O my Father! verily I beheld eleven stars and the sun and the moon – beheld them make obeisance to me!'[3]

He said, 'O my son! tell not thy vision to thy brethren, lest they plot a plot against thee: for Satan is the manifest foe of man.

It is thus that thy Lord shall choose thee and will teach thee the interpretation of dark sayings, and will perfect his favours on thee and on the family of Jacob, as of old he perfected it on thy fathers Abraham and Isaac; verily thy Lord is Knowing, Wise!'

Now in JOSEPH and his brethren are signs for the enquirers;[4]

When they said, 'Surely better loved by our Father, than we, who are more in number, is Joseph and his brother; verily, our father hath clearly erred.

Slay ye Joseph! or drive him to some other land, and on you alone shall your father's face be set! and after this, ye shall live as upright persons.'

10 One of them said, 'Slay not Joseph, but cast him down to the bottom of the well; if ye do so, some wayfarers will take him up.'

They said, 'O our Father! why dost thou not entrust us with Joseph? indeed we mean him well.

Send him with us to-morrow that he may enjoy himself and sport: we will surely keep him safely.'

He said, 'Verily, your taking him away will grieve me; and I fear lest while ye are heedless of him the wolf devour him.'

They said, 'Surely if the wolf devour him, and we so many, we must in that case be weak indeed.'

And when they went away with him they agreed to place him at the bottom of the well. And We revealed to him, 'Thou wilt yet tell them of this their deed, when they shall not know thee.'

And they came at nightfall to their father weeping.

They said, 'O our Father! of a truth, we went to run races, and we left Joseph with our clothes, and the wolf devoured him: but thou wilt not believe us even though we speak the truth.'

And they brought his shirt with false blood upon it. He said, 'Nay, but yourselves have managed this affair.[5] But patience is seemly: and the help of God is to be implored that I may bear what you tell me.'

And wayfarers came and sent their drawer of water,[6] and he let down his bucket. 'Good news!' said he, 'This is a youth!' And they kept his case secret, to make merchandise of him. But God knew what they did.

20 And they sold him for a paltry price – for some dirhems counted down, and at no high rate did they value him.

And he who bought him – an Egyptian – said to his wife,

'Treat him hospitably; haply he may be useful to us, or we may adopt him as a son.' Thus did we settle Joseph in the land, and we instructed him in the interpretation of dark sayings, for God is equal to his purpose; but most men know it not.

And when he had reached his age of strength we bestowed on him judgment and knowledge; for thus do we recompense the well doers.

And she in whose house he was conceived a passion for him, and she shut the doors and said, 'Come hither.' He said, 'God keep me! Verily, my lord hath given me a good home: and the injurious shall not prosper.'

But she longed for him; and he had longed for her had he not seen a token from his lord.[7] Thus we averted evil and defilement from him, for he was one of our sincere servants.

And they both made for the door, and she rent his shirt behind; and at the door they met her lord. 'What,' said she, 'shall be the recompense of him who would do evil to thy family, but a prison[8] or a sore punishment?'

He said, 'She solicited me to evil.' And a witness out of her own family[9] witnessed: 'If his shirt be rent in front she speaketh truth, and he is a liar:

But if his shirt be rent behind, she lieth and he is true.'

And when his lord saw his shirt torn behind, he said, 'This is one of your devices! verily your devices are great!

Joseph! leave this affair. And thou, O *wife*, ask pardon for thy crime, for thou hast sinned.'

30 And in the city, the women said, 'The wife of the Prince hath solicited her servant: he hath fired her with his love: but we clearly see her manifest error.'

And when she heard of their cabal, she sent to them and got ready a banquet for them, and gave each one of them a knife, and said, '*Joseph* shew thyself to them.' And when they saw him they were amazed at him, and cut their hands,[10] and said, 'God keep us! This is no man! This is no other than a noble angel!'

She said, 'This is he about whom ye blamed me. I wished him to yield to my desires, but he stood firm. But if he obey not my command, he shall surely be cast into prison, and become one of the despised.'

He said, 'O my Lord! I prefer the prison to compliance with their bidding: but unless thou turn away their snares from me, I shall play the youth with them, and become one of the unwise.'

And his Lord heard him and turned aside their snares from him: for he is the Hearer, the Knower.

Yet resolved they, even after they had seen the signs *of his innocence*, to imprison him for a time.

And there came into the prison with him two youths. Said one of them, 'Methought in my dream that I was pressing grapes.' And the other said, 'I dreamed that I was carrying bread on my head, of which the birds did eat. Declare to us the interpretation of this, for we see thou art a virtuous person.'

He said, 'There shall not come to you *in a dream* any food wherewith ye shall be fed, but I will acquaint you with its interpretation ere it come to pass to you. This is *a part* of that which my Lord hath taught me: for I have abandoned the religion of those who believe not in God and who deny the life to come;

And I follow the religion of my fathers, Abraham and Isaac and Jacob. We may not associate aught with God. This is of God's bounty towards us and towards mankind: but the greater part of mankind are not thankful.

O my two fellow prisoners! are sundry lords best, or God, the One, the Mighty?

40 Ye worship beside him mere names which ye have named, ye and your fathers, for which God hath not sent down any warranty. Judgment belongeth to God alone. He hath bidden you worship none but Him. This is the right faith: but most men know it not.

O my two fellow prisoners! as to one of you, he will serve wine unto his Lord: but as to the other, he will be crucified and the birds shall eat from off his head. The matter is decreed concerning which ye enquire.'

And he said unto him who he judged would be set at large, 'Remember me with thy lord.' But Satan caused him to forget the remembrance of his Lord,[11] so he remained some years in prison.

And the King said, 'Verily, I saw *in a dream* seven fat kine which seven lean devoured; and seven green ears and other withered. O nobles, teach me my vision, if a vision ye are able to expound.'

They said, 'They are confused dreams, nor know we aught of the unravelling of dreams.'

And he of the twain who had been set at large, said, 'I will tell you the interpretation; let me go for it.'

'Joseph, man of truth! teach us of the seven fat kine which seven lean devoured, and of the seven green ears, and other withered, that I may return to the men, and that they may be informed.'

He said, 'Ye shall sow seven years as is your wont, and the corn which ye reap leave ye in its ear, except a little of which ye shall eat.

Then after that shall come seven grievous years which shall eat what ye have stored for them, except a little which ye shall have kept.

Then shall come after this a year, in which men shall have rain, and in which they shall press the grape.'

50 And the King said, 'Bring him to me.'[12] And when the messenger came to Joseph, he said, 'Go back to thy lord, and ask him what meant the women who cut their hands, for my lord well knoweth the snare they laid.'

Then said the Prince to the women, 'What was your purpose when ye solicited Joseph?' They said, 'God keep us! we know not any ill of him.' The wife of the Prince said, 'Now doth the truth appear. It was I who would have led him into unlawful love, and he is one of the truthful.'

'By this' (said Joseph) 'may my lord know that I did not in his absence play him false, and that God guideth not the machinations of deceivers.

Yet I hold not myself clear, for the heart is prone to evil, save theirs on whom my Lord hath mercy; for gracious is my Lord, Merciful.'

And the King said, 'Bring him to me: I will take him for my special service.' And when he had spoken with him he said, 'From this day shalt thou be with us, invested with place and trust.'

He said, 'Set me over the granaries of the land,[13] I will be their prudent keeper!'

Thus did we stablish Joseph in the land that he might house himself therein at pleasure. We bestow our favours on whom we will, and suffer not the reward of the righteous to perish.

And truly the recompense of the life to come is better, for those who have believed and feared God.

And Joseph's brethren came and went in to him and he knew them, but they recognised him not.

And when he had provided them with their provision, he

said, 'Bring me your brother from your father. See ye not that I
fill the measure, and am the best of hosts?
60 But if ye bring him not to me, then no measure of corn shall
there be for you from me, nor shall ye come near me.'

They said, 'We will ask him of his father, and we will surely
do it.'

Said he to his servants, 'Put their money into their camel-
packs, that they may perceive it when they have returned to
their family: haply they will come back to us.'

And when they returned to their father, they said, 'O, our
father! corn is withholden from us: send, therefore, our brother
with us and we shall have our measure; and all care of him will
we take.'

He said, 'Shall I entrust you with him otherwise than as I
before entrusted you with his brother? But God is the best
guardian, and of those who shew compassion He is the most
compassionate.'

And when they opened their goods they found their money
had been returned to them. They said, 'O, our father, what
more can we desire? Here is our money returned to us; we will
provide corn for our families, and will take care of our brother,
and shall receive a camel's burden more of corn. This is an
easy quantity.'[14]

He said, 'I will not send him with you but on your oath before
God that ye will, indeed, bring him back to me, unless
hindrances encompass you.' And when they had given him
their pledge, he said, 'God is witness of what we say.'

And he said, 'O, my sons! Enter not by one gate, but enter
by different gates.[15] Yet can I not help you against aught
decreed by God: judgment belongeth to God alone. In Him put
I my trust, and in Him let the trusting trust.'

And when they entered as their father had bidden them, it did
not avert from them anything decreed of God; but it only *served
to satisfy* a desire in the soul of Jacob which he had charged
them to perform; for he was possessed of knowledge which we
had taught him; but most men have not that knowledge.

And when they came in to Joseph, he took his brother to
him. He said, 'Verily, I am thy brother. Be not thou grieved
for what they did.'[16]
70 And when he had provided them with their provisions,
he placed his drinking cup in his brother's camel-pack.

Then a crier cried after them, 'O travellers! ye are surely thieves.'

They turned back to them and said, 'What is that ye miss?'

'We miss,' said they, 'the prince's cup. For him who shall restore it, a camel's load of corn! I pledge myself for it.'

They said, 'By God! ye know certainly that we came not to do wrong[17] in the land and we have not been thieves.'

'What,' said *the Egyptians*, 'shall be the recompense of him *who hath stolen it*, if ye be found liars?'

They said, 'That he in whose camel-pack it shall be found be given up to you in satisfaction for it. Thus recompense we the unjust.'

And Joseph began with their sacks, before the sack of his brother, and then from the sack of his brother he drew it out. This stratagem did we suggest to Joseph. By the King's law he had no power to seize his brother, had not God pleased. We uplift into grades *of wisdom* whom we will. And there is one knowing above every one else endued with knowledge.

They said, 'If he steal, a brother of his hath stolen heretofore.'[18] But Joseph kept his secret, and did not discover it to them. Said he, *aside*, 'Ye are in the worse condition. And God well knoweth what ye state.'

They said, 'O Prince! Verily he hath a very aged father; in his stead, therefore, take one of us, for we see that thou art a generous person.'

He said, 'God forbid that we should take but him with whom our property was found, for then should we act unjustly.'

80 And when they despaired of Benjamin, they went apart for counsel. The eldest of them said, 'Know ye not how that your father hath taken a pledge from you before God, and how formerly ye failed in duty with regard to Joseph? I will not quit the land till my father give me leave, or God decide for me; for of those who decide is He the best.

Return ye to your father and say, "O our father! Verily, thy son hath stolen: we bear witness only of what we know: we could not guard against the unforeseen.

Enquire for thyself in the city where we have been, and of the caravan with which we have arrived; and we are surely speakers of the truth."

He said, 'Nay, ye have arranged all this among yourselves:

But patience is seemly: God, may be, will bring them back to me together; for he is the Knowing, the Wise.'

And he turned away from them and said, 'Oh! how I am grieved for Joseph!' and his eyes became white with grief, for he bore a silent sorrow.

They said, 'By God thou wilt only cease to think of Joseph when thou art at the point of death, or dead.'

He said, 'I only plead my grief and my sorrow to God: but I know from God what ye know not:[19]

Go, my sons, and seek tidings of Joseph and his brother, and despair not of God's mercy, for none but the unbelieving despair of the mercy of God.'

And when they came in to Joseph, they said, 'O Prince, distress hath reached us and our family, and little is the money that we have brought. But give us full measure, and bestow it as alms, for God will recompense the almsgivers.'

He said, 'Know ye what ye did to Joseph and his brother in your ignorance?'

90 They said, 'Canst thou indeed be Joseph?' He said, 'I am
Joseph, and this is my brother. Now hath God been gracious to us. For whoso feareth God and endureth . . . God verily will not suffer the reward of the righteous to perish!'

They said, 'By God! now hath God chosen thee above us, and we have indeed been sinners!'

He said, 'No blame be on you this day. God will forgive you, for He is the most merciful of those who shew mercy.

Go ye with this my shirt and throw it on my father's face, and he shall recover his sight: and bring me all your family.'

And when the caravan was departed, their father said, 'I surely perceive the smell of Joseph:[20] think ye that I dote?'

They said, 'By God, it is thy old mistake.'

And when the bearer of good tidings came, he cast it on his face, and Jacob's eyesight returned.

Then he said, 'Did I not tell you that I knew from God what ye knew not?'

They said, 'Our father, ask pardon for our crimes for us, for we have indeed been sinners.'

He said, 'I will ask your pardon of my Lord, for he is Gracious, Merciful.'

100 And when they came into Joseph he took his parents[21] to
him, and said, 'Enter ye Egypt, if God will, secure.'

And he raised his parents to the seat of state, and they fell down bowing themselves unto him. Then said he, 'O my father, this is the meaning of my dream of old. My Lord hath now made it true, and he hath surely been gracious to me, since he took me forth from the prison, and hath brought you up out of the desert, after that Satan had stirred up strife between me and my brethren; for my Lord is gracious to whom He will; for He is the Knowing, the Wise.

O my Lord, thou hast given me dominion, and hast taught me to expound dark sayings. Maker of the Heavens and of the Earth! My guardian art thou in this world and in the next! Cause thou me to die a Muslim, and join me with the just.'

This is one of the secret histories[22] which we reveal unto thee. Thou wast not present with Joseph's brethren when they conceived their design and laid their plot: but the greater part of men, though thou long for it, will not believe.

Thou shalt not ask of them any recompense for this *message*. It is simply an instruction for all mankind.

And many as are the signs in the Heavens and on the Earth, yet they will pass them by, and turn aside from them:

And most of them believe not in God, without also joining other deities with Him.

What! Are they sure that the overwhelming chastisement of God shall not come upon them, or that that Hour shall not come upon them suddenly, while they are unaware?

SAY: This is my way: resting on a clear proof, I call you to God, I and whoso followeth me: and glory be to God! I am not one of those who add other deities to Him.

Never before thee have we sent any but men, chosen out of the people of the cities, to whom we made revelations. Will they not journey through the land, and see what hath been the end of those who were before them? But the mansions of the next life shall be better for those who fear God. Will they not then comprehend?

110 When at last the Apostles lost all hope, and deemed that they were reckoned as liars, our aid reached them, and we delivered whom we would; but our vengeance was not averted from the wicked.

Certainly in their histories is an example for men of understanding. This is no new tale of fiction, but a confirmation of previous scriptures, and an explanation of all things, and guidance and mercy to those who believe.

SURA 13 – THUNDER

MECCA – 43 VERSES

In the Name of God, the Compassionate, the Merciful

Elif. Lam. Mim. Ra.[1] These, the signs of the Book! And that which hath been sent down to thee from thy Lord is the very truth: But the greater part of men will not believe.

It is God who hath reared the Heavens without pillars thou canst behold; then mounted his throne, and imposed laws on the sun and moon: each travelleth to its appointed goal. He ordereth all things. He maketh his signs clear, that ye may have firm faith in a meeting with your Lord.

And He it is who hath outstretched the earth, and placed on it the firm mountains, and rivers: and of every fruit He hath placed on it two kinds: He causeth the night to enshroud the day. Verily in this are signs for those who reflect.

And on the earth hard by each other are its various portions: gardens of grapes and corn, and palm trees single or clustered. Though watered by the same water, yet some make we more excellent as food than other: Verily in all this are signs for those who understand.

If ever thou dost marvel, marvellous surely is their saying, 'What! when we have become dust, shall we be restored in a new creation?'

These are they who in their Lord believe not: these! the collars shall be on their necks; and these shall be inmates of the fire, to abide therein for aye.

To hasten evil rather than good will they challenge thee: but, before their time have been like examples. Full, truly, of mercy is thy Lord unto men, despite their sins; but verily, thy Lord is right vehement to punish.

And they who believe not say: 'If a sign from his Lord be not sent down to him . . . !' Thou art a warner only. And every people hath its guide.

God knoweth the burden of every female, and how much their wombs lessen and enlarge: with Him everything is by measure:
10 Knower of the Hidden and the Manifest! the Great! the Most
High!

Alike to Him is that person among you who concealeth his words, and he that telleth them abroad: he who hideth him in the night, and he who cometh forth in the day.

Each hath a succession *of Angels* before him and behind him, who watch over him by God's behest. Verily, God will not change his gifts to men, till they change what is in themselves: and when God willeth evil unto men, there is none can turn it away, nor have they any protector beside Him.

He it is who maketh the lightning to shine unto you; for fear and hope: and who bringeth up the laden clouds.

And the THUNDER uttereth his praise, and the Angels also, for awe of Him: and he sendeth his bolts and smiteth with them whom he will, while they are wrangling about God! Mighty is he in prowess.

Prayer is His of right: but these *deities* to whom they pray beside Him give them no answer, otherwise than as he is answered who stretcheth forth his hands to the water that it may reach his mouth, when it cannot reach it! The prayer of the Infidels only wandereth, *and is lost.*

And unto God doth all in the Heavens and on the Earth bow down in worship, willingly or by constraint: their very shadows also morn and even!

SAY: Who is Lord of the Heavens and of the Earth? SAY: God. SAY: Why then have ye taken beside Him protectors, who even for their own selves have no power for help or harm? SAY: What! shall the blind and the seeing be held equal? Shall the darkness and the light be held equal? Or have they given associates to God who have created as He hath created, so that their creation appear to them like His? SAY: God is the Creator of all things! He is the One! the Conquering!

He sendeth down the rain from Heaven: then flow the torrents in their due measure, and the flood beareth along a swelling foam. And from the *metals* which are molten in the fire for the sake of ornaments or utensils, a like scum ariseth. In this way doth God depict (set forth) truth and falsehood. As to the foam, it is quickly gone: and as to what is useful to man, it remaineth on the earth. Thus doth God set forth comparisons! To those who respond to their Lord shall be an excellent reward; but those who respond not *to his call*, had they all that the earth containeth twice over, they would surely give it for their ransom. Evil their reckoning! and Hell their home! And wretched the bed!

Shall he then who knoweth that what hath been sent down to thee from thy Lord is the truth, act like him who is blind? Men of insight only will bear this in mind,

20 Who fulfil their pledge to God, and break not their compact:

And who join together what God hath bidden to be joined, and who fear their Lord, and dread an ill reckoning;

And who, from desire to see the face of their Lord, are constant amid trials, and observe prayer and give alms, in secret and openly, out of what we have bestowed upon them, and turn aside evil by good: for these is the recompense of that abode,

Gardens of Eden – into which they shall enter together with the just of their fathers, and their wives, and their descendants: and the angels shall go in unto them at every portal:

'Peace be with you!' *say they*, 'because ye have endured all things!' Charming the recompense of their abode!

But those who, after having contracted it, break their covenant with God, and cut asunder what God hath bidden to be united, and commit misdeeds on the earth, these, a curse awaiteth them, and an ill abode!

God is open-handed with supplies to whom he will, or is sparing. They rejoice in the life that now is, but this present life is but a passing good, in respect of the life to come![2]

And they who believe not say, 'Unless a sign be sent down to him from his Lord . . .' SAY: God truly will mislead whom he will; and He will guide to Himself him who turneth to Him,

Those who believe, and whose hearts rest securely on the thought of God. What! Shall not men's hearts repose in the thought of God? They who believe and do the things that be right – blessedness awaiteth them, and a goodly home.

Thus have we sent thee to a people whom other peoples have preceded, that thou mightest rehearse to them our revelations to thee. Yet they believe not on the God of Mercy.[3] SAY: He is my Lord. There is no God but He. In Him do I put my trust. To Him must I return.

30 If there were a Koran by which the mountains could be set
in motion, or the earth cleft, or the dead be made to speak . . .
! But all sovereignty is in the hands of God. Do then believers doubt[4] that had He pleased God would certainly have guided all men aright?

Misfortune shall not cease to light on the unbelievers for what they have done, or to take up its abode hard by their dwellings, until the threat of God come to pass. Verily, God will not fail his plighted word.

Before thee indeed have apostles been mocked at; but though I bore long with the unbelievers, at last I seized upon them; –and how severe was my punishment!

Who is it then that is standing over every soul to mark its actions? Yet have they set up associates with God. SAY: Name them. What! Would ye inform God of that which He knoweth not on the Earth? Or are they not a mere empty name? But prepared of old for the infidels was this fraud of theirs; and they are turned aside from the path; and whom God causeth to err, no guide shall there be for him!

Chastisement awaiteth them in this present life, and more grievous shall be the chastisement of the next: and none shall screen them from God.

A picture of the Paradise which God hath promised to them that fear Him. The rivers flow beneath its *bowers:* its food and its shades are perpetual. This is the reward of those who fear God; but the reward of the unbelievers is the Fire.

They to whom we have given the Book rejoice[5] in what hath been sent down to thee; yet some are banded together who deny a part of it. SAY: I am commanded to worship God, and not to associate any creature with Him. On Him do I call, and to Him shall I return.

Thus, then, as a code in the Arabic tongue have we sent down the Koran; and truly, if after the knowledge that hath reached thee thou follow their desires, thou shalt have no guardian nor protector against God.

Apostles truly have we already sent before thee, and wives and offspring have we given them. Yet no apostle had come with miracles unless by the leave of God. To each age its Book.

What He pleaseth will God abrogate or confirm: for with Him is the source of revelation.[6]

40 Moreover, whether we cause thee to see the fulfilment of part of our menaces, or whether we take thee hence, verily, thy work is preaching only, and ours to take account.

See they not that we come into their land and cut short its borders?[7] God pronounceth a doom, and there is none to reverse his doom. And swift is He to take account.

Those who lived before them made plots: but all plotting is controlled by God: He knoweth the works of every one, and the infidels shall know whose will be the recompense of the abode.

The infidels, moreover, will say; Thou art not sent *of God*. SAY: God is witness enough betwixt me and you, and, whoever hath knowledge of the Book.

SURA 14 – ABRAHAM, ON WHOM BE PEACE

MECCA – 52 VERSES

In the Name of God, the Compassionate, the Merciful

Elif. Lam. Ra.[1] This Book have we sent down to thee that by their Lord's permission thou mayest bring men out of darkness into light, into the path of the Mighty, the Glorious –

Of God; to whom belongeth whatever is in the Heavens and whatever is on the Earth: and woe! for their terrible punishment, to the infidels,

Who love the life that now is, above that which is to come, and mislead from the way of God, and seek to make it crooked. These are in a far-gone error.

And in order that He might speak plainly to them, we have not sent any Apostle, save with the speech of his own people; but God misleadeth whom He will, and whom He will he guideth: and He is the mighty, the Wise.

Of old did we send Moses with our signs: *and said to him*, 'Bring forth thy people from the darkness into the light, and remind them of the days of God.' Verily, in this are signs for every patient, grateful person:

When Moses said to his people, 'Remember the kindness of God to you, when he rescued you from the family of Pharaoh who laid on you a cruel affliction, slaughtering your male children, and suffering only your females to live.' In this was a sore trial from your Lord –

And when your Lord caused it to be heard *that*, 'If ye render thanks then will I surely increase you more and more: but if ye be thankless . . . Verily, right terrible my chastisement.'

And Moses said, 'If ye and all who are on the Earth be thankless, yet truly God is passing Rich, and worthy of all praise.'

Hath not the story reached you of those who were before you, the people of Noah, and Ad, and Themoud,

10 And of those who lived after them? None knoweth them but God. When their prophets came to them with proofs of their mission, they put their hands on their mouths and said, 'In sooth, we believe not your message; and in sooth, of that to which you bid us, we are in doubt, as of a thing suspicious.'

Their prophets said: 'Is there any doubt concerning God, maker of the Heavens and of the Earth, who calleth you that He may pardon your sins, and respite you until an appointed time?'

They said, 'Ye are but men like us: fain would ye turn us from our fathers' worship. Bring us therefore some clear proof.'

Their Apostles said to them, 'We are indeed but men like you. But God bestoweth favours on such of his servants as he pleaseth, and it is not in our power to bring you any *special* proof,

But by the leave of God. In God therefore let the faithful trust.

And why should we not put our trust in God, since He hath already guided us in our ways. We will certainly bear with constancy the harm you would do to us. In God let the trustful trust.'

And they who believed not said to their Apostles, 'Forth from our land will we surely drive you, or, to our religion shall ye return.' Then their Lord revealed to them, 'We will certainly destroy the wicked doers,

And we shall certainly cause you to dwell in the land after them. This for him who dreadeth the appearance at my judgment-seat and who dreadeth my menace!'

Then sought they help from God, and every proud rebellious one perished:

Hell is before him: and of tainted water shall he be made to
drink:
20 He shall sup it and scarce swallow it for loathing; and Death
shall assail him on every side, but he shall not die: and before
him shall be seen a grievous torment.

A likeness of those who believe not in their Lord. Their works are like ashes which the wind scattereth on a stormy day: no advantage shall they gain from their works. This is the far-gone wandering.

Seest thou not that in truth[2] hath God created the Heavens and the Earth? Were such his pleasure He could make you pass away, and cause a new creation to arise.

And this would not be hard for God.

All mankind shall come forth before God; and the weak shall say to the men of might, 'Verily, we were your followers: will ye not then relieve us of some part of the vengeance of God?'

They shall say, 'If God had guided us, we surely had guided you. It is now all one whether we be impatient, or endure with patience. We have no escape.'

And after doom hath been given, Satan shall say, 'Verily, God promised you a promise of truth: I, too, made you a promise, but I deceived you. Yet I had no power over you:

But I only called you and ye answered me. Blame not me then, but blame yourselves: I cannot aid you, neither can ye aid me. I never believed that I was His equal with whom ye joined me.'[3] As for the evil doers, a grievous torment doth await them.

But they who shall have believed and done the things that be right, shall be brought into gardens beneath which the rivers flow: therein shall they abide for ever by the permission of their Lord: their greeting therein shall be 'Peace.'

Seest thou not to what God likeneth a good word?[4] To a
good tree: its root firmly fixed, and its branches in the Heaven:
30 Yielding its fruit in all seasons by the will of its Lord. God
setteth forth these similitudes to men that haply they may
reflect.

And an evil word is like an evil tree torn up from the face of the earth, and without strength to stand.

Those who believe shall God stablish by his steadfast word both in this life and in that which is to come: but the wicked shall He cause to err: God doth his pleasure.

Hast thou not beholden those who repay the goodness of God with infidelity, and sink their people into the abode of perdition –

Hell? Therein shall they be burned; and wretched the dwelling!

They set up compeers with God in order to mislead man from his way. SAY: Enjoy your pleasures yet awhile, but assuredly, your going hence shall be into the fire.

Speak to my servants who have believed, that they observe prayer, and give alms of that with which we have supplied them, both privately and openly, ere the day come when there shall be neither traffic nor friendship.

It is God who hath created the Heavens and the Earth, and sendeth down water from the Heaven, and so bringeth forth the fruits for your food: And He hath subjected to you the ships, so that by His command, they pass through the sea; and He hath subjected the rivers to you: and He hath subjected to you the sun and the moon in their constant courses: and He hath subjected the day and the night to you: of everything which ye ask Him, giveth He to you; and if ye would reckon up the favours of God, ye cannot count them! Surely man is unjust, ungrateful!

ABRAHAM said, 'O Lord make this land secure, and turn aside me and my children from serving idols:

For many men, O my Lord, have they led astray. But whosoever shall follow me, he truly shall be of me; and whosoever shall disobey me . . . Thou truly art Gracious, Merciful.

40 O our Lord! verily I have settled some of my offspring in an unfruitful valley, nigh to thy holy house;[5] O our Lord, that they may strictly observe prayer! Make thou therefore the hearts of men to yearn towards them, and supply them with fruits that they may be thankful.

O our Lord! thou truly knowest what we hide and what we bring to light; nought on earth or in heaven is hidden from God. Praise be to God who hath given me, in my old age, Ismael and Isaac! My Lord is the hearer of prayer.

Lord! grant that I and my posterity may observe prayer. O our Lord! and grant this my petition. O our Lord! forgive me and my parents and the faithful, on the day wherein account shall be taken.'

Think thou not that God is regardless of the deeds of the wicked. He only respiteth them to the day on which all eyes shall stare up with terror:

They hasten forward in fear; their heads upraised in supplication; their looks riveted; and their hearts a blank. Warn men therefore of the day when the punishment shall overtake them,

And when the evil doers shall say, 'O our Lord! respite us yet a little while:[6]

To thy call will we make answer; thine Apostles will we follow.' 'Did ye not once swear that no change should befal you?

Yet ye dwelt in the dwellings of those[7] who were the authors of their undoing[8] and it was made plain to you how we had dealt with them; and we held them up to you as examples. They plotted their plots: but God could master their plots, even though their plots had been so powerful as to move the mountains.'

Think not then that God will fail his promise to his Apostles: aye! God is mighty, and Vengeance is His.

On the day when the Earth shall be changed into another Earth, and the Heavens also, men shall come forth unto God, the Only, the Victorious.

50 And thou shalt see the wicked on that day linked together in chains –

Their garments of pitch, and fire shall enwrap their faces – that God may reward every soul as it deserveth; verily God is prompt to reckon.

This is a message for mankind, that they may thereby be warned: and that they may know that there is but one God; and that men of understanding may ponder it.

SURA 15 – HEDJR[1]

MECCA – 99 VERSES

In the Name of God, the Compassionate, the Merciful

Elif. Lam. Ra.[2] These are the signs of the Book, and of a lucid recital [Koran].

Many a time will the infidels wish that they had been Muslims.

Let them feast and enjoy themselves, and let hope beguile them: but they shall know *the truth* at last.

We never destroyed a city whose term was not perfixed:[3]

No people can forestall or retard its destiny.

They say: 'O thou to whom the warning hath been sent down, thou art surely possessed by a djinn:

Wouldst thou not have come to us with the angels, if thou wert of those who assert the truth?'

– We will not send down the angels without due cause.[4] *The Infidels* would not in that case have been respited.

Verily, We have sent down the warning, and verily, We will
be its guardian;
10 And already have We sent Apostles, before thee, among the
sects of the ancients;

But never came Apostles to them whom they did not deride.

In like manner will We put it into the hearts of the sinners *of Mecca* to do the same:

They will not believe on him though the example of those of old hath gone before.

Even were We to open above them a gate in Heaven, yet all the while they were mounting up to it,

They would surely say: It is only that our eyes are drunken: nay, we are a people enchanted.

We have set the signs of the zodiac[5] in the Heavens, and adorned and decked them forth for the beholders,

And We guard them from every stoned[6] Satan,

Save such as steal a hearing:[7] and him doth a visible flame pursue.

And the Earth have We spread forth, and thrown thereon the mountains, and caused everything to spring forth in it in balanced measure:

20 And We have provided therein sustenance for you, and for the creatures which not ye sustain:

And no one thing is there, but with Us are its storehouses; and We send it not down but in settled measure:

And We send forth the fertilising winds, and cause the rain to come down from the heaven, and give you to drink of it; and it is not ye who are its storers:

And We cause to live and We cause to die,[8] and We are the heir *of all things:*

We know those of you who flourish first and We know those who come later:

And truly thy Lord will gather them together again, for He is Wise, Knowing.

We created man of dried clay, of dark loam moulded;

And the djinn had We before created of subtle fire.

Remember when thy Lord said to the Angels, 'I create man of dried clay, of dark loam moulded:

And when I shall have fashioned him and breathed of my spirit into him, then fall ye down and worship him.'

30 And the Angels bowed down in worship, all of them, all together,

Save Eblis: he refused to be with those who bowed in worship.

'O Eblis,'[9] said God, 'wherefore art thou not with those who bow down in worship?'

He said, 'It beseemeth not me to bow in worship to man whom thou hast created of clay, of moulded loam.'

He said, 'Begone then hence; thou art a stoned one,[10]

And the curse shall be on thee till the day of reckoning.'

He said, 'O my Lord! respite me till the day when man shall be raised from the dead.'

He said, 'One then of the respited shalt thou be

Till the day of the predestined time.'

He said, 'O my Lord! because thou hast beguiled me, I will surely make all fair seeming to them[11] on the earth; I will surely beguile them all;

40 Except such of them as shall be thy sincere servants.'

He said, 'This is the right way with me;

For over none of my servants shalt thou have power, save those beguiled ones who shall follow thee.'

And verily, Hell is the promise for them one and all.

It hath seven Portals;[12] at each Portal is a separate band of them;

But 'mid gardens and fountains shall the pious dwell:

'Enter ye therein in peace, secure –'

And all rancour will We remove from their bosoms: they shall sit as brethren, face to face, on couches:

Therein no weariness shall reach them, nor forth from it shall they be cast for ever.

Announce to my servants that I am the Gracious, the Merciful,

50 And that my chastisement is the grievous chastisement.

And tell them of Abraham's guests.

When they entered in unto him, and said, 'Peace.' 'Verily,' said he, 'We fear you.'

They said, 'Fear not, for of a sage son we bring thee tidings.'

He said, 'Bring ye me such tidings now that old age hath come upon me? What, therefore, are your tidings really?'

They said, 'We announce them to thee in very truth. Be not then one of the despairing.'

'And who,' said he, 'despaireth of the mercy of his Lord, but they who err?'

He said, 'What is your business then, O ye Sent Ones?'

They said, 'We are sent unto a people who are sinners,

Except the family of Lot, whom verily we will rescue all,

60 Except his wife. We have decreed that she shall be of those who linger.'

And when the Sent Ones came to the family of Lot

He said, 'Ye are persons unknown to me.'

They said, 'Yes; but we have come to thee for a purpose about which thy people doubt:

We have come to thee with very truth, and we are truthful *envoys*.

Lead forth therefore thy family in the dead of the night; follow thou on their rear: and let no one of you turn round, but pass ye on whither ye are bidden.'

And this command we gave him because to the last man should these people be cut off at morning.

Then came the people of the city rejoicing at the news[13] –

He said, 'These are my guests: therefore disgrace me not.

And fear God and put me not to shame.'

70 They said, 'Have we not forbidden thee *to entertain* any one whatever?'[14]

He said, 'Here are my daughters, if ye will thus act.'

As thou livest, O Muhammad, they were bewildered in the drunkenness *of their lust.*

So a tempest overtook them at their sunrise,

And we turned the city upside down, and we rained stones of baked clay upon them.

Verily, in this are signs for those who scan heedfully;

And these *cities* lay on the high road.[15]

Verily, in this are signs for the faithful.

The inhabitants also of El Aika[16] were sinners:

So we took vengeance on them, and they both became a plain example.

80 And the people of HEDJR treated God's messengers as liars.

And we brought forth our signs to them, but they drew back from them:

And they hewed them out abodes in the mountains to secure them:

But a tempest surprised them at early morn,

And their labours availed them nothing.

We have not created the heavens and the earth and all that between them is, but for a worthy end.[17] And verily, 'the hour' shall surely come. Wherefore do thou, *Muhammad,* forgive with kindly forgiveness,

For thy Lord! He is the Creator, the Wise.

We have already given thee the seven verses of repetition[18] and the glorious Koran.

Strain not thine eyes after the good things we have bestowed on some of *the unbelievers:* afflict not thyself on their account, and lower thy wing to the faithful.[19]

And SAY: I am the only plain-*spoken* warner.

90 We will punish those who foster divisions,[20]

Who break up the Koran into parts:

By thy Lord! we will surely take account from them one and all,

Concerning that which they have done.

Profess publicly then what thou hast been bidden,[21] and withdraw from those who join gods to God.

Verily, We will maintain thy cause against those who deride *thee,*

Who set up gods with God: and at last shall they know their folly.

Now know We that thy heart is distressed[22] at what they say:
But do thou celebrate the praise of thy Lord, and be of those
who bow down in worship;
And serve thy Lord till the certainty[23] o'ertake thee.

SURA 16 – THE BEE

MECCA – 128 VERSES

In the Name of God, the Compassionate, the Merciful

The doom of God cometh to pass. Then hasten it not. Glory
be to Him! High let Him be exalted above the gods whom they
join with Him!
By His own behest will He cause the angels to descend with
the Spirit on whom he pleaseth among his servants, bidding
them, 'Warn that there is no God but me; therefore fear me.'
He hath created the Heavens and the Earth to set forth his
truth;[1] high let Him be exalted above the gods they join with Him!
Man hath He created from a moist germ;[2] yet lo! man is an
open caviller.
And the cattle! for you hath He created them: in them ye have
warm garments and gainful uses; and of them ye eat:
And they beseem you well[3] when ye fetch them home and
when ye drive them forth to pasture:
And they carry your burdens to lands which ye could not else
reach but with travail of soul: truly your Lord is full of
goodness, and merciful:
And *He hath given you* horses, mules, and asses, that ye may
ride them, and for your ornament: and things of which ye have
no knowledge hath he created.
Of God it is to point out 'the Way.' Some turn aside from it:
but had He pleased, He had guided you all aright.
10 It is He who sendeth down rain out of Heaven: from it is your
drink; and from it are the plants by which ye pasture.
By it He causeth the corn, and the olives, and the palm-trees,
and the grapes to spring forth for you, and all kinds of fruits;
verily, in this are signs for those who ponder.

And He hath subjected to you the night and the day; the sun and the moon and the stars too are subjected to you by his behest; verily, in this are signs for those who understand:

And all of varied hues that He hath created for you over the earth: verily, in this are signs for those who remember.

And He it is who hath subjected the sea to you, that ye may eat of its fresh fish, and take forth from it ornaments to wear – thou seest the ships ploughing its billows – and that ye may go in quest of his bounties, and that ye might give thanks.

And He hath thrown firm mountains on the earth, lest it move with you; and rivers and paths for your guidance,

And way marks. By the stars too are men guided.

Shall He then who hath created be as he who hath not created? Will ye not consider?

And if ye would reckon up the favours of God, ye could not count them. Aye! God is right Gracious, Merciful!

And God knoweth what ye conceal, and what ye bring to light,

20 While the gods whom they call on beside God, create nothing, but are themselves created:

Dead are they, lifeless! and they know not
When they shall be raised!

Your God is the one God: and they who believe not in a future life, have hearts given to denial, and are men of pride:–

Beyond a doubt God knoweth what they conceal and what they manifest:–

He truly loveth not the men of pride.

For when it is said to them, 'What is this your Lord hath sent down?' they say, 'Fables of the ancients,' –

That on the day of resurrection they may bear their own entire burden, and the burden of those whom they, in their ignorance, misled. Shall it not be a grievous burden for them?

They who were before them did plot of old. But God attacked their building at its foundation – the roof fell on them from above; and, whence they looked not for it, punishment overtook them:[4]

On the day of resurrection, too, will He shame them. He will say, 'Where are the gods ye associated with me, the subjects of your disputes?' They to whom 'the knowledge' hath been given will say, Verily, this day shall shame and evil fall upon the infidels.

30 The sinners against their own souls whom the angels shall
cause to die will proffer the submission, 'No evil have we
done.' Nay! God knoweth what ye have wrought:
Enter ye therefore the gates of Hell to remain therein for ever:
and horrid the abiding place of the haughty ones!
But to those who have feared God it shall be said, 'What is
this that your Lord hath awarded?' They shall say, 'That
which is best. To those who do good, a good reward in this
present world; but better the mansion of the next, and right
pleasant the abode of the God-fearing!'
Gardens of Eden into which they shall enter; rivers shall flow
beneath their shades; all they wish for shall they find there-
in! Thus God rewardeth those who fear Him;
To whom, as righteous persons, the angels shall say, when
they receive their souls, 'Peace be on you! Enter Paradise as
the meed of your labours.'
What can the infidels expect but that the angels *of death*
come upon them, or that a sentence of thy Lord take effect?
Thus did they who flourished before them. God was not
unjust to them, but to their ownselves were they unjust;
And the ill which they had done recoiled upon them, and that
which they had scoffed at encompassed them round about.
They who have joined other gods with God say, 'Had He
pleased, neither we nor our fathers had worshipped aught but
him; nor should we, apart from him, have forbidden aught.'
Thus acted they who were before them. Yet is the duty of the
apostles other than public preaching?
And to every people have we sent an apostle *saying:* –
Worship God and turn away from Taghout. Some of them
there were whom God guided, and there were others decreed to
err. But go through the land and see what hath been the end of
those who treated my apostles as liars!
If thou art anxious for their guidance, *know* that God will
not guide him whom He would lead astray, neither shall they
have any helpers.
40 And they swear by God with their most sacred oath that
'God will never raise him who once is dead.' Nay, but on Him
is a promise binding, though most men know it not, –
That He may clear up to them the subject of their disputes,
and that the infidels may know that they are liars.

Our word to a thing when we will it, is but to say, 'Be,' and it is.[5]

And as to those who when oppressed have fled their country for the sake of God, we will surely provide them a goodly abode in this world, but greater the reward of the next life, did they but know it

They who bear ills with patience and put their trust in the Lord!

None have we sent before thee but men inspired – ask of those who have Books of Monition,[6] if ye know it not –

With proofs *of their mission* and Scriptures: and to thee have we sent down this Book of Monition that thou mayest make clear to men what hath been sent down to them, and that they may ponder it.

What! Are they then who have plotted mischiefs, sure that God will not cause the earth to cleave under them? or that a chastisement will not come upon them whence they looked not for it?

Or that He will not seize upon them in their comings and goings, while they shall not be able to resist him?

Or that he will not seize them with some slowly wasting scourge? But verily your Lord is Good, Gracious.

50 Have they not seen how everything which God hath created turneth its shadow right and left, prostrating itself before God in all abasement?

And all in the Heavens and all on the Earth, each thing that moveth, and the very angels, prostrate them in adoration before God, and are free from pride;

They fear their Lord who is above them, and do what they are bidden:

For God hath said, 'Take not to yourselves two gods, – for He is one God: me, therefore! yea, me revere!

All in the Heavens and in the Earth is His! His due unceasing service! Will ye then fear any other than God?

And all your blessings are assuredly from God: then, when trouble befalleth you, to Him ye turn for help:

Then when He relieveth you of the trouble, lo! some of you join associates with your Lord:–

To prove how thankless are they for our gifts! Enjoy yourselves then: but in the end ye shall know *the truth*.

And for *idols*, of which they know nothing, they set apart a share of our bounties! By God ye shall be called to account for your devices!

And they ascribe daughters unto God! Glory be to Him! But they desire them not for themselves:[7]

60 For when the birth of a daughter is announced to any one of
them, dark shadows settle on his face, and he is sad:

He hideth him from the people because of the ill tidings: shall he keep it with disgrace or bury it in the dust?[8] Are not their judgments wrong?

To whatever is evil may they be likened who believe not in a future life;[9] but God is to be likened to whatever is loftiest: for He is the Mighty, the Wise.

Should God punish men for their perverse doings, he would not leave on earth a moving thing! but to an appointed term doth He respite them; and when their term is come, they shall not delay or advance it an hour.

Yet what they loathe themselves do they assign to God: and their tongues utter the lie, that theirs shall be a goodly lot. But beyond a doubt is it that the fire awaiteth them, and that they shall be the first sent into it.

By God we have sent Apostles to nations before thee, but Satan prepared their work for them, and this day is he their liege; and a woeful punishment doth await them.

And we have sent down the Book to thee only, that thou mightest clear up to them the subject of their wranglings, and as a guidance and a mercy to those who believe.

And God sendeth down water from Heaven, and by it giveth life to the Earth after it hath been dead; verily, in this is a sign to those who hearken.

Ye have also teaching from the cattle. We give you drink of the pure milk, between dregs and blood, which is in their bellies; the pleasant beverage of them that quaff it.

And among fruits ye have the palm and the vine, from which ye get wine and healthful nutriment: in this, verily, are signs for those who reflect.

70 And thy Lord hath taught the BEE, saying: 'Provide thee
houses in the mountains, and in the trees, and in *the hives* which
men do build *thee*:

Feed, moreover, on every kind of fruit, and walk the beaten paths of thy Lord.' From its belly cometh forth a fluid of varying hues,[10] which yieldeth medicine to man. Verily in this is a sign for those who consider.

And God hath created you; by and bye will he take you to himself; and some among you will he carry on to abject old age, when all that once was known is known no longer. Aye, God is Knowing, Powerful.

And God hath abounded to some of you more than to others in the supplies of life; yet they to whom He hath abounded, impart not thereof to the slaves whom their right hands possess, so that they may share alike. What! will they deny, then, that these boons are from God?

God, too, hath given you wives of your own race, and from your wives hath He given you sons and grandsons, and with good things hath he supplied you. What, will they then believe in vain idols? For God's boons they are ungrateful!

And they worship beside God those who neither out of the Heavens or Earth can provide them a particle of food, and have no power in themselves!

Make no comparisons, therefore, with God.[11] Verily, God hath knowledge, but ye have not.

God maketh comparison between a slave[12] the property of his lord, who hath no power over anything, and *a free* man whom we have ourselves supplied with goodly supplies, and who giveth alms therefrom both in secret and openly. Shall they be held equal? No: praise be to God! But most men know it not.

God setteth forth also a comparison between two men, one of whom is dumb from his birth, and hath no power over anything, and is a burden to his lord: send him where he will, he cometh not back with success. Shall he and the man who enjoineth what is just, and keepeth in the straight path, be held equal?

God's are the secrets of the Heavens and of the Earth! and the business of the last hour will be but as the twinkling of an eye, or even less. Yes! for all things is God Potent.

80 God hath brought you out of your mothers' wombs devoid of all knowledge; but hath given you hearing, and sight, and heart, that haply ye might render thanks.

Have they never looked up at the birds subjected to Him in Heaven's vault? None holdeth them in hand but God! In this are signs for those who believe.

And God hath given you tents to dwell in: and He hath given you the skins of beasts for tents, that ye may find them light when ye shift your quarters, or when ye halt; and from their wool and soft fur and hair, hath He supplied you with furniture and goods for temporary use.

And from the things which He hath created, hath God provided shade for you, and hath given you the mountains for places of shelter, and hath given you garments to defend you from the heat, and garments to defend you in your wars. Thus doth He fill up the measure of His goodness towards you, that you may resign yourselves to Him.

But if they turn their backs, still thy office is only plain *spoken* preaching.

They own the goodness of God – then they disown it – and most of them are infidels.

But one day, we will raise up a witness out of every nation: then shall the infidels have no permission *to make excuses*, and they shall find no favour.

And when they who have acted thus wrongly shall behold their torment, it shall not be made light to them, nor will God deign to look upon them.

And when they who had joined associates with God shall see those their associate-gods, they shall say, 'O our Lord! these are our associate-gods whom we called upon beside Thee.' But they shall retort on them, 'Verily, ye are liars.'

And on that day shall they proffer submission to God; and the *deities* of their own invention shall vanish from them.

90 As for those who were infidels and turned others aside from the way of God, to them we will add punishment on punishment for their corrupt doings.

And one day we will summon up in every people a witness against them from among themselves; and we will bring thee up as a witness against these *Meccans:* for to thee have we sent down the Book which cleareth up everything, a guidance, and mercy, and glad tidings to those who resign themselves to God (to Muslims).

Verily, God enjoineth justice and the doing of good and gifts to kindred; and he forbiddeth wickedness and wrong and oppression. He warneth you that haply ye may be mindful.

Be faithful in the covenant of God when ye have covenanted, and break not your oaths after ye have pledged them: for now have ye made God to stand surety for you. Verily, God hath knowledge of what ye do.

And, because you are a more numerous people than some other people, be not like her who unravelleth the thread which she had strongly spun, by taking your oaths with mutual perfidy. God is making trial of you in this: and in the day of resurrection he will assuredly clear up to you that concerning which ye are now at variance.

Had God pleased, He could have made you one people: but He causeth whom He will to err, and whom He will He guideth: and ye shall assuredly be called to account for your doings.

Therefore take not your oaths with mutual fraud, lest your foot slip after it hath been firmly fixed, and ye taste of evil because ye have turned others aside from the way of God, and great be your punishment.

And barter not the covenant of God for a mean price; for with God is that which is better for you, if ye do but understand.

All that is with you passeth away, but that which is with God abideth. With a reward meet for their best deeds will we surely recompense those who have patiently endured.

Whoso doeth that which is right, whether male or female, if a believer, him will we surely quicken to a happy life, and recompense them with a reward meet for their best deeds.

100 When thou readest the Koran, have recourse to God for help against Satan the stoned,[13]

For no power hath he over those who believe, and put their trust in their Lord,

But only hath he power over those who turn away from God, and join other deities with Him.

And when we change one (sign) verse for another, and God knoweth best what He revealeth, they say, 'Thou art only a fabricator.' Nay! but most of them have no knowledge.

SAY: The Holy Spirit[14] hath brought it down with truth from thy Lord, that He may stablish those who have believed, and as guidance and glad tidings to the Muslims.

We also know that they say, 'Surely a certain person teacheth him.' But the tongue of him at whom they hint is foreign,[15] while this *Koran* is in the plain Arabic.

As for those who believe not in the signs of God, God will not guide them, and a sore torment doth await them.

Surely they invent a lie who believe not in the signs of God –
and they are the liars.
Whoso, after he hath believed in God denieth him, if he were
forced to it and if his heart remain steadfast in the faith, *shall be*
guiltless:[16] but whoso openeth his breast to infidelity – on such
shall be wrath from God, and a severe punishment awaiteth
them.
This, because they have loved this present life beyond the
next, and because God guideth not the unbelievers!
110 These are they whose hearts and ears and eyes God hath
sealed up: these are the careless ones: in the next world shall
they perish beyond a doubt.
To those also who after their trials fled their country,[17] then
fought and endured with patience, verily, thy Lord will in the
end be forgiving, gracious.
On a certain day shall every soul come to plead for itself, and
every soul shall be repaid according to its deeds; and they shall
not be wronged.
God proposeth the instance of a city,[18] secure and at ease, to
which its supplies come in plenty from every side. But she was
thankless for the boons of God; God therefore made her taste
the woe[19] of famine and of fear, for what they had done.
Moreover, an apostle of their own people came to them, and
they treated him as an impostor. So chastisement overtook
them because they were evil doers.
Of what God hath supplied you eat the lawful and good, and
be grateful for the favours of God, if ye are his worshippers.
Forbidden to you is that only which dieth of itself, and blood,
and swine's flesh, and that which hath been slain in the name of
any other than God: but if any be forced, and neither lust for it
nor wilfully transgress, then verily God is forgiving, gracious.[20]
And say not with a lie upon your tongue, 'This is lawful and
this is forbidden:' for so will ye invent a lie concerning God: but
they who invent a lie of God shall not prosper:
Brief their enjoyment, but sore their punishment!
To the Jews[21] we have forbidden that of which we before told
thee; we injured them not, but they injured themselves.
120 To those who have done evil in ignorance, then afterwards
have repented and amended, verily thy Lord is in the end right
gracious, merciful.
Verily, Abraham was a leader in religion:[22] obedient to

God, sound in faith:[23] he was not of those who join gods with God.

Grateful was he for His favours: God chose him and guided him into the straight way;

And we bestowed on him good things in this world: and in the world to come he shall be among the just.

We have moreover revealed to thee that thou follow the religion of Abraham, the sound in faith. He was not of those who join gods with God.

The Sabbath was only ordained for those who differed about it: and of a truth thy Lord will decide between them on the day of resurrection as to the subject of their disputes.

Summon thou to the way of thy Lord with wisdom and with kindly warning: dispute with them in the kindest manner: thy Lord best knoweth those who stray from his way, and He best knoweth those who have yielded to his guidance.

If ye make reprisals, then make them to the same extent that ye were injured: but if ye can endure patiently, best will it be for the patiently enduring.

Endure then with patience. But thy patient endurance must be sought in none but God. And be not grieved about the infidels, and be not troubled at their devices; for God is with those who fear him and do good deeds.

SURA 17 – THE NIGHT JOURNEY

MECCA[1] – 111 VERSES

In the Name of God, the Compassionate, the Merciful

Glory be to Him who carried his servant by night[2] from the sacred temple *of Mecca* to the temple[3] that is more remote, whose precinct we have blessed, that we might show him of our signs! for He is the Hearer, the Seer.

And we gave the Book to Moses and ordained it for guidance to the children of Israel – 'that ye take no other Guardian than me.'

O posterity of those whom we bare with Noah! He truly was a grateful servant!

And we solemnly declared to the children of Israel in the Book, 'Twice surely will ye enact crimes in the earth, and with great loftiness *of pride* will ye surely be uplifted.'

So when the menace for the first *crime*[4] came *to be inflicted*, we sent against you our servants endued with terrible prowess; and they searched the inmost part of your abodes, and the menace was accomplished.

Then we gave you the mastery over them[5] in turn, and increased you in wealth and children, and made you a most numerous host.

We said, 'If ye do well, to your own behoof will ye do well: and if ye do evil, against yourselves will ye do it. And when the menace for your latter crime[6] came to be inflicted, *then we sent an enemy* to sadden your faces, and to enter the temple as they entered it at first, and to destroy with utter destruction that which they had conquered.

Haply your Lord will have mercy on you! but if ye return we will return:[7] and we have appointed Hell – the prison of the infidels.

Verily, this Koran guideth to what is most upright; and it announceth to believers

10 Who do the things that are right, that for them is a great reward;

And that for those who believe not in the life to come, we have got ready a painful punishment.

Man prayeth for evil as he prayeth for good; for man is hasty.

We have made the night and the day for two signs: the sign of the night do we obscure, but the sign of the day cause we to shine forth, that ye may seek plenty from your Lord, and that ye may know the number of the years and the reckoning *of time;* and we have made everything distinct by distinctiveness.

And every man's fate[8] have we fastened about his neck: and on the day of resurrection will we bring forth to him a book which shall be proffered to him wide open:

– 'Read thy Book:[9] there needeth none but thyself to make out an account against thee this day.'

For his own good only shall the guided yield to guidance, and to his own loss only shall the erring err; and the heavy laden shall not be laden with another's load. We never punished until we had first sent an apostle:

And when we willed to destroy a city, to its affluent ones did we address our bidding; but when they acted criminally therein, just was its doom, and we destroyed it with an utter destruction.

And since Noah, how many nations have we exterminated! And of the sins of his servants thy Lord is sufficiently informed, observant.

Whoso chooseth this quickly passing life, quickly will we bestow therein that which we please – even on him we choose; afterwards we will appoint hell for him, in which he shall burn – disgraced, outcast:

20 But whoso chooseth the next life, and striveth after it as it should be striven for, being also a believer, – these! their striving shall be grateful *to God:*

To all – both to these and those – will we prolong the gifts of thy Lord; for not to any shall the gifts of thy Lord be denied.

See how we have caused some of them to excel others! but the next life shall be greater in its grades, and greater in excellence.

Set not up another god with God, lest thou sit thee down disgraced, helpless.[10]

Thy Lord hath ordained that ye worship none but him; and, kindness to your parents, whether one or both of them attain to old age with thee: and say not to them, 'Fie!' neither reproach them; but speak to them both with respectful speech;

And defer humbly to them[11] out of tenderness; and say, 'Lord, have compassion on them both, even as they reared me when I was little.'

Your Lord well knoweth what is in your souls; *he knoweth* whether ye be righteous:

And gracious is He to those who return to Him.

And to him who is of kin render his due, and also to the poor and to the wayfarer; yet waste not wastefully,

For the wasteful are brethren of the Satans, and Satan was ungrateful to his Lord:

30 But if thou turn away from them, while thou thyself seekest boons from thy Lord for which thou hopest, at least speak to them with kindly speech:

And let not thy hand be tied up to thy neck; nor yet open it with all openness, lest thou sit thee down in rebuke, in beggary.

Verily, thy Lord will provide with open hand for whom he pleaseth, and will be sparing. His servants doth he scan, inspect.

Kill not your children for fear of want:[12] for them and for you will we provide. Verily, the killing them is a great wickedness.

Have nought to do with adultery; for it is a foul thing and an evil way:

Neither slay any one whom God hath forbidden you to slay, unless for a just cause: and whosoever shall be slain wrongfully, to his heir[13] have we given powers; but let him not outstep bounds in putting the manslayer to death, for he too, in his turn, will be assisted *and avenged*.

And touch not the substance of the orphan, unless in an upright way, till he attain his age of strength: And perform your covenant; verily the covenant shall be enquired of:

And give full measure when you measure, and weigh with just balance. This will be better, and fairest for settlement:

And follow not that of which thou hast no knowledge;[14] because the hearing and the sight and the heart, – each of these shall be enquired of:

And walk not proudly on the earth, for thou canst not cleave the earth, neither shalt thou reach to the mountains in height:

40 All this is evil; odious to thy Lord.

This is a part of the wisdom which thy Lord hath revealed to thee. Set not up any other god with God, lest thou be cast into Hell, rebuked, cast away.

What! hath your Lord prepared sons for you, and taken for himself daughters from among the angels? Indeed, ye say a dreadful saying.

Moreover, for man's warning have we varied[15] this Koran: Yet it only increaseth their flight from it.

SAY: If, as ye affirm, there were other gods with Him, they would in that case seek occasion against the occupant of the throne:

Glory to Him! Immensely high is He exalted above their blasphemies!

The seven heavens[16] praise him, and the earth, and all who are therein; neither is there aught which doth not celebrate his praise; but their utterances of praise ye understand not. He is kind, indulgent.

When thou recitest the Koran we place between thee and those who believe not in the life to come, a dark veil;

And we put coverings over their hearts lest they should understand it, and in their ears a heaviness;

And when in the Koran thou namest thy One Lord, they turn
their backs in flight.
50 We well know why they hearken, when they hearken unto
thee, and when they whisper apart; when the wicked say, 'Ye
follow no other than a man enchanted.'
See what likenesses they strike out for thee! But they are in
error, neither can they find the path.
They also say, 'After we shall have become bones and dust,
shall we in sooth be raised a new creation?'
SAY: 'Yes, though ye were stones, or iron, or any other
creature, to your seeming, yet harder *to be raised*.' But they will
say, 'Who shall bring us back?' SAY: 'He who created you at
first.' And they will wag their heads at thee, and say, 'When
shall this be?' SAY: 'Haply it is nigh.'
On that day shall God call you forth, and ye shall answer by
praising Him; and ye shall seem to have tarried but a little
while.
Enjoin my servants to speak in kindly sort: Verily Satan
would stir up strifes among them, for Satan is man's avowed
foe.
Your Lord well knoweth you: if He please He will have
mercy on you; or if He please He will chastise you: and we have
not sent thee to be a guardian over them.
Thy Lord hath full knowledge of all in the heavens and the
earth. Higher gifts have we given to some of the prophets than
to others, and the Psalter we gave to David.
SAY: Call ye upon those whom ye fancy to be Gods beside
Him; yet they will have no power to relieve you from trouble, or
to shift it elsewhere.
Those whom ye call on, themselves desire union with their
Lord,[17] striving which of them shall be nearest to him: they also
hope for his mercy and fear his chastisement. Verily the
chastisement of thy Lord is to be dreaded.
60 There is no city which we will not destroy before the day of
Resurrection, or chastise it with a grievous chastisement. This
is written in the Book.
Nothing hindered us from sending *thee* with the power of
working miracles, except that the peoples of old treated them as
lies. We gave to Themoud[18] the she-camel before their very
eyes, yet they maltreated her! We send not a prophet with
miracles but to strike terror.

And *remember* when we said to thee, Verily, thy Lord is round about mankind; we ordained the vision[19] which we shewed thee, and likewise the cursed tree of the Koran, only for men to dispute of; we will strike them with terror; but it shall only increase in them enormous wickedness:

And when we said to the Angels, 'Prostrate yourselves before Adam:' and they all prostrated them, save Eblis. 'What!' said he, 'shall I bow me before him whom thou hast created of clay?

Seest thou this man whom thou hast honoured above me? Verily, if thou respite me till the day of Resurrection, I will destroy his offspring, except a few.'

He said, 'Begone; but whosoever of them shall follow thee, verily, Hell shall be your recompense; an ample recompense!

And entice such of them as thou canst by thy voice; assault them with thy horsemen and thy footmen;[20] be their partner in their riches and in their children, and make them promises: but Satan shall make them only deceitful promises.

As to my servants, no power over them shalt thou have; And thy Lord *will be their* sufficient guardian.'

It is your Lord who speedeth onward the ships for you in the sea, that ye may seek of his abundance; for he is merciful towards you.

When a misfortune befalleth you out at sea, they whom ye invoke are not to be found: God alone is there: yet when he bringeth you safe to dry land, ye place yourselves at a distance from Him. Ungrateful is man.

70 What! are ye sure, then, that he will not cleave the sides of the
earth for you? or that he will not send against you a whirlwind charged with sands? Then shall ye find no protector.

Or are ye sure that he will not cause you to put back to sea a second time, and send against you a storm blast, and drown you, for that ye have been thankless? Then shall ye find no helper against us therein.

And now have we honoured the children of Adam: by land and by sea have we carried them: food have we provided for them of good things, and with endowments beyond many of our creatures have we endowed them.

One day we will summon all men with their leaders: they whose book shall be given into their right hand, shall read their book, and not be wronged a thread:

And he who has been blind here, shall be blind hereafter, and wander yet more from the way.

And, verily, they had well nigh beguiled thee from what we revealed to thee, and caused thee to invent some other thing in our name: but in that case they would surely have taken thee as a friend;[21]

And had we not settled thee, thou hadst well nigh leaned to them a little:

In that case we would surely have made thee taste of woe[22] in life and of woe in death: then thou shouldest not have found a helper against us.

And truly they had almost caused thee to quit the land, in order wholly to drive thee forth from it:[23] but then, themselves should have tarried but a little after thee.

This was our way with the Apostles we have already sent before thee, and in this our way thou shalt find no change.

80 Observe prayer at sunset, till the first darkening of the night, and the daybreak reading – for the daybreak reading hath its witnesses,

And watch unto it in the night: this shall be an excess in service:[24] it may be that thy Lord will raise thee to a glorious station:

And say, 'O my Lord, cause me to enter[25] with a perfect entry, and to come forth with a perfect forthcoming, and give me from thy presence a helping power:'

And SAY: Truth is come and falsehood is vanished. Verily, falsehood is a thing that vanisheth.

And we send down of the Koran that which is a healing and a mercy to the faithful: But it shall only add to the ruin of the wicked.

When we bestow favours on man, he withdraweth and goeth aside; but when evil toucheth him, he is despairing.

SAY: Every one acteth after his own manner: but your Lord well knoweth who is best guided in his path.

And they will ask thee of the Spirit.[26] SAY: The Spirit *proceedeth* at my Lord's command: but of knowledge, only a little to you is given.

If we pleased, we could take away what we have revealed to thee: none couldst thou then find thee to undertake thy cause with us,

Save as a mercy from thy Lord; great, verily, is his favour
towards thee.
90 Say: Verily, were men and Djinn assembled to produce the
like of this Koran, they could not produce its like, though the
one should help the other.

And of a truth we have set out to men every kind of similitude
in this Koran, but most men have refused everything except
unbelief.

And they say, 'By no means will we believe on thee till thou
cause a fountain to gush forth for us from the earth;

Or, till thou have a garden of palm-trees and grapes, and
thou cause forth-gushing rivers to gush forth in its midst;

Or thou make the heaven to fall on us, as thou hast given out,
in pieces; or thou bring God and the angels to vouch for thee;

Or thou have a house of gold; or thou mount up into Heaven;
nor will we believe in thy mounting up, till thou send down to
us a book which we may read.' Say: Praise be to my Lord! Am I
more than a man, an apostle?

And what hindereth men from believing, when the guidance
hath come to them, but that they say, 'Hath God sent a man as
an apostle?'

Say: Did angels walk the earth as its familiars, we had surely
sent them an angel-apostle out of Heaven.

Say: God is witness enough between you and me. His
servants He scanneth, eyeth.

And He whom God shall guide will be guided indeed; and
whom he shall mislead thou shalt find none to assist, but Him:
and we will gather them together on the day of the resurrection,
on their faces, blind and dumb and deaf: Hell shall be their
abode: so oft as its fires die down, we will rekindle the flame.
100 This shall be their reward for that they believed not our signs
and said, 'When we shall have become bones and dust, shall we
surely be raised a new creation?'

Do they not perceive that God, who created the Heavens and
the Earth, is able to create their like? And he hath ordained
them a term; there is no doubt of it: but the wicked refuse
everything except unbelief.

Say: If ye held the treasures of my Lord's mercy ye would
certainly refrain *from them* through fear of spending them: for
man is covetous.

We therefore gave to Moses nine clear signs. Ask thou,

therefore, the children of Israel *how it was* when he came unto them, and Pharaòh said to him, 'Verily, I deem thee, O Moses, a man enchanted.'

Said Moses, 'Thou knowest that none hath sent down these clear signs but the Lord of the Heavens and of the Earth; and I surely deem thee, O Pharaoh, a person lost.'

So Pharaoh sought to drive them out of the land; but we drowned him and all his followers.

And after his death, we said to the children of Israel, 'Dwell ye in the land:' and when the promise of the next life shall come to pass, we will bring you both up together *to judgment*. In truth have we sent down the Koran, and in truth hath it descended, and we have only sent thee to announce and to warn.

And we have parcelled out the Koran into sections, that thou mightest recite it unto men by slow degrees, and we have sent it down piecemeal.

SAY: Believe ye therein or believe ye not? They verily to whom knowledge had been given previously, fall on their faces worshipping when it is recited to them, and say: 'Glory be to God! the promise of our Lord is made good!'

They fall down on their faces weeping, and It increaseth their humility.

110 SAY: Call upon God (Allah), or call upon the God of Mercy (Arrahman),[27] by whichsoever ye will invoke him: He hath most excellent names. And be not loud in thy prayer, neither pronounce it too low;[28] but between these follow a middle way:

And SAY: Praise be to God who hath not begotten a son, who hath no partner in the Kingdom, nor any protector on account of weakness. And magnify him by proclaiming His greatness.[29]

SURA 18 – THE CAVE

MECCA – 110 VERSES

In the Name of God, the Compassionate, the Merciful

Praise be to God, who hath sent down the Book to his servant, and hath not made it tortuous[1]

But direct; that it may warn of a grievous woe from him, and announce to the faithful who do the things that are right, that a goodly reward, wherein they shall abide for ever, awaiteth them;

And that it may warn those who say, 'God hath begotten a Son.'

No knowledge of this have either they or their fathers! A grievous saying to come out of their mouths! They speak no other than a lie!

And haply, if they believe not in this new revelation, thou wilt slay thyself, on their very footsteps, out of vexation.

Verily, we have made all that is on earth as its adornment, that we might make trial who among mankind would excel in works:

But we are surely about to reduce all that is thereon to dust!

Hast thou reflected that the Inmates of THE CAVE and of Al Rakim[2] were one of our wondrous signs?

When the youths betook them to the cave they said, 'O our Lord! grant us mercy from before thee, and order for us our affair aright.'

10 Then struck we upon their ears *with deafness* in the cave for many a year:

Then we awaked them that we might know which of the two parties could best reckon the space of their abiding.

We will relate to thee their tale with truth. They were youths who had believed in their Lord, and in guidance had we increased them;

And we had made them stout of heart, when they stood up and said, 'Our Lord is Lord of the Heavens and of the Earth: we will call on no other God than him; for in that case we had said a thing outrageous.

These our people have taken other gods beside Him, though

they bring no clear proof for them; but, who more iniquitous than he who forgeth a lie of God?

So when ye shall have separated you from them and from that which they worship beside God, then betake you to the cave: Your Lord will unfold his mercy to you, and will order your affairs for you for the best.'

And thou mightest have seen the sun when it arose, pass on the right of their cave, and when it set, leave them on the left, while they were in its spacious chamber. This is one of the signs of God. Guided indeed is he whom God guideth; but for him whom He misleadeth, thou shalt by no means find a patron, director.

And thou wouldst have deemed them awake,[3] though they were sleeping: and we turned them to the right and to the left. And in the entry lay their dog with paws outstretched.[4] Hadst thou come suddenly upon them, thou wouldst surely have turned thy back on them in flight, and have been filled with fear at them.

So we awaked them that they might question one another. Said one of them, 'How long have ye tarried here?' They said, 'We have tarried a day or part of a day.' They said, 'Your Lord knoweth best how long ye have tarried: Send now one of you with this your coin into the city, and let him mark who therein hath purest food, and from him let him bring you a supply: and let him be courteous, and not discover you to any one.

For they, if they find you out, will stone you or turn you back to their faith, and in that case it will fare ill with you for ever.'

20 And thus made we their adventure known to *their fellow citizens*, that they might learn that the promise of God is true, and that as to 'the Hour' there is no doubt of its coming. When they disputed among themselves concerning what had befallen them, some said, 'Build a building over them; their Lord knoweth best about them.' Those who prevailed in the matter said, 'A place of worship will we surely raise over them.'

Some say, 'They were three; their dog the fourth:' others say, 'Five; their dog the sixth,' guessing at the secret: others say, 'Seven; and their dog the eighth.' SAY: My Lord best knoweth the number: none, save a few, shall know them.

Therefore be clear in thy discussions about them,[5] and ask not any *Christian* concerning them.

Say not thou of a thing, 'I will surely do it to-morrow;'

without, 'If God will.'[6] And when thou hast forgotten, call thy Lord to mind; and say, 'Haply my Lord will guide me, that I may come near to *the truth* of this *story* with correctness.'

And they tarried in their cave 300 years, and 9 years over.[7]

SAY: God best knoweth how long they tarried: With Him are the secrets of the Heavens and of the Earth: Look thou and hearken unto Him alone.[8] Man hath no guardian but Him, and none may bear part in his judgments:–

And publish what hath been revealed to thee of the Book of thy Lord – none may change his words, – and thou shalt find no refuge beside Him.

Be patient with those who call upon their Lord at morn and even, seeking his face: and let not thine eyes be turned away from them in quest of the pomp of this life;[9] neither obey him[10] whose heart we have made careless of the remembrance of Us, and who followeth his own lusts, and whose ways are unbridled.

And SAY: the truth is from your Lord: let him then who will, believe; and let him who will, be an infidel. But for the offenders we have got ready the fire whose smoke shall enwrap them: and if they implore help, helped shall they be with water like molten brass which shall scald their faces. Wretched the drink! and an unhappy couch!

But as to those who have believed and done the things that are right, – Verily we will not suffer the reward of him whose works were good, to perish!

30 For them, the gardens of Eden, under whose shades shall rivers flow: decked shall they be therein with bracelets of gold, and green robes of silk and rich brocade shall they wear, reclining them therein on thrones. Blissful the reward! and a pleasant couch![11]

And set forth to them as a parable two men; on one of whom we bestowed two gardens of grape vines, and surrounded both with palm-trees, and placed corn fields between them: Each of the gardens did yield its fruit, and failed not thereof at all:

And we caused a river to flow in their midst: And this man received his fruit, and said, disputing with him, to his companion, 'More have I than thou of wealth, and my family is mightier.'

And he went into his garden – to his own soul unjust. He said, 'I do not think that this will ever perish:

And I do not think that "the Hour" will come: and even if I be taken back to my Lord, I shall surely find a better than it in exchange.'

His fellow said to him, disputing with him, 'What! hast thou no belief in him who created thee of the dust, then of the germs of life,[12] then fashioned thee a perfect man?

But God is my Lord; and no other being will I associate with my Lord.

And why didst thou not say when thou enteredst thy garden, 'What God willeth! There is no power but in God.' Though thou seest that I have less than thou of wealth and children,

Yet haply my Lord may bestow on me better than thy garden, and may send his bolts upon it out of Heaven, so that the next dawn shall find it barren dust;

Or its water become deep sunk, so that thou art unable to find it.'

40 And his fruits were encompassed *by destruction.* Then
began he to turn down the palms of his hands at what he had spent on it; for its vines were falling down on their trellises, and he said, 'Oh that I had not joined any other god to my Lord!'

And he had no host to help him instead of God, neither was he able to help himself.

Protection in such a case is of God – the Truth: He is the best rewarder, and He bringeth to the best issue.

And set before them a similitude of the present life. It is as water which we send down from Heaven, and the herb of the Earth is mingled with it, and on the morrow it becometh dry stubble which the winds scatter: for God hath power over all things.

Wealth and children are the adornment of this present life: but good works, which are lasting, are better in the sight of thy Lord as to recompense, and better as to hope.

And *call to mind* the day when we will cause the mountains to pass away,[13] and thou shalt see the earth a levelled plain, and we will gather *mankind* together, and not leave of them any one.

And they shall be set before thy Lord in ranks: – 'Now are ye come unto us as we created you at first: but ye thought that we should not make good to you the promise.'

And each shall have his book put *into his hand:* and thou shalt see the wicked in alarm at that which is therein: and they shall say, 'O woe to us! what meaneth this Book? It leaveth neither small nor great unnoted down!' And they shall find all that they have wrought present to them, and thy Lord will not deal unjustly with any one.

When we said to the angels, 'Prostrate yourselves before Adam,' they all prostrated them save Eblis, who was of the Djinn,[14] and revolted from his Lord's behest. – What! will ye then take him and his offspring as patrons rather than Me? and they your enemies? Sad exchange for the ungodly!

I made them not witnesses of the creation of the Heavens and of the Earth, nor of their own creation, neither did I take seducers as my helpers.

50 On a certain day, God shall say, 'Call ye on the companions ye joined with me, deeming them *to be gods:*' and they shall call on them, but they shall not answer them: then will we place a valley of perdition between them:

And the wicked shall see the fire, and shall have a foreboding that they shall be flung into it, and they shall find no escape from it.

And now in this Koran we have presented to man similitudes of every kind: but, at most things is man a caviller.

And what, now that guidance is come to them, letteth men from believing and from asking forgiveness of their Lord – unless they wait till that the doom of the ancients overtake them, or the chastisement come upon them in the sight of the universe?

We send not our Sent Ones but to announce and to warn: but the infidels cavil with vain words in order to refute the truth; and they treat my signs and their own warnings with scorn.

But who is worse than he who when told of the signs of his Lord turneth him away and forgetteth what in time past his hands have wrought? Truly we have thrown veils over their hearts lest they should understand this *Koran*, and into their ears a heaviness:

And if thou bid them to 'the guidance' yet will they not even then be guided ever.

The gracious one, full of compassion, is thy Lord! if he would have chastised them for their demerits he would have hastened their chastisement. But they have a time fixed for the accomplishment of our menaces: and beside God they shall find no refuge.

And those cities did we destroy when they became impious; and of their *coming* destruction we gave them warning.

Remember when Moses said to his servant, 'I will not stop till I reach the confluence of the two seas,[15] or for years will I journey on.'

60 But when they reached their confluence, they forgot their fish, and it took its way in the sea at will.

And when they had passed on, said Moses to his servant, 'Bring us our morning meal; for now have we incurred weariness from this journey.'

He said, 'What thinkest thou? When we repaired to the rock for rest I forgot the fish; and none but Satan made me forget it, so as not to mention it; and it hath taken its way in the sea in a wondrous sort.'

He said, 'It is this we were in quest of.'[16] And they both went back retracing their footsteps.

Then found they one of our servants to whom we had vouchsafed our mercy, and whom we had instructed with our knowledge.

And Moses said to him, 'Shall I follow thee that thou teach me, for guidance, of that which thou too hast been taught?'

He said, 'Verily, thou canst not have patience with me;

How canst thou be patient in matters whose meaning thou comprehendest not?'

He said, 'Thou shalt find me patient if God please, nor will I disobey thy bidding.'

He said, 'Then, if thou follow me, ask me not of aught until I have given thee an account thereof.'

70 So they both went on, till they embarked in a ship, and he – *the unknown* – staved it in. 'What!' said *Moses*, 'hast thou staved it in that thou mayest drown its crew? a strange thing now hast thou done!'

He said, 'Did I not tell thee that thou couldst not have patience with me?'

He said, 'Chide me not that I forgat, nor lay on me a hard command.'

Then went they on till they met a youth, and he slew him. Said Moses, 'Hast thou slain him who is free from guilt of blood? Now hast thou wrought a grievous thing!'

He said, 'Did I not tell thee that thou couldst not have patience with me?'

Moses said, 'If after this I ask thee aught, then let me be thy comrade no longer; but now hast thou my excuse.'

They went on till they came to the people of a city. Of this people they asked food, but they refused them for guests. And they found in it a wall that was about to fall, and he set it upright. Said Moses, 'If thou hadst wished, for this thou mightest have obtained pay.'

He said, 'This is the parting point between me and thee. But I will first tell thee the meaning of that which thou couldst not await with patience.

As to the vessel, it belonged to poor men who toiled upon the sea, and I was minded to damage it, for in their rear was a king who seized every ship by force.

As to the youth his parents were believers, and we feared lest he should trouble them by error and infidelity.

80 And we desired that their Lord might give them in his place a child, better than he in virtue, and nearer to filial piety.

And as to the wall, it belonged to two orphan youths in the city, and beneath it was their treasure: and their father was a righteous man: and thy Lord desired that they should reach the age of strength, and take forth their treasure through the mercy of thy Lord. And not of mine own will have I done this. This is the interpretation of that which thou couldst not bear with patience.'

They will ask thee of Dhoulkarnain [the two-horned[17]]. SAY: I will recite to you an account of him.

We stablished his power upon the earth, and made for him a way to everything. And a route he followed,

Until when he reached the setting of the sun, he found it to set in a miry fount; and hard by he found a people.

We said, 'O Dhoulkarnain! either chastise or treat them generously.'

'The impious,' said he, 'will we surely chastise;' then shall he be taken back to his Lord, and he will chastise him with a grievous chastisement.

But as to him who believeth and doeth that which is right, he shall have a generous recompense, and we will lay on them our easy behests.

Then followed he a route

Until when he reached the rising of the sun he found it to rise on a people to whom we had given no shelter from it.

90 Thus *it was*. And we had full knowledge of the forces that
were with him.

Then followed he a route.

Until he came between the two mountains, beneath which he found a people who scarce understood a language.

They said, 'O Dhoulkarnain! verily, Gog and Magog[18] waste this land; shall we then pay thee tribute, so thou build a rampart[19] between us and them?'

He said, 'Better *than your tribute* is the might wherewith my Lord hath strengthened me; but help me strenuously, and I will set a barrier between you and them.

Bring me blocks of iron,' – until when it filled the space between the mountain sides – 'Ply,' said he, 'your bellows,' – until when he had made it red with heat (fire), he said, – 'Bring me molten brass that I may pour upon it.'

And Gog and Magog were not able to scale it, neither were they able to dig through it.

'This,' said he, 'is a mercy from my Lord:

But when the promise of my Lord shall come to pass, he will turn it to dust; and the promise of my Lord is true.'

On that day we will let them dash like billows one over another; and there shall be a blast on the trumpet, and we will gather them together in a body.

100 And we will set Hell on that day close before the infidels,

Whose eyes were veiled from my warning, and who had no power to hear.

What! do the infidels think that they can take my servants as their patrons, beside Me? Verily, we have got Hell ready as the abode of the infidels.

SAY: Shall we tell you who they are that have lost their labour most?

Whose aim in the present life hath been mistaken, and who deem that what they do is right?

They are those who believe not in the signs of the Lord, or that they shall ever meet him. Vain, therefore, are their works; and no weight will we allow them on the day of resurrection.

This shall be their reward – Hell.[20] Because they were unbelievers, and treated my signs and my Apostles with scorn.

But as for those who believe and do the things that are right, they shall have the gardens of Paradise[21] for their abode:

They shall remain therein for ever: they shall wish for no change from it.

SAY: Should the sea become ink, to write the words of my Lord, the sea would surely fail ere the words of my Lord would fail, though we brought its like in aid.

110 SAY: In sooth I am only a man like you. It hath been revealed to me that your God is one only God: let him then who hopeth to meet his Lord work a righteous work: nor let him give any other creature a share in the worship of his Lord.

SURA 19[1] – MARY

MECCA – 98 VERSES

In the Name of God, the Compassionate, the Merciful

Kaf. Ha. Ya. Ain. Sad.[2] A recital of thy Lord's mercy to his servant Zachariah;

When he called upon his Lord with secret calling,

And said: 'O Lord, verily my bones are weakened, and the hoar hairs glisten on my head,

And never, Lord, have I prayed to thee with ill success.

But now I have fears for my kindred after me;[3] and my wife is barren:

Give me, then, a successor as thy special gift, who shall be my heir and an heir of the family of Jacob: and make him, Lord, well pleasing to thee.'

'O Zachariah! verily we announce to thee a son, – his name John:

That name We have given to none before him.[4]

He said: 'O my Lord! how when my wife is barren shall I have a son, and when I have now reached old age, failing in my powers?'

10 He said: So shall it be. Thy Lord hath said, Easy is this to me, for I created thee aforetime when thou wast nothing.'

He said: 'Vouchsafe me, O my Lord! a sign.' He said: 'Thy sign shall be that for three nights, though sound in health, thou speakest not to man.'

And he came forth from the sanctuary to his people, and made signs to them to sing praises morn and even.

We said: 'O John! receive the Book with purpose of heart:'[5] – and We bestowed on him wisdom while yet a child;

And mercifulness from Ourself, and purity; and pious was he, and duteous to his parents; and not proud, rebellious.

And peace was on him on the day he was born, and the day of his death, and *shall be* on the day when he shall be raised to life!

And make mention in the Book, of Mary, when she went apart from her family, eastward,[6]

And took a veil *to shroud herself* from them: and we sent our spirit[7] to her, and he took before her the form of a perfect man.[8]

She said: 'I fly for refuge from thee to the God of Mercy! If thou fearest Him, *begone from me.*'

He said: 'I am only a messenger of thy Lord, that I may bestow on thee a holy son.'

20 She said: 'How shall I have a son, when man hath never touched me? and I am not unchaste.'

He said: 'So shall it be. Thy Lord hath said: "Easy is this with me;" and we will make him a sign to mankind, and a mercy from us. For it is a thing decreed.'

And she conceived him,[9] and retired with him to a far-off place.

And the throes came upon her[10] by the trunk of a palm. She said: 'Oh, would that I had died ere this, and been a thing forgotten, forgotten quite!'

And one cried to her from below her:[11] 'Grieve not thou, thy Lord hath provided a streamlet at thy feet:–

And shake the trunk of the palm-tree towards thee:[12] it will drop fresh ripe dates upon thee.

Eat then and drink, and be of cheerful eye:[13] and shouldst thou see a man,

Say, – Verily, I have vowed abstinence to the God of mercy. – To no one will I speak this day.'

Then came she with the babe to her people, bearing him. They said, 'O Mary! now hast thou done a strange thing!

O sister of Aaron![14] Thy father was not a man of wickedness, nor unchaste thy mother.'

30 And she made a sign *to them, pointing* towards the babe. They said, 'How shall we speak with him who is in the cradle, an infant?'

It said,[15] 'Verily, I am the servant of God; He hath given me the Book, and He hath made me a prophet;

And He hath made me blessed wherever I may be, and hath enjoined me prayer and almsgiving so long as I shall live;

And to be duteous to her that bare me: and he hath not made me proud, depraved.

And the peace of God was on me the day I was born, and will be the day I shall die, and the day I shall be raised to life.'

This is Jesus, the son of Mary; this is a statement of the truth concerning which they doubt.

It beseemeth not God to beget a son. Glory be to Him! when he decreeth a thing, He only saith to it, Be, and it Is.

And verily, God is my Lord and your Lord; adore Him then. This is the right way.

But the Sects have fallen to variance among themselves *about Jesus:* but woe, because of the assembly of a great day, to those who believe not!

Make them hear, make them behold the day when they shall come before us! But the offenders this day are in a manifest error.

40 Warn them of the day of sighing when the decree shall be accomplished, while they are *sunk* in heedlessness and while they believe not.

Verily, we will inherit the earth and all who are upon it. To us shall they be brought back.

Make mention also in the Book of Abraham; for he was a man of truth, a Prophet.[16]

When he said to his Father, 'O my Father! why dost thou worship that which neither seeth nor heareth, nor profiteth thee aught?

O my Father! verily now hath knowledge come to me which hath not come to thee. Follow me therefore – I will guide thee into an even path.

O my Father! worship not Satan, for Satan is a rebel against the God of Mercy.

O my Father! indeed I fear lest a chastisement from the God of Mercy light upon thee, and thou become Satan's vassal.'

He said, 'Castest thou off my Gods, O Abraham? If thou forbear not, I will surely stone thee. Begone from me for a length of time.'

He said, 'Peace be on thee! I will pray my Lord for thy forgiveness, for he is gracious to me:

But I will separate myself from you, and the gods ye call on beside God, and on my Lord will I call. Haply, my prayers to my Lord will not be with ill success.'

50 And when he had separated himself from them and that which they worshipped beside God, we bestowed on him Isaac and Jacob, and each of them we made a prophet:

And we bestowed gifts on them in our mercy, and gave them the lofty tongue of truth.'[17]

And commemorate Moses in 'the Book;' for he was a man of purity: moreover he was an Apostle, a Prophet:

From the right side of the mountain we called to him, and caused him to draw nigh to us for secret converse:

And we bestowed on him in our mercy his brother Aaron, a Prophet.

And commemorate Ismael in 'the Book;' for he was true to his promise, and was an Apostle, a Prophet;

And he enjoined prayer and almsgiving on his people, and was well pleasing to his Lord.

And commemorate Edris[18] in 'the Book;' for he was a man of truth, a Prophet:

And we uplifted him to a place on high.[19]

These are they among the prophets of the posterity of Adam, and among those whom we bare with Noah, and among the posterity of Abraham and Israel, and among those whom we have guided and chosen, to whom God hath shewed favour. When the signs of the God of Mercy were rehearsed to them, they bowed them down worshipping and weeping.

60 But others have come in their place after them: they have made an end of prayer, and have gone after their own lusts; and in the end they shall meet with evil:–

Save those who turn and believe and do that which is right, these shall enter the Garden, and in nought shall they be wronged:

The Garden of Eden, which the God of Mercy hath promised to his servants, though yet unseen:[20] for his promise shall come to pass:

No vain discourse shall they hear therein, but only 'Peace;' and their food shall be given them at morn and even:

This is the Paradise which we will make the heritage of those our servants who fear us.

We[21] come not down *from Heaven* but by thy Lord's command. His, whatever is before us and whatever is behind us, and whatever is between the two! And thy Lord is not forgetful, –

Lord of the Heavens and of the Earth, and of all that is between them! Worship Him, then, and abide thou steadfast in his worship. Knowest thou any other of the same name?[22]

Man saith: 'What! after I am dead, shall I in the end be brought forth alive?'

Doth not man bear in mind that we made him at first, when he was nought?

And I swear by thy Lord, we will surely gather together them and the Satans: then will we set them on their knees round Hell:

70 Then will we take forth from each band those of them who have been stoutest in rebellion against the God of Mercy:

Then shall we know right well to whom its burning is most due:

No one is there of you who shall not go down unto it[23] – This is a settled decree with thy Lord –

Then will we deliver those who had the fear of God, and the wicked will we leave in it on their knees.

And when our clear signs are rehearsed to them, the infidels say to those who believe: 'Which of the two parties[24] is in the best plight? and which is the most goodly company?'

But how many generations have we brought to ruin before them, who surpassed them in riches and in splendour!

SAY: As to those who are in error, the God of Mercy will lengthen out to them a length of days

Until they see that with which they are threatened, whether it be *some present* chastisement, or whether it be 'the Hour,' and they shall then know which is in the worse state, and which the more weak in forces:

But God will increase the guidance of the already guided.

And good works which abide, are in thy Lord's sight better in respect of guerdon, and better in the issue *than all worldly good*.

80 Hast thou marked him who believeth not in our signs, and saith, 'I shall surely have riches and children bestowed upon me?'

Hath he mounted up into the secrets of God? Hath he made a compact with the God of Mercy?

No! we will certainly write down what he saith, and will lengthen the length of his chastisement:

And We will inherit what he spake of, and he shall come before us all alone.

They have taken other gods beside God to be their help.[25]

But it shall not be. Those gods will disavow their worship and will become their enemies.

Seest thou not that we send the Satans against the Infidels to urge them into sin?

Wherefore be not thou in haste with them;[26] for a small number *of days* do we number to them.

One day we will gather the God-fearing before the God of Mercy with honours due:[27]

But the sinners will we drive unto Hell, like flocks driven to the watering.

90 None shall have power to intercede, save he who hath received permission at the hands of the God of Mercy.

They say: 'The God of Mercy hath gotten offspring.' Now have ye done a monstrous thing!

Almost might the very Heavens be rent thereat, and the Earth cleave asunder, and the mountains fall down in fragments,

That they ascribe a son to the God of Mercy, when it beseemeth not the God of Mercy to beget a son!

Verily there is none in the Heavens and in the Earth but shall approach the God of Mercy as a servant. He hath taken note of them, and numbered them with *exact* numbering:

And each of them shall come to Him, on the day of Resurrection, singly:

But love will the God of Mercy vouchsafe to those who believe and do the things that be right.

Verily we have made this *Koran* easy and in thine own tongue, that thou mayest announce glad tidings by it to the God-fearing, and that thou mayest warn the contentious by it.

How many generations have we destroyed before them! Canst thou search out one of them? or canst thou hear a whisper from them?

SURA 20[1] – TA. HA.

MECCA – 135 VERSES

In the Name of God, the Compassionate, the Merciful

TA. HA.[2] Not to sadden thee have we sent down this Koran
to thee,
But as a warning for him who feareth;
It is a missive *from* Him who hath made the earth and the
lofty heavens!
The God of Mercy sitteth on his throne:
His, whatsoever is in the heavens and whatsoever is in the
earth, and whatsoever is between them both, and whatsoever is
beneath the humid soil!
Thou needest not raise thy voice:[3] for He knoweth the secret
whisper, and the yet more hidden.
God! There is no God but He! Most excellent His titles!
Hath the history of Moses reached thee?
When he saw a fire, and said to his family, 'Tarry ye *here*, for I
perceive a fire:
10 Haply I may bring you a brand from it, or find at the fire a
guide.[4]
And when he came to it, he was called to, 'O Moses!
Verily, I am thy Lord: therefore pull off thy shoes: for thou
art in the holy valley of Towa.
And I have chosen thee: hearken then to what shall be
revealed.
Verily, I am God: there is no God but me: therefore worship
me, and observe prayer for a remembrance of me.
Verily the hour is coming: – I all but manifest it –
That every soul may be recompensed for its labours.
Nor let him who believeth not therein and followeth his lust,
turn thee aside from this *truth*, and thou perish.
Now, what is that in thy right hand, O Moses?'
Said he, 'It is my staff on which I lean, and with which I beat
down leaves for my sheep, and I have other uses for it.'
20 He said, 'Cast it down, O Moses!'
So he cast it down, and lo! it became a serpent that ran along.
He said, 'Lay hold on it, and fear not: to its former state will
we restore it.

Now place thy right hand to thy arm-pit: it shall come forth white, *but* unhurt: – another sign! –
That We may shew thee the greatest of our signs.
Go to Pharaoh, for he hath burst all bounds.'
He said, 'O my Lord! enlarge my breast for me,
And make my work easy for me,
And loose the knot of my tongue,[5]
That they may understand my speech.
30 And give me a counsellor[6] from among my family,
Aaron my brother;
By him gird up my loins,[7]
And make him a colleague in my work,
That we may praise thee oft and oft remember thee,
For thou regardest us.'
He said, 'O Moses, thou hast obtained thy suit:
Already, at another time, have we showed thee favour,
When we spake unto thy mother what was spoken:
"Cast him into the ark:[8] then cast him on the sea [the river], and the sea shall throw him on the shore: and an enemy to me and an enemy to him shall take him up." And I myself have made thee an object of love,
40 That thou mightest be reared in mine eye.
When thy sister went and said, "Shall I shew you one who will nurse him?"[9] Then We returned thee to thy mother that her eye might be cheered, and that she might not grieve. And when thou slewest a person, We delivered thee from trouble, and We tried thee with *other* trial.
For years didst thou stay among the people of Midian; then camest thou hither by *my* decree, O Moses:
And I have chosen thee for Myself.
Go thou and thy brother with my signs and be not slack to remember me.
Go ye to Pharaoh, for he hath burst all bounds:
But speak ye to him with gentle speech; haply he will reflect or fear.'
They said, 'O our Lord! truly we fear lest he break forth against us, or act with exceeding injustice.'
He said, 'Fear ye not, for I am with you both. I will hearken and I will behold.
Go ye then to him and say, "Verily we are Sent ones of thy Lord; send therefore the children of Israel with us and vex them

not: now are we come to thee with signs from thy Lord, and, Peace shall be on him who followeth the right guidance.
50 For now hath it been revealed to us, that chastisement shall be on him who chargeth with falsehood, and turneth him away." '

And he said, 'Who is your Lord, O Moses?'

He said, 'Our Lord is He who hath given to everything its form and then guideth it aright.'

'But what,' said he, 'was the state of generations past?'[10]

He said, 'The knowledge thereof is with my Lord in the Book of his decrees. My Lord erreth not, nor forgetteth.

He hath spread the earth as a bed, and hath traced out paths for you therein, and hath sent down rain from Heaven, and by it we bring forth the kinds[11] of various herbs:

– "Eat ye, and feed your cattle." Of a truth in this are signs unto men endued with understanding.

From it have we created you, and into it will we return you, and out of it will we bring you forth a second time.'[12]

And we shewed him all our signs: but he treated them as falsehoods, and refused *to believe*.

He said, 'Hast thou come, O Moses, to drive us from our land by thine enchantments?
60 Therefore will we assuredly confront thee with like enchantments: so appoint a meeting between us and you – we will not fail it, we, and do not thou – in a place alike for both.'

He said, 'On the feast day[13] be your meeting, and in broad daylight let the people be assembled.'

And Pharaoh turned away, and collected his craftsmen and came.

Said Moses to them, 'Woe to you! devise not a lie against God:

For then will he destroy you by a punishment. They who have lied have ever perished.'

And the magicians discussed their plan, and spake apart in secret:

They said, 'These two are surely sorcerers: fain would they drive you from your land by their sorceries, and lead away in their paths your chiefest men:

So muster your craft: then come in order: well this day shall it be for him, who shall gain the upper hand.'

They said, 'O Moses, wilt thou first cast down *thy rod*, or shall we be the first who cast?'

He said, 'Yes, cast ye down first.' And lo! by their enchantment their cords and rods seemed to him as if they ran.
70 And Moses conceived a secret fear within him.
We said, 'Fear not, for thou shalt be the uppermost:
Cast forth then what is in thy right hand: it shall swallow up what they have produced: they have only produced the deceit of an enchanter: and come where he may, ill shall an enchanter fare.'
And the magicians fell down and worshipped. They said, 'We believe in the Lord of Aaron and of Moses.'
Said Pharaoh, 'Believe ye on him ere I give you leave? He, in sooth, is your Master who hath taught you magic. I will therefore cut off your hands and your feet on opposite sides, and I will crucify you on trunks of the palm, and assuredly shall ye learn which of us is severest in punishing, and who is the more abiding.'[14]
They said, 'We will not have more regard to thee than to the clear tokens which have come to us, or than to Him who hath made us: doom the doom thou wilt: Thou canst only doom as to this present life: of a truth we have believed on our Lord that he may pardon us our sins and the sorcery to which thou hast forced us, for God is better, and more abiding than thou.[15]
As for him who shall come before his Lord laden with crime – for him verily is Hell: he shall not die in it and he shall not live.
But he who shall come before Him, a believer, with righteous works, – these! the loftiest grades await them:
Gardens of Eden, beneath whose trees[16] the rivers flow: therein shall they abide for ever. This, the reward of him who hath been pure.'
Then revealed we to Moses, 'Go forth by night with my servants and cleave for them a dry path in the sea;
80 Fear not thou to be overtaken, neither be thou afraid.'
And *Pharaoh* followed them with his hosts, and the whelming billows of the sea overwhelmed them,[17] for Pharaoh misled his people, and did not guide them.
O children of Israel! we rescued you from your foes; and We appointed a meeting with you on the right side of the mountain; and We caused the manna and the quail to descend upon you:
'Eat,' *said We*, 'of the good things with which we have supplied you; but without excess, lest my wrath fall upon you; for on whom my wrath doth fall, he perisheth outright.

Surely however will I forgive him who turneth to God and believeth, and worketh righteousness, and then yieldeth to guidance.

But what hath hastened thee on apart from thy people,[18] O Moses?'

He said, 'They are hard on my footsteps: but to thee, O Lord, have I hastened, that thou mightest be well pleased with me.'

He said, 'Of a truth now have we proved thy people since thou didst leave them, and Samiri[19] had led them astray.'

And Moses returned to his people, angered, sorrowful.

He said, 'O my people! did not your Lord promise you a good promise? Was the time *of my absence* long to you? or desired ye that wrath from your Lord should light upon you, that ye failed in your promise to me?'

90 They said, 'Not of our own accord have we failed in the promise to thee, but we were made to bring loads of the people's trinkets, and we threw them *into the fire* – and Samiri likewise cast them in, and brought forth to them a corporeal lowing[20] calf: and they said, "This is your God and the God of Moses, whom he hath forgotten." '

What! saw they not that it returned them no answer, and could neither hurt nor help them?

And Aaron had before said to them, 'O my people! by this calf are ye only proved: surely your Lord is the God of Mercy: follow me therefore and obey my bidding.'

They said, 'We will not cease devotion to it, till Moses come back to us.'

He said, 'O Aaron! when thou sawest that they had gone astray, what hindered thee from following me? Hast thou then disobeyed my command?'

He said, 'O Son of my mother! seize me not by my beard, nor by my head: indeed I feared lest thou shouldst say, "Thou hast rent the children of Israel asunder, and hast not observed my orders." '

He said, 'And what was thy motive, O Samiri?' He said, 'I saw what they saw not: so I took a handful *of dust* from the track[21] of the messenger *of God*, and flung it *into the calf*, for so my soul prompted me.'

He said, 'Begone then: verily thy doom even in this life shall be to say, "Touch me not."[22] And there is a threat against thee, which thou shalt not escape *hereafter*. Now look at thy god to which thou hast continued so devoted: we will surely burn it and reduce it to ashes, which we will cast into the sea.

Your God is God, beside whom there is no God: In his knowledge he embraceth all things.'

Thus do We recite to thee histories of what passed of old; and from ourself have we given thee admonition.

100 Whoso shall turn aside from it shall verily carry a burden on
the day of Resurrection:

Under it shall they remain: and grievous, in the day of Resurrection, shall it be to them to bear.

On that day there shall be a blast on the trumpet, and We will gather the wicked together on that day with leaden[23] eyes:

They shall say in a low voice, one to another, – 'Ye tarried but ten *days on earth*.'

We are most knowing with respect to that which they will say when the most veracious[24] of them will say. 'Ye have not tarried above a day.'

And they will ask thee of the mountains: SAY: scattering my Lord will scatter them in dust;

And he will leave them a level plain: thou shalt see in it no hollows or jutting hills.

On that day shall men follow their summoner[25] – he marcheth straight on: and low shall be their voices before the God of Mercy, nor shalt thou hear *aught* but the light footfall.

No intercession shall avail on that day, save his whom the God of Mercy shall allow to intercede, and whose words he shall approve.

He knoweth their future and their past; but in their own knowledge they comprehend it not:–

110 And humble shall be their faces before Him that Liveth, the
Self-subsisting: and undone he, who shall bear the burden of
iniquity;

But he who shall have done the things that are right and is a believer, shall fear neither wrong nor loss.

Thus have We sent down to thee an Arabic Koran, and have set forth menaces therein diversely, that haply they may fear God, or that it may give birth to reflection in them.

Exalted then be God, the King, the Truth! Be not hasty in its recital[26] while the revelation of it to thee is incomplete. Say rather, 'O my Lord, increase knowledge unto me.'

And of old We made a covenant with Adam; but he forgat *it;* and we found no firmness *of purpose* in him.

And when We said to the angels, 'Fall down and worship Adam,' they worshipped all, save Eblis, *who* refused: and We said, 'O Adam! this truly is a foe to thee and to thy wife. Let him not therefore drive you out of the garden, and ye become wretched;

For to thee *is it granted* that thou shalt not hunger therein, neither shalt thou be naked;

And that thou shalt not thirst therein, neither shalt thou parch with heat;'

But Satan whispered him: said he, 'O Adam! shall I shew thee the tree of Eternity,[27] and the Kingdom that faileth not?'

And they both ate thereof, and their nakedness appeared to them, and they began to sew of the leaves of the Garden to cover them, and Adam disobeyed his Lord and went astray.

120 Afterwards his Lord chose him for himself, and was turned towards him, and guided him.

And God said, 'Get ye all down hence, the one of you a foe unto the other. Hereafter shall guidance come unto you from me;

And whoso followeth my guidance shall not err, and shall not be wretched:

But whoso turneth away from my monition, his truly shall be a life of misery:

And We will assemble him *with others* on the day of Resurrection, blind.'[28]

He will say, 'O my Lord! why hast thou assembled me *with others*, blind? whereas I was endowed with sight.'

He will answer, 'Thus is it, because our signs came unto thee and thou didst forget them, and thus shalt thou be forgotten this day.'

Even thus will We recompense him who hath transgressed and hath not believed in the signs of his Lord; and assuredly the chastisement of the next world will be more severe and more lasting.

Are not they, who walk the very places where they dwelt, aware how many generations we have destroyed before them? Verily in this are signs to men of insight.

And had not a decree *of respite* from thy Lord first gone forth, *their chastisement had at once ensued.* Yet the time is fixed.

130 Put up then with what they say; and celebrate the praise of thy Lord before the sunrise, and before its setting; and some time in the night do thou praise Him, and in the extremes[29] of the day, that thou haply mayest please Him.

And strain not thine eye after what We have bestowed on divers of them – the braveries of this world – that we may thereby prove them. The portion which thy Lord will give, is better and more lasting.

Enjoin prayer on thy family, and persevere therein. We ask not of thee to find thine own provision – we will provide for thee, and a *happy* issue shall there be to piety.

But they say, 'If he come not to us with a sign from his Lord . . . !'[30] But have not clear proofs *for the Koran* come to them, in what is in the Books of old?

And had We destroyed them by a chastisement before its time, they would surely have said, 'O our Lord! *How could we believe* if thou didst not send unto us an Apostle that we might follow thy signs ere that we were humbled and disgraced.'

SAY: Each one of us awaiteth the end. Wait ye then, and ye shall know which of us have been followers of the even way, and who hath been the rightly guided.

SURA 21 – THE PROPHETS

MECCA – 112 VERSES

In the Name of God, the Compassionate, the Merciful

This people's reckoning hath drawn nigh, yet, *sunk* in carelessness, they turn aside.

Every fresh warning that cometh to them from their Lord they only hear to mock it, –

Their hearts set on lusts: and they who have done this wrong say in secret discourse, 'Is He more than a man like yourselves? What! will ye, with your eyes open,[1] accede to sorcery?'

SAY: 'My Lord knoweth what is spoken in the heaven and on the earth: He is the Hearer, the Knower.'

'Nay,' say they, 'it is the medley of dreams: nay, he hath forged it: nay, he is a poet: let him come to us with a sign as *the prophets* of old were sent.'

Before their time, none of the cities which we have destroyed, believed: will these men, then, believe?

And we sent none, previous to thee, but men to whom we had revealed ourselves. Ask ye the people who are warned by Scriptures,[2] if ye know it not.

We gave them not bodies which could dispense with food: and they were not to live for ever.

Then made we good our promise to them; and we delivered them and whom we pleased, and we destroyed the transgressors.

10 And now have we sent down to you 'the book,' in which is your warning: What, will ye not then understand?

And how many a guilty city have we broken down, and raised up after it other peoples:

And when they felt our vengeance, lo! they fled from it.

'Flee not,' *said the angels in mockery*, 'but come back to that wherein ye revelled, and to your abodes! Questions will haply be put to you.'

They said, 'Oh, woe to us! Verily we have been evil doers.'

And this ceased not to be their cry, until we made them like reaped corn, extinct.

We created not the heaven and the earth, and what is between them, for sport:

Had it been our wish to find a pastime, we had surely found it in ourselves; – if to do so had been our will.

Nay, we will hurl the truth at falsehood, and it shall smite it, and lo! it shall vanish. But woe be to you for what ye utter *of God!*

All beings in the heaven and on the earth are His: and they who are in his presence disdain not his service, neither are they wearied:

20 They praise Him night and day: they rest not.[3]

Have they taken gods from the earth who can quicken the dead?

Had there been in either *heaven or earth* gods besides God, both surely had gone to ruin. But glory be to God, the Lord of the throne, beyond what they utter!

He shall not be asked of his doings, but they shall be asked.

Have they taken other gods beside Him? SAY: Bring forth your proofs *that they are gods.* This is the warning of those who are with me, and the warning of those who were before me: but most of them know not the truth, and turn aside.

No apostle have we sent before thee to whom we did not reveal that 'Verily there is no God beside me: therefore worship me.'

Yet they say, 'The God of Mercy hath begotten issue *from the angels.*' Glory be to Him! Nay, they are *but* His honoured servants:

They speak not till He hath spoken;[4] and they do His bidding.

He knoweth what is before them and what is behind them; and no plea shall they offer

Save for whom He pleaseth; and they tremble for fear of Him.

30 And *that angel* among them who saith 'I am a god beside Him,' will we recompense with hell: in such sort will we recompense the offenders.

Do not the infidels see that the heavens and the earth were both a solid mass, and that we clave them asunder, and that by means of water we give life to everything? Will they not then believe?

And we set mountains on the earth lest it should move with them, and we made on it broad passages between them as routes for their guidance;

And we made the heaven a roof strongly upholden; yet turn they away from its signs.

And He it is who hath created the night and the day, and the sun and the moon, each moving swiftly in its sphere.

At no time[5] have we granted to man a life that shall last for ever: if thou then die, shall they live for ever?

Every soul shall taste of death:[6] and for trial will we prove you with evil and with good; and unto Us shall ye be brought back.

And when the infidels see thee they receive thee only with scoffs: – 'What! is this he who maketh such mention of your gods?' Yet when mention is made to them of the God of Mercy, they believe not.

'Man,' *say they*, 'is made up of haste.'[7] But I will shew you my signs:[8] desire them not then to be hastened.

They say, 'When will this threat *be made good?* Tell us, if ye be men of truth?'

40 Did the infidels but know the time when they shall not be able to keep the fire of hell from their faces or from their backs, neither shall they be helped!

But it shall come on them suddenly and shall confound them; and they shall not be able to put it back, neither shall they be respited.

Other apostles have been scoffed at before thee: but that *doom* at which they mocked encompassed the scoffers.

SAY: Who shall protect you by night and by day from the God of Mercy? Yet turn they away from the warning of their Lord.

Have they gods beside Us who can defend them? For their own succour have they no power; neither shall the gods they join with God screen them from Us.

Yes! we have given these men and their fathers enjoyments so long as their life lasted. What! see they not that we come to a land and straiten its borders? Is it they who are the conquerors?

SAY: I only warn you of what hath been revealed to me: but the deaf will not hear the call, whenever they are warned;

Yet if a breath of thy Lord's chastisement touch them, they will assuredly say, 'Oh! woe to us! we have indeed been offenders.'

Just balances will we set up for the day of the resurrection, neither shall any soul be wronged in aught; though, were a work but the weight of a grain of mustard seed, we would bring it forth *to be weighed:* and our reckoning will suffice.

We gave of old to Moses and Aaron the illumination,[9] and a light and a warning for the God-fearing,

50 Who dread their Lord in secret, and who tremble for 'the Hour.'

And this *Koran* which we have sent down is a blessed warning: will ye then disown it?

Of old we gave unto Abraham his direction,[10] for we knew him worthy.

When he said to his Father and to his people, 'What are these images to which ye are devoted?'

They said, 'We found our fathers worshipping them.'

He said, 'Truly ye and your fathers have been in a plain mistake.'

They said, 'Hast thou come unto us in earnest? or art thou of those who jest?'

He said, 'Nay, your Lord is Lord of the Heavens and of the Earth, who hath created them both; and to this am I one of those who witness:

– And, by God, I will certainly lay a plot against your idols, after ye shall have retired and turned your backs.'

So, he broke them all in pieces, except the chief of them, that to it they might return, *inquiring*.

60 They said, 'Who hath done this to our gods? Verily he is *one* of the unjust.'

They said, 'We heard a youth make mention of them: they call him Abraham.'

They said, 'Then bring him before the people's eyes, that they may witness *against him*.'

They said, 'Hast thou done this to our gods, O Abraham?'

He said, 'Nay, that their chief hath done it: but ask ye them, if they can speak.'

So they turned their *thoughts* upon themselves, and said, 'Ye truly are the impious persons:'

Then became headstrong in their former error[11] and exclaimed, 'Thou knowest that these speak not.'

He said, 'What! do ye then worship, instead of God, that which doth not profit you at all, nor injure you? Fie on you and on that ye worship instead of God! What! do ye not then understand?'

They said:[12] 'Burn him, and come to the succour of your gods: if ye will do *anything at all*.'

We said, 'O fire! be thou cold, and to Abraham a safety!'[13]

70 And they sought to lay a plot against him, but we made them the sufferers.

And we brought him and Lot in safety to the land which we have blessed for all human beings:

And we gave him Isaac and Jacob as a farther gift, and we made all of them righteous:

We also made them models who should guide *others* by our command, and we inspired them with good deeds and constancy in prayer and almsgiving, and they worshipped us.

And unto Lot we gave wisdom, and knowledge; and we rescued him from the city which wrought filthiness; for they were a people, evil, perverse:

And we caused him to enter into our mercy, for he was of the righteous.

And *remember* Noah when aforetime he cried to us and we heard him, and delivered him and his family from the great calamity;

And we helped him against the people who treated our signs as impostures. An evil people verily were they, and we drowned them all.

And David and Solomon; when they gave judgment concerning a field when some people's sheep had caused a waste therein; and we were witnesses of their judgment.

And we gave Solomon insight into the affair; and on both of them we bestowed wisdom and knowledge. And we constrained the mountains and the birds to join with David in our praise: Our doing was it!

80 And we taught David the art of making mail[14] for you, to defend you from each other's violence: will ye therefore be thankful?

And to Solomon we subjected the strongly blowing wind: it sped at his bidding to the land we had blessed; for we know all things:

And sundry Satans[15] who should dive for him and perform other work beside: and we kept watch over them.

And *remember* Job: When he cried to his Lord, 'Truly evil hath touched me: but thou art the most merciful of those who shew mercy.'

So we heard him, and lightened the burden of his woe; and we gave him back his family, and as many more with them, – a mercy from us, and a memorial for those who serve us:

And Ismael, and Edris[16] and Dhoulkefl[17] – all steadfast in patience.

And we caused them to enter into our mercy; for they were of the righteous:

And Dhoulnoun;[18] when he went on his way in anger, and thought that we had no power over him. But in the darkness he cried 'There is no God but thou: Glory be unto Thee! Verily, I have been one of the evil doers:'

So we heard him and rescued him from misery: for thus rescue we the faithful:

And Zacharias; when he called upon his Lord saying, 'O my

Lord, leave me not childless: but there is no better heir than Thyself.'[19]

90 So we heard him, and gave him John, and we made his wife fit for child-bearing. Verily, these vied in goodness, and called upon us with love and fear, and humbled themselves before us:

And her who kept her maidenhood, and into whom[20] we breathed of our spirit, and made her and her son a sign to all creatures.

Of a truth, this, your religion, is the one[21] Religion, and I your Lord; therefore serve me:

But they have rent asunder this their *great* concern among themselves *into sects*. All of them shall return to us.

And whoso shall do the things that are right, and be a believer, his efforts shall not be disowned: and surely will we write them down for him.

There is a ban on every city which we shall have destroyed, that they shall not rise again,

Until a way is opened for Gog and Magog,[22] and they shall hasten from every high land,

And this sure promise shall draw on. And lo! the eyes of the infidels shall stare amazedly; *and they shall say*, 'Oh, our misery! of this were we careless! yea, we were impious persons.'

Verily, ye, and what ye worship beside God,[23] shall be fuel for hell: ye shall go down into it.

Were these gods, they would not go down into it; but they shall all abide in it for ever.

100 Therein shall they groan; but nought therein shall they hear *to comfort them*.

But they for whom we have before ordained good things, shall be far away from it:

Its slightest sound they shall not hear: in what their souls longed for, they shall abide for ever:

The great terror shall not trouble them; and the angel shall meet them with, 'This is your day which ye were promised.'

On that day we will roll up the heaven as one rolleth up[24] written scrolls. As we made the first creation, so will we bring it forth again. This promise bindeth us; verily, we will perform it.

And now, since the Law was given, have we written in the Psalms that 'my servants, the righteous, shall inherit the earth.'[25]

Verily, in this *Koran* is teaching for those who serve *God*.

We have not sent thee otherwise than as mercy unto all creatures.

SAY: Verily it hath been revealed to me that your God is one God; are ye then resigned to Him? (Muslims.)

But if they turn their backs, then SAY: I have warned you all alike; but I know not whether that with which ye are threatened be nigh or distant.

110 God truly knoweth what is spoken aloud, and He also knoweth that which ye hide.

And I know not whether haply this *delay* be not for your trial, and that ye may enjoy yourselves for a time.

My Lord saith: Judge *ye* with truth; for our Lord is the God of Mercy – whose help is to be sought against what ye utter.

SURA 22 – THE PILGRIMAGE

MEDINA[1] – 78 VERSES

In the Name of God, the Compassionate, the Merciful

O Men *of Mecca*, fear your Lord. Verily, the earthquake of the *last* Hour will be a tremendous thing!

On the day when *ye* shall behold it, every suckling woman shall forsake her sucking babe; and every woman that hath a burden in her womb shall cast her burden; and thou shalt see men drunken, yet are they not drunken: but it is the mighty chastisement of God!

There is a man who, without knowledge, wrangleth about God, and followeth every rebellious Satan;

Concerning whom it is decreed, that he shall surely beguile and guide into the torment of the Flame, whoever shall take him for his Lord.

O men! if ye doubt as to the resurrection, yet, of a truth, have We created you of dust, then of the moist germs of life, then of clots of blood, then of pieces of flesh shapen and unshapen, that We might give you proofs *of our power!* And We cause *one sex or the other*, at our pleasure, to abide in the womb until the appointed time; then We bring you forth infants; then permit you to reach your age of strength; and one of you dieth, and another of you liveth on to an age so abject that all his former knowledge is clean forgotten![2] And thou hast seen the earth dried up and barren: but when We send down the rain upon it, it stirreth and swelleth, and groweth every kind of luxuriant herb.

This, for that God is the Truth, and that it is He who quickeneth the dead, and that He hath power over everything:

And that 'the Hour' will *indeed* come – there is no doubt of it – and that God will wake up to life those who are in the tombs.

A man there is who disputeth about God without knowledge or guidance or enlightening Book,

Turning aside *in scorn* to mislead *others* from the way of God! Disgrace shall be his in this world; and on the day of the resurrection, We will make him taste the torment of the burning: –

10 'This, for thy handywork of old! for God is not unjust to His servants.'

There are some who serve God in a single point. If good come upon one of them, he resteth in it; but if trial come upon him, he turneth him round (to infidelity) with the loss both of this world and of the next! This same is the clear ruin!

He calleth upon that beside God which can neither hurt him nor profit him. This same is the far-gone error!

He calleth on him who would sooner hurt than profit him. Surely, bad the lord, and, surely, bad the vassal!

But God will bring in those who shall believe and do the things that are right, into gardens 'neath which the rivers flow: for God doth that which He pleaseth.

Let him who thinketh that God will not help *His Apostle* in this world and in the next, stretch a cord aloft as if to *destroy himself;* then let him cut it, and see whether his devices can bring that[3] to nought at which he was angry!

Thus send we down *the Koran with its* clear signs (verses): and because God guideth whom He pleaseth.

As to those who believe, and the Jews, and the Sabeites,[4] and the Christians, and the Magians, and those who join other gods with God, of a truth, God shall decide between them on the day of resurrection: for God is witness of all things.

Seest thou not that all in the Heavens and all on the Earth

adoreth God? the sun and the moon and the stars, and the mountains, and the trees, and the beasts, and many men? But of many is chastisement the due:

And whom God shall disgrace there shall be none to honour: God doth that which pleaseth Him.

20 These, *the Faithful and the Infidels*, are the two disputants who dispute concerning their Lord: but for those who have disbelieved, garments of fire shall be cut out; the boiling water shall be poured down upon their heads:

All that is in their bowels, and their skins, shall be dissolved: and there are maces of iron for them!

So oft as they, for very anguish, would fain come forth thence, back shall they be turned into it: and – 'Taste ye the torment of the burning.'

But God will bring in those who shall have believed, and done the things that are right, into gardens 'neath which the rivers flow. Adorned shall they be therein with golden bracelets and with pearls, and their raiment therein shall be of silk;

For they were guided to the best of words; guided to the glorious path!

But those who believe not, and seduce others from the way of God, and from the Holy Mosque which we have appointed to all men, alike for those who abide therein, and for the stranger;

And those who seek impiously to profane it, we will cause to taste a grievous punishment.

And *call to mind* when we assigned the site of the House[5] to Abraham *and said:* 'Unite not aught with Me in worship, and cleanse My House for those who go in procession round it, and who stand or bow in worship:' –

And proclaim to the peoples a PILGRIMAGE: Let them come to thee on foot and on every fleet[6] camel, arriving by every deep defile:

That they may bear witness of its benefits to them, and may make mention of God's name on the appointed days,[7] over the brute beasts with which He hath supplied them for sustenance: Therefore eat thereof yourselves, and feed the needy, the poor:

30 Then let them bring the neglect of their persons to a close,[8] and let them pay their vows, and circuit the ancient House.

This *do*. And he that respecteth the sacred ordinances of God, this will be best for him with his Lord. The flesh of cattle is allowed you, save of those *already* specified to you. Shun ye, therefore, the pollutions of idols; and shun ye the word of falsehood;

Sound in faith Godward, uniting no god with Him; for whoever uniteth gods with God, is like that which falleth from on high, and the birds snatch it away, or the wind wafteth it to a distant place.

This *do*. And they who respect the rites of God, *perform an action* which proceedeth from piety of heart.

Ye may obtain advantages from the *cattle* up to the set time *for slaying them:* then, the place for sacrificing them is at the ancient House.

And to every people have we appointed rites, that they may commemorate the name of God over the brute beasts which He hath provided for them. And your God is the one God. To Him, therefore, surrender yourselves: and bear thou good tidings to those who humble them, –

Whose hearts, when mention is made of God, thrill with awe; and to those who remain steadfast under all that befalleth them, and observe prayer, and give alms of that with which we have supplied them.

And the camels have we appointed you for the sacrifice to God: *much* good have ye in them. Make mention, therefore, of the name of God over them *when ye slay them*, as they stand in a row; and when they are fallen over on their sides, eat of them, and feed him who is content *and asketh not*, and him who asketh. Thus have We subjected them to you, to the intent ye should be thankful.[9]

By no means can their flesh reach unto God, neither their blood; but piety on your part reacheth Him. Thus hath He subjected them to you, that ye might magnify God for His guidance: moreover, announce to those who do good deeds –

That God will ward off *mischief* from believers: for God loveth not the false, the Infidel.

40 A sanction is given to those who, because they have suffered outrages, have taken up arms; and verily, God is well able to succour them:

Those who have been driven forth from their homes wrongfully, only because they say 'Our Lord is the God.' And if God had not repelled some men by others, cloisters, and churches, and oratories, and mosques, wherein the name of

God is ever commemorated, would surely have been destroyed. And him who helpeth God will God surely help:[10] for God is right Strong, Mighty: –

Those who, if we establish them in this land, will observe prayer, and pay the alms of obligations, and enjoin what is right, and forbid what is evil. And the final issue of all things is unto God.

Moreover, if they charge thee with imposture, then already, before them, the people of Noah, and Ad and Themoud, and the people of Abraham, and the people of Lot, and the dwellers in Madian, have charged their prophets with imposture! Moses, too, was charged with imposture! And I bore long with the unbelievers; then seize on them: and how great was the change I wrought!

And how many cities which had been ungodly, and whose roofs are now laid low in ruin, have We destroyed! And wells have been abandoned and lofty castles!

Have they not journeyed through the land? Have they not hearts to understand with, or ears to hear with? It is not that these *sights* their eyes are blind, but the hearts in their breasts are blind!

And they will bid thee to hasten the chastisement. But God cannot fail His threat. And verily, a day with thy Lord is a thousand years,[11] as ye reckon them!

How many cities have I long borne with, wicked though they were, yet then laid hold on them to chastise them! Unto Me shall all return.

SAY: O men! I am only your open warner:

And they who believe and do the things that are right, shall have forgiveness and an honourable provision;

50 But those who strive to invalidate our signs shall be inmates of Hell.

We have not sent any apostle or prophet before thee, among whose desires Satan injected not some *wrong* desire, but God shall bring to nought that which Satan had suggested. Thus shall God affirm His revelations[12] for God is Knowing, Wise!

That He may make that which Satan hath injected, a trial to those in whose hearts is a disease, and whose hearts are hardened. – Verily, the wicked are in a far-gone severance from the truth! –

And that they to whom 'the Knowledge' hath been given,

may know that *the Koran* is the truth from thy Lord and may believe in it, and their hearts may acquiesce in it for God is surely the guider of those who believe, into the straight path.

But the Infidels will not cease to doubt concerning it, until 'the Hour' come suddenly upon them, or until the chastisement of the day of desolation come upon them.

On that day the Kingdom shall be God's: He shall judge between them: and they who shall have believed and done the things that are right, *shall be* in gardens of delight:

But they who were Infidels and *treated* our signs as lies – these then – their's a shameful chastisement!

And as to those who fled their country for the cause of God, and were afterwards slain, or died, surely with goodly provision will God provide for them! for verily, God! He, surely, is the best of providers!

He will assuredly bring them in with an in-bringing that shall please them well: for verily, God is right Knowing, Gracious.

So shall it be. And whoever in making exact reprisal for injury done him, shall again be wronged, God will assuredly aid him: for God is most Merciful, Gracious.

60 So shall it be; for that God causeth the night to enter in upon the day, and He causeth the day to enter in upon the night: and for that God Heareth, Seeth.

So shall it be, for that God is the truth; and because what they call on beside Him is vanity: and because God is the Lofty, the Mighty!

Seest thou not that God sendeth down water from Heaven, and that on the morrow the earth is clad with verdure? for God is benignant, cognisant of all.

His, all in the Heavens and all on Earth: and verily, God! He assuredly is the Rich, the Praiseworthy!

Seest thou not that God hath put under you whatever is in the earth; and the ships which traverse the sea at His bidding? And He holdeth back the heaven that it fall not on the earth, unless He permit it! for God is right Gracious to mankind, Merciful.

And He it is who hath given you life, then will cause you to die, then will give you life – of a truth man is all ungrateful.

To every people have we appointed observances which they observe. Therefore, let them not dispute this matter with thee, but bid them to thy Lord, for thou art on the right way:

But if they debate with thee, then SAY: God best knoweth what ye do!

God will judge between you on the day of resurrection, as to the matters wherein ye differ.

Knowest thou not that God knoweth whatever is in the Heaven and on the Earth? This truly is *written* in the Book: this truly is easy for God.

70 They worship beside God, that for which He hath sent down no warranty, and that of which they have no knowledge: but for those who commit this wrong, no helper!

And when our clear signs are rehearsed to them, thou mayst perceive disdain in the countenances of the Infidels. Scarce can they refrain from rushing to attack those who rehearse our signs to them! SAY: Shall I tell you of worse than this? The fire which God hath threatened to those who believe not! Wretched the passage thither!

O men! a parable is set forth to you, wherefore hearken to it. Verily, they on whom ye call beside God, cannot create a fly, though they assemble for it; and if the fly carry off aught from them, they cannot take it away from it! Weak the suppliant and the supplicated!

Unworthy the estimate they form of God![13] for God is right Powerful, Mighty!

God chooseth messengers from among the angels and from among men: verily, God Heareth, Seeth.

He knoweth what is before them and what is behind them; and unto God shall *all* things return.

Believers! bow down and prostrate yourselves and worship your Lord, and work righteousness that you may fare well.

And do valiantly in *the cause of* God as it behoveth you to do for Him. He hath elected you, and hath not laid on you any hardship in religion, the Faith of your father Abraham. He hath named you the Muslims.

Heretofore and in this *Book*, that the Apostles may be a witness against you, and that ye may be witnesses against the rest of mankind. Therefore observe prayer, and pay the legal impost, and cleave fast to God. He is your liege Lord – a goodly Lord, and a goodly Helper!

SURA 23 – THE BELIEVERS

MECCA[1] – 118 VERSES

In the Name of God, the Compassionate, the Merciful

Happy now the BELIEVERS,

Who humble them in their prayers,

And who keep aloof from vain words,[2]

And who are doers of alms deeds,

And who restrain their appetites,

(Save with their wives, or the slaves whom their right hands possess: for *in that case* they shall be free from blame:

But they whose desires reach further than this are transgressors:)

And who tend well their trusts and their covenants,

And who keep them strictly to their prayers:

10 These shall be the heritors,

Who shall inherit the paradise, to abide therein for ever.

Now of fine clay have we created man:

Then we placed him, a moist germ,[3] in a safe abode;

Then made we the moist germ a clot of blood: then made the clotted blood into a piece of flesh; then made the piece of flesh into bones: and we clothed the bones with flesh: then brought forth man of yet another make[4] – Blessed therefore be God, the most excellent of Makers[5] –

Then after this ye shall surely die:

Then shall ye be waked up on the day of resurrection.

And we have created over you seven heavens:[6] – and we are not careless of the creation.

And we send down water from the Heaven in its due degree, and we cause it to settle on the earth; – and we have power for its withdrawal: –

And by it we cause gardens of palm trees, and vineyards to spring forth for you, in which ye have plenteous fruits, and whereof ye eat;

20 And the tree that groweth up on Mount Sinai; which yieldeth oil and a juice for those who eat.

And there is a lesson for you in the cattle: We give you to drink of what is in their bellies, and many advantages do ye derive from them, and for food they serve you;

And on them and on ships are ye borne.

We sent Noah heretofore unto his people, and he said, 'O my people! serve God: ye have no other God than He: will ye not therefore fear Him?

But the chiefs of the people who believed not said, 'This is but a man like yourselves: he fain would raise himself above you: but had it pleased God *to send*, He would have sent angels: We heard not of this with our sires of old; –

Verily he is but a man possessed; leave him alone therefore for a time.'

He said, 'O my Lord! help me against their charge of imposture.'

So we revealed unto him, 'Make the ark under our eye, and as we have taught, and when our doom shall come on, and the earth's surface shall boil up,[7]

Carry into it of every kind a pair, and thy family, save him on whom sentence hath already passed: and plead not with me for the wicked, for they shall be drowned.

And when thou, and they who shall be with thee, shall go up into the ark; say, "Praise be unto God, who hath rescued us from the wicked folk."

30 And say, "O my Lord! disembark me with a blessed
disembarking: for thou art the best to disembark."'

Verily in this were signs, and verily we made proof *of man*.

We then raised up other generations after them;

And we sent among them an apostle from out themselves, with, 'Worship ye God! ye have no other God than He: will ye not therefore fear Him?'

And the chiefs of His people who believed not, and who deemed the meeting with us in the life to come to be a lie, and whom we had richly supplied in this present life, said, 'This is but a man like yourselves; he eateth of what ye eat,

And he drinketh of what ye drink:

And if ye obey a man like yourselves, then ye will surely be undone.

What! doth he foretell you, that after ye shall be dead and become dust and bones, ye shall be brought forth?

Away, away with his predictions!

There is no life beyond our present life; we die, and we live, and we shall not be quickened again!

40 This is merely a man who forgeth a lie about God: and we
will not believe him.'

He said, 'O my Lord! help me against this charge of imposture.'

He said, 'Yet a little, and they will soon repent them!'

Then did the shout *of the destroying angel* in justice surprise them, and we made them like leaves swept down by a torrent. Away then with the wicked people!

Then raised we up other generations after them –

Neither too soon, nor too late, shall a people reach its appointed time –

Then sent we our apostles one after another. Oft as their apostle presented himself to a nation, they treated him as a liar; and we caused one nation to follow another; and we made them the burden of a tale. Away then with the people who believe not!

Then sent we Moses and his brother Aaron, with our signs and manifest power,

To Pharaoh and his princes; but they behaved them proudly, for they were a haughty people.

And they said, 'Shall we believe on two men like ourselves, whose people are our slaves?'

50 And they treated them both as impostors; wherefore they
became of the destroyed.

And we gave Moses the Book for *Israel's* guidance.

And we appointed the Son of Mary, and His mother for a sign; and we prepared an abode for both in a lofty spot,[8] quiet, and watered with springs.

'O ye apostles! eat of things that are good: and do that which is right: of your doings I am cognisant.

And truly this your religion is the one religion;[9] and I am your Lord: therefore fear me.'

But men have rent their great concern, one among another, into sects; every party rejoicing in that which is their own;

Wherefore leave them till a certain time, in their depths of error.

What! think they that what we largely bestow on them of wealth and children,

We hasten to them for their good? Nay, they have no knowledge.

But they who are awed with the dread of their Lord,

60 And who believe in the signs of their Lord,

And who join no other gods with their Lord,

And who give that which they give with hearts thrilled with dread because they must return unto their Lord,

These hasten after good, and are the first to win it.

We will not burden a soul beyond its power: and with us is a book, which speaketh the truth; and they shall not be wronged:

But as to this Book, their hearts are plunged in error, and their works are far other than those *of Muslims*, and they will work those works,

Until when we lay hold on their affluent ones with punishment; lo! they cry for help:

– 'Cry not for help this day, for by Us ye shall not be succoured:

Long since were my signs rehearsed to you, but ye turned back on your heels,

Puffed up with pride, discoursing foolishly by night.'

70 Do they not then heed the things spoken – whether that hath come to them which came not to their fathers of old?

Or do they not recognise their apostle; and therefore disavow him?

Or say they, 'A Djinn is in him?' Nay! he hath come to them with the truth; but the truth do most of them abhor.

But if the truth had followed in the train of their desires, the heavens and the earth, and all that therein is, had surely come to ruin! But we have brought them their warning; and from their warning they withdraw.

Dost thou ask them for remuneration? But, remuneration from thy Lord is best; and He is the best provider.

And thou indeed biddest them to the right path;

But verily they who believe not in the life to come, from that path do surely wander!

And if we had taken compassion on them, and relieved them from their trouble, they would have plunged on in their wickedness, wildly wandering.[10]

We formerly laid hold on them with chastisement, yet they did not humble them to their Lord, nor did they abase them;

Until, when we have opened upon them the door of a severe punishment, lo! they are in despair at it.

80 It is He who hath implanted in you hearing, and sight, and heart; how few of you give thanks!

It is He who hath caused you to be born on the earth: and unto Him shall ye be gathered.

And it is He who maketh alive and killeth, and of Him is the change of the night and of the day: Will ye not understand?

But they say, as said those of old: –

They say, 'What! When we shall be dead, and have become dust and bones, shall we, indeed, be waked to life?

This have we been promised, we and our fathers aforetime: but it is only fables of the ancients.'

SAY: Whose is the earth, and all that is therein; – if ye know?

They will answer, 'God's.' SAY: Will ye not then reflect?

SAY: Who is the Lord of the seven heavens, and the Lord of the glorious throne?

They will say, 'They are God's.' SAY: Will ye not, then, fear Him?

90 SAY: In whose hand is the empire of all things, who protecteth but is not protected? if ye know:

They will answer, 'In God's.' SAY: How, then, can ye be so spell-bound?

Yea, we have brought them the truth; but they are surely liars:

God hath not begotten offspring; neither is there any other God with Him: else had each god assuredly taken away that which he had created,[11] and some had assuredly uplifted themselves above others! Far from the glory of God, be what they affirm of Him!

He knoweth *alike* the unseen and the seen: far be He uplifted above the gods whom they associate with Him!

SAY: O my Lord! If thou wilt let me witness *the infliction of that* with which they have been threatened!

O my Lord! place me not among the ungodly people.

Verily, we are well able to make thee see the punishment with which we have threatened them.

Turn aside evil with that which is better: we best know what they utter *against thee*.

And SAY: 'O my Lord! I betake me to Thee, against the promptings of the Satans:

100 And I betake me to Thee, O my Lord! that they gain no hurtful access to me.'

When death overtaketh one of the *wicked*, he saith, 'Lord, send me back again,

That I may do the good which I have left undone.'[12] 'By no means.' These are the very words which he shall speak: But behind them shall be a barrier, until the day when they shall be raised again.

And when the trumpet shall be sounded, the ties of kindred between them shall cease on that day; neither shall they ask each other's help.

They whose balances shall be heavy, shall be the blest.

But they whose balances shall be light, – these are they who shall lose their souls, abiding in hell for ever:

The fire shall scorch their faces, and their lips shall quiver therein: –

– 'What! Were not my signs rehearsed unto you? and did ye not treat them as lies?'

They shall say, 'O our Lord! our ill-fortune prevailed against us, and we became an erring people.

O our Lord! Bring us forth hence: if we go back again *to our sins*, we shall indeed be evil doers.'

110 He will say; 'Be ye driven down into it; and, address me not.'

A part truly of my servants was there, who said, 'O our Lord! we believe: forgive us, then, and be merciful to us, for of the merciful art thou the best.'

But ye received them with such scoffs that they suffered you to forget my warning, and ye laughed them to scorn.

Verily this day will I reward them, for their patient endurance: the blissful ones shall they be!

He will say, 'What number of years tarried ye on earth?'

They will say, 'We tarried a day, or part of a day;[13] but ask the recording *angels*.'[14]

God will say, 'Short indeed was the time ye tarried, if that ye knew it.

What! Did ye then think that we had created you for pastime, and that ye should not be brought back again to us?' Wherefore let God be exalted, the King, the Truth! There is no god but He! Lord of the stately throne! And whoso, together with God, shall call on another god, for whom he hath no proof, shall surely have to give account to his Lord. Aye, it shall fare ill with the infidels.

And SAY: 'O my Lord, pardon, and have mercy; for of those who show mercy, art thou the best.'

SURA 24 – LIGHT

MEDINA – 64 VERSES

In the Name of God, the Compassionate, the Merciful

A Sura which we have sent down and sanctioned! Clear signs have we sent down therein, that ye may take warning.

The whore and the whoremonger – scourge each of them with an hundred stripes; and let not compassion keep you from *carrying out* the sentence of God, if ye believe in God and the last day: And let some of the faithful witness their chastisement.[1]

The whoremonger shall not marry other than a whore or an idolatress; and the whore shall not marry other than a whoremonger or an idolater. Such *alliances* are forbidden to the faithful.

They who defame virtuous women, and bring not four witnesses, scourge them with *fourscore* stripes, and receive ye not their testimony for ever, for these are perverse persons –

Save those who afterwards repent and live virtuously; for truly God is Lenient, Merciful!

And they who shall accuse their wives, and have no witnesses but themselves, the testimony of each of them shall be a testimony by God four times repeated, that he is indeed of them that speak the truth.[2]

And the fifth time that the malison of God be upon him, if he be of them that lie.

But it shall avert the chastisement from her if she testify a testimony four times repeated, by God, that he is of them that lie;

And a fifth time *to call down* the wrath of God on her, if he have spoke the truth.

10 And but for the goodness and mercy of God towards you, and that God is He who loveth to turn, Wise . . . !

Of a truth, they who advanced that lie[3] were a large number of you; but regard it not as an evil to you. No, it is an advantage to you.[4] To every man among them shall it be done according to the offence he hath committed; and as to that person[5] among them who took on himself to aggravate it, a sore punishment doth await him.

Did not the faithful of both sexes, when ye heard of this, form a favourable judgment in their own minds, and say, 'This is a manifest lie?'

Have they brought four witnesses of the fact? If they cannot produce the witnesses, they are the liars in the sight of God.

And but for the goodness of God towards you, and His mercy in this world and in the next, a severe punishment had come upon you for that which ye spread abroad, when ye uttered with your tongues, and spake with your mouths that of which ye had no knowledge. Ye deemed it to be a light matter, but with God it was a grave one.

And did ye say when ye heard it, 'It is not for us to talk of this affair! *O God!* By thy Glory, this is a gross calumny?'

God hath warned you that ye go not back to the like of this for ever, if ye be believers:

And God maketh His signs clear to you: for God is Knowing, Wise.

But as for those who love that foul calumnies should go forth against those who believe, a grievous chastisement awaits them

In this world and in the next. And God hath knowledge, but ye have not.

20 And but for the goodness of God towards you and His Mercy, and that God is Kind, Merciful . . . !

O ye who believe! follow not the steps of Satan, for whosoever shall follow the steps of Satan, he will enjoin on him what is base and blameworthy; and but for the goodness of God towards you,[6] and His mercy, no one of you had been cleansed for ever: but God maketh whom He will to be clean, and God Heareth, Knoweth.

And let not persons of wealth and means among you swear that they will not give to their kindred, to the poor, and to those who have fled their homes in the cause of God; let them rather pardon and pass over *the offence.*[7] Desire ye not that God should forgive you? And God is Gracious, Merciful!

Verily, they who throw out charges against virtuous but careless women, who *yet* are believers, shall be cursed in this world and in the world to come; and a terrible punishment doth await them.

Their own tongues, and hands, and feet, shall one day bear witness against them of their own doings.[8]

On that day will God pay them their just due, and they shall know that God is the clear Truth itself.

Bad women for bad men, and bad men for bad women; but virtuous women for virtuous men, and virtuous men for virtuous women! These shall be cleared from calumnies; theirs shall be forgiveness and an honourable provision.

O ye who believe! enter not into other houses[9] than your own, until ye have asked leave, and have saluted its inmates. This will be best for you: haply ye will bear this in mind.

And if ye find no one therein, then enter it not till leave be given you; and if it be said to you, 'Go ye back,' then go ye back. This will be more blameless in you, and God knoweth what ye do.

There shall be no harm in your entering houses in which no one dwelleth, for the supply of your needs: and God knoweth what ye do openly and what ye hide.

30 Speak unto the believers that they restrain their eyes and observe continence. Thus will they be more pure. God is well aware of what they do.

And speak to the believing women that they refrain their eyes, and observe continence; and that they display not their ornaments, except those which are external; and that they throw their veils over their bosoms, and display not their ornaments, except to their husbands or their fathers, or their husbands' fathers, or their sons, or their husbands' sons, or their brothers, or their brothers' sons, or their sisters' sons, or their women, or their slaves, or male domestics who have no natural force, or to children who note not women's nakedness. And let them not strike their feet together, so as to discover their hidden ornaments.[10] And be ye all turned to God, O ye Believers! that it may be well with you.

And marry those among you who are single, and your good servants, and the handmaidens. If they are poor, God of His bounty will enrich them. God is all-bounteous, Knowing.

And let those who cannot find a match[11] live in continence till God of His bounty shall enrich them. And to those of your slaves who desire a deed of manumission, execute it for them, if ye know good in them, and give them a portion of the wealth of God which He hath given you.[12] Force not your female slaves into sin, in order that ye may gain the casual fruitions of this world, if they wish to preserve their modesty. Yet if any one compel them, then Verily to them, after their compulsion, will God be Forgiving, Merciful.

And now have we sent down to you clear signs, and an instance from among those who flourished before you, and a caution for the God-fearing.[13]

God is the LIGHT of the Heavens and of the Earth. His Light is like a niche in which is a lamp – the lamp encased in glass – the glass, as it were, a glistening star. From a blessed tree is it lighted, the olive neither of the East nor of the West, whose oil would well nigh shine out, even though fire touched it not! It is light upon light. God guideth whom He will to His light, and God setteth forth parables to men, for God knoweth all things.

In the temples which God hath allowed to be reared, that His name may therein be remembered, do men praise Him morn and even.

Men whom neither merchandise nor traffic beguile from the remembrance of God, and from the observance of prayer, and the payment of the stated alms, through fear of the day when hearts *shall throb* and eyes shall roll:

That for their most excellent works may God recompense them, and of His bounty increase it to them more and more: for God maketh provision for whom He pleaseth without measure.

But as to the infidels, their works are like the vapour in a plain which the thirsty dreameth to be water, until when he cometh unto it, he findeth it not aught, but findeth that God is with him; and He fully payeth him his account: for swift to take account is God:

40 Or like the darkness on the deep sea when covered by billows riding upon billows, above which are clouds: darkness upon darkness. When a man reacheth forth his hand, he cannot nearly see it! He to whom God shall not give light, no light at all hath he!

Hast thou not seen how all in the Heavens and in the Earth uttereth the praise of God? – the very birds as they spread their wings? Every creature knoweth its prayer and its praise! and God knoweth what they do.

God's, the Kingdom of the Heavens and of the Earth: and unto God the *final* return!

Hast thou not seen that God driveth clouds lightly forward, then gathereth them together, then pileth them in masses? And then thou seest the rain forthcoming from their midst; and He causeth *clouds like* mountains charged with hail, to descend from the heaven, and He maketh it to fall on whom He will, and from whom He will He turneth it aside. – The brightness of His lightning all but taketh away the sight!

God causeth the day and the night to take their turn. Verily in this is teaching for men of insight. And God hath created every animal of water.[14] Some go upon the belly; some go upon two feet; some go upon four feet. God hath created what He pleased. Aye, God hath power over all things.

Now have we sent down distinct signs. – and God guideth whom He will into the right path:

For there are who say 'We believe on God and on the Apostle, and we obey;' yet, after this, a part of them turn back.[15] But these are not of the faithful.

And when they are summoned before God and His Apostle that He may judge between them, lo! a part of them withdraw:

But had the truth been on their side, they would have come to Him, obedient.

What! are they diseased of heart? Do they doubt? Are they afraid that God and His Apostles will deal unfairly with them? Nay, themselves are the unjust doers.

50 The words of the believers, when called to God and His Apostle that He may judge between them, are only to say, 'We have heard, and we obey:' these are they with whom it shall be well.

And whoso shall obey God, and His Apostle, and shall dread God and fear Him, these are they that shall be the blissful.

And they have sworn by God, with a most solemn oath, that if thou give them the word, they will certainly march forth. SAY: swear ye not: of more worth is obedience. Verily, God is well aware of what ye do.

SAY: Obey God and obey the Apostle. Suppose that ye turn back, still the burden of his duty is on him only, and the burden of your duty rests on you. If ye obey Him, ye shall have guidance: but plain preaching is all that devolves upon the Apostle.

God hath promised to those of you who believe and do the things that are right, that He will cause them to succeed others in the land, as He gave succession to those who were before them, and that He will establish for them that religion which they delight in, and that after their fears He will give them security in exchange. They shall worship Me: nought shall they join with Me: And whoso, after this, believe not, they will be the impious.

But observe prayer, and pay the stated alms, and obey the Apostle, that haply ye may find mercy.

Let not the Infidels think that they can weaken *God on His own* Earth: their dwelling place shall be the Fire! and right wretched the journey!

O ye who believe! let your slaves, and those of you who have not come of age, ask leave of you, three times a day, ere they come into your presence; – before the morning prayer, and when ye lay aside your garments at mid-day, and after the evening prayer. These are your three times of privacy. No blame shall attach to you or to them, *if* after these *times*, when ye go your rounds of *attendance* on one another, *they come in without permission*. Thus doth God make clear to you His signs: and God is Knowing, Wise!

And when your children come of age, let them ask leave to come into your presence, as they who were before them asked it. Thus doth God make clear to you his signs: and God is Knowing, Wise.

As to women who are past childbearing, and have no hope of marriage, no blame shall attach to them if they lay aside their *outer* garments, but so as not to shew their ornaments. Yet if they abstain from this, it will be better for them: and God Heareth, Knoweth.

60 No crime[16] shall it be in the blind, or in the lame, or in the
sick, *to eat at your tables:* or in yourselves, if ye eat in your own houses, or in the houses of your fathers, or of your mothers, or of your brothers, or of your sisters, or of your uncles on the father's side, or of your aunts on the father's side, or of your uncles on the mother's side, or of your aunts on the mother's side, or in those of which ye possess the keys, or in the house of your friend. No blame shall attach to you whether ye eat together or apart.

And when ye enter houses, salute one another with a good and blessed greeting as from God. Thus doth God make clear to you His signs, that haply ye may comprehend them.

Verily, they only are believers who believe in God and His Apostle, and who, when they are with him upon any affair of common interest, depart not until they have sought his leave. Yes, they who ask leave of thee, are those who believe in God and His Apostle. And when they ask leave of Thee on account of any affairs of their own, then grant it to those of them whom thou wilt, and ask indulgence for them of God: for God is Indulgent, Merciful.

Address not the Apostle as ye address one another.[17] God knoweth those of you who withdraw quietly *from the assemblies*, screening themselves behind others. And let those who transgress his command beware, lest some present trouble befal them, or a grievous chastisement befal them, *hereafter*.

Is not whatever is in the Heavens and the Earth God's? He knoweth your state; and one day shall men be assembled before Him, and He will tell them of what they have done: for God knoweth all things.

SURA 25 – AL FURKAN

MECCA – 77 VERSES

In the Name of God, the Compassionate, the Merciful

Blessed be He who hath sent down AL FURKAN[1] (the illumination) on his servant, that to all creatures he may be a warner.

His the Kingdom of the Heavens and of the Earth! No son hath He begotten! No partner hath He in his Empire! All things hath He created, and decreeing hath decreed their destinies.

Yet have they adopted gods beside Him which have created nothing, but were themselves created:

And no power have they over themselves for evil or for good, nor have they power of death, or of life, or of raising the dead.

And the infidels say, 'This *Koran* is a mere fraud of his own devising, and others have helped him with it,[2] who had come *hither* by outrage and lie.'

And they say, 'Tales of the ancients that he hath put in writing! and they were dictated to him morn and even.'

SAY: He hath sent it down who knoweth the secrets of the Heavens and of the Earth. He truly is the Gracious, the Merciful.

And they say, 'What sort of apostle is this? He eateth food and he walketh the streets! Unless an angel be sent down and take part in his warnings,

Or a treasure be thrown down to him, or he have a garden that supplieth him with food . . .'[3] and those unjust persons say, 'Ye follow but a man enchanted.'

10 See what likenesses they strike out for thee! But they err, and cannot find their way.

Blessed be He who if he please can give thee better than that *of which they speak* – Gardens, 'neath which the rivers flow: and pavilions will He assign thee.

Aye, they have treated the coming of 'the Hour' as a lie. But a flaming fire have we got ready for those who treat the coming of the Hour as a lie.

When it shall see them from afar, they shall hear its raging and roaring, –

And when they shall be flung into a narrow space thereof bound together, they shall invoke destruction on the spot:

– 'Call not this day for one destruction, but call for destructions many.'

SAY: Is this, or the Paradise of Eternity which was promised to the God-fearing, best? Their recompense shall it be and their retreat;

Abiding therein for ever, they shall have in it all that they desire! It is a promise to be claimed of thy Lord.

And on the day when he shall gather them together, and those whom they worshipped beside God, he will say, 'Was it ye who led these my servants astray, or of themselves strayed they from the path?'

They will say, 'Glory be to thee! It beseemed not us to take other lords than thee. But thou gavest them and their fathers their fill of good things, till they forgat the remembrance *of thee*, and became a lost people.'

20 *Then will God say to the Idolaters*, 'Now have they made you liars in what ye say,[4] and they have no power to avert *your doom*, or to succour you.'

And whosoever of you *thus* offendeth, we will make him taste a great punishment.

Never have we sent Apostles before thee who ate not *common* food, and walked not the streets. And we test you by means of each other. Will ye be steadfast? Thy Lord is looking on!

They who look not forward to meet Us say, 'If the angels be not sent down to us, or unless we behold our Lord . . .' Ah! they are proud of heart, and exceed with great excess!

On the day when they shall see the angels, no good news shall there be for the guilty ones, and they shall cry out, 'A barrier that cannot be passed!'[5]

Then will we proceed to the works which they have wrought, and make them as scattered dust.

Happier, on that day, the inmates of the Garden as to abode, and better off as to place of noontide slumber!

On that day shall the heaven with its clouds be cleft, and the angels shall be sent down, descending.

On that day shall all empire be in very deed with the God of Mercy, and a hard day shall it be for the Infidels.

And on that day shall the wicked one[6] bite his hands, *and* say, 'Oh! would that I had taken the *same* path with the Apostle!

30 'Oh! woe is me! would that I had not taken such an one[7] for my friend!

It was he who led me astray from the Warning which had reached me! and Satan is man's betrayer.'[8]

Then said the Apostle, 'O my Lord! truly my people have esteemed this Koran to be vain babbling.'

Thus have we given to every Prophet an enemy from among the wicked ones – But thy Lord is a sufficient guide and helper.

And the infidels say, 'Unless the Koran be sent down to him all at once . . .' But in this way would we stablish thy heart by it; in parcels have we parcelled it out to thee;[9]

Nor shall they come to thee with puzzling questions,[10] but we will come to thee with the truth, and their best solution.

They who shall be gathered upon their faces into hell, shall have the worst place, and be farthest from the path *of happiness*.

Heretofore we gave the law to Moses, and appointed his brother Aaron to be his counsellor:[11]

And we said, 'Go ye to the people who treat our signs as lies.' And them destroyed we with *utter* destruction.

And as to the people of Noah! when they treated their

Apostles as impostors, we drowned them; and we made them a sign to mankind: – A grievous chastisement have we prepared for the wicked!
40 And Ad and Themoud, and the men of Rass,[12] and divers
generations between them:

Unto each of them did we set forth parables *for warnings*, and each of them did we utterly exterminate.

Oft ere this have *the unbelieving Meccans* passed by the city on which was rained a fatal rain. 'What! Have they not seen it? Yet have they no hope of a resurrection!

And when they see thee, they do but take thee as the subject of their railleries. 'What! Is this he whom God has sent as an Apostle?

Indeed he had well nigh led us astray from our gods, had we not persevered steadfastly in their service.' But in the end they shall know, when they shall see the punishment, who hath most strayed from the path.

What thinkest thou? He who hath taken his passions as a god – wilt thou be a guardian over him?

Thinkest thou that the greater part of them hear or understand? They are just like the brutes! Yes! they stray even further from the *right* way.

Hast thou not seen how thy Lord lengtheneth out the shadow? Had He pleased he had made it motionless.[13] But we made the sun to be its guide;

Then draw it in unto Us with easy indrawing.

He it is who ordaineth the night as a garment, and sleep for rest, and ordaineth the day for waking up to life:
50 He it is who sendeth the winds as the forerunner of his mercy
(rain); and pure water send we down from Heaven,

That we may revive by it a dead land: and we give it for drink to our creation, beasts and men in numbers;

And we distribute it among them on all sides, that they may reflect: but most men refuse to be aught but thankless.

Had we pleased, we had raised up a warner in every city.

Give not way therefore to the Infidels, but by means of this *Koran* strive against them with a mighty strife.

And He it is who hath let loose the two seas,[14] the one sweet, fresh; and the other salt, bitter; and hath put an interspace between them, and a barrier that cannot be passed.

And it is He who hath created man of water,[15] and

established between them the ties of kindred and affinity: and potent is thy Lord.

Yet beside God do they worship what can neither help nor hurt them: and the Infidel is *Satan's* helper against his Lord:

Still we have sent thee only as a herald and a warner.

SAY: I ask of you no recompense for it,[16] except *from* him who is willing to take the way to his Lord.

60 And put thou thy trust in Him that liveth and dieth not, and celebrate his praise; (He fully knoweth the faults of his servants) who in six days created the Heavens and the Earth, and whatever is between them, then mounted his Throne: the God of Mercy! Ask now of the Wise concerning Him.

But when it is said to them, 'Bow down before the God of Mercy,' they say, 'Who is the God of Mercy? Shall we bow down to what thou biddest?' And they fly from thee the more.

Blessed be He who hath placed in the Heaven the sign of the Zodiac![17] who hath placed in it the Lamp *of the Sun*, and the light-giving Moon!

And it is He who hath ordained the night and the day to succeed one another for those who desire to think on God or desire to be thankful.

And the servants of the God of Mercy are they who walk upon the Earth softly; and when the ignorant[18] address them, they reply, 'Peace!'

They that pass the night in the worship of their lord prostrate and standing: –

And that say, 'O our Lord! turn away from us the torment of Hell, for its torment is endless: it is indeed an ill abode and resting place!

Those who when they spend are neither lavish nor niggard, but keep the mean: –

Those who call on no other gods with God, nor slay whom God hath forbidden to be slain, except for a just cause, and who commit not fornication (for he who doth this shall meet the reward of his wickedness:

Doubled to him shall be the torment on the day of Resurrection; and in it shall he remain, disgraced, for ever: –

70 Save those who shall repent and believe and do righteous works – for them God will change their evil things into good things, for God is Gracious, Merciful –

And whoso turneth *to God* and doeth what is right, he verily will convert with a *true* conversion):

And they who bear not witness to that which is false, and when they pass by frivolous sport, pass on with dignity: –

And they who, when monished by the signs of their Lord, fall not down thereat, *as if* deaf and blind: –

And who say, 'O our Lord! give us in our wives and offspring the joy of our eyes, and make us examples to those who fear thee:'

These shall be rewarded with the High Places of Paradise for their steadfast endurance, and they shall meet therein with – Welcome and Salutation: –

For ever shall they remain therein: a fair abode and resting-place!

SAY: Not on your account doth my Lord care if ye call not on Him! ye have treated his Apostle as an impostor: but bye and bye a punishment shall cleave to them.

SURA 26 – THE POETS[1]

MECCA – 228 VERSES

In the Name of God, the Compassionate, the Merciful

Ta. Sin. Mim.[2] These are the signs of the lucid Book.

Haply thou wearest thyself away with grief because they will not believe.

Were it our will we could send down to them a sign from Heaven, before which they would humbly bow.[3]

But from each fresh warning that cometh to them from the God of Mercy they have only turned aside,

And treated it as a lie: But tidings shall reach them which they shall not laugh to scorn.

Have they not beheld the earth – how we have caused every kind of noble plant to spring up therein?

Verily, in this is a sign: but most of them believe not.

And assuredly, thy Lord! – He is the Mighty, the Merciful.

And *remember* when thy Lord called to Moses, 'Go to the wicked people,

10 The people of Pharaoh. What! will they not fear me?'

He said, 'My Lord, in sooth I fear lest they treat me as a liar:

And my breast is straitened, and I am slow of speech:[4] send therefore to Aaron *to be my helpmate*.

For they have a charge[5] against me, and I fear lest they put me to death.'

He said, 'Surely not. Go ye therefore with our signs: we will be with you and will hearken.

And go to Pharaoh and say: "Verily we are the messengers of the Lord of the Worlds —

Send forth with us the children of Israel." '

He said, 'Did we not rear thee among us when a child? And hast thou not passed years of thy life among us?

And yet what a deed is that which thou hast done![6] Thou art one of the ungrateful.'

He said, 'I did it indeed, and I was one of those who erred:

20 And I fled from you because I feared you; but my Lord hath given me wisdom and hath made me one of his Apostles.

And is this the favour thou hast conferred on me, that thou hast enslaved the children of Israel?'

Said Pharaoh, 'Who then is the Lord of the Worlds?'

He said, 'The Lord of the Heavens and of the Earth and of all that is between them, if only ye believe it.'

Said Pharaoh to those around him, 'Hear ye this?'

'Your Lord,' said Moses, 'and the Lord of your sires of old.'

'In sooth, your Apostle whom He hath sent to you,' said Pharaoh, 'is certainly possessed.'

He said, 'Lord is He of the East and of the West, and of all that is between them, if ye can understand.'

He said, 'If ye take any God beside me, I will surely put thee in ward.'

Said Moses, 'What! if I shew thee that which shall be a proof *of my mission?*'

30 He said, 'Forth with it then, if thou speakest truth.'

Then threw he down his staff, and lo! an undoubted serpent:

And he drew out his hand, and lo! it was white[7] to the beholders.

He said to his nobles around him, 'This truly is a right cunning sorcerer:

Fain would he drive you out of your land by his Sorcery. But what do ye suggest?'

They said, 'Put him and his brother off awhile, and send summoners to all the cities,

Who shall bring to thee every cunning magician.'

So the magicians were mustered at a set time, on a solemn day:

And it was said to the people, 'Are ye all assembled?'

– 'Yes! and we will follow the magicians if they gain the day.'

40 And when the magicians were arrived they said to Pharaoh, 'Shall we have a reward if we gain the day?'

He said, 'Yes. And verily in that case ye shall be of those who are near my person.'

Moses said to them, 'Throw down what ye have to throw.'

So they cast down their ropes and rods, and said, 'By Pharaoh's might we shall surely win.'

Then Moses threw down his rod, and lo! it swallowed up their cheating wonders.

Then the magicians threw themselves down in worship:

They said, 'We believe on the Lord of the Worlds,

The Lord of Moses and of Aaron.'

Said Pharaoh, 'Have ye then believed on him ere I gave you leave? He truly is your master who hath taught you magic.[8] But bye and bye ye shall surely know *my power*.

I will cut off your hands and feet on opposite sides, and I will have you all crucified.'

50 They said, 'It cannot harm us, for to our Lord shall we return:

Assuredly we trust that our Lord will forgive us our sins, since we are of the first who believe.'

Then revealed we this order to Moses: 'Go forth by night with my servants, for ye will be pursued.'

And Pharaoh sent summoners through the cities: –

'These *Israelites*,' said they, 'are a scanty band;

Yet are they enraged against us –

But we truly are numerous, wary.'

Thus we caused them to quit gardens and fountains,

And treasures and splendid dwellings;

So was it; and we gave them to the children of Israel for an heritage.[9]

60 Then at sunrise the Egyptians followed them:

And when the hosts came in view of one another, the comrades of Moses said, 'We are surely overtaken.'

He said, 'By no means: – for my Lord is with me – He will guide me.'

And we revealed this order to Moses, 'Strike the sea with thy rod.' And it clave asunder, and each part became like a huge mountain.

Then made we the others to draw on;
And we saved Moses, and those who were with him, all;
But we drowned the others.
Truly in this was a sign; but most of them did not believe.
But verily thy Lord, – He is the Mighty, the Merciful!
And recite to them the story of Abraham

70 When he said to his Father and to his people, 'What worship ye?'

They said, 'We worship idols, and constant is our devotion to them.'

He said, 'Can they hear you when ye cry to them?
Or help you or do you harm?'
They said, 'But we found our Fathers do the like.'
He said, 'How think ye? They whom ye worship,
Ye and your fathers of early days,
Are my foes: but not so[10] the Lord of the Worlds,
Who hath created me, and guideth me,
Who giveth me food and drink;
80 And when I am sick, he healeth me,
And who will cause me to die and again quicken me,

And who, I hope, will forgive me my sins in the day of reckoning.

My Lord! bestow on me wisdom and join me to the just,
And give me a good name[11] among posterity,
And make me one of the heirs of the garden of delight,
And forgive my father, for he was one of the erring,

And put me not to shame on the day when mankind shall be raised up,

The day when neither wealth nor children shall avail,
Save to him who shall come to God with a sound heart:
90 When Paradise shall be brought near the pious,
And Hell shall lay open for those who have gone astray.

And it shall be said to them, "Where are they whom ye worshipped

Beside God? Can they harm you or help themselves?"
And they shall be cast into it – the seducers and the seduced,
And all the host of Eblis.
They shall say, as they wrangle therein together,
"By God, we were in a plain error,
When we equalled you with the Lord of the Worlds:
And none misled us but the wicked,
100 And we have none to plead for us,
Nor friend who careth for us.
Could we but return, we would be of the believers." '
Verily, in this was a sign: but most of them believed not.
And truly thy Lord! – He is the Mighty, the Merciful!
The people of Noah gainsaid the Apostles,
When their brother Noah said to them, 'Will ye not fear God?
Of a truth am I your faithful Apostle;
Fear God then and obey me.
I ask of you no reward for this, for my reward is of the Lord of the Worlds alone:
110 Fear God then and obey me.'
They said, 'Shall we believe on thee when the meanest only are thy followers?'
He said, 'But I have no knowledge of that they did:[12]
To my Lord only must their account be given: would that ye understood this!
And I will not thrust away those who believe,
For I am only one charged with plain warnings.'
They said, 'Now unless thou desist, O Noah, one of the stoned shalt thou surely be.'
He said, 'Lord! my people treat me as a liar:
Decide thou therefore a decision between me and them, and rescue me and the faithful who are with me.'
So we saved him and those who were with him in the fully-laden ark,
120 And afterwards we drowned the rest.
Herein truly was a sign, but most of them believed not.
But thy Lord! – He is the Mighty, the Merciful.
The Adites[13] treated their Apostles as liars,
When their brother Houd said to them, 'Will ye not fear God?
I am your Apostle, worthy of all credit;

Fear God then and obey me:

I ask for no reward for this; for my reward is of the Lord of the Worlds alone.

What! build ye landmarks on all heights in mere pastime?

And raise ye structures to be your lasting abodes?[14]

130 And when ye put forth your power do ye put it forth with harshness?

Fear ye God then and obey me;

And fear ye Him who hath plenteously bestowed on you ye well know what:

Plenteously bestowed on you flocks and children,

And gardens and fountains;

Indeed I fear for you the punishment of a tremendous day.'

They said, 'It is the same to us whether thou warn or warn us not.

This is but a tale of the ancients,

And we are not they who shall be punished.'

And they charged him with imposture; and we destroyed them. In this was a sign: but most of them believed not.

140 But thy Lord! – He is the Mighty, the Merciful!

The Themoudites also treated their Apostles as liars,

When their brother Saleh said to them, 'Will ye not fear God?

I am your Apostle worthy of all credit:

Fear God, then, and obey me.

I ask of you no reward for this: my reward is of the Lord of the Worlds alone.

Shall ye be left secure amid these things here?

Amid gardens and fountains,

And corn-fields and palm-trees, with flower-sheathing branches?

And, insolent that ye are, will ye hew out your dwellings in the mountains?

150 But fear God and obey me,

And obey not the bidding of those who commit excess,

Who act disorderly on the earth and reform it not.'

They said, 'Certainly thou art a person bewitched;

Thou art only a man like us: produce now a sign if thou art a man of truth.'

He said, 'This she-camel, then – drink shall there be for her, and drink shall there be for you, on a several day for each.

But harm her not, lest the punishment of a tremendous day overtake you.'

But they ham-strung her, and repented of it on the morrow;

For the punishment overtook them. In this truly was a sign, but most of them believed not.

But thy Lord! – He is the Powerful, the Merciful!

160 The people of Lot treated their apostles as liars,

When their brother Lot said to them, 'Will ye not fear God?

I am your Apostle worthy of all credit:

Fear God, then, and obey me.

For this I ask you no reward: my reward is of the Lord of the Worlds alone.

What! with men, of all creatures, will ye have commerce?

And leave ye your wives whom your Lord hath created for you? Ah! ye are an erring people!'

They said, 'O Lot, if thou desist not, one of the banished shalt thou surely be.'

He said, 'I utterly abhor your doings:

My Lord! deliver me and my family from what they do.'

170 So we delivered him and his whole family –

Save an aged one among those who tarried –

Then we destroyed the rest –

And we rained a rain upon them, and fatal was the rain to those whom we had warned.

In this truly was a sign; but most of them did not believe.

But thy Lord! He is the Powerful, the Merciful!

The dwellers in the forest of Madian[15] treated the Apostles as liars.

When Shoaib their brother said to them, 'Will ye not fear God?

I truly am your trustworthy Apostle.

Fear God, then, and obey me:

180 No reward ask I of you for this: my reward is of the Lord of the Worlds alone.

Fill the measure, and be not of those who minish:

Weigh with exact balance:

And defraud not men in their substance, and do no wrong on the earth by deeds of licence;

And fear Him who made you and the races of old.'

They said, 'Certainly thou art a person bewitched.

Thou art but a man like us, and we deem thee liar –

Make now a part of the heaven to fall down upon us, if thou art a man of truth.'

He said, 'My Lord best knoweth your doings.'

And when they treated him as a liar, the chastisement of the day of cloud overtook them. This truly was the chastisement of a dreadful day!

190 In this was a sign, but most of them believed not.

But thy Lord! – He is the Mighty, the Merciful!

Verily from the Lord of the Worlds hath this *Book* come down;

The faithful spirit[16] hath come down with it

Upon thy heart, that thou mightest become a warner –

In the clear Arabic tongue:

And truly it is *foretold* in the Scriptures of them of yore.[17]

Was it not a sign to them[18] that the learned among the children of Israel recognised it?

If we had sent it down unto any foreigner,

And he had recited it to them, they had not believed.

200 In such sort have we influenced[19] the heart of the wicked ones,

That they will not believe it till they see the grievous chastisement?

And it shall come upon them on a sudden when they look not for it:

And they will say, 'Can we be respited?'

What! will they seek to hasten on our chastisement?

How thinkest thou? If after we have given them their fill for years,

That with which they are menaced come upon them at last,

Of what avail will their enjoyments be to them?

We never destroyed a city which had not first its warners

With admonition; nor did we deal unjustly.

210 The Satans were not sent down with this *Koran:*

It beseemed them not, and they had not the power,

For they are far removed from hearing it.[20]

Call not thou on any other god but God, lest thou be of those consigned to torment:

But warn thy relatives of nearer kin,[21]

And kindly lower thy wing over the faithful who follow thee.

And if they disobey thee, then say: 'I will not be answerable for your doings;' –

And put thy trust in Him that is the Mighty, the Merciful,
Who seeth thee when thou standest *in prayer*,
And thy demeanour amongst those who worship;
220 For He heareth, knoweth all.
Shall I tell you on whom Satan descend?
They descend on every lying, wicked person:
They impart what they have heard;[22] – but most of them are liars.
It is the POETS[23] whom the erring follow:
Seest thou not how they rove distraught in every valley?
And that they say that which they do not?
Save those who believe and do good works, and oft remember God;
And who defend themselves when unjustly treated. But they who treat them unjustly shall find out what a lot awaiteth them.

SURA 27 – THE ANT

MECCA – 95 VERSES

In the Name of God, the Compassionate, the Merciful

Ta. Sad.[1] These are the signs (verses) of the Koran and of the lucid Book;
Guidance and glad tidings to the believers who observe prayer and pay the stated alms, and believe firmly – do they – in the life to come.
As to those who believe not in the life to come, we have made their own doings fair seeming to them, and they are bewildered *therein*.
These are they whom the woe of chastisement awaiteth; and in the next life they shall suffer – yes shall they – greatest loss;
But thou hast certainly received the Koran from the Wise, the Knowing.
Bear in mind when Moses said to his family, 'I have perceived a fire;
I will bring you tidings from it, or will bring you a blazing brand, that ye may warm you.'

And when he came to it, he was called to, 'Blessed, He who is in the fire, and He who is about it; and glory be to God, the Lord of the Worlds!

O Moses! verily, I am God, the Mighty, the Wise!

10 Throw down now thy staff.' And when he saw that it moved itself as though it were a serpent, he retreated backward and returned not. 'O Moses, fear not; for the Sent Ones fear not in my presence,

Save he who having done amiss shall afterwards exchange the evil for good; for I am Forgiving, Merciful.

Put now thy hand into thy bosom: it shall come forth white, yet free from hurt:[2] one of nine signs to Pharaoh and his people; for a perverse people are they.'

And when our signs were wrought in their very sight,[3] they said, 'This is plain magic.'

And though in their souls they knew them to be true, yet in their wickedness and pride they denied them. But see what was the end of the corrupt doers!

And of old we gave knowledge to David and Solomon: and they said, 'Praise be to God, who hath made us to excel many of his believing servants!'

And *in knowledge* Solomon was David's heir. And he said, 'O men, we have been taught the speech of birds,[4] and are endued with everything. This is indeed a clear boon *from God*.'

And to Solomon were gathered his hosts of Djinn[5] and men and birds, and they were marched on in bands,

Till they reached the Valley of Ants. Said AN ANT, 'O ye ants, enter your dwellings, lest Solomon and his army crush you and know it not.'

Then smiled *Solomon*, laughing at her words, and he said, 'Stir me up, O Lord, to be thankful for thy favour which thou hast shewed upon me and upon my parents, and to do righteousness that shall be well pleasing to thee, and bring me in, by thy mercy, among thy servants the righteous.'

20 And he reviewed the birds, and said, 'How is it that I see not the lapwing? Is it one of the absent?

Surely, with a severe chastisement will I chastise it, or I will certainly slaughter it, unless it bring me a clear excuse.'

Nor tarried it long ere it came and said, 'I have gained the knowledge that thou knowest not, and with sure tidings have I come to thee from Saba:

I found a woman reigning over them, gifted with everything, and she hath a splendid throne;

And I found her and her people worshipping the sun instead of God; and Satan hath made their works fair seeming to them, so that he hath turned them from the Way: wherefore they are not guided,

To the worship of God, who bringeth to light the secret things of heaven and earth, and knoweth what *men* conceal and what they manifest:

God! there is no god but He! the lord of the glorious throne!'

He said, 'We shall see whether thou hast spoken truth, or whether thou art of them that lie.

Go with this my letter and throw it down to them: then turn away from them and await their answer.'

She said, 'O my nobles! an honourable letter hath been thrown down to me:

30 It is from Solomon; and it is *this:* "In the name of God, the Compassionate, the Merciful!

Set not yourselves against me, but come to me submitting (Muslims)." '

She said, 'O my nobles, advise me in mine affair: I decide it not without your concurrence.'[6]

They said, 'We are endued with strength and are endued with mighty valour. – But to command is thine: See therefore what thou wilt command us.'

She said, 'Kings when they enter a city spoil it, and abase the mightiest of its people: and in like manner will these also do.

But I will send to them with a gift, and await what my envoys bring back.'

And when *the messenger* came to Solomon, he said, 'Aid ye me with riches? But what God hath given to me is better than what he hath given you: yet ye glory in your gifts:

Return to them: for we will surely come to them with forces which they cannot withstand, and we will drive them from *their land* humbled and contemptible.'

Said he, 'O nobles, which of you will bring me her throne before they come to me, submitting? (Muslims).'

An Efreet[7] of the Djinn said: 'I will bring it thee ere thou risest from thy place: I have power for this and am trusty.'

40 And one who had the knowledge of Scripture said, 'I will bring it to thee in the twinkling of an eye.'[8] And when he saw

it set before him, he said, 'This is of the favour of my Lord, to try me whether I will be thankful or unthankful. And he who is thankful is thankful to his own behoof; and as for him who is unthankful – truly my Lord is self-sufficient, bounteous!'

Said he, 'Make her throne so that she know it not: we shall see whether she hath or hath not guidance.'

And when she came he said, 'Is thy throne like this?' She said, 'As though it were the same.' 'And we,' said he, 'have had knowledge given us before her, and have been Muslims.'

But the gods she had worshipped instead of God had led her astray: for she was of a people who believe not.

It was said to her, 'Enter the Palace:' and when she saw it, she thought it a lake of water, and bared her legs. He said, 'It is a palace paved with glass.'

She said, 'O my Lord! I have sinned against my own soul, and I resign myself, with Solomon, to God the Lord of the Worlds.'

And of old we sent to Themoud their brother Saleh, with 'Serve ye God:' but lo! they became two sets of disputants wrangling with each other.

He said, 'O my people, why, if ye ask not pardon of God that ye may find mercy, hasten ye on evil rather than good?'

They said, 'We augur[9] ill concerning thee and those who are with thee.' He said, 'The ills of which ye augur[10] depend on God. But ye are a people on your trial.'

And there were in the city nine persons who committed excesses in the land and did not that which is right.

50 They said, 'Swear ye to one another by God that we will surely fall on him and on his family by night: then will we say to the avenger of blood, we witnessed not the destruction of his family: and verily we speak the truth.'

And they devised a device, and we devised a device, and they were not aware of it –

And see what was the end of their device! We destroyed them and their whole people:

And for their sin these their houses are empty ruins: Verily in this is a sign to those who understand;

And we delivered those who believed and feared.

And Lot, when he said to his people, 'What! proceed ye to such filthiness with your eyes open?

What! come ye with lust unto men rather than to women? Surely ye are an ignorant people.'

And the answer of his people was but to say, 'Cast out the family of Lot from your city: they, forsooth, are men of purity!'

So we rescued him and his family: but as for his wife, we decreed her to be of them that lingered:

And we rained a rain upon them, and fatal was the rain to those who had had their warning.

60 SAY: Praise be to God and peace be on His servants whom He hath chosen! Is God the more worthy or the gods they join with Him?

Is not He who hath made the Heavens and the Earth, and hath sent down rain to you from Heaven, by which we cause the luxuriant groves to spring up? It is not in your power to cause its trees to spring up! What! A god with God? Yet they find equals for Him!

Is not He, who hath set the earth so firm, and hath made rivers in its midst, and hath placed mountains upon it, and put a barrier between the two seas?[11] What! a god with God? Yet the greater part of them have no knowledge!

Is not He *the more worthy* who answereth the oppressed when they cry to him, and taketh off their ills, and maketh you to succeed your sires on the earth? What! a god with God? How few bear these things in mind!

Is not He, who guideth you in the darkness of the land and of the sea, and who sendeth forth the winds as the forerunners of His mercy? What! a god with God? Far from God be what ye join with Him!

Is not He, who created a Being, then reneweth it, and who supplieth you out of the Heaven and the Earth? What! a god with God? SAY: Bring forth your proofs if you speak the truth.

SAY: None either in the Heavens or in the Earth knoweth the unseen but God. And they know not

When they shall be raised.

– Yet they have attained to a knowledge of the life to come:[12] – yet are they in doubt about it: – yet are they blind about it!

And the unbelievers say: 'When we and our fathers have been dead shall we be taken forth?

70 Of old have we been promised this, we and our sires of old: it is but fables of the ancients.'

SAY: Go ye through the land, and see what hath been the end of the wicked.

And grieve not thou for them, nor be in distress at their devisings.

And they say, 'When will this promise be made good, if ye speak true?'

SAY: Haply a part of what ye desire to be hastened may be close behind you.

And truly thy Lord is full of goodness towards men: But most of them are not thankful.

And thy Lord knoweth well what their breasts enshroud, and what they bring to light,

And there is no secret thing in the Heaven or on the Earth, but it is in the clear Book.

Truly this Koran declareth to the children of Israel most things wherein they disagree:

And it is certainly guidance and a mercy to the faithful.

80 Verily, by his wisdom will thy Lord decide between them: for He is the Mighty, the Knowing.

Put thou then thy trust in God: for thou hast clear truth on thy side.[13]

Thou shalt not make the dead to hear; neither shalt thou make the deaf to hear the call, when they turn away backward;

Neither art thou the guide of the blind out of their errors: none truly shalt thou make to hear but those who believe our signs: and they are Muslims.

When the doom shall be ready to light upon them, we will cause a monster[14] to come forth to them out of the earth, and cry to them, 'Verily men have not firmly believed our signs.'

And on that day shall be gathered out of every nation a company of those who have gainsaid our signs, in separate bands;

Till they come before God, who will say, 'Treated ye my signs as impostures, although ye embraced them not in your knowledge? or what is it that ye were doing?

And doom shall light upon them for their evil deeds, and nought shall they have to plead.

See they not that we have ordained the night that they may rest in it, and the day with its gift of light? Of a truth herein are signs to people who believe.

On that day there shall be a blast on the trumpet, and all that are in the heavens, and all that are on the earth shall be terror-stricken, save him whom God pleaseth *to deliver;* and all shall come to him in humble guise.

90 And thou shalt see the mountains, which thou thinkest so firm, pass away with the passing of a cloud! 'Tis the work of God, who ordereth all things! of all that ye do is He well aware.

To him who shall present himself with good works, shall be a reward beyond their desert,[15] and they shall be secure from the terror on that day;

And they who shall present themselves with evil shall be flung downward on their faces into the fire. Shall ye be rewarded but as ye have wrought?

SAY: Specially am I commanded to worship the Lord of this land, which He hath sanctified. All things are His: and I am commanded to be one of those who surrender them *to God* (a Muslim)

And to recite the Koran: and whoever is rightly guided, assuredly will be rightly guided to his own behoof.

And as to him who erreth, SAY, I truly am a warner only. And SAY, Praise be to God! He will shew you His signs, and ye shall acknowledge them: and of what ye do, thy Lord is not regardless.

SURA 28 – THE STORY

MECCA – 88 VERSES

In the Name of God, the Compassionate, the Merciful

Ta. Sin. Mim.[1] These are the signs of the lucid Book.

We will recite to thee portions of the History of Moses and Pharaoh with truth, for *the teaching of* the faithful.

Now Pharaoh lifted himself up in the earth, and divided his people into parties: one portion of them he brought low – He slew their male children, and let their females only live; for he was one of those who wrought disorders.

And we were minded to shew favour to those who were brought low in the land, and to make them spiritual chiefs,[2] and to make them *Pharaoh's* heirs,

And to stablish them in the land;[3] and to make Pharaoh and

Haman and their hosts, the eye-witnesses of what they dreaded from them.

And we said by revelation to the mother of Moses, 'Give him suck; and if thou fearest for him, launch him on the sea; and fear not, neither fret; for we will restore him to thee, and make him one of the apostles.'

And Pharaoh's family took him up to be a foe, and a sorrow to them, for sinners were Pharaoh and Haman and their hosts!

And Pharaoh's wife said, 'Joy of the eye[4] to me and thee! put him not to death: haply he will be useful to us, or we may adopt him as a son.' But they knew not *what they did*.

And the heart of Moses' mother became a blank *through fear:* and almost had she discovered him, but that we girt up her heart with constancy, in order that she might be one of those who believe.

10 She said to his sister, 'Follow him.' And she watched him from afar: and they perceived it not.

And we caused him to refuse the nurses,[5] until *his sister came* and said, Shall I point out to you the family of a house that will rear him for you, and will be careful of him?

So we restored him to his mother, to be the joy of her eyes, and that she might not fret, and that she might know that the promise of God was true. But most men knew it not.

And when he had reached his age of strength, and had become a man, we bestowed on him wisdom and knowledge; for thus do we reward the righteous.

And he entered a city at the time when its inhabitants would not observe him,[6] and found therein two men fighting: the one, of his own people; the other, of his enemies. And he who was of his own people asked his help against him who was of his enemies. And Moses smote him with his fist and slew him. Said he, 'This is a work of Satan; for he is an enemy, a manifest misleader.'

He said, 'O my Lord, I have sinned to mine own hurt:[7] forgive me.' So God forgave him; for He is the Forgiving, the Merciful.

He said, 'Lord, because thou hast shewed me this grace, I will never again be the helper of the wicked.'

And in the city at noon he was full of fear, casting furtive glances round him: and lo! the man whom he had helped the day before, cried out to him *again* for help. Said Moses to him, 'Thou are plainly a most depraved person.'

And when he would have laid violent hands on him who was their common foe, he said to him, 'O Moses, dost thou desire to slay me, as thou slayedst a man yesterday? Thou desirest only to become a tyrant in this land, and desirest not to become a peacemaker.'

But a man came running up from the city's end. He said, 'O Moses, of a truth, the nobles consult to slay thee – Begone then – I counsel thee as a friend.'

20 So forth he went from it in fear, looking warily about him. He said, 'O Lord, deliver me from the unjust people.'

And when he was journeying towards Madian, he said, 'Haply my Lord will direct me in an even path.'

And when he arrived at the water of Madian, he found at it a company of men watering.

And he found beside them, two women[8] keeping back their flock: 'Why do ye,' said he, 'thus?' They said, 'We shall not water till the shepherds shall have driven off; for our father is very aged.'

So he watered for them – then retired to the shade and said, 'O my Lord, of the good thou hast caused me to meet with I stand in need.'[9]

And one of them came to him, walking bashfully. Said she, 'My father calleth thee, that he may pay thee wages for thy watering for us.' And when he came to him and had told him his STORY, 'Fear not,' said he, 'thou hast escaped from an unjust people.'

One of them said, 'O my father, hire him: for the best thou canst hire is the strong, the trusty.'

He said, 'Truly to one of these my two daughters I desire to marry thee, if for eight years thou wilt be my hired servant: and if thou fulfil ten, it shall be of thine own accord, for I wish not to deal hardly with thee. Thou wilt find me, if God will, one of the upright.'

He said, 'Be it so between me and thee: Whichever of the two terms I fulfil, there will be no injustice to me. And God is witness of what we say.'

And when Moses had fulfilled the term, and was journeying with his family, he perceived a fire on the mountainside. He said to his family, 'Wait ye, for I perceive a fire. Haply I may bring you tidings from it, or a brand from the fire to warm you.'

30 And when he came up to it, a Voice cried to him[10] out of the

bush from the right side of the valley in the sacred hollow, 'O Moses, I truly am God, the Lord of the Worlds:

Throw down now thy rod.' And when he saw it move as though it were a serpent, he retreated and fled and returned not. 'O Moses,' *cried the Voice*, 'draw near and fear not, for thou art in safety.

Put thy hand into thy bosom; it shall come forth white, but unharmed: and draw back thy hand[11] to thee without fear. These shall be two signs from thy Lord to Pharaoh and his nobles; for they are a perverse people.'

He said, 'O my Lord! truly I have slain one of them, therefore fear I lest they slay me.

My brother Aaron is clearer of speech than I. Send him, therefore, with me as a help, and to make good my cause, for I fear lest they treat me as an impostor.'

He said, 'We will strengthen thine arm with thy brother, and we will give power unto you both, and they shall not equal you in our signs. Ye twain and they who shall follow you, shall gain the day.'

And when Moses came to him with our demonstrative signs they said, 'This is nought but magical device. We never heard the like among our sires of old.'

And Moses said, 'My Lord best knoweth on whom He hath bestowed His guidance, and whose shall be the recompense of the abode *of Paradise*. Verily, the wicked shall not prosper.'

And Pharaoh said, 'O ye nobles, ye have no other God that I know of but myself. Burn me then, Haman, bricks of clay,[12] and build me a tower that I may mount up to the God of Moses, for in sooth, I deem him a liar.'

And he and his hosts behaved themselves proudly and unjustly on the earth, and thought that they should never be brought back to us.

40 But we seized on him and his hosts and cast them into the sea: Behold, then, the end of the wrongful doers:

And we made them Imâms who invite to the fire of hell, and on the day of Resurrection they shall not be helped.

We followed them with a curse in this world, and covered shall they be with shame on the day of Resurrection.

And after we had destroyed the former generations, we gave the book *of the Law* to Moses for man's enlightening, and a guidance and a mercy, that haply they might reflect.

And thou wast not on the western slope *of Sinai* when we laid his charge on Moses, nor wast thou one of the witnesses;

But we raised up generations *after Moses*, men whose days were lengthened;[13] neither didst thou dwell among the inhabitants of Madian to rehearse to them our signs, but we sent *Apostles* to them.[14]

Nor wast thou on the slope *of Sinai* when we called *to Moses*, but it is of the mercy of thy Lord that thou warnest a people, to whom no warner had come before thee, to the intent that they should reflect:

And that they should not say when a calamity shall befal them for their previous handy work, 'O our Lord! why hast thou not sent an Apostle to us? Then we should have followed thy signs and have been of the believers.'

Yet when the truth came to them from our very presence, they said, 'Unless the like *powers* be given to him that were given to Moses. . .'[15] But did they not disbelieve in what of old was given to Moses? They said, 'Two works of sorcery[16] have helped each other;' and they said, 'We disbelieve them both.'

SAY: Bring then a Book from before God which shall be a better guide than these, that I may follow it; if ye speak the truth.

50 And if they answer thee not, then know that verily they are following their own caprices; and who goeth more widely astray than he who followeth his own caprice without guidance from God? for God guideth not the wicked.

And now have we caused our word to come unto them, that they may be warned:

They[17] to whom we gave the Scriptures before IT, do in IT believe.

And when it is recited to them they say, 'We believe in it, for it is the truth from our Lord. We were Muslims before it came.'

Twice shall their reward be given them, for that they suffered with patience, and repelled evil with good, and gave alms out of that with which we provided them.

And when they hear light discourse they withdraw from it, and say, 'Our works for us and your works for you! Peace be on you! We are not in quest of fools!'

Thou truly canst not guide whom thou desirest; but God guideth whom He will; and He best knoweth those who yield to guidance.

But they say, 'If we follow the way in which thou art guided,[18] we shall be driven from our country.' But have we not established for them a sacred secure precinct, to which fruits of every kind, our gift for their support, are gathered together? But most of them have no knowledge.

And how many cities have we destroyed that flourished in wanton ease! And these their dwellings have not been inhabited since their time save by a few, and it is we who became their heirs.

But thy Lord did not destroy the cities till He had sent an apostle to their mother-city to rehearse our signs to its people: nor did we destroy the cities unless its people were unjust.

60 And all that hath been bestowed on you is merely for enjoyment and pomp of this life present: but that which is with God is better and more lasting. Will ye not be wise?

Shall he then to whom we have promised a goodly promise and who obtaineth it, be as he on whom we have bestowed the enjoyments of this life present, and who on the day of Resurrection shall be brought up *for punishment?*

On that day will *God* cry to them and say, 'Where are my companions, as ye supposed them?'

They on whom doom shall be justly pronounced will say, 'O our Lord! these are they whom we led astray: we led them astray even as we had been led astray ourselves: Thou hast no cause of blame against us: It was not we whom they worshipped.[19]

And it shall be said, 'Call now on those whom ye made God's companions:' and they shall call on them, but they will not answer them. And they shall see the punishment, and wish that they had been guided aright.

And on that day shall *God* call to them and say, 'How answered ye the apostles?'

But on that day they shall be too blinded *with confusion* to give an account,[20] nor shall they ask it of one another.

Yet as to him who shall turn *to God* and believe and do the thing that is right, it may come to pass that he shall be among the happy.

And thy Lord createth what he will and hath a free choice. But they, *the false gods*, have no power to choose. Glory be to God! and high let him be exalted above those whom they associate with him.

And thy Lord knoweth what their breasts conceal and what they bring to light.
70 And He is God! There is no god but He! His, all praise in
this life and in the next, and His the power supreme,[21] and to Him shall ye be brought back!

SAY: What think ye? If God should enshroud you with a long night until the day of resurrection, what god beside God would bring you light? Will ye not then hearken?

SAY: What think ye? If God should make it one long day for you until the day of resurrection, what god but God could bring you the night in which to take your rest? Will ye not then see?

Of His mercy he hath made for you the night that ye may take your rest in it; and the day that ye may seek what ye need out of his bounteous supplies, and that ye may give thanks.

One day God will call to them and say, 'Where are my companions as ye supposed them?'

And we will bring up a witness out of every nation and say, 'Bring your proofs.' And they shall know that the truth is with God *alone*, and the gods of their own devising shall desert them.

Now Korah[22] was of the people of Moses: but he behaved haughtily towards them; for we had given him such treasure that its keys would have burdened a company of men of strength. When his people said to him, 'Exult not, for God loveth not those who exult;

But seek, by means of what God hath given thee, to attain the future Mansion; and neglect not thy part in this world, but be bounteous to others as God hath been bounteous to thee, and seek not to commit excesses on the earth; for God loveth not those who commit excesses:'

He said, 'It hath been given me only on account of the knowledge that is in me.' Did he not know that God had destroyed before him generations that were mightier than he in strength and had amassed more abundant wealth? But the wicked shall not be asked of their crimes.

And Korah went forth to his people in his pomp. Those who were greedy for this present life said, 'Oh that we had the like of that which hath been bestowed on Korah! Truly he is possessed of great good fortune.'
80 But they to whom knowledge had been given said, 'Woe to

you! the reward of God is better for him who believeth and worketh righteousness, and none shall win it but those who have patiently endured.'

And we clave the earth for him and for his palace, and he had no forces, in the place of God,[23] to help him, nor was he among those who are succoured.

And in the morning those who the day before had coveted his lot said, 'Aha! God enlargeth supplies to whom he pleaseth of his servants, or is sparing. Had not God been gracious to us, He had caused it to cleave for us. Aha! the ungrateful can never prosper.'

As to this future mansion, we will bestow it on those who seek not to exalt them in the earth or to do wrong: And there is a happy issue for the God-fearing.

Whoso doeth good shall have reward beyond its merits, and whoso doeth evil, they who do evil shall be rewarded only as they shall have wrought.

He who hath sanctioned the Koran to thee will certainly bring thee to thy home.[24] SAY: My Lord best knoweth who hath guidance, and who is in undoubted error.

Thou didst never expect that the Book would be given thee. Of thy Lord's mercy only *hath it been sent down*. Be not thou helpful then to the unbelievers:

Neither let them turn thee aside from the signs of God after they have been sent down to thee, but bid men to thy Lord; and be not among those who add gods to God:

And call not on any other god with God. There is no god but He! Everything shall perish except Himself! Judgment is His, and to Him shall ye return!

SURA 29 – THE SPIDER

MECCA – 69 VERSES

In the Name of God, the Compassionate, the Merciful

Elif. Lam. Mim.[1] Think men that when they say, 'We
believe,' they shall be let alone and not be put to proof?
We put to proof those who lived before them; for God will
surely take knowledge of those who are sincere, and will surely
take knowledge of the liars.
Think they who work evil that they shall escape Us? Ill do
they judge.
To him who hopeth to meet God, the set time of God will
surely come. The Hearer, the Knower, He!
Whoso maketh efforts for the faith, maketh them for his own
good only. Verily God is rich enough to dispense with all
creatures.
And as to those who shall have believed and done the things
that are right, their evil deeds will we surely blot out from them,
and according to their best actions will we surely reward them.
Moreover we have enjoined on man to shew kindness to
parents: but if they strive with thee that thou join that with Me
of which thou hast no knowledge,[2] obey them not. To me do
ye return, and then will I tell you of your doings:
And those who shall have believed and done the things that
are right, we will surely give them an entering in among the just.
But some men say, 'We believe in God,' yet when they meet
with sufferings in the cause of God, they regard trouble from
man as chastisement from God. Yet if a success come from thy
Lord they are sure to say, 'We were on your side!' Doth not God
well know what is in the breasts of his creatures?
10 *Yes*, and God well knoweth those who believe, and He well
knoweth the Hypocrites.
The unbelievers say to the faithful, 'Follow ye our way, and
we will surely bear your sins.' But not aught of their sins will
they bear – verily they are liars!
But their own burdens, and burdens beside their own
burdens shall they surely bear: and inquisition shall be made of
them on the day of Resurrection as to their false devices.
Of old sent we Noah to his people: a thousand years save fifty

did he tarry among them; and the flood overtook them in their wrongful doings:

But we rescued him and those who were in the vessel; and we made it a sign to all men:

And Abraham; when he said to his people, 'Worship God and fear Him. This will be best for you, if ye have knowledge;'

Ye only worship idols beside God, and are the authors of a lie. Those whom ye worship beside God can give you no supplies: seek, then, your supplies from God; and serve Him and give Him thanks. To Him shall ye return.

Suppose that ye treat me as a liar! nations before you have treated God's messenger as a liar; but open preaching is his only duty.

See they not how God bringeth forth creation? and then causeth it to return again? Thus truly is easy for God.

SAY,[3] Go through the earth, and see how he hath brought forth created beings. Hereafter, with a second birth will God cause them to be born again; for God is Almighty.

20 Whom He pleaseth will He chastise, and on whom He pleaseth will He have mercy, and to Him shall ye be taken back.

And ye shall not invalidate his power either in the Earth or in the Heaven:[4] and, save God, ye shall have neither patron nor helper.

As for those who believe not in the signs of God, or that they shall ever meet him, these of my mercy shall despair, and these doth a grievous chastisement await.'

And the only answer of his people was to say, 'Slay him or burn him.' But from the fire did God save him! Verily, herein are signs to those who believe.

And Abraham said, 'Of a truth ye have taken idols along with God as your bond of union[5] in this life present;

But on the day of resurrection some of you shall deny the others, and some of you shall curse the others; and your abode shall be the fire, and ye shall have none to help.'

But Lot believed on him,[6] and said, 'I betake me to my Lord, for He truly is the Mighty, the Wise.'

And we bestowed on him Isaac and Jacob, and placed the gift of prophecy and the Scripture among his posterity; And we gave him his reward in this world, and in the next he shall be among the just.

We sent also Lot: when he said to his people, 'Proceed ye to a filthiness in which no people in the world hath ever gone before you?

Proceed ye even to men? attack ye them on the highway? and proceed ye to the crime in your assemblies?' But the only answer of his people was to say, 'Bring God's chastisement upon us, if thou art a man of truth.'

He cried: My Lord! help me against this polluted people.

And when our messengers came to Abraham with the tidings *of a son*, they said, 'Of a truth we will destroy the in-dwellers in this city, for its in-dwellers are evil doers.'

He said, 'Lot is therein.' They said, 'We know full well who therein is. Him and his family will we save, except his wife; she will be of those who linger.

And when our messengers came to Lot, he was troubled for them, and his arm was too weak[7] to protect them; and they said, 'Fear not, and distress not thyself, for thee and thy family will we save, except thy wife; she will be of those who linger.[8]

We will surely bring down upon the dwellers in this city vengeance from Heaven for the excesses they have committed.'

And in what we have left of it is a clear sign to men of understanding.

And to Madian *we sent* their brother Shoaib. And he said, 'Oh! my people! worship God, and expect the latter day, and enact not in the land deeds of harmful excess.'

But they treated him as an impostor: so an earthquake assailed them; and at morn they were found prostrate *and dead* in their dwellings.

And *we destroyed* Ad and Themoud. Already is this made plain to you in *the ruins* of their dwellings. For Satan had made their own works fair seeming to them, and drew them from the right path, keen-sighted though they were.

And Corah and Pharaoh and Haman. With proofs of his mission did Moses come to them, and they behaved proudly on the earth; but us they could not outstrip;[9]

For, every one of them did we seize in his sin. Against some of them did we send a stone-charged wind: Some of them did the terrible cry of Gabriel surprise: for some of them we cleaved the earth; and some of them we drowned. And it was not God who would deal wrongly by them, but they wronged themselves.

40 The likeness for those who take to themselves guardians

instead of God is the likeness of the SPIDER who buildeth her a house: But verily, frailest of all houses surely is the house of the spider. Did they but know this!

God truly knoweth all that they call on beside Him; and He is the Mighty, the Wise.

These similitudes do we set forth to men: and none understand them except the wise.

God hath created the Heavens and the Earth for a serious end.[10] Verily in this is a sign to those who believe.

Recite the portions of the Book which have been revealed to thee and discharge the duty of prayer: for prayer restraineth from the filthy and the blame-worthy. And the gravest duty is the remembrance of God; and God knoweth what ye do.

Dispute not, unless in kindly sort, with the people of the Book;[11] save with such of them as have dealt wrongfully with you: And say ye, 'We believe in what hath been sent down to us and hath been sent down to you. Our God and your God is one, and to him are we self-surrendered' (Muslims).

Thus have we sent down the Book *of the Koran* to thee: and they to whom we have given the Book *of the law* believe in it: and of these *Arabians* there are those who believe in it: and none, save the Infidels, reject our signs.

Thou didst not recite any book (of revelation) before it: with that right hand of thine thou didst not transcribe one: else might they who treat it as a vain thing have justly doubted:

But it is a clear sign in the hearts of those whom 'the knowledge' hath reached. None except the wicked reject our signs.

And they say, 'Unless a sign be sent down to him from his Lord. . .' SAY: Signs are in the power of God alone. I am only a plain spoken warner.

50 Is it not enough for them that we have sent down to thee the Book to be recited to them? In this verily is a mercy and a warning to those who believe.

SAY: God is witness enough between me and you.

He knoweth all that is in the Heavens and the Earth, and they who believe in vain things[12] and disbelieve in God – these shall be the lost ones.

They will challenge thee to hasten the punishment: but had there not been a season fixed for it, that punishment had already come upon them. But it shall overtake them suddenly when they look not for it.

They will challenge thee to hasten the punishment: but verily Hell shall be round about the infidels.

One day the punishment shall wrap them round, both from above them and from beneath their feet; and *God* will say, 'Taste ye your own doings.'

O my servants who have believed! Vast truly is my Earth:[13] me, therefore! yea worship me.

Every soul shall taste of death. Then to us shall ye return.

But those who shall have believed and wrought righteousness will we lodge in gardens with palaces, beneath which the rivers flow. For ever shall they abide therein. How goodly the reward of those who labour,

Who patiently endure, and put their trust in their Lord!

60 How many animals are there which provide not[14] their own food! God feedeth them and you. He Heareth, Knoweth all things.

If thou ask them who hath created the Heavens and the Earth, and hath imposed laws on the sun and on the moon, they will certainly say, 'God.' How then can they devise lies?

God lavisheth supplies on such of his servants as He pleaseth or giveth to them by measure. God knoweth all things.

If thou ask them who sendeth rain from heaven, and by it quickeneth the earth, after it hath been dead, they will certainly answer, 'God.' SAY: Praise be to God! Yet most of them do not understand.

This present life is no other than a pastime and a disport: but truly the future mansion is life indeed! Would that they knew this!

Lo! when they embark on shipboard, they call upon God, vowing him sincere worship, but when He bringeth them safe to land, behold they join partners with Him.

In our revelation they believe not, yet take their fill of good things. But in the end they shall know *their folly*.

Do they not see that we have established a safe precinct[15] while all around them men are being spoiled? Will they then believe in vain idols, and not own the goodness of God?

But who acteth more wrongly than he who deviseth a lie against God, or calls the truth when it hath come to him, a lie? Is there not an abode for the infidels in Hell?

And whoso maketh efforts for us, in our ways will we guide them: for God is assuredly with those who do righteous deeds.

SURA 30 – THE GREEKS

MECCA – 60 VERSES

In the Name of God, the Compassionate, the Merciful

Elif. Lam. Mim.[1] THE GREEKS have been defeated[2]

In a land hard by: But after their defeat they shall defeat their foes,

In a few years.[3] First and last is the affair with God. And on that day shall the faithful rejoice

In the aid of their God: He aideth whom He will; and He is the Mighty, the Merciful.

It is the promise of God: To his promise God will not be untrue: but most men know it not.

They know the outward shews of this life present, but of the next life are they careless.

Have they not considered within themselves that God hath not created the Heavens and the Earth and all that is between them but for a serious end, and for a fixed term? But truly most men believe not that they shall meet their Lord.

Have they never journeyed through the land, and seen what hath been the end of those who were before them? Mightier were they than these in strength; and they broke up the land, and dwelt in it in greater numbers than they who dwell there now; and their apostles came to them with proofs of their mission: and it was not God who would wrong them, but they wronged themselves.

Then evil was the end of the evil doers; because they had treated our signs as lies, and laughed them to scorn.

10 God bringeth forth the creation – then causeth it to return again – then to Him shall ye come back.[4]

And on the day when the hour shall arrive, the guilty shall be struck dumb for despair,

And they shall have no intercessors from among the gods whom they have joined with God, and they shall deny the gods they joined with Him.

And on that day when the Hour shall arrive, shall men be separated one from another;

And as for those who shall have believed and done the things that are right, they shall enjoy themselves in a flowery mead;

But as for those who shall not have believed, but treated our signs and the meeting of the next life as lies, they shall be given over to the torment.

Glorify God therefore when ye reach the evening, and when ye rise at morn:

And to Him be praise in the Heavens and on the Earth; and at twilight, and when ye rest at noon.

He bringeth forth the living out of the dead, and He bringeth forth the dead out of the living: and He quickeneth the earth when dead. Thus is it that ye too shall be brought forth.[5]

And one of his signs it is that He hath created you out of dust; then lo! ye become men who spread themselves far and wide:

20 And one of his signs it is, that He hath created wives for you of your own species,[6] that ye may dwell with them, and hath put love and tenderness between you. Herein truly are signs for those who reflect.

And among his signs are the creation of the Heavens and of the Earth, and your variety of tongues and colour. Herein truly are signs for all men.

And of his signs are your sleep by night and by day, and your goings in quest of his bounties. Herein truly are signs to those who hearken.

And of his signs are, that He sheweth you the lightning, a source of awe and hope; and that He sendeth down rain from the heaven and giveth life by it to the earth when dead. Herein truly are signs to those who understand.

And of his signs also one is that the Heaven and the Earth stand firm at his bidding: hereafter, when with one summons He shall summon you out of the earth, – lo! forth shall ye come.

His, whatsoever is in the Heavens and on the Earth: all are obedient to him.

And He it is who bringeth a creature forth, then causeth it to return again; and to him is this most easy. To whatever is loftiest in heaven and earth is He to be likened; and He is the Mighty, the Wise.

He setteth forth to you an instance drawn from yourselves. Have ye among the slaves whom your right hands have won, any partner in what we have bestowed on you, so that ye share alike? Fear ye them as ye fear each other? (Thus make we our signs clear to men of understanding.)

No, *ye do not*. But the wicked, devoid of knowledge, follow their own desires:[7] and those whom God shall mislead, who shall guide, and who shall be their protector?

Set thou thy face then, as a true convert,[8] towards the Faith which God hath made, and for which He hath made man. No change is there in the creation of God. This is the right Faith, but the greater part of men know it not.

30 And be ye turned to Him, and fear Him, and observe prayer, and be not of those who unite gods with God:

Of those who have split up their religion, and have become sects, where every party rejoices in what is their own.[9]

When some evil toucheth men, they turn to their Lord and call upon him: then when he hath made them taste his mercy, lo, a part of them join other gods with their Lord,

Ungrateful for our favours! Enjoy yourselves then. But in the end ye shall know *your folly*.

Have we sent down to them any mandate which speaketh *in favour* of what they join with God?

When we cause men to taste mercy they rejoice in it; but if, for that which their hands have aforetime wrought, evil befal them, they despair.

See they not that God bestoweth full supplies on whom He pleaseth and giveth sparingly to whom He pleaseth? Signs truly are there herein to those who believe.

To him who is of kin to thee give his due, and to the poor and to the wayfarer: this will be best for those who seek the face of God; and with them it shall be well.

Whatever ye put out at usury to increase it with the substance of others shall have no increase from God:[10] but whatever ye shall give in alms, as seeking the face of God, shall be doubled to you.

It is God who created you – then fed you – then will cause you to die – then will make you alive. Is there any of your companion-gods who can do aught of these things? Praise be to Him! and far be He exalted above the gods they join with Him.

40 Destruction hath appeared by land and by sea on account of what men's hands have wrought, that it might make them taste somewhat of *the fruit* of their doings, that haply they might turn *to God*.

SAY: Journey through the land, and see what hath been the end of those who were before you! The greater part of them joined other gods with God.

Set thy face then towards the right faith, ere the day come which none can hinder God from bringing on.[11] On that day shall they be parted in twain:

Unbelievers on whom shall be their unbelief; and they who have wrought righteousness, and prepared for themselves couches of repose:

That of his bounty He may reward those who have believed and wrought righteousness; for the unbelievers He loveth not.

And one of his signs is that He sendeth the winds with glad tidings *of rain*, both that He may cause you to taste his mercy, and that ships may sail at his command, that out of his bounties ye may seek *wealth*, and that haply ye may render thanks.

We have sent apostles before thee to their peoples, and they presented themselves to them with clear proofs of their mission; and while it behoved us to succour the faithful, we took vengeance on the guilty.

It is God who sendeth the winds and uplifteth the clouds, and, as He pleaseth, spreadeth them on high, and breaketh them up; and thou mayest see the rain issuing from their midst; and when He poureth it down on such of his servants as He pleaseth, lo! they are filled with joy,

Even they who before it was sent down to them, were in mute despair.

Look then at the traces of God's mercy – how after its death he quickeneth the earth! This same *God* will surely quicken the dead, for to all things His might is equal.

50 Yet should we send a blast, and should they see their *harvest* turn yellow, they would afterwards shew themselves ungrateful.

Thou canst not make the dead to hear, neither canst thou make the deaf to hear the call, when they withdraw and turn their backs:

Neither canst thou guide the blind out of their error: in sooth, none shalt thou make to hear, save him who shall believe in our signs: for they are resigned to our will (Muslims).

It is God who hath created you in weakness, then after weakness hath given you strength: then after strength, weakness and grey hairs: He createth what He will; and He is the Wise, the Powerful.

And on the day whereon the Hour shall arrive, the wicked will swear

That not above an hour have they waited: Even so did they utter lies *on earth:*

But they to whom knowledge and faith have been given will say, 'Ye have waited, in accordance with the book of God, till the day of Resurrection: for this is the day of the Resurrection – but ye knew it not.'

On that day their plea shall not avail the wicked, neither shall they again be bidden to seek acceptance with God.

And now have we set before men, in this Koran, every kind of parable: yet if thou bring them a single verse of it, the infidels will surely say, 'Ye are only utterers of vain things.'

It is thus that God hath sealed up the hearts of those who are devoid of knowledge.

60 But do thou, *Muhammad*, bear with patience, for true is the promise of God; and let not those who have no firm belief, unsettle thee.

SURA 31 – LOKMAN[1]

MECCA – 34 VERSES

In the Name of God, the Compassionate, the Merciful

Elif. Lam. Mim.[2] These are the verses (signs) of the wise Book,

A guidance and a mercy to the righteous,

Who observe prayer, and pay the impost,[3] and believe firmly in the life to come: –

These *rest* on guidance from their Lord, and with these it shall be well.

But a man there is who buyeth an idle tale, that in his lack of knowledge he may mislead others from the way of God, and turn it to scorn. For such is prepared a shameful punishment!

And when our signs are rehearsed to him, he turneth away disdainfully, as though he heard them not, – as though his ears were heavy with deafness. Announce to him therefore tidings of an afflictive punishment!

But they who shall have believed and wrought good works, shall enjoy the gardens of delight:

For ever shall they dwell therein: it is God's true promise! and He is the Mighty, the Wise.

Without pillars that can be seen hath He created the heavens, and on the earth hath thrown mountains lest it should move with you;[4] and He hath scattered over it animals of every sort: and from the Heaven we send down rain and cause every kind of noble plant to grow up therein.

10 This is the creation of God: Shew me now what others than He have created. Ah! the ungodly are in a manifest delusion.

Of old we bestowed wisdom upon LOKMAN, *and taught him thus* – 'Be thankful to God: for whoever is thankful, is thankful to his own behoof; and if any shall be thankless . . . God truly is self-sufficient, worthy of all praise!'

And *bear in mind* when Lokman said to his son by way of warning, 'O my son! join not other gods with God, for the joining gods with God is the great impiety.'

(We have commanded man concerning his parents. His mother carrieth him with weakness upon weakness; nor until after two years is he weaned.[5] Be grateful to me, and to thy parents. Unto me shall all come.

But if they importune thee to join that with Me of which thou hast no knowledge, obey them not: comport thyself towards them in this world as is meet and right; but follow the way of him who turneth unto me. Unto me shall ye return at last, and then will I tell you of your doings;)

'Oh my son! verily God will bring everything to light, though it were but the weight of a grain of mustard-seed, and hidden in a rock or in the heavens or in the earth; for, God is subtile, informed of all.

O my son! observe prayer, and enjoin the right and forbid the wrong, and be patient under whatever shall betide thee: for this is a bounden duty.

And distort not thy face at men; nor walk thou loftily on the earth; for God loveth no arrogant vain-glorious one.

But let thy pace be middling; and lower thy voice: for the least pleasing of voices is surely the voice of asses.'

See ye not how that God hath put under you all that is in the heavens and all that is on the earth, and hath been bounteous to you of his favours, both for soul and body.[6] But some are there

who dispute of God without knowledge, and have no guidance and no illuminating Book:
20 And when it is said to them, Follow ye what God hath sent
down, they say, 'Nay; that religion in which we found our fathers will we follow.' What! though Satan bid them to the torment of the flame?

But whoso setteth his face towards God with self-surrender, and is a doer of that which is good, hath laid hold on a sure handle; for unto God is the issue of all things.

But let not the unbelief of the unbelieving grieve thee: unto us shall they return: then will we tell them of their doings; for God knoweth the very secrets of the breast.

Yet a little while will we provide for them: afterwards will we force them to a stern punishment.

If thou ask them who hath created the heavens and the earth, they will certainly reply, 'God.' SAY: God be praised! But most of them have no knowledge.

God's, whatever is in the Heavens and the Earth! for God, He is the Rich,[7] the Praiseworthy.

If all the trees that are upon the earth were to become pens, and if God should after that swell the sea into seven seas *of ink*, His words would not be exhausted: for God is Mighty, Wise.[8]

Your creation and your quickening *hereafter*, are but as those of a single individual. Verily, God Heareth, Seeth!

Seest thou not that God causeth the night to come in upon the day, and the day to come in upon the night? and that he hath subjected the sun and the moon to laws by which each speedeth along to an appointed goal? and that God *therefore* is acquainted with that which ye do?

This, for that God is the truth; and that whatever ye call upon beside Him is a vain thing; and that God – He is the High, the Great.
30 Seest thou not how the ships speed on in the sea, through
the favour of God, that he may shew you of his signs? for herein are signs to all patient, grateful ones.

When the waves cover them like dark shadows they call upon God as with sincere religion; but when He safely landeth them, some of them there are who halt between two opinions.[9] Yet none reject our signs but all deceitful, ungrateful ones.

O men! fear ye your Lord, and dread the day whereon father shall not atone for son, neither shall a son in the least atone for his father.

Aye! the promise of God is a truth. Let not this present life then deceive you; neither let the deceiver deceive you concerning God.

Aye! God! – with Him is the knowledge of the Hour: and He sendeth down the rain – and He knoweth what is in the wombs – but no soul knoweth what it shall have gotten on the morrow: neither knoweth any soul in what land it shall die. But God is knowing, informed of all.

SURA 32 – ADORATION

MECCA – 30 VERSES

In the Name of God, the Compassionate, the Merciful

Elif. Lam. Mim.[1] This Book is without a doubt a Revelation sent down from the Lord of the Worlds.

Will they say, He hath forged it? Nay, it is the truth from thy Lord that thou mayest warn a people to whom no warner hath come before thee, that haply they may be guided.

God it is who hath created the Heavens and the Earth and all that is between them in six days; then ascended his throne. Save Him ye have no patron, and none to plead for you. Will ye not then reflect?

From the Heaven to the Earth He governeth all things: hereafter shall they come up to Him on a day whose length shall be a thousand of such years as ye reckon.[2]

This is He who knoweth the unseen and the seen; the Mighty, the Merciful,

Who hath made everything which He hath created most good; and began the creation of man with clay;

Then ordained his progeny from germs of life,[3] from sorry water:

Then shaped him, and breathed of His Spirit into him, and gave you hearing and seeing and hearts: what little thanks do ye return!

And they say, 'What! when we shall have lain hidden in the earth, shall we become a new creation?'

10 Yea, they deny that they shall meet their Lord.

SAY: The angel of death who is charged with you shall cause you to die: then shall ye be returned to your Lord.

Couldst thou but see when the guilty shall droop their heads before their Lord, *and cry*, 'O our Lord! we have seen and we have heard: return us then *to life:* we will do that which is right. Verily we believe firmly!'

(Had we pleased we had certainly given to every soul its guidance. But true shall be the word which hath gone forth from me – I will surely fill hell with Djinn and men together.)

'Taste then the recompense of your having forgotten the meeting with this your day. We, too, we have forgotten you: taste then an eternal punishment for that which ye have wrought.'

They only believe in our signs, who, when mention is made of them, fall down in ADORATION, and celebrate the praise of their Lord, and are not puffed up with disdain:

Who, as they raise them[4] from their couches, call on their Lord with fear and desire, and give alms of that with which we have supplied them.

No soul knoweth what joy of the eyes is reserved *for the good* in recompense of their works.

Shall he then who is a believer be as he who sinneth grossly? they shall not be held alike.

As to those who believe and do that which is right, they shall have gardens of eternal abode as the meed of their works:

20 But as for those who grossly sin, their abode shall be the fire: so oft as they shall desire to escape out of it, back shall they be turned into it. And it shall be said to them, Taste ye the torment of the fire, which ye treated as a lie.

And we will surely cause them to taste a punishment yet nearer at hand, besides the greater punishment, that haply they may turn to us *in penitence*.

Who acteth worse than he who is warned by the signs of his Lord, then turneth away from them? We will surely take vengeance on the guilty ones.

We heretofore gave the Book *of the law* to Moses: have thou no doubt as to our meeting with him: and we appointed it for the guidance of the children of Israel.

And we appointed Imâms from among them who should guide after our command when they had themselves endured with constancy, and had firmly believed in our signs.

Now thy Lord! He will decide between them on the day of resurrection as to the subject of their disputes.

Is it not notorious to them how many generations, through whose abodes they walk, we have destroyed before them? Truly herein are signs: will they not then hear?

See they not how we drive the rain to some parched land and thereby bring forth corn of which their cattle and themselves do eat? Will they not then behold?

They say, 'When will this decision take place? Tell us, if ye are men of truth?'

SAY: On the day of that decision, the faith of infidels shall not avail them, and they shall have no further respite.

30 Stand aloof from them then, and wait thou, for they too wait.[5]

SURA 33 – THE CONFEDERATES[1]

MEDINA – 73 VERSES

In the Name of God, the Compassionate, the Merciful

O Prophet, fear thou God, and obey not the unbelievers and the hypocrites; – Truly God is Knowing, Wise:

But follow what is revealed to thee from thy Lord: Cognisant truly is He of all your actions –

And put thou thy trust in God, for a sufficient guardian is God.

God hath not given a man two hearts within him; neither hath he made your wives whom ye divorce[2] to be as your mothers; nor hath he made your adopted sons to be as your own sons. Such words are indeed in your mouths; but God speaketh the truth, and in the right way He guideth.

Name them after their fathers: this will be more right before God. But if ye know not who their fathers are, then let them be your brethren in the faith, and your comrades. And unless made with intent of heart, mistakes in this matter shall be no crime in you: for God is Lenient, Merciful.

Nearer of kin to the faithful is the Prophet, than they are to their own selves. His wives are their mothers. According to the Book of God, they who are related by blood, are nearer the one to the other than other believers, and than those who have fled their country[3] for the cause of God: but whatever kindness ye shew to your kindred, shall be noted down in the Book.

And remember that we have entered into covenant with the Prophets, and with thee, and with Noah, and Abraham, and Moses, and Jesus, Son of Mary: and we formed with them a strict covenant,

That God may question the men of truth as to their truth.[4] But a sore torment hath He prepared for the unbelievers.

O believers![5] remember the goodness of God towards you, when the armies came against you, and we sent against them a blast, and hosts that ye saw not; for the eye of God was upon your doings:

10 When they assailed you from above you, and from below you,[6] and when your eyes became distracted, and your hearts came up into your throat, and ye thought divers thoughts of God:

Then were the faithful tried, and with strong quaking did they quake:

And when the disaffected and the diseased[7] of heart said, 'God and his Apostle have made us but a cheating promise:'

And when a party of them said, 'O people of Yathrib![8] there is no place of safety for you here;[9] therefore return *into the city*.' And another party of you asked the prophet's leave to return, saying, 'Our houses are left defenceless.' No! they were not left defenceless: but their sole thought was to flee away.

If the enemy had effected an entry at all points, and they (the disaffected) had been asked to promote confusion, they would have done so; but only a short time would they have remained in it. – (Medina).[10]

They had before pledged themselves to God that they would not turn their backs; and a pledge given to God must be enquired of.

SAY: Flight shall not profit you; if ye have fled the death or the slaughter, yet even then, but a little while shall ye enjoy *your good things!*

SAY: Who is he that will screen you from God, whether He choose to bring evil on you, or to shew you mercy? None beside God shall they find to be their patron or helper.

God well knoweth those among you who cause hindrances, and those who say to their brethren, 'Come hither to us;' and who come not to the fight except a little.

It is out of covetousness in your regard: for when an alarm cometh, thou mayest see them look to thee, and roll their eyes like him on whom the shadows of death have fallen! Yet, when the alarm is passed, with sharp tongues will they assail you, covetous of the best of the spoil. No faith have these! God will make their doings of no avail! And easy is this with
God.
20 They thought that the CONFEDERATES would never
retire:[11] and were the confederates to come again, they would fain be dwelling among the Arabs of the desert, *and there* ask news about you! for though they were with you, they fought not except a little.

A noble pattern had ye in God's Apostle, for all who hope in God, and in the latter day, and oft remember God!

And when the faithful saw the confederates, they said, 'This is what God and His Apostle promised us,[12] and God and His Apostle spoke truly:' and it only increased their faith and self-devotion.

Some were there among the faithful who made good what they had promised to God. Some have fulfilled their course, and others await *its fulfilment*, and have not been changelings who change –

That God may reward the faithful for their faithfulness, and may punish the hypocrites, if He so please, or be turned unto them: for God is Forgiving, Merciful.

And God drove back the infidels in their wrath; they won no advantage; God sufficed the faithful in the fight: for God is Strong, Mighty!

And He caused those of the people of the Book (the Jews), who had aided *the confederates*, to come down out of their fortresses, and cast dismay into their hearts: some ye slew, others ye took prisoners.[13]

And He gave you their land, and their dwellings, and their wealth, for an heritage – even a land on which ye had never set foot: for the might of God is equal to all things.

O Prophet! say to thy wives,[14] If ye desire this present life and its braveries, come then, I will provide for you, and dismiss you with an honourable dismissal.

But if ye desire God and His Apostle, and a home in the next life, then, truly, hath God prepared for those of you who are virtuous, a great reward.

30 O wives of the Prophet! should any of you be guilty of a proven lewdness, doubly shall her chastisement be doubled: and with God this is easy.

But whoever of you shall obey God and His Apostle, and shall do that which is right, twice over will we give her her reward, and we have prepared for her a noble provision.

O wives of the Prophet! ye are not as other women. If ye fear God, be not too complaisant of speech, lest the man of unhealthy heart should lust after you, but speak with discreet speech.

And abide still in your houses, and go not in public decked as in the days of your former ignorance,[15] but observe prayer, and pay the impost, and obey God and the Apostle: for God only desireth to put away filthiness from you[16] as his household, and with cleansing to cleanse you.

And recollect what is rehearsed to you in your houses of the Book of God, and of wisdom: for God is keen-sighted, cognisant *of all*.

Truly the men who resign themselves to God (Muslims), and the women who resign themselves, and the believing men and the believing women, and the devout men and the devout women, and the men of truth, and the women of truth, and the patient men and the patient women, and the humble men and the humble women, and the men who give alms and the women who give alms, and the men who fast and the women who fast, and the chaste men and the chaste women, and the men and the women who oft remember God: for them hath God prepared forgiveness and a rich recompense.

And it is not for a believer, man or woman, to have any choice in their affairs, when God and His Apostle have decreed a matter: and whoever disobeyeth God and His Apostle, erreth with palpable error.

And, *remember*, when thou saidst to him unto whom God had shewn favour,[17] and to whom thou also hadst shewn favour, 'Keep thy wife to thyself, and fear God;' and thou didst hide in thy mind what God would bring to light,[18] and thou didst fear man; but more right had it been to fear God. And when Zaid had settled concerning her to divorce her, we married her to thee, that it might not be a crime in the faithful to marry the wives of their adopted sons, when they have settled the affair concerning them. And the behest of God is to be performed.

No blame attacheth to the prophet where God hath given him a permission. Such was the way of God with those prophets who flourished before thee; for God's behest is a fixed decree –

Who fulfilled the mission with which God had charged them,[19] and feared Him, and feared none but God. And God taketh a sufficient account.

40 Muhammad is not the father of any man among you, but he is the Apostle of God, and the seal of the prophets: and God knoweth all things.

O Believers! remember God with frequent remembrance, and praise Him morning and evening.

He blesseth you, and His angels *intercede for you*, that He may bring you forth out of darkness into light: and Merciful is He to the Believers.

Their greeting on the day when they shall meet Him shall be 'Peace!' And He hath got ready for them a noble recompense.

O Prophet! we have sent thee to be a witness, and a herald of glad tidings, and a warner;

And one who, through His own permission, summoneth to God, and a light-giving torch.

Announce, therefore, to believers, that great boons do await them from God;

And obey not the Infidels and Hypocrites – yet abstain from injuring them: and put thou thy trust in God, for God is a sufficient guardian.

O Believers! when ye marry believing women, and then divorce them before ye have consummated the marriage, ye have no term prescribed you, which ye must fulfil towards them: provide for them, and dismiss them with a reputable dismissal.

O Prophet! we allow thee thy wives whom thou hast dowered, and the slaves whom thy right hand possesseth out of the booty which God hath granted thee, and the daughters of thy uncle, and of thy paternal and maternal aunts who fled with thee *to Medina*, and any believing woman who hath given herself up to the Prophet, if the Prophet desired to wed her – a Privilege for thee above the rest of the Faithful.

50 We well know what we have settled for them, in regard to their
wives and to the slaves whom their right hands hold, that there
may be no fault on thy part:[20] and God is Indulgent, Merciful!

Thou mayst decline for the present whom thou wilt of them, and thou mayest take to thy *bed* her whom thou wilt, and whomsoever thou shalt long for of those thou shalt have before neglected; and this shall not be a crime in thee. Thus will it be easier to give them the desire of their eyes, and not to put them to grief, and to satisfy them with what thou shalt accord to each of them. God knoweth what is in your hearts, and God is Knowing, Gracious.

It is not permitted thee to take *other* wives hereafter,[21] nor to change thy present wives for other women, though their beauty charm thee, except slaves whom thy right hand shall possess.[22] And God watcheth all things.

O Believers! enter not into the houses of the Prophet,[23] save by his leave, for a meal, without waiting his time. When ye are invited then enter, and when ye have eaten then disperse at once. And engage not in familiar talk, for this would cause the Prophet trouble, and he would be ashamed to bid you go; but God is not ashamed to say the truth. And when ye would ask any gift of his wives, ask it from behind a veil. Purer will this be for your hearts and for their hearts. And ye must not trouble the Apostle of God, nor marry his wives, after him, for ever. This would be a grave *offence* with God.

Whether ye bring a matter to the light or hide it, God truly hath knowledge of all things.

No blame shall attach to them (your wives) for speaking to their fathers unveiled, or to their sons, or to their brothers, or to their brothers' sons, or to their sisters' sons, or to their women, or to the slaves whom their right hands hold. And fear ye God: for God witnesseth all things.

Verily, God and His Angels bless the Prophet! Bless ye Him, O Believers, and salute Him with salutations of Peace.

Verily, they who affront God and His Apostle, the curse of God is on them in this world, and in the world to come: and He hath prepared for them a shameful chastisement.

And they who shall affront believing men and believing women, for no fault of theirs, they shall surely bear the guilt of slander, and of a clear wrong.

O Prophet! speak to thy wives and to thy daughters,[24] and to the wives of the Faithful, that they let their veils fall low. Thus will they more easily be known, and they will not be affronted. God is Indulgent, Merciful!

60 If the Hypocrites, and the men of tainted heart, and the
stirrers of sedition in Medina desist not, we will surely stir thee up against them. Then shall they not be suffered to dwell near thee therein, but a little while:

Cursed wherever they are found; they shall be seized and slain with slaughter!

Such hath been the way of God with those who lived before them; and no change canst thou find in the way of God.

Men will ask thee of 'the Hour.' SAY: The knowledge of it is with God alone: and who can tell thee whether haply the Hour be not nigh at hand?

Verily, God hath cursed the Infidels, and hath got ready for them the flame:

For aye shall they abide therein; none to befriend them, no helper shall they find!

On the day when their faces shall be rolled in the fire, they shall cry: 'Oh! would that we had obeyed God, and obeyed the Apostle!'

And they shall say: 'Oh our Lord! indeed we obeyed our chiefs and our great ones, and they misled us from the way *of God* –

O our Lord! give them a double chastisement, and curse them with a heavy curse.'

O Believers! be not like those who affronted Moses.[25] But God cleared him from what they said of him, and of God was he highly esteemed.

70 O Believers! fear God, and speak with well-guided speech.

That God may bless your doings for you, and forgive you your sins. And whoso obeyeth God and His Apostle with great bliss shall he be blessed.

Verily, we proposed to the Heavens, and to the Earth, and to the Mountains *to receive* the Faith, but they refused the burden, and they feared to receive it. Man undertook to bear it, but hath proved unjust, senseless!

Therefore will God punish the hypocritical men and the hypocritical women, and the men and the women who join gods with God; but to the believing men and women will God turn him: for God is Indulgent, Merciful!

SURA 34 – SABA[1]

MECCA – 54 VERSES

In the Name of God, the Compassionate, the Merciful

Praise be to God! to whom belongeth all that is in the Heavens and all that is on the Earth; and to Him be praise in the next world: for he is the All-wise, the All-informed!

He knoweth what entereth into the earth, and what proceedeth from it; and what cometh down from heaven, and what goeth up into it: and He is the Merciful, the Forgiving!

'Never,' say the unbelievers, 'will the Hour come upon us!' SAY: Yea, by my Lord who knoweth the unseen, it will surely come upon you! not the weight of a mote either in the Heavens or in the Earth escapeth him; nor is there aught less than this or aught greater, which is not in the clear Book; –

To the intent that God may reward those who have believed and done the things that are right: Pardon and a noble provision shall they receive:

But as for those who aim to invalidate our signs, – a chastisement of painful torment awaiteth them!

And they to whom knowledge hath been given see that what hath been sent down to thee from thy Lord is the truth, and that it guideth into the way of the Glorious one, the Praiseworthy.

But the unbelievers say *to those whom they fall in with*, 'Shall we shew you a man who will foretell you that when ye shall have been utterly torn and rent to pieces, ye shall be restored in a new form?

He deviseth a lie about God, or there is a djinn in him,' but they who believe not in the next life, shall incur the chastisement, and be lost in the mazes of estrangement *from God*.

What! have they never contemplated that which is before

them and behind them, the Heaven and the Earth? If such were our pleasure, we could sink them into that Earth, or cause a portion of that Heaven to fall upon them! herein truly is a sign for our every returning servant.

10 Of old bestowed we on David a gift, our special boon: – 'Ye mountains and ye birds answer his songs of praise.' And we made the iron soft for him: – 'Make coats of mail, and arrange its plates; and work ye righteousness; for I behold your actions.'

And unto Solomon *did we subject* the wind, which travelled in the morning a month's journey, and a month's journey in the evening. And we made a fountain of molten brass to flow for him. And of the Djinn were some who worked in his presence, by the will of his Lord; and such of them as swerved from our bidding will we cause to taste the torment of the flame.

They made for him whatever he pleased, of lofty halls, and images, and dishes large as tanks for watering camels, and cooking pots that stood firmly. 'Work,' *said we*, 'O family of David with thanksgiving:' But few of my servants are the thankful!

And when we decreed the death *of Solomon*, nothing shewed them that he was dead but a reptile of the earth that gnawed the staff *which supported his corpse*.[2] And when it fell, the Djinn perceived that if they had known the things unseen, they had not continued in this shameful affliction.[3]

A sign there was to SABA, in their dwelling places: – two gardens, the one on the right hand and the other on the left: – 'Eat ye of your Lord's supplies, and give thanks to him: Goodly is the country, and gracious is the Lord!'

But they turned aside: so we sent upon them the flood of Irem;[4] and we changed them their gardens into two gardens of bitter fruit and tamarisk and some few jujube trees.

Such was our retribution on them for their ingratitude: but do we thus recompense any except the ungrateful?

And we placed between them and the cities which we have blessed, conspicuous cities, and we fixed easy stages: 'Travel ye through them by night and day, secure.'

But they said, 'O Lord! make the distance between our journeys longer,'[5] – and against themselves did they act unjustly: so we made them a tale, and scattered them with an utter scattering. Truly herein are signs to everyone that is patient, grateful.

And Eblis found that he had judged truly of them: and they
all except a remnant of the faithful, followed him:
20 Yet no power had he over them. Only we would discern
him who believed in the life to come, from him who doubted of
it; for thy Lord watcheth all things.

SAY: Call ye upon those whom ye deem gods, beside God:
their power in the Heavens and in the Earth is not the weight of
an atom – neither have they any share in either; nor hath He a
helper from among them.

No intercession shall avail with Him but that which He shall
Himself allow. Until when at last their hearts shall be relieved
from terror, they shall say, 'What saith your Lord?' they shall
say, 'The Truth; and He is the High, the Great.'

SAY: Who supplieth you out of the Heavens and the
Earth? SAY: God. And either we or ye have guidance, or are
in palpable error!

SAY: Not as to our faults shall ye be questioned; neither shall
we be questioned as to your actions.

SAY: Our Lord will gather us together: then will He judge
between us in justice; for He is the Judge, the Knowing!

SAY: Shew me those whom ye have united with Him as
associates: Nay, rather, He is God, the Mighty, the Wise!

And we have sent thee to mankind at large, to announce and
to threaten. But most men understand not.

And they say, 'When will this threat come to pass? *Tell us*, if
ye be men of truth.'

SAY: Ye are menaced with a day, which not for an hour shall
ye retard or hasten on.
30 The unbelievers say, 'We will not believe in this Koran, nor in
the Books which preceded it.' But couldst thou see when the
wicked shall be set before their Lord! With reproaches will
they answer one another. The weak shall say to the mighty
ones, 'But for you we had been believers:'

Then shall the mighty ones say to the weak, 'What! was it we
who turned you aside from the guidance which had reached
you? Nay, but ye acted wickedly yourselves.'

And the weak shall say to the mighty ones, 'Nay, but there
was a plot by night and by day, when ye bad us believe not in
God, and gave him peers.' And they shall proclaim their
repentance after they have seen the punishment! And yokes

will we place on the necks of those who have not believed! Shall they be rewarded but as they have wrought?

And never have we sent a warner to any city whose opulent men did not say, 'In sooth we disbelieve your message.'

And they said, 'We are the more abundant in riches and in children, nor shall we be among the punished.'

SAY: Of a truth my Lord will be liberal or sparing in his supplies to whom he pleaseth: but the greater part of men acknowledge it not.

Neither by your riches nor by your children shall you bring yourselves into nearness with Us; but they who believe and do the thing that is right shall have a double reward for what they shall have done: and in the pavilions of Paradise shall they *dwell* secure!

But they who shall aim to invalidate our signs, shall be consigned to punishment.

SAY: Of a truth my Lord will be liberal in supplies to whom he pleaseth of his servants, or will be sparing to him: and whatever ye shall give in alms he will return; and He is the best dispenser of gifts.

One day he will gather them all together: then shall he say to the angels, 'Did these worship you?'

40 They shall say, 'Glory be to thee! Thou art our master, not these! But they worshipped the Djinn: it was in them that most of them believed.

On this day the one of you shall have no power over others for help or hurt. And we will say to the evil doers, 'Taste ye the torment of the fire, which ye treated as a delusion.'

For when our distinct signs are recited to them, they say, 'This is merely a man who would fain pervert you from your father's Worship.' And they say, 'This (Koran) is no other than a forged falsehood.' And the unbelievers say to the truth when it is presented to them, ''Tis nothing but palpable sorcery.'

Yet have we given them no books in which to study deeply, nor have we sent any one to them before thee, charged with warnings.

They also flourished before them, treated our apostles as impostors in like sort: but not to the tenth part of what we bestowed on them,[6] have these attained. And yet when they charged my apostles with deceit, how terrible was my vengeance:

SAY: One thing in sooth do I advise you: – that ye stand up before God two and two, or singly,[7] and then reflect that in your fellow citizen is no djinn:[8] he is no other than your warner before a severe punishment.

SAY: I ask not any wage from you: keep it for yourselves: my wage is from God alone. And He is witness over all things!

SAY: Truly my Lord sendeth forth the Truth: – Knower of things unseen!

SAY: Truth is come, and falsehood shall vanish and return no more.

SAY: If I err, verily to my own cost only shall I err: but if I have guidance, it will be of my Lord's revealing, for He is the Hearer, the near at hand.

50 Couldst thou see how they shall tremble and find no escape, and be taken forth from the place that is so near;[9]

And shall say, 'We believe in Him!' But how, in their present distance, shall they receive the faith,

When they had before denied it, and aimed their shafts at the mysteries from afar?[10]

And a gulf shall be between them and that which they shall desire –

As was done unto their likes of old, who were *lost* in the questionings of doubt.

SURA 35 – THE CREATOR, OR THE ANGELS

MECCA – 45 VERSES

In the Name of God, the Compassionate, the Merciful

Praise be to God, Maker of the Heavens and of the Earth! Who employeth the ANGELS as envoys, with pairs of wings, two, three, and four: He addeth to his creature what He will! Truly God hath power for all things.

The mercy which God layeth open for man, no one can keep back; and what He shall keep back, none can afterwards send forth. And He is the Mighty, the Wise.

O men! bear in mind the favour of God towards you. Is

there a creator other than God, who nourisheth you with the gifts of heaven and earth? There is no God but He! How then are ye turned aside *from Him?*

If they treat thee as an impostor, then before thee have apostles been treated as impostors. But to God shall all things return.

O men! assuredly the promise of God is true: let not then the present life deceive you: and let not the Deceiver deceive you as to God.

Yes, Satan is your foe. For a foe then hold him. He calleth his followers to him that they may become inmates of the flame.

The unbelievers, – for them a terrible punishment!

But believers and doers of good works, for them is mercy, and a great reward!

Shall he, the evil of whose deeds are so tricked out to him that he deemeth them good, *be treated like him who seeth things aright?* Verily God misleadeth whom He will, and guideth whom He will. Spend not thy soul in sighs for them: God knoweth their doings.

10 It is God who sendeth forth the winds which raise the clouds aloft: then drive we them on to some land dead *from drought*, and give life thereby to the earth after its death. So shall be the resurrection.

If any one desireth greatness, all greatness is in God. The good word riseth up to Him, and the righteous deed will He exalt. But a severe punishment awaiteth the plotters of evil things; and the plots of such will He render vain.

Moreover, God created you of dust – then of the germs of life – then made you two sexes: and no female conceiveth or bringeth forth without his knowledge; and the aged ageth not, nor is aught minished from man's age, but in accordance with the Book. An easy thing truly is this to God.

Nor are the two seas[1] alike: the one fresh, sweet, pleasant for drink, and the other salt, bitter; yet from both ye eat fresh fish, and take forth for you ornaments to wear, and thou seest the ships cleaving their waters that ye may go in quest of his bounties, and that ye may be thankful.

He causeth the night to enter in upon the day, and the day to enter in upon the night; and He hath given laws to the sun and to the moon, so that each journeyeth to its appointed goal: This is God your Lord: All power is His: But the gods whom ye call on beside Him have no power over the husk of a date stone!

If ye cry to them they will not hear your cry; and if they heard they would not answer you, and in the day of resurrection they will disown your joining them with God: and none can instruct thee like Him who is informed of all.

O men! ye are but paupers in need of God; but God is the Rich, the Praiseworthy!

If He please, He could sweep you away, and bring forth a new creation!

Nor will this be hard for God.

And the burdened soul shall not bear the burden of another: and if the heavy laden soul cry out for its burden to be carried, yet shall not aught of it be carried, even by the near of kin! Thou shalt warn those who fear their Lord in secret, and observe prayer. And whoever shall keep himself pure, he purifieth himself to his own behoof: for unto God shall be the final gathering.

20 And the blind and the seeing are not alike; neither darkness
and light; nor the shade and the hot wind;

Nor are the living and the dead the same thing! God indeed shall make whom He will to hearken, but thou shalt not make those who are in their graves to hearken; for only with warning art thou charged.

Verily we have sent thee with the truth; a bearer of good tidings and a warner; nor hath there been a people unvisited by its warner.

And if they treat thee as a liar, so did those who were before them treat their Apostles who came to them with the proofs *of their mission*, and with the Scriptures and with the enlightening Book:[2]

Then chastised I the unbelievers: and how great was my vengeance!

Seest thou not how that God sendeth down water from the Heaven, and that by it we cause the up-growth of fruits of varied hues, and that on the mountains[3] are tracks of varied hues, white and red, and others are of a raven black? And of men and reptiles and animals, various likewise are the hues. Such only of his servants as are possessed of knowledge fear God. Lo! God is Mighty, Gracious!

Verily they who recite the Book of God, and observe prayer, and give alms in public and in private from what we have bestowed upon them, may hope for a merchandise that shall not perish:

God will certainly pay them their due wages, and of his bounty increase them: for He is Gracious, Grateful,

And that which we have revealed to thee of the Book is the very Truth, confirmatory of previous Scriptures: for God knoweth and beholdeth his servants.

Moreover, we have made the Book an heritage to those of our servants whom we have chosen. Some of them injure themselves by evil deeds; others keep the midway *between good and evil*; and others, by the permission of God, outstrip in goodness; this is the great merit!

30 Into the gardens of Eden shall they enter: with bracelets of gold and pearl shall they be decked therein, and therein shall their raiment be of silk:

And they shall say, 'Praise be to God who hath put away sorrow from us. Verily our Lord is Gracious, Grateful,

Who of His bounty hath placed us in a mansion that shall abide for ever: therein no toil shall reach us, and therein no weariness shall touch us.'

But for infidels is the fire of Hell; to die shall never be decreed them, nor shall aught of its torment be made light to them. Thus reward we every infidel!

And therein shall they cry aloud, 'Take us hence, O our Lord! righteousness will we work, and not what we wrought of old.' – 'Prolonged we not your days that whoever would be warned might be warned therein? And the preacher came to you –

Taste it then.' – There is no protector for the unjust.

God truly knoweth the hidden things both of the Heavens and of the Earth: for He knoweth the very secrets of the breast.

He hath appointed you his vicegerents in the earth: And whoever believeth not, on him shall be his unbelief; and their unbelief shall only increase for the unbelievers, hatred at the hands of their Lord: – and their unbelief shall only increase for the unbelievers their own perdition!

SAY: What think ye of the gods whom ye invoke beside God? Shew me what part of the earth they have created? Had they a share *in the creation* of the Heavens? Have we given them a Book in which they can find proofs *that they are to be called on?* Nay, the wicked promise one another only deceits.

Verily God holdeth fast the Heavens and the Earth that they

pass not away: and if they were passing away none could hold them back but He: for He is Kind, Gracious.

40 They swore by God with their mightiest oath that should a preacher come to them they would yield to guidance more than any people: but when the preacher came to them it only increased in them their estrangement,

Their haughtiness on earth and their plotting of evil! But the plotting of evil shall only enmesh those who make use of it.[4] Look they then for aught but God's way[5] *of dealing* with the peoples of old? Thou shalt not find any change in the way of God, –

Yea, thou shalt not find any variableness in the way of God.

Have they never journeyed in the land and seen what hath been the end of those who flourished before them, though mightier in strength than they? God is not to be frustrated by aught in the Heavens or in the Earth; for He is the All-knowing, the All-mighty.

If, moreover, God should chastise men according to their deserts, He would not leave even a reptile on the back *of the earth!* But to an appointed time doth He respite them.

And when their time shall come, then verily God's eye is on his servants.

SURA 36 – YA. SIN.

MECCA – 83 VERSES

In the Name of God, the Compassionate, the Merciful

YA. SIN.[1] By the wise Koran!

Surely of the Sent Ones, Thou,

Upon a right path!

A revelation of the Mighty, the Merciful,

That thou shouldest warn a people whose fathers were not warned and therefore lived in heedlessness!

Just, now, is our sentence[2] against most of them; therefore they shall not believe.

On their necks have we placed chains which reach the chin, and forced up are their heads:

Before them have we set a barrier and behind them a barrier, and we have shrouded them in a veil, so that they shall not see.

Alike is it to them if thou warn them or warn them not: they will not believe.

10 Him only shalt thou really warn, who followeth the monition and feareth the God of mercy in secret: him cheer with tidings of pardon, and of a noble recompense.

Verily, it is We who will quicken the dead, and write down the works which they have sent on before them, and the traces which they shall have left behind them: and everything have we set down in the clear Book of our decrees.[3]

Set forth to them the instance of the people of the city[4] when the Sent Ones came to it.

When we sent two unto them and they charged them both with imposture – therefore with a third we strengthened them: and they said, 'Verily we are the Sent unto you *of God*.'

They said, 'Ye are only men like us: Nought hath the God of Mercy sent down. Ye do nothing but lie.'

They said, 'Our Lord knoweth that we are surely sent unto you;

To proclaim a clear message is our only duty.'

They said, 'Of a truth we augur ill from you:[5] if ye desist not we will surely stone you, and a grievous punishment will surely befal you from us.'

They said, 'Your augury of ill is with yourselves. Will ye be warned?[6] Nay, ye are an erring people.'

Then from the end of the city a man came running:[7] He said, 'O my people! follow the Sent Ones;

20 Follow those who ask not of you a recompense, and who are rightly guided.

And why should I not worship Him who made me, and to whom ye shall be brought back?

Shall I take gods beside Him? If the God of Mercy be pleased to afflict me, their intercession will not avert from me aught, nor will they deliver:

Truly then should I be in a manifest error.

Verily, in your Lord have I believed; therefore hear me.'

– It was said to him, 'Enter thou into Paradise:' And he said, 'Oh that my people knew

How gracious God hath been to me, and that He hath made me one of *His* honoured ones.'

But no army sent we down out of heaven after his *death*, nor were we then sending down *our angels* –

There was but one shout *from Gabriel*, and lo! they were extinct.

Oh! the misery *that rests* upon my servants! No apostle cometh to them but they laugh him to scorn.

30 See they not how many generations we have destroyed before them?

Not to *false gods* is it that they shall be brought[8] back,

But all, gathered together, shall be set before Us.

Moreover, the dead earth is a sign to them: we quicken it and bring forth the grain from it, and they eat thereof:

And we make in it gardens of the date and vine; and we cause springs to gush forth in it;

That they may eat of its fruits and of the labour of their hands. Will they not therefore be thankful?

Glory be to Him, who hath created all the sexual pairs of such things as Earth produceth,[9] and of *mankind* themselves; and of things beyond their ken!

A sign to them also is the Night. We withdraw the day from it, and lo! they are plunged in darkness;

And the Sun hasteneth to her place of rest. This, the ordinance of the Mighty, the Knowing!

And as for the Moon, We have decreed stations for it, till it change like an old and crooked palm branch.

40 To the Sun it is not given to overtake the Moon, nor doth the night outstrip the day; but each in its own sphere doth journey on.

It is also a sign to them that we bare their posterity in the full-laden Ark;

And that we have made for them vessels like it on which they embark;

And if we please, we drown them, and there is none to help them, and they are not rescued,

Unless through our mercy, and that they may enjoy themselves for yet awhile.

And when it is said to them, Fear what is before you and what is behind you,[10] that ye may obtain mercy. . .

Aye, not one sign from among the signs of their Lord dost thou bring them, but they turn away from it!

And when it is said to them, Give alms of what God hath bestowed on you,[11] they who believe not say to the believers, 'Shall we feed him whom God can feed if He will? Truly ye are in no other than a plain error.'

And they say, 'When will this promise be fulfilled, if what ye say be true?'

They await but a single blast: as they are wrangling shall it assail them:

50 And not a bequest shall they be able to make, nor to their families shall they return.

And the trumpet shall be blown, and, lo! they shall speed out of their sepulchres to their Lord:

They shall say, 'Oh! woe to us! who hath roused us from our sleeping place? 'Tis what the God of Mercy promised; and the Apostles spake the truth.'

But one blast shall there be,[12] and, lo! they shall be assembled before us, all together.

And on that day shall no soul be wronged in the least: neither shall ye be rewarded but as ye shall have wrought.

But joyous on that day shall be the inmates of Paradise, in their employ;

In shades, on bridal couches reclining, they and their spouses:

Therein shall they have fruits, and shall have whatever they require –

'Peace!' shall be the word on the part of a merciful Lord.

'But be ye separated this day, O ye sinners!

60 Did I not enjoin on you, O sons of Adam, "Worship not Satan, for that he is your declared foe,"

But "Worship Me: this is a right path"?

But now hath he led a vast host of you astray. Did ye not then comprehend?

This is Hell with which ye were threatened:

Endure its heat this day, for that ye believed not.'

On that day will we set a seal upon their mouths; yet shall their hands speak unto us, and their feet[13] shall bear witness of that which they shall have done.

And, if we pleased, we would surely put out their eyes: yet even then would they speed on with rivalry in their path: but how should they see?

And, if we pleased, we would surely transform them as they

stand,[14] and they would not be able to move onward, or to return.

Him cause we to stoop *through age* whose days we lengthen. Will they not understand?

We have not taught him (Muhammad) poetry,[15] nor would it beseem him. This *Book* is no other than a warning and a clear Koran,

70 To warn whoever liveth; and, that against the Infidels sentence may be justly given.

See they not that we have created for them among the things which our hands have wrought, the animals of which they are masters?

And that we have subjected them unto them? And on some they ride, and of others they eat;

And they find in them profitable uses and beverages:

Yet have they taken other gods beside God that they might be helpful to them.

No power have they to succour them: yet are *their votaries* an army at their service.

Let not their speech grieve thee: We know what they hide and what they bring to light.

Doth not man perceive that we have created him of the moist germs of life? Yet lo! is he an open caviller.

And he meeteth us with arguments,[16] and forgetteth his creation: 'Who,' saith he, 'shall give life to bones when they are rotten?'

SAY: He shall give life to them who gave them being at first, for in all creation is he skilled:

80 Who even out of the green tree hath given you fire,[17] and lo! ye kindle flame from it.

What! must not He who hath created the Heavens and the Earth be mighty enough to create your likes? Yes! and He is the skilful creator.

His command when He willeth aught, is but to say to it, BE, and IT IS.

So glory be to Him in whose hand is sway over all things! And to Him shall ye be brought back.

SURA 37 – THE RANKS

MECCA – 182 VERSES

In the Name of God, the Compassionate, the Merciful

By the angels ranged in order for Songs of Praise,
And by those who repel demons,[1]
And by those who recite *the Koran* for warning,
Truly your God is but one,
Lord of the Heavens and of the Earth, and of all that is between them, and Lord of the East.[2]
We have adorned the lower heaven with the adornment of the stars.
They serve also as a guard against every rebellious Satan,
That they overhear not what passeth in the assembly on high, for they are darted at from every side,[3]
Driven off and consigned to a lasting torment;
10 While, if one steal *a word by* stealth, a glistening flame pursueth him.
Ask the *Meccans* then, Are they, or *the angels* whom we have made, the stronger creation? Aye, of coarse clay have we created them.
But while thou marvellest they mock;
When they are warned, no warning do they take;
And when they see a sign, they fall to mocking,
And say, 'This is no other than clear sorcery:
What! when dead, and turned to dust and bones, shall we indeed be raised?
Our sires also of olden times?'
SAY, Yes; and ye shall be covered with disgrace.
For, one blast only, and lo! they shall gaze around them,
20 And shall say, 'Oh! woe to us! this is the day of reckoning;
This is the day of decision which ye gainsaid as an untruth.'
Gather together those who have acted unjustly, and their consorts,[4] and the gods whom they adored
Beside God; and guide them to the road for Hell.
Set them forth: they shall be questioned.
'How now, that ye help not one another?'
But on this day they shall submit themselves to God,
And shall address one another with mutual reproaches.

They shall say, 'In sooth, ye came to us in well-omened sort:'[5]

But they will answer, 'Nay, it was ye who would not believe; and we had no power whatever over you. Nay, ye were people given to transgress;

30 Just, therefore, is the doom which our Lord hath passed upon us.[6] We shall surely taste it:

We made you err, for we had erred ourselves.'

Partners therefore shall they be in punishment on that day.

Truly, thus will we deal with the wicked,

Because when it was said to them, There is no God but God, they swelled with pride,

And said, 'Shall we then abandon our gods for a crazed poet?'

Nay, he cometh with truth and confirmeth the Sent Ones of old.

Ye shall surely taste the painful punishment,

And ye shall not be rewarded but as ye have wrought,

Save the sincere servants of God!

40 A stated banquet shall they have

Of fruits; and honoured shall they be

In the gardens of delight,

Upon couches face to face.

A cup shall be borne round among them from a fountain,

Limpid, delicious to those who drink;

It shall not oppress the sense, nor shall they therewith be drunken.

And with them are the large-eyed ones with modest refraining glances, fair like the sheltered egg.[7]

And they shall address one another with mutual questions.

Saith one of them, 'I truly had a bosom friend,

50 Who said, "Art thou of those who credit it?

What! when we shall have died, and become dust and bones, shall we indeed be judged?"'

He shall say *to those around him*, 'Will ye look?'

And he shall look and see him in the midst of Hell.

And he shall say to him, 'By God, thou hadst almost caused me to perish;

And, but for the favour of my Lord, I had surely been of those who have been brought *with thee into torment*.'

'But do we not die,' *say the blessed*,

'Any other than our first death? and have we escaped the torment?'[8]

This truly is the great felicity!
For the like of this should the travailers travail!
60 Is this the better repast or the tree Ez-zakkoum?
Verily, we have made it for a subject of discord to the wicked.
It is a tree which cometh up from the bottom of hell;
Its fruits is as it were the heads of Satans;
And, lo! the *damned* shall surely eat of it and fill their bellies with it:
Then shall they have, thereon, a mixture of boiling water:
Then shall they return to hell.
They found their fathers erring,
And they hastened on in their footsteps.
Also before them the greater number of the ancients had erred,
70 Though we had sent warners among them.
But see what was the end of these warned ones,
Except of God's true servants.
Noah called on us of old, and right prompt were we to hear him,[9]
And we saved him and his family out of the great distress,
And we made his offspring the survivors;
And we left for him with posterity,
'Peace be on Noah throughout the Worlds!'
Thus do we reward the well-doers,
For he was one of our believing servants; –
80 And the rest we drowned.
And truly, of his faith was Abraham,
When he brought to his Lord a perfect heart,
When he said to his father and to his people, 'What is this ye worship?
Prefer ye with falsehood gods to God?
And what deem ye of the Lord of the worlds?'
So gazing he gazed towards the stars,
And said, 'In sooth I am ill:[10]
And they turned their back on him and departed.
He went aside to their gods and said, 'Do ye not eat?
90 What aileth you that ye do not speak?'
He broke out upon them, with the right hand striking:
When his tribesmen came back to him with hasty steps –
He said, 'Worship ye what ye carve,
When God hath created you, and that ye make?'

They said, 'Build up a pyre for him and cast him into the glowing flame.'
Fain would they plot against him, but we brought them low.
And he said, 'Verily, I repair to my Lord who will guide me:
O Lord give me *a son*, of the righteous.'
We announced to him a youth of meekness.
100 And when he became a full-grown youth,[11]
His father said to him, 'My son, I have seen in a dream that I should sacrifice thee; therefore, consider what thou seest *right*.'
He said, 'My father, do what thou art bidden; of the patient, if God please, shalt thou find me.'
And when they had surrendered them to the will of God, he laid him down upon his forehead:
We cried unto him, 'O Abraham!
Now hast thou satisfied the vision.' See how we recompense the righteous.
This was indeed a decisive test.
And we ransomed his *son* with a costly[12] victim,
And we left this[13] for him among posterity,
'PEACE BE ON ABRAHAM!'
110 Thus do we reward the well-doers,
For he was of our believing servants.
And we announced Isaac to him – a righteous Prophet –
And on him and on Isaac we bestowed our blessing. And among their offspring were well-doers, and others, to their own hurt undoubted sinners.
And of old,[14] to Moses and to Aaron shewed we favours:
And both of them, and their people, we rescued from the great distress:
And we succoured them, and they became the conquerors:
And we gave them (Moses and Aaron) each the lucid book:
And we guided them each into the right way:
And we left *this* for each among posterity,
120 'PEACE BE ON MOSES AND AARON.'
Thus do we reward the well-doers,
For they were two of our believing servants.
And Elias truly was of our Sent Ones,
When he said to his people, 'Fear ye not God?
Invoke ye Baal and forsake ye the most skilful Creator?
God is your Lord, and the Lord of your sires of old?'

But they treated him as a liar, and shall therefore be consigned *to punishment*,
Except God's faithful servants.
And we left this for him among posterity,
130 'PEACE BE ON ELIASIN!'[15]
Thus do we reward the well-doers,
For he was one of our believing servants.
And Lot truly was of our Sent Ones,
When we rescued him and all his family,
Save an aged woman among those who tarried.
Afterward we destroyed the others.
And ye indeed pass by their *ruined dwellings* at morn
And night: will ye not then reflect?
Jonas, too, was one of the Apostles,
140 When he fled unto the laden ship,
And lots were cast[16] and he was doomed,
And the fish swallowed him, for he was blameworthy.
But had he not been of those who praise Us,
In its belly had he surely remained, till the day of resurrection.
And we cast him on the bare *shore* – and he was sick; –
And we caused a gourd-plant to grow up over him,
And we sent him to a hundred thousand persons, or even more,
And because they believed, we continued their enjoyments for a season.
Inquire then of the *Meccans* whether thy Lord hath daughters, and they, sons?
150 Have we created the angels females? and did they witness it?
Is it not a falsehood of their own devising, when they say,
'God hath begotten'? They are indeed liars.
Would he have preferred daughters to sons?
What reason have ye for thus judging?
Will ye not then receive this warning?
Have ye a clear proof *for them?*
Produce your Book if ye speak truth.
And they make him to be of kin with the Djinn: but the Djinn have long known that *these idolaters* shall be brought up before God.
Far be the glory of God from what they impute to him.
160 'His faithful servants do not thus.

Moreover, ye and what ye worship
Shall not stir up any against God,[17]
Save him who shall burn in Hell.
And verily each one of us hath his appointed place,
And we range ourselves in order,
And we celebrate His praises.'[18]
And if those *infidels* say,
'Had we a revelation transmitted to us from those of old,[19]
We had surely been God's faithful servants.'

170 Yet they believe not *the Koran.* But they shall know *its truth* at last.
Our word came of old to our servants the apostles,
That they should surely be the succoured,
And that our armies should procure the victory for them.
Turn aside therefore from them for a time,
And behold them, for they too shall in the end behold *their doom.*
Would they then hasten our vengeance?
But when it shall come down into their courts, an evil morning shall it be to those who have had their warning.
Turn aside from them therefore for a time.
And behold; for they too shall in the end behold *their doom.*

180 Far be the glory of thy Lord, the Lord of all greatness, from what they impute to him,
And peace be on his Apostles!
And praise be to God the Lord of the Worlds.

SURA 38 – SAD

MECCA – 88 VERSES

In the Name of God, the Compassionate, the Merciful

SAD.[1] By the Koran full of warning! In sooth the Infidels are *absorbed* in pride, in contention *with thee.*
How many generations have we destroyed before them! And they cried *for mercy* but no time was it of escape!

And they marvel that a warner from among themselves hath come to them; and the Infidels say, 'This is a sorcerer, a liar:

Maketh he the gods to be but one god? A strange thing forsooth is this!'

And their chiefs took themselves off. 'Go, *said they*, and cleave steadfastly[2] to your gods. Ye see the thing aimed at.

We heard not of this in the previous creed.[3] It is but an imposture:

To him alone of us all hath a *book of* warning been sent down?' Yes! they are in doubt as to my warnings, for they have not yet tasted my vengeance.

Are the treasures of the mercy of thy Lord, the Mighty, the bounteous, in their hands?

Is the kingdom of the heavens and of the earth and of all that is between them theirs? Then let them mount up by cords!

10 Any army of the confederates[4] shall here be routed.

Before them the people of Noah and Ad and Pharaoh the impaler[5] treated their prophets as impostors;

And Themoud, and the people of Lot, and the dwellers in the forest: these were the confederates.

Nought did they all but charge the apostles with falsehood: Just, therefore, the retribution.

And these (Meccans) await but one single trumpet blast – There shall be no delaying it –

Yet they *dare to* say, 'O our Lord! hasten our lot to us, before the day of reckoning.'

Put thou up with what they say: and remember our servant David, a man strong of hand,[6] one who turned him to Us in penitence:

We constrained the mountains[7] to join with him in lauds at even and at sunrise;

And the birds which flocked *to him*, and would all return to him oft;

And we stablished his kingdom: and wisdom, and skill to pronounce clear decisions, did we bestow on him.

20 Hath the story of the two pleaders[8] reached thee, O *Muhammad*, when they mounted the walls of *his* closet?

When they entered in upon David, and he was frightened at them, they said, 'Be not afraid; we are two opposing parties: one of us hath wronged the other. Judge therefore with truth between us, and be not unjust, but guide us to the right way.

Now this my brother had ninety and nine ewes, and I had but a single ewe; and he said, make me her keeper. And he over-persuaded me in the dispute.'

He said, 'Certainly he hath wronged thee in asking for thine ewe *to add her* to his own ewes: and truly many associates do one another wrong – except those who believe and do the things that are right; and few indeed are they!' And David perceived that we had tried him; so he asked pardon of his Lord, and fell down and bowed himself and repented.

So we forgave him that *his sin;* and truly he shall have a high rank with Us, and an excellent retreat *in Paradise.*

O David! verily we have made thee our vicegerent upon earth. Judge therefore between men with truth, and follow not thy passions, lest they cause thee to err from the way of God. For they who err from the way of God shall meet with a grievous chastisement, for that they have forgotten the day of reckoning.

We have not created the heaven and the earth and what is between them for nought. That is the thought of infidels; but woe to the infidels because of the fire!

Shall we treat those who believe and do the things that are right like those who propagate evil on earth? Shall we treat the God-fearing like the impious?

A blessed Book[9] have we sent down to thee, that *men* may meditate its verses, and that those endued with understanding may bear it in mind.

And Solomon gave we unto David. An excellent servant, for he loved to turn him Godward.

30 *Remember* when at eventide the prancing[10] chargers were displayed before him,

And he said, 'Truly I have loved the love of earthly goods above the remembrance of my Lord, till the sun hath been hidden by the veil of darkness.[11]

Bring them back to me.' And he began to sever the legs and necks.

We also made trial of Solomon, and placed a phantom[12] on his throne: whereupon he returned *to Us* (in penitence).

He said, O my Lord! pardon me, and give me a dominion that may not be to any one beside me, for thou art the liberal giver.

So we subjected the wind to him; it ran softly at his bidding, whithersoever he directed it:

And the Satans – every builder and diver –

And others bound in chains:[13]

'This,' said we, 'is our gift: be bounteous then, or withhold thy favours; no account shalt thou render.'

And his rank also is high with Us, and an excellent retreat.

40 And remember our servant Job when he cried to his Lord, 'Verily, Satan hath laid on me disease and pain.'

'Stamp,' said we, 'with thy foot. This[14] is to wash with; cool, and to drink.'

And we gave him back his family, and as many more with them in our mercy; and for a monition to men of judgment.

And *we said*, 'Take in thine hand a rod, and strike[15] with it, nor break thine oath.' Verily, we found him patient!

How excellent a servant, one who turned to Us was he!

And remember our servants Abraham and Isaac and Jacob, men of might and vision.[16]

With this cleansing did we cleanse them – the remembrance of the abode of *Paradise*.

And verily, they were, in our sight, of the elect and of the good.

And remember Ishmael and Elisha and Dhoulkefl, for all these were of the just.

This is a monition: and verily, the pious shall have a goodly retreat:

50 Gardens of Eden, whose portals shall stand open to them:

Therein reclining, they shall there call for many a fruit and drink:

And with them shall be *virgins* of their own age, with modest retiring glances:

'This is what ye were promised at the day of reckoning.'

'Yes! this is our provision: it shall never fail.'

Even so. But for the evil doers is a wretched home –

Hell – wherein they shall be burned: how wretched a bed!

Even so. Let them then taste it – boiling water and gore,

And other things of kindred sort!

To their leaders it shall be said, 'This company shall be thrown in headlong with you. No greetings shall await them, for they shall be burned in the fire.'

60 They shall say: 'But ye, too! there shall be no welcome for you. It was ye who prepared this for us, and wretched is the abode!'

They will say: 'O our Lord! increase twofold in the fire, the punishment of him who hath brought this upon us.'

And they will say: 'Why see we not the men whom we numbered among the wicked –

Whom we used to treat with scorn? Have they escaped our eyes?'[17]

Verily this is truth – the wrangling together of the people of the fire.

SAY: I am but a warner; and there is no God but God the One, the Almighty!

Lord of the Heavens and of the Earth, and of all that is between them,[18] the Potent, the Forgiving!

SAY: this is a weighty message,[19]

From which ye turn aside!

Yet had I no knowledge of *what passed* among the celestial chiefs when they disputed,[20]

70 – Verily, it hath been revealed to me only because I am a public preacher –

When thy Lord said to the angels, 'I am about to make man of clay,[21]

And when I have formed him and breathed my spirit into him, then worshipping fall down before him.'

And the angels prostrated themselves, all of them with one accord,

Save Eblis. He swelled with pride, and became an unbeliever.

'O Eblis,' said God, 'what hindereth thee from prostrating thyself before him whom my hands have made?

Is it that thou are puffed up with pride? or art thou a being of lofty merit?'

He said: 'I am more excellent than he; me hast thou created of fire:[22] of clay hast thou created him.'

He said: 'Begone then hence: thou art accursed,[23]

And lo! my ban shall be on thee till the day of the reckoning.'

80 He said: 'O my Lord! respite me till the day of Resurrection.'

He said, 'One then of the respited shalt thou be,

Till the day of the time appointed.'

He said: '*I swear* by thy might then that all of them will I seduce,

Save thy sincere servants among them.'

He said: 'It is truth, and the truth I speak. From thee will I surely fill Hell, and with such of them as shall follow thee, one and all.

SAY: I ask no wage of you for this, nor am I one who intermeddleth.

Of a truth *the Koran* is no other than a warning to all creatures.

And after a time shall ye surely know its message.

SURA 39 – THE TROOPS

MECCA – 75 VERSES

In the Name of God, the Compassionate, the Merciful

The Book[1] sent down from God, the Mighty, the Wise!

We have sent down the Book to thee with the truth: serve thou God then, and be sincere in thy worship:

Is not a sincere worship due to God?

But they who take others beside him as lords *saying*, 'We serve them only that they may bring us near to God' – God will judge between them *and the faithful*, concerning that wherein they are at variance.

Verily God will not guide him who is a liar, an infidel.

Had God desired to have had a son, he had surely chosen what he pleased out of his own creation. But praise be to Him! He is God, the One, the Almighty.

For truth[2] hath he created the Heavens and the Earth: It is of Him that the night returneth upon the day and that the day returneth upon the night: and He controlleth the sun and the moon so that each speedeth to an appointed goal. Is He not the Mighty, the Gracious?

He created you all of one man, from whom He afterwards formed his wife; and of cattle He hath sent down to you four pairs.[3] In the wombs of your mothers did He create you by creation upon creation in triple darkness. It is He who is God your Lord: the kingdom is His: There is no God but He. How then are ye so turned aside from Him?

Suppose ye render him no thanks! yet forsooth is God rich

without you: but He is not pleased with thanklessness in His servants: yet if ye be thankful He will be pleased with you. The soul burdened *with its own works* shall not be burdened with the burden of another: hereafter shall ye return to your Lord, and he will tell you of all your works,

10 For he knoweth the very secrets of your breasts.

When some trouble toucheth a man, he turneth to his Lord and calleth on him: yet no sooner hath He enriched him with his favour than he forgetteth Him on whom he before had called, and setteth up peers with God, that he may beguile others from His way. SAY: Enjoy thou thyself yet a little in thine ingratitude! but thou shalt surely be one of the inmates of the fire.

Shall he who observeth the hours of the night, prostrate or standing in devotion, heedful of the life to come, and hoping for the mercy of his Lord . . . ? SAY: Shall they who have knowledge and they who have it not, be treated alike? In sooth, men of understanding *only* will take the warning.

SAY: O my believing servants, fear your Lord. For those who do good in this world there is good: and broad is God's earth[4] – verily those who endure with patience shall be repaid: their reward shall not be by measure.

SAY: I am bidden to serve God with a sincere worship: and I am bidden to be the first of those who surrender themselves to him (Muslims).

SAY: Verily I fear if I rebel against my Lord the punishment of a great day.

SAY: God will I serve, presenting him with a sincere worship:

And serve ye what ye choose beside Him. SAY: The losers truly will they be who shall lose their own souls and their families on the day of resurrection: Is not this the clear ruin?

Canopies of fire shall be over them, and floors *of fire* beneath them. With this doth God alarm his servants: Fear ye me, then, O my servants!

But good tidings are there for those who shun the worship of Thagout and are turned to God. Cheer then with good tidings those my servants who hearken to my word and follow its excellence. These are they whom God guideth, and these are men of insight.

20 Him then on whom the sentence of punishment hath justly lighted – him who is *doomed* to the fire canst thou rescue?

But for those who fear their Lord are storied pavilions beneath which shall the rivers flow: it is the promise of God, and God will not fail in his promise.

Seest thou not that God sendeth down water from heaven, and guideth it along so as to form springs in the earth – then bringeth forth by it corn of varied sorts – then causeth he it to wither, and thou seest it become yellow – then crumbleth it away? Lo! herein is teaching for men of insight.

Shall he then whose breast God hath opened to Islam, and who hath light from his Lord . . . ? But woe to those whose hearts are hardened against the remembrance of God! They plainly err.

The best of recitals hath God sent down – a book in unison with itself, and teaching by iteration.[5] The very skins of those who fear their Lord do creep at it! Then do their skins and their hearts soften at the remembrance of their Lord! This is God's guidance: by it will He guide whom He pleaseth; and, whom God shall mislead, no guide shall there be for him.

Shall he who shall have nought but his own face to shelter him with from the torment of the punishment on the day of the resurrection . . . ? Aye, to the evil doers it shall be said, 'Taste what ye have earned.'

They who were before them said it was a lie; but a punishment came upon them whence they looked not for it:

And God made them taste humiliation in this present life: but greater surely will be the punishment of the life to come. Did they but know it!

Now have we set before man in this Koran every kind of parable for their warning:

An Arabic Koran, free from tortuous wording, to the intent that they may fear God.

30 God setteth forth the comparison of a man with associates[6] at variance among themselves, and of a man devoted wholly to a man. Are these to be held alike? No, praise be to God! But the greater part of them understand not.

Thou truly shall die, O *Muhammad*, and they too shall die:

Then, at the day of resurrection, ye shall wrangle with one another in the presence of your Lord.

And who acteth more unjustly than he who lieth of God, and treateth the truth when it cometh to him as a lie? Is there not a dwelling-place in Hell for the infidels?

But he who bringeth the truth, and he who believeth it to be the truth: these are the God-fearing.

Whatever they shall desire, awaiteth them with their Lord! This is the reward of the righteous;

That God may do away the guilt of their worst actions, and for their best actions render them their reward.

Is not God all-sufficient for his servant? Yet would they scare thee by their idols. But no guide shall there be for him whom God misleadeth:

And he whom God guideth shall have none to mislead him. Is not God, all-mighty, able to revenge?

And if thou ask them who hath created the Heavens and the Earth, they will surely answer, God. SAY: Think ye, then, that they[7] on whom ye call beside God, if God choose to afflict me, could remove his affliction? or if he choose to show me mercy, could they withhold His mercy? SAY: God sufficeth me: in Him let the trusting trust.

40 SAY: O my people, act your part as best ye can, I too will act mine; and in the end ye shall know

On whom shall light a punishment that shall shame him, and on whom a lasting punishment shall fall.

Assuredly we have sent down the Book to thee for man and for the ends of truth. Whoso shall be guided by it – it will be for his own advantage, and whoso shall err, shall only err to his own loss. But not to thy keeping are they entrusted.

God taketh souls unto Himself at death; and during their sleep those who do not die:[8] and he retaineth those on which he hath passed a decree of death, but sendeth the others back till a time that is fixed. Herein are signs for the reflecting.

Have they taken aught beside God as intercessors? SAY: What! though they have no power over anything, neither do they understand?

SAY: Intercession is wholly with God:[9] His the kingdom of the Heavens and of the Earth! To him shall ye be brought back hereafter!

But when the One God is named, the hearts of those who believe not in the life to come, shrivel up: but when the deities who are adored beside Him are named, lo! they are filled with joy.

SAY: O God, creator of the Heaven and of the Earth, who knowest the hidden and the manifest, thou shalt judge between thy servants as to the subject of their disputes.

If the wicked possessed all that is in the earth and as much again therewith, verily they would ransom themselves with it from the pain of the punishment on the day of the resurrection; and there shall appear to them, from God, things they had never reckoned on:

And their own ill deeds shall be clearly perceived by them, and
that *fire* at which they mocked shall encircle them on every side.
50 When trouble befalleth a man he crieth to Us; afterwards,
when we have vouchsafed favour to him, he saith, 'God knew
that I deserved it.'[10] Nay, it is a trial. But the greater part of
them knew it not.

The same said those who flourished before them; but their deeds profited them not.

And their own ill deeds recoiled upon them. And whoso among these (Meccans) shall do wrong, on them likewise their own misdeeds shall light, neither shall they invalidate God.

Know they not that God giveth supplies with open hand, and that He is sparing to whom He will? Of a truth herein are signs to those who believe.

SAY: O my servants who have transgressed to your own hurt,[11] despair not of God's mercy, for all sins doth God forgive. Gracious, Merciful is He!

And return ye to your Lord, and to Him resign yourselves, ere the punishment come on you, for then ye shall not be helped:

And follow that most excellent *thing* which hath been sent down to you from your Lord, ere the punishment come on you suddenly, and when ye look not for it:

So that a soul say, 'Oh misery! for my failures in duty towards God! and verily I was of those who scoffed:'

Or say, 'Had God guided me, I had surely been of those who feared Him:'

Or say, when it seeth the punishment, 'Could I but return,
then I would be of the righteous.'
60 Nay! my signs had already come to thee, and thou didst treat
them as untruths, and wast arrogant, and becamest of those
who believe not.

And on the resurrection day, thou shalt see those who have lied of God, with their faces black. Is there not an abode in Hell for the arrogant?

But God shall rescue those who fear him into their safe retreat: no ill shall touch them, neither shall they be put to grief.

God is the creator of all things, and of all things is He the guardian! His the keys of the Heavens and of the Earth! and – who believe not in the signs of God – these! they shall perish!

SAY: What! do ye then bid me worship other than God, O ye ignorant ones?

But now hath it been revealed to thee and to those who flourished before thee, – 'Verily, if thou join partners with God, vain shall be all thy work, and thyself shalt be of those who perish.

Nay, rather worship God! and be of those who render thanks.'

But they have not deemed of God as is His due;[12] for on the resurrection day the whole Earth shall be but his handful, and in his right hand shall the Heavens be folded together. Praise be to Him! and high be He uplifted above the partners they join with Him!

And there shall be a blast on the trumpet, and all who are in the Heavens and all who are in the Earth shall expire, save those whom God shall vouchsafe *to live*. Then shall there be another blast on it, and lo! arising they shall gaze around them:

And the earth shall shine with the light of her Lord, and the Book shall be set, and the prophets shall be brought up, and the witnesses; and judgment shall be given between them with equity; and none shall be wronged:

70 And every soul shall receive as it shall have wrought, for well knoweth He men's actions.

And by TROOPS shall the unbelievers be driven towards Hell, until when they reach it, its gates shall be opened, and its keepers shall say to them, 'Came not apostles from among yourselves to you, reciting to you the signs of your Lord, and warning you of the meeting with Him on this your day?' They shall say, 'Yes.' But just is the sentence of punishment on the unbelievers.

It shall be said to them, 'Enter ye the gates of Hell, therein to dwell for ever;' and wretched the abode of the arrogant!

But those who feared their Lord shall be driven on by troops to Paradise, until when they reach it, its gates shall be opened, and its keepers shall say to them, 'All hail! virtuous have ye been: enter then in, to abide herein for ever.'

And they shall say, 'Praise be to God who hath made good to us His promise, and hath given to us the earth as our heritage, that we may dwell in Paradise wherever we please!' And goodly is the reward of those who travailed *virtuously*.

And thou shalt see the Angels circling around the Throne with praises of their Lord: and judgment shall be pronounced between them with equity: and it shall be said, 'Glory be to God the Lord of the Worlds.'

SURA 40 – THE BELIEVER

MECCA – 85 VERSES

In the Name of God, the Compassionate, the Merciful

Ha. Mim. The Revelation (sending down) of the Book is from God the Almighty, the All-knowing,[1]

Forgiver of sin, and receiver of penitence, – vehement in chastisement,

Long-suffering! There is no God but He: to Him shall be the final gathering.

None but infidels gainsay the signs of God: but let not their prosperity in the land deceive thee.

The people of Noah, and the confederates after them, have brought the charge of imposture before these *Meccans:* each nation schemed against their apostle to lay violent hold on him, and disputed with vain words to refute the truth. Therefore did I lay violent hold on them; and how great was my chastisement!

Thus is it that thy Lord's sentence, that inmates shall they be of the fire, was accomplished upon the infidels.

They who bear the throne[2] and they who encircle it, celebrate the praise of their Lord and believe in Him, and implore forgiveness for the believers: – 'O our Lord! thou embracest all things in mercy and knowledge; forgive, therefore, those who turn to thee and follow thy path; keep them from the pains of hell:

O our Lord! and bring them into the Gardens of Eden which thou hast promised to them, and to the righteous ones of their fathers and their wives and their children; for thou art the All-mighty, the All-wise:

And keep them from evil: for on him hast thou mercy whom on that day thou shalt keep from evil;' and this will be the great felicity.

10 But to the infidels shall a voice cry, 'Surely the hatred of God is more grievous than your hatred of yourselves, when ye were called to the faith, and remained unbelievers.'

They shall say, 'Twice, O our Lord, hast thou given us death, and twice hast thou given us life:[3] and we acknowledge our sins: is there no way to escape?'

'This hath befallen you, for that when One God was proclaimed to you, ye believed not: but when partners had been united with him, ye believed: But judgment belongeth unto God, the High, the Great.'

It is He who sheweth you his signs, and sendeth down supplies to you from Heaven: but none will receive warning save he who turneth to God.

Call then on God, offering him a pure worship, though the infidels abhor it.

Of exalted grade, of the throne possessed, He sendeth forth the Spirit at His own behest on whomsoever of His servants He pleaseth, that He may warn of the day of meeting,

The day when they shall come forth *from their graves*, when nought that concerneth them shall be hidden from God. With whom shall be the power supreme on that day? With God, the One, the Almighty.

On that day shall every soul be recompensed as it hath deserved: no injustice on that day! Verily, God will be swift to reckon.

Warn them, then, of the approaching day, when *men's* hearts shall rise up, choking them, into their throats.

The evil doers shall have no friend or intercessor who shall prevail.

20 God knoweth the deceitful of eye, and what men's breasts conceal.

And everything will God decide with truth: But nothing shall those gods whom men call on beside him, decide. Verily, God! the Hearer, the Beholder, He!

Have they never journeyed in this land, and seen what hath been the end of those who flourished before them? Mightier were they in strength than these *Meccans*, and their traces *remain* in the land: Yet God took them in their sins, and there was none to defend them against God.

This, because their apostles had come to them with proofs *of their mission*, and they believed not: so God took them in hand; for He is mighty, vehement in punishing.

Moreover we had sent Moses of old with our signs and with clear authority.

To Pharaoh, and Haman, and Karun:[4] and they said, 'Sorcerer, impostor.'

And when he came to them from our presence with the truth, they said, 'Slay the sons of those who believe as he doth, and save their females alive;' but the stratagem of the unbelievers issued only in failure.

And Pharaoh said, 'Let me alone, that I may kill Moses; and let him call upon his Lord: I fear lest he change your religion, or cause disorder to shew itself in the land.'

And Moses said, 'I take refuge with my Lord and your Lord from every proud one who believeth not in the day of reckoning.'

And a man of the family of Pharaoh, who was a BELIEVER,[5] but hid his faith, said, 'Will ye slay a man because he saith my Lord is God, when he hath already come to you with proofs *of his mission* from your Lord? and if he be a liar, on him will be his lie:[6] but if he be a man of truth, part at least of what he threateneth will fall upon you. Truly God guideth not him who is a transgressor, a liar.

30 O my people! this day is the kingdom yours, the eminent of the earth! but who shall defend us from the vengeance of God if it come on us?' Pharaoh said, 'I would have you see only what I see; and in a right way only will I guide you.'

Then said he who believed, 'O my people! truly I fear for you the like of the day of the allies,[7]

The like of the state of the people of Noah and Ad and Themoud,

And of those who came after them; yet God willeth not injustice to his servants.

And, O my people! I indeed fear for you the day of mutual outcry –

The day when ye shall be turned back *from the Judgment into hell*. No protector shall ye have then against God. And he whom God shall mislead no guide shall there be for him.

Moreover, Joseph had come to you before with clear tokens, but ye ceased not to doubt of the message with which he came to you, until when he died, ye said, "God will by no means raise up an apostle after him."' Thus God misleadeth him who is the transgressor, the doubter.

They who gainsay the signs of God without authority having come to them, are greatly hated by God and by those who believe. Thus God sealeth up every proud, contumacious heart.

And Pharaoh said, 'O Haman,[8] Build for me a tower that I may reach the avenues,

The avenues of the heavens, and may mount to the God of Moses, for I verily deem him a liar.'

40 And thus the evil of his doings was made fair-seeming to Pharaoh, and he turned away from the path *of truth;* but the artifice of Pharaoh ended only in his ruin.

And he who believed said, 'O my people! follow me: into the right way will I guide you.

O my people! this present life is only a passing joy, but the life to come is the mansion that abideth.

Whoso shall have wrought evil shall not be recompensed but with its like; but whoso shall have done the things that are right, whether male or female, and is a believer – these shall enter paradise: good things unreckoned shall they enjoy therein.

And, O my people! how is it that I bid you to salvation, but that ye bid me to the fire?

Ye invite me to deny God, and to join with him gods of whom I know nothing; but I invite you to the Mighty, the Forgiving.

No doubt is there that they to whom ye invite me are not to be invoked either in this world or in the world to come: and that unto God is our return, and that the transgressors shall be the inmates of the fire.

Then shall ye remember what I am saying unto you: and to God commit I my case: Verily, God beholdeth his servants.'

So God preserved him from the evils which they had planned, and the woe of the punishment encompassed the people of Pharaoh.

It is the fire to which they shall be exposed morning and evening, and on the day when 'the Hour' shall arrive – 'Bring in the people of Pharaoh into the severest punishment.'

50 And when they shall wrangle together in the fire, the weak

shall say to those who had borne themselves so proudly, 'It is you we followed: will ye therefore relieve us from aught of the fire?'

And those proud ones shall say, 'Verily we are all in it; for now hath God judged between his servants.'

And they who are in the fire shall say to the keepers of Hell, 'Implore your Lord that he would give us ease but for one day from this torment.'

They shall say, 'Came not your apostles to you with the tokens?' They shall say, 'Yes.' They shall say, 'Cry ye then aloud *for help:*' but the cry of the unbelievers shall be only in vain.

Assuredly, in this present life will we succour our apostles and those who shall have believed, and on the day when the witnesses shall stand forth;

A day whereon the plea of the evil doers shall not avail them; but theirs shall be a curse, and theirs the woe of the abode *in Hell.*

And of old gave we Moses the guidance, and we made the children of Israel the heritors of the Book, – a guidance and warning to men endued with understanding.

Therefore be steadfast thou and patient; for true is the promise of God: and seek pardon for thy fault,[9] and celebrate the praise of thy Lord at evening and at morning.

As to those who cavil at the signs of God without authority having reached them, nought is there but pride in their breasts: but they shall not succeed. Fly thou for refuge then to God, for He is the Hearer, the Beholder.

Greater surely than the creation of man is the creation of the heavens and of the earth: but most men know it not.

60 Moreover, the blind and the seeing, and the evil doer and they who believe and do the things that are right, shall not be deemed equal. How few ponder this!

Aye, 'the Hour' will surely come: there is no doubt of it: but most men believe it not.

And your Lord saith, 'Call upon me – I will hearken unto you: but they who turn in disdain from my service shall enter Hell with shame.'

It is God who hath ordained the night for your rest, and the day to give you light: verily God is rich in bounties to men: but most men render not the tribute of thanks.

This is God your Lord, Creator of all things: no god is there but He: why then do ye turn away from Him?

Yet thus are they turned aside who gainsay the signs of God.

It is God who hath given you the earth as a sure foundation, and over it built up the Heaven, and formed you, and made your forms beautiful, and feedeth you with good things. This is God your Lord. Blessed then be God the Lord of the Worlds!

He is the Living One. No God is there but He. Call then upon Him and offer Him a pure worship. Praise be to God the Lord of the Worlds!

SAY: Verily I am forbidden to worship what ye call on beside God, after that the clear tokens have come to me from my Lord, and I am bidden to surrender myself to the Lord of the Worlds.

He it is who created you of the dust, then of the germs of life, then of thick blood, then brought you forth infants: then he letteth you reach your full strength, and then become old men (but some of you die first), and reach the ordained term. And this that haply ye may understand.

70 It is He who giveth life and death; and when He decreeth a
thing, He only saith of it, 'Be,' and it is.

Seest thou not those who cavil at the signs of God? how are they turned aside!

They who treat 'the Book,' and the message with which we have sent our Sent Ones, as a lie, shall know *the truth* hereafter,

When the collars shall be on their necks and the chains to drag them into Hell: then in the fire shall they be burned.

Then shall it be said to them, 'Where are they whom ye made the objects of joint worship with God?' They shall say, 'They have vanished away from us. Yea, it was nought on which we called heretofore.' Thus God leadeth the unbelievers astray.

– 'This for you, because of your unrighteous insolence and immoderate joys on earth.

Enter ye the portals of Hell to abide therein for ever. And, wretched the abode of the haughty ones!'

Therefore be thou steadfast in patience: for the promise of God is truth: and whether we shall make thee see part of the woes with which we threatened them, or whether we cause thee first to die, unto us shall they be brought back.

And we have already sent apostles before thee: of some we have told thee, and of others we have told thee nothing: but no apostle had the power to work a miracle unless by the leave of God. But when God's behest cometh, *everything* will be decided with truth: and then they perish who treated it as a vain thing.

It is God who hath given you the cattle that on some of them ye may ride, and of some may eat:
80 (Other advantages too do ye derive from them) – and that by
them ye may effect the projects ye cherish in your breasts; for on them, and on ships are ye borne:

And He sheweth you His signs: which, then, of the signs of God will ye deny?

Have they not journeyed in this land, and seen what hath been the end of those who flourished before them? More were they than these in number and mightier in strength, and greater are the traces *of their power* remaining in the land: yet their labours availed them nothing.

And when their apostles had come to them with the tokens of *their mission*, they exulted in what they possessed of knowledge; but that *retribution* at which they scoffed, encompassed them.

And when they beheld our vengeance they said, 'We believe in God alone, and we disbelieve in the deities we once associated with Him.'

But their faith, after they had witnessed our vengeance, profited them not. Such the procedure of God with regard to his servants who flourished of old. And then the unbelievers perished.

SURA 41[1] – THE MADE PLAIN

MECCA – 54 VERSES

In the Name of God, the Compassionate, the Merciful

Ha. Mim.[2] A Revelation from the Compassionate, the Merciful!

A Book whose verses (signs) are MADE PLAIN – an Arabic Koran, for men of knowledge;

Announcer of glad tidings and charged with warnings! But most of them withdraw and hearken not:

And they say, 'Our hearts are under shelter from thy teachings, and in our ears is a deafness, and between us and thee there is a veil. Act *as thou thinkest right:* we verily shall act *as we think right.*'

SAY: I am only a man like you.[3] It is revealed to me that your God is one God: go straight then to Him, and implore his pardon. And woe to those who join gods with God;

Who pay not the alms of obligation, and in the life to come believe not!

But they who believe and do the things that are right shall receive a perfect[4] recompense.

SAY: Do ye indeed disbelieve in Him who in two days created the earth? and do ye assign Him peers? The Lord of the Worlds is He!

And he hath placed on the earth the firm mountains which tower above it; and He hath blessed it, and distributed food throughout it, for the cravings of all alike, in four days:

10 Then He applied himself to the Heaven, which then was but smoke: and to it and to the Earth He said, 'Come ye, whether in obedience or against your will?' and they both said, 'We come obedient.'

And He made them seven heavens in two days, and in each heaven made known its office: And we furnished the lower heaven with lights and guardian angels. This, the disposition of the Almighty, the All-knowing.

If they turn away, then SAY: I warn you of a tempest, like the tempest of Ad and Themoud!

When the apostles came to them on every side,[5] *saying*, 'Worship none but God,' they said, 'Had our Lord been pleased *to send down*, He had surely sent down angels; and in sooth, your message we do not believe.'

As to Ad, they bore them proudly and unjustly in the land, and said, 'Who more mighty than we in prowess?' Saw they not that God their creator was mightier than they in prowess? And they rejected our signs.

Therefore on ill-omened days did we send against them an impetuous blast that we might make them taste the chastisement of shame in this world: – but more shameful shall be the chastisement of the life to come; and they shall not be protected.

And as to Themoud, we had vouchsafed them guidance; but to guidance did they prefer blindness; wherefore the tempest of a shameful punishment overtook them for their doings:

But we rescued the believing and the God-fearing:

And *warn* of the day when the enemies of God shall be gathered[6] unto the fire urged on in bands:

Until when they reach it, their ears and their eyes and their skins shall bear witness against them of their deeds:

20 And they shall say to their skins, 'Why witness ye against
us?' They shall say, 'God, who giveth a voice to all things,
hath given us a voice: He created you at first, and to Him are ye
brought back.

And ye did not hide yourselves so that neither your ears nor your eyes nor your skins should witness against you: but ye thought that God knew not many a thing that ye did!

And this your thought which ye did think of your Lord hath ruined you, so that ye are become of those who perish.'

And be they patient, still the fire shall be their abode: or if they beg for favour, yet shall they not be of the favoured.

And we will appoint *Satans* as their fast companions; for it was they who made their present and future state seem fair and right to them; and the sentence passed on the peoples of Djinn and men who flourished before them hath become their due, and they shall perish.

Yet the unbelievers say, 'Hearken not to this Koran, but keep up a talking, that ye may overpower *the voice of the reader*.'

Surely therefore will we cause the unbelievers to taste a terrible punishment;

And recompense them according to the worst of their actions.

This the reward of the enemies of God, – the Fire! it shall be their eternal abode, in requital for their gainsaying our signs.

And they who believed not shall say, 'O our Lord! shew us those of the Djinn and men who led us astray: both of them will we put under our feet, that they may be of the humbled.'

30 But as for those who say, 'Our Lord is God;' and who go
straight to Him,[7] the angels shall descend to them *and say*, 'Fear
ye not, neither be ye grieved, but rejoice ye in the paradise
which ye have been promised.

We are your guardians in this life and in the next: yours therein shall be your soul's desire, and yours therein whatever ye shall ask for,

The hospitality of a Gracious, a Merciful One.'

And who speaketh fairer than he who biddeth to God and doth the thing that is right, and saith, 'I for my part am of the Muslims'?

Moreover, good and evil are not to be treated as the same thing. Turn away evil by what is better, and lo! he between whom and thyself was enmity, shall be as though he were a warm friend.

But none attain to this save men steadfast in patience, and none attain to it except the most highly favoured.[8]

And if an enticement from Satan entice thee, then take refuge in God, for He is the Hearing, the Knowing.

And among his signs are the night, and the day, and the sun, and the moon. Bend not in adoration to the sun or the moon, but bend in adoration before God who created them both, if ye would serve Him.

But if they are too proud *for this*, yet they who are with thy Lord do celebrate His praises night and day,[9] and cease not.

And among His signs *is this*, that thou seest the earth drooping: but, when we send down the rain upon it, it is stirred and swelleth; verily He who giveth it life, will surely give life to the dead; for His might extendeth over all things.[10]

40 They truly who with obloquy disown our signs are not hidden from us. Is he then who shall be cast into the fire, or he who shall come forth secure on the day of resurrection, in the better position? Do what ye will: but His eye is on all your doings.

Verily, they who believe not in 'the warning,' after it hath come to them . . . and yet *the Koran* is a glorious book!

Falsehood, from whatever side it cometh, shall not come nigh it;[11] it is a missive down from the Wise, the Praiseworthy.

Nothing hath been said to thee which hath not been said of old to apostles before thee. Verily with thy Lord is forgiveness, and with Him is terrible retribution.

Had we made it a Koran in a foreign tongue, they had surely said, 'Unless its signs be made clear . . . ![12] What! in a foreign tongue? and the people Arabian?' SAY: It is to those who believe a guide and a medicine;[13] but as to those who believe not, there is a thickness in their ears, and to them it is a blindness: they are *like* those who are called to from afar.

Of old we gave the Book to Moses, and disputes arose about

it: and if a decree *of respite* from thy Lord had gone before, there would surely have been a decision between them: for great were their doubts and questionings about it.[14]

He who doth right – it is for himself:[15] and he who doth evil – it is for himself: and thy Lord will not deal unfairly with his servants.

With Him alone[16] is the knowledge of 'the Hour.' No fruit cometh forth from its coverings, neither doth any female conceive, nor is she delivered, but with His knowledge. And on that day He shall call men to Him, *saying*, 'Where are the companions ye gave me?' They shall say, 'We own to thee, there is no one of us can witness *for them*.'

And what they erst called on shall pass away from them, and they shall perceive that there will be no escape for them.

Man ceaseth not to pray for good: but if evil betide him he despondeth, despairing.

50 And if we cause him to taste our mercy after affliction hath touched him, he is sure to say, 'This is my due: and I take no thought of the Hour of Resurrection: and if I be brought back to my Lord, I shall indeed attain with Him my highest good.' But we will then certainly declare their doings to the Infidels, and cause them to taste a stern punishment.

When we are gracious to man, he withdraweth and turneth him aside: but when evil toucheth him, he is a man of long prayers.

SAY: What think ye? If this *Book* be from God and ye believe it not, who will have gone further astray than he who is at a distance *from it?*

We will shew them our signs in *different* countries and among themselves, until it become plain to them that it is the truth. Is it not enough for thee that thy Lord is witness of all things?

Are they not in doubt as to the meeting with their Lord? But doth he not encompass all things?

SURA 42 – COUNSEL

MECCA – 53 VERSES

In the Name of God, the Compassionate, the Merciful

Ha. Mim. Ain. Sin. Kaf. Thus unto thee as unto those who preceded thee doth God, the Mighty, the Wise, reveal!

All that is in the Heavens and all that is in the Earth is His: and He is the High, the Great!

Ready are the Heavens to cleave asunder from above *for very awe:* and the angels celebrate the praise of their Lord, and ask forgiveness for the dwellers on earth: Is not God the Indulgent, the Merciful?

But whoso take aught beside Him as lords – God watcheth them! but thou hast them not in thy charge.

It is thus moreover that we have revealed to thee an Arabic Koran, that thou mayest warn the mother city[2] and all around it, and that thou mayest warn them of that day of the Gathering, of which there is no doubt – when part shall be in Paradise and part in the flame.

Had God so pleased, He had made them one people *and of one creed:* but He bringeth whom He will within His mercy; and as for the doers of evil, no patron, no helper shall there be for them.

Will they take other patrons than Him? But God is man's only Lord: He quickeneth the dead; and He is mighty over all things.

And whatever the subject of your disputes, with God doth its decision rest. This is God, my Lord: in Him do I put my trust, and to Him do I turn in penitence;

Creator of the Heavens and of the Earth! he hath given you wives from among your own selves, and cattle male and female – by this means to multiply you: Nought is there like Him! the Hearer, the Beholder He!

10 His, the keys of the Heavens and of the Earth! He giveth with open hand, or sparingly, to whom He will: He knoweth all things.

To you hath He prescribed the faith which He commanded unto Noah, and which we have revealed to thee, and which we commanded unto Abraham and Moses and Jesus, saying,

'Observe this faith, and be not divided into sects therein.' Intolerable to those who worship idols jointly with God

Is that faith to which thou dost call them. Whom He pleaseth will God choose for it, and whosoever shall turn to Him in penitence will He guide to it.

Nor were they divided into sects through mutual jealousy, till after that 'the knowledge' had come to them: and had not a decree from thy Lord gone forth *respiting them* to a fixed time, verily, there had at once been a decision between them.[3] And they who have inherited 'the Book' after them, are in perplexity of doubt concerning it.

For this cause summon thou *them to the faith*, and go straight on as thou hast been bidden, and follow not their desires: and SAY: In whatsoever Books God hath sent down do I believe: I am commanded to decide justly between you: God is your Lord and our Lord: we have our works and you have your works: between us and you let there be no strife: God will make us all one: and to Him shall we return.

And as to those who dispute about God, after pledges of obedience given to Him, their disputings shall be condemned by their Lord, and wrath shall be on them, and theirs shall be a sore torment.

It is God who hath sent down the Book with truth, and the Balance:[4] but who shall inform thee whether haply 'the Hour' be nigh?

They who believe not in it, challenge its speedy coming:[5] but they who believe are afraid because of it, and know it to be a truth. Are not they who dispute of the Hour, in a vast error?

Benign is God towards his servants: for whom He will doth He provide: and He is the Strong, the Mighty.

Whoso will choose the harvest field of the life to come, to him will we give increase in this his harvest field: and whoso chooseth the harvest field of this life, thereof will we give him: but no portion shall there be for him in the life to come.[6]

20 Is it that they have gods who have sanctioned for them aught in the matter of religion which God hath not allowed? But had it not been for a decree *of respite till the day* of severance, judgment had ere now taken place among them; and assuredly the impious shall undergo a painful torment.

On that day thou shalt see the impious alarmed at their own works, and the consequence thereof shall fall upon them: but they who believe and do the things that are right, shall dwell in the meadows of paradise: whatever they shall desire awaiteth them with their Lord. This, the greatest boon.

This is what God announceth to his servants who believe and do the things that are right. SAY: For this ask I no wage of you, save the love of my kin. And whoever shall have won the merit of a good deed, we will increase good to him therewith; for God is forgiving, grateful.

Will they say he hath forged a lie of God? If God pleased, He could then seal up thy very heart.[7] But God will bring untruth to nought, and will make good the truth by his word: for He knoweth the very secrets of the breast.

He it is who accepteth repentance from his servants, and forgiveth their sins and knoweth your actions:

And to those who believe and do the things that are right will he hearken, and augment his bounties to them:[8] but the unbelievers doth a terrible punishment await.

Should God bestow abundance upon his servants, they might act wantonly on the earth: but He sendeth down what He will by measure; for he knoweth, beholdeth his servants.

He it is who after that men have despaired of it, sendeth down the rain, and spreadeth abroad his mercy: He is the Protector, the Praiseworthy.

Among his signs is the creation of the Heavens and of the Earth, and the creatures which he hath scattered over both: and, for their gathering together when he will, He is all-powerful!

Nor happeneth to you any mishap, but it is for your own handy-work: and yet he forgiveth many things.

30 Ye cannot weaken him on the earth: neither, beside God, patron or helper shall ye have.

Among his signs also are the sea-traversing ships like mountains: if such be his will, He lulleth the wind, and they lie motionless on the back of the waves: – truly herein are signs to all the constant, the grateful; –

Or if, for their ill deserts, He cause them to founder, still He forgiveth much:

But they who gainsay our signs shall know that there will be no escape for them.

All that you receive is but for enjoyment in this life present: but better and more enduring is a portion with God, for those who believe and put their trust in their Lord;

And who avoid the heinous things of crime, and filthiness, and when they are angered, forgive;

And who hearken to their Lord, and observe prayer, and whose affairs are guided by mutual COUNSEL, and who give alms of that with which we have enriched them;

And who, when a wrong is done them, redress themselves: – Yet let the recompense of evil be only a like evil – but he who forgiveth and is reconciled, shall be rewarded by God himself; for He loveth not those who act unjustly.

And there shall be no way *open* against those who, after being wronged, avenge themselves;

40 But there shall be a way *open* against those who unjustly wrong others, and act insolently on the earth in disregard of justice. These! a grievous punishment doth await them.

And whoso beareth wrongs with patience and forgiveth; – this verily is a bounden duty;

But he whom God shall cause to err, shall thenceforth have no protector. And thou shalt behold the perpetrators of injustice,

Exclaiming, when they see the torment, 'Is there no way to return?'

And thou shalt see them when set before it, downcast for the shame: they shall look at it with stealthy glances: and the believers shall say, 'Truly are the losers they who have lost themselves and their families on the day of Resurrection! Shall not the perpetrators of injustice be in lasting torment?'

And no other protectors shall there be to succour them than God; and no pathway for him whom God shall cause to err.

Hearken then to your Lord ere the day come, which none can put back when God doth ordain its coming. No place of refuge for you on that day! no denying *your own works!*

But if they turn aside from thee, yet we have not sent thee to be their guardian. 'Tis thine but to preach. When we cause man to taste our gifts of mercy, he rejoiceth in it; but if for their by-gone handy-work evil betide them, then lo! is man ungrateful.

God's, the kingdom of the Heavens and of the Earth! He createth what He will! and he giveth daughters to whom He will, and sons to whom He will:

Or He giveth them children of both sexes, and He maketh whom He will to be childless; for He is Wise, Powerful!

50 It is not for man that God should speak with him but by
vision, or from behind a veil:
Or, He sendeth a messenger to reveal, by his permission,
what He will: for He is Exalted, Wise!
Thus have we sent the Spirit (Gabriel[9]) to thee with a
revelation, by our command. Thou knewest not, ere this,
what 'the Book' was, or what the faith. But we have ordained
it for a light: by it will we guide whom we please of our
servants. And thou shalt surely guide into the right way,
The way of God, whose is all that the Heaven and the Earth
contain. Shall not all things return to God?

SURA 43 – ORNAMENTS OF GOLD

MECCA – 89 VERSES

In the Name of God, the Compassionate, the Merciful

Ha. Mim.[1] By the Luminous Book!
We have made it an Arabic Koran that ye may understand:
And it is a transcript of the archetypal Book,[2] kept by us; it is
lofty, filled with wisdom,
Shall we then turn aside this warning from you because ye are
a people who transgress?
Yet how many prophets sent we among those of old!
But no prophet came to them whom they made not the object
of their scorn:
Wherefore we destroyed nations mightier than these
Meccans in strength; and the example of those of old hath gone
before!
And if thou ask them who created the Heavens and the Earth,
they will say: 'The Mighty, the Sage, created them both,'
Who hath made the Earth as a couch for you, and hath traced
out routes therein for your guidance;
10 And who sendeth down out of Heaven the rain in due degree,
by which we quicken a dead land; thus shall ye be brought forth
from the grave:

And who hath created the sexual couples, all of them, and hath made for you the ships and beasts whereon ye ride:

That ye may sit balanced on their backs and remember the goodness of your Lord as ye sit so evenly thereon, and say: 'Glory to Him who hath subjected these to us! We could not have attained to it of ourselves:

And truly unto our Lord shall we return.'

Yet do they assign to him some of his own servants for offspring! Verily man is an open ingrate!

Hath God adopted daughters from among those whom he hath created, and chosen sons for you?

But when that[3] is announced to any one of them, which he affirmeth to be the case with the God of Mercy,[4] his face settleth into darkness and he is silent-sad.

What! make they a being to be the offspring of God who is brought up among trinkets, and is ever contentious without reason?

And they make the angels who are the servants of God of Mercy, females. What! did they witness their creation? Their witness shall be taken down, and they shall hereafter be enquired at.

And they say: 'Had the God of Mercy so willed it we should never have worshipped them.' No knowledge have they in this: they only lie.

20 Have we ere this given them a Book?[5] and do they possess it still?

But say they: 'Verily we found our fathers of that persuasion, and verily, by their footsteps do we guide ourselves.'

And thus never before thy time did we send a warner to any city but its wealthy ones said: 'Verily we found our fathers with a religion, and in their tracks we tread.'

SAY, – *such was our command to that apostle* – 'What! even if I bring you a religion more right than that ye found your fathers following?' And they said, 'Verily we believe not in your message.'

Wherefore we took vengeance on them, and behold what hath been the end of those who treated our messengers as liars!

And bear in mind when Abraham said to his father and to his people, 'Verily I am clear of what ye worship,

Save Him who hath created me; for he will vouchsafe me guidance.'

And this he stablished as a doctrine that should abide among his posterity, that to God might they be turned.

In sooth to these *idolatrous Arabians* and to their fathers did I allow their full enjoyments, till the truth should come to them, and an undoubted apostle:

But now that the truth hath come to them, they say, ''Tis sorcery, and we believe it not.'

30 And they say, 'Had but this Koran been sent down to some *great* one of the two cities[6] . . . !'

Are they then the distributors of thy Lord's Mercy?[7] It is we who distribute their subsistence among them in this world's life; and we raise some of them by grades above others, that the one may take the other to serve him: but better is the mercy of thy Lord than all their hoards.

But for fear that all mankind would have become a single people of *unbelievers*, verily we would certainly have given to those who believe not in the God of Mercy roofs of silver to their houses, and *silver* stairs to ascend by;

And doors *of silver* to their houses, and couches *of silver* to recline on;

And ORNAMENTS OF GOLD: for all these are merely the good things of the present life; but the next life doth thy Lord reserve for those who fear Him.

And whoso shall withdraw from the Warning of the God of M ercy, we will chain a Satan to him, and he shall be his fast companion:

For the Satans will turn men aside from the Way, who yet shall deem themselves rightly guided;

Until when man shall come before us, he shall say, 'O *Satan*, would that between me and thee were the distance of the East and West.'[8] And a wretched companion *is a Satan*.

But it shall not avail you on that day, because ye were unjust: partners shall ye be in the torment.

What! Canst thou then make the deaf to hear, or guide the blind and him who is in palpable error?

40 Whether therefore we take thee off by death, surely will we avenge ourselves on them;

Or whether we make thee a witness of *the accomplishment of* that with which we threatened them, we will surely gain the mastery over them.[9]

Hold thou fast therefore what hath been revealed to thee, for thou art on a right path:

For truly to thee and to thy people it is an admonition; and ye shall have an account to render for it at last.[10]

And ask our Sent Ones whom we have sent before thee, 'Appointed we gods beside the God of Mercy whom they should worship?'[11]

Of old sent we Moses with our signs to Pharaoh and his nobles: and he said, 'I truly am the Apostle of the Lord of the Worlds.'

And when he presented himself before them with our signs, lo! they laughed at them,

Though we shewed them no sign that was not greater than its fellow:[12] and therefore did we lay hold on them with chastisement, to the intent that they might be turned *to God*.

Then they said, 'O Magician! call on thy Lord on our behalf to do as he hath engaged with thee, for truly we would fain be guided.'

But when we relieved them from the chastisement, lo! they broke their pledge.

50 And Pharaoh made proclamation among his people. Said he, 'O my people! is not the kingdom of Egypt mine, and these rivers which flow at my feet?[13] Do ye not behold?

Am I not mightier than this despicable fellow,

And who scarce can speak distinctly?

Have bracelets of gold[14] then been put upon him, or come there with him a train of Angels?'

And he inspired his people with levity, and they obeyed him; for they were a perverse people:

And when they had angered us, we took vengeance on them, and we drowned them all.

And we made them a precedent and instance of divine judgments to those who came after them.

And when the Son of Mary was set forth as an instance *of divine power*, lo! thy people cried out for *joy* thereat:

And they said, 'Are our gods or is he the better?'[15] They put this forth to thee only in the spirit of dispute. Yea, they are a contentious people.

Jesus is no more than a servant whom we favoured, and proposed as an instance *of divine power* to the children of Israel.

60 (And if we pleased, we could from yourselves bring forth Angels to succeed you on earth:)[16]

And he shall be a sign of the *last* hour;[17] doubt not then of it, and follow ye me: this is the right way;

And let not Satan turn you aside from it, for he is your manifest foe.

And when Jesus came with manifest proofs, he said, 'Now am I come to you with wisdom; and a part of those things about which ye are at variance I will clear up to you; fear ye God therefore and obey me.

Verily, God is my Lord and your Lord; wherefore worship ye him: this is a right way.'

But the different parties[18] fell into disputes among themselves; but woe to those who thus transgressed, because of the punishment of an afflictive day!

For what wait they but for the hour 'to come suddenly on them, while they expect it not'?

Friends on that day shall become foes to one another, except the God-fearing: –

'O my servants! on this day shall no fear come upon you, neither shall ye be put to grief,

Who have believed in our signs and become Muslims:

70 Enter ye and your wives into Paradise, delighted.'

Dishes and bowls of gold shall go round unto them: there shall they enjoy whatever their souls desire, and whatever their eyes delight in; and therein shall ye abide for ever.

This is Paradise, which ye have received as your heritage in recompense for your works;

Therein shall ye have fruits in abundance, of which ye shall eat.

But in the torment of Hell shall the wicked remain for ever:

It shall not be mitigated to them, and they shall be mute for despair therein,

For it is not we who have treated them unjustly, but it was they who were unjust to themselves.

And they shall cry: 'O Malec![19] would that thy Lord would make an end of us!' He saith: 'Here must ye remain.'

We have come to you with the truth (O Meccans), but most of you abhor the truth.

Have they drawn tight their toils *for thee?*[20] We too will tighten ours.

80 Think they that we hear not their secrets and their private talk? Yes, and our angels who are at their sides write them down.

SAY: If the God of Mercy had a son, the first would I be to worship him:

But far be the Lord of the Heavens and of the Earth, the Lord of the Throne, from that which they impute to Him!

Wherefore let them alone, to plunge on, and sport, until they meet the day with which they are menaced.

He who is God in the Heavens is God in Earth also: and He is the Wise, the Knowing.

And Blessed be He whose is the kingdom of the Heavens and of the Earth and of all that is between them; for with Him is the knowledge of the Hour, and to Him shall ye be brought back.

The gods whom they call upon beside Him shall not be able to intercede for others: they only shall be able who bore witness to the truth and[21] knew it.'

If thou ask them who hath created them, they will be sure to say, 'God.' How then hold they false opinions?

And one[22] saith, 'O Lord! verily these are people who believe not.'

Turn thou then from them, and say, 'Peace:' In the end they shall know *their folly.*

SURA 44 – SMOKE

MECCA – 59 VERSES

In the Name of God, the Compassionate, the Merciful

Ha. Mim.[1] By this clear Book!

See! on a blessed night[2] have we sent it down, for we would warn *mankind:*

On the night wherein all things are disposed in wisdom,[3]

By virtue of our behest. Lo! we have ever sent forth Apostles,

A mercy from thy Lord: he truly heareth and knoweth all things –

Lord of the Heavens and of the Earth and of all that is between them, – if ye be firm in faith –

There is no God but He! – He maketh alive and killeth! – Your Lord and the Lord of your sires of old!

Yet with doubts do they disport them.

But mark them on the day when the Heaven shall give out a palpable SMOKE,

10 Which shall enshroud mankind: this will be an afflictive torment.

They will cry, 'Our Lord! relieve us from this torment: see! we are believers.'

But how did warning avail them, when an undoubted apostle had come to them;

And they turned their backs on him, and said, 'Taught by others, possessed?'

Were we to relieve you from the plague even a little, ye would certainly relapse.[4]

On the day when we shall fiercely put forth our great fierceness, we will surely take vengeance on them!

Of old, before their time, had we proved the people of Pharaoh, when a noble apostle presented himself to them.

'Send away with me,' cried he, 'the servants of God; for I am an apostle worthy of all credit:

And exalt not yourselves against God, for I come to you with undoubted power;

And I take refuge with Him who is my Lord and your Lord, that ye stone me not:

20 And if ye believe me not, at least separate yourselves from me.'

And he cried to his Lord, 'That these are a wicked people.'

'March forth then, *said God*, with my servants by night, for ye will be pursued.

And leave behind you the cleft sea: they are a drowned host.'

How many a garden and fountain did they quit!

And corn-fields and noble dwellings!

And pleasures in which they rejoiced them!

So was it: and we gave them as a heritage to another people.

Nor Heaven nor Earth wept for them, nor was their sentence respited;

And we rescued the children of Israel from a degrading affliction –

30 From Pharaoh, for he was haughty, given to excess.
And we chose them, in our prescience, above all peoples,[5]
And we shewed them miracles wherein was *their* clear trial.
Yet these *infidels* say,
'There is but our first death, neither shall we be raised again:
Bring back our sires, if ye be men of truth.'
Are they better than the people of Tobba,[6]
And those who flourished before them whom we destroyed
for their evil deeds?
We have not created the Heavens and the Earth and whatever
is between them in sport:
We have not created them but for a serious end:[7] but the
greater part of them understand it not.
40 Verily the day of severing[8] shall be the appointed time of all:
A day when the master shall not at all be aided by the servant,
neither shall they be helped;
Save those on whom God shall have mercy: for He is the
mighty, the merciful.
Verily the tree of Ez-zakkoum[9]
Shall be the sinner's[10] food:
Like dregs of oil shall it boil up in their bellies,
Like the boiling of scalding water.
'– Seize ye him, and drag him into the mid-fire;
Then pour on his head of the tormenting boiling water.
– "Taste this:" for thou forsooth art the mighty, the
honourable!
50 Lo! this is that of which ye doubted.'
But the pious shall be in a secure place,
Amid gardens and fountains,
Clothed in silk and richest robes, facing one another:
Thus shall it be: and we will wed them to the *virgins* with
large dark eyes:
Therein shall they call, secure, for every kind of fruit;
Therein, their first death passed, shall they taste death no
more; and He shall keep them from the pains of Hell: –
'Tis the gracious bounty of thy Lord! This is the great
felicity.
We have made this Koran easy for thee in thine own tongue,
that they may take the warning.
Therefore wait thou, for they are waiting.[11]

SURA 45 – THE KNEELING

MECCA – 36 VERSES

In the Name of God, the Compassionate, the Merciful

Ha. Mim.[1] This Book is sent down[2] from God, the Mighty, the Wise!

Assuredly in the Heavens and the Earth are signs for those who believe:

And in your own creation, and in the beasts which are scattered abroad are signs to the firm in faith:

And in the succession of night and day, and in the supply which God sendeth down from the Heaven whereby He giveth life to the earth when dead, and in the change of the winds, are signs for a people of discernment.

Such are the signs of God: with truth do we recite them to thee. But in what teaching will they believe, if they reject[3] God and his signs?

Woe to every lying sinner,

Who heareth the signs of God recited to him, and then, as though he heard them not, persisteth in proud disdain! Apprise him of an afflictive punishment.

And when he becometh acquainted with any of our signs he turneth them into ridicule. These! a shameful punishment for them!

Hell is behind them! and neither their gains nor the lords whom they have adopted beside God shall avail them in the least: and theirs, a great punishment!

10 This is 'Guidance:' and for those who disbelieve the signs of their Lord is the punishment of an afflictive torment.

It is God who hath subjected the sea to you that the ships may traverse it at his bidding, and that ye may go in quest of the gifts of his bounty, and that ye may be thankful.

And he hath subjected to you all that is in the Heavens and all that is on the Earth: all is from him. Verily, herein are signs for those who reflect.

Tell the believers to pardon those who hope not for the days of God[4] in which He purposeth to reward men according to their deeds.

He who doth that which is right, doth it to his own behoof, and whoso doth evil, doth it to his own hurt. Hereafter, to your Lord shall ye be brought back.

To the children of Israel gave we of old the Book and the Wisdom, and the gift of Prophecy, and we supplied them with good things, and privileged them above all peoples:

And we gave them clear sanctions for our behests: neither did they differ, through mutual envy, till after they had become possessed of knowledge; but thy Lord will judge between them on the day of resurrection, as to the subject of their disputes.

Afterwards we set thee over our divine law:[5] follow it then: and follow not the wishes of those who have no knowledge,

For against God shall they avail thee nothing. And in sooth, the doers of evil are one another's patrons; but the patron of them that fear Him is God himself.

This *Book* hath insight for mankind, and a Guidance and
Mercy to a people who are firm in faith.
20 Deem they whose gettings are only evil, that we will deal
with them as with those who believe and work righteousness,
so that their lives and deaths shall be alike? Ill do they judge.

In all truth hath God created the Heavens and the Earth, that he may reward every one as he shall have wrought; and they shall not be wronged.

What thinkest thou? He who hath made a God of his passions, and whom God causeth wilfully to err, and whose ears and whose heart he hath sealed up, and over whose sight he hath placed a veil – who, after *his rejection by* God, shall guide such a one? Will ye not then be warned?

And they say, 'There is only this our present life: we die and we live, and nought but time destroyeth us.' But in this they have no knowledge: it is merely their own conceit.

And when our clear signs are recited to them, their only argument is to say, 'Bring back our fathers, if ye speak the truth.'

SAY: God giveth you life, then causeth you to die: then will He assemble you on the day of resurrection: there is no doubt of it: but most men have not this knowledge.

And God's is the kingdom of the Heavens and of the Earth; and on the day when the Hour shall arrive, on that day shall the despisers[6] perish.

And thou shalt see every nation KNEELING: to its own book

shall every nation be summoned: – 'This day shall ye be repaid as ye have wrought.

This our Book will speak of you with truth: therein have we written down whatever ye have done.'

As to those who have believed and wrought righteously, into his mercy shall their Lord cause them to enter. This shall be undoubted bliss!

30 But as to the Infidels – 'Were not my signs recited to you? but
ye proudly scorned them, and became a sinful people.'

And when it was said, 'Verily the Promise of God is truth; and as to the Hour, there is no doubt of it;' ye said, 'We know not what the hour is – we conceive it a mere conceit, – we have no assurance of it.'

And the evils they have wrought shall rise up into their view, and that at which they mocked shall hem them in on every side.

And it shall be said to them, 'This day will we forget you as ye forgat your meeting with us this day, and your abode shall be the fire, and none shall there be to succour you: –

This, because ye received the signs of God with mockery, and this present life deceived you.' On that day therefore they shall not come out from it; and they shall not be asked to win the favour of God.

Praise then be to God, Lord of the Heavens and Lord of the Earth; the Lord of the Worlds!

And His be the greatest in the Heavens and on the Earth; for He is the Mighty, the Wise!

SURA 46 – AL AHKAF

MECCA – 35 VERSES

In the Name of God, the Compassionate, the Merciful

Ha. Mim.[1] The Revelation (sending down) of this Book is from the Mighty, the Wise!

We have not created the Heavens and the Earth and all that is between them otherwise than in truth and for a settled term. But they who believe not, turn away from their warning.

SAY: What think ye? As for those whom ye invoke beside God, shew me what part of the earth it is which they have created? Had they a share in the Heavens? Bring me a Book sent down *by them* before this *Koran*, or traces of their knowledge;[2] – if ye are men of truth.

And who erreth more than he who, beside God, calleth upon that which shall not answer him until the day of Resurrection? Yes, they regard not their invocations;

And when mankind shall be assembled together, they will become their enemies, and ungratefully disown their worship.

And when our clear signs are recited to them, they who believe not say of the truth when it cometh to them, 'This is plain sorcery.'

Will they say, 'He hath devised It?' SAY: If I have devised *the Koran*, then not one single thing shall ye *ever* obtain for me from God! He best knoweth what ye utter in its regard! Witness enough is He between me and you! And He is the Gracious, the Merciful.

SAY: I am no apostle of new doctrines: neither know I what will be done with me or you. Only what is revealed to me do I follow, and I am only charged to warn openly.

SAY: What think ye? If *this Book* be from God, and ye believe it not, and a witness of the children of Israel witness to its conformity *with the Law*, and believe, while ye proudly disdain it . . . ? Ah! God guideth not the people guilty of such a wrong!

10 But the infidels say of the believers, 'If it were a good *Book*
they would not have been before us in believing it:'[3] And not having submitted to guidance, they proceed to say, 'It is an old lying legend!'

But before the Koran was the Book of Moses, a rule and a mercy; and this Book confirmeth it (the Pentateuch) – in the Arabic tongue – that those who are guilty of that wrong may be warned, and as glad tidings to the doers of good.

Assuredly they who say, 'Our Lord is God,' and take the straight way *to Him* – no fear shall come on them, neither shall they be put to grief:

These shall be the inmates of Paradise to remain therein for ever, – the recompense of their deeds!

Moreover, we have enjoined on man to shew kindness to his parents. With pain his mother beareth him; with pain she bringeth him forth: and his bearing and his weaning is thirty months; until when he attaineth his strength, and attaineth to forty years,[4] he saith, 'O my Lord! stir me up to be grateful for thy favours wherewith thou hast favoured me and my parents, and to do good works which shall please thee: and prosper me in my offspring: for to thee am I turned, and am resigned to thy will' (am a Muslim).

These are they from whom we will accept their best works, and whose evil works we will pass by; among the inmates shall they be of Paradise: – a true promise which they are promised.

But he who saith to his parents, 'Fie on you both! Promise ye me that I shall be taken forth *from the grave* alive, when whole generations have already passed away before me?' But they both will implore the help of God, *and say*, 'Alas for thee! Believe: for the promise of God is true.' But he saith, 'It is no more than a fable of the ancients.'

These are they in whom the sentence passed on the nations, djinn and men, who flourished before them, is made good. They shall surely perish.[5]

And there are grades for all, according to their works, that God may repay them for their works; and they shall not be dealt with unfairly.

And they who believe not shall one day be set before the fire. 'Ye made away your precious gifts during your life on earth; and ye took your fill of pleasure in them: This day, therefore, with punishment of shame shall ye be rewarded, for that ye behaved you proudly and unjustly on the earth, and for that ye were given to excesses.'

20 Remember, too, the brother of Ad[6] when he warned his
people in AL AHKAF[7] – and before and since his time there have been warners – 'Worship none but God: verily I fear for you the punishment of the great day.'

They said, 'Art thou come to us to turn us away from our Gods? Bring on us now the woes which thou threatenest if thou speakest truth.'

'That knowledge,' said he, 'is with God alone: I only proclaim to you the message with which I am sent. But I perceive that ye are a people sunk in ignorance.'

So when they saw a cloud coming straight for their valleys, they said, 'It is a passing cloud that shall give us rain.' 'Nay, it is that whose speedy coming ye challenged – a blast wherein is an afflictive punishment: –

It will destroy everything at the bidding of its Lord!' And at morn nought was to be seen but their *empty* dwellings! Thus repay we a wicked people.

With power had we endued them, even as with power have we endued you; and we had given them ears and eyes and hearts: yet neither their eyes, nor their ears, nor their hearts aided them at all, when once they gainsaid the signs of God; but that punishment which they had mocked at enveloped them on all sides.

Of old, too, did we destroy the cities which were round about you; and, in order that they might return to us, we varied our signs before them.

But did those whom they took for gods beside God as his kindred deities, help them?[8] Nay, they withdrew from them. Such was their delusion, and their device!

And *remember* when we turned aside a company of the djinn to thee, that they might hearken to the Koran: and no sooner were they present at its reading than they said to each other, 'Hist;' and when it was ended, they returned to their people with warnings.

They said, 'O our people! verily we have been listening to a book sent down since the days of Moses, affirming the previous scriptures; it guideth to the truth, and to the right way.

30 O our people! Obey the Summoner of God, and believe in him, that He may forgive your sins, and rescue you from an afflictive punishment.

And he who shall not respond to God's preacher, yet cannot weaken God's power on earth, nor shall he have protectors beside Him. These are in obvious error.'

See they not that God who created the Heavens and the Earth, and was not wearied with their creation, is of power to quicken the dead? Yea, he is for all things Potent.

And a day is *coming* when the infidels shall be set before the fire. 'Is not this it in truth?' They shall say, 'Aye, by our Lord.' He said, 'Taste then the punishment for that ye would not believe.'

Bear thou up, then, with patience, as did the Apostles endued with firmness, and seek not to accelerate their doom. *For*, on the day when they shall see that with which they have been menaced,

It shall be as though they had waited but an hour of the day. Enough! shall any perish save they who transgress?

SURA 47[1] – MUHAMMAD

MEDINA – 40 VERSES

In the Name of God, the Compassionate, the Merciful

Whoso believe not, and prevent others from the way of God – their works will He cause to miscarry;[2]

But whoso believe, and do things that are right, and believe in what hath been sent down to MUHAMMAD – for it is the truth from their Lord – their sins will He cancel, and dispose their hearts aright.

This – because the infidels followed vanity, while those who believe, followed the truth from their Lord. Thus to men doth God set forth their likenesses.

When ye encounter the infidels,[3] strike off their heads till ye have made a great slaughter among them, and *of the rest* make fast the fetters.

And afterwards let there either be free dismissals or ransomings, till the war hath laid down its burdens. Thus do. Were such the pleasure of God, he could himself take vengeance upon them: but He would rather prove the one of you by the other. And whoso fight for the cause of God, their works he will not suffer to miscarry;

He will vouchsafe them guidance, and dispose their hearts aright;

And he will bring them into the Paradise, of which he hath told them.

Believers! if ye help God, God will help you, and will set your feet firm:

But as for the infidels, let them perish: and their works shall God bring to nought:

10 This – because they were averse from the command which
God sent down; Fruitless, therefore, shall their works become!

Have they not journeyed through the land, and seen what

hath been the end of those who flourished before them? God brought destruction on them: and the like of this doth await the infidels.

This – because God is the protector of those who believe, and because the infidels have no protector.

Verily God will bring those who believe, and do the things that are right, into the Gardens, beneath whose *shades* the rivers flow: but they who believe not, take their fill, and eat as the beasts eat! And their dwelling-place the fire!

And how many cities were mightier in strength than thy city, which hath thrust thee forth![4] We destroyed them, and there was none to help them.

Shall he who followeth the clear teaching of his Lord be as he, the evil of whose doings hath been made to seem good to him, or *like those* who follow their own lusts?

A picture of the Paradise which is promised to the God-fearing! Therein are rivers of water, which corrupt not: rivers of milk, whose taste changeth not: and rivers of wine, delicious to those who quaff it;

And rivers of honey clarified: and therein are all kinds of fruit for them from their Lord! Is this like the lot of those who must dwell for ever in the fire? and shall have draughts of boiling water forced on them which will rend their bowels asunder?

Some of them indeed hearken to thee, until when they go out from thee, they say with sneers to those to whom 'the knowledge' hath been given, 'What is this he said?' These are they whose hearts God hath sealed up, and who follow their own lusts.

But as to those who have the guidance, He will increase their guidance, and He will teach them what to fear.

20 For what do the *infidels* wait, but that the Hour come suddenly on them? Already are its signs come,[5] and when it hath come on them indeed, how can they be warned then?

Know, then, that there is no god but God: and ask pardon for thy sin, and for believers, both men and women. God knoweth your busy movements, and your final resting-places.

The believers say, 'Oh, would that a Sura were sent down!'[6] but when a peremptory Sura is revealed, whose burden is war, thou mayest see the diseased of heart look towards thee, with a look of one on whom the shadows of death have fallen! But better in them would be obedience and becoming language.

And if, when the command for war is issued, they are true to God, it will be assuredly best for them.

Were ye not ready, if ye had turned back from Him, to spread disorder in the land, and violate the ties of blood?

These are they whom God hath cursed, and made deaf, and blinded their eyes!

Will they not then meditate on the Koran? Are locks upon their hearts?

But as to those who return to their errors after 'the guidance' hath been made plain to them, Satan shall beguile them, and fill them *with his suggestions*.

This – because they say to those who abhor what God hath sent down, 'We will comply with you in part of what ye enjoin.' But God knoweth their secret reservations.

But how? When the angels, in causing them to die, shall
smite them on the face and back!
30 This – because they follow that which angereth God, and abhor
what pleaseth Him: therefore will He make their works fruitless.

Think these men of diseased hearts, that God will not bring out their malice to light?

If such were our pleasure, we could point them out to thee, and thou surely know them by their tokens: and know them thou shalt, by the strangeness of their words.[7] God knoweth your doings.

And we will surely test you, until we know the valiant and the steadfast among you: and we will test the reports *of your conduct*.

Verily they who believe not, and turn others from the way of God, and separate from the Apostle after that 'the guidance' hath been clearly shewn them, shall in no way injure God: but their works shall he bring to nought.

Believers! obey God and the Apostle: and render not your works vain.

Verily those who believe not, and who pervert others from the way of God, and then die in unbelief, God will not forgive.

Be not fainthearted then; and invite not the *infidels* to peace when ye have the upper hand: for God is with you, and will not defraud you *of the recompense* of your works.

Surely this present life is only a play, and pastime! but if ye believe, fear God; He will give you your rewards: but He will not ask *all* your riches of you.

Should He ask them of you, and urge you, ye would shew yourself niggards: and He would bring your grudges to light.
40 Lo! ye are they, who are called to expend for the cause of God: and some of you are niggards: but whoso is niggardly shall be niggard only to his own loss; for God is the Rich, and ye are the poor: and if ye turn back, He will change you for another people,[8] and they shall not be your like!

SURA 48[1] – THE VICTORY

MEDINA – 29 VERSES

In the Name of God, the Compassionate, the Merciful

Verily, We have won for thee an undoubted VICTORY –

In token that God forgiveth thy earlier and later faults, and fulfilleth His goodness to thee, and guideth thee on the right way,

And that God succoureth thee with a mighty succour.

He it is who sendeth down a spirit of secure repose into the hearts of the faithful that they might add faith to their faith; (for God's are the armies of the Heavens and of the Earth: and God is Knowing, Wise:)

And that He may bring the believing men and the believing women into gardens 'neath whose *trees* the rivers flow, to dwell therein for ever, and that He may cancel their evil deeds: for this is the great bliss with God:

And that He may punish the hypocritical men and the hypocritical women, and the men and women who join other gods with God, and think evil thoughts of Him. Theirs *shall be* a round of evil; and God is angry with them and curseth them, and hath prepared Hell for them: and, an evil journey thither!

The armies of the Heavens and of the Earth are God's, and God is Mighty, Wise!

Verily, we have sent thee to be a witness and a herald of good (an announcer), and a warner,

That ye may believe on God and on His Apostle; and may

assist Him, and honour Him, and praise him, morning and evening.

10 In truth, they who plighted fealty to thee, really plighted that fealty to God: the hand of God was over their hands! Whoever, therefore, shall break his oath shall only break it to his own hurt; but whoever shall be true to his engagement with God, He will give him a great reward.

The Arabs who took not the field with you,[2] will say to thee,[3] 'We were engaged with our property and our families; therefore ask thou pardon for us.' They speak with their tongues what is not in their hearts. SAY: And who can have any power over God in your behalf, whether he will you some loss, or whether he will you an advantage? Yes, God is acquainted with your doings.

But ye thought that the Apostle and the faithful could never more come back to their families; and your hearts were pleased at this; and ye thought an evil thought *of this expedition*, and ye became an undone people:

For, whoso believeth not in God, and His Apostle . . . Verily, we have got ready the flame for the Infidels!

And God's is the kingdom of the Heavens and of the Earth: Whom He will He forgiveth, and whom He will He punisheth: and God is Gracious, Merciful!

They who took not the field with you will say, when ye go forth to the spoil to take it, 'Let us follow you.' Fain would they change the word of God.[4] SAY: Ye shall by no means follow us: thus hath God said already. They will say, 'Nay, ye are jealous of us.' Nay! they are men of little understanding.

SAY to those Arabs of the desert, who took not the field, ye shall be called forth against a people of mighty valour. Ye shall do battle with them, or they shall profess Islam. If ye obey, a goodly recompense will God give you; but if ye turn back, as ye turned back aforetime, He will chastise you with a sore chastisement.

It shall be no crime on the part of the blind, the lame, or the sick, *if they go not to the fight*. But whoso shall obey God and His Apostle, He shall bring him into the gardens 'neath which the rivers flow: but whoso shall turn back, He will punish him with a sore punishment.

Well pleased now hath God been with the believers when they plighted fealty to thee under the tree;[5] and He knew what was in their hearts: therefore did He send down upon them a spirit of secure repose, and rewarded them with a speedy victory,

And with the rich booty which they took: for God is Mighty, Wise!

20 God promised you the taking of a rich booty[6] and sped it to
you; and He withheld men's hands from you, for a sign to the faithful, and that He might guide you along the right way: –

And other booty, over which ye have not yet had power: but now hath God compassed them for you; for God is over all things Potent.

If the Infidels shall fight against you, they shall assuredly turn their backs; then, neither protector nor helper shall they find!

Such is God's method carried into effect of old; no change canst thou find in God's mode of dealing.

And He it was who held their hands from you and your hands from them in the valley of Mecca, after that He had given you the victory over them: for God saw what ye did.

These are they who believed not, and kept you away from the sacred Mosque, as well as the offering which was prevented from reaching the place of sacrifice. And had it not been that ye would have trodden down believers, both men and women, whom ye knew not, so that a crime might have lighted on you without your knowledge on their account, and that God would bring whom He will within His mercy, *this would have been otherwise ordered.* Had they been apart,[7] we had surely punished such of them as believed not, with a sore punishment.

When the unbelievers had fostered rage in their hearts – the rage of ignorance (of heathens) – God sent down His peace on His Apostle and on the faithful, and stablished in them the word of piety, for they were most worthy and deserving of it: and God knoweth all things.

Now hath God in truth made good to His Apostle the dream[8] *in which he said*, 'Ye shall surely enter the sacred Mosque, if God will, in full security, having your heads shaved and your hair cut: ye shall not fear; for He knoweth what ye know not; and He hath ordained you, beside this, a speedy victory.'

It is He who hath sent His Apostle with 'the Guidance,' and the religion of truth, that He may exalt it above every religion. And enough *for thee* is this testimony on the part of God.

Muhammad is the Apostle of God; and his comrades are vehement against the infidels, *but* full of tenderness among themselves. Thou mayst see them bowing down, prostrating themselves, imploring favours from God, and His acceptance. Their tokens[9] are on their faces, the marks of their prostrations. This is their picture in the Law, and their picture in the Evangel:[10] they are as the seed which putteth forth its stalk; then strengtheneth it, and it groweth stout, and riseth upon its stem,[11] rejoicing the husbandman – that the infidels may be wrathful at them. To such of them as believe and do the things that are right, hath God promised forgiveness and a noble recompense.

SURA 49 – THE APARTMENTS

MEDINA – 18 VERSES

In the Name of God, the Compassionate, the Merciful

O Believers! enter not upon any affair ere God and His Apostle[1] permit you; and fear ye God: for God Heareth, Knoweth.[2]

O Believers! raise not your voices above the voice of the Prophet, neither speak loud to him as ye speak loud one to another, lest your works come to nought, and ye unaware of it.

They who lower their voices in the presence of the Apostle of God, are the persons whose hearts God hath inclined to piety. Forgiveness shall be theirs and a rich reward.

They who call out to thee while thou art within[3] thine APARTMENTS, have most of them no right perception *of what is due to thee.*

But if they wait patiently till thou come forth to them, it were far better for them. But God is Indulgent, Merciful.

O Believers! if any bad man[4] come to you with news, clear it up at once, lest through ignorance ye harm others, and speedily have to repent of what ye have done.

And know that an Apostle of God is among you! should he give way to you in many matters ye would certainly become guilty of a crime. But God hath endeared the faith to you, and hath given it favour in your hearts, and hath made unbelief, and wickedness, and disobedience hateful to you. Such are they who pursue a right course.

Through the bounty and grace *which is* from God: and God is Knowing, Wise.

If two bodies of the faithful are at war, then make ye peace between them: and if the one of them wrong the other, fight against that party which doth the wrong, until they come back to the precepts of God: if they come back, make peace between them with fairness, and act impartially; God loveth those who act with impartiality.

10 Only the faithful are brethren; wherefore make peace between your brethren; and fear God, that ye may obtain mercy.

O Believers! let not men laugh men to scorn who haply may be better than themselves; neither let women laugh women to scorn who may haply be better than themselves![5] Neither defame one another, nor call one another by nicknames. Bad is it to be called wicked after *having professed* the faith:[6] and whoso repent not *of this* are doers of wrong.

O Believers! avoid frequent suspicions, for some suspicions are a crime; and pry not: neither let the one of you traduce another in his absence. Would any one of you like to eat the flesh of his dead brother? Surely ye would loathe it. And fear ye God: for God is Ready to turn, Merciful.

O men! verily, we have created you of a male, and a female; and we have divided you into peoples and tribes that ye might have knowledge one of another. Truly, the most worthy of honour in the sight of God is he who feareth Him most.[7] Verily, God is Knowing, Cognisant.

The Arabs of the desert[8] say, 'We believe.' SAY thou: Ye believe not; but rather say, 'We profess Islam;' for the faith hath not yet found its way into your hearts. But if ye obey God and His Apostle, he will not allow you to lose any of your actions: for God is Indulgent, Merciful.

The true believers are those only who believe in God and His Apostle, and afterwards doubt not; and who contend with their substance and their persons on the path of God. These are the sincere.

SAY: Will ye teach God about your religion? when God

knoweth whatever is in the Heavens and on the Earth: yea, God hath knowledge of all things.

They taunt thee with their having embraced Islam.[9] SAY: Taunt me not with your having embraced Islam: God rather taunteth you with His having guided you to the faith: *acknowledge this* if ye are sincere.

Verily, God knoweth the secrets of the Heavens and of the Earth: and God beholdeth what ye do.

SURA 50 – KAF

MECCA – 45 VERSES

In the Name of God, the Compassionate, the Merciful

KAF.[1] By the glorious Koran:

They marvel forsooth that one of themselves hath come to them charged with warnings. 'This,' say the infidels, 'is a marvellous thing:

What! when dead and turned to dust shall we. . . ? Far off is such a return as this?'

Now know we what the earth consumeth of them, and with us is a Book in which account is kept.

But they have treated the truth which hath come to them as falsehood; perplexed therefore is their state.

Will they not look up to the heaven above them, and consider how we have reared it and decked it forth, and that there are no flaws therein?

And as to the earth, we have spread it out, and have thrown the mountains upon it, and have caused an upgrowth in it of all beauteous kinds of plants,

For insight and admonition to every servant who loveth to turn to God:

And we send down the rain from Heaven with its blessings, by which we cause gardens to spring forth and the grain of harvest,

10 And the tall palm-trees with date-bearing branches one above the other

For man's nourishment: And life give we thereby to a dead country. So also shall be the resurrection.

Ere the days of these (Meccans) the people of Noah, and the men of Rass[2] and Themoud, treated their prophets as impostors:

And Ad and Pharaoh, and the brethren of Lot and the dwellers in the forest, and the people of Tobba,[3] all gave the lie to their prophets: justly, therefore, were the menaces inflicted.

Are we wearied out with the first creation? Yet are they in doubt with regard to a new creation![4]

We created man: and we know what his soul whispereth to him, and we are closer to him than his neck-vein.

When the two *angels* charged with taking account shall take it, one sitting on the right hand, the other on the left:

Not a word doth he utter, but there is a watcher with him ready *to note it down:*

And the stupor of certain death cometh upon him: – 'This is what thou wouldst have shunned' –

And there shall be a blast on the trumpet, – it is the threatened day!

20 And every soul shall come, – an *angel* with it urging it along, and an *angel* to witness against it[5] –

Saith he, 'Of this day didst thou live in heedlessness: but we have taken off thy veil from thee, and thy sight is becoming sharp this day.'

And he who is at this side[6] shall say, 'This is what I am prepared with against thee.'

And God will say, 'Cast into Hell, ye twain, every infidel, every hardened one,

The hinderer of the good, the transgressor, the doubter,

Who set up other gods with God. Cast ye him into the fierce torment.'

He who is at his side shall say, 'O our Lord! I led him not astray, yet was he in an error wide of truth.'

He shall say, 'Wrangle not in my presence. I had plied you beforehand with menaces:

My doom changeth not, and I am not unjust to man.'

On that day will we cry to Hell, 'Art thou full?' And it shall say, 'Are there more?'[7]

30 And not far from thence shall Paradise be brought near unto the Pious:

–'This is what ye have been promised: to every one who hath
turned in penitence to God and kept his laws;
Who hath feared the God of Mercy in secret, and come to
him with a contrite heart:
Enter it in peace: this is the day of Eternity.'
There shall they have all that they can desire: and ours will it
be to augment their bliss:
And how many generations have we destroyed ere the days of
these (Meccans), mightier than they in strength! Search ye
then the land. Is there any escape?
Lo! herein is warning for him who hath a heart, or giveth ear,
and is himself an eye-witness.[8]
We created the heavens and the earth and all that is between
them in six days, and no weariness touched us.[9]
Wherefore put up with what they say, and celebrate the
praise of thy Lord before sunrise and before sunset:
And praise Him in the night: and perform the *two* final
prostrations.
40 And list for the day whereon the crier shall cry from a place
near to every one alike:
The day on which men shall in truth hear that shout will be
the day of their coming forth *from the grave*.
Verily, we cause to live, and we cause to die. To us shall all
return.
On the day when the earth shall swiftly cleave asunder over
the *dead*, will this gathering be easy to Us.
We know best what the infidels say: and thou art not to
compel them.
Warn then by the Koran those who fear my menace.

SURA 51 – THE SCATTERING

MECCA – 60 VERSES

In the Name of God, the Compassionate, the Merciful

By the *clouds*[1] which scatter with SCATTERING,
And those which bear their load,
And by those which speed lightly along,

And those which apportion by command!
True, indeed, is that with which ye are threatened,
And lo! the judgment will surely come.[2]
By the star-tracked heaven!
Ye are discordant in what ye say;
But whoso turneth him *from the truth*, is turned from it *by a divine decree.*
10 Perish the liars,
Who are bewildered in the depths *of ignorance!*
They ask, 'When this day of judgment?'
On that day they shall be tormented at the fire.
'Taste ye of this your torment, whose speedy coming ye challenged.'
But the God-fearing *shall dwell* amid gardens and fountains,
Enjoying what their Lord hath given them, because, aforetime they were well-doers:
But little of the night was it that they slept,
And at dawn they prayed for pardon,
And gave due *share* of their wealth to the suppliant and the outcast.
20 On Earth are signs for men of firm belief,
And also in your own selves: Will ye not then behold them?
The Heaven hath sustenance for you, and *it containeth* that which you are promised.
By the Lord then of the heaven and of the earth, *I swear* that this is the truth, even as ye speak yourselves.[3]
Hath the story reached thee of Abraham's honoured guests?[4]
When they went in unto him and said, 'Peace!' he replied, 'Peace: – they are strangers.'
And he went apart to his family, and brought a fatted calf,
And set it before them. He said, 'Eat ye not?'
And he conceived a fear of them. They said to him, 'Fear not;' and announced to him a wise son.
His wife came up with outcry: she smote her face and said, '*What I*, old and barren!'
30 They said, 'Thus saith thy Lord. He truly is the Wise, the Knowing.'
Said he, 'And what, O messengers, is your errand?'
They said, 'To a wicked people are we sent,
To hurl upon them stones of clay,

Destined[5] by thy Lord for men guilty of excesses.'

And we brought forth the believers who were in the city:

But we found not in it but one family of Muslims.

And signs we left in it for those who dread the afflictive chastisement, –

And in Moses: when we sent him to Pharaoh with manifest power:

But relying on his forces[6] he turned his back and said, 'Sorcerer, or Possessed.'

40 So we seized him and his hosts and cast them into the sea; for of all blame was he worthy.

And in Ad: when we sent against them the desolating blast:

It touched not aught over which it came, but it turned it to dust.

And in Themoud:[7] when it was said to them, 'Enjoy yourselves for yet a while.'

But they rebelled against their Lord's command: so the tempest took them as they watched its coming.[8]

They were not able to stand upright, and could not help themselves.

And *we destroyed* the people of Noah, before them; for an impious people were they.

And the Heaven – with our hands have we built it up, and given it its expanse;

And the Earth – we have stretched it out like a carpet; and how smoothly have we spread it forth!

And of everything have we created pairs: that haply ye may reflect.

50 Fly then to God: I come to you from him a plain warner.

And set not up another god with God: I come to you from him a plain warner.

Even thus came there no apostle to those who flourished before them, but they exclaimed, 'Sorcerer, or Possessed.'

Have they made a legacy to one another of this scoff? Yes, they are a rebel people.

Turn away, then, from them, and thou shalt not incur reproach:

Yet warn them, for, in truth, warning will profit the believers.

I have not created Djinn and men, but that they should worship me:

I require not sustenance from them, neither require I that they feed me:

Verily, God is the sole sustainer: possessed of might: the unshaken!

Therefore to those who injure thee shall be a fate like the fate of their fellows of old. Let them not challenge me to hasten it.

60 Woe then to the infidels, because of their threatened day.

SURA 52 – THE MOUNTAIN

MECCA – 49 VERSES

In the Name of God, the Compassionate, the Merciful

By the MOUNTAIN,
And by the Book written
On an outspread roll,
And by the frequented fane,[1]
And by the lofty vault,
And by the swollen sea,
Verily, a chastisement from thy Lord is imminent,
And none shall put it back.
Reeling on that day the Heaven shall reel,
10 And stirring shall the mountains stir.[2]
And woe, on that day, to those who called the apostles liars,
Who plunged for pastime into vain disputes –
On that day shall they be thrust with thrusting to the fire of Hell: –
'This is the fire which ye treated as a lie.
What! is this magic, then? or, do ye not see it?
Burn ye therein: bear it patiently or impatiently 'twill be the same to you: for ye shall assuredly receive the reward of your doings.'
But mid gardens and delights shall they dwell who have feared God,
Rejoicing in what their Lord hath given them; and that from the pain of hell-fire hath their Lord preserved them.
'Eat and drink with healthy enjoyment, in recompense for your deeds.'

20 On couches ranged in rows shall they recline; and to the damsels with large dark eyes will we wed them.

And to those who have believed, whose offspring have followed them in the faith, will we again unite their offspring; nor of the meed of their works will we in the least defraud them. Pledged *to God* is every man for his actions and their desert.[3]

And fruits in abundance will we give them, and flesh as they shall desire:

Therein shall they pass to one another the cup which shall engender no light discourse, no motive to sin:

And youths shall go round among them beautiful as imbedded pearls:

And shall accost one another and ask mutual questions.

'A time indeed there was,' will they say, 'when we were full of care as to *the future lot of* our families;

But kind hath God been to us, and from the pestilential torment hath he preserved us;

For, heretofore we called upon Him – and He is the Beneficent, the Merciful.'

Warn thou, then. For thou by the favour of thy Lord art neither soothsayer nor possessed.

30 Will they say, 'A poet! let us await some adverse turn of his fortune?'

SAY, wait ye, and in sooth I too will wait with you.

Is it their dreams which inspire them with this? or is it that they are a perverse people?

Will they say, 'He hath forged it (the Koran) himself?' Nay, rather it is that they believed not.

Let them then produce a discourse like it, if they speak the Truth.

Were they created by nothing? or were they the creators of themselves?

Created they the Heavens and Earth? Nay, rather, they have no faith.

Hold they thy Lord's treasures? Bear they the rule supreme?

Have they a ladder for hearing the angels? Let any one who hath heard them bring a clear proof of it.

Hath God daughters and ye sons?

40 Asketh thou pay of them? they are themselves weighed down with debts.

Have they such a knowledge of the secret things that they can write them down?

Desire they to lay snares for thee? But the snared ones shall be they who do not believe.

Have they any God beside God? Glory be to God above what they join with Him.

And should they see a fragment of the heaven falling down, they would say, 'It is only a dense cloud.'

Leave them then until they come face to face with the day when they shall swoon away:

A day in which their snares shall not at all avail them, neither shall they be helped.

And verily, beside this is there a punishment for the evil doers: but most of them know it not.

Wait thou patiently the judgment of thy Lord, for thou art in our eye; and celebrate the praise of thy Lord when thou risest up,

And in the night-season: Praise him when the stars are setting.

SURA 53[1] – THE STAR

MECCA – 62 VERSES

In the Name of God, the Compassionate, the Merciful

By the STAR when it setteth,
Your compatriot erreth not, nor is he led astray,
Neither speaketh he from mere impulse.
The *Koran* is no other than a revelation revealed to him:
One terrible in power[2] taught it him,
Endued with wisdom. With even balance stood he
In the highest part of the horizon:
Then came he nearer and approached,
And was at the distance of two bows, or even closer, –
10 And he revealed to his servant what he revealed.
His heart falsified not what he saw.
What! will ye then dispute with him as to what he saw?

He had seen him also another time,

Near the Sidrah-tree, which marks the boundary.[3]

Near which is the garden of repose.

When the Sidrah-tree[4] was covered with what covered it,[5]

His eye turned not aside, nor did it wander:

For he saw the greatest of the signs of his Lord.

Do you see Al-Lat and Al-Ozza,[6]

20 And Manat the third idol besides?[7]

What? shall ye have male progeny and God female?

This were indeed an unfair partition!

These are mere names: ye and your fathers named them thus: God hath not sent down any warranty in their regard. A mere conceit and their own impulses do they follow. Yet hath 'the guidance' from their Lord come to them.

Shall man have whatever he wisheth?

The future and the present are in the hand of God:

And many as are the Angels in the Heavens, their intercession shall be of no avail[8]

Until God hath permitted it to whom he shall please and will accept.

Verily, it is they who believe not in the life to come, who name the angels with names of females:

But herein they have no knowledge: they follow a mere conceit; and mere conceit can never take the place of truth.

30 Withdraw then from him who turneth his back on our warning and desireth only this present life.

This is the sum of their knowledge. Truly thy Lord best knoweth him who erreth from his way, and He best knoweth him who hath received guidance.

And whatever is in the Heavens and in the Earth is God's, that he may reward those who do evil according to their deeds: and those who do good will He reward with good things.

To those who avoid great crimes and scandals but commit only lighter faults, verily, thy Lord will be diffuse of mercy. He well knew you when he produced you out of the earth, and when ye were embryos in your mother's womb. Assert not then your own purity. He best knoweth who feareth him.

Hast thou considered him who turned his back?

Who giveth little and is covetous?

Is it that he hath the knowledge and vision of the secret things?

Hath he not been told of what is in the pages of Moses?
And of Abraham faithful to his pledge?
That no burdened soul shall bear the burdens of another,
40 And that nothing shall be reckoned to a man but that for which he hath made efforts:
And that his efforts shall at last be seen *in their true light:*
That then he shall be recompensed with a most exact recompense,
And that unto thy Lord is the term of all things,
And that it is He who causeth to laugh and to weep,
And that He causeth to die and maketh alive,
And that He hath created the sexes, male and female,
From the diffused germs of life,[9]
And that with Him is the second creation,
And that He enricheth and causeth to possess,
50 And that He is the Lord of Sirius,[10]
And that it was He who destroyed the ancient Adites,
And the people of Themoud and left not *one survivor*,
And before them the people of Noah who were most wicked and most perverse.
And it was He who destroyed the cities that were overthrown.
So that that which covered them covered them.
Which then of thy Lord's benefits wilt thou make a matter of doubt?[11]
He who warneth you is one of the warners of old.
The day that must draw nigh, draweth nigh already: and yet none but God can reveal *its time.*
Is it at these sayings that ye marvel?
60 And that ye laugh and weep not?
And that ye are triflers?
Prostrate yourselves then to God and worship.

SURA 54 – THE MOON

MECCA – 55 VERSES

In the Name of God, the Compassionate, the Merciful

The hour hath approached and the MOON hath been cleft:

But whenever they see a miracle they turn aside and say, This is well-devised magic.

And they have treated the prophets as impostors, and follow their own lusts; but everything is unalterably fixed.

A message of prohibition had come to them –

Consummate wisdom – but warners profit them not.

Quit them then. On the day when the summoner shall summon to a stern business,

With downcast eyes shall they come forth from their graves, as if they were scattered locusts,

Hastening to the summoner. 'This,' shall the infidels say, 'is the distressful day.'

Before them the people of Noah treated the truth as a lie. Our servant did they charge with falsehood, and said, 'Demoniac!' and he was rejected.

10 Then cried he to his Lord, 'Verily, they prevail against me; come thou therefore to my succour.'

So we opened the gates of Heaven with water which fell in torrents,

And we caused the earth to break forth with springs, and their waters met by settled decree.

And we bare him on a *vessel* made with planks and nails.

Under our eyes it floated on: a recompense to him who had been rejected with unbelief.

And we left it a sign: but, is there any one who receives the warning?

And how great was my vengeance and my menace!

Easy for warning have we made the Koran – but, is there any one who receives the warning?

The Adites called the truth a lie: but how great was my vengeance and my menace;

For we sent against them a roaring wind in a day of continued distress:

20 It tore men away as though they were uprooted palm stumps.
And how great was my vengeance and my menace!
Easy for warning have we made the Koran – but, is there any one who receives the warning?
The tribe of Themoud treated the threatenings as lies:
And they said, 'Shall we follow a single man from among ourselves? Then verily should we be in error and in folly.
To him alone among us is the office of warning entrusted? No! he is an impostor, an insolent person.'
To-morrow shall they learn who is the impostor, the insolent.
'For we will send the she-camel to prove them: do thou mark them well, O *Saleh*, and be patient:
And foretell them that their waters shall[1] be divided between themselves and her, and that every draught shall come by turns to them.'
But they called to their comrade, and he took *a knife* and ham-strung her.
30 And how great was my vengeance and my menace!
We sent against them a single shout; and they became like the dry sticks of the fold-builders.
Easy have we made the Koran for warning – but, is there any one who receives the warning?
The people of Lot treated his warning as a lie;
But we sent a stone-charged wind against them all, except the family of Lot, whom at daybreak we delivered,
By our special grace – for thus we reward the thankful.
He, indeed, had warned them of our severity, but of that warning they doubted.
Even this guess did they demand: therefore we deprived them of sight,
And said, 'Taste ye my vengeance and my menace;'
And in the morning a relentless punishment overtook them.
40 Easy have we made the Koran for warning – but, is there any one who receives the warning?
To the people of Pharaoh also came the threatenings:
All our miracles did they treat as impostures. Therefore seized we them as he only can seize, who is the Mighty, the Strong.
Are your infidels, O *Meccans*, better men than these? Is there an exemption for you in the sacred Books?

Will they say, 'We are a host that lend one another aid?'
The host shall be routed, and they shall turn them back.
But, that Hour is their threatened time, and that Hour shall be most severe and bitter.
Verily, the wicked are sunk in bewilderment and folly.
On that day they shall be dragged into the fire on their faces. 'Taste ye the touch of Hell.'
All things have we created after a fixed decree:
50 Our command was but one word, swift as the twinkling of an eye.
Of old, too, have we destroyed the like of you – yet is any one warned?
And everything that they do is in the Books;[2]
Each action, both small and great, is written down.
Verily, amid gardens[3] and rivers shall the pious dwell.
In the seat of truth, in the presence of the potent King.

SURA 55 – THE MERCIFUL

MECCA – 78 VERSES

In the Name of God, the Compassionate, the Merciful

The God of MERCY hath taught the Koran,
Hath created man,
Hath taught him articulate speech.
The Sun and the Moon have each their times,
And the plants and the trees bend in adoration.
And the Heaven, He hath reared it on high, and hath appointed the balance;
That in the balance ye should not transgress.
Weigh therefore with fairness, and scant not the balance.
And the Earth, He hath prepared it for the living tribes:
10 Therein are fruits, and the palms with sheathed clusters,
And the grain with its husk, and the fragrant plants.
Which then of the bounties of your Lord will ye twain[1] deny?
He created man of clay like that of the potter.
And He created the djinn of pure fire:

Which then of the bounties, etc.
He is the Lord of the East,[2]
He is the Lord of the West:
Which, etc.
He hath let loose the two seas[3] which meet each other:
20 Yet between them is a barrier which they overpass not:
Which, etc.
From each he bringeth up pearls both great and small:
Which, etc.
And His are the ships towering up at sea like mountains:
Which, etc.
All on the earth shall pass away,
But the face of thy Lord shall abide resplendent with majesty and glory:
Which, etc.
To Him maketh suit all that is in the Heaven and the Earth. Every day doth some new work employ Him:
30 Which, etc.
We will find leisure *to judge* you, O ye men and djinn:[4]
Which, etc.
O company of djinn and men, if ye can overpass the bounds of the Heavens and the Earth, then overpass them. But by *our* leave only shall ye overpass them:
Which, etc.
A bright flash of fire shall be hurled at you both, and molten brass, and ye shall not defend yourselves from it:
Which, etc.
When the Heaven shall be cleft asunder, and become rose red, like stained leather:
Which, etc.
On that day shall neither man nor djinn be asked of his sin:
40 Which, etc.
By their tokens shall the sinners be known, and they shall be seized by their forelocks and their feet:
Which, etc.
'This is Hell which sinners treated as a lie.'
To and fro shall they pass between it and the boiling water:
Which, etc.
But for those who dread the majesty of their Lord shall be two gardens:
Which, etc.

With o'erbranching trees in each:
Which, etc.
50 In each two fountains flowing:
Which, etc.
In each two kinds of every fruit:
Which, etc.
On couches with linings of brocade shall they recline, and the fruit of the two gardens shall be within easy reach:
Which, etc.
Therein shall be the damsels with retiring glances, whom nor man nor djinn hath touched before them:
Which, etc.
Like jacynths and pearls:
Which, etc.
60 Shall the reward of good be aught but good?
Which, etc.
And beside these shall be two other gardens:[5]
Which, etc.
Of a dark green:
Which, etc.
With gushing fountains in each:
Which, etc.
In each fruits and the palm and the pomegranate:
Which, etc.
70 In each, the fair, the beauteous ones:
Which, etc.
With large dark eyeballs, kept close in their pavilions:
Which, etc.
Whom man hath never touched, nor any djinn:
Which, etc.
Their spouses on soft green cushions and on beautiful carpets shall recline:
Which, etc.
Blessed be the name of thy Lord, full of majesty and glory.

SURA 56 – THE EVENT

MECCA – 96 VERSES

In the Name of God, the Compassionate, the Merciful

When the EVENT that must come shall have come suddenly,[1]
None shall treat that sudden coming as a lie:
Day that shall abase! Day that shall exalt!
When the earth shall be shaken with a shock,
And the mountains shall be crumbled with a crumbling,
And shall become scattered dust,
And into three bands shall ye be divided:[2]
Then the people of the right hand[3] – Oh! how happy shall be the people of the right hand!
And the people of the left hand – Oh! how wretched shall be the people of the left hand!
10 And they who were foremost *on earth* – the foremost still.[4]
These are they who shall be brought nigh to God,
In gardens of delight;
A crowd of the former
And few of the latter generations;
On inwrought couches
Reclining on them face to face:
Aye-blooming youths go round about to them
With goblets and ewers and a cup of flowing wine;
Their brows ache not from it, nor fails the sense:
20 And with such fruits as shall please them best,
And with flesh of such birds, as they shall long for:
And theirs shall be the Houris, with large dark eyes, like pearls hidden in their shells,
In recompense of their labours past.
No vain discourse shall they hear therein, nor charge of sin,
But only the cry, 'Peace! Peace!'
And the people of the right hand – oh! how happy shall be the people of the right hand!
Amid thornless sidrahs[5]
And talh[6] trees clad with fruit,
And in extended shade,
30 And by flowing waters,

And with abundant fruits,[7]
Unfailing, unforbidden,
And on lofty couches.
Of a *rare* creation have we created the Houris,
And we have made them ever virgins,
Dear to their spouses, of equal age *with them*,[8]
For the people of the right hand,
A crowd of the former,
And a crowd of the latter generations.[9]
40 But the people of the left hand – oh! how wretched shall be the people of the left hand!
Amid pestilential[10] winds and in scalding water,
And in the shadow of a black smoke,
Not cool, and horrid to behold.[11]
For they truly, ere this, were blessed with worldly goods,
But persisted in heinous sin,
And were wont to say,
'What! after we have died, and become dust and bones, shall we be raised?
And our fathers, the men of yore?'
SAY: Aye, the former and the latter:
50 Gathered shall they all be for the time of a known day.
Then ye, O ye the erring, the gainsaying,
Shall surely eat of the tree Ez-zakkoum,
And fill your bellies with it,
And thereupon shall ye drink boiling water,
And ye shall drink as the thirsty camel drinketh.
This shall be their repast in the day of reckoning!
We created you, will ye not credit us?[12]
What think ye? The germs of life[13] –
Is it ye who create them? or are we their creator?
60 It is we who have decreed that death should be among you;
Yet are we not *thereby* hindered[14] from replacing you with others, your likes, or from producing you again in a form which ye know not!
Ye have known the first creation: will ye not then reflect?
What think ye? That which ye sow –
Is it ye who cause its upgrowth, or do we cause it to spring forth?
If we pleased we could so make your harvest dry and brittle that ye would ever marvel *and* say,

'Truly we have been at cost,[15] yet are we forbidden *harvest*.'
What think ye of the water ye drink?
Is it ye who send it down from the clouds, or send we it down?
Brackish could we make it, if we pleased: will ye not then be thankful?
70 What think ye? The fire which ye obtain *by friction* –
Is it ye who rear its tree, or do we rear it?
It is we who have made it for a memorial and a benefit to the wayfarers of the desert,
Praise therefore the name of thy Lord, the Great.
It needs not that I swear by the setting of the stars,
And it is a great oath, if ye knew it,
That this is the honourable Koran,
Written in the preserved Book:[16]
Let none touch it but the purified,[17]
It is a revelation from the Lord of the Worlds.
80 Such tidings as these will ye disdain?
Will ye make it your daily bread to gainsay them?
Why, at the moment when *the soul of a dying man* shall come up into his throat,
And when ye are gazing at him,
Though we are nearer to him than ye, although ye see us not:–
Why do ye not, if ye are to escape the judgment,
Cause that soul to return? Tell me, if ye speak the truth.
But as to him who shall enjoy near access to God,
His shall be repose, and pleasure, and a garden of delights.
Yea, for him who shall be of the people of the right hand,
90 *Shall be the greeting* from the people of the right hand – 'Peace be to thee.'
But for him who shall be of those who treat the prophets as deceivers,
And of the erring,
His entertainment shall be of scalding water,
And the broiling of hell-fire.
Verily this is a certain truth:
Praise therefore the name of thy Lord, the Great.

SURA 57 – IRON

MEDINA[1] – 29 VERSES

In the Name of God, the Compassionate, the Merciful

All that is in the Heavens and in the Earth praiseth God, and He is the Mighty, the Wise!

His the Kingdom of the Heavens and of the Earth; He maketh alive and killeth; and He hath power over all things!

He is the first and the last; the Seen and the Hidden;[2] and He knoweth all things!

It is He who in six days created the Heavens and the Earth, then ascended His throne. He knoweth that which entereth the earth, and that which goeth forth from it, and what cometh down from Heaven, and what mounteth up to it; and wherever ye are, He is with you; and God beholdeth all your actions!

His the kingdom of the Heavens and the Earth; and to God shall all things return!

He causeth the night to pass into the day, and He causeth the day to pass into the night: and He knoweth the very secrets of the bosom!

Believe in God and his apostle, and bestow in alms of that whereof God hath made you heirs: for whoever among you believe and give alms – theirs shall be a great recompense.

What hath come to you that ye believe not in God, although the apostle exhorteth you to believe in your Lord, and He hath accepted your alliance – if ye are *true* believers?

He it is who hath sent down clear tokens upon His servant, that He may bring you out of darkness into light; and truly, Kind, Merciful to you is God.

10 And what hath come to you that ye expend not for the cause of God? since the heritage of the Heavens and of the Earth is God's only! Those among you who contributed before the victory, and fought, shall be differently treated *from* certain others among you! Such shall have a nobler grade than those who contributed and fought after it. But a goodly recompense hath God promised to all; and God is fully informed of your actions.

Who is he that will lend a generous loan to God? So will He double it to him, and he shall have a noble reward.

One day thou shalt see the believers, men and women, with their light running before them, and on their right hand.[3] *The angels shall say to them*, 'Good tidings for you this day of gardens beneath whose *shades* the rivers flow, in which ye shall abide for ever!' This the great bliss!

On that day the hypocrites, both men and women, shall say to those who believe, 'Tarry for us, that we may kindle our light at yours.' It shall be said, 'Return ye back, and seek light for yourselves.' But between them shall be set a wall with a gateway, within which shall be the Mercy, and in front, without it, the Torment. They shall cry to them, 'Were we not with you?' They shall say, 'Yes! but ye led yourselves into temptation, and ye delayed, and ye doubted, and the good things ye craved deceived you, till the doom of God arrived: – and the deceiver deceived you in regard to God.'

On that day, therefore, no ransom shall be taken from you or from those who believe not: – your abode the fire! – This shall be your master![4] and wretched the journey thither!

Hath not the time come, for those who believe, to humble their hearts at the warning of God and at the truth which he hath sent down? and that they be not as those to whom the Scriptures were given heretofore, whose lifetime was prolonged, but whose hearts were hardened, and many of them were perverse?

Know that God quickeneth the earth after its death! Now have we made these signs clear to you, that ye may understand.

Verily, they who give alms, both men and women, and they who lend a generous loan to God, – doubled shall it be to them – and they shall have a noble recompense.

And they who believed in God and his apostle are the men of truth, and the witnesses in the presence of their Lord;[5] They shall have their recompense and their light: But as for the infidels, and those who give the lie to our signs, these shall be the inmates of Hell.

Know ye that this world's life is only a sport, and pastime, and show, and a cause of vainglory among you! And the multiplying of riches and children is like the plants which spring up after rain – Their growth rejoiceth the husbandman; then they wither away, and thou seest them all yellow; then they
become stubble. And in the next life is a severe chastisement,
20 Or else pardon from God and His satisfaction: and this
world's life is but a cheating fruition.[6]

Vie in hasting after pardon from your Lord, and Paradise – whose outspread is as the outspread of the Heaven and of the Earth: Prepared is it for those who believe in God and His apostles: Such is the bounty of God: to whom He will He giveth it: and of immense bounty is God!

No mischance chanceth either on earth or in your own persons, but ere we created them, it was in the Book;[7] – for easy is this to God –

Lest ye distress yourselves *if good things* escape you, and be over joyous for what falleth to your share. God loveth not the presumptuous, the boaster,

Who are covetous themselves and incite others to covetousness. But whoso turneth away *from almsgiving* – Ah! God is the Rich, the Praiseworthy.

We have sent our apostles with the clear tokens, and we have caused the Book and the balance[8] to descend with them, that men might observe fairness. And we have sent down IRON. Dire evil[9] resideth in it, as well as advantage, to mankind! God would know who will assist Him and his apostle in secret. Verily, God is Powerful, Strong.

And of old sent we Noah and Abraham, and on their seed conferred the gift of prophecy, and the Book; and some of them we guided aright; but many were evil doers.

Then we caused our apostles to follow in their footsteps; and we caused Jesus the son of Mary to follow them; and we gave him the Evangel,[10] and we put into the hearts of those who followed him kindness and compassion: but as to the monastic life, they invented it themselves. The desire only of pleasing God did we prescribe to them, and this they observed not as it ought to have been observed: but to such of them as believed gave we their reward, though many of them were perverse.

O ye who believe! fear God and believe in his apostle: two portions of his mercy will He give you. He will bestow on you light to walk in, and He will forgive you: for God is Forgiving, Merciful;

That the people of the Book may know that they have no control over aught of the favours of God, and that these gifts of grace[11] are in the hands of God, and that He vouchsafeth them to whom he will; for God is of immense bounty.

SURA 58 – SHE WHO PLEADED

MEDINA – 22 VERSES

In the Name of God, the Compassionate, the Merciful

God hath heard the words of HER WHO PLEADED with thee against her husband, and made her plaint to God; and God hath heard your mutual intercourse: for God Heareth, Beholdeth.

As to those of you who put away their wives *by saying*, '*Be thou to me as my mother's back*' – their mothers[1] they are not; they only are their mothers who gave them birth! they certainly say a blameworthy thing and an untruth:

But truly, God is Forgiving, Indulgent.

And those who *thus* put away their wives, and afterwards would recall their words, must free a captive before they can come together *again*. To this are ye warned to conform: and God is aware of what ye do.

And he who findeth not a *captive to set free*, shall fast two months in succession before they two come together. And he who shall not be able *to do so*, shall feed sixty poor men. This, that he may believe in God and His Apostle. These are the statues of God: and for the unbelievers is an afflictive chastisement!

Truly they who oppose God and His Apostle shall be brought low, as those who were before them were brought low. And now have we sent down demonstrative signs: and, for the Infidels is a shameful chastisement.

On the day when God shall raise them all to life, and shall tell them of their doings. God hath taken count of them, though they have forgotten them! and God is witness over all things.

Dost thou not see that God knoweth all that is in the Heavens and all that is in the Earth? Three persons speak not privately together, but He is their fourth; nor five, but He is their sixth; nor fewer nor more, but wherever they be He is with them. Then on the day of resurrection He will tell them of their deeds: for God knoweth all things.

Hast thou not marked those who have been forbidden secret talk, and return to what they have been forbidden, and talk privately together with wickedness, and hate, and disobedience towards the Apostle? And when they come to thee, they greet thee not as God greeteth thee:[2] and they say among themselves, 'Why doth not God punish us for what we say?' Hell shall be their meed:[3] they shall be burned at its fire: and a wretched passage *thither!*

10 O Believers! when ye hold private converse together, let it not be with wickedness, and hate, and disobedience towards the Apostle; but let your private talk be with justice and the fear of God: aye, fear ye God unto whom ye shall be gathered!

Only of Satan is this clandestine talk, that he may bring the faithful to grief: but, unless by God's permission, not aught shall he harm them! in God then let the faithful trust.

O ye who believe! when it is said to you, 'Make room in your assemblies,' then make ye room. God will make room for you *in Paradise!* And when it is said to you, 'Rise up,' then rise ye up. God will uplift those of you who believe, and those to whom 'the Knowledge' is given, to lofty grades! and God is cognisant of your actions.

O ye who believe! when ye go to confer in private with the Apostle, give alms before such conference. Better will this be for you, and more pure. But if ye have not the means, then truly God is Lenient, Merciful.

Do ye hesitate to give alms previously to your private conference? Then if ye do it not (and God will excuse it in you), at least observe prayer, and pay the stated impost, and obey God and His Apostle: for God is cognisant of your actions.

Hast thou not remarked those who make friends of that people with whom God is angered? They are neither of your party nor of theirs; and they swear to a lie,[4] knowing it to be such.

God hath got ready for them a severe torment: for, evil is that they do.

They make a cloak of their faith, and turn others aside from the way of God: wherefore a shameful torment awaiteth them.

Not at all shall their wealth or their children avail them aught against God. Companions shall they be of the fire: they shall abide therein for ever.

On the day when God shall raise them all, they will swear to Him as they *now* swear to you, deeming that it will avail them. Are they not – yes they – the liars?

20 Satan hath gotten mastery over them, and made them forget
the remembrance of God. These are Satan's party. What!
shall not verily the party of Satan be for ever lost.

Verily, they who oppose God and His Apostle shall be among the most vile. God hath written *this decree:* 'I will surely prevail, and my Apostles also.' Truly God is Strong, Mighty.

Thou shalt not find that any of those who believe in God, and in the last day, love him who opposeth God and His Apostle, even though they be their fathers, or their sons, or their brethren, or their nearest kin. On the hearts of these hath God graven the Faith, and with His own Spirit hath He strengthened them; and He will bring them into gardens, beneath whose *shades* the rivers flow, to remain therein eternally. God is well pleased in them, and they in Him. These are God's party! Shall not, of a truth, a party of God be for ever blessed?

SURA 59 – THE EMIGRATION

MEDINA – 24 VERSES

In the Name of God, the Compassionate, the Merciful

All that is in the Heavens and all that is on the Earth praiseth God! He, the Mighty, the Wise!

He it is who caused the unbelievers among the people of the Book to quit their homes and join those who had EMIGRATED previously.[1] Ye did not think that they would quit them; and they on their part thought that their fortresses would protect them against God: But God came upon them whence they looked not for Him, and cast such fear into their hearts that by their own hands as well as by the hands of the *victorious* believers they demolished their houses! Profit by this example ye who are men of insight!

And were it not that God had decreed their exile, surely in this world would he have chastised them: but in the world to come the chastisement of the fire awaiteth them.

This because they set them against God and his apostle; and

whoso setteth him against God. . . ! God truly is vehement in punishing.

Your cutting down some of their palm-trees and sparing others was by God's permission, and to put the wicked to shame.

After the spoils of these *Jews* which God hath assigned to his apostle, ye pressed not with horse or camel.[2] But God giveth his apostles power over what he will. God is Almighty.

The spoil taken from the people of the towns and assigned by God to his apostle, belongeth to God, and to the apostle, and to his kindred, and to the orphan, and to the poor, and to the wayfarer, that none of it may circulate among such of you only as are rich: What the apostle hath given you, take: What he hath refused you, refuse: And fear ye God, for God is severe in punishing.

To the poor refugees (Mohadjerin) also doth a part belong, who have been driven from their homes and their substance, and who seek favour from God and his good will, and aid God and his apostle. These are the men of genuine virtue.

They *of Medina* who had been in possession of their abodes and embraced the faith before them, cherish those who take refuge with them; and they find not in their breasts any desire for what hath fallen to their share: they prefer them before themselves, though poverty be their own lot. And with such as are preserved from their own covetousness shall it be well.

10 And they who have come after them *into the faith* say, 'O our Lord! forgive us and our brethren who have preceded us in the faith, and put not into our hearts ill-will against those who believe. O our Lord! thou verily art Kind, Merciful.'

Hast thou not observed the disaffected saying to their unbelieving brethren[3] among the people of the Book, 'If ye be driven forth, we will go forth with you; and in what concerneth you, never will we obey any one; and if ye be attacked we will certainly come to your help.' But God is witness that they are liars.

No! if they were driven forth, they would not share their banishment; if they were attacked they would not help them, or if they help them they will surely turn their backs: then would they remain unhelped.

Assuredly the fear of you is more intense in their hearts than the fear of God! This because they are a people devoid of discernment.

They (the Jews) will not fight against you in a body except in fenced towns or from behind walls. Mighty is their valour among themselves! thou thinkest them united – but their hearts are divided. This for that they are a people who understand not.

They act like those who lately preceded them, *who also* tasted the result of their doings; and a grievous chastisement awaiteth them –

Like Satan when he saith to a man, 'Be an infidel:' and when he hath become an infidel, he saith, 'I share not thy guilt:[4] verily, I fear God the Lord of the Worlds.'

Of both, therefore, shall the end be that they dwell for ever in the fire: This is the recompense of the evil doers.

O ye who believe! fear God. And let every soul look well to what it sendeth on before for the morrow. And fear ye God: Verily, God is cognisant of what ye do.

And be ye not like those who forget God, and whom He hath therefore caused to forget their proper selves. Such men are the evil doers.

20 The inmates of the Fire and the inmates of Paradise are not to be held equal. The inmates of Paradise only shall be the blissful.

Had we sent down this Koran on some mountain, thou wouldst certainly have seen it humbling itself[5] and cleaving asunder for the fear of God. Such are the parables we propose to men in order that they may reflect.

He is God beside whom there is no god. He knoweth things visible and invisible: He is the Compassionate, the Merciful.

He is God beside whom there is no god: He is the King, the Holy, the Peaceful, the Faithful, the Guardian, the Mighty, the Strong, the Most High! Far be the Glory of God from that which they unite with Him!

He is God, the Producer, the Maker, the Fashioner! To Him are ascribed excellent titles. Whatever is in the Heavens and in the Earth praiseth Him. He is the Mighty, the Wise!

SURA[1] 60 – SHE WHO IS TRIED

MEDINA – 13 VERSES

In the Name of God, the Compassionate, the Merciful

O ye who believe! take not my foe and your foe for friends, shewing them kindness, although they believe not that truth which hath come to you: they drive forth the Apostles and yourselves because ye believe in God your Lord! If ye go forth to fight on my way, and from a desire to please me, and shew them kindness in private, I well know what ye conceal, and what ye discover! Whoso doth this hath already gone astray from the even way.

If they meet with you they will prove your foes: hand and tongue will they put forth for your hurt, and will desire that you become infidels *again*.

Neither your kindred nor your children shall at all avail you on the day of the resurrection. A severance between you will it make! and your actions doth God behold.

A good example had ye in Abraham,[2] and in those who followed him, when they said to their people, 'Verily, we are clear of you, and of what ye worship beside God: we renounce you: and between us and you hath hatred and enmity sprung up for ever, until ye believe in God alone.' Yet *imitate not* the language of Abraham to his Father, 'I will pray for thy forgiveness, but not aught shall I obtain for thee from God.'[3] O our Lord! in thee do we trust! to thee do we turn! to thee we shall come back at the last.

O our Lord! expose us not for trial to the unbelievers, and forgive us: for thou art the Mighty, the Wise!

A good example had ye in them, for all who hope in God and in the last day. But let who will turn back, God truly is the Rich, the Praiseworthy!

God will, perhaps, establish good will between yourselves and those of them whom ye take to be your enemies:[4] God is Powerful: and God is Gracious, Merciful.

God doth not forbid you to deal with kindness and fairness towards those who have not made war upon you on account of your religion, or driven you forth from your homes: for God loveth those who act with fairness.

Only doth God forbid you to make friends of those who, on account of your religion, have warred against you, and have driven you forth from your homes, and have aided those who drove you forth: and whoever maketh friends of them are wrong doers.

10 O Believers![5] when believing women come over to you as
refugees (Mohadjers), then make TRIAL of them. God best knoweth their faith; but if ye have also ascertained their faith, let them not go back to the infidels; they are not lawful for them, nor are the unbelievers lawful for these women. But give them back what they have spent *for their dowers*. No crime shall it be in you to marry them, provided ye give them their dowers. Do not retain any right in the infidel women, but demand back what you have spent *for their dowers*, and let *the unbelievers* demand back what they have spent *for their wives*.[6] This is the ordinance of God which He ordaineth among you: and God is Knowing, Wise.

And if any of your wives escape from you to the Infidels from whom ye afterwards take any spoil, then give to those whose wives shall have fled away, the like of what they shall have spent *for their dowers;* and fear God in whom ye believe.

O Prophet! when believing women come to thee, and pledge themselves that they will not associate aught with God, and that they will not steal or commit adultery, nor kill their children, nor bring scandalous charges,[7] nor disobey thee in what is right, then plight thou thy faith to them, and ask pardon for them of God: for God is Indulgent, Merciful!

O Believers! enter not into amity with those against whom God is angered; they despair of the life to come, even as the Infidels despair of the inmates of the tombs.

SURA 61 – BATTLE ARRAY

MEDINA – 14 VERSES

In the Name of God, the Compassionate, the Merciful

All that is in the Heavens and all that is on the Earth praiseth God. He is the Mighty, the Wise!

Believers! why profess ye that which ye practise not?[1]

Most hateful is it to God that ye say that which ye do not.

Verily God loveth those who, as though they were a solid wall, do battle for his cause in serried lines!

And *bear in mind* when Moses said to his people, 'Why grieve ye me, O my people, when ye know that I am God's apostle unto you?' And when they went astray, God led their hearts astray; for God guideth not a perverse people:

And *remember* when Jesus the son of Mary said, 'O children of Israel! of a truth I am God's apostle to you to confirm the law which was given before me, and to announce an apostle that shall come after me whose name shall be Ahmad!'[2] But when he (Ahmad) presented himself with clear proofs of his mission, they said, 'This is manifest sorcery!'

But who more impious than he who when called to Islam deviseth a falsehood concerning God? God guideth not the wicked!

Fain would they put out the light of God with their mouths! but though the Infidels hate it, God will perfect his light.

He it is who hath sent his apostle with guidance and the religion of truth, that, though they hate it who join other gods with God, He may make it victorious over every other religion.

10 O ye who believe! shall I shew you a merchandise that shall deliver you from the sore torment?

Believe in God and his apostle, and do valiantly in the cause of God with your wealth and with your persons! This, did ye but know it, will be best for you.

Your sins will He forgive you, and He will bring you into gardens beneath whose shades the rivers flow – into charming abodes in the gardens of Eden: This shall be the great bliss. –

And other things which ye desire *will he bestow*, Help from God and speedy conquest![3] Bear thou these tidings to the faithful.

O ye who believe! be helpers (ansars) of God; as said Jesus the son of Mary to his apostles, 'Who will come to the help of God?' 'We,' said the apostles, 'will be helpers of God.' And a part of the children of Israel believed, and a part believed not. But to those who believed gave we the upperhand over their foes, and soon did they prove victorious.

SURA 62 – THE ASSEMBLY

MEDINA – 11 VERSES

In the Name of God, the Compassionate, the Merciful

All that is in the Heavens, and all that is on the Earth, uttereth the Praise of God, the King! the Holy! the Mighty! the Wise!

It is He who hath sent to the pagan folk (Arabs) an Apostle from among themselves, to rehearse His signs to them, and to purify them, and to impart to them a knowledge of 'the Book' and wisdom; for aforetime were they in manifest error.

And others among them have not yet overtaken those *who preceded them in the faith*. But He is the Mighty, the Wise!

This is the goodness of God: He bestoweth it on whom He will: God is of immense goodness!

They on whom the burden of the law was laid, and would not bear it, are like an ass beneath a load of books. A sorry likeness this, for the people who give the lie to the signs of God! God guideth not the people who do this wrong!

SAY: O ye Jews, if ye profess that ye rather than other men are the friends of God, then wish for death if ye are men of truth.

But never on account of their previous handywork will they wish for it, and God knoweth the wrong doers.

SAY: Verily the death from which ye flee will surely meet you. Then shall ye be brought back to Him who knoweth alike the things done in secret and openly: and He will tell you of your actions.

O ye who believe! When ye are summoned to prayer on the

day of THE ASSEMBLY,[1] haste to the commemoration of God,
and quit your traffic. This, if ye knew it, will be best for you.
10 And when the Prayer is ended, then disperse yourselves
abroad and go in quest of the bounties of God; and, that it may
be well with you, oft remember God.

But when they get a sight of merchandise or sport, they disperse after it, and leave thee standing alone.[2] SAY: God hath in reserve what is better than sport or wares. And God is the best provider!

SURA 63[1] – THE HYPOCRITES

MEDINA – 11 VERSES

In the Name of God, the Compassionate, the Merciful

When the Hypocrites come to thee, they say, 'We bear witness that thou art the Sent One of God.' God knoweth that thou art His Sent One: but God beareth witness that the HYPOCRITES do surely lie.

Their faith[2] have they used as a cloak, and they turn aside others from the way of God! Evil are all their doings.

This, for that they believed, then became unbelievers! Therefore hath a seal been set upon their hearts, and they understand not.

When thou seest them, their persons make thee marvel; and if they speak, thou listenest *with pleasure* to their discourse. Like timbers are they leaning against a wall![3] They think that every shout is against them. They are enemies – Beware of them then – God do battle with them! How false are they!

And when it is said to them, 'Come, the Apostle of God will ask pardon for you,' they turn their heads aside, and thou seest them withdraw in their pride.

Alike shall it be to them whether thou ask forgiveness for them, or ask it not. By no means will God forgive them: God hath no guidance for a perverse people.

These are they who say *to you of Medina*, 'Spend not aught upon those who are with the Apostle of God, and they will be forced to quit him.' Yet the treasures of the Heavens and of the Earth are God's! But the Hypocrites have no understanding.

They say: 'If we return to the city, the mightier will assuredly drive out the weaker from it.' But might is with God, and with the Apostle, and with the Faithful! Yet the Hypocrites understand not.

O ye who believe! let not your wealth and your children delude you into forgetfulness of God. Whoever shall act thus, shall surely suffer loss.

10 And expend *in the cause of God* out of that with which we have supplied you, ere death surprise each one of you, and he say, 'O Lord! wilt thou not respite me to a term not far distant, that I may give alms, and become one of the just?'

And by no means will God respite a soul when its hour hath come! And God is fully cognisant of what ye do.

SURA 64 – MUTUAL DECEIT

MEDINA[1] – 18 VERSES

In the Name of God, the Compassionate, the Merciful

All that is in the Heavens, and all that is in the Earth, praiseth God: His the Kingdom and His the Glory! And He hath power over all things!

It is He who hath created you *all;* yet some of you are infidel and others believers: but God beholdeth all your actions.

He hath created the Heavens and the Earth in Truth; and He hath fashioned you and given you goodly forms; and to Him must ye all return.

He knoweth all that passeth in the Heavens and in the Earth; and He knoweth what ye hide and what ye bring to light; and God knoweth the very secrets of *men's* breasts.

Hath not the story reached you of those who disbelieved of yore, and therefore tasted the evil consequences of their doings? And a sore punishment doth await them.

This, for that when their apostles came to them with the clear tokens, they said, 'What! shall men be our guides?' And they believed not and turned their backs. But God can dispense with them; for God is the Rich, the Praiseworthy!

The infidels pretend that they shall not be raised from the dead. SAY: Yea, by my Lord, ye shall surely be raised; then shall ye surely be told of your deeds! And easy is this for God.

Believe then in God and his apostle and in the light which we have sent down; for God is fully aware of all ye do.

The day when He shall gather you together for the day of mutual gathering, will be the day of MUTUAL DECEIT,[2] and whoso shall have believed in God and done what is right, for him will He cancel his deeds of evil; and He will bring him into the gardens beneath whose *shades* the rivers flow, to abide therein for evermore. This will be the great bliss!

10 But the unbelieving – those who gave the lie to our signs – shall be the inmates of the fire, wherein they shall remain for ever. And a wretched passage *thither!*

No mischance chanceth but by God's permission; and whoso believeth in God, that man's heart will he guide: and God knoweth all things.

Obey God then and obey the apostle: but if ye turn away, our apostle *is not to blame, for he* is only charged with plain preaching.

God! there is no God but He! On God, then, let the faithful trust.

O ye who believe! Verily, in your wives and your children ye have an enemy: wherefore beware of them. But if ye pass it[3] over and pardon, and are lenient, then God too is Lenient, Merciful.

Your wealth and your children are only a source of trial! but God! with Him is the great recompense.

Fear God, then, with all your might, and hear and obey: and give alms for your own weal; for such as are saved from their own greed, shall prosper.

If ye lend God a generous loan, He will double it to you and will forgive you, for God is Grateful, Long-suffering.

He knoweth *alike* the Hidden and the Manifest: the Mighty, the Wise!

SURA 65 – DIVORCE[1]

MECCA – 12 VERSES

In the Name of God, the Compassionate, the Merciful

O Prophet! when ye divorce women, divorce them at their special times. And reckon those times exactly, and fear God your Lord. Put them not forth from their houses, nor allow them to depart, unless they have committed a proven adultery. This is the precept of God; and whoso transgresseth the precept of God, assuredly imperilleth his own self. Thou knowest not whether, after this, God may not cause something new to occur *which may bring you together again.*

And when they have reached their set time, then either keep them with kindness, or in kindness part from them. And take upright witnesses from among you, and bear witness as unto God. This is a caution for him who believeth in God and in the latter day. And whoso feareth God, to him will He grant a prosperous issue, and will provide for him whence he reckoned not upon it.

And for him who putteth his trust in Him will God be all-sufficient. God truly will attain his purpose. For everything hath God assigned a period.

As to such of your wives as have no hope of the recurrence of their times, if ye have doubts in regard to them, then reckon three months, and let the same be the term of those who have not yet had them. And as to those who are with child, their period shall be until they are delivered of their burden. God will make His command easy to him who feareth Him.

This is God's command which He hath sent down to you: Whoso feareth God, his evil deeds will He cancel and will increase his reward.

Lodge *the divorced* wherever ye lodge, according to your means; and distress them not by putting them to straits. And if they are pregnant, then be at charges for them till they are delivered of their burden; and if they suckle your children, then pay them their hire and consult among yourselves, and act generously: And if herein ye meet with obstacles, then let another female suckle for him.

Let him who hath abundance give of his abundance; let him, too, whose store is scanty, give of what God hath vouchsafed to him. God imposeth burdens only according to the means which He hath given. God will cause ease to succeed difficulties.

How many cities have turned aside from the command of their Lord and of his apostles! Therefore did we reckon with them in a severe reckoning, and chastised them with a stern chastisement;

And they tasted the harmfulness of their own conduct: and the end of their conduct was ruin.

10 A vehement chastisement hath God prepared for them! Fear God, then, O ye men of understanding![2]

Believers! Now hath God sent down to you a warning! a prophet, who reciteth to you the clear signs of God, that he may bring those who believe, and do the things that are right, out of the darkness into the light. And whoso believeth in God, and doeth the things that are right, God will cause them to enter the gardens beneath which the rivers flow, to remain therein for aye! A goodly provision now hath God made for him.

It is God who hath created seven heavens and as many earths.[3] The Divine command cometh down through them all, that ye may know that God hath power over all things, and that God in his knowledge embraceth all things!

SURA 66 – THE FORBIDDING

MEDINA – 12 VERSES

In the Name of God, the Compassionate, the Merciful

Why,[1] O Prophet! dost thou hold that to be FORBIDDEN which God hath made lawful to thee, from a desire to please thy wives, since God is Lenient, Merciful?

God hath allowed you release from your oaths; and God is your master: and He is the Knowing, Wise.

When the prophet told a recent occurrence as a secret to one of his wives, and when she divulged it and God informed him of this, he acquainted her with part and withheld part.[2] And when he had told her of it, she said, 'Who told thee this?' He said, 'The Knowing, the Sage hath told it me.

'If ye both be turned to God in penitence, for now have your hearts gone astray. . .[3] but if ye conspire against the Prophet, then *know* that God is his Protector, and Gabriel, and every just man among the faithful; and the angels are his helpers besides.

'Haply if he put you both away, his Lord will give him in exchange other wives better than you, Muslims, believers, devout, penitent, obedient, observant of fasting, both known of men and virgins.'

O Believers! save yourselves and your families from the fire whose fuel is men and stones, over which are set angels fierce and mighty: they disobey not God in what He hath commanded them, but execute His behests.

O ye Infidels! make no excuses for yourselves this day; ye shall surely be recompensed according to your works.

O Believers! turn to God with the turning of true penitence; haply your Lord will cancel your evil deeds, and will bring you into the gardens 'neath which the rivers flow, on the day when God will not shame the Prophet, nor those who have shared his faith: their light shall run before them, and on their right hands! they shall say, 'Lord perfect our light, and pardon us: for thou hast power over all things.'

O Prophet! make war on the infidels and hypocrites, and deal rigorously with them. Hell shall be their abode! and wretched the passage to it!

10 God setteth forth as an example to unbelievers the wife of Noah and the wife of Lot; they were under two of our righteous servants, both of whom they deceived: but their husbands availed them nought against God: and it shall be said 'Enter ye into the fire with those who enter.'

God also holdeth forth to those who believe the example of the wife of Pharaoh, when she said, 'Lord, build me an house with thee in Paradise, and deliver me from Pharaoh and his doings; and deliver me from the wicked:'

And Mary, the daughter of Imran, who kept her maidenhood, and into whose womb[4] we breathed of our spirit, and who believed in the words of her Lord and His Scriptures, and was one of the devout.

SURA 67 – THE KINGDOM

MECCA – 30 VERSES

In the Name of God, the Compassionate, the Merciful

Blessed be He in whose hand is the KINGDOM! and over all things is He potent:

Who hath created death and life to prove which of you will be most righteous in deed; and He is the Mighty, the Forgiving!

Who hath created seven Heavens one above another: No defect canst thou see in the creation of the God of Mercy: Repeat the gaze: seest thou a single flaw?

Then twice more repeat the gaze: thy gaze shall return to thee dulled and weary.

Moreover we have decked the lowest heaven with lights, and have placed them *there* to be hurled at the Satans, for whom we have prepared the torment of the flaming fire.

And for those who believe not in their Lord is the torment of Hell; and horrid the journey thither!

When they shall be thrown into it, they shall hear it braying:[1] and it shall boil –

Almost shall it burst for fury. So oft as a crowd shall be thrown into it, its keepers shall ask them, 'Came not the warner to you?'

They shall say, Yes! there came to us one charged with warnings; but we treated him as a liar, and said, 'Nothing hath God sent down: ye are in nothing but a vast delusion.'

10 And they shall say, 'Had we but hearkened or understood, we had not been among the dwellers in the flames;'

And their sin shall they acknowledge: but, 'Avaunt, ye dwellers in the flame.'

But pardon and a great reward for those who fear their Lord in secret!

Be your converse hidden or open, He truly knoweth the inmost recess of your breasts!

What! shall He not know who hath created? for He is the Subtil,[2] the Cognizant.

It is He who hath made the earth level for you: traverse then its broad sides, and eat of what He hath provided. – Unto Him shall be the resurrection.

What! are ye sure that He who is in Heaven will not cleave the Earth beneath you? And lo, it shall quake.

Or are ye sure that He who is in Heaven will not send against you a stone-charged whirlwind? Then shall ye know what my warning *meant!*

And verily, those who flourish before you treated their prophets as liars: and how grievous my wrath!

Behold they not the birds over their heads, outstretching and drawing in their wings? None, save the God of Mercy, upholdeth them: for he regardeth all things.

20 Who is he that can be as an army to you, to succour you, except the God of Mercy? Truly, the infidels are in the merest delusion.

Or who is he that will furnish you supplies, if He withhold His supplies? Yet do they persist in pride and in fleeing from Him!

Is he who goeth along grovelling on his face, better guided than he who goeth upright on a straight path?

SAY: It is He who hath brought you forth, and gifted you with hearing and sight and heart: yet how few are grateful!

SAY: It is He who hath sown you in the earth, and to Him shall ye be gathered.

And they say, 'When shall this threat be put in force, if ye speak the truth?'

SAY: Nay truly, this knowledge is with God alone: and I am only an open warner.

But when they shall see it nigh, sad shall wax the countenances of the infidels: and it shall be said, 'This is what ye have been calling for.'

SAY: What think ye? Whether God destroy me or not, and those who follow me, or whether he have mercy on us, yet who will protect the infidels from a woeful torment?

SAY: He is the God of Mercy: in Him do we believe, and in Him put we our trust; and ye shall know hereafter who is in a manifest error.

30 SAY: What think ye? If at early morn your waters shall have sunk away, who then will give you clear running water?

SURA 68 – THE PEN

MECCA – 52 VERSES

In the Name of God, the Compassionate, the Merciful

Nun.[1] By the PEN and by what they write,

Thou, *O Prophet;* by the grace of thy Lord art not possessed![2]

And truly a boundless recompense doth await thee,

For thou art of a noble nature.[3]

But thou shalt see and they shall see

Which of you is the demented.

Now thy Lord! well knoweth He the man who erreth from his path, and well doth he know those who have yielded to Guidance;

Give not place, therefore, to those who treat thee as a liar:

They desire thee to deal smoothly with them: then would they be smooth as oil with thee:

10 But yield not to the man of oaths, a despicable person,

Defamer, going about with slander,

Hinderer of the good, transgressor, criminal,

Harsh – beside this, impure by birth,

Though a man of riches and blessed with sons.

Who when our wondrous verses are recited to him saith – 'Fables of the ancients.'

We will brand him on the nostrils.

Verily, we have proved them (the Meccans) as we proved the owners of the garden, when they swore that at morn they would cut its fruits;

But added no reserve.[4]

Wherefore an encircling desolation from thy Lord swept round it while they slumbered,

20 And in the morning it was like a garden whose fruits had all been cut.

Then at dawn they called to each other,

'Go out early to your field, if ye would cut your dates.'

So on they went whispering to each other,

'No poor man shall set foot this day within your garden;'

And they went out at daybreak with this settled purpose.

But when they beheld it, they said, 'Truly we have been in
fault:
Yes! we are forbidden our fruits.'
The most rightminded of them said, 'Did I not say to you,
Will ye not give praise to God?'
They said, 'Glory to our Lord! Truly we have done amiss.'
30 And they fell to blaming one another:
They said, 'Oh woe to us! we have indeed transgressed!
Haply our Lord will give us in exchange a better garden than
this: verily we crave it of our Lord.'
Such hath been our chastisement – but heavier shall be the
chastisement of the next world. Ah! did they but know it.
Verily, for the God-fearing are gardens of delight in the
presence of their Lord.
Shall we then deal with those who have surrendered them-
selves to God, as with those who offend him?
What hath befallen you that ye thus judge?
Have ye a Scripture wherein ye can search out
That ye shall have the things ye choose?
Or have ye received oaths which shall bind Us even until the day
of the resurrection, that ye shall have what yourselves judge right?
40 Ask them which of them will guarantee this?
Or is it that they have joined gods with God? let them
produce those associate-gods of theirs, if they speak truth.
On the day when *men's* legs shall be bared,[5] and they shall be
called upon to bow in adoration, they shall not be able:
Their looks shall be downcast: shame shall cover them:
because, while yet in safety, they were invited to bow in
worship, *but would not obey.*
Leave me alone therefore with him who chargeth this
revelation with imposture. We will lead them by degrees to
their ruin; by ways which they know not;
Yet will I bear long with them; for my plan is sure.
Askest thou any recompense from them? But they are
burdened with debt.
Are the secret things within their ken? Do they copy them
from the Book of God?
Patiently then await the judgment of thy Lord, and be not like
him who was in the fish,[6] when in deep distress he cried *to God.*
Had not favour from his Lord reached him, cast forth would
he have been on the naked shore, overwhelmed with shame:

50 But his Lord chose him and made him of the just.

Almost would the infidels strike thee down with their very looks when they hear the warning *of the Koran*. And they say, 'He is certainly possessed.'

Yet is it nothing less than a warning for all creatures.

SURA 69 – THE INEVITABLE

MECCA – 52 VERSES

In the Name of God, the Compassionate, the Merciful

The INEVITABLE!

What is the Inevitable?

And who shall make thee comprehend what the Inevitable is?

Themoud and Ad treated the day of Terrors[1] as a lie.

So as to Themoud,[2] they were destroyed by crashing thunder bolts;

And as to Ad, they were destroyed by a roaring and furious blast.

It did the bidding of God[3] against them seven nights and eight days together, during which thou mightest have seen the people laid low, as though they had been the trunks of hollow palms;

And couldst thou have seen one of them surviving?

Pharaoh also, and those who flourished before him, and the overthrown cities, committed sin, –

10 And disobeyed the Sent one of their Lord; therefore did he chastise them with an accumulated chastisement.

When the Flood rose high, we bore you in the Ark,

That we might make that event a warning to you, and that the retaining ear might retain it.

But when one blast shall be blown on the trumpet,

And the earth and the mountains shall be upheaved, and shall both be crushed into dust at a single crushing,

On that day the woe that must come suddenly shall suddenly come,[4]

And the heaven shall cleave asunder, for on that day it shall be fragile;

And the angels shall be on its sides, and over them on that day eight shall bear up the throne of thy Lord.

On that day ye shall be brought before Him: none of your hidden deeds shall remain hidden:

And he who shall have his book given to him in his right hand, will say to his friends, 'Take ye it; read ye my book;

20 I ever thought that to this my reckoning I should come.'

And his shall be a life that shall please him well,

In a lofty garden,

Whose clusters shall be near at hand:

'Eat ye and drink with healthy relish, as the meed of what ye sent on beforehand in the days which are past.'

But he who shall have his book given into his left hand, will say, 'O that my book had never been given me!

And that I had never known my reckoning!

O that death had made an end of me!

My wealth hath not profited me!

My power hath perished from me!'

30 'Lay ye hold on him and chain him,

Then at the Hell-fire burn him,

Then into a chain whose length is seventy cubits thrust him;

For he believed not in God, the Great,

And was not careful to feed the poor;

No friend therefore shall he have here this day,

Nor food, but corrupt stores,

Which none shall eat but the sinners.'

It needs not that I swear by what ye see,

And by that which ye see not,

40 That this verily is the word of an apostle worthy of all honour!

And that it is not the word of a poet – how little do ye believe!

Neither is it the word of a soothsayer (Kahin) – how little do ye receive warning!

It is a missive from the Lord of the worlds.

But if Muhammad had fabricated concerning us any sayings,

We had surely seized him by the right hand,

And had cut through the vein of his neck.

Nor would We have withheld any one of you from him.

But, verily, It (the Koran) is a warning for the God-fearing;

And we well know that there are of you who treat it as a falsehood.

50 But it shall be the despair of infidels,
For it is the very truth of sure knowledge.
Praise, then, the name of thy Lord, the Great.

SURA 70 – THE STEPS OR ASCENTS

MECCA – 44 VERSES

In the Name of God, the Compassionate, the Merciful

A suitor sued[1] for punishment to light suddenly
On the infidels: none can hinder
God from inflicting it, the master of those ASCENTS,
By which the angels and the spirit ascend to him in a day,
whose length is fifty thousand years.[2]
Be thou patient therefore with becoming patience;
They forsooth regard *that day* as distant,
But we see it nigh:
The day when the heavens shall become as molten brass,
And the mountains shall become like flocks of wool:
10 And friend shall not question of friend,
Though they look at one another. Fain would the wicked
redeem himself from punishment on that day at the price of his
children,
Of his spouse and his brother,
And of his kindred who shewed affection for him,
And of all who are on the earth *that* then it might deliver him.
But no. For the fire,
Dragging by the scalp,
Shall claim him who turned his back and went away,
And amassed and hoarded.
Man truly is by creation hasty;
20 When evil befalleth him, impatient;
But when good falleth to his lot, tenacious.
Not so the prayerful,
Who are ever constant at their prayers;
And of whose substance there is a due and stated portion
For him who asketh, and for him who is ashamed[3] to beg;

And who own the judgment-day a truth,
And who thrill with dread at the chastisement of their Lord –
For there is none safe from the chastisement of their Lord –
And who control their desires,
30 (Save with their wives or the slaves whom their right hands have won, for there they shall be blameless;
But whoever indulge their desires beyond this are transgressors);
And who are true to their trusts and their engagements,
And who witness uprightly,
And who keep strictly *the hours of* prayer:
These *shall dwell*, laden with honours, amid gardens.
But what hath come to the unbelievers that they run at full stretch around thee,
On the right hand and on the left, in bands?
Is it that every man of them would fain enter that garden of delights?
Not at all. We have created them, they know of what.
40 It needs not that I swear by the Lord of the East and of the West[4] that we have power
To replace them with better than themselves: neither are we to be hindered.
Wherefore let them flounder on and disport them, till they come face to face with their threatened day,
The day on which they shall flock up out of their graves in haste like men who rally to a standard: –
Their eyes downcast; disgrace shall cover them. Such their threatened day.

SURA 71 – NOAH

MECCA – 29 VERSES

In the Name of God, the Compassionate, the Merciful

We sent NOAH to his people, and said to him, 'Warn thou thy people ere there come on them an afflictive punishment.'
He said, 'O my people! I come to you a plain-spoken warner:

Serve God and fear Him, and obey me:
Your sins will He forgive you, and respite you till the fixed Time; for when God's fixed Time hath come, it shall not be put back. Would that ye knew this!'
He said, 'Lord I have cried to my people night and day; and my cry doth but make them flee from me the more.
So oft as I cry to them, that thou mayest forgive them, they thrust their fingers into their ears, and wrap themselves in their garments, and persist *in their error*, and are disdainfully disdainful.
Then I cried aloud to them:
Then again spake I with plainness, and in private did I secretly address them:
And I said, "Beg forgiveness of your Lord, for He is ready to forgive.
10 He will send down the very Heaven upon you in plenteous rains;
And will increase you in wealth and children; and will give you gardens, and will give you watercourses: –
What hath come to you that ye hope not for goodness from the hand of God?
For He it is who hath formed you by successive steps.[1]
See ye not how God hath created the seven heavens one over the other?
And He hath placed therein the moon as a light, and hath placed *there* the sun as a torch;
And God hath caused you to spring forth from the earth like a plant;
Hereafter will He turn you back into it again, and will bring you forth anew –
And God hath spread the earth for you like a carpet,
That ye may walk therein along spacious paths."'
20 Said Noah, 'O my Lord! they rebel against me, and they follow those whose riches and children do but aggravate their ruin.'
And they plotted a great plot;
And they said, 'Forsake not your Gods; forsake not Wadd nor Sowah,
Nor Yaghuth and Yahuk and Nesr;'
And they caused many to err;[2] – and thou, too, O Muhammad! shalt be the means of increasing only error in the wicked –

Because of their sins they were drowned, and made to go into the Fire;

And they found that they had no helper save God.

And Noah said, 'Lord, leave not one single family of Infidels on the Earth:

For if thou leave them they will beguile thy servants and will beget only sinners, infidels.

O my Lord, forgive me, and my parents, and every one who, being a believer, shall enter my house, and believers men and women: and add to the wicked nought but perdition.'

SURA 72 – DJINN

MECCA – 28 VERSES

In the Name of God, the Compassionate, the Merciful

SAY: It hath been revealed to me that a company of DJINN[1] listened, and said, – 'Verily, we have heard a marvellous discourse (Koran);

It guideth to the truth; wherefore we believed in it, and we will not henceforth join any *being* with our Lord;

And He, – may the majesty of our Lord be exalted! – hath taken no spouse neither hath he any offspring.

But the foolish among us hath spoken of God that which is unjust:

And we verily thought that no one amongst men or Djinn would have uttered a lie against God.

There are indeed people among men, who have sought for refuge unto people among Djinn: but they only increased their folly:

And they thought, as ye think, that God would not raise any from the dead.

And the Heavens did we essay, but found them filled with a mighty garrison, and with flaming darts;

And we sat on some of the seats to listen, but whoever listeneth findeth an ambush *ready* for him of flaming darts.

10 And truly we know not whether evil be meant for them that are on earth, or whether their Lord meaneth guidance for them.

And there are among us good, and *others* among us of another kind; – we are of various sorts:

And verily we thought that no one could weaken God on earth, neither could we escape from him by flight:

Wherefore as soon as we had heard "the guidance" we believed in it; and whoever believeth in his Lord, need not fear either loss or wrong.

There are some among us who have resigned themselves to God (the Muslims); and there are others of us who have gone astray. And whoso resigneth himself to God pursueth the way of truth;

But they who go astray from it shall be fuel for Hell.'

Moreover, if they (the Meccans) keep straight on in that way, we will surely give them to drink of abundant waters,

That we may prove them thereby: but whoso withdraweth from the remembrance of his Lord, him will He send into a severe torment.

It is unto God that the temples are set apart: call not then on any other therein with God.

When the servant of God stood up to call upon Him, the *Djinn* almost jostled him by their crowds.

20 SAY: I call only upon my Lord, and I join no other being with Him.

SAY: No control have I over what may hurt or benefit you.

SAY: Verily none can protect me against God;

Neither shall I find any refuge beside Him.

My sole work is preaching from God, and His message: and for such as shall rebel against God and his apostle is the fire of Hell! they shall remain therein alway, – for ever!

Until they see their threatened vengeance *they will be perverse!* but then shall they know which side was the weakest in a protector and the fewest in number.

SAY: I know not whether that with which ye are threatened be nigh, or whether my Lord hath assigned it to a distant day: He knoweth the secret, nor doth He divulge his secret to any,

Except to that Apostle who pleaseth Him; and before him and behind him He maketh a guard to march:

That He may know if his Apostles have verily delivered the

messages of their Lord: and He embraceth *in his knowledge* all their ways, and taketh count of all that concerneth them.

SURA 73 – THE ENFOLDED[1]

MECCA – 20 VERSES

In the Name of God, the Compassionate, the Merciful

O Thou ENFOLDED in thy mantle,

Stand up all night, except a small portion of it, for prayer:

Half; or curtail the half a little, –

Or add to it: And with measured tone intone the Koran,[2]

For we shall devolve on thee weighty words.

Verily, at the oncoming of night are *devout* impressions strongest, and words are most collected;[3]

But in the day time thou hast continual employ –

And commemorate the name of thy Lord, and devote thyself to Him with entire devotion.

Lord of the East and of the West! No God is there but He! Take Him for thy protector,

10 And endure what they say with patience, and depart from them with a decorous departure.

And let Me alone with the gainsayers, rich in the pleasures of this life; and bear thou with them yet a little while:

For with Us are strong fetters, and a flaming fire,

And food that choketh, and a sore torment.

The day cometh when the earth and the mountains shall be shaken; and the mountains shall become a loose sand heap.

Verily, we have sent you an Apostle to witness against you, even as we sent an Apostle to Pharaoh:

But Pharaoh rebelled against the Apostle, and we therefore laid hold on him with a severe chastisement.

And how, if ye believe not, will you screen yourselves from the day that shall turn children greyheaded?

The very heaven shall be reft asunder by it: this threat shall be carried into effect.

Lo! this is a warning. Let him then who will, take the way to his Lord.

20 Of a truth,[4] thy Lord knoweth that thou prayest almost
two-thirds, or half, or a third of the night, as do a part of thy followers. But God measureth the night and the day: – He knoweth that ye cannot count its hours aright, and therefore, turneth to you mercifully. Recite then so much of the Koran as may be easy to you. He knoweth that there will be some among you sick, while others travel through the earth in quest of the bounties of God; and others do battle in his cause. Recite therefore so much of it as may be easy. And observe the Prayers and pay the legal Alms, and lend God a liberal loan: for whatever good works ye send on before for your own behoof, ye shall find with God. This will be best and richest in the recompense. And seek the forgiveness of God: verily, God is Forgiving, Merciful.

SURA 74 – THE ENWRAPPED[1]

MECCA – 55 VERSES

In the Name of God, the Compassionate, the Merciful

O thou, ENWRAPPED in thy mantle!
Arise and warn!
Thy Lord – magnify Him!
Thy raiment – purify it!
The abomination – flee it!
And bestow not favours that thou mayest receive again with increase;
And for thy Lord wait thou patiently.
For when there shall be a trump on the trumpet,[2]
That shall be a distressful day,
10 A day, to the Infidels, devoid of ease.
Leave me alone to deal with him[3] whom I have created,
And on whom I have bestowed vast riches,
And sons dwelling before him,
And for whom I have smoothed all things smoothly down; –

Yet desireth he that I should add more!
But no! because to our signs he is a foe
I will lay grievous woes upon him.
For he plotted and he planned!
May he be cursed! How he planned!
20 Again, may he be cursed! How he planned!
Then looked he around him,
Then frowned and scowled,
Then turned his back and swelled with disdain,
And said, 'This is merely magic that will be wrought;
It is merely the word of a mortal.'
We will surely cast him into Hell-fire.
And who shall teach thee what Hell-fire is?
It leaveth nought, it spareth nought,
Blackening the skin.
30 Over it are nineteen *angels*.

None but angels have we made guardians of the fire:[4] nor have we made this to be their number but to perplex the unbelievers, and that they who possess the Scriptures may be certain of the truth *of the Koran*, and that they who believe may increase their faith;

And that they to whom the Scriptures have been given, and the believers, may not doubt;

And that the infirm of heart and the unbelievers may say, What meaneth God by this parable?

Thus God misleadeth whom He will, and whom He will doth He guide aright: and none knoweth the armies of thy Lord but Himself: and this is no other than a warning to mankind.

Nay, by the Moon!
By the Night when it retreateth!
By the Morn when it brighteneth!
Hell is one of the most grievous woes,
Fraught with warning to man,
40 To him among you who desireth to press forward, or to remain behind.[5]

For its own works lieth every soul in pledge. But they of *God's* right hand
In their gardens shall ask of the wicked; –
'What hath cast you into Hell-fire?'[6]
They will say, 'We were not of those who prayed,
And we were not of those who fed the poor,

And we plunged into vain disputes with vain disputers,
And we rejected as a lie, the day of reckoning,
Till the certainty[7] came upon us' –
And intercession of the interceders shall not avail them.
50 Then what hath come to them that they turn aside from the Warning
As if they were affrighted asses fleeing from a lion?
And every one of them would fain have open pages given to him out of Heaven.
It shall not be. They fear not the life to come.
It shall not be. For this *Koran* is warning *enough*. And whoso will, it warneth him.
But not unless God please, shall they be warned. Meet is He to be feared. Meet is forgiveness in Him.

SURA 75 – THE RESURRECTION

MECCA – 40 VERSES

In the Name of God, the Compassionate, the Merciful

It needeth not that I swear by the day of the RESURRECTION,
Or that I swear by the self-accusing soul.
Thinketh man that we shall not re-unite his bones?
Aye! his very finger tips are we able evenly to replace.
But man chooseth to deny what is before him:
He asketh, 'When this day of Resurrection?'
But when the eye shall be dazzled,
And when the moon shall be darkened,
And the sun and the moon shall be together,[1]
10 On that day man shall cry, 'Where is there a place to flee to?'
But in vain – there is no refuge –
With thy Lord on that day shall be the sole asylum.
On that day shall man be told of all that he hath done first and last;
Yea, a man shall be the eye witness against himself:
And even if he put forth his plea. . .[2]

(Move not thy tongue in haste *to follow and master this revelation:*[3]
For we will see to the collecting and the recital of it;
But when we have recited it, then follow thou the recital,
And, verily, afterwards it shall be ours to make it clear to thee.)
20 Aye, but ye love the transitory,
And ye neglect the life to come.
On that day shall faces beam with light,
Outlooking towards their Lord;
And faces on that day shall be dismal,
As if they thought that some great calamity would befal them.
Aye, when *the soul* shall come up into the throat,
And there shall be a cry, 'Who hath a charm that can restore him?'
And the man feeleth that the time of his departure is come,
And when one leg shall be laid over the other,[4]
30 To thy Lord on that day shall he be driven on;
For he believed not, and he did not pray,
But he called the truth a lie and turned his back,
Then, walking with haughty men, rejoined his people.
That Hour is nearer to thee and nearer,[5]
It is ever nearer to thee and nearer still.
Thinketh man that he shall be left supreme?
Was he not a mere embryo?[6]
Then he became thick blood of which God formed him and fashioned him;
And made him twain, male and female.
40 Is not He powerful enough to quicken the dead?

SURA 76 – MAN

MECCA – 31 VERSES

In the Name of God, the Compassionate, the Merciful

Doth not a long time pass over MAN, during which he is a thing unremembered?[1]

We have created man from the union of the sexes that we might prove him; and hearing, seeing, have we made him:

In a right way have we guided him, be he thankful or ungrateful.

For the Infidels we have got ready chains and collars and flaming fire.

But a wine cup tempered at the camphor fountain[2] the just shall quaff:

Fount whence the servants of God shall drink, and guide by channels from place to place;

They who fulfilled their vows, and feared the day whose woes will spread far and wide;

Who though longing for it themselves, bestowed their food on the poor and the orphan and the captive:

'We feed you for the sake of God: we seek from you neither recompense nor thanks:[3]

10 A stern and calamitous day dread we from our Lord.'

From the evil therefore of that day hath God delivered them and cast on them brightness of face and joy:

And hath rewarded their constancy, with Paradise and silken robes:

Reclining therein on bridal couches, nought shall they know of sun or piercing cold:

Its shades shall be close over them, and low shall its fruits hang down:

And vessels of silver and goblets like flagons shall be borne round among them:

Flagons of silver whose measure themselves shall mete.

And there shall they be given to drink of the cup tempered with zendjebil (ginger)

From the fount therein whose name is Selsebil (the softly flowing).

Aye-blooming youths go round among them. When thou lookest at them thou wouldest deem them scattered pearls;

20 And when thou seest *this*, thou wilt see delights and a vast kingdom:

Their clothing green silk robes and rich brocade: with silver bracelets shall they be adorned; and drink of a pure beverage shall their Lord give them.

This shall be your recompense. Your efforts shall meet with thanks.

We ourselves have sent down to thee the Koran as a missive from on high.

Await then with patience the judgments of thy Lord, and obey not the wicked among them and the unbelieving:

And make mention of the name of thy Lord at morn, at even,

And at night. Adore him, and praise him the livelong night.

But these men love the fleeting present, and leave behind them the heavy day of doom.

Ourselves have we created them, and strengthened their joints; and when we please, with others like unto themselves will we replace them.

This truly is a warning: And whoso willeth, taketh the way to his Lord;

30 But will it ye shall not, unless God will it, for God is Knowing, Wise.

He causeth whom He will to enter into his mercy. But for the evil doers, He hath made ready an afflictive chastisement.

SURA 77 – THE SENT

MECCA – 50 VERSES

In the Name of God, the Compassionate, the Merciful

By the train of THE SENT ones,[1]
And the swift in their swiftness;
By the scatterers who scatter,
And the distinguishers who distinguish;
And by those that give forth the word

To excuse or warn;
Verily that which ye are promised is imminent.
When the stars, therefore, shall be blotted out,
And when the heaven shall be cleft,
10 And when the mountains shall be scattered in dust,
And when the Apostles shall have a time assigned them;
Until what day shall that time be deferred?
To the day of severing!
And who shall teach thee what the day of severing is?
Woe on that day to those who charged with imposture!
Have we not destroyed them of old?
We will next cause those of later times to follow them.[2]
Thus deal we with the evil doers.
Woe on that day to those who charged with imposture!
20 Have we not created you of a sorry germ,
Which we laid up in a secure place,
Till the term decreed *for birth?*
Such is our power! and, how powerful are We!
Woe on that day to those who charged with imposture!
Have we not made the earth to hold
The living and the dead?
And placed on it the tall firm mountains, and given you to drink of sweet water.
Woe on that day to those who charged with imposture!
Begone to that Hell which ye called a lie: –
30 Begone to the shadows that lie in triple masses;
'But not against the flame shall they shade or help you:' –
The sparks which it casteth out are like towers –
Like tawny camels.
Woe on that day to those who charged with imposture!
On that day they shall not speak,
Nor shall it be permitted them to allege excuses.
Woe on that day to those who charged with imposture!
This is the day of severing, when we will assemble you and your ancestors.
If now ye have any craft try your craft on me.
40 Woe on that day to those who charged with imposture!
But the god-fearing shall be placed amid shades and fountains,
And fruits, whatsoever they shall desire:
'Eat and drink, with health, as the meed of your toils.'

Thus recompense we the good.
Woe on that day to those who charged with imposture!
'Eat ye and enjoy yourselves a little while. Verily, ye are doers of evil.'
Woe on that day to those who charged with imposture!
For when it is said to them, bend the knee, they bend it not.
Woe on that day to those who charged with imposture
50 In what other revelation after this will they believe?

SURA 78 – THE NEWS

MECCA – 41 VERSES

In the Name of God, the Compassionate, the Merciful

Of what ask they of one another?
Of the great NEWS.[1]
The theme of their disputes.
Nay! they shall certainly know its *truth!*
Again. Nay! they shall certainly know it.
Have we not made the Earth a couch?
And the mountains its tent-stakes?
We have created you of two sexes,
And ordained your sleep for rest,
10 And ordained the night as a mantle,
And ordained the day for gaining livelihood,
And built above you seven solid[2] heavens,
And placed therein a burning lamp;
And we send down water in abundance from the rain-clouds,
That we may bring forth by it corn and herbs,
And gardens thick with trees.
Lo! the day of Severance is fixed;
The day when there shall be a blast on the trumpet, and ye shall come in crowds,
And the heaven shall be opened and be full of portals,
20 And the mountains shall be set in motion, and melt into thin vapour.
Hell truly shall be a place of snares,

The home of transgressors,
To abide therein ages;
No coolness shall they taste therein nor any drink,
Save boiling water and running sores;
Meet recompense!
For they looked not forward to their account;
And they gave the lie to our signs, charging them with falsehood;
But we noted and wrote down all:
30 'Taste this then: and we will give you increase of nought but
torment.'
But, for the God-fearing is a blissful abode,
Enclosed gardens and vineyards;
And damsels with swelling breasts, their peers in age,
And a full cup:
There shall they hear no vain discourse nor any falsehood:
A recompense from thy Lord – sufficing gift! –
Lord of the heavens and of the earth, and of all that between[3] them lieth – the God of Mercy! But not a word shall they obtain from Him.

On the day whereon the Spirit[4] and the Angels shall be ranged in order, they shall not speak: save he whom the God of Mercy shall permit, and who shall say that which is right.

This is the sure day. Whoso then will, let him take the path
of return to his Lord.
40 Verily, we warn you of a chastisement close at hand:
The day on which a man shall see the deeds which his hands have sent before him; and when the unbeliever shall say, 'Oh! would I were dust!'

SURA 79[1] – THOSE WHO DRAG FORTH

MECCA – 46 VERSES

In the Name of God, the Compassionate, the Merciful

By those *angels* who DRAG FORTH souls with violence,
And by those who with joyous release release them;
By those who swim swimmingly along;

By those who are foremost with foremost speed;[2]
By those who conduct the affairs of the universe!
One day, the disturbing trumpet-blast shall disturb it,
Which the second blast shall follow:
Men's hearts on that day shall quake: –
Their looks be downcast.
10 The infidels will say, 'Shall we indeed be restored as at first?
What! when we have become rotten bones?'
'This then,' say they, 'will be a return to loss.'
Verily, it will be but a single blast,
And lo! they are on the surface of the earth.
Hath the story of Moses reached thee?
When his Lord called to him in Towa's holy vale:
Go to Pharaoh, for he hath burst all bounds:
And say, 'Wouldest thou become just?
Then I will guide thee to thy Lord that thou mayest fear him.'
20 And he showed him a great miracle, –
But he treated him as an impostor, and rebelled;
Then turned he his back all hastily,
And gathered an assembly and proclaimed,
And said, 'I am your Lord supreme.'
So God visited on him the punishment of this life and of the other.
Verily, herein is a lesson for him who hath the fear of God.
Are ye the harder to create, or the heaven which he hath built?
He reared its height and fashioned it,
And gave darkness to its night, and brought out its light,
30 And afterwards stretched forth the earth, –
He brought forth from it its waters and its pastures;
And set the mountains firm
For you and your cattle to enjoy.
But when the grand overthrow shall come,
The day when a man shall reflect on the pains that he hath taken,
And Hell shall be in full view of all who are looking on;
Then, as for him who hath transgressed
And hath chosen this present life,
Verily, Hell – that shall be his dwelling-place:
40 But as to him who shall have feared the majesty of his Lord, and shall have refrained his soul from lust,

Verily, Paradise – that shall be his dwelling-place.
They will ask thee of 'the Hour,' when will be its fixed time?
But what knowledge hast thou of it?
Its period is *known only* to thy Lord;
And thou art only charged with the warning of those who fear it.
On the day when they shall see it, *it shall seem to them* as though they had not tarried *in the tomb*, longer than its evening or its morn.

SURA 80 – HE FROWNED

MECCA – 42 VERSES

In the Name of God, the Compassionate, the Merciful

He FROWNED, and he turned his back,[1]
Because the blind man came to him!
But what assured thee that he would not be cleansed *by the Faith*,
Or be warned, and the warning profit him?
As to him who is wealthy –
To him thou wast all attention:
Yet is it not thy concern if he be not cleansed:[2]
But as to him who cometh to thee in earnest,
And full of fears –
10 Him dost thou neglect.
Nay! but it (the Koran) is a warning;
(And whoso is willing beareth it in mind)
Written on honoured pages,
Exalted, purified,
By the hands of Scribes, honoured, righteous.
Cursed be man! What hath made him unbelieving?
Of what thing did God create him?
Out of moist germs.[3]
He created him and fashioned him,
20 Then made him an easy passage *from the womb*,
Then causeth him to die and burieth him;

Then, when he pleaseth, will raise him again to life.
Aye! but man hath not yet fulfilled the bidding of his Lord.
Let man look at his food:
It was We who rained down the copious rains,
Then cleft the earth with clefts,
And caused the upgrowth of the grain,
And grapes and healing herbs,
And the olive and the palm,
30 And enclosed gardens thick with trees,
And fruits and herbage,
For the service of yourselves and of your cattle.
But when the stunning trumpet-blast shall arrive,
On that day shall a man fly from his brother,
And his mother and his father,
And his wife and his children;
For every man of them on that day his own concerns shall be enough.
There shall be faces on that day radiant,
Laughing and joyous:
40 And faces on that day with dust upon them:
Blackness shall cover them!
These are the Infidels, the Impure.

SURA 81 – THE FOLDED UP

MECCA – 29 VERSES

In the Name of God, the Compassionate, the Merciful

When the sun shall be FOLDED UP,[1]
And when the stars shall fall,
And when the mountains shall be set in motion,
And when the she-camels shall be abandoned,
And when the wild beasts shall be gathered together,[2]
And when the seas shall boil,
And when souls shall be paired *with their bodies*,
And when the female child that had been buried alive shall be asked
For what crime she was put to death,[3]

10 And when the leaves of the Book shall be unrolled,
And when the Heaven shall be stripped away,[4]
And when Hell shall be made to blaze,
And when Paradise shall be brought near,
Every soul shall know what it hath produced.
It needs not that I swear by the stars[5] of retrograde motions
Which move swiftly and hide themselves away,
And by the night when it cometh darkening on,
And by the dawn when it brighteneth,
That this is the word of an illustrious Messenger,[6]
20 Endued with power, having influence with the Lord of the Throne,
Obeyed there by *Angels*, faithful to his trust,
And your compatriot is not one possessed by djinn;
For he saw him in the clear horizon:[7]
Nor doth he grapple with heaven's secrets,[8]
Nor doth he teach the doctrine of a cursed[9] Satan.
Whither then are ye going?
Verily, this is no other than a warning to all creatures;
To him among you who willeth to walk in a straight path:
But will it ye shall not, unless as God willeth it,[10] the Lord of the worlds.

SURA 82 – THE CLEAVING

MECCA – 19 VERSES

In the Name of God, the Compassionate, the Merciful

When the Heaven shall CLEAVE asunder,
And when the stars shall disperse,
And when the seas[1] shall be commingled,
And when the graves shall be turned upside down,
Each soul shall recognise its earliest and its latest actions.
O man! what hath misled thee against thy generous Lord,
Who hath created thee and moulded thee and shaped thee aright?
In the form which pleased Him hath He fashioned thee.
Even so; but ye treat the Judgment as a lie.

10 Yet truly there are guardians over you –
Illustrious recorders –
Cognisant of your actions.
Surely amid delights *shall* the righteous *dwell*,
But verily the impure in Hell-fire:
They shall be burned at it on the day of doom,
And they shall not be able to hide themselves from it.
Who shall teach thee what the day of doom is?
Once more. Who shall teach thee what the day of doom is?
It is a day when one soul shall be powerless for another soul: all sovereignty on that day shall be with God.

SURA 83 – THOSE WHO STINT

MECCA – 36 VERSES

In the Name of God, the Compassionate, the Merciful

Woe to those who STINT the measure:
Who when they take by measure from others, exact the full;
But when they mete to them or weigh to them, minish –
What! have they no thought that they shall be raised again
For the great day?
The day when mankind shall stand before the Lord of the worlds.
Yes! the register of the wicked is in Sidjin.[1]
And who shall make thee understand what Sidjin is?
It is a book distinctly written.
10 Woe, on that day, to those who treated *our signs* as lies,
Who treated the day of judgment as a lie!
None treat it as a lie, save the transgressor, the criminal,
Who, when our signs are rehearsed to him, saith, 'Tales of the Ancients!'
Yes; but their own works have got the mastery over their hearts.
Yes; they shall be shut out as by a veil from their Lord on that day;
Then shall they be burned in Hell-fire:

Then shall it be said *to them*, 'This is what ye deemed a lie.'
Even so. But the register of the righteous is in Illiyoun.
And who shall make thee understand what Illiyoun is?
20 A book distinctly written;
The angels who draw nigh unto God attest it.
Surely, among delights *shall* the righteous *dwell!*
Seated on bridal couches they will gaze around;
Thou shalt mark in their faces the brightness of delight;
Choice sealed wine shall be given them to quaff,
The seal of musk. For this let those pant who pant for bliss –
Mingled therewith shall be the waters of Tasnim –[2]
Fount whereof they who draw nigh to God shall drink.
The sinners indeed laugh the faithful to scorn:
30 And when they pass by them they wink at one another, –
And when they return to their own people, they return jesting,
And when they see them they say, 'These are the erring ones.'
And *yet* they have no mission to be their guardians.
Therefore, on that day the faithful shall laugh the infidels to scorn,
As reclining on bridal couches they behold them.
Shall not the infidels be recompensed according to their works?

SURA 84 – THE SPLITTING ASUNDER

MECCA – 25 VERSES

In the Name of God, the Compassionate, the Merciful

When the Heaven shall have SPLIT ASUNDER
And duteously obeyed its Lord;[1]
And when Earth shall have been stretched out *as a plain*,
And shall have cast forth what was in her and become empty,
And duteously obeyed its Lord;
Then verily, O man, who desirest to reach thy Lord, shalt thou meet him.
And he into whose right hand his Book shall be given,

Shall be reckoned with in an easy reckoning,
And shall turn, rejoicing, to his kindred.
10 But he whose Book shall be given him behind his back[2]
Shall invoke destruction:
But in the fire shall he burn,
For that he lived joyously among his kindred,
Without a thought that he should return *to God*.
Yea, but his Lord beheld him.
It needs not therefore that I swear by the sunset redness,
And by the night and its gatherings,
And by the moon when at her full,
That from state to state shall ye be surely carried onward.[3]
20 What then hath come to them that they believe not?
And that when the Koran is recited to them they adore not?
Yea, the unbelievers treat it as a lie.
But God knoweth their secret hatreds:
Let their only tidings[4] be those of painful punishment;
Save to those who believe and do the things that be right. An
unfailing recompense shall be theirs.

SURA 85 – THE STARRY

MECCA – 22 VERSES

In the Name of God, the Compassionate, the Merciful

By the star-spangled Heaven![1]
By the promised Day!
By the witness and the witnessed![2]
Cursed the masters of the trench[3]
Of the fuel-fed fire,
When they sat around it
Witnesses of what they inflicted on the believers!
Nor did they torment them but for their faith in God, the
Mighty, the Praiseworthy:[4]
His the kingdom of the Heavens and of the Earth; and God is
the witness of everything.
10 Verily, those who vexed the believers, men and women, and

repented not, doth the torment of Hell, and the torment of the burning, await.

But for those who shall have believed and done the things that be right, are the Gardens beneath whose shades the rivers flow. This the immense bliss!

Verily, right terrible will be thy Lord's vengeance!
He it is who produceth *all* things, and causeth them to return;
And is He the Indulgent, the Loving;
Possessor of the Glorious throne;
Worker of that he willeth.
Hath not the story reached thee of the hosts
Of Pharaoh and Themoud?
Nay! the infidels are all for denial:
20 But God surroundeth them from behind.
Yet it is a glorious Koran,
Written on the preserved Table.

SURA 86 – THE NIGHT-COMER

MECCA – 17 VERSES

In the Name of God, the Compassionate, the Merciful

By the heaven, and by the NIGHT-COMER!
But who shall teach thee what the night-comer is?
'Tis the star of piercing radiance.
Over every soul is set a guardian.
Let man then reflect out of what he was created.
He was created of the poured-forth germs,
Which issue from the loins and breastbones:
Well able then is God to restore him to life, –
On the day when all secrets shall be searched out,
10 And he shall have no *other* might or helper.
I swear by the heaven which accomplisheth its cycle,
And by the earth which openeth her bosom,
That this *Koran* is a discriminating discourse,
And that it is not frivolous.
They plot a plot *against thee*,

And I will plot a plot *against them.*
Deal calmly therefore with the infidels; leave them awhile alone.

SURA 87 – THE MOST HIGH

MECCA – 19 VERSES

In the Name of God, the Compassionate, the Merciful

Praise the name of thy Lord THE MOST HIGH,
Who hath created and balanced *all things*,
Who hath fixed their destinies and guideth them,
Who bringeth forth the pasture,
And reduceth it to dusky stubble.
We will teach thee to recite *the Koran*, nor aught shalt thou forget,
Save what God pleaseth; for he knoweth alike things manifest and hidden;
And we will make easy to thee our easy ways.
Warn, therefore, for the warning is profitable:
10 He that feareth God will receive the warning, –
And the most reprobate only will turn aside from it,
Who shall be exposed to the terrible fire,
In which he shall not die, and shall not live.
Happy he who is purified *by Islam*,
And who remembereth the name of his Lord and prayeth.
But ye prefer this present life,
Though the life to come is better and more enduring.
This truly is in the Books of old,
The Books of Abraham[1] and Moses.

SURA 88 – THE OVERSHADOWING

MECCA – 26 VERSES

In the Name of God, the Compassionate, the Merciful

Hath the tidings of the day that shall OVERSHADOW, reached thee?
Downcast on that day shall be the countenances of some,
Travailing and worn,
Burnt at the scorching fire,
Made to drink from a fountain fiercely boiling.
No food shall they have but the fruit of Darih,[1]
Which shall not fatten, nor appease their hunger.
Joyous too, on that day, the countenances of others,
Well pleased with their labours past,
10 In a lofty garden:
No vain discourse shalt thou bear therein:
Therein shall be a gushing fountain,
Therein shall be raised couches,
And goblets ready placed,
And cushions laid in order,
And carpets spread forth.
Can they not look up to the clouds, how they are created;
And to the heaven how it is upraised;
And to the mountains how they are rooted;
20 And to the earth how it is outspread?
Warn thou then; for thou art a warner only:
Thou hast no authority over them:
But whoever shall turn back and disbelieve,
God shall punish him with the greater punishment.
Verily to Us shall they return;
Then shall it be Ours to reckon with them.

SURA 89 – THE DAYBREAK

MECCA – 30 VERSES

In the Name of God, the Compassionate, the Merciful

By the DAYBREAK and ten nights.[1]
By that which is double and that which is single,
By the night when it pursues its course!
Is there not in this an oath becoming a man of sense?
Hast thou not seen how thy Lord dealt with Ad,
At Irem adorned with pillars,
Whose like have not been reared in these lands!
And with Themoud who hewed out the rocks in the valley;
And with Pharaoh the impaler;
10 Who all committed excesses in the lands,
And multiplied wickedness therein.
Wherefore thy Lord let loose on them the scourge of chastisement,[2]
For thy Lord standeth on a watch tower.
As to man, when his Lord trieth him and honoureth him and is bounteous to him,
Then saith he, 'My Lord honoureth me:'
But when he proveth him and limiteth his gifts to him,
He saith, 'My Lord despiseth me.'
Aye. But ye honour not the orphan,
Nor urge ye one another to feed the poor,
20 And ye devour heritages, devouring greedily,
And ye love riches with exceeding love.
Aye. But when the earth shall be crushed with crushing, crushing,
And thy Lord shall come and the angels rank on rank,
And Hell on that day shall be moved up, – Man shall on that day remember himself. But how shall remembrance help him?
He shall say, Oh! would that I had prepared for this my life! On that day none shall punish as God punisheth,
And none shall bind with such bonds as He.
Oh, thou soul which art at rest,
Return to thy Lord, pleased, and pleasing him:
Enter thou among my servants,
30 And enter thou my Paradise.

SURA 90 – THE SOIL

MECCA – 20 VERSES

In the Name of God, the Compassionate, the Merciful

I need not to swear by this SOIL,
This soil on which thou dost dwell,
Or by sire and offspring![1]
Surely in trouble have we created man.
What! thinketh he that no one hath power over him?
'I have wasted,' saith he, 'enormous riches!'
What! thinketh he that no one regardeth him?
What! have we not made him eyes,
And tongue, and lips,
And guided him to the two highways?[2]
Yet he attempted not the steep.
And who shall teach thee what the steep is?
It is to ransom the captive,[3]
Or to feed in the day of famine,
The orphan who is near of kin, or the poor that lieth in the dust;
Beside this, to be of those who believe, and enjoin stedfastness on each other, and enjoin compassion on each other.
These shall be the people of the right hand:
While they who disbelieve our signs,
Shall be the people of the left.
Around them the fire shall close.

SURA 91 – THE SUN

MECCA – 15 VERSES

In the Name of God, the Compassionate, the Merciful

By the SUN and his noonday brightness!
By the Moon when she followeth him!
By the Day when it revealeth his glory!

By the Night when it enshroudeth him!
By the Heaven and Him who built it!
By the Earth and Him who spread it forth!
By a Soul and Him who balanced it,
And breathed into it its wickedness and its piety,
Blessed now is he who hath kept it pure,
10 And undone is he who hath corrupted it!
Themoud[1] in his impiety rejected the message of the Lord,
When the greatest wretch among them rushed up: –
Said the Apostle of God to them, – 'The Camel of God! let her drink.'
But they treated him as an impostor and hamstrung her.
So their Lord destroyed them for their crime, and visited all alike:
Nor feared he the issue.

SURA 92 – THE NIGHT

MECCA – 21 VERSES

In the Name of God, the Compassionate, the Merciful

By the NIGHT when she spreads her veil;
By the Day when it brightly shineth;
By Him who made male and female;
At different ends truly do ye aim!
But as to him who giveth *alms* and feareth God,
And yieldeth assent to the Good;
To him will we make easy the path to happiness.
But as to him who is covetous and bent on riches,
And calleth the Good a lie,
10 To him will we make easy the path to misery:
And what shall his wealth avail him when he goeth down?
Truly man's guidance is with Us
And Ours, the Future and the Past.
I warn you therefore of the flaming fire;
None shall be cast to it but the most wretched, –
Who hath called the truth a lie and turned his back.

But the God-fearing shall escape it, –
Who giveth away his substance that he may become pure;[1]
And who offereth not favours to any one for the sake of recompense,
20 But only as seeking the face of his Lord the Most High.
And surely in the end he shall be well content.

SURA 93 – THE BRIGHTNESS

MECCA – 11 VERSES

In the Name of God, the Compassionate, the Merciful

By the noon-day BRIGHTNESS,
And by the night when it darkeneth!
Thy Lord hath not forsaken thee, neither hath he been displeased.
And surely the Future shall be better for thee than the Past,
And in the end shall thy Lord be bounteous to thee and thou be satisfied.
Did he not find thee an orphan[1] and gave thee a home?
And found thee erring and guided thee,[2]
And found thee needy and enriched thee.
As to the orphan therefore wrong him not;
10 And as to him that asketh of thee, chide him not away;
And as for the favours of thy Lord tell them abroad.

SURA 94 – THE OPENING

MECCA – 8 VERSES

In the Name of God, the Compassionate, the Merciful

Have we not OPENED thine heart for thee?
And taken off from thee thy burden,
Which galled thy back?

And have we not raised thy name for thee?
Then verily along with trouble cometh ease.
Verily along with trouble cometh ease.
But when thou art set at liberty, then prosecute thy toil.
And seek thy Lord with fervour.

SURA 95 – THE FIG

MECCA – 8 VERSES

In the Name of God, the Compassionate, the Merciful

I swear by the FIG and by the olive,
By Mount Sinai,
And by this inviolate soil![1]
That of goodliest fabric we created man,
Then brought him down to be the lowest of the low; –
Save who believe and do the things that are right, for theirs shall be a reward that faileth not.
Then, who after this shall make thee treat the Judgment as a lie?
What! is not God the most just of judges?

SURA 96 – CLOTS OF BLOOD

MECCA – 18 VERSES

In the Name of God, the Compassionate, the Merciful

Recite[1] thou, in the name of thy Lord who created; –[2]
Created man from CLOTS OF BLOOD: –
Recite thou! For thy Lord is the most Beneficent,
Who hath taught the use of the pen; –
Hath taught Man that which he knoweth not.
Nay, verily,[3] Man is insolent,

Because he seeth himself possessed of riches.
Verily, to thy Lord is the return of all.
What thinkest thou of him that holdeth back
10 A servant[4] *of God* when he prayeth?
What thinkest thou?[5] Hath he followed the *true* Guidance, or enjoined Piety?
What thinkest thou? Hath he treated the truth as a lie and turned his back?
What! doth he not know how that God seeth?
Nay, verily, if he desist not, We shall seize him by the forelock.
The lying sinful forelock!
Then let him summon his associates;[6]
We too will summon the guards of Hell:
Nay! obey him not; but adore, and draw nigh *to God*.[7]

SURA 97 – POWER

MECCA – 5 VERSES

In the Name of God, the Compassionate, the Merciful

Verily, we have caused It[1] to descend on the night of POWER.
And who shall teach thee what the night of power is?
The night of power excelleth a thousand months:
Therein descend the angels and the spirit by permission of their Lord for every matter;
And all is peace till the breaking of the morn.

SURA 98 – CLEAR EVIDENCE

MEDINA – 8 VERSES

In the Name of God, the Compassionate, the Merciful

The unbelievers among the people of the Book, and the Polytheists, did not waver, until the CLEAR EVIDENCE had come to them;

A messenger from God, reciting to them the pure pages wherein are true Scriptures!

Neither were they to whom the Scriptures were given divided into sects, till after *this* clear evidence had reached them!

Yet was not aught enjoined on them but to worship God with sincere religion, sound in faith; and to observe prayer and pay the stated alms. For this is true religion.

But the unbelievers among the people of the Book, and among the Polytheists, shall go into the fire of Gehenna to abide therein for aye. Of all creatures are they the worst!

But they who believe and do the things that are right – these of all creatures are the best!

Their recompense with their Lord shall be gardens of Eden, 'neath which the rivers flow, in which they shall abide for evermore.

God is well pleased in them and they in Him! This, for him who feareth his Lord.

SURA 99 – THE EARTHQUAKE

MECCA – 8 VERSES

In the Name of God, the Compassionate, the Merciful

When the Earth with her quaking shall quake
And the Earth shall cast forth her burdens,
And man shall say, What aileth her?
On that day shall she tell out her tidings,
Because thy Lord shall have inspired her.

On that day shall men come forward in throngs to behold their works,

And whosoever shall have wrought an atom's weight of good shall behold it,

And whosoever shall have wrought an atom's weight of evil shall behold it.

SURA 100 – THE CHARGERS

MECCA – 11 VERSES

In the Name of God, the Compassionate, the Merciful

By the snorting CHARGERS!
And those that dash off sparks of fire!
And those that scour to the attack at morn!
And stir therein the dust aloft;
And cleave therein their midway through a host!
Truly, Man is to his Lord ungrateful.
And of this he is himself a witness;
And truly, he is vehement in the love of this world's good.
Ah! knoweth he not, that when that which is in the graves shall be laid bare,
10 And that which is in men's breasts shall be brought forth,
Verily their Lord shall on that day be informed concerning them?

SURA 101 – THE BLOW

MECCA – 8 VERSES

In the Name of God, the Compassionate, the Merciful

The BLOW! what is the Blow?
Who shall teach thee what the Blow is?
The Day when men shall be like scattered moths,
And the mountains shall be like flocks of carded wool,
Then as to him whose balances are heavy – his shall be a life that shall please him well:
And as to him whose balances are light – his dwelling-place[1] shall be the pit.
And who shall teach thee what the pit (El-Hawiya) is?
A raging fire!

SURA 102 – DESIRE

MECCA – 8 VERSES

In the Name of God, the Compassionate, the Merciful

The DESIRE of increasing riches occupieth you,
Till ye come to the grave.
Nay! but in the end ye shall know –
Nay! once more, in the end ye shall know *your folly*.
Nay! would that ye knew it with knowledge of certainty!
Surely ye shall see hell-fire.
Then shall ye surely see it with the eye of certainty;
Then shall ye on that day be taken to task concerning pleasures.

SURA 103 – THE AFTERNOON

MECCA – 3 VERSES

In the Name of God, the Compassionate, the Merciful

I swear by the declining day!
Verily, man's lot is cast amid destruction,
Save those who believe and do the things which be right, and enjoin truth and enjoin stedfastness on each other.

SURA 104 – THE BACKBITER

MECCA – 9 VERSES

In the Name of God, the Compassionate, the Merciful

Woe to every BACKBITER, Defamer!
Who amasseth wealth and storeth it against the future!
He thinketh surely that his wealth shall be with him for ever.
Nay! for verily he shall be flung into the Crushing Fire;
And who shall teach thee what the Crushing Fire is?
It is God's kindled fire,
Which shall mount above the hearts *of the damned;*
It shall verily rise over them like a vault,
On outstretched columns.

SURA 105 – THE ELEPHANT

MECCA – 5 VERSES

In the Name of God, the Compassionate, the Merciful

Hast thou not seen[1] how thy Lord dealt with the army of the ELEPHANT?

Did he not cause their strategem to miscarry?

And he sent against them birds in flocks (ababils),

Claystones did they hurl down upon them,

And he made them like stubble eaten down!

SURA 106 – THE KOREISCH

MECCA – 4 VERSES

In the Name of God, the Compassionate, the Merciful

For the union of the KOREISCH: –

Their union in equipping caravans winter and summer.

And let them worship the Lord of this house, who hath provided them with food against hunger,

And secured them against alarm.[1]

SURA 107 – RELIGION

MECCA – 7 VERSES

In the Name of God, the Compassionate, the Merciful

What thinkest thou of him who treateth our RELIGION as a lie?

He it is who thrusteth away the orphan,

And stirreth not *others* up to feed the poor.

Woe to those who pray,
But in their prayer are careless;
Who make a shew of devotion,
But refuse help to the needy.

SURA 108 – THE ABUNDANCE

MECCA – 3 VERSES

In the Name of God, the Compassionate, the Merciful

Truly we have given thee an ABUNDANCE;
Pray therefore to the Lord, and slay the victims.
Verily whoso hateth thee shall be childless.[1]

SURA 109 – UNBELIEVERS

MECCA – 6 VERSES

In the Name of God, the Compassionate, the Merciful

SAY: O ye UNBELIEVERS!
I worship not that which ye worship,
And ye do not worship that which I worship;
I shall never worship that which ye worship,
Neither will ye worship that which I worship.
To you be your religion; to me my religion.[1]

SURA 110 – HELP

MEDINA – 3 VERSES

In the Name of God, the Compassionate, the Merciful

When the HELP of God and the victory arrive,
And thou seest men entering the religion of God by troops;
Then utter the praise of thy Lord, implore His pardon; for He loveth to turn *in mercy*.

SURA 111 – ABU LAHAB

MECCA – 5 VERSES

In the Name of God, the Compassionate, the Merciful

Let the hands of ABU LAHAB[1] perish, and let himself perish!
His wealth and his gains shall avail him not.
Burned shall he be at the fiery flame,[2]
And his wife laden with fire wood, –
On her neck a rope of palm fibre.

SURA 112 – THE UNITY

MECCA – 4 VERSES

In the Name of God, the Compassionate, the Merciful

SAY: He is God alone:
God the eternal!
He begetteth not, and He is not begotten;
And there is none like unto Him.

SURA 113 – THE DAYBREAK

MECCA OR MEDINA – 5 VERSES

In the Name of God, the Compassionate, the Merciful

SAY: I betake me for refuge to the Lord of the DAYBREAK
Against the mischiefs of his creation;
And against the mischief of the night when it overtaketh me;
And against the mischief of weird women;[1]
And against the mischief of the envier when he envieth.

SURA 114 – MEN

MECCA OR MEDINA – 6 VERSES

In the Name of God, the Compassionate, the Merciful

SAY: I betake me for refuge to the Lord of MEN,
The King of men,
The God of men,
Against the mischief of the stealthily withdrawing whisperer,[1]
Who whispereth in man's breast –
Against djinn and men.

NOTES

Though Rodwell's notes have been pruned, no attempt has been made to suppress his standpoint, which is that of a Victorian Christian clergyman. His cross-references to Jewish and Christian material are particularly important.

Sura 1

1 The word Sura occurs nine times in the Koran, viz. Sur. 9. 65, 87, 125, 128; 24. 1; 47. 22 (twice); 2. 21; 10. 39; but it is not easy to determine whether it means a whole chapter, or part only of a chapter, or is used in the sense of 'revelation.' See Weil's *Mohammed der Prophet*, pp. 361–363. It is understood by the Muhammadan commentators to have a primary reference to the succession of subjects or parts, like the *rows* of bricks in a wall. The titles of the Suras are generally taken from some word occurring in each, which is printed in capital letters throughout, where practicable.

It should be observed that, including the auspicatory formula, there are the same number of petitions in this Sura as in the Lord's Prayer. It is recited several times in each of the five daily prayers, and on many other occasions, as in concluding a bargain, etc. It is termed 'the Opening of the Book,' 'the Completion,' 'the Sufficing Sura,' 'the Sura of Praise, Thanks, and Prayer,' 'the Healer,' 'the Remedy,' 'the Basis,' 'the Treasure,' 'the Mother of the Book,' 'the Seven Verses of Repetition.' The Muhammadans always say 'Amen' after this prayer, Muhammad having been instructed, says the Sonna, to do so by the Angel Gabriel.

2 This formula – *Bismillahi 'rrahmani 'rrahim* – is prefixed to each Sura except the ninth. The former of the two epithets implies that the mercy of God is exercised as occasions arise, towards all his creatures; the latter that the quality of mercy is inherent in God and permanent, – so that there is only a shade of difference between the two words. Maracci well renders, *In Nomine Dei Miseratoris, Misericordis*. The rendering I have adopted is that of Mr Lane in his extracts from the Koran. Perhaps, *In the name of Allah, the God of Mercy, the Merciful*, would more fully express the original Arabic.

Sura 2

1 The greater part of this, the oldest of the Medina Suras, was revealed in the early part of the second year of the Hejira and previously to the

battle of Bedr. – The Hejira took place in the beginning of Muharram, or middle of April, A.D. 622. The numbers who emigrated with Muhammad at first, were about 150 persons. Medina is 250 miles north of Mecca, and ten days' journey.

2 A group of the mystical letters that are prefixed to twenty-nine of the Suras.

3 Death, Resurrection, Judgment, etc.

4 The Jews.

5 The Jews and Christians, hostile to the mission of Muhammad.

6 Lit. *the similitude of them is as the similitude of*, etc.

7 The people of Medina are generally addressed with 'O ye who believe;' the Meccans, with 'O men.' Hence it has been inferred that from verse 19 (O men) to 37 inclusively, is of the Meccan period. The subjects treated of also lead to this conclusion.

8 The statues of false gods.

9 It will be an agreeable surprise to the blessed to have fruits, which at first sight resemble those of earth, but are infinitely more delicious.

10 Muhammad had been reproached for having drawn illustrations from the Ant, Bee, Spider, etc.

11 Concerning faith in Muhammad. See verse 39 below, note.

12 The number of the Heavens is borrowed from the Talmud, or traditions based upon it; but the idea probably has its root in the Scriptural expression, 'Heaven of Heavens.'

13 Lit. *a caliph, vicegerent.* 'When the Holy One, Blessed be He, would create man, He took counsel with the Angels and said to them, We will make man in our image.' Midr. Rabbah on Numb. iv. par. 19. Comp. Midr. on Gen. 1, par. 8, 17. Sanhedr. 38.

14 'God said to the Angels, "His wisdom is greater than yours." Then brought he before them beasts, cattle, and birds, and asked for their names, but they knew them not. But when he had created man,' etc. Midr. as above.

15 Or, *if ye are truthful*, or can *make good* a better claim to the vicegerency.

16 In the name Eblis (diabolos) and in the honour claimed for Adam as a kind of God-man, there are traces of a Christian original, as well as in the identification of the serpent with Satan. Comp. Ps. civ. 4; Heb. i. 6. The Talmudists also enlarge on the honour paid to Adam. 'Adam sat in the garden and the Angels brought him flesh and cooling wine.' Sanhedr. 29. 'In the hour when the Holy One, Blessed be He, created man, the Angels went astray in regard to him, and essayed to say before him, "O Holy One!" then God permitted sleep to fall on him, and all knew that he was of earth.' Midr. Rabbah on Gen. par. 8. It is possible that the Arabic word *balas*, a profligate, wicked person, may have influenced the formation of the word Eblis. *Eblis* is used in the Arabic version of the New Testament, for the probable date of which, see Tischendorf, Prol. p. 78.

17 Observe the change from Eblis, *the calumniator*, to Satan, *the hater*.
18 See Sura 7. 168, and v. 73 below.
19 See Sura 21. 49.
20 Lit. *slay one another*.
21 The Talmudists relate how the Israelites who had died, on hearing the divine voice, etc., were restored by the intercession of the Law itself. Sanh. 5.
22 By storing them up in violation of God's command.
23 Jericho according to some commentators, Jerusalem according to others, but see verse 58.
24 See Sura 7. 162.
25 Lit. *all men*. This incident is perhaps inadvertently borrowed from Ex. xv. 27.
26 This passage (comp. 26. 59) is one of the numerous anachronisms which abound in the Koran and prove the gross ignorance of the Arabian Prophet.
27 The Sabeites are identical with the Mendaites, residing in the marshy district at the mouth of the Euphrates, but are not the same with the star-worshipping Sabians of Harran in Mesopotamia.
28 See Sura 7. 170.
29 See Sura 7. 164.
30 Compare Numb. xix.; Deut. xxii. 1–9. The cow was to be sacrificed in order that a murderer might be discovered through the miracle to be wrought on the corpse by a piece of her flesh.
31 To please you, O Muslims.
32 This is one of the passages which shews great familiarity with the habits of the Jews.
33 The Pentateuch. This passage shews that the art of writing was known in Medina shortly after the Hejira.
34 Forty days; the period during which they worshipped the calf.
35 The blood of those who are as your own flesh.
36 Two Jewish tribes (Koreidha and Nadhir) in alliance with certain Arab tribes who were at war, destroyed one another's abodes, but redeemed the Jewish captives, professing that they were commanded to do this by the Law. So the commentators.
37 Gabriel.
38 The gift of the prophetic office, etc., to a pagan Arab and not to a Jew.
39 Matt. xxiii. 37.
40 See Sura 7. 170.
41 Comp. 1 Tim. v. 24.
42 'Babel is regarded by the Muslims as the fountain head of the science of magic. They suppose Haroot and Maroot to be two angels who, in consequence of their want of compassion for the frailties of mankind, were sent down to earth to be tempted. They both sinned; and being

permitted to choose whether they would be punished now or hereafter, chose the former, and are still suspended by the feet at Babel in a rocky pit, and are the great teachers of magic.' (Lane on ch. iii. note 14 of the *1001 Nights*.)

43 *Raina*, as *pronounced* in Hebrew, '*our bad one*;' but in Arabic, '*look upon us*,' a kind of salutation of the same signification as *ondhorna*, which, however, does not admit of any secondary bad sense like *raina*.

44 Comp. Sura 4. 84; 16. 103. The Muslims admit that there are 225 verses cancelled by later ones. The doctrine of 'abrogation' is taught in the Talmud. Thus Hilchoth Mamrim, ii. 1, 2, etc.

45 That is, does not weigh the evidence for Muhammad's mission already given, but demands, as the Jews did, to see God himself.

46 In all Muslim countries the first time of prayer is the *moghreb* or sunset, or rather, four minutes later; the second the *eshe*, when it has become quite dark; the third the *soobh* or *fegr*, the daybreak; the fourth, *doohr*, or a little after noon, when the sun has begun to decline; the fifth, the *asr*, midway between noon and nightfall. The obligatory legal alms or impost are called, as here, *zekah* (lit. purity), the voluntary, *sadackah*. It is, however, left to the conscience of individuals to give and to apply them as they think fit.

47 The idolatrous Arabs.

48 If this verse is aimed at the Meccans who, in the 6th year of the Hejira, forbad Muhammad and his followers to enter the temple of Mecca in the expedition of Hodeibiya, it is misplaced here.

49 Abrogated by verse 139 below.

50 The Caaba.

51 See note on Sura 3. 90.

52 Deut. xviii. 15.

53 'At the time when our father Jacob quitted this world, he summoned his twelve sons and said to them, Hearken to your father Israel (Gen. xlix. 2). Have ye any doubts in your hearts concerning the Holy One, Blessed be He! They said, Hear, O Israel, our Father. As there is no doubt in thy heart, so neither is there in ours. For the Lord is our God, and He is one.' Midr. Rabbah on Gen. par. 98, and on Deut. par. 2. Comp. also Targ. Jer. on Deut. vi. 4. Tract. Pesachim, 56.

54 See Sura 16. 121, n., p. 179.

55 Ibn Batutah assures us (vol. ii. 10) that when in the 14th century he visited Basra, he saw in the mosque the copy of the Koran which the Caliph Othman had in his hands when murdered, and that the marks of his blood were still visible at the words of this verse. Othman's originals are also said to be preserved in Egypt, Morocco, Damascus, Mecca, and Medina.

56 Or, *intermediate*, i.e. according to the commentators, not addicted to excess, just.

57 In having prayed towards Jerusalem.

58 Of Mecca. This change of the Kebla from Jerusalem to Mecca shows that this part of the Sura was revealed at a time when the breach between Muhammad and the Jews was past healing; i.e. in the first half of the second year of the Hejira.

59 That is, the Jews are really convinced of the truth of Muhammad's mission.

60 That is, warring with the infidels. The precise date of verses 148–152 depends upon whether this passage refers to the battle of Bedr or Ohod.

61 These words are constantly used by the pious Muslims when in any trouble.

62 Hills in the sacred territory of Mecca, which had long been objects of superstitious reverence to the idolatrous Arabs, on which account the Muslims were at first unwilling to include them among the sacred places.

63 The Pentateuch. See verse 141.

64 This and the three following verses are probably Meccan, as also verses 167–171.

65 The ringleaders of infidelity and idolatrous faiths.

66 *To whom his brother*, that is, any Arab or believer, shall remit the penalty of death.

67 Of the stricter Mosaic lex talionis, as well of the ante-Islamitic Arabian custom, by which the killing of a slave was avenged by the death of a free man, and the killing of a woman by taking the life of a man. Comp. Ex. xxi. 23.

68 That is, by killing the manslayer.

69 On the word *Furqan*, see Sura 21. 49.

70 A mutual comfort to each other.

71 Thus Misch. Berachoth, 1, 2, 'Prayer is to be said as soon as one *can distinguish between a blue and white thread.*'

72 Judging from the minuteness of the precepts laid down in this and the following verses to 193, it would appear that they were added at a late period of Muhammad's residence at Medina.

73 Such appears to have been the superstitious custom of the Arabs after their return from pilgrimages to Mecca.

74 Their driving you out of Mecca; or, *the temptation* (*to idolatry*).

75 Lit. *the sacred month for the sacred month, and the sacred precincts* or *things* (for) *reprisals*. The meaning of this difficult passage is that in wars for the cause of religion, the sacred month and the temple of Mecca may be made the time and scene of contests, which then and there are usually prohibited.

76 The greater Pilgrimage, which every Muslim is bound to perform once in his life, is the Hadjat el Farz (the one obligatory Pilgrimage), or the Hadjat el Islam. The Umrah, or little pilgrimage, may be performed at any time except the pilgrimage season, and its ceremonies are much fewer. They are described by Lieut. Burton in his 'Pilgrimage,' vol. iii. ch. xxviii.

77 Namely, Shawâl, Dhu'lkaada, and Dhu'lhijja.

78 By trading during the Hadj.

79 The pilgrims move on very rapidly when in the immediate neighbourhood of the Holy Places.

80 From the valley of Mina.

81 Verses 204–210 are probably addressed to those Muslims who were desirous to observe certain parts of the Jewish law.

82 The Koran.

83 That is, there was originally but one religion in the world.

84 Comp. Sura 4. 42, and 5. 99, 100.

85 *Limits, fences*. The word is Talmudic. Thus Pirke Aboth, i. 'The men of the great synagogue said . . . Make a fence for the law;' and iii. 13, 'Tradition is a fence to the law.'

86 Comp. Sura 31. 13.

87 Within the four months and ten days.

88 Either the *asr*, midway between noon and nightfall (see note 46 above) or the prayer immediately after midday. See note on Sura 4. 46.

89 This verse is certainly older than the commencement of Sura 4. which alters the law here laid down.

90 Comp. Ezek. xxxvii. 1–10. These Jews are said by some commentators to have abandoned their dwellings through fear of a pestilence (comp. Talmud Sanhed. 92); by others, for fear of being compelled to serve in the wars of God.

91 This and the seven following verses shew that Muhammad, foreseeing an open rupture with the people of Medina at no distant period, felt it necessary to stimulate the zeal and courage of his partisans by examples from Jewish history.

92 Ar. *Shechinah*. This word, as well as the Arabic word for *ark* betray in their form a Rabbinic origin.

93 The shoes and rod of Moses, the mitre of Aaron, the vase of manna, the fragments of the two tables of the law.

94 Observe the confusion between Gideon and Saul.

95 See verse 81.

96 The drift of these words, which are of such frequent recurrence in the Koran, is, that the former revelations had been abused, and instead of leading them to Islam broke them up into sects and dissentient parties.

97 This verse must have been revealed before Muhammad felt himself secure in his new position at Medina.

98 A name applied to an idol or idols – especially Allat and Ozza, the ancient idols of the Meccans. The termination of the word Thagout is more Hebraic than pure Arabic, and literally means *error*.

99 Nimrod.

100 Ozair or Esdras doubted whether Jerusalem could be rebuilt after its destruction by Nebuchadnezzar, and the miracle here narrated, was

wrought for his assurance. The fable has its origin in the circuit made by Nehemiah around the ruined city. Neh. ii. 13.

101 Lit. *it was falling on its roofs.*

102 Comp. Gen. xv. 9.

103 That is, Satan would dissuade you from liberal contributions by instilling the fear of poverty.

104 Comp. Matt. vi. 3, 4.

105 This contradicts verse 254, as well as several verses in Sura 19.

Sura 3

1 Verses 1–87 probably belong to the period between the battle of Bedr and Hej. 6: – Muhammad supposed Imran or Amran to be the father of the Virgin Mary (Sura 66. 12) – Mary and Elizabeth to be sisters; who, with Jesus, John, and Zacharias, make up the family of Imran. It is difficult to avoid the conclusion that Muhammad is guilty of the anachronism of confounding Miriam with the Virgin Mary. On the other hand is the difficulty of conceiving that as the sequence of time and fact is observed with tolerable accuracy in regard to the main features of Jewish and Christian History, he should have fallen into so serious an error, or have so inadvertently adopted, as Mr Muir supposes, the phraseology of his Jewish informants (amongst whom the only well-known Mary (Miriam) was the daughter of Imran and the sister of Moses) as to have overlooked the discrepancy in their respective dates. But it is possible that Muhammad believed, as some Muslim writers assert, that Miriam's soul and body were miraculously preserved till the time of Jesus in order to become Mary his mother. Certainly the Talmudists fabled that the Angel of Death and the worm of corruption had no power over Miriam. Comp. Babha Bathra, 17. Jos. Ant. iv. 4, 6.

2 See Sura 2. 1.

3 See Sura 21. 49.

4 Lit. *mother.*

5 In the battle of Bedr, Muhammad, with 319 followers routed 1,000 Meccans, A.H. 2.

6 That is, knowledge, or revelation, became the cause of disputings.

7 That is, will ye receive Islam? The *Ummiin*, or *common folk*, the heathen Arabians destitute of Revelation.

8 Evang. de Nat. Mar. 7: Quotidie ab angelis frequentabatur, quotidie divinâ visione fruebatur, quæ eam a malis omnibus custodiebat et bonis omnibus redundare faciebat. See also Protev. Jac. 8: and also Hist. Nativ. Mar. 6: Quotidie escâ, quam de manu angeli accipiebat, ipsâ tantum reficiebatur.

9 The word rendered *descendants* is a collective noun.

10 Lit. *chamber*. Comp. Luke i. 21.

11 Luke i. 28.

12 Hist. de Nativ. Mar. 6: Abierunt simul Joachim et Anna uxor ejus ad templum domini, et . . . tradiderunt . . . Mariam in contubernio virginum quæ die noctuque in Dei laudibus manebant.

13 These reeds, say the commentators, were written over with passages from the law, and cast into Jordan. That of Zacharias alone swam, and was the token that the charge of Mary was to devolve on him. Others render, *their divining arrows*. Hist. Nat. Mar. ib. p. 359 *sqq*.

14 Ar. *El-Mesich Isa ben Mariam*, illustrious in this world as a Prophet, in the next as an Intercessor. Beidh.

15 Evang.Thomæ, ch. 2 (Thilo. p. 281) and Evang. Infantiæ Arab. ch. 36, 46. (Thilo. p. 111, 123.)

16 See Sura 5. 111.

17 Muslims believe that God took the dead body of Jesus to Heaven – for three hours according to some – while the Jews crucified a man who resembled him. Sura 4. 156. The word *motewaffika* (comp. Sura 39. 156) means, in speaking of God, *to cause to die, take to himself*. It would also seem from Sura 19. 34, that Jesus died a natural death, though it is nowhere said how long he continued in that state. Muslims also believe that Jesus on his return to earth at the end of the world will slay the Antichrist, die, and be raised again. A vacant place is reserved for his body in the Prophet's tomb at Medina. See Lieut. Burton's 'Pilgrimage,' vol. ii.

18 Lit. *verily the similitude* or *analogy of Isa is as the similitude* or *analogy of Adam*, i.e. neither of them had a human father.

19 This refers to an embassy from the Christians in Nedjran in Arabia, with their Bishop, Abu Hareth, at their head, to Muhammad at Medina, who had now acquired political power. The embassy declined to be parties to the strange mode of settling the dispute here proposed, but consented to pay tribute on condition of not being molested in their religion or lands.

20 If this be not a mere figure of speech, it must mean *let us call over and curse the names*, the persons being at a distance.

21 As the Christians do their Bishops and Priests.

22 Whether he were a Jew or Christian.

23 About Moses and Jesus, and their respective faiths.

24 See Sura 16. 121.

25 i.e. the claim to be equal with God could never have been made by Jesus himself, but by his followers, in ignorance of the Scriptures and of his true nature.

26 That is, to call them *rabb* – a title due only to God.

27 Assembled on Mount Sinai. Compare the Jewish legend, that all the prophets, even those who were not yet born, were present on Mount Sinai, when God gave the law to Moses. See Shemoth Rabba. Parashah

28, according to which, not only the Prophets but the Rabbis of every generation, were present at the giving of the Law.

28 Becca, *place of crowding*, i.e. Mecca. This sentence, together with other Suras – the Cave, Mary, Imran, Repentance, T. H. Sura 20, are woven into the Kiswah or covering of the Caaba, which is renewed annually.

29 The Makam Ibrahim (praying place of Abraham) is a small building supported by six pillars about 8 ft. high, four of which are surrounded from top to bottom by a fine iron railing, while they leave the space between the two hind pillars open; within the railing is a frame about 5 ft. square, said to contain the sacred stone on which Ibrahim stood when he built the Caaba. Burckhardt. Lieut. Burton ('Pilgrimage,' iii. 336) says that as the Arab tradition speaks clearly and consistently as to the fact of Abraham having visited Mecca to build the Caaba, it may be considered an open question.

30 The Koran.

31 Or, *they are smitten with*. Sale.

32 This probably refers to the battle of Ohod.

33 The Arabic word occurs at verse 13 of horses as known by certain marks. So here these angels would be known by their accoutrements, etc.

34 This and the following verses to 154 were probably revealed shortly after the reverse of Ohod.

35 This verse and 39. 31 were recited at Muhammad's death by Abu Bekr, in order to convince Omar and the other Muslims of the possibility of that event.

36 That is, return to idolatry. A report had been spread in the battle of Ohod that Muhammad had been slain.

37 Lit. *according to a writing* (i.e. of God) *definite*. The Rabbins also teach (Com. Tract. Rosch. Haschanah) that there are books in which God has written down the lifetime of every individual. Lit. *No soul can die*.

38 Lit. *and their saying was no other than that they said*.

39 To relapse into infidelity. The Koreisch attempted to seduce the Muslims to renounce their faith after the battle of Ohod.

40 The command to abstain from taking the spoils. This disobedience turned the scale of victory against the Muslims.

41 Victory and plunder.

42 Some took to flight, others stood firm, and were not careful of their lives.

43 That is, in confused rout.

44 Muhammad had been accused of having secretly appropriated a portion of the spoil.

45 At Ohod.

46 See Sura 2. 149.

47 At Ohod; lit. *wound*.

48 Lit. *that Satan*. Said to refer to Abu Sofian, the leader of the Koreisch.

49 This is an answer to the taunt that Muhammad could not distinguish true believers from hypocrites.

50 This was the taunt of the Jews of the tribe of Kainoka, when Muhammad demanded tribute of them in the name of God.

51 That is, who rejoice in their successful corruptions of their own sacred books, especially the testimony of Moses to Muhammad, and in their own fancied righteousness. Thus some of the commentators.

52 Lit. *some of you are from others*. These words were occasioned by one of the Prophet's wives having told him that God often praised the men, but not the women, who had fled their country for the faith. Beidh.

Sura 4

1 Most of the events alluded to in this Sura fall between the end of the third and the close of the fifth year after the Flight to Medina.

2 Verses 8 and 12 are said by the commentators to have been revealed in consequence of the complaints of Omm Kuhha that, in accordance with the ante-Islamitic custom, she had been excluded from any portion of her deceased husband's property. The unsatisfactory nature of the Muhammadan traditions may be inferred from the fact that no less than six different names are assigned to him. It is, however, probable that these and similar laws relative to inheritances were given at a time when many heads of families had fallen, as at Ohod, in battle. This remark applies to verses 33–45.

3 Women found guilty of adultery and fornication were punished at the first rise of Islam, by being literally immured. But this was exchanged, in the case of a maiden, for one year's banishment and 100 stripes; and in the case of a married woman, for stoning.

4 What took place in the times of ignorance, previous to the revelation of the Koran.

5 By marrying without means adequate to the support of a free wife, or by remaining single.

6 From marrying slaves.

7 Games of chance, usury, etc.

8 By providing for them a home and the protection of a husband. Or, *of that which God would have them care for*.

9 An undutiful child is very seldom heard of among the Egyptians, or the Arabs in general. Sons scarcely ever sit, or eat, or smoke, in the presence of the father unless bidden to do so; and they often wait upon him and upon his guests at meals and on other occasions: they do not cease to act thus when they have become men. Lane's Mod. Egypt. vol. i. p. 69.

10 The Koranic precepts as to prayer savour of Jewish origin. Thus, 'Prayer should be said standing,' is a Rabbinic precept – Comp. Sura 2. 240. – Misch. Berachoth 10 – may be shortened in dangerous places, ib. iv. 10 – is forbidden to the drunken, ib. 31, 2. Erubin, 64 – and to the polluted; Berachoth iii. 4 – and is to be preceded, in this case, by washings with water or sand. See Sura 17. 110. 1 Cor. xi. 21.

11 The Jews and their Rabbis.

12 See Sura 2. 98.

13 Lit. *the companions of the sabbath*. See 2. 61.

14 This refers to certain renegade Jews, who out of hatred against Muhammad, went over to the Koreisch.

15 Lit. *ripened*.

16 Mecca.

17 And therefore a fit subject for plunder.

18 Some of the Meccans after embracing Islam did not thoroughly break with the infidels and fly their country. These persons were miraculously slain by angels at Bedr. Others suppose the angels to be Nakir and Monkir, who examine the dead in the grave.

19 That is, to what religion did ye belong?

20 And therefore could not resist the unbelievers.

21 Thus the Rabbins Tr. Berachoth, iv. 4, 'He that goeth in a dangerous place may pray a short prayer.'

22 See Mischna Tr. Berachoth, 10.

23 This verse is said to have been revealed when Muhammad was about to acquit a Muslim who had committed theft, and laid the guilt at the door of a Jew. But the particulars are given in a very contradictory manner.

24 In allusion to an idolatrous and superstitious custom of the old Arabians.

25 By the mutilation of slaves, branding their bodies, filing the teeth, etc.

26 See Sura 84. 24.

27 Sura 6.

28 See Sura 2. 7.

29 Lit. *one was made to appear to them like* (*Jesus*). Comp. 3. 48.

30 By believing too much, like the Christians who regarded Jesus as God; or too little, like the Jews who would not believe on Muhammad.

31 That is, a Being possessing a Spirit.

Sura 5

1 The garlands, etc., attached to the victims offered at Mecca.

2 When you have again returned to your common and everyday life by laying aside the *ihram*, or pilgrim's robe. This generally consists of two

pieces of cotton, or linen, or woollen cloth, without seam or ornament, one of which is wrapped round the loins, and the other thrown over the shoulders. The instep, heel, and head must be bare.

3 The Koreisch sent to meet Muhammad, who was on his way to visit the Caaba with 1, 400 men, at Hudaibiya (An. Hej. 6) to prohibit his nearer approach. A truce for ten years was ultimately concluded.

4 By making war in the holy month.

5 Comp. Tract Cholin, c. 3.

6 Lit. *on blocks or shafts of stone*. These were set up by the pagan Arabs in front of their houses for the purpose of sacrificing thereon. See Tr. Cholin, p. 39, 40, 41.

7 It was the custom to draw lots for joints of a camel with arrows, some feathered and others unfeathered, kept for this purpose in the temple of Mecca.

8 In the sense of sound, healthful.

9 Thus Talm. Tr. Berachoth, 46.

10 This refers to the oath of fidelity which Muhammad's followers took at Al Akaba.

11 It is quite uncertain to what events this refers. The commentators narrate, and have doubtless invented, various incidents as having occasioned it.

12 Verses 15–38 belong probably to the period shortly before the taking of Chaibar in the beginning of Hej. 7.

13 The space between the mission of different prophets.

14 Called by the Arabians Habeel and Kabeel. The dialogue between Cain and Abel is slightly varied from that given in Targ. Jerus. on Gen. iv. 8, and Jonath. Ben Uzziel.

15 Or, *the sin against me*, i.e. of slaying me.

16 In the Jewish tradition the raven shews the mode of burial to Adam, not to Cain. Pirke R. Elieser, c. 21. Midr. fol. 11 ap. Weil (Legenden, p. 39).

17 Or, *corpse*.

18 Thus Mischn. Sanhedr. iv. 5, 'We find it said in the case of Cain who murdered his brother – "the voice of thy brother's bloods crieth" – It is not said, *blood of thy brother*, but *bloods*, i.e. his blood and the blood of his seed. Therefore was man created single, in order to shew that to him who kills a single individual of Israel it shall be reckoned as if he had slain the whole race, and that he, etc.' precisely as in the text. Comp. also the same form of expression in Bab. Tal, Kidush, § 1, 'If one fulfil but one commandment, he causes the scale of innocence to preponderate for himself and the whole world; but if he commit one sin, he causes the scale of guilt to preponderate for himself and the whole world.'

19 Muhammad is said by the early traditionists to have punished a woman who had been guilty of theft in this manner while on the route to

Mecca previous to its capture. We are, therefore, able to fix the date of verses 39–44.

20 Usury, bribes.

21 Ex. xxi. 23–27.

22 This may refer to proposals made to the Muslims to enter into alliance with the Jews and Christians against the heathen, after the reverse at Ohod. Lane observes (Mod. Egyptians, i. 358) with regard to this precept, that 'of the leading features of the character of the Mooslims none is more remarkable than their religious pride. They regard persons of every other faith as the children of perdition; and such the Mooslim is early taught to despise.' They are, however, 'as remarkable for their toleration as for their contempt of unbelievers.'

23 Weil suggests that verses 64–88 were revealed subsequently to contests with the Jews, but before Muhammad had broken with the Christians, i.e. between Hej. 4 and 8.

24 That is, God has ceased to be bounteous. The Muslims believe that at the day of judgment all the Jews will appear with the right hand tied to the neck.

25 That is, the Koran. The Jew was to retain a faith in the Towrât, or Law; the Christian in the Injil, or Gospel; but both Jews and Christians were to receive the Koran as the complement of both.

26 See Sura 2. 59. p. 8.

27 1 Thess. ii. 15.

28 Did not give herself out to be a goddess. Djelal.

29 That is, were human beings, and subject to the usual wants and liabilities of ordinary persons.

30 See Sura 2. 61. Mark viii. 30.

31 Comp. Sura 66. 2. The date of verses 89–91 is therefore probably Hej. 7.

32 If you violate it.

33 See verse 4. Tradition has expanded the word *ansab*, so as to include all figures, and hence the strict observers of the letter of the Koran forbid the game of chess. The Persians, however, and Indians generally interpret this verse more liberally.

34 This and the two following verses are placed by the commentators in the year of Hudaibiya, as also 98, 99, 100.

35 That is, Cube-House. Maison Carrée. It is also commonly called the Bait Ullah, *House of God*. The Caaba is an oblong massive structure 55 ft. in length, 45 in breadth, and the height somewhat greater than the length. At the S.E. corner is the famous Hajar El-Aswad, or Black Stone, according to Lieut. Burton, an undoubted aerolite. The Caaba stands in an open parallelogram of about 500 ft. by 530 ft. and is surrounded by colonnades, the pillars of which, made of various marbles, some Egyptian but mostly Meccan, stand in a quadruple row on the east side, and three deep on the other sides, and

amount to 554. It has been rebuilt several times, but has not been materially altered since A.H. 1040.

36 Names given to the sacred animals which were marked and allowed to range for pasture at liberty. The dedicated mother-camel was the *Saiba*; the *Wasila* included also goats or ewes; the eleventh female offspring of the camel was *Bahira*; the dedicated stallion was *Hami*. These forms of superstition grew up, obviously, from a remote period, out of the intense affection of the Bedouin for his flocks, especially his horses and camels.

37 Lit. *on you your souls*.

38 Lit. *upon its face*, i.e. according to its plain scope.

39 See Evang. Infant. c. τ, Invenimus in libro Josephi Pontificis qui vixit tempore Christi, Jesum locutum esse, et quidem cum in cunis jaceret, etc. The date of verse 108 to the end is uncertain.

40 Precisely the same expression is applied to our Lord in the Arabic Evang. Infantiæ, c. 36 at the end, which also relates the story of the Birds.

41 Ar. *El-hawariyin*, a different word from that used for Jesus, Hud, Saleh, and the other apostles par excellence. The root of the word is the Æthiopic *hawyra*, to go, send; hence the Church is called in Æthiopic the *Beth chrestyan ant hawariyat*, i.e. Apostolic. See, however, the note on Thilo's Cod. Apoc. p. 152, who derives from the root *hur, to be white, pure*; hence, *friends, helpers*.

42 Comp. 1 Cor. xi. 27, sqq.

43 *Thou hast a right to do so as their Lord.*

Sura 6

1 Lit. *their affair would have been decided*. In that case there would no longer have been an opportunity for the warnings of the prophets and for repentance, but the angels would at once have executed the divine judgments.

2 See Sura 41. 13.

3 See Sura 13. 36.

4 This denunciation is repeated in eleven other passages of the Koran, and coupled with the known reverence of the early Muslims for what they considered as the word of God, must have greatly tended to secure the revelations of the Prophet from being in any way tampered with and corrupted.

5 They are self-convicted of their own hypocrisy and of the hollowness of their professions.

6 The Resurrection, etc.

7 See Sura 52. 38.

8 A community. Comp. Prov. xxx. 25, 26. Animals as well as mankind are under the control of God, are held within the limits of his

decrees, are accountable to him, and will stand before him in the judgment.

9 Of the Eternal decrees.

10 Or, *embellished, made it fair-seeming.*

11 Lit. *openly*, i.e. preceded by some sign.

12 The Rabbins speak of the three keys in the hand of God. Tr. Tanith, fol. 1.

13 On the preserved tablet, on which are written the decrees of God.

14 That is, during sleep. See Sura 39. 43. Or, *layeth to rest.* Mar. renders literally, *defungi faciet vos*, id est, obdormiscere. Thus also Beidh. But see the use of the same word in the next verse.

15 Or, *to perplex you (by dividing you into) sects.*

16 Comp. Sura 60. 13.

17 Compare a similar narrative (Midr. Rabbah on Gen. par. 17) in which Abraham is given over by his idolatrous father Zarah to Nimrod, who says, 'We will adore the Fire:' 'Rather,' said Abraham, 'the water which puts out fire.' 'The Water then' – 'Rather the clouds that bear the water.' 'The Clouds then' – 'Rather the wind which scatters the clouds.' 'The Wind then' – 'Rather man who endures the wind.' Whereupon Abraham was thrown into the furnace. – It is quite possible that in what follows, Muhammad may have intended to imply that Abraham had renounced the Sabian star-worship of his fathers, and to vindicate him from the habit of consulting the stars attributed to him by the Talmudists. Shabbath, fol. 156, coi. 1. 'Abraham replied, I have consulted my Astrology.' Comp Rashi on Gen. xv. 5. See Maim. Yad Hachaz. vii. 6.

18 Comp. Gen. xv. 5.

19 See Sura 21. 52.

20 Lit. *unless that my Lord shall will anything.*

21 Or, *confuse not their faith with wrong, injustice*, i.e. idolatry.

22 Koran.

23 This verse and the following were probably added at Medina after the Hejira; at least it is difficult to conceive that Muhammad would have ventured thus to have written at Mecca.

24 This verse is said to have been revealed at Medina and to be aimed at the false prophets Moseilama and Aswad al-Ansi; also at Abdallah Ibn Saad, Muhammad's secretary, who for corrupting the sacred text and apostacy, was one of the ten proscribed at the taking of Mecca.

25 In the womb.

26 Of all sorts.

27 Lit. *attaineth to.* Lane renders, 'the eyes see not Him, but He seeth the eyes.'

28 The verses of the Koran.

29 Comp. Ex. xxii. 28.

30 Notwithstanding this disclaimer, the Muslim tradition, etc. speak of many of their Prophet's miracles.

31 Lit. *the outside of iniquity and its inside.* Some understand these words of open sins, and secret sins.

32 That is, God's method of dealing with the guilty was to send apostles previous to the execution of his judgments.

33 It appears to have been the custom of the idolatrous Arabs to set apart one portion of their fields for the Supreme God, and the other for the inferior gods represented by their idols. If any of the fruit happened to fall from the part consecrated to the idols into that consecrated to God, they restored it, but if the reverse occurred, they gave it to the idols. God, said they, is rich and can dispense with it. The secret, however, was that the idols' portion was reserved for the priests, Beidhawi.

34 Comp. Sura 5. 102.

35 Comp. Sura 17. 33.

36 See verse 120 above.

37 This very abrupt transition to Jewish history seems to indicate that a passage between this and the preceding verse is lost.

38 Lit. *we were careless of their studies.*

Sura 7

1 See Sura 2. 1. The first part of this Sura was perhaps revealed when the Arabians were assembled at the Pilgrimage. See verse 29.

2 A figure of frequent occurrence in the Talmud. See Tr. Rosh. Haschana, 17*a*.

3 Comp. Sura 20. 118.

4 Gen. iii. 15.

5 Lit. *towards each Mosque*, i.e. towards the kïbla of each Mosque. The word mosque, *mesjid*, however, is usually applied only to that of Mecca. The common term in use for larger places of worship is *djami*, a word unknown, in that sense, to the Koran.

6 The Koreisch (we are told in Sirat Arrasul, fol. 26, and Beidh.), in order to instil a deep respect for the Caaba and other holy places into the minds of the Arabians, had forbidden all food during the processions, and required that no clothes, except those borrowed from Meccans, should be worn, or that those who wore their own should devote them to God as holy vestments. The consequence was that most of the pilgrims visited the holy places in perfect nudity. Hence the precept in the text.

7 The Angels of Death.

8 Comp. Matth. xix. 24; Mark x. 25; Luke xviii. 25.

9 'On this wall (the name of which is derived from *Arafa*, "to know," with allusion to the employment of those upon it) will stand those whose good and evil works are equal, and are not, therefore, deserving of either Paradise or Gehenna. The idea, which is analogous to that of Purgatory, may be derived from the Talmud. Thus in the Midrasch on Eccl. vii. 14,

"How much space is there between the two" (Paradise and Hell)? R. Jochanan saith, a wall; R. Acha, a span: others hold them to be so close that a person may see from one into the other.'

10 That is, they will know the inmates of Paradise by their whiteness, and the people of Hell by the blackness of their faces.

11 That is, ye believers: to whom the speakers on Al Araf are supposed to turn.

12 The fruits of Paradise. Comp. Luke xvi. 19.

13 The fulfilment of its promises and threats.

14 The rain. Thus, the Rabbins call the rain 'the might and power of God,' Comp. Tract Tanith, fol. 1, and connect it with the Resurrection, Tract Berachoth, fol. 33.

15 The Rabbins in like manner describe the mission of Noah. Comp. Sanhedr. 108. Midr. Rabbah on Gen. par. 30, 33; and on Eccl. 9, 14. See Sura 11. 40.

16 The two tribes of Ad and Themoud – the latter of whom is mentioned by Diod. Sic. and Ptolemy – lay to the north of Mecca in the direct line of traffic between the countries to the north and to the south, and both probably disappeared with its cessation, when the Arabs were no longer held in check by the Romans. Popular tradition attributed this to the divine vengeance, and so too the Koran.

17 On Houd, see Geiger, pp. 113–119. He supposes him to be the Eber of the Bible. But Mr Muir suggests that both Houd and Saleh may have been persecuted Jewish or Christian emissaries and teachers, whose rejection was thus recast by Muhammad. See note on verse 71.

18 Or, *entrusted*, i.e. with the office of apostle.

19 See Sura 24. 176.

20 This verse may contain an implied reference to the famine with which Mecca had been visited, and fix the date of this part of the Sura. Comp. verse 127.

21 Lit. *plot, stratagem.*

22 Comp. the passage from Pirke R. Eliezer, c. 48, who makes Moses perform this miracle in the presence of Pharaoh, which the Scripture (Ex. vii.) account does not.

23 Lit. *cause him to hope, temporise with him.*

24 They traced their calamities to Moses. So Sale. Kas.

25 In Suras 17. and 27. the text speaks of *nine* plagues. The *flood* is not mentioned in the Scripture.

26 Lit. *when we removed from them the plague until a period at which they should arrive.*

27 Lit. *that in which these are.*

28 Lit. *the set time of his Lord was fulfilled in forty nights.*

29 Sale and others render *having a body, corporeal*, of which the commentators give no satisfactory explanation. That the calf lowed in

consequence of Samaël having entered into it, is one of the traditions of the Talmud. Pirke R. Eliezer, c. 45.

30 Compare Sura 29. 47, 72. 2, 2. 73. The word *ummiyy* is derived from *ummah*, a nation, and means Gentile; it here refers to Muhammad's ignorance, previous to the revelation of Islam, of the ancient Scriptures. It is equivalent to the Gr. *laic, ethnic*, and to the term *gojim*, as applied by the Jews to those unacquainted with the Scriptures. There can, however, be no doubt that Muhammad – in spite of assertions to the contrary, with the view of proving his inspiration – was well acquainted with the Bible histories.

31 If these words contain an allusion to the Ansars, it is likely that this verse was added at Medina. The epithet Al-Ummiyy (the unlettered) does not, thus, occur in Meccan Suras.

32 The Koran.

33 Pirke R. Eliezer, 45, explains Ex. xxxii. 26, of the tribe of Levi, as not having been implicated with the other tribes in the sin of the golden calf.

34 The Jews changed *hittat*, absolution, indulgence, into *habbat*, corn.

35 This and the next six verses are supposed to have been added at Medina.

36 Comp. Sura 2. 61. No trace of this legend is to be found in the Talmudists. The city is said to have been Aila (Elath) on the Red Sea.

37 Perhaps in allusion to Deut. xxviii. 49, 50.

38 As bribes to pervert Scripture, etc.

39 Sinai – which, however, is not mentioned in the Koran as the place where the law was given. Comp. 'I will cover you with the mountain like a roof.' Abodah Sar. 2, 2. Thus also in Tract Sabbath, f. 88, 1, 'R. Avdimi . . . saith, These words teach us that the Holy One, blessed be He, turned the mountain over them like a vessel, and said to them, If ye will receive the law, well; but if not, there shall be your grave.' This tradition is still held by the Jews. See D. Lewis Pent. Prayers, fol. 150. Its origin is a misunderstanding of Ex. xix. 17, rightly rendered in the E. version *at the nether part of the mountain*.

40 To the Jews.

41 Balaam. But according to others, a Jew who renounced his faith in Muhammad.

42 The 99 titles of God, taken from the Koran, are to be found in Maracci, vol. 11, p. 414, or in Macbride's Religion of the Mohammedans, p. 121. To facilitate the repetition of these names, the Muslims use a rosary.

43 In altering the names of God, changing Allah into Allat, Elaziz into Alozza, Mennan into Menat, etc.

44 Lit. *and in what declaration after it will they believe?*

45 That is, it weighs heavily on the hopes and fears of men, djinn, and angels.

46 Probably the usual final clause, *whence ye looked not for it*, should here be added to make good the rhyme, which is otherwise interrupted in the original.

47 Some render *salihan, well made, rightly shaped*; others, *virtuous, morally perfect*.

48 And their idolatrous posterity. Beidh.

49 *Take* or *use indulgence*; i.e. take men and their actions as they are, and make all due allowances. Some understand it, of Muhammad's accepting such voluntary and superfluous alms as the people could spare.

50 That is, those under Satanic influence.

51 Collected *or* sought it out. Beidh.

Sura 8

1 This Sura relates mainly to the battle of Bedr, A.H. 2.

2 At Medina.

3 The necessity for the combat and its probable result.

4 Muhammad had conceived the design of attacking an unarmed caravan belonging to the Koreisch on its way from Syria to Mecca. Abu Sofian, who had charge of it, sent to Mecca for succour, whence a body of nearly 1,000 armed men at once set out to his assistance. Some of the Muslims were anxious to attack the caravan: others, notwithstanding the disparity of numbers, proposed to throw themselves upon the succours.

5 Idolatry.

6 In Sura 3. the angels are said to be 3,000.

7 Lit. *thou didst not cast when thou didst cast, but God cast.* This is explained of the miracle of the gravelstones and sand cast by God into the eyes of the Meccans at Bedr.

8 That is, by our victory over you.

9 Specially addressed to the Mohadjers, i.e. those who had fled with Muhammad to Medina.

10 Twelve of the Koreisch had given camels and a large sum of money in aid of the Meccan succours.

11 Lit. *hath preceded.*

12 Before Islam it had been the custom among the Arabians to assign a fourth part of the booty to the leader of an expedition.

13 That is, on the day of the battle of Bedr. See Sura 21. 49.

14 The mission of Gabriel to Muhammad with the promise of victory.

15 Compare the different account in Sura 3. 11. The commentators, however, get over the discrepancy by explaining the apparent diminution of the Muslims at the commencement only of the battle, which had the effect of drawing on the enemy in self-confidence.

16 The angels fighting for the Muslims.

17 By inducing them to attack so greatly superior a force.

18 Thus Beidh. Or, more simply, *render them the like.*
19 Comp. Lev. xxvi. 8; Josh. xxiii. 10.
20 Authorising the ransom of captives.
21 That is, a disposition to become Muslims.
22 That is, on account of their infidelity.
23 See Weil. Life of M. p. 84, n.

Sura 9

1 The 'Immunity' is said by some commentators to have formed originally one Sura with the eighth, p. 112, and that on this account the usual formula of invocation is not prefixed. The Caliph Othman accounted for this omission of the Bismillah from the fact of this Sura having been revealed, with the exception of a few verses, shortly before the prophet's death, who left no instructions on the subject. (Mishcat 1, p. 526.) The former verses from 1–12, or, according to other traditions, from 1–40, were recited to the pilgrims at Mecca by Ali, Ann. Hej. 9.

2 Lit. *that ye cannot weaken God.*

3 Shawâl, Dhu'lkaada, Dhu'lhajja, Muharram. These months were observed by the Arabians previous to the time of Muhammad.

4 Al Abbas, Muhammad's uncle, when taken prisoner, had defended his unbelief, and declared that he had performed these two important duties. Beidh.

5 Or, *shall issue his behest.*

6 At the battle of Honein, a valley three miles from Mecca (A.H. 8), the Muhammadans, presuming upon the great superiority of their numbers, 12,000 men, over the enemy who were only 4,000 strong, were seized with a panic throughout their ranks. Order was restored and victory obtained through the bravery and presence of mind of Muhammad and his kindred.

7 The enemy attacked and routed you on all sides.

8 See 2. 249.

9 Through the breaking off commercial relations.

10 Or, *by right of subjection*, Sale; *in cash*, Wahl.; *all without exception*, K. i.e. as if by counting hands.

11 Thus Hilchoth Melachim, vi. 4. The Jews are commanded, in case of war with the Gentiles, to offer peace on two conditions: – that they become tributaries, and renounce idolatry. Thus also chap. viii. 4.

12 The Muhammadan tradition is that Ezra was raised to life after he had been 100 years dead, and dictated from memory the whole Jewish law, which had been lost during the captivity, to the scribes. That the Jews regarded Ezra as a son of God is due to Muhammad's own invention. See Sonna, 462 v. H. v. Purgstall's Fundgruben des Orients, i. 288. The Talmudists, however, use very exaggerated language

concerning him. Thus, Sanhedrin, 21, 22, 'Ezra would have been fully worthy to have been the lawgiver, if Moses had not preceded him.' Josephus, Ant. xi. 5, 5, speaks of his high repute with the people, and of his honourable burial. Muhammad probably represents the Jews as having deified Ezra with the view of showing that they, as well as the Christians, had tampered with the doctrine of the Divine unity.

13 An allusion to the word Rabbi, used by Jews and Christians, of their priests, etc., but *in Arabic of God only.* Comp. Matt. xxiii. 7, 8.

14 See Sura 5. 85.

15 The pre-Islamic intercalation of a month every third year, in order to reduce the lunar to the solar years, was ended by this passage.

16 See Sura, 13. 26.

17 With Abubekr. lit. *second of two.*

18 Wahk. *reich oder arm.* Savary, *young or old.* Ibn Hisam (924) pronounces this to be the oldest verse of the Sura.

19 This refers to the expedition of Tabouk, a town half-way between Medina and Damascus, against the Greeks, A.H. 9. Muhammad was now at the head of an army of 30,000 men. Verses 42–48 are said to have been revealed during the march.

20 Lit. *prepared a preparation.*

21 Lit. *written.*

22 That is, victory or martyrdom.

23 Compare Sura 3. 172.

24 *The poor,* i.e. absolute paupers; *the needy,* i.e. those in some temporary distress.

25 The petty Arab chiefs with whom Muhammad made terms after the battle of Honein, in order to secure their followers.

26 There seems to be a play, in the original, upon the similarity of the words for *injure* and *ear.*

27 Lit. (are) *the one from the other.*

28 From giving alms.

29 Comp. Sura 54. The traditions as to the collection of pitch from wood of the Ark, in the time of Berosus (B.C. 250?) for amulets, and of the wood itself, in the time of Josephus (Ant. i. 3, 6, c. Apion, i. 19) must have reached Muhammad through his Jewish informants. Fragments are said to have existed in the days of Benjamin of Tudela, and to have been carried away by the Chalif Omar, from the mountain al Djoudi to the mosque of Gazyrat Ibn Omar.

30 To kill Muhammad. Lit. *they had nothing to avenge but that,* etc.

31 Prayers for the dead were customary among the Arabians before Muhammad.

32 The *Mohadjers* were those who fled with Muhammad from Mecca to Medina, the *Ansars* his auxiliaries in Medina.

33 The commentators are not agreed as to the nature of this double punishment.

34 The fine of a third part of all their substance was imposed upon seven of those who had held back from the expedition to Tabouk. This is the *fault* spoken of in the preceding verse.

35 The tribe of Beni Ganim had built a mosque, professedly from religious motives, which they invited Muhammad on his way to Tabouk to dedicate by a solemn act of prayer. Muhammad, however, discovered that the real motive of the Beni Ganim was jealousy of the tribe of Beni Amru Ibn Auf, and of the mosque at Kuba, and that there existed an understanding between them and his enemy the monk Abu Amir, who was then in Syria, for the purpose of urging the Greeks to attack the Muslims and their mosque. It is to him that the word *irsâdan* refers.

36 To the dwellers at Kuba. Verses 108–111 were probably promulged on the return from Tabouk previous to the entry into Medina.

37 Abu Amir.

38 Or, *never stand thou in it* (*to pray*).

39 The mosque of Kuba, about three miles S.S.E. of Medina. The spot where this verse was revealed is still pointed out, and called 'Makam el Ayat,' or 'the place of signs.' Burton's 'Pilgrimage,' ii. p. 214. Muhammad laid the first brick, and it was the first place of public prayer in El Islam. Ib. p. 209.

40 The Beni Ganim.

41 That is, up to the time of their death they will never reflect on what they have done without bitter pangs of conscience.

42 Lit. *limits*, i.e. laws.

43 Shall have their recompense.

44 See verse 101.

45 Lit. *turned aside, swerved.*

46 Three Ansars who did not accompany Muhammad to Tabouk, and who on his return were put under interdict, and not released from it till after fifty days of penance.

47 Verses 120–128 probably belong to the period after the return from Tabouk to Medina.

48 While fighting for the cause of God.

Sura 10

1 See Sura 2. 1.

2 That is, for a serious end, to manifest the Divine Unity.

3 Gen. xi. 1.

4 This refers to the seven years of scarcity with which Mecca had been visited.

5 Paradise.

6 Verses 27, 28 are to be noted, as defining the proportion to be observed in rewards and punishments, the severity of the latter being only

in proportion to the crime, the excellence of the former being above and beyond its strict merits.

7 *But rather your own lusts.*

8 The ordinary Arabic word for *to die* seems to be avoided in speaking of Jesus and Muhammad.

9 This is the doctrine of the Rabbins. Comp. Midrasch Rabba, and Midr. Jalkut on Numb. xxii. 2.

10 The preaching of Noah is mentioned by the Rabbins. Sanhedrin, 108. Comp. Midr. Rabbah on Gen. Par. 30 and 33, on Eccl. ix. 14, and in the probably sub. Apostolic 2 Pet. ii. 5.

11 This is in accordance with Talmudic legend. 'Recognise the power of repentance, in the case of Pharaoh, King of Egypt, who rebelled excessively against the most High; *Who is God that I should hearken to his voice?* (Ex. v. 2). But with the same tongue that sinned he did penance: *Who is like thee, O Lord, among the Gods?* (xv. 11). The Holy One, Blessed be He, delivered him from the dead, . . . so that he should not die (ix. 15, 16). – For now have I stretched forth my hand, and verily thee have I raised up from among the dead, to proclaim my might.' Ex. ix. 15, 16. A strange comment! Pirke R. Eliezer, § 43. Comp. Midr. on Ps. cvi. Midr. Jalkut, ch. 238.

12 That is, whether thou art not foretold in the Law and Gospel, and whether the Koran is not in unison with, and confirmatory of, them.

Sura 11

1 See Sura 2. 1.

2 Or, *will bestow his grace on every gracious one,* or *will bestow his abundance on every one who hath abundance* (*of merit*). The difficulty of rendering this passage arises from the word *fadhl*, which means *merit* as applied to man, *favour* as applied to God.

3 That is, before the Creation. Precisely the same statement occurs in Raschi on Gen. i. 2, as also in the modern catechism. *Tsenah ur'enah b'noth Tsion*, authoritatively put forth by the Polish and German *Talmudist* Rabbins. 'At the first creation of Heaven and Earth . . . the throne of glory of the Blessed God stood in the air above the waters.' Comp. Ps. civ. 3.

4 Men, heaven, and earth. Comp. Tr. Aboth, v. Mischna 1.

5 Comp. verse 37 and Sura 2. 21. It should be observed that the challenge in these passages is not to produce a book which shall equal the Koran in point of poetry or rhetoric, but in the importance of its subject-matter, with reference to the Divine Unity, the future retribution, etc. Upon these topics Muhammad well knew that he had preoccupied the ground. And we may infer from the fragments of the Revelations of Musailima and Sajâh (Hisam. 946; Attabâri (ed. Kosegarten) i. 134, 136, 152; Tab. Agâni, 339), which are mere imitations of the Koran, that he felt this to be the case.

6 'They laughed and jeered at him in their words.' Midr. Tanchuma. 'The passage Job xii. 5, refers to the righteous Noah who taught them and spake to them words severe as flames: but they scorned him, and said, "Old man! for what purpose is this ark?"' Sanhedr. 108. Comp. Midr. Rabbah on Gen. 30, and 33 on Eccl. ix. 14.

7 Or, *oven:* according to others, *reservoir*. Geiger thinks that the expression *the oven boiled up* may be a figurative mode of expressing the Rabbinic idea that 'the generation of the Deluge were punished by hot water.' Rosch. Haschanah, 16, 2; Sanhedr. 108.

8 According to another reading: *He hath done amiss*. The origin of this story is probably Gen. ix. 20–25.

9 That is, we had intended to make thee our chief. Beidh.

10 Thus, in contradiction to Gen. xviii. 8, the Rabbins; comp. Tr. Baba Mezia, fol. 86, 'They made as though they ate.'

11 Or, *menstrua passa est*, in token of the possibility of her bearing a child.

12 Lit, *his arm was straitened concerning them*.

13 Lit. *column*.

14 With the name, it is said, of the person each should strike.

15 See Sura 26. 176.

16 That is, after giving fair measure.

17 *Seizure*, for punishment. Hence, *the punishment* itself.

Sura 12

1 See Sura 2. 1. In no other Sura beside this is one subject treated of throughout. It was recited to the first eight of the Ansars who were converted, and clearly proves that Muhammad must have been in confidential intercourse with learned Jews.

2 The word Koran is here used in the same sense as Sura.

3 Muhammad was either unaware of the previous dream mentioned, Gen. xxxvii. 7, or passes it by in silence.

4 The captious and unbelieving Koreisch.

5 Lit. *your minds have made a thing seem pleasant to you*.

6 According to Gen. xxxvii. 24, the well or pit had 'no water in it.'

7 The apparition of his father, who said, 'Hereafter shall the names of thy brethren, engraven on precious stones, shine on the breast of the High Priest. Shall thine be blotted out?' Tr. Sotah, fol. 36.

8 Lit. *that he be imprisoned*.

9 An infant in the cradle. Sepher Hadjaschar, as below on v. 31.

10 Instead of their food, through surprise at his beauty. Seph. Hadj. in Midr. Jalkut. See also Midr. Abkhir, ib. ch. 146.

11 Satan induced Joseph to place his confidence in man, rather than in

God alone, in punishment of which sin the imprisonment was continued. Thus Midr. Rabba. Gen. Par. 89. Midr. Jalkut, ib. ch. 147.

12 In Gen. xli. 14, Joseph is released from prison *before* the interpretation of the dreams. But the Koran makes him decline to quit it till his character is cleared.

13 According to Gen. xli. 39, Pharaoh of his own accord sets Joseph over his house and land.

14 For the king to bestow.

15 Thus we read in Mid. Rab. on Gen. Par. 91, 'Jacob said to them, Enter ye not all by one gate.' See also Midr. Jalkut, ch. 148.

16 Thus also, in the Sepher Hadjaschar, Joseph first discovers himself to Benjamin, in opposition to Gen. xlv. 1.

17 Comp. Gen. xlii. 9.

18 Joseph is said by the Muslim commentators to have stolen an idol of gold belonging to his mother's father, which he broke, that he might not worship it. But this comment, as well as the text of the Koran, is probably based upon some such tradition as that of Midr. Rabba, Par. 92, 'He is a thief and the son of a thief' (Comp. Gen. xxxi. 19). – spoken of Benjamin.

19 That is, that Joseph was still alive. Thus Midr. Tanchumah on Gen. xlii. 1.

20 Comp. Gen. xxvii. 27.

21 Joseph's mother had long been dead. See Gen. xxxv. 19. But the object of Muhammad was probably to bring the event into strict accordance with the prediction of the dream. Gen. xxxvii. 10. Some, however, suppose that Bilhah is here meant, and her appearance before Joseph is also asserted to be the fulfilment of the dream by some of the Rabbins. Comp. Raschi on Gen. xxxvii. 10.

22 Lit. *This is of the announcements of the things unseen* (by thee, Muhammad). Compare the manner in which the story of the Creation and of Moses in the mount is introduced. Sura 28. 45; 38. 70.

Sura 13

1 See Sura 2. 1.

2 Thus, 'one hour of bliss in the world to come is better than all life in this world.' Mischnah Aboth, iv. 17. Comp. Sura 9. 38.

3 See Sura 17. 109. This verse is said to have been occasioned by the refusal of the Meccans at Hudaibiya to adopt the formula prescribed by Muhammad – *In the Name of the God of Mercy, the Merciful* – declaring that they knew not who the God of Mercy (Arrahman) was. This was in Hej. 6.

4 Lit. *despair.*

5 That is, the Jews, who at this period of Muhammad's prophetic

function, must have been highly gratified at the strong leaning towards, and respect for, their Scriptures and Histories, which shews itself increasingly in the later Meccan Suras.

6 Lit. *Mother*, or *Prototype of the Book*. Either God's knowledge or Prescience, or the fabled preserved tablet, on which is written the original of the Koran, and all God's decrees. The Jews have a tradition that the Law existed before the Creation. Midr. Jalkut, 7.

7 That is, the progressive conquests of the Muslims trench more and more on the territories of the idolatrous Arabians.

Sura 14

1 See Sura 2. 1.

2 See Sura 10. 5.

3 Lit. *I truly renounce your having associated me* (*with God*) *heretofore*.

4 The preaching and the profession of Islam. Comp. Ps. i. 3, 4.

5 The Caaba.

6 Lit. *to a term near at hand*.

7 Of the anciently destroyed cities of Themoud, Ad, etc.

8 Lit. *were unjust to their own souls*.

Sura 15

1 Hedjr, a valley in the route between Medina and Syria, originally the country of the Themoudites.

2 See Sura 2. 1.

3 Lit. *which had not a known writing*.

4 That is, not merely to gratify the curiosity of the doubting, but to execute prompt punishment. It might also be rendered, *save with justice*.

5 Ar. *bourdj*, i.e. Signs of the Zodiac.

6 See Sura 15. 34.

7 Comp. Sura 37. 6. In Chagiga 16, 1, the Demons (schedim) are said to learn the secrets of the future by listening behind the veil (pargôd).

8 Compare precisely a similar association of subjects, the Rain, Food, God, as Lord of life and death in Tr. Taanith, fol. 1 *a*.

9 Comp. Sura 2. 32. There is much in this dialogue between Eblis and Allah which reminds of the dialogue between Jehovah and Satan in the opening of the Book of Job.

10 That is, accursed. According to the Muslim tradition, Abraham drove Satan away with stones when he would have hindered him from sacrificing Ismael. Hence the custom during the pilgrimage of throwing

a certain number of stones as if at Satan, in the valley of Mina, near Mecca. The spot where the apparition of Satan to Abraham took place is marked by three small pillars, at which the stones are now thrown. Comp. Gen. xv. 11.

11 Lit. *I will embellish, prepare.*

12 Thus, in Sota, 10, David is said to have rescued Absalom from 'the seven dwellings of Hell;' in Midr. on Ps. xi. 'There are seven houses of abode for the wicked in Hell;' and in Sohar ii. 150, 'Hell hath seven gates.'

13 At the arrival of strangers.

14 Comp. Midr. Rabbah on Gen. Par. 50.

15 From Arabia to Syria. The pronoun in the fem. sing. may refer to the Pentapolis as to a single city, or to Sodom alone.

16 See Sura 26. 176.

17 See Sura 16. 3.

18 That is, the seven verses of Sura 1. Others understand, the seven long Suras; or, the fifteen Suras which make a seventh of the whole; or, this Sura (Hedjr) as originally the seventh. This verse and Sura 10. 10 shew that a part at least of the Koran was known under that name and existed as a whole in the time of Muhammad.

19 Comp. Sura 26. 215, i.e. demean thyself gently.

20 Lit. *as we sent down upon the dividers*, i.e. the Jews and Christians, who receive part of the Scriptures and reject part. Others render *obstructors* and explain the passage of twelve idolaters, who in order to intimidate the Meccans, seized upon the public revenues of Mecca during the pilgrimage.

21 In this, the fourth year of his mission, Muhammad is said to have hazarded the step of mounting the Safa, a slight eminence in one of the streets of Mecca, and publicly preached to the Koreisch.

22 Lit. *contracted.*

23 Death.

Sura 16

1 See Sura 10. 5, n.

2 *Ex gutta spermatis.* Pirke Aboth iii. *Unde venisti? ex guttá fœtidâ.* This verse is said to be an allusion to a difficulty proposed by an idolatrous Arab, who brought a carious leg-bone to Muhammad, and asked whether it could be restored to life. Compare a similar argument for the Resurrection, Tr. Sanhedrin, fol. 91 *a.*

3 Lit. *there is beauty in them for you*, i.e. they win you credit.

4 In allusion to Gen. xi. 1–10.

5 Ps. xxxv. 9.

6 Lit. *the family of the admonition*, i.e. Jews and Christians versed in the Pentateuch and Gospel.

7 The idolatrous Arabians regarded Angels as females and daughters of God. But their own preference was always for male offspring.

8 See Sura 81. 8.

9 Lit. *the likeness of evil to those*, etc.

10 The Arabs are curious in and fond of honey: Mecca alone affords eight or nine varieties – green, white, red, and brown. Burton's 'Pilgrimage', iii. 110.

11 Ex. xx. 4.

12 The *slave*, and the *dumb* in verse following, are the idols.

13 See Sura 3. 34.

14 Gabriel.

15 This passage has been supposed to refer to Salman the Persian. He did not, however, embrace Islam till a much later period, at Medina.

16 This is to be understood of the persecutions endured by the more humble and needy Muslims by their townspeople of Mecca.

17 From Mecca to Medina, i.e. the Mohadjers, to whom also verse 43 refers. Both passages, therefore, are of a later date than the rest of this Sura.

18 Mecca.

19 Lit. *the garment*.

20 Comp. Sura 6. 119.

21 Comp. Sura 6. 147. This verse as well as the following, and verse 125, were probably added at Medina.

22 *Antistes*, Maracci. Or the text may be literally rendered *Abraham was a people*, i.e. the people of Abraham; from whom the idolatrous Koreisch pretended to derive their origin.

23 Ar. *a Hanyf*. According to a tradition in Waquidi, fol. 255, Zaid (who died only five years before Muhammad received his first inspiration, and undoubtedly prepared the way for many of his subsequent announcements) adopted this term at the instance of a Christian and a Jew, who exhorted him to become a *Hanyf*. Zaid having at this time renounced idolatry, and being unable to receive either Judaism or Christianity, 'What,' said he, 'is a Hanyf?' They both told him, it was the religion of Abraham, who worshipped nothing but God. On this Zaid exclaimed, 'O God, I bear witness that I follow the religion of Abraham.' The root, whence *Hanyf* is derived, means generally to *turn* from good to bad, or vice versa, and is equivalent to the verbs *convert* and *pervert*.

Sura 17

1 Verses 12, 23–41, 75–82, 87 are supposed by many commentators to have originated at Medina.

2 Waquidy says the night-journey took place on the 17th of Rabhy' 1, a twelvemonth before the Hejira.

3 Of Jerusalem; and thence through the seven heavens to the throne of God on the back of *Borak*, accompanied by Gabriel, according to some traditions; while others, and those too of early date, regard it as no more than a vision. It was, however, in all probability a dream.

4 According to the commentators the slaughter of Isaiah and the imprisonment of Jeremiah, punished by the invasion of the Assyrians.

5 Over Sennacherib.

6 The slaying Zacharias, John Baptist, and Jesus, punished by the destruction of Jerusalem by the Romans. Comp. Tr. Gittin, fol. 57, where we read of the sufferings drawn down upon the Jews in consequence of the former of these crimes.

7 That is, if ye return to sin, we will return to punish.

8 Lit. *bird*.

9 Comp. Mischnah Aboth, 3, 20.

10 Comp. in Heb. Isai. liii. 3.

11 Lit. *lower a wing of humility*.

12 Comp. Sura 6. 151; 81. 8. Zaid, the sceptical seeker after truth, is reported to have discouraged the killing of daughters, saying, 'I will support them.' Kitâb al Wackidi, p. 255.

13 Or, *next of kin*.

14 Or, *run not after vain things which will avail nought*. Or, *accuse not any of a crime if thou art not sure of his guilt*.

15 Used a variety of arguments and illustrations.

16 Thus Tr. Chagiga, fol. 9 *b*. 'There are seven heavens (*rakian*): the veil, the firmament, the clouds, the habitation, the abode, the fixed seat, the araboth.' See Wetst. on 2 Cor. xii. 2.

17 In obvious allusion to the saint-worship of the Christians.

18 See Sura 7. 71.

19 See note on 5. 1. The tree is Zakkoum, Sura 56. The Rabbins teach that food of the bitterest herbs is one of the punishments of Hell. See Schröder's Rabb. und. Talm. Judenthum, p. 403.

20 That is, with all thy might.

21 Zamakshary relates that this passage was revealed when the Thaqyfites in framing the document of agreement between themselves and Muhammad, required that the words requiring the prostrations in worship should not be added. The writer looked at the prophet, who stood by in silence, when Omar stood up and drew his sword with menacing words. They replied, We speak not to thee but to Muhammad. Then this verse was revealed.

22 Lit. *weakness, languors.*

23 'The Jews, envious of Muhammad's good reception and stay there, told him, by way of counsel, that Syria was the land of the Prophets, and that if he was really a prophet, he ought to go there.' Sale from Djelal Eddin ap. Mar.

24 A work of supererogation, and therefore doubly meritorious. Thus Tr. Berachoth, fol. 4. The word station (*mekam*) is still used of the nearness to God, attained in spiritual ecstacies, etc.

25 That is, to enter the Grave or Mecca. Lit. *with an entry of truth.*

26 The word *spirit* is probably to be understood of the Angel Gabriel. Comp. 1 Kings xxii. 21. Others understand it of the immaterial soul of man. See note on Sura 2. 81.

27 The infidels hearing Muhammad say, Ya Allah! Ya Rahman! in his prayers, imagined that he was addressing two Deities; hence this passage. Comp. 16. 52; 25. 61. The title Arrahman was applied to their deities by the Himyarites; and it occurs in Ps. lxxviii. 38, and Ex. xxxiv. 6. The root is not found in Æthiopic.

28 The Talm. Tr. Berachoth, 31, 2, forbids loudness in prayer by the example of Hannah.

29 Lit. *magnify Him by magnifying.*

Sura 18

1 Lit. *hath not put crookedness into it.*

2 The valley, or mountain, in which the Cave of the Seven Sleepers was situated. See Gibbon's Decline and Fall, ch. xxxiii., especially the concluding sentences.

3 Because they slept with their eyes open. Beidh.

4 Muslims believe that this dog will be admitted into Paradise. One of its traditional names is Katmir, a word whose letters, it should be observed, are with one exception identical with Rakim.

5 Lit. *dispute not about them unless with clear disputation.*

6 Muhammad had omitted to use the qualifying phrase when, in reply to the Jews who asked for the History of the Seven Sleepers, he simply promised to give it on the morrow; hence, this verse. Comp. James iv. 13–15.

7 They entered the cavern under Decius and awoke in the time of Theodosius, according to the tradition; which cannot be reconciled with the number of years given in the text.

8 The words may be taken with Beidh. and Sale, as ironical. *Make thou him to see and hear.*

9 Said to have been promulgated at Medina.

10 Omaya Ibn Chalf, who advised Muhammad to cast off all his poorer followers, out of respect to the Koreisch.

11 It is probable that this and the numerous similar descriptions of the enjoyments in Paradise are based upon Muhammad's knowledge, or possibly personal observation, of the luxurious habits of the Persians, to whom many Arabian tribes owed allegiance, and with whom they had mercantile transactions by means of caravans. The word *Paradise*, the names of *cups* and *brocade* in Sura 56, and the word *sundus* in this passage, are all Persian.

12 Lit. *ex spermate*.

13 Comp. Isai. xl. 4, etc.

14 Muhammad appears, according to this text, to have considered Eblis not only as the father of the Djinn, but as one of their number. The truth appears to be that Muhammad derived his doctrines of the Genii from the Persian and Indian mythology, and attempted to identify them with the Satan and demons of the Semitic races. Both the Satans and Djinn represent in the Koran the principle of Evil. See Sura 2. 32, n.

15 The sea of Greece and the sea of Persia. But as no literal interpretation of the passage seems satisfactory, the Commentators have devised a spiritual or metaphorical one, and explain it of the two oceans of natural and supernatural knowledge. There is no trace of this legend in the Rabbinic writings.

16 The loss of our fish is a sign to us of our finding him whom we seek, namely, El-Khidr, or El-Khadir, the reputed vizier of Dhoulkarnain, and said to have drunk of the fountain of life, by virtue of which he still lives, and will live till the day of judgment. He is also said to appear, clad in *green* robes, to Muslims in distress, whence his name. Perhaps the name *Khidr* is formed from *Jethro*.

17 Probably Alexander the Great – so called from his expeditions to the East and West. He seems to be regarded in this passage as invested with a divine commission for the extirpation of impiety and idolatry. Comp. Dan. viii. and Tr. Tanith, fol. 32.

18 Ar. *Yadjoudj* and *Madjoudj* – the barbarous people of E. Asia. See Ibn Batoutah's Travels, iv. p. 274 (Par. ed.)

19 This rampart has been identified with fortifications which extended from the W. shore of the Caspian Sea to the Pontus Euxinus, made, as it is said, by Alexander, and repaired by Yezdegird II. See Sura 21. 96.

20 The form of this word in the Arabic, with the *h* in the second syllable and the final *m*, shews that the word was borrowed from the Hebrew, and not from the Greek or Syriac.

21 Observe in this expression the same admixture of the Semitic and Indo-Persian elements as was noticed above in the identification of Satans and Djinn; verse 48.

Sura 19

1 Comp. the first 37 verses of this Sura with Sura 3. 35–57 with reference to the different style adopted by Muhammad in the later Suras. This Sura is one of the fullest and earliest Koranic Gospel Histories, and is said to have been recited to the Nagash or King of Æthiopia, in the presence of the ambassadors of the Koreisch. His. 220.

2 See Sura ii. 1.

3 Lest they should desert the worship of the God of Israel.

4 Ar. *Yahia.* It may be true that the name in this form had never been given. Otherwise, we have in this passage a misunderstanding of Luke i. 61, as well as ignorance of the Jewish Scriptures. Comp. 2 Kings xxv. 23; 1 Chron. iii. 16; Ezra viii. 12; Jerem. xl. 8. Some commentators try to avoid the difficulty by rendering *samiyan, deserving of the name.*

5 Or, *with firm resolve.* See Sura 3. 36. The speaker is God.

6 To an eastern chamber in the temple to pray. Or it may mean, to some place eastward from Jerusalem, or from the house of her parents.

7 Gabriel.

8 See Sura 6. 9.

9 It is quite clear from this passage, and from verse 36, that Muhammad believed Jesus to have been conceived *by an act of the divine will.* Comp. Sura 3. 52; see also note at Sura 2. 81.

10 Or, *the throes urged her to the trunk of*, etc.

11 This was either the Infant which spoke as soon as born, or Gabriel. Comp. Thilo Cod. Apoc. 136–139 on this passage. Beidhawi explains: *from behind the palm tree.*

12 See Thilo Cod. Apoc. N.T. p. 138, and the Hist. Nat. Mar. c. 20, which connects similar incidents with the flight into Egypt.

13 Or, *settle, calm thine eye, refresh thine eye.* The birth of a son is still called *korrat ol ain.*

14 The anachronism is probably only apparent. See Sura 3. 1, n. Muhammad may have supposed that this Aaron (or Harun) was the son of Imran and Anna. Or, if Aaron the brother of Moses be meant Mary may be called his sister, either because she was of the Levitical race, or by way of comparison.

15 See Sura 5. 109.

16 The title *Nabi*, prophet, is used of Abraham, Isaac, and Jacob, as depositaries of the worship of the one true God, but with a mission restricted to their own families; whereas Houd, Saleh, Shoaib, etc., are designated as (*Resoul*) apostles and envoys, charged with a more extended mission to the tribes of Arabia. In Moses, Jesus, and Muhammad, etc., are united the office and gift both of prophet (*nabi*) and apostle (*resoul*).

17 Made them to be highly praised. Beidh.

18 Enoch. Beidhawi derives the name Edris from the Ar. *darasa, to*

search out, with reference to his knowledge of divine mysteries. The Heb. *Enoch*, in like manner, means *initiated*.

19 Comp. Gen. v. 24, and the tract Derek Erez in Midr. Jalkut, c. 42, where Enoch is reckoned among the *nine* – according to other Talmudists, *thirteen* (Schroder's Talm. und Rabb. Judenthum) – individuals who were exempted from death and taken straight to Paradise. It should be observed that both here and Sura 21. 85, Edris is named after Ismael.

20 Beidhawi, *in absentiâ*. Sale, *as an object of faith*. Beidhawi ad f. *in reward for their secret faith*.

21 This verse is to be understood as an answer on the part of Gabriel to Muhammad's complaints of the long intervals between the revelations.

22 The idolaters called their deities *Gods*, but as Polytheists were unused to the singular *Allah*, *God*.

23 Even the pious on their way to Paradise are to pass the confines of Hell.

24 The Koreisch, or the Muslims.

25 Or, *glory, strength*.

26 To call down judgments upon them.

27 As ambassadors come into the presence of a prince. Sale. This is implied in the original.

Sura 20

1 The first 14 or 16 verses of this Sura are said to have induced Omar to embrace Islam (His. 226. Ibn Sâd, i. and v.) in the sixth year before the Hejira.

2 See Sura 2. 1.

3 Lit. *if thou raise thy voice*.

4 Lit. *guidance*. Moses had lost his way, say the Commentators, when journeying to Egypt to visit his mother.

5 The Muslim Commentators tell how Moses when a child burnt his tongue with a live coal. The same story is found in Midr. Jalkut on Ex. c. 166, and in Shalsheleth Hakabalah, p. 5, *b*. Ed. Amsterd.

6 Lit. *vizir*.

7 Or, *strengthen my back*.

8 The form of the word in the original is not the pure Hebraic, but the later Rabbinic form.

9 See Sura 28. 11, 12.

10 What is their condition after their death as to happiness or misery. Beidh. whom Sale follows. But the word *state*, which Mar. renders *mens*, refers rather to their creed. 'How,' enquires Pharaoh, 'do you explain the fact that the generations of men have always practised a different worship?'

11 Lit. *pairs.*

12 The Midrasch Tanchumah on Ex. vii. gives a very similar dialogue between Pharaoh and Moses.

13 Lit. *the day of ornament.*

14 In punishing. Beidh.

15 To recompense. Beidh.

16 As the garden is said in Sura 88. to be lofty in point of situation, this frequently recurring phrase may mean that rivers run at its base. The Commentators, however, generally understand it to imply that the rivers flow beneath its shades or pavilions.

17 Lit. *and there overwhelmed them of the sea that which overwhelmed them.*

18 The 70 elders who were to have accompanied him.

19 That is, *the Samaritan.*

20 'The calf came forth (Ex. xxxii. 24) lowing and the Israelites beheld it. R. Jehuda saith, Samuel entered into it and lowed in order to mislead Israel.' Pirke R. Eliezer, § 45.

21 From the track of Gabriel's horse, or of Gabriel himself.

22 Lit. *no touch.*

23 I have adopted the word *leaden* as expressive of the *idea* implied in the original word, viz. *grey* or *greyish blue*; hence, *dulled, dimmed.* The Arabians have a great aversion to blue and grey eyes as characteristics of their enemies the Greeks. The word, however, may also mean *blind.* Comp. v. 124, 5.

24 Lit. *the most excellent or just of them in his way: dignitate*, Mar. But Kam. in Freyt. (iii. 150) *justissimus eorum, simillimus veracibus.* The sense of the last clause is, 'Ye have not tarried even so much as ten days, such, now that we look back upon it, is the brevity of life.' See Sura 23. 115.

25 The angel Israfil.

26 Compare Sura 55. 16–19.

27 It should be observed that here and in Sura 7. 19 there is no distinction between the tree of knowledge and the tree of life, as given in Gen. ii. 9, and iii. 5.

28 From the intensity of the light, mentioned Sura 39. 69.

29 In order to reconcile this passage with the prescribed hours, some understand *the extremes* to mean the *mid-day*, when the day is as it were divided.

30 Supply, *we will not believe.*

Sura 21

1 Lit. *while ye see it to be such.*

2 Lit. *the people* or *family of the admonition.* Itq. 34 considers this verse to have been revealed at Medina.

3 Or, *they invent not* (*concerning Him*). Comp. Rev. iv. 8.

4 Lit. *they precede him not in speech.*

5 Lit. *before thee*, which might seem to imply that the grant of immortality had been made to Muhammad. I have therefore rendered, as in the text, to avoid the ambiguity. Comp. Suras 3. 182; 29. 57.

6 Comp. Matt. xvi. 28; Heb. ii. 9. Hist. Josephi Fabr. Lign. c. 22 at the end.

7 See the index under the word *Man.* The Rabbins teach that man was created with innate evil propensities. See Schroder's Talm. und Rabb. Judenthum, p. 378.

8 That is, my teaching as to the future lot of the infidels, etc.

9 Ar. *furqan* – a word derived from the Jews, constantly used in the Talmud, and meaning as in Syr. and Æth. *deliverance, liberation.* Thus, Sura 8. 29, 42, and hence, *illumination, revelation*, generally. The usual interpretation here and in other passages is *the distinction*, i.e. between good and evil, lawful and unlawful. The title is applied to the Koran and Pentateuch alike.

10 This story is taken in part verbatim from Midr. Rabbah on Gen. par. 17. See also Schalscheleth Hakabala, 2; Maimon de Idol. ch. 1; and Yad Hachazakah, vii. 6, who makes Abraham – in his 40th year – renounce star-worship, break images, escape the wrath of the king by a miracle, and preach that there is one God of the whole universe.

11 Lit. They were turned down upon their heads.

12 The Rabbins make Nimrod to have been the persecutor of Abraham. Comp. Targ. Jon. on Gen. xv. 7. Tr. Bava Bathra, fol. 91 *a.* Maimon. More Nevochim, iii. 29.

13 Or, *let peace be upon Abraham.* Comp. Targ. Jon. on Gen. xi. 28, from the mistranslation of which this legend took its rise, the word *ur* in Heb. meaning *fire.* See also Targ. Jon, on Gen. xv. 7. The legend was adopted by some of the Eastern Christians; and commemorated in the Syrian Calendar on Jan. 29 (Hyde de Rel. V. Pers. 74). Comp. the Abyssinian Calendar on Jan. 25 (Ludolf. Hist. p. 409).

14 It has been observed that the blacksmith has ever been looked upon with awe by barbarians on the same principle that made Vulcan a deity. In Abyssinia all artisans are Budah, sorcerers, especially the blacksmith, and he is a social outcast, as among the Somal; . . . Throughout the rest of El-Islam, the blacksmith is respected as treading in the path of David, the father of the craft. Burton. First Footsteps in E. Africa, p. 33. The numerous wars in which David was engaged, may have given rise to the myth of his being the inventor of mail.

15 See Sura 38. 37.

16 See Sura 19. 55, 6.

17 The man of the *lot* or *portion.* Or, of *care, support.* According to some Elias, as others say, Isaiah. It is more probable, however, that he is the Obadiah of 1 Kings xviii. 4, who *supported* 100 prophets in the cave, or

Ezechiel, who is called Kephil by the Arabs. See Niebuhr, Travels, ii. 265.

18 The man of the fish – Jonah.

19 See Suras 3. 33; 19. p. 19. 1–11, for the story of Zacharias in full. The concluding sentence of this clause is obscure. It probably means that even if no heir were vouchsafed to Zacharias, yet since God will be the heir of all things he would take Zacharias to himself and thus abundantly recompense him. See Sura 28. 58.

20 See Sura 66. 12. It is quite clear from these two passages that Muhammad believed in the Immaculate and miraculous conception of Jesus.

21 That is, identical with that of the previous prophets, etc.

22 See Sura 18. 93. Thus, the ancient Jewish and Christian legend connects Gog and Magog with the end of the world. Rev. xx. 8. Pseudojon on Lev. xxvi. 44. Comp. Numb. xi. 27.

23 'Whenever a people is punished (for idolatry) the beings honoured by them as gods, shall also be punished, for so it is written, on all the gods also of Egypt will I inflict judgments.' (Sakkah, 29.)

24 Ar. *Sidjill*, which is supposed by some to be the name of the angel who writes down the actions of every man's life upon a scroll, which is *rolled up* at his death (comp. Isai. xxxiv. 4); by others, to be the name of one of Muhammad's secretaries.

25 Ps. xxxvii. 29. This is the only text quoted in the Koran.

Sura 22

1 This Sura is generally said to have been revealed at Mecca, – but this is probably only the case with verses 1–24; 43–56; 60–65; 67–75.

2 Lit. *so that after knowledge he knoweth not aught.*

3 The teachings and progress of Islam.

4 See Sura 2. 59.

5 The Kaaba. Sharastani informs us that there was an opinion prevalent among the Arabs, that the walking round the Kaaba, and other ceremonies, were symbolic of the motion of the planets and of other astronomical facts. The people of Saba worshipped the Sun, the tribes of Asad and Kaninah the Moon, etc. etc. At a later period they all sunk into idolatry, and in the time of Muhammad, the idols round the Kaaba amounted to 360.

6 Lit. *thin*, with the implied sense of *fleet.*

7 The ten first days of the Dhu'lhijja. For the ceremonies, see Lieut. Burton's 'Pilgrimage,' vol. iii.; Sale's Notes and Prelim. Disc.

8 That is, the uncut beards, nails, etc.

9 Offerings of animals are by no means confined to Mecca and the Pilgrimage. Five or six thousand animals are said to have been slain in the valley of Mina by the pilgrims of the year 1854. (See Lieut. Burton's

'Pilgrimage,' iii. p. 313.) The victim is considered by the devout as an expression of their conviction that death is their desert at the hands of God.

10 See Ibn Batoutah, iv. 106. (Par. ed.)

11 Comp. Sur. 32. 4.

12 The ayats, signs or verses of the Koran. It is said by tradition that Muhammad was consoled by this revelation for the Satanic suggestion mentioned Sur. 53. 20. But in this view of the text, for *among whose desires*, or *affections*, we should render *when he recited.*

13 Lit. *they measure not God with truth of His measurement.*

Sura 23

1 This Sura is said by Wahidi Intr, and by Assuyûti, 55, to be the last Meccan revelation. But there seems to be no reason for this opinion.

2 In prayer. Eccl. v. 1; Matt. vi. 7. But it may be understood of *idle talk* generally.

3 See Sura 22. 5.

4 That is, a perfect man at last, composed of soul and body. The verb *halaka*, *to create*, is used throughout, for which I have necessarily substituted *to make*, in order to retain the same word throughout the verse.

5 These words are said by most commentators on Sura 6. 93, to have been uttered by Muhammad's scribe, Abdallah, on hearing the previous part of this verse, and to have been adopted by the prophet, at the same moment, as identical with his own inspirations.

6 Lit. *seven paths* – a Talmudic expression.

7 See Sura 11. 42, n.

8 Comp. Sura 19. 22 ff.

9 Comp. Sura 21. 92.

10 There is no reliable tradition as to the nature of the visitation here alluded to.

11 That is, each would have formed a separate and independent kingdom.

12 Or, *in the* (*world*) *which I have left.*

13 That is, our past life seems brevity itself in comparison with eternal torment.

14 Lit. *those who number*, or *keep account*, i.e. our torments distract us too much to allow us to compute.

Sura 24

1 With this verse commences the reference to the scandal against Ayesha, to which verses 6–9 read like a later addition. See His. 731 ff. Albuhari, passim. Muslim ii. 628 ff. Tirm. 524.

2 Comp. Numb. v. 11, 31, with which Muhammad must have been acquainted.

3 The rumour of improper intimacy between Ayesha and Safwan Ibn El Moattal, during Muhammad's return from the expedition against the tribe of Mostaliq (an. Hej. 9), in which he was separated from her for an entire day, which she passed in the company of Safwan, who had found her when accidentally left behind. Verses 4–26 were revealed shortly after the return.

4 Whose characters are cleared.

5 Abdallah Ibn Ubayy.

6 Comp. verse 10, 11 (n.).

7 Abubekr had been desirous to punish one of his relatives, Mestah, who had propagated the scandal against Ayesha, by refusing him gifts or alms.

8 'The very members of a man shall testify against him, for thus we read (Jer. xliii. 12), Ye are yourselves my witnesses saith the Lord.' Chagiga, 16. Thaanith, 11*a*.

9 It was the custom in Arabia, before Islam, to enter houses without permission.

10 That is, the anklets. Comp. Isai. iii. 16, 18.

11 On account of poverty.

12 Comp. Deut. xv. 12–15.

13 The meaning probably is, that the scandal raised against Ayesha resembled the scandal in the case of Joseph in Egypt, and of the Virgin Mary, detailed in previous suras.

14 An idea perhaps derived from Gen. i. 20, 21. Comp. Tr. Cholin, fol. 27*a*.

15 Verses 46–56 obviously refer to a period, perhaps that between the battle of Ohod and the end of the war of the Ditch, when Muhammad's prospects were overclouded and the confidence of his followers shaken.

16 This verse was intended to relieve the scruples of the Muslims, who, following the superstitious customs of the Arabs, thought that they ought not to admit the blind, etc. to their tables, to eat alone, or in a house of which they were entrusted with the key, etc.

17 Lit. *make not the calling of the Apostle among you, like the calling of some of you to others*, i.e., address him by some respectful and honourable title. Thus in the Talmud, 'It is forbidden to a disciple to call his Rabbi by name even when he is not in his presence;' and again: 'Neither is he to salute his Rabbi, nor to return his salutation, in the same way that salutations are given and returned among friends.' 'Whoever despises the wise men hath no portion in the world to come.' See Hilchoth Torah, c. 5.

Sura 25

1 See Sura 21. 49.

2 Comp. Sura 16. 105. The frequency with which Muhammad feels it necessary to rebut this charge by mere denial is strongly indicative of its truth.

3 Supply, *we will not believe.*

4 In your ascriptions of divinity to them. Beidh.

5 Or, *far, far be they removed.* The same words occur at the end of verse 55. The Commentators doubt whether they are spoken by the wicked of the impossibility of their attaining Paradise, or by the angels to the wicked.

6 Said by Beidh. to be the polytheist Okbeh, the son of Abu Mo'eyt, who by Muhammad's persuasion professed Islam, but afterwards retracted to please Ubei ben Khalaf.

7 Ar. *fulan* (whence the Spanish *fulano*).

8 Or, *abandoner.*

9 This verse shews that the Koran was of gradual growth in the time of Muhammad himself.

10 Lit. *parables.*

11 Lit. *vizier.*

12 It is uncertain whether *Rass* is the name of a city in Yemama; or merely, as some interpret it, of a well near Midian; or, according to others, in the territory of Hadramawt.

13 Lit. *quiescent*, i.e. always the same.

14 According to some commentators, the waters of the Tigris, which do not mingle with the salt water of the sea till they have reached a considerable distance from the river-mouth. See Zech. xiv. 8.

15 See Sura 24. 44.

16 'Thou art taught that whoever would make a profit by the Law depriveth himself of life.' Pirke Aboth, i. 4. This precept is of frequent occurrence in the Talmud.

17 Comp. Sura 13. 29 and Sura 17. 109.

18 The idolaters.

Sura 26

1 This Sura belongs to about the seventh year of Muhammad's prophetic life.

2 See Sura 2. 1.

3 Lit. *to which their necks would humble themselves.*

4 Lit. *my tongue is not free.* This verse appears to be a studied simplification of Ex. iv. 10–13.

5 The murder of the Egyptian.

6 Lit. *and thou hast done thy deed which thou hast done.* See 28. 15.

7 Thus Pirke R. Elieser § 48. 'He placed his hand in his bosom, and drew it forth, white as snow with leprosy.'

8 'The Pharaoh who lived in the days of Moses was a great magician.' Mid. Jalkut, c. 182. Comp. Sura 28. 38, where, in accordance with the Rabbinic traditions Pharaoh claims to be a God.

9 See 2. 58, and Midr. Jalkut on Ex. xii. c. 208.

10 Lit. *except.*

11 Lit. *a tongue of truth*, i.e. high repute. Or, *grant that my words may be believed among posterity.* See 19. 47.

12 Of their motives in embracing Islam.

13 The Adites are mentioned in 7. and 11.

14 This is to be understood of the small forts erected by the nomads of the Hejaz along the route of the caravans to guarantee their safety. Comp. Gen. xi. 1–10, and Sura 89. 6, p. 417.

15 The Madian and the El-Aika of other Suras are unquestionably one and the same place, as they have the same prophet Shoaib (or Sho'eyb), the Jethro of Scripture – a name perhaps altered from Hobab (Numb. x. 29) – and because the same sin is laid to the charge of both. See Winer's Realwörterbuch on Jethro. The Midr. Rabbah on Ex. ii. 16, Par. 1, makes Jethro renounce idolatry, and his office of Priest, and undergo banishment from the Midianites.

16 Gabriel. See Sura 81. 19.

17 See Sura 13. 36. This verse is said to have been revealed at Medina by Itq. 34.

18 The unbelieving Meccans. Lit. *that the knowing* (*Doctors, Uhlemas*) *knew it.*

19 Lit. *have introduced it.* i.e. infidelity; or, the Koran. Beidh. The latter interpretation seems most accordant with the context.

20 Comp. Sura 37. 7, 8.

21 It is probable that within three or four years from his entry upon the prophetic office, Muhammad had made about 40 converts.

22 They impart to their votaries on earth what they have learned by stealth and partially, in heaven.

23 Muhammad found it necessary to employ the pens of certain poets to defend himself and his religion from the ridicule and satire of other poets, whose productions were recited at the great annual fair held at Okatz, the Olympus of the Hejaz.

Sura 27

1 See Sura 2. 1.

2 Not really leprous.

3 Lit. *when our visible signs came to them.*

4 This tradition may be derived from 1 Kings iv. 33. The legend of Solomon's power over the Genii originates in a mistranslation of Eccl. ii. 8. Comp. also for other points in this story Prov. vi. 6; 1 Kings x. 1–10.

5 'Demons obeyed him (Solomon) . . . and evil spirits were subjected to him.' Targ. 2. on Esther 1, 2. From the same source Muhammad has adopted, with slight variations, the whole story of Solomon's intercourse with the Queen of Saba. Comp. also Tr. Gittin, fol. 68, and Midr. Jalkut on 1 Kings vi. ch. 182.

6 Lit. *unless ye bear me witness.*

7 That is, *malignant.* 'The efreets are generally believed to differ from the other djinn in being very powerful and always malicious; but to be in other respects of a similar nature' (Lane's Modern Egyptians, i. 285). 'The ghosts of dead persons are also called by this name' (ib. 289).

8 Or, *before thy glance can be withdrawn from an object.*

9 Lit. *we have consulted the flight of birds*: hence *presage.*

10 Lit. *your bird*, augury.

11 Comp. Sura 25. 55.

12 Lit. *their knowledge attaineth to the next life.*

13 Lit. *art on clear truth.*

14 *Al Jassaca*, the Spy.

15 Or, *shall derive advantage from them.*

Sura 28

1 See Sura 2. 1.

2 *Lit.* Imâms.

3 Comp. 2. 58.

4 That is, This child will be a comfort to us. See Sura. 19. 26.

5 'Why must the nurse be a Hebrew woman? (Ex. ii. 7.) This shews that he refused the breast of all the Egyptian women. For the Holy, blessed be He, had said, Shall the mouth that is to speak with me suck an unclean thing?' Sotah. xii. 2.

6 Lit. *in the time of neglect on the part of its people*, i.e. at the hour of the noon sleep.

7 Lit. *I have acted unjustly to my soul.*

8 Comp. Ex. ii. 16, 17, where the daughters are said to be *seven.*

9 That is, of a wife.

10 Lit. *he was cried to.* According to Muhammad, Moses had resolved to quit Madian previously to the Vision of the Bush, which, according to Ex. iii., was the real occasion.

11 Lit. *thy wing.*

12 Lit. *kindle upon the clay.* Comp. 40. 38–49. 'He (Pharaoh) said to them: From the first have ye spoken an untruth, for Lord of the Worlds am I. I created myself and the Nile, as it is said (Ez. xxix. 3), "My river is

mine own and I have made it for myself."' (E.T.) Mid. Rab. on Ex. Par. 5.

13 So that the oral traditions would be easily handed down.

14 Or, *yet have we sent thee as an Apostle to them.*

15 Supply, *we will not believe.*

16 That is, the Pentateuch and the Koran.

17 The Meccan Jews and Christians who had formerly embraced Islam, and could now affirm that they had always held the same faith. This passage could not have been written after Muhammad's experience of Jewish unbelief at Medina.

18 Lit. *the guidance with thee.*

19 But their own imaginations and passions.

20 Lit. *the account shall be blind* or *dark to them.*

21 *Potestas judiciaria.*

22 Ar. *Karun.* 'Joseph concealed three treasures in Egypt, one of which became known to Korah ... the keys of Korah's treasure chambers were a burden for 300 white mules.' Midr. Jalkut on Eccl. v. 12, 'Riches kept for the owners thereof to their hurt,' – which may have furnished Muhammad with the nucleus of this story. Compare also Tract. Psachim fol. 119 *a.*

23 Or, *against God.*

24 Probably to Paradise, according to others to Mecca, as a conqueror. But this latter interpretation involves the revelation of this verse at least, at Medina.

Sura 29

1 See Sura 2. 1. The first ten verses of this Sura were revealed at Medina, after the battles of Bedr and Ohod.

2 Deities for whose worship thou canst shew no authority. Comp. Tr. Jebhamoth, fol. 6. If a father saith to his son, 'Defile thyself,' or saith, 'Make not restitution,' shall he obey him? It is said (Lev. xix. 3), Let every man reverence his father and mother, but keep my Sabbaths all of you: ye are all bound to honour me. Thus also Midr. Jalkut, 604. Comp. Sura 31. v. 13.

3 The word SAY – the usual address of God or Gabriel to Muhammad – must either be considered as spoken by God to Abraham, in which case we have a curious instance of the manner in which Muhammad identifies himself with Abraham, and makes Abraham speak in words which he constantly elsewhere uses himself; or, with Wahl, we must suppose that from v. 17 to v. 22 are misplaced.

4 Comp. Ps. cxxxix. 7.

5 Lit. *for love among yourselves*, or *as an object of love*, i.e. devout worship.

6 Thus Sura 21. 71. The Midr. Rabbah on Gen. Par. 18, says that Haran, the father of Lot, was brought by Abraham's deliverance from the furnace to the adoption of his doctrines. Muhammad may have transferred this idea to Lot.

7 Lit. *was straitened in regard to them.*

8 See 11. 83.

9 So as to fly from our vengeance.

10 Lit. *in truth.*

11 With the Jews. This passage is quoted by modern Muslims in justification of their indifference with respect to the propagation of their religion. 'The number of the faithful,' said one of them to Mr Lane, 'is decreed by God, and no act of man can increase or diminish it.' Mod. Egypt. i. p. 364.

12 Idols.

13 That is, you may find places of refuge where you may worship the true God in some other parts of the earth, if driven forth from your native city. This verse is very indicative of a late Meccan origin. Flight from Mecca must have been imminent when Muhammad could thus write.

14 Lit. *carry not.* Comp. Matth. vi. 26; Luke xii. 24.

15 At Mecca.

Sura 30

1 See Sura 2. 1.

2 By the Persians; probably in Palestine in the 6th year before the Hejira, under Khosrou Parviz. (Ann. 615. See Gibbon's Decline and Fall, ch. xlvi.)

3 This alludes to the defeat of the Persians by Heraclius, ann. 625. Muslims appeal to this passage as a clear proof of the inspiration of their prophet. But it should be borne in mind that the vowel points of the consonants of the Arabic word for *defeated* in verse 1, not being originally written, and depending entirely on the speaker or reader, would make the prophecy true in either event, according as the verb received an active or passive sense in pronunciation. The whole passage was probably constructed with the view of its proving true in any event.

4 Comp. Psalm xc. 30, in the Arabic version.

5 The Talmudists apply the description of God of the *sender of the rain* to the divine command which shall cause the dead to arise. Taanith (init.).

6 Lit. *from yourselves*, i.e. either from the side of Adam or of human, and of no other kind of being. Beidh.

7 By worshipping idols conjointly with God.

8 Lit. *as a Hanyf.* See note 23 on Sura 16.

9 Peculiar to and distinctive of themselves. Muhammad had a just

appreciation of that narrowness of mind which is the characteristic of sectarians in every age, who seize upon some one point of truth, through inability to grasp the whole in its due proportions and bearing, and glory in it, as if the fragment were the whole.

10 Comp. Ps. xv. 5.

11 Lit. *which none can put back from God.*

Sura 31

1 Nothing certain is known concerning the history of this fabulist and philosopher. The opinion most generally received is that Lokman is the same person whom the Greeks, not knowing his real name, have called Æsop, i.e. Æthiops. This Sura shews the high degree of respect entertained for Lokman in Arabia at the time of Muhammad, who doubtless aimed to promote the interests of his new religion by connecting the Koran with so celebrated a name.

2 See Sura 2. 2.

3 Beidh. and Itq. suppose this verse to have been revealed at Medina, on account of the precept to pay the *impost*, required by Muhammad of his followers as a religious duty, and different from the *alms*. The former is usually coupled with the duty of observing prayer.

4 Comp. Ps. civ. 5.

5 Comp. Talm. Kethuboth, 60, 1, 'A woman is to suckle her child two years.' Comp. Jos. Ant. ii. 9, 6.

6 Or, *the seen and unseen*, lit., *outwardly and inwardly.*

7 Or as rendered in verse 11, '*the self-sufficient.*'

8 Wah. Omar ben Muhammad, Zam. and Beidh. suppose this and the three following verses to have been revealed at Medina, in answer to the Jews, who had affirmed that all knowledge was contained in their own Law. But the accuracy of this supposition is very doubtful, if considered with regard to the preceding and following context.

9 Between idolatry and Islam.

Sura 32

1 See Sura 2. 1.

2 Comp. Sura xxii. 46, and Ps. xc. 4, which is taken literally by many of the Talmudists. Comp. e.g. Sanhed. 96, 2.

3 Lit. *ex spermate genitali.*

4 Lit. *their sides are raised.*

5 Wait thou for their punishment as they wait for thy downfall.

Sura 33

1 Medina was besieged, when this Sura was revealed, by certain *confederate* tribes at the instigation of the Jews, an. Hej. 5. The first nine verses, however, have no immediate reference to this event, but to Muhammad's contemporary marriage with Zeinab. See verse 37.

2 The Arabians had been accustomed, before the time of Muhammad, to divorce their wives with the words, – *thy back be to me as the back of my mother*. The drift and motive of this passage is explained by verse 37. It had also been the custom to hold adopted sons to be as nearly related to them as their natural ones.

3 The Mohadjers – those who had emigrated with Muhammad from Mecca. This verse abrogates Sura 8. 73.

4 How they have discharged their prophetic functions.

5 Verses 9–33 have reference to the events of the year Hej. 5, towards the close. See next note. His. 688; Waq. 4 *f*.

6 In the engagement which took place under the walls of Medina, some of the enemy were posted on a height to the east of the city, others in a valley on the west. The besiegers were 12,000, the Muslims 3,000 strong, when a violent storm, which upset the tents, put out the camp fires, and blinded the eyes of the confederates with sand, turned the scale of victory against them. Muhammad ascribes the storm to angelic agency.

7 That is, with infidelity.

8 The ancient name of El-Medina.

9 In the trenches which had been dug around the city by the advice of Salmân, the Persian.

10 They would speedily have quitted the city to attack the faithful in the trenches.

11 That is, raise the siege.

12 That is, that through trials we should attain to Paradise, v. 29.

13 After the siege of Medina had been raised, Muhammad made a successful expedition against the Jews of Koreidha, for their treason and violation of treaties.

14 Muhammad's wives having caused him much annoyance by demands of rich dresses, etc., he gave them the choice of continuing with him as before, or of divorce. They chose the former.

15 That is, Idolatry. Acts xvii. 30.

16 The pronoun is in the pl. masc., whereas the pl. fem. is used in the previous part of the verse. The partisans of Ali quote this passage to prove the intimate union of Ali and his posterity with the Prophet.

17 That is, to Zaid. The favour of God to Zaid consisted in having caused him to become a Muslim: the favour of Muhammad in adopting him as his son. Zaid and Abu Lahab (Sura 111.) are the only contemporaries of Muhammad mentioned by name in the Koran.

18 Thy plan to obtain Zeinab, Zaid's wife, as thy wife.

19 Lit. *who brought the messages of God.*

20 If thou makest use of the special prerogative (conferred in verse 49).

21 He had nine wives at this period, beside slaves. The number of wives allowed to the faithful is four.

22 The first slave whom Muhammad took to wife was Raihana, at the conquest of the Banu Koreidha. His. 693.

23 Verses 53–55 refer to the conduct of the guests at Muhammad's house after his marriage with Zeinab. Albuhari passim. Muslim i. 824 ff.

24 This verse cannot be of later date than Hej. 8, when Muhammad's daughter Omm Kulthum died, leaving only Fatima.

25 This may refer to the charge of adultery said by the Rabbins to have been brought by Korah against Moses. Comp. Tr. Sanhedrin, fol. 110*a*. and Numbers xii. 1. The verse is said to have been revealed on account of aspersions thrown on Muhammad for unfairly dividing spoils, whereupon he said, 'God be merciful to my brother Moses. He was wronged more than this, and bore it with patience.'

Sura 34

1 In Arabia Felix, three days' journey from Sanaa.

2 The Talmud mentions the worm Shameer, used by Solomon to cut the stones for building the temple. Pirke Aboth. v. See Buxt. Lex. Talmud, p. 2456. Tr. Gittin, fol. 68; and Midr. Jalkut on 1 Kings, vi. 7. This passage of Scripture may have suggested the idea that Solomon built, etc., by the aid of Spirits.

3 That is, in their difficult toils.

4 Possibly in the second century of our era.

5 The *Saba* of verse 14 formed an important branch of the trading population of Yemen. This whole passage, 14–18, alludes to the cessation of traffic between them and Syria, which led to the desire to lengthen the stages and diminish the expense of the journey.

6 That is, of strength and material prosperity.

7 That is, so as to form a judgment free from the influence of others.

8 It is very remarkable, that when the power of Muhammad became firmly established, he never reverts to the insinuations against the soundness of his mind which in the earlier Suras he so often rebuts.

9 That is, their graves.

10 That is, when in this life.

Sura 35

1 Not only *seas*, properly so called, but the great masses of fresh water in the Nile, Tigris, inland lakes, etc.

2 The Gospel.

3 This idea was probably suggested by Muhammad's reminiscences of the view from the Cave of Hira, to the north and west of which there is a prospect thus described by Burckhardt (Travels, p. 176). 'The country before us had a dreary aspect, not a single green spot being visible; barren, black, and grey hills, and white sandy valleys were the only objects in sight.'

4 Lit. *shall encompass its people*.

5 Method *of dealing*, i.e. first warning, then punishing.

Sura 36

1 This Sura is said to have been termed by Muhammad 'the heart of the Koran.' It is recited in all Muslim countries to the dying, at the tombs of saints, etc. On Ya. Sin., see Sura 2. 1.

2 Sura 38. 85.

3 Lit. *in the clear prototype*, that is, in the Preserved Table, on which all the actions of mankind are written down.

4 Antioch, to which Jesus is said to have sent two disciples to preach the unity of God, and subsequently Simon Peter. This vague story, and that of the seven sleepers in Sura 18., are the only traces to be found in the Koran of any knowledge, on the part of Muhammad of the history of the Church subsequent to the day of Pentecost, or of the spread of the Christian religion.

5 Comp. Sura 7. 128; 27. 48, where, as in this passage, the word *augur* refers to the mode of divination practised previous to Islam, by the flight of birds.

6 Lit. *if ye have been warned* (*will ye still disbelieve?*).

7 Habib, the carpenter, who, as implied at verse 25, was martyred, and whose tomb at Antioch is still an object of veneration to the Muhammadans.

8 Or, *the Apostles shall not return to them again*.

9 For instance, date trees, the female blossoms of which were carefully impregnated, when requisite, by branches of the male plant.

10 The chastisements of this world and of the next.

11 On account of this precept, Itq. 35, and Omar b. Muhammad suppose the verse to have originated at Medina.

12 The Muslims affirm that a space of forty years will intervene between two blasts of the Trumpet. Maracci suggests that the idea of the two blasts is derived from 1 Thess. iv. 16, 'the voice of the archangel and . . . the trump of God.'

13 Thus Chagiga, 16; Taanith, 11. 'The very members of a man bear witness against him, for thus is it written (Is. xliii. 12), Ye yourselves are my witnesses, saith the Lord.' See also Sura 41. 19, 20.

14 Lit. *in their place.*

15 See Sura 26. 225.

16 Lit. *he setteth forth to us comparisons.*

17 The form of the Arabic word is Rabbinic Hebrew.

Sura 37

1 I have given in the text the sense of these first two verses according to the Muhammadan commentators. The original, literally translated, viz. *By the ranks which rank themselves, and by the repellers who repel*, would not convey an intelligible idea to the English reader. Mar. renders, *Per ordinantes ordinando et agitantes agitando.*

2 Ar. *Easts. Errat in pluralitate mundorum.* Mar. But the allusion probably is to the different points of the horizon at which the sun rises and sets in the course of the year.

3 See Sura 15. 18.

4 Or, *comrades*, i.e. the demons.

5 Lit. *on the right hand*, the sign of good omen, i.e. with semblance of truth.

6 See Sura 36. 6.

7 The ostrich egg carefully protected from dust.

8 Lit. *and are we not among the punished?*

9 Lit. *et sane euge auditores.* Mar.

10 And therefore unable to assist at your sacrifices.

11 Lit. *cum igitur pervenisset eum eo ad ætatem cui competit operandi studium.* Mar. Beidh. When he had attained to the age when he could work with him. Lane.

12 Brought, says Rabbi Jehoshua, from Paradise by an angel. Midr. fol. 28.

13 This salutation.

14 The Arabic particle which is here and elsewhere rendered *of old* (also, *already, certainly*) serves to mark the position of a past act or event as prior to the time present, and in all such passages merely gives a fullness and intensity to our perfect, or pluperfect tense.

15 The form of this word is altered in the original for the sake of the rhyme.

16 Lit. *he cast lots* (with the sailors).

17 *Nequequam vos ad illud colendum estis Seducturi.* Mar.

18 This verse and the six preceding are the words of the Angel.

19 Compare verse 69.

Sura 38

1 The letter S. See Sura 2. 1.

2 These verses are said to have been revealed when, upon the conversion of Omar, the Koreisch went in a body to Abu Talib and requested him to withdraw his protection from Muhammad, but being put to silence by the latter, departed in great confusion.

3 That is, in the Christian religion, which teaches, Muhammad ironically implies, a plurality of Gods.

4 This may allude to the so-called 'confederacy' of the Koreisch against Muhammad.

5 This term is also applied to Pharaoh, Sura 89. 9. He is said to have fastened the Israelites to stakes, and then subjected them to various torments.

6 *Prædititi (manibus) virtute.* Mar.

7 Comp. Ps. cxlviii. 9, 10.

8 Two angels who pretended to appeal to David in order to convince him of his sin in the matter of Uriah's wife. Comp. 1 Sam. xii.

9 The Psalms, if we suppose with Nöldeke, p. 99, that David is still addressed: the Koran, if with Sale we refer the passage to Muhammad.

10 The Commentators say that the word used in the original implies that the mares stood on three feet, and touched the ground with the edge of the fourth foot.

11 Solomon, in his admiration of these horses, the result, we are told, of David's or his own conquests, forgot the hour of evening prayer, and when aware of his fault commenced their slaughter. The Tr. Sanhedr. fol. 21, mentions Solomon's love for horses, and that he determined to have a large stud; yet not to send the people to Egypt (Deut. xvii. 16) but to have them *brought* to him out of Egypt (1 Kings x. 28).

12 One of the Djinn. See Sale. Compare Tr. Sanhedr. fol. 20, *b.* and Midr. Jalkut on 1 Kings vi. § 182.

13 Thus the second Targum on Esther i. 2, mentions the four different kinds of Demons which were 'given into the hand' of Solomon – a legend derived from a misunderstanding of Eccl. ii. 8.

14 The fountain which had sprung up. To this history the Talmudists have no allusion.

15 Thy wife; – on whom he had sworn that he would inflict an hundred blows, because she had absented herself from him when in need of her assistance, or for her words (Job ii. 9). The oath was kept, we are told, by his giving her one blow with a rod of a hundred stalks. This passage is often quoted by the Muslims as authorising any similar manner of release from an oath inconsiderately taken.

16 Lit. *men of hand and of sight.*

17 Lit. *or do our eyes wander from them.*

18 See verses 9, 26, above.

19 The connection between the concluding episode and the preceding part of the Sura does not seem very clear. It probably originated at a different but uncertain period.

20 About the creation of man.

21 Comp. Sura 2. 28, ff.

22 Comp. Ps. civ. 4.

23 Lit. *stoned.* See Sura 15. 34.

Sura 39

1 Lit. *the sending down*, or *revelation, of the Book is*, etc.

2 Lit. *in truth*, i.e. for a serious and earnest purpose, and not as mere pastime.

3 That is, camels, oxen, sheep and goats.

4 The wording of this verse would seem to indicate a period when Muhammad was meditating flight from Mecca. Comp. 29. 56.

5 For the word *Mathani*, see also Sura 15. 87.

6 The word *associates* contains an implied allusion to the deities associated with God, and who distract the idolaters in their worship.

7 In the fem. gender in the Ar. This passage was revealed shortly after the circumstances mentioned, 53. 20.

8 See Sura 6. 60.

9 That is, none may intercede with Him but those whom He permits to do so.

10 Lit. *It was only given to me on account of knowledge.*

11 By becoming apostates from Islam. Comp. Sura 16. 108. This and the two following verses are said to have originated at Medina. His. 230, Wah. Omar ben Muhammad. Beidh. Itq. 19.

12 Lit. *they have not esteemed God according to the truth of His estimation.*

Sura 40

1 See Sura 2. 1.

2 The Cherubic beings of Scripture are said to be *above* the throne of God (Is. vi. 1), *beneath* it (Ezek. x.); and the mystical beasts in the Revelations are said to be *in the midst of the throne and round about it.*

3 Probably the union of life and death in the womb, and the subsequent life followed by death.

4 See Sura 28. 76.

5 Thus Sura 28. 20, and Sura 36. 19, we have a similar character introduced into the narrative.

6 Comp. Acts v. 38, 39.

7 These tribes no doubt constantly formed temporary alliances. Muhammad implies that they were confederate against their prophets.

8 Haman, the favourite of Ahasuerus and the enemy of the Jews, is thus made the vizier of Pharaoh. The Rabbins make this vizier to have been Korah, Jethro, or Balaam. Midr. Jalkut on Ex. ch. 1, Sect. 162–168; and Tr. Solah, fol. 11. See Sura 28. 5.

9 Thy remissness in propagating Islam. Beidh.

Sura 41

1 In some MSS. this Sura is entitled *Adoration*. Thus Beidh. According to His. 186, comp. Caussin 1, 375 f., Muhammad's aim in this Sura was the conversion of a noble Meccan, Utba ben Rabia, to Islam. The precise year is uncertain.

2 See Sura 2. 1.

3 Thus SS. Paul and Barnabas, Acts xiv. 15.

4 Or, *never failing*.

5 Lit. *from before them and from behind them.*

6 See Sura 36. 64, n.

7 Comp. Sura 46. 12.

8 Lit. *the possessor of great good fortune.*

9 Comp. Rev. iv. 8 in the original.

10 Thus Tr. Taanith (init.).

11 Lit. *vanity shall not come to it from before it, or from behind it.*

12 *We will not receive it.* The literal rendering of the following words is *what! foreign and Arabian?*

13 Comp. Sura 17. 83, 84.

14 Lit. *verily they were in suspicious doubting about it.*

15 Lit. *for his soul.* See Sura 45, v. 14.

16 Lit. *to Him is referred.*

Sura 42

1 See Sura 2. 1.

2 Mecca.

3 Jews and Christians.

4 The law contained in the Koran.

5 Isai. v. 19.

6 Comp. Gal. vi. 7, 8.

7 That is, deprive thee of the Prophetic mission.

8 Lit. *he will increase them.* Comp. Ps. cxv. 14.

9 Thus Beidhawi.

Sura 43

1 See Sura 2. 1.

2 Lit. *it is in the Mother of the Book*, i.e. the original of the Koran, preserved before God.

3 That is, of the birth of a female.

4 Lit. *which he imputeth to the God of Mercy, as his likeness.*

5 To authorise angel-worship.

6 Supply, *Mecca and Taief, we would have received it.*

7 Lit. *mercy*, i.e. the gift and office of prophecy.

8 Lit. *the two Easts*, by which some understand the distance between the two solstices.

9 Comp. Suras 10. 47; 13. 42; 23. 97; 29. 53; 37. 179; 40. 77. These passages clearly show that Muhammad had at this period – towards the close of his Meccan period – full faith in his ultimate success, and in the fulfilment of his menaces against the unbelievers.

10 Lit. *ye shall be examined in the end.*

11 This verse is said to have been revealed in the temple at Jerusalem on the occasion of the night journey thither.

12 Lit. *sister.*

13 See Sura 28. 39, n.

14 Comp. Gen. xli. 42.

15 This was a captious objection made to Muhammad by the idolaters of Mecca when he condemned their gods (Sura 21. 98), as if they had said, 'Jesus is worshipped as a God by the Christians: does he come under your anathema equally with our idols? we shall be content for our gods to be with him.'

16 That is, as we caused Jesus to be born without a human father.

17 At his return to this earth. Some refer this to the Koran as revealing the last Hour. Lit. *He* (or *It*) *is for knowledge of the Hour.*

18 Jewish and Christian sects.

19 Malec is one of the keepers of Hell, who specially presides over the torments of the damned.

20 Lit. *if they have twisted tight* or *set firmly the affair*, i.e. their plots against thee and the truth.

21 Or, *and they* (*the Infidels*). The Commentators say that Jesus, Ezra, and the angels, will be allowed to intercede.

22 Muhammad.

Sura 44

1 See Sura 2. 1.

2 Of the 23rd and 24th of Ramadhan, in which, according to the Muslim creed, all the events of the year subsequent are arranged. See Sura 97.

3 Lit. *We settle each wise affair* – called *wise*, because proceeding direct from the will of Him who is absolute wisdom.

4 Beidh. and others suppose this verse to have been revealed at Medina. This opinion, however, is based upon the supposition that it refers to the famine with which Mecca was visited after the Hejira.

5 Comp. Ex. xx. 20; Deut. viii. 16.

6 Tobba, title of the Kings of Yemen.

7 Lit. *in truth*.

8 That is, Of the good from the bad.

9 See Sura 37. 60.

10 The commentators suppose this *sinner* to be Abu Jahl, one of the chief of the Koreisch, and the bitter enemy of Muhammad.

11 To see the turn which events may take.

Sura 45

1 See Sura 2. 1.

2 Lit. *the sending down*, i.e. the revelation of the Book.

3 Lit. *after God*.

4 That is, the days of victory. In Scripture phrase, 'the days of the right hand of the Most High.'

5 The Arabic *amri* may be rendered either *command* or *business*, i.e. of religion.

6 Lit. *the makers vain*.

Sura 46

1 See Sura 2. 1.

2 Of a divine revelation, authorising the worship of other gods than God.

3 Comp. John vii. 48.

4 Thus Mischn. Aboth, v. 21, 'at forty years of age a man comes to intelligence.' This verse refers, it is said by the Sonnites, to Abu Bekr, afterwards Chalif, who embraced Islam in his 40th year.

5 Lit. *suffer loss*.

6 The Prophet Houd.

7 That is, *Sandhills*; at Taief, to which Muhammad had retired in consequence of the opposition, etc., of the Meccans. Verses 20–31 are probably misplaced, as they interrupt the connection between 19 and 32, but appear to belong to the same period as the rest of the Sura.

8 *Ad appropinquandum* (*magis ipsi Deo*), by intercession. Mar. Beidh.

Sura 47

1 This Sura was revealed at a period after the victory at Bedr, when there was still some hesitation on the part of Muhammad's followers to take decided steps for securing their position.

2 Lit. *will He cause to wander*, that is, from their proper aim and end, the rewards of Paradise. See verse 5 ad f.

3 The Meccans and other unbelievers of Muhammad's time. The Hanefites suppose this law to apply only to the battle of Bedr. The Shiites take it as of universal obligation.

4 This verse is said (by Omar b. Muhammad, and Itq. 43) to be the expression of Muhammad's feelings at the injuries inflicted on Mecca. He is reported to have wept over it.

5 The first sign being the mission of Muhammad; the second, the splitting of the moon; the third, the smoke mentioned in Sura 44.

6 That is, commanding war against the infidels.

7 Unintelligible or affected words, applied to the new religion in contempt. See Sura 2. 56.

8 Matt. xxi. 43.

Sura 48

1 This Sura was probably revealed shortly after the peace of Hudaibiya. Ann. Hej. 6. Some commentators, however, understand the *Victory* of the taking of Mecca two years later – the preterite being used in the prophetic style for the future – others of the taking of Chaibar, or Mùta, a town of the Roman empire.

2 Lit. *were left behind*.

3 On the return to Medina.

4 The law relative to booty, viz. that those who were not at Hudaibiya should have no share in the booty to be obtained from the Jews at Chaibar. Muhammad marched against them in Hej. 7.

5 When the rumour reached Muhammad at Hudaibiya that Othman Ibn Affan, whom he had sent to inform the Meccans that he was merely coming to visit their temple, and with peaceable intentions, had been slain by them.

6 At Chaibar.

7 Had the believers been separate from the infidels.

8 This dream Muhammad had at Medina, before he set out for al Hudaibiya. His followers expected its fulfilment within the year, but when the truce frustrated their hopes, this verse was revealed to pacify them.

9 Dust from the pavement. The Muhammadans who say their

prayers on carpets often place little bricks before them which they touch in prostration with their forehead.

10 Comp. Mark iv. 28.

11 Lit. *legs.*

Sura 49

1 Or *anticipate not, take not the lead of God and His Apostle.*

2 All the ancient Interpreters refer from 1–5 to the disrespectful demeanour, in Muhammad's presence, of the envoys of the Banu Tamim in Hej. 9 or 10.

3 Lit. *from without.*

4 The commentators explain this verse of Al Walid ben Uqba, who had brought a false report of the refusal of the Banu'lmustaliq to pay certain alms which Muhammad had sent him to demand. This Al Walid became governor of Kufa under Othman. He probably was never really converted to Islam.

5 Said to refer to Safia, one of Muhammad's wives, who had been taunted by his other wives with being a Jewess.

6 Lit. *Bad the name, wickedness, after faith.*

7 That is, not the most nobly born, like the Koreisch. This verse is said to have been revealed in Mecca on the day of its conquest.

8 The Banû Asad had come to Medina in a year of famine to seek support for themselves and families, and made profession of Islamism. Beidh. – Thus, also Ibn Sad. Tabari. Wah.

9 As if by so doing they had conferred a favour on the Prophet.

Sura 50

1 See Sura 2. 1.

2 See 25. 40.

3 See 44. 36.

4 The Resurrection.

5 Lit. *a driver and a witness.*

6 The Satan who is chained to him. Sura 41. 24.

7 Lit. *is there any addition?* which some explain as if Hell enquired whether, being already full, any addition could be made to its size. Comp. Prov. xxx. 15, and Othioth Derabbi Akiba, 8, 1: 'That the Prince of Hell saith daily, Give me food enough, is clear from what is said (Is. v. 14). Therefore Shaol hath enlarged herself, and opened her mouth without measure, etc.'

8 That is, of the ruins of the destroyed cities, etc.

9 This verse is said (by Omar b. Muhammad, Itq. 36, Djelal Eddin, ap.

Maracc. and Beidh.) to have been revealed in answer to the Jews who told the Prophet that if God rested on the Sabbath, it was because he was weary. But a connection with verse 14 seems more natural.

Sura 51

1 Lit. (*I swear*) *by those which scatter* (i.e., the rain) *with a scattering*, (2) *and by those which carry a burden*, (3) *and by those which run lightly*, (4) *and by those which divide a matter*, or, *by command*. The participles are all in the feminine: hence some interpret verse 1 of winds; verse 2 of clouds; verse 3 of ships; verse 4 of angels.

2 Comp. note at Sura 56. 1.

3 That is, this oath is for the confirmation of the truth, as ye are wont to confirm things one among another by an oath.

4 Comp. Sura 11. 72, and 15. 51. From the want of connection with what precedes, it is highly probablc that the whole passage from verse 24–60 did not originally form a part of this Sura, but was added at a later period.

5 Lit. *marked*, with the names of the individuals to be slain, say the commentators.

6 Or, *with his nobles*.

7 For Ad and Themoud, see Sura 11.

8 That is, in broad daylight. Thus Beidh. Comp. Sura 46. 22.

Sura 52

1 Of the Caaba.

2 Comp. Psalm lxviii. 9.

3 The more prosaic style of this verse indicates a later origin than the context.

Sura 53

1 This Sura was revealed at about the time of the first emigration of Muhammad's followers to Abyssinia, A. 5. The manner in which the Prophet cancelled the objectionable verses 19, 20, is the strongest proof of his sincerity (as also is the opening of Sura 80.) at this period. Had he not done so, nothing would have been easier for him than to have effected a reconciliation with the powerful party in Mecca, who had recently compelled his followers to emigrate.

2 The Angel Gabriel, to the meaning of whose name, as *the strong one of God*, these words probably allude.

3 That is, Beyond which neither men nor angels can pass (Djelal). The original word is also rendered, the *Lote-Tree of the extremity*, or of the loftiest spot in Paradise, in the seventh Heaven, on the right hand of the throne of God. Its leaves are fabled to be as numerous as the members of the whole human family, and each leaf to bear the name of an individual. This tree is shaken on the night of the 15th of Ramadan every year a little after sunset, when the leaves on which are inscribed the names of those who are to die in the ensuing year fall, either wholly withered, or with more or less green remaining, according to the months or weeks the person has yet to live.

4 The Sidrah is a prickly plum, which is called *Ber* in India, the *zizyphus jujuba* of Linnæus. A decoction of the leaves is used in India to wash the dead, on account of the sacredness of the tree.

5 Hosts of adoring angels, by which the tree was masked.

6 Al-Lat or El-Lat, probably the Alilat of Herodotus (iii. 8) was an idol at Nakhlah, a place east of the present site of Mecca. Al-Ozza was an idol of the Kinanah tribe; but its hereditary priests were the Banu Solaym, who were stationed along the mercantile road to Syria in the neighbourhood of Chaibar.

7 When at the first recital of this Sura, the prophet had reached this verse, he continued,

> These are the exalted females, [or, sublime swans, i.e. mounting nearer and nearer to God]
> And truly their intercession may be expected.

These words, however, which were received by the idolaters with great exultation, were disowned by Muhammad in the course of a few days as a Satanic suggestion, and replaced by the text as it now stands. The probability is that the difficulties of his position led him to attempt a compromise of which he speedily repented. In the Suras subsequent to this period the denunciations of idolatry become much sterner and clearer. The authorities are given by Weil, Sprenger and Muir. See Sura 17. 74–76.

8 Verses 26–33 are probably later than the previous part of the Sura, but inserted with reference to it. Some (as Omar b. Muhammad and Itq.) consider verse 33, or (as Itq. 36) verses 34–42, or (as Omar b. Muhammad) the whole Sura to have originated at Medina.

9 Ex spermate cum seminatum fuerit.

10 The Dog-star, worshipped by the Arabians.

11 Compare the refrain in Sura 55. pp. 362–4.

Sura 54

1 See Sura 26. 155; also Sura 7. 71.

2 Kept by the Guardian Angels.

3 The Talmudic descriptions of the Gardens – for the later Jews believed in more than one paradise – and of the rivers and the trees therein, will be found in Schroder Talm. und Rabb. Judenthum, pp. 418–32.

Sura 55

1 Men and djinn. The verb is in the dual.

2 Lit. *of the two easts, of the two wests*, i.e. of all that lies between the extreme points at which the sun rises and sets at the winter and summer solstices.

3 Lit. *he hath set at large*, poured forth over the earth the masses of fresh and salt water which are in contact at the mouths of rivers, etc. See Sura 27. 62; 35. 13.

4 Lit. O *ye two weights*; hence, treasures; and, generally, any collective body of men or things.

5 One for men, the other for the Genii; or, two for each man and Genius; or, both are for the inferior classes of Muslims. Beidh.

Sura 56

1 The renderings of Mar. *cum inciderit casura*, or as in Sur. 69. 15, *ingruerit ingruens* nearly express the peculiar force of the Arabic verb and of the noun formed from it; i.e. *a calamity that falls suddenly and surely.* Weil renders, wenn der Auferstehung's Tag eintritt (p. 389). Lane, when the calamity shall have happened.

2 Comp. Tr. Rosch Haschanah, fol. 16, 6.

3 Lit. *the companions of the right hand, what shall be the companions of the right hand!* and thus in verses 9, 37, 40.

4 Lit. *the preceders, the preceders.*

5 See Sura 53. 14, p. 69.

6 Probably the *banana* – according to others, the *acacia gummifera.*

7 'A Muslim of some learning professed to me that he considered the descriptions of Paradise in the Koran to be, in a great measure, figurative; "like those," he said, "in the book of the Revelation of St. John;" and he assured me that many learned Muslims were of the same opinion.' Lane's Modern Egyptians, i. p. 75, note.

8 Like them, grow not old.

9 This seems a direct contradiction to verse 14, unless we suppose with Beidhawi that an inferior and more numerous class of believers are here spoken of.

10 Or, *scorching.*

11 Lit. *not noble, agreeable in appearance.*

12 As to the resurrection.
13 Lit. *semen quod emittitis.*
14 Lit. *forestalled, anticipated.*
15 Lit. *have incurred debt.*
16 That is, The Prototype of the Koran written down in the Book kept by God himself.
17 This passage implies the existence of copies of portions at least of the Koran in common use. It was quoted by the sister of Omar when at his conversion he desired to take her copy of Sura 20. into his hands.

Sura 57

1 The general tone of this Sura shews it to have been revealed at Medina, and from verse 22 it may be inferred that its true date lies between the battle of Ohod and the battle of the Ditch.
2 Lit. *the exterior and the interior.*
3 To guide them on their route to paradise.
4 Or, *what ye have deserved.*
5 Against the infidels.
6 *Supellex deceptionis.* Mar.
7 Of our eternal decrees.
8 Brought by Gabriel to Noah, who imparted its use to his posterity. So say the commentators. But the expression seems rather to be figurative. Comp. Sura 55. 6.
9 Or, *mighty warlike strength*, but the antithesis requires the rendering given in the text. Comp. Gen. iv. 22, and Michna Tr. Aboth, 5, 9.
10 We are not to understand by the word Evangel the actual volume of the New Testament, or any one of its component parts, but rather the revelation made to Jesus by God himself, which Muhammad may have imagined to have been committed to writing subsequently, in the same way as his own Koran.
11 The word in the original is the same for *favours, gifts of grace, bounty*. The reference is to the gift of prophecy (Beidh.) mentioned verse 27.

Sura 58

1 See Sura 33. 4.
2 Instead of saying, *Es-salam aleika*, 'Peace be on thee,' the Infidels and Jews said, *Es-sam aleika*, 'a plague, or poison on thee.'
3 Lit. *sufficiency.*
4 The Jews swear that they are Muslims.

Sura 59

1 The Jews of Nadhir, three miles from Medina, had broken a treaty made with Muhammad, and in the month Rabî of the fourth year of the Hejira were besieged by him and driven first to the Jews of Kainoka, who had emigrated previously, under compulsion after the battle of Bedr, and subsequently out of Arabia.

2 On which account these spoils were entirely assigned to Muhammad, and not divided in the usual manner. See Sura 8. 42.

3 To the Jews of the tribe of Nadhir.

4 Lit. *I am clear of thee.*

5 This may be derived from the Rabbinical idea that Mount Sinai was chosen, on account of its lowness, to be the scene of the revelation to Moses, in order to shew that God loves the humble.

Sura 60

1 Revealed probably as far as verse 9 (Ramadhan Hej. 8) shortly before the taking of Mecca.

2 Speaking of the representatives of the different religious systems prevalent in the Roman Empire, as Orpheus, Abraham, Christ, Apollonius of Tyana, enshrined among the household deites of Alexander Severus, Mr Milman remarks (Hist. of Christianity, ii. p. 231) that 'It is singular that Abraham, rather than Moses, was placed at the head of Judaism: it is possible that the traditionary sanctity which attached to the first parent of the Jewish people, and of many of the Arab tribes, and which was afterwards embodied in the Koran, was floating in the East, and would comprehend, as it were, the opinions, not only of the Jews, but of a much wider circle of the Syrian natives.'

3 Sura 9. 115.

4 That is, by their conversion hereafter.

5 Said to have been revealed at, or shortly after, the peace of Hudaibiya. According to the terms then agreed upon, a mutual restitution of property was to take place.

6 Who are converted to Islam.

7 Lit. *with a calumny which they have devised between their hands and their feet.* Said to have been revealed at the taking of Mecca. Tab. Beidh.

Sura 61

1 Addressed to the Muslims who had turned their backs to the enemy at Ohod.

2 Equated by Muslims with Muhammad.

3 If this allude to a meditated attack on the Banu Nadir (see Sura 59) we have a clue to the probable date of the Sura. The promise, however, may be general. But the tone of verse 9 evidently points to a period when, as at Medina, the prospects of Islam were becoming hopeful.

Sura 62

1 Friday; the day on which Muhammad made his first entry into Medina, and the day on which creation was finished.

2 It is said that when Muhammad was preaching, Dahya Alkalbi, while yet a heathen, came, on a Friday, into Medina at the head of a caravan, and that all the congregation, attracted by the music of the tambours which preceded it, left the sermon for the spectacle. Muquâtil ap. Alfarrâ. If this account be accurate, we may approximate to the date of this Sura as in Hej. 5 (towards the close). Dahya is known to have fought in the ranks of the Muslims at the battle of the Ditch. And as the former part is aimed at the Jews, it is probably at the same period as Sura 2.

Sura 63

1 Revealed shortly after the expedition against the Banu 'l Mustaliq in Hej. 6. The 'Hypocrites' mentioned in the later Suras are the disaffected portion of the population of Medina, who covertly opposed the claims of Muhammad to temporal authority over that city. They were gradually absorbed, as the authority of Islam increased.

2 Or, in accordance with another reading, *oaths*. Comp. Ps. cix. 18.

3 Like timbers or joists supported in a wall or leaned against it, i.e. their persons are bulky, but their hearts so hypocritical and cowardly that they are afraid of the slightest noise. In the original, *saïkat* is perhaps an allusion to the *shout* of Gabriel, that is to exterminate the wicked.

Sura 64

1 The first verse of this Sura, and the phrase *obey God and the Apostle* (verses 8, 12), which usually occurs only in Medina Suras, the phrases in verse 16 compared with Sura 59. 9, as well as the subject matter, incline me to follow those Muslim commentators who are of opinion that the whole Sura was revealed at Medina.

2 That is, the day on which it will be found that if the just had been wicked they would have taken the place of the reprobates, while the

reprobates will see that if they had been just persons they would have gone to Paradise.

3 Their occasionally beguiling you from your duty, especially that of contending for the faith. Comp. 1 Cor. vii. 32.

Sura 65

1 Comp. Sura 2. 228, which this Sura is perhaps intended to supplement. Wahidi and Beidhawi state that it was revealed on account of Ibn Omar who had divorced his wife at improper time, and was obliged to take her again.

2 In order to make good the rhyme, verse 10 ought to be continued to the end of the first clause of verse 11.

3 Lit. *and of the earth, their likes*. The style of this verse resembles that of the Meccan Suras. Hence, probably, a tradition in Omar ben Muhammad makes the whole Sura Meccan.

Sura 66

1 The first verses of this Sura were revealed (Hej. 7.) on occasion of Muhammad's reviving affection for Mary, a Copt slave sent him by the governor of Egypt, from whom he had recently (verse 3) sworn to his wife Hafsa to separate entirely. Hafsa, who had been greatly incensed at their amour, of which Muhammad had himself informed her, communicated the matter in confidence to Ayesha, from whose altered manner, probably, the prophet found that his secret had been betrayed. To free Muhammad from his obligation to Hafsa was the object of this chapter.

2 Muhammad *withheld* the fact that Ayesha, as well as God, was his informant, but taxed Hafsa with not having kept his secret.

3 Supply *God will pardon you*.

4 See Sura 21. 91. Lit. *quæ rimam suam tuita est, in quam* (*rimam*) *inflavimus Spiritus nostri partem*. Thus Beidh.

Sura 67

1 Thus Shakespeare uses the word *braying* of *clamours of Hell*; and Milton speaks of *braying horrible discord*. Comp. Sura 25. 12–21.

2 *Sagacious*. Sale. The primary meaning of the Arabic root is *to draw near*; hence the above signification, in the sense of God's presence as *interpenetrating all things*: hence also the other sense of *benign*, as in Sura 42. 18.

Sura 68

1 It has been conjectured that as the word Nun means *fish*, there may be a reference to the fish which swallowed Jonas (v. 48).

2 By djinn. Comp. Sur. 34. 45.

3 In bearing the taunts of the unbelievers with patience.

4 They did not add the restriction, *if God will.*

5 An expression implying a grievous calamity; borrowed probably from the action of stripping previous to wrestling, swimming, etc.

6 Lit. *the companion of the fish*. Comp. on Jonah Sura 37. 139–148, and Sura 21. 87.

Sura 69

1 Thus Beidh., Sale, etc. But with reference to another sense of the root *karaa*, it may be rendered *the day of decision, the day on which man's lot shall be decided.*

2 On Ad and Themoud. See Sura 7. 63–77.

3 Lit. *God subjected it to himself*, availed himself of it against them.

4 *El-wakia*, the sudden event, the calamity; the woe that must break in upon Heaven and Earth. The same word is used, Sura 1 for the Resurrection and Day of Judgment.

Sura 70

1 Lit. *asking one asked*; probably some unbeliever, with reference to the opening of Sura 56 p. 365, or like statements in some previous Sura.

2 The expression is hyperbolical, and, as such, identical with Sura 32. 4. Compare also Sura 97, p. 422, where the descent is said to take place in a single night.

3 Lit. *forbidden* or *prevented* by shame.

4 See Sura 55 v. 16.

Sura 71

1 See Sura 22. 5.

2 Or, *the idols had seduced many.* Thus Kas. Beidh. gives both interpretations. – See on these idols Freytag's Einleitung, p. 349.

Sura 72

1 This interview with the Djinn took place at Nakhla, probably the 'Wady Mohram' of Burckhardt, midway between Mecca and Taïef, when Muhammad was driven from Mecca. A.D. 620.

Sura 73

1 From the first line of this Sura, and its expressions concerning the Koran, Prayer, and Future Punishment: from the similarity of the tradition with regard to its having been preceded by a vision of Gabriel (Beidh., etc.), it seems to belong to, or at least to describe, a period, perhaps immediately succeeding the Fatrah, during which the hours of night were spent by Muhammad in devotion and in the labour of working up his materials in rhythmical and rhyming Suras, and in preparation for the public assumption of the prophetic office. Comp. especially verses 11, 19, 20, at the end, with 11, 54, 55, of Sura 74.

2 Singe den Koran laut. H. v. P. Psalle Alcoranum psallendo. Mar Singe den Koran mit singender und lauter Stimme ab. Ullm.

3 Lit. *most firm*, perhaps, *distinct*.

4 This verse, according to a tradition of Ayesha, was revealed one year later than the previous part of the Sura. Nöldeke says it is 'offenbar ein Medinischer.'

Sura 74

1 According to most commentaries it was the next revealed after the Fatrah, and the designation to the prophetic office. The main features of the tradition are, that Muhammad while wandering about in the hills near Mecca, distracted by doubts and by anxiety after truth, had a vision of the Angel Gabriel seated on a throne between heaven and earth, that he ran to his wife, Chadijah, in the greatest alarm, and desired her, perhaps from superstitious motives (and believing that if covered with clothes he should be shielded from the glances of evil spirits) to envelope him in his mantle; that then Gabriel came down and addressed him as in v. 1.

2 The Arabic words are not those used in *later* Suras to express the same idea.

3 Said to be Walid b. Mogheira, a person of note among the unbelieving Meccans. This portion of the Sura seems to be of a different date from the first seven verses, though very ancient, and the change of subject is similar to that at v. 9 of the previous Sura.

4 This and the three following verses wear the appearance of having been inserted at a later period to meet objections respecting the number of

the angels who guard hell, raised by the Jews; perhaps at Medina, as the four classes of persons specified are those whom Muhammad had to deal with in that city, viz., the Jews, Believers, th Hypocrites, or undecided, and Idolaters. These are constantly mentioned together in the Medina Suras.

5 That is, who believe, and do not believe.

6 As the word *sakar* disturbs the rhyme, it may have been inserted by a mistake of the copyist for the usual word, which suits it.

7 That is, death. Beidh. Comp. Sura 15. 99.

Sura 75

1 Lit. *shall be united.* In the loss of light, or in the rising in the west. – Beidh.

2 Supply, *it shall not be accepted.*

3 Verses 16–19 are parenthetic, and either an address to Muhammad by Gabriel desiring him (1) not to be overcome by any fear of being unable to follow and retain the revelation of this particular Sura; (2) or, not to interrupt him, but to await the completion of the entire revelation before he should proceed to its public recital. In either case we are led to the conclusion that, from the first, Muhammad had formed the plan of promulging a written book. Comp. Sura 20. 112.

4 In the death-struggle.

5 Or, *Therefore woe to thee, woe! And, again, woe to thee, woe.* Thus Sale, Ullm. Beidhawi; who also gives the rendering in the text, which is that of Maracci.

6 *Nonne fuit humor ex spermate quod spermatizatur.*

Sura 76

1 When in the womb.

2 With (the water of) Kafoor. Lane.

3 Desire no recompense from you.

Sura 77

1 Lit. *by the sent* (fem.) *one after another. Per missas.* Mar. Either *angels* following in a continued series; or, *winds*, which disperse rain over the earth; or the successive verses of the Koran which *disperse* truth and *distinguish* truth from error.

2 Sura 44. 40.

Sura 78

1 Of the Resurrection.

2 See Sura 2. 27. This is the title given by the Talmudists to the fifth of the seven heavens.

3 This phrase is of constant recurrence in the Talmud. Maimonides, Yad Hach. i. 3, makes it one of the positive commands of the Rabbins to believe 'that there exists a first Being . . . and that all things existing, Heaven and Earth, and whatever is between them, exist only through the truth of his existence.'

4 Gabriel.

Sura 79

1 This Sura obviously consists of three portions, verses 1–14, 15–26, 27–46, of which the third is the latest in point of style, and the second, more detailed than is usual in the Suras of the early period, which allude to Jewish and other legend only in brief and vague terms. It may therefore be considered as one of the short and early Suras.

2 Or, *By those angels which precede*, i.e. the souls of the pious into Paradise. Or, are beforehand with the Satans and djinn in learning the decrees of God.

Sura 80

1 We are told in the traditions, etc., that when engaged in converse with Walid, a chief man among the Koreisch, Muhammad was interrupted by the blind Abdallah Ibn Omm Maktûm, who asked to hear the Koran. The Prophet spoke very roughly to him at the time, but afterwards repented, and treated him ever after with the greatest respect. So much so, that he twice made him Governor of Medina.

2 That is, if he does not embrace Islam, and so become pure from sin, thou wilt not be to blame; thou art simply charged with the delivery of a message of warning.

3 *Ex spermate.*

Sura 81

1 Or, *thrown down.*

2 Thus Bab. Talm. Erchin, 3. 'In the day to come (i.e. of judgment) all the beasts will assemble and come, etc.'

3 See Sura 16. 61; 17. 33.

4 Like a skin from an animal when flayed. The idea is perhaps borrowed from the Sept. V. of Psalm civ. 2. Vulg. *sicut pellem.*

5 Mercury, Venus, Jupiter, Mars, Saturn.

6 Gabriel; of the meaning of whose name the next verse is probably a paraphrase.

7 Sura 53. 7.

8 Like a mere Kahin, or soothsayer.

9 Lit. stoned. Sura 3. 31. This vision or hallucination is one of the few clearly stated miracles, to which Muhammad appeals in the Koran. According to the tradition of Ibn-Abbas in Waquidi he was preserved by it from committing suicide by throwing himself down from Mount Hira, and that after it, God cheered him and strengthened his heart, and one revelation speedily followed another.

10 Comp, the doctrine of predestination in Sura 76. v. 25 to end.

Sura 82

1 Salt water and fresh water.

Sura 83

1 Sidjin is a prison in Hell which gives its name to the register of actions there kept, as Illiyoun, a name of the *lofty* apartments of Paradise, is transferred to the register of the righteous.

2 Derived from the root *sanima*, to be high: this water being conveyed to the highest apartments in the Pavilions of Paradise.

Sura 84

1 Lit. *and obeyed its Lord, and shall be worthy*, or *capable*, i.e. of obedience.

2 That is, into his left hand. The Muhammadans believe that the right hand of the damned will be chained to the neck; the left chained behind the back.

3 From Life to Death, from the Grave to Resurrection, thence to Paradise.

4 The expression is ironical. See Freyt. on the word. Lit. *tell them glad tidings*.

Sura 85

1 Lit. *By the Heaven furnished with towers*, where the angels keep watch; also, *the signs of the Zodiac*: this is the usual interpretation. See Sura 15. 15.

2 That is, by Muhammad and by Islam; or, angels and men. See, however, v. 7.

3 Prepared by Dhu Nowas, King of Yemen, A.D. 523, for the Christians. See Gibbon's Decline and Fall, chap. xii. towards the end. Pocock Sp. Hist. Ar. p. 62. And thus the comm. generally. But Geiger (p. 192) and Nöldeke (p. 77 n.) understand the passage of Dan. iii. But it should be borne in mind that the Suras of this early period contain very little allusion to Jewish or Christian legends.

4 Verses 8–11 wear the appearance of a late insertion, on account of their length, which is a characteristic of the more advanced period. Observe also the change in the rhymes.

Sura 87

1 Thus the Rabbins attribute the Book Jezirah to Abraham. See Fabr. Cod. Apoc. V. T. p. 349.

Sura 88

1 The name of a bitter, thorny shrub.

Sura 89

1 Of the sacred month Dhu'lhajja.

2 Or, *poured on them the mixed cup of chastisement.*

Sura 90

1 Lit. *and begetter and what he hath begotten.*

2 Of good and evil.

3 Thus we read in Hilchoth Matt'noth Aniim, c. 8, 'The ransoming of captives takes precedence of the feeding and clothing of the poor, and there is no commandment so great as this.'

Sura 91

1 See Sura 7. 33, for the story of Themoud.

Sura 92

1 Comp. Luke xi. 41. Muhammad perhaps derived this view of the meritorious nature of almsgiving from the Jewish oral law.

Sura 93

1 The charge of the orphaned Muhammad was undertaken by Abd-al-Mutalib, his grandfather, A.D. 576. Hishami, p. 35; Kitab al Wakidi, p. 22, have preserved traditions of the fondness with which the old man of fourscore years treated the child, spreading a rug for him under the shadow of the Kaaba, protecting him from the rudeness of his own sons, etc.

2 Up to his 40th year Muhammad followed the religion of his countrymen.

Sura 95

1 In allusion to the sacredness of the territory of Mecca. This valley in about the fourth century of our æra was a kind of sacred forest of 37 miles in circumference, and called Haram – a name applied to it as early as the time of Pliny (vi. 32). It had the privilege of asylum, but it was not lawful to inhabit it, or to carry on commerce within its limits, and its religious ceremonies were a bond of union to several of the Bedouin tribes of the Hejaz. The Koreisch had monopolised most of the offices and advantages of the Haram in the time of Muhammad. See Sprenger's Life of Mohammad, pp. 7–20.

Sura 96

1 The usual rendering is *read*. But the word *qaraa*, which is the root of the word Koran, analogous to the Rabbinic *mikra*, rather means *to address, recite*; and with regard to its etymology and use in the kindred dialects *to call, cry aloud, proclaim*. Compare Isai. lviii. 1; 1 Kings xviii. 37; and Gesen. Thesaur, on the Hebrew root. I understand this passage to mean, 'Preach to thy fellow men what thou believest to be true of thy Lord who has created man from the meanest materials, and can in like manner prosper the truth which thou proclaimest. He has taught man the art of writing – (recently introduced at Mecca) – and in this thou wilt find a powerful help for propagating the knowledge of the divine Unity.' The speaker in this, as in all the Suras, is Gabriel, of whom Muhammad had, as he believed, a vision on the mountain Hirâ, near Mecca.

2 The first five verses of this Sura are, in the opinion of nearly all commentators, ancient and modern, the earliest revelations made to Muhammad, in the 40th year of his life, and the starting point of El-Islam.

3 This, and the following verses, may have been added at a later period, though previous to the Flight, and with special reference, if we are to believe the commentators Beidhawi, etc., to the opposition which Muhammad experienced at the hands of his opponent, Abu Jahl, who had threatened to set his foot on the Prophet's neck when prostrate in prayer. But the whole passage admits of application to mankind in general.

4 That is Muhammad.

5 Lit. *hast thou seen if he be upon the guidance.*

6 The principal men of the Koreisch who adhered to Abu Jahl.

7 During a period variously estimated from six months to three years from the revelation of this Sura, or of its earliest verses, the prophetic inspiration and the revelation of fresh Suras is said to have been suspended. This interval is called the *Fatrah* or *intermission*; and the Meccan Suras delivered at its close show that at or during this period Muhammad had gained an increasing and more intimate acquaintance with the Jewish and Christian Scriptures. 'The accounts, however,' says Mr Muir (vol. ii. 86) 'are throughout confused, if not contradictory; and we can only gather with certainty that there was a time during which his mind hung in suspense, and doubted the divine mission.' The idea of any supernatural influence is of course to be entirely excluded; although there is no doubt that Muhammad himself had a full belief in the personality and influence of Satans and Djinn. Profound meditation, the struggles of an earnest mind anxious to attain to truth, visions, disgust at Meccan idolatry, and a desire to teach his countrymen the divine Unity – will sufficiently account for the period of indecision termed the *Fatrah*, and for the determination which led Muhammad, in all sincerity, but still self-deceived, to take upon himself the office and work of a Messenger from God. We may perhaps infer from such passages as Sura 2. 123, what had ever been the leading idea in Muhammad's mind.

Sura 97

1 The night of Al Kadr is one of the last ten nights of Ramadhan, and as is commonly believed the seventh of those nights reckoning backward.

Sura 101

1 Lit. *Mother.*

Sura 105

1 This Sura is probably Muhammad's appeal to the Meccans, intended at the same time for his own encouragement, on the ground of their deliverance from the army of Abraha, the Christian King of Abyssinia and Arabia Felix, said to have been lost in the year of Muhammad's birth in an expedition against Mecca for the purpose of destroying the Caaba. This army was cut off by small-pox (Wakidi; Hishami), and there is no doubt, as the Arabic word for small-pox also means 'small stones,' in reference to the hard gravelly feeling of the pustules, what is the true interpretation of the fourth line of this Sura, which, like many other poetical passages in the Koran, has formed the starting point for the most extravagant legends. *Vide* Gibbon's Decline and Fall, c. 1. The small-pox first shewed itself in Arabia at the time of the invasion by Abraha.

Sura 106

1 In allusion to the ancient inviolability of the Haram, or precinct round Mecca. See Sura, 95. This Sura, therefore, like Sura 105., is a brief appeal to the Meccans on the ground of their peculiar privileges.

Sura 108

1 A reply to those who had taunted Muhammad with the death of his sons, as a mark of the divine displeasure.

Sura 109

1 This Sura is said to have been revealed when Walîd urged Muhammad to consent that his God should be worshipped at the same time with the old Meccan deities, or alternately every year. Hishâmi, p. 79; Tabari, p. 139. It is a distinct renunciation of Meccan idolatry.

Sura 111

1 Undoubtedly one of the earliest Suras, and refers to the rejection of Muhammad's claim to the prophetic office by his uncle, Abu Lahab, at the instigation of his wife, Omm Djemil, who is said to have strewn the path of Muhammad on one occasion with thorns.

2 In allusion to the meaning of Abu Lahab, *father of flame.*

Sura 113

1 Lit. *who blow on knots.* According to some commentators an allusion to a species of charm. Suras 113 and 114 are called the *el mouwwidhetani*, or preservative chapters, are engraved on amulets, etc.

Sura 114

1 Satan.

INDEX

The index used here is that of Rodwell, with minor corrections. The numbers indicate, respectively, the sura, the verse and the page, which appears in brackets.